AMERICAN HISTORICAL SPOONS
The American Story in Spoons

AMERICAN HISTORICAL SPOONS

The American Story in Spoons

by ALBERT STUTZENBERGER

CHARLES E. TUTTLE COMPANY
Rutland, Vermont

Representatives
Continental Europe: BOXERBOOKS, INC., *Zurich*
British Isles: PRENTICE-HALL INTERNATIONAL, INC., *London*
Australasia: PAUL FLESCH & CO., PTY. LTD., *Melbourne*
Canada: M. G. HURTIG LTD., *Edmonton*

Published by the Charles E. Tuttle Company, Inc.
of Rutland, Vermont & Tokyo, Japan
with editorial offices at
Suido 1-chome, 2-6, Bunkyo-ku, Tokyo, Japan

Copyright in Japan, 1971 by Charles E. Tuttle Co., Inc.

Library of Congress Catalog Card No. 77-116483

International Standard Book No. 0-8048-0903-8

First edition published 1953 at Springdale Springs as a Bookmaster Book
First Tuttle edition published 1971

PRINTED IN JAPAN

To

WILLIAM MARSHALL BULLITT
friend of long standing, a true American,
who has fought long and valiantly to
preserve inviolate his beloved Oxmoor—
where I was born.

PLATE 1

THE CORONATION OR ANOINTING SPOON

TABLE OF CONTENTS

FOREWORD

It seems like a monstrous bit of conceit to say that this book is entirely different from any other, yet the statement, while a global contract, is not such an asinine exaggeration as it sounds on the surface. Nor is it a rebellious outcry against the specious reasoning which claims there is nothing newly different under the sun. It simply means that this is the first book devoted exclusively to a lowly domestic utensil, the spoon, which has been used by man, from the cradle to the grave, three times daily, for every sort of soup or sop, from the very rude beginnings of human destiny in cave-hideouts down through the ages to the present glittering modes of civilization. Now there have been books containing meager paragraphs or at most a chapter on the subject of the spoon, sandwiched between other more widely discussed topics, in volumes dealing ponderously with every conceivable object wrought out of silver, but nothing has ever been written with a direct floodlight emphasis on the spoon at the apogee of its glory, that is, in that era when American makers of silver were employing all their ingenuity to create lovely pieces of art, as souvenirs, which would bring before our people visual representations of the precious heritage that was theirs by birthright or adoption.

This book attempts to be more than just another dry-as-dust manual. True, while it has been pioneered primarily for that avid-eyed person, the collector, scouting around in old shops—his idea of seventh heaven— for another item to stockpile, it is intended equally as well for the general reader, that very commendable citizen who holds an abiding curiosity in and a strong affection for the historical characters, events, and places that have gone toward making our country, about all other nations, the "land of the free and the home of the brave." In this restricted sense the author does feel justified in saying categorically that his book, being thus an experimental entry into an untrodden field, is on a new and entirely different tack.

The essential viewpoint espoused by the author is, that every American souvenir spoon is a "talking spoon," and has a story behind it, one worth telling and one worth knowing. As it stands, this volume is by no means the complete record of our past, since that necessarily cannot be contained in a single piece of writing, but enough of the facets are showing in the narration to indicate the richness and multiplicity of the ores from which our nation is compounded. Delving deep into the mines of historical research has been a graciously-rewarding process. Some of the factual ores unearthed may be little more than dross, while others brought to light have contained much matter of sterling substance.

The essay-stories explaining the various souvenir spoons are not arranged according to any chronological sequence, because to do so would mislead the reader into expecting something like the general run of textbook histories, and he would be disappointed in finding some one or other subject missing. The arrangement simply follows a pattern deemed most expedient for exhibiting the individual spoons to their best advantage, and then allowing the "spoonographies" or sketches to fit in like pieces of a jig-saw puzzle. The development of our country has proceeded along similar lines. Moreover, such topics as Grand Canyon (No. 1), Kentucky Thoroughbred (No. 12), Tampa Strawberries (No. 72), and Rocky Ford Melons (No. 75) would dovetail into no historical sequence. Those spoons accompanying the introductory sketch, however, are placed as approximately correct as possible in chronological order.

Experts will doubtless find errors here and there in the presentation of the facts involved; the author will humbly plead guilty to the charge as readily as the famous Doctor Johnson when a lady once accosted him about some erroneous definitions in his dictionary: he admitted everything, attributing all mistakes to "ignorance, madam, sheer ignorance."

Let not the prospector be dismayed if he discovers that certain spoons are not represented here: granted time and sufficient encouragement for the effort, the hopes for a continuance of this endeavor will materialize.

In regard to the general type of spoon used by many small towns, the collector is apt to find some in his possession representing one place in the bowl, whereas the one used in this volume pictures a scene in another locality. It is well to remember that many of such spoons were selected from catalogs, and there occurred considerable duplication, the same spoon serving for many places. One spoon of this type is purposely included for illustration, namely, the one displaying Union Station (No. 49), Hot Springs Hostelry (No. 50), and Ramona's Wedding Place (No. 51), to show how widely a spoon can travel. This seems to have been a very popular spoon, having turned up for at least a half-dozen other communities.

Then again, criticism might justifiably be leveled at the reading matter in the form of this question: "Why was much more space allotted to the discussion of the subject found on one spoon than to that on another?" In answering that, the author can only ask for a little indulgence. The Actors' Fund Fair spoon is a typical example of this liberty. His defense for making a prolonged study of these once-famous but now almost-forgotten actors and actresses rests with this naïve confession: his research on the American theatre in the heyday of its greatest glory proved to be too utterly fascinating, too vitally refreshing, and too sadly neglected by others to be passed over lightly by him. The old American sense of "fair play" cried out for justice, that is, for letting a little more light beam in on these once-dear faces of people who brought pleasure in bygone days to thousands of seekers after good entertainment.

Since there were previously no names whatsoever for any of these spoons, such as are indicated for regular sets of tableware silver, a nomenclature was adopted to accord with the most salient feature of the spoon. As a rule, this was usually taken from the handle, though common sense sometimes dictated that it be taken from the bowl. Notable people pictured anywhere on the spoon were given preference to other features.

❋   ❋   ❋   ❋

The names of those persons who have assisted, by and large, in the preparation of this work are multiple. A host of authorities was consulted for the discussion of the various essays. A list of their books appears in the bibliography after the reading matter. Footnotes were generally avoided, but wherever credit was thought due in connection with quoted material, mention of the author was made within the written page, thus furnishing to the exacting reader, if he is zealous enough, a sufficient key to the arcana of sources listed in the bibliography.

Above all, the author wishes to make grateful acknowledgment to those "dear hearts and gentle people" with whom he came into contact, either personally or by correspondence, for the invaluable assistance they so unstintingly gave to help make THE AMERICAN STORY IN SPOONS a living reality. Their names are as follows:

Mr. A. V. Ansel of the Jewelers' Circular Keystone Co., New York City; Miss Catharine S. Thayer, Robbins Company, Attleboro, Mass.; Miss Ann Holbrook, The Gorham Company, Providence, R. I.; Mr. E. P. Hogan, Assistant Advertising Manager, International Silver Co., Meriden, Conn.; Mr. Ralph C. Potter, Advertising Department, Alvin Corporation, Providence, R. I.; Miss Emily McGrath, Acting Secretary, Sterling Silversmiths Guild of America, New York City; Mr. H. H. Harrison, The Williams Bros. Silver Co., Glastonbury, Conn.; Mrs. W. H. Marquess, III, Advertising Manager, Samuel Kirk & Son, Inc., Baltimore, Md.; Mr. A. F. Swanton, The Watson Company, Attleboro, Mass.; Mr. A. A. Gordon, Paye & Baker Mfg. Co., North Attleboro, Mass.; Mr. William T. Hurley, Jr., Advertising Manager, Reed & Barton, Taunton, Mass.; Mr. Harry E. Stahl, Dept. of Public Relations, General Motors Corporation, Detroit; Mr. Jerome Kempler, Kudner Agency, Inc., New York City; Mr. Frank B. Marshall, Jr., Advertising Manager, Samuel Kirk & Son, Inc., Baltimore, Md.; Mr. W. J. F., Tiffany & Co., New York City; Shreve & Co., San Francisco, Cal.; Miss Gwendolen A. Haste, Advertising Dept., General Foods Corporation, New York City; Mr. C. Sauer, Lange Jewelry Co., Cincinnati, Ohio; Mr. Robert Campbell, Secretary of the Actors' Fund of America, New York City; Mr. E. B. Bedford, Publicity Manager, Oneida Ltd., Oneida, N. Y.; Mr. Herbert H. Hewitt, Chief of Reference Dept., Chicago Public Library; Miss Helen Louis, Flesh Public Library, Piqua, Ohio; Miss Ethel L. Hutchins, Reference Dept., Public Library of Cincinnati; Carnegie-Lawther Library, Red Wing, Minnesota; Miss Johnnie Elizabeth Riner, Public Library of Jefferson City, Missouri; Mr. Paul North Rice, Chief of the Reference Dept., New York Public Library; Mrs. Emma W. MacMillan, Librarian, Public Library, Wilmington, N. C.; Mrs. J. W. Simmons, Orange Chamber of Commerce, Orange, Texas; Mrs. Gordorelle Williams, Librarian, Hot Springs, Arkansas; Mr. James W. Tufts, Pinehurst, N. C.; Mrs. Louella B. Albee, Nokomis, Fla.; Miss Marget Tompkins, Assistant Western History Dept., Denver Public Library; Mrs. Mildred N. Freeman, Lending Dept., Cincinnati Public Library; Mrs. Anna Neal Muller, Librarian, Free Public Library, Topeka, Kansas; Miss Helen M. McFarland, Librarian, Kansas State Historical Society, Topeka, Kansas; Miss Pauline D. Weedon, Reference Dept., Tampa Public Library; Miss Helga H. Eason, Reference Librarian, Miami Public Library; Mrs. Alys Freeze,

First Assistant Western History Dept., Denver Public Library; Miss Evelyn R. Dale, Filson Club, Louisville, Ky.; the late Mr. Howland Dudley, Harvard, Mass.; Mrs. Alyse D. Westbrook, Hayward High School, Hayward, California; Mr. A. T. White, Manager, Chamber of Commerce, Southern Pines, N. C.; Miss Margaret Lucille Stull, Reference Librarian, Des Moines Public Library; Miss Flora Hartsook, Assistant Librarian, Public Library, Marion, Indiana; Mrs. Elizabeth McCrory, Louisville, Ky.; Misses Edna Grauman, Hattie Burrell, Nanette Crutcher, Ruth Rinehart, Amy Lutes, Helen Frantz, and Mrs. Alene Christine, Louisville Public Library; Senator Paul H. Douglas, of Illinois; Mr. B. P. C. Bridgewater, Secretary, British Museum, London, England; and Mr. Robert A. K. Stevenson, Keeper, National Museum of Antiquities of Scotland, Edinburgh, Scotland.

For permission to use copyrighted materials grateful acknowledgment is hereby made to:

The American Home, for line drawings of two monkey spoons.

Houghton Mifflin Co., for the lines of poetry from "The Children's Hour," "Courtship of Miles Standish," "Wreck of the Hesperus," and "Paul Revere's Ride," by Longfellow; "The Sandpiper" and "Good-By, Sweet Day," by Celia Thaxter; "Old Ironsides," by Holmes; "Song of the Kansas Emigrant," by Whittier; and "The New Colossus," by Emma Lazarus.

Charles Scribner's Sons, for selected lines of poetry from "The Jamestown Celebration," from *Poems,* by John R. Thompson.

The Macmillan Co., for selected lines of poetry from "Ode to the North-East Wind," by Charles Kingsley; and "Mother and Son," by Dinah Mulock Craik.

Doubleday & Co., Inc., for selected lines from "Crossing Brooklyn Ferry," in *Leaves of Grass,* by Walt Whitman.

Harcourt, Brace & Co., for brief quotations from *Main Currents in American Thought,* by Vernon Louis Parrington.

Brandt & Brandt, for quotation from "The Devil and Daniel Webster" from *Selected Works of Stephen Vincent Benet,* published by Rinehart & Co., Inc., copyright, 1936, by Stephen Vincent Benet.

E. P. Dutton & Co., Inc., for quotations from *The World of Washington Irving,* by Van Wyck Brooks, and copyright, 1944, by Van Wyck Brooks; and also from *The Alamo,* by John Myers Myers, and copyright, 1948, by John Myers Myers.

The Caxton Printers, Ltd., Caldwell, Idaho, for quoted material from *Pony Trails in Wyoming,* by John K. Rollinson, published by The Caxton Printers, Ltd.

Mrs. Michelle Ticknor Furlow, for the stanzas from "The Sword in the Sea," by Francis O. Ticknor.

S. J. Bloch Publishing Co., Detroit, Michigan, for quoted material from *Doctor and I,* by Louella B. Albee.

Above all, I owe a debt of gratitude to the trustees, and also to Mr. Ll. Davies, agent, of the Jackson Estates, Cardiff, Glamorganshire, Wales, for their kind permission in allowing me to use drawings and illustrations of many rare spoons from the private collection of the late Sir Charles James Jackson, as shown in his *Illustrated History of English Plate,* and here accompanying my introductory chapter.

The line drawings in this book were made by Miss Henrietta Baker, Middletown, Ky.; the photographs, by Mr. and Mrs. Richard G. Potter, Mrs. Ruth Howard, and Mr. Herbert Leopold, all of Louisville, Ky.

LIST OF SPOONS ILLUSTRATED

I Historical Types of Spoons

II American Souvenir Spoons

AMERICAN HISTORICAL SPOONS
The American Story in Spoons

THE ANOINTING SPOON THAT FOUNDED
A CAR MAKERS' CRAFT

A hush descends on the great cathedral on this glad day in the seventeenth century.

A shaft of sunlight dances on the rich silver spoon as the prelate dips his fingers into the precious oil it bears. He is preparing to anoint a new king of England.

This is the great ceremony of coronation, blazing with ritual handed down from Biblical times. And it is fitting that an important part of it be the magnificent silver spoon, created with painstaking care by the best craftsmen in the realm . . .

☆   ☆   ☆   ☆

These anointing or coronation spoons were among the earliest examples of the silversmith's art in pieces of this kind.

In the old days, silverware had very limited uses since, as you learn in history, even royalty used their hands while eating. But when spoons, forks, and knives began coming into their own, the silversmith rated high as an artist — seldom hurrying, always working to achieve perfection in line and balance.

Today, you can see many examples of the silversmith's work right in your own home — in mother's best dinner-table setting, for example. You may also see it, surprisingly enough, right in the family car . . .

Reprinted from an advertisement of GENERAL MOTORS CORPORATION and used through their courteous permission.

PLATE 2

CORONATION SCENE IN WESTMINSTER ABBEY

INTRODUCING THE SPOON

The old nursery rhyme beginning "Hey-dey-diddle" and winding up with this confession, "The dish ran away with the spoon," expresses by inference the romantic nature of the spoon. The pie-faced, homely dish obviously passed up the keen-edged knife and the sharp-pointed fork, both common-sense, hard-working worthies, to grow spoony and elope with the more handsome, likeable spoon.

The dish, thus personified, is not unusual in showing an honest preference for the spoon. A great many people, passing up knives and forks, have gone about collecting and treasuring a wide variety of spoons. Evidence that many fine folk have a flair for this particular utensil may be deduced from the fact that, if any one piece is missing from an old set of family silver, it is sure to be a spoon. Four centuries ago Robert William Chapman naïvely admitted: "When I dine out and find my soup embellished by a notable Spoon, as may often happen to those who dine in Colleges and Inns of Court, my Manners are seldom proof against Temptation." Boswell records Doctor Samuel Johnson's pronouncement on a fellow of lax principles: "If he does really think that there is no distinction between virtue and vice, why, sir, when he leaves our house, let us count our spoons."

The temptation to purloin spoons gradually led people to an associated idea, that the devil often appeared to certain persons in the guise of a shapely spoon, and this article, accordingly, had to be long and ungainly before one could hope to keep the devil at a safely respectable distance. Chaucer, in *The Squire's Tale*, declares of a weak-willed character: "Therefore bihoveth hire a ful long spoon." Shakespeare makes mention of this superstition twice. In *The Tempest*—

> Mercy, Mercy, this is a devil.
> I will leave him; I have no long spoon.

And in *the Comedy of Errors,* he repeats the idea as it usually appeared in the old proverb—

> Bespeak a long spoon. Why, Dromio?
> Marry, he must have a long spoon
> that must eat with the devil.

John Heyward, an Elizabethan dramatist slightly earlier than Shakespeare, also repeats this old adage in one of his plays.

Shelley pictures the devil and the stealer of spoons as identical creatures—

3

The Devil, I safely can aver,
Has neither hoof, nor tail, nor sting;
Nor is he as some sages swear,
A spirit, neither here nor there,
In nothing—yet in everything.

He is—what we are; for sometimes
The Devil is a gentleman;
At others a bard bartering rhymes
For sack; a statesman spinning crimes;
A swindler, living as he can;

A thief, who cometh in the night,
With whole boots and net pantaloons,
Like some one whom it were not right
To mention—or the luckless wight
From whom he steals nine silver spoons.

Spoons have always made pleasing gifts. The giving of spoons by godparents to children at christenings appears to have been a well-established custom already under the Tudor and early Stuart kings. In one scene of *Henry VIII*, Shakespeare has the king urging Cranmer, Archbishop of Canterbury, to be the godfather of the infant Elizabeth. The archbishop declines on the grounds that he is unworthy of such a great honor, being only a "poor and humble subject," without the blood of royalty in his veins. Whereupon the king chided him on his parsimoniousness: "Come, come, my lord, you'd spare your spoons."

The story is told that Shakespeare himself once stood godfather to one of Ben Jonson's children. After the christening he appeared to be in such a meditative mood that Jonson inquired for the cause. "I have been considering a great while," he replied, "what would be the fittest gift to bestow upon my godchild, and I have resolved it at last." "I prithee what?" asked Ben. "I' faith, Ben, I'll give him a dozen good latten spoons," rejoined Shakespeare, "and thou shalt translate them." Lowes astutely asserts that this witticism "cut two ways: first, a dig at the erudition of the father, by the play upon the word latten (Latin); and lastly, the gift of a set of tinned-iron spoons, which were used by the poorer classes, instead of a set of Apostle spoons such as Shakespeare might be expected to give."

The spoon was one of the earliest inventions of man. Being a kind of ladle, it was always a prime necessity for conveying liquids or hot foods to the mouth. A French courtier, De la Borde, truthfully remarked that "spoons are old, I will not say, as the world but certainly as soup." Probably the earliest dipper used by cavemen of the Stone Age was the palm of the hand. With the discovery of fire and the heating of food, a better receptacle than the hand was needed. It is only natural that shells

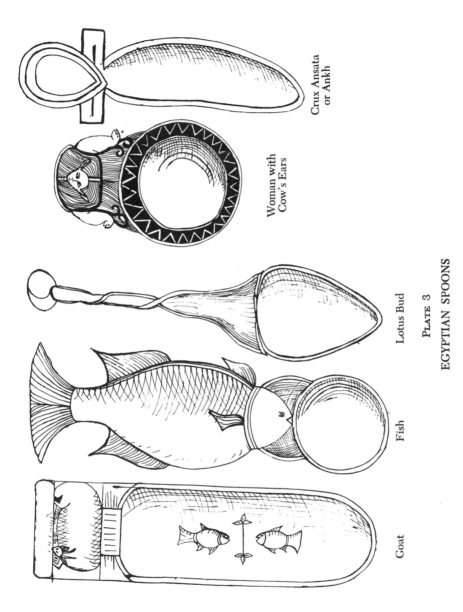

Goat

Fish

Lotus Bud

Woman with
Cow's Ears

Crux Ansata
or Ankh

PLATE 3

EGYPTIAN SPOONS

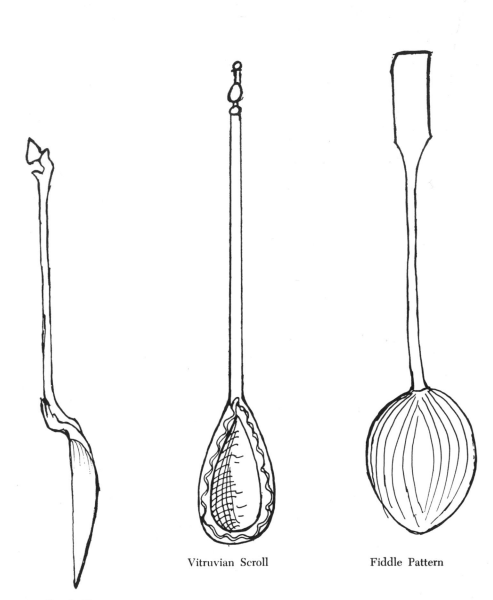

Vitruvian Scroll

Fiddle Pattern

Goat's Foot

PLATE 4

GREEK AND ROMAN SPOONS

should be the readiest substitute, for they lay accessible in all sizes and shapes along river banks and ocean beaches. Bivalve mollusks, like the cockle, oyster, and clam, supplied the most natural form of spoons. Indeed, the Greek word for spoon meant the same as valve, wedge, or shell. The cylindrical handle with knobby ends found in early Greek spoons suggests a carved wooden stick or the leg-bone of an animal attached to one end of a shell to form a dipper useful in stirring hot foods. The English word for spoon is derived from the Anglo-Saxon *spon*, meaning a chip of wood, and has cognate forms in Dutch, Danish, Swedish, and German. In Northern Europe the first spoons were carved from wood. Later specimens were devised from the horns of cattle, ivory tusks, bronze, and eventually from silver and gold.

The earliest mention of spoons made from precious metals occurs in the Book of Exodus, when Moses is commanded to make dishes and spoons of pure gold for the Tabernacle. When the altar was dedicated and anointed by the heads of the twelve tribes of Israel, we are told in Numbers VII, 84-86, that "twelve chargers of silver, twelve silver bowls, [and] twelve spoons of gold" were used. We learn further: "The golden spoons were twelve, full of incense, weighing ten shekels apiece . . . all the gold of the spoons was an hundred and twenty shekels." As a shekel of gold is estimated at $10.88 in modern money, it would mean that these spoons were worth more than thirteen hundred dollars. Fortunately we are given the name of the goldsmith who made the spoons. In Exodus XXXI, 1-5, it is stated that Moses commanded Bezalel "to devise cunning works, to work in gold, and in silver, and in brass." Thus, Bezalel becomes the first spoon maker definitely known to us by name in history.

Since Bezalel had come with his native people under the leadership of Moses out of Egypt, it is obvious that he must have learned his trade in the land along the Nile. While time has effaced all of Bezalel's handiwork, we can easily conjecture what specimens of his craftsmanship were like by the spoons which have been preserved in the tombs of Egyptian pharaohs dating back more than four thousand years.

The most striking feature about Egyptian spoons is their unconventionality of form. Most of those that have come down to us are commonly made of flint, slate, wood, ivory and bronze, occasionally bearing hieroglyphics with religious connotations. Since those wrought of gold and silver are rarely unearthed, it is likely that marauders entering the pyramids long ago carried off the more valuable spoons once deposited in the tombs. Many Egyptian spoons were cast in the form of paterae or handled dishes, with covered bowls, annular feet, and a spout or lip features which made it possible for them to stand safely as receptacles for sweet-smelling perfumes and incense. The movable cover was contained by a pin on one side.

The crux ansata, or ankh, shown on Plate 3, is hewn out of slate in the form of a tall cross with a loop at one end. The ankh was a sacred emblem of motherhood and fertility to the Egyptians, and symbolized Isis, the queen of Heaven. Sometimes Isis is represented as a woman with cow's ears. In this state she is supposed to be shedding the tears which cause the Nile River to overflow its banks, thus creating the fertility for an abundant harvest and sustenance of life. The lotus, which grows in the marshy banks of the Nile, is the sacred flower of Egypt. The fish, goat, ram, dove, and serpent, being integral features of the life of ancient Egypt, are frequently pictured on spoons, many of them painted and having richly ornamented borders. The handles of these diversified spoons are extremely unpractical.

Greek and Roman spoons begin to assume a modern appearance and sometimes it is difficult to distinguish clearly between them. Bronze and silver were the metals most commonly used, although gold implements were occasionally employed for sacred services in the temple. Pan, the god of field and flocks, and the patron of huntsmen and shepherds, is popularly represented as having the hoofs, ears, and horns of a goat. No god was held in higher esteem by the Greeks, and hence he was honored by the goat's foot on numerous spoons. The one illustrated here has a tripartite lobe running from the bowl into the handle-drop, on which the stem has been affixed. Examples of the goat's-foot spoon have been unearthed at Cyzicus, Pompeii, Herculaneum and Berthonville (Normandy). At the latter place sixty pieces of silverware weighing fifty-five pounds and belonging once to the treasury of a temple dedicated to Mercury six centuries before Christ came to light in 1830. Some of the pieces were chased with battle scenes from the *Iliad;* others featured the exploits of Achilles. Forty-two persons are distinguished on a single ewer. These exquisitely embossed pieces, of varying date, are now in the Bibliothèque Nationale at Paris. Spoons of Greek workmanship have been found as far distant as the Crimea in burial grounds of the Scythians.

The influence of Marcus Vitruvius Pollio, a Roman architect living in the Augustan era, is seen in the ivory convolutions ornamenting the flattened rim of the Vitruvian scroll spoon. This rim is about one-fourth of an inch in width and runs entirely around the bowl. The Vitruvian scroll was revived with success during the Renaissance by Andrea Palladio, who followed closely the styles pictured in *De Architectura,* a scholarly compendium by Marcus Vitruvius.

The fiddle-pattern spoon, of Roman origin in the first or second century after Christ, resembles the modern type known by the same name, differing only in that the stem-head is squared off in the Puritan style instead of being arched.

The keel-and-disk style appears on both Greek and Roman spoons, with many modifications. On those of Greek provenance a rectangular strip or keel projects in increasing thickness from the convex center of the bowl till it meets the stem under which it coils or convolves into a disk. The stem is accordingly attached to the upper surface of the disk, causing

Anglo-Saxon   Coronation (obverse)   Coronation (reverse)

PLATE 5

EARLY ENGLISH SPOONS

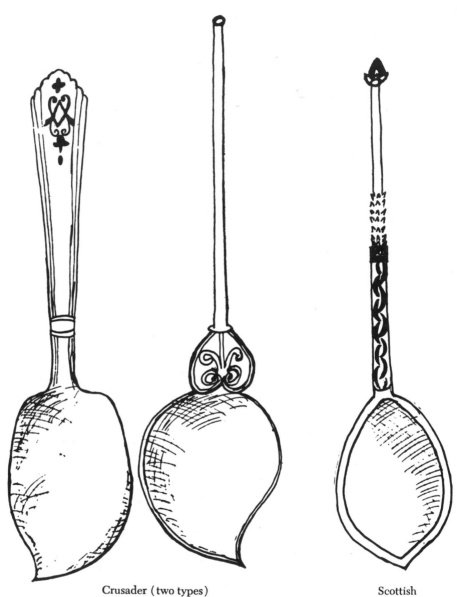

Crusader (two types)   Scottish

PLATE 6

MEDIEVAL SPOONS

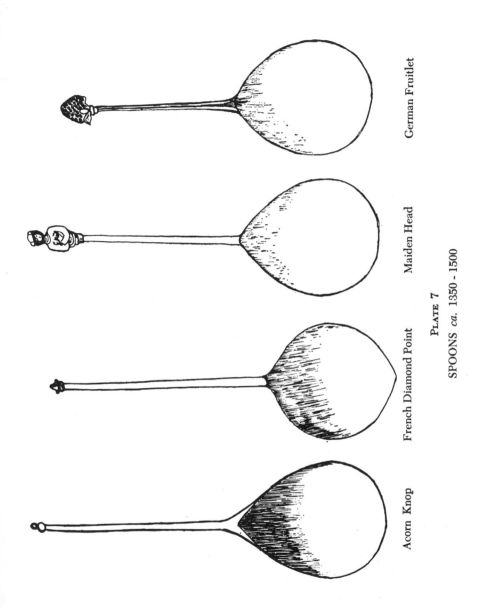

Acorn Knop   French Diamond Point   Maiden Head   German Fruitlet

PLATE 7

SPOONS *ca.* 1350 - 1500

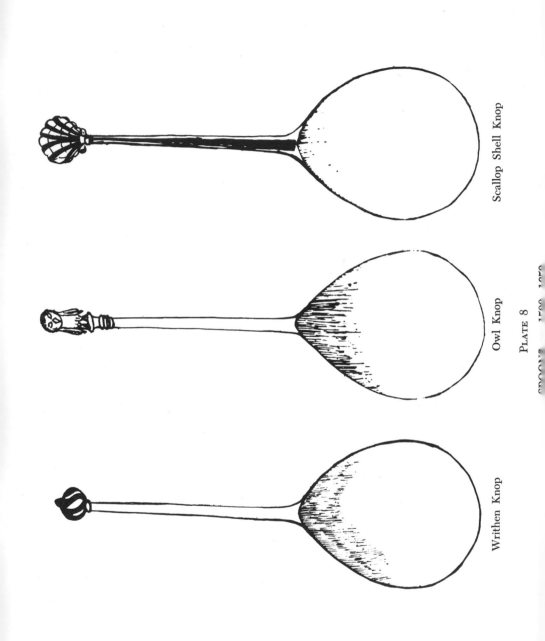

Writhen Knop   Owl Knop   Scallop Shell Knop

PLATE 8

the handle to repose, when placed horizontally, about one-half an inch above the bowl. The Roman variations of this spoon generally show the disk placed between stem and bowl almost on an even level. The stem-ends are often sharp spikes useful for spearing morsels of meat or gouging the edible parts out of lobsters, oysters, or clams baked in the shell. Numerous Greek and Roman spoons have been found in Britain. One located in Monmouthshire bears the monogram of Christ, the Greek letters *Ch (i)* and *R (ho)*, the first two letters in *Christos,* the Greek name for Christ.

The earliest English spoons were undoubtedly imitations of those brought in by the Roman encampments in Britain. The Angles and Saxons, however, on arriving from the Continent introduced a spoon with small, pear-shaped bowl and a long rectangular or a hexagonal stem. The illustration in this book shows a slender handled spoon, eight and a half inches long, with a flattened disk in the middle and a decoration of interlaced reeding along the handle and around the edges of the bowl. It lay buried with a cache of seventy silver coins, dated from the ninth century, in Wiltshire, south-central England. Most of the early English spoons were made of horn or wood; by the fourteenth century castings of bronze, brass, pewter, and latten (or sheet tin) were fairly common. A beautiful silver spoon, set with garnets and encased in gold foil, but showing signs of great wear and mended fractures, was discovered among the bones of an atheling buried at Chatham about the time of the Norman Conquest.

The finest and undoubtedly the most priceless spoon in existence is the Coronation or Anointing spoon, ten and a half inches in length, which has been employed at the crowning of all English sovereigns since the days of the Plantagenets in the twelfth century. The heart-shaped bowl is divided perpendicularly through the middle by an intersecting ridge, the entire surface being ornamented by a stately swirl of arabesque engraving. The stem is divided into three sections, the lower one of which is joined to the bowl by a monster's head simulating the characteristic features of gargoyles found in the frieze-work of Gothic cathedrals.

The lower section of the stem is centered about a large amethyst rosette of royal purple, encircled by a beaded band, touching which are four large pearls, two above and two below, like pairs of watchful eyes. Above and below the pearls are rings of enamelled work, through veins of which a fine tracery of gold leaf is interlaced. The central section is embellished by a cartouche of finely-enamelled foliations. The upper section, joined to the middle area by a monster's head of smaller size than the one below, is composed of swirled cable terminating in a seal knop on top of which appears a minute scroll-work similar to that found in the central section.

The reverse side of the spoon presents several interesting features. In the first place, the junction of bowl and stem is effected by means of a modified keel-and-disk construction, a feature that suggests a definitely early genesis. Chased rosettes and interweaving incisions ornament the lower section on this side. Zigzagging lines and dots are engraved features of the central section.

The anointing of a sovereign at his coronation is a long-established rite, having had its origin in the symbolistic rituals of the most ancient peoples. We learn in the Old Testament that Saul, David, and Solomon were anointed with oil poured from horns by the high priests of their time. French kings were anointed by oil from a vial preserved in the cathedral at Rheims. English monarchs have been anointed for seven centuries in Westminster Abbey by oil poured from an ampulla into the coronation spoon, over which the Archbishop of Canterbury presides.

Some authorities maintain that the original anointing spoon was destroyed along with all the other royal regalia when Oliver Cromwell became master of England during the Protectorate. It is true that the coronation of Charles II was held up for two years because the old regalia could not readily be located, and some of the crown jewels, decorations, and robes were irretrievably lost, but there is documentary evidence that the anointing spoon was mended for the coronation of Charles II at the small sum of two pounds, the spoon being one item discovered on a repair bill after that monarch's death. Henry Shaw, an expert on old English dress and decoration, asserts: "We can have little hesitation in considering our spoon as having belonged to the ancient regalia. There can, of course, be no doubt of its antiquity; and it is not at all probable than an article of this kind should have been obtained from any other source."

Belief in the authenticity of the coronation spoon was strengthened when, late in the nineteenth century, four spoons wrapped in a gold crown-like snood were by accident uncovered from beneath the stone ruins of the floor that had once been part of a nunnery on the island of Iona, off the west coast of Scotland. All the spoons bore a distinguishable likeness in style, configuration, and length to the English coronation spoon, and one of them, showing fewer signs of use than the others, is well preserved. The history of the nunnery confirms the belief that the spoons belong to the thirteenth century, when the Western Isles, hitherto independent and Celtic in spirit, were brought into subjection by the Scottish Crown. During the long reigns of Alexander II (1214-1249) and Alexander III (1249-1286) the convents and monasteries in the islands off the west coast were repeatedly the scenes of sieges and battles. Commander G. E. How, of the Royal Navy, believes that the spoons and the gold snood were concealed for safe keeping under the large stone during that period. Sir Edward James Jackson, the notable English authority on old silver, tends to believe they belong to a somewhat later period, perhaps to the troubled times attendant on the wars of the disputed succession and independence following the death of Alexander III. The genesis of these spoons is purely conjectural.

An interesting type of spoon that has survived out of the Middle Ages is the Crusader spoon, of which two specimens are herewith given, brought back by European warriors who went on Crusades to the Near East to recover the Holy Land from the Turks. These spoons present an unusual feature in the shape of their shallow bowls, fashioned somewhat like shields, with an angular base and a sharp edge on one side, thus making a handy combination of knife, fork, and spoon, all in one, very serviceable for soldiers compelled to eat frequently on the run and in the open. The spatulate handle of the one shown on the left precedes by several centuries its general acceptance for flatware in Western Europe. These Crusader spoons, from a Parisian collection, probably originated in Persia.

It may well be worth noting here that forks were not introduced to the table service till the time of the Crusades, when the Doge Domenice Silvie, of Venice, and his Dogess at the beginning of the twelfth century astonished their guests by placing a fork beside each plate at one of their banquets. It required more than three centuries to accustom the people of Northern Europe to the use of a fork, instead of fingers, for conveying food to the mouth from their plates.

Knives had long been carried in the belts of hunters and soldiers employed more extensively for the dispatching of meat on the hoof than on the platter. In England and France knives were not universally used by individual diners at the table until the middle of the seventeenth century. "Fingers were made before knives and forks" was no idle adage even at the festive boards of kings and their most elegant courtiers. The rise of factories, however, for the production of tableware on a wide scale in England after 1650 effected a profound revolution for the better in table etiquette. During the next fifty years a general code for the observance of more genteel manners at the table was evolved.

Spoons made of silver appeared on the continent before they did in England, although frequently in the guise of a hard wood inlaid or overlaid with silver. In time, strict laws demanding high standards greatly improved the quality of silverware, and the necessity for stamping the name of the maker, the place, and the date-letter very effectively curbed the imposition of slipshod work on the public. In England, where the finest articles of silver were produced, the word "sterling" came to mean "of unexcelled quality."

From an inquiry into old legal documents it is apparent that spoons, especially those made of silver, were prize possessions, if the frequency with which they are mentioned in wills is a reliable indication. The first of such references is found in the will of Martin St. Croix, dated 1259, leaving a dozen silver spoons among his chattels. On the wardrobe expense —inventories of Edward 1 for the year 1300 several gold and silver spoons with the fleur-de-lis (Paris) hallmark are listed. The Court of Husting records for 1305-06 mention the bequest of thirteen silver spoons by Edith Panmer to her daughter Edith—could this have been an early set of Apostle spoons? An inventory of the crown jewels of Edward III for 1329 lists thirty-six silver spoons valued at 59 s 10 d and five of gold at 9£ 12 s 6 d. After 1400 the mention of spoons in wills is a common occurrence. Eventually, it became a custom for those possessing silverware to bequeath their spoons to grandchildren or friends in a wide and varied distribution. A particular instance is the will (1634) of Alice Williams, mother of Roger Williams, who left among other things: to Anne Williams, grandchild, two gilt spoons; to James Wightman, grandchild, two silver spoons; to Hester Davies, two spoons.

A form of folding pocket-spoon, first developed on the continent, spread to the British Isles; it was popular everywhere because it enabled the traveler to have his chief eating implement with him at all times. Most of the folding spoons that have come down to us are of French or German origin, and are wrought from the cheaper materials—pewter, copper or latten—but a few made of the more precious metals have also survived. These often display an elaborate ornamentation—perhaps having been made to order.

During the fourteenth century, spoons began to be characterized by the different styles of knops, that is, their modes of "head-dress." There was little variation otherwise, the stems being hexagonal and the bowls fig-shaped. The first mention of the acorn knop occurs in 1351, when John de Halegh willed a dozen silver spoons "with akernes" to Thomas Taillour. Its popularity continued for nearly a century. Spoons "with dyamond poynts" seem to have originated in France, where they were most prevalent, but the style spread elsewhere, and lasted a great while, from the latter part of the fourteenth to the beginning of the sixteenth century. The knop was faceted like a diamond with a gleaming gold-leaf tip, creating the semblance of a previous gem scintillating in the sunlight. Even folding spoons of the better type were diamond pointed.

The maidenhead spoon assumes its name from the image of the Virgin Mary adorning the stem-caput or knop. One testament as early as 1446 lists this spoon, though no further mention of it is found for several decades, that is, through the terrible period of the Wars of the Roses; then it sprang into popularity and continued in evidence till the time of Queen Elizabeth. Changes in styles of head-dress to follow the prevailing fashions render this spoon unique. Usually meek and mild, the "mayden" began to look like the devil during the reign of Henry VIII, when women drew their hair out in conical peaks resembling horns. Sometimes the bust was armless; again, the arms would be folded or allowed to hang suspended beside the body. The idea that this spoon originated in honor of either Mary I or Elizabeth is erroneous.

The fruitlet spoon, although mentioned as such in a bequest of six silver spoons as early as 1440 in England, was never too common there. It was probably made before that time on the continent, where many specimens have been found dating throughout the fifteenth and sixteenth centuries. In France the mulberry appears most often as the finial while the strawberry and blackberry were exceedingly popular in Germany.

Spoons with a writhen or twisted knop were somewhat of a fad for about a quarter-century following 1487, and then disappeared completely. Sir Charles Jackson likens this bulbous-shaped finial to a pellet around which several strands of wire were twisted thick in the middle and smaller at the extremities. Duhousset, the Frenchman, compares this finial to a mint drop coated with a swirled-rib-icing. Since similes are in order, I might suggest an onion in petticoats doing a round waltz.

In the beginning of the sixteenth century birds, and infrequently animals, found a perch at the stem end of a spoon. In England the lion sejant, dove, and owl were devised most frequently; in France, the columbine (dove) and the falcon; in Germany and the Low Countries, the stork and the eagle. The owl-knop spoon in the illustration, one of a half-dozen sets presented to Oxford College by Bishop Foxe, bears the London hallmark for 1506-07.

Sundry other types of spoons made their appearance in the first part of the sixteenth century, the most frequent knops being the pine cone, the pineapple, a bunch of grapes, those with seal tops bearing family crests, a spear point, and the "slipped-in-the-stalk," the last-named having an end rounding off to an edge and thus being devoid of any finial. Ribbed and fluted balls were in vogue during the reigns of Henry VIII and Edward VI. Sometimes an English silversmith, hoping to encourage in his countrymen the Italian custom of eating with a fork, introduced that implement on the end opposite a spoon. Many of the seal tops, plentifully made from the accession of Elizabeth till the execution of Charles I, displayed a new style in the handle known as the baluster stem, especially in the later examples. Legend ascribes the Pudsey spoon, the most famous of seal tops, to the middle of the fifteenth century, far ahead in time of any other spoon of this type.

The scallop-shell spoon shown here was made by Hans Koppel of Nuremberg in 1549. The scallop appears on both the obverse and reverse sides, and along the stem in front runs a shallow groove widening as it approaches the bowl. Koppel was a contemporary of Hans Sachs and Wenzel Jamnitzer in the heyday of Nuremberg's great cultural prosperity. Jamnitzer, a migrant from Vienna, is sometimes called the Cellini of Germany for his versatility in all the fine arts. Both Koppel and Jamnitzer utilized various kinds of shells for the thematic enrichment of silver, the nautilus, scallop, and limpet being especially favored. Even replicas of the shells themselves were skillfully artificed—one of the few instances where articles of silver were made for other than utilitarian purposes.

Spoons cast for the Apostles were the first genuine souvenir spoons, since they were presented by sponsors as gifts at the baptism of godchildren. Apostle spoons enjoyed a long and continuing popularity for two centuries. The earliest mention of them occurs in 1494-95, in a Yorkshire will of thirteen spoons "cum Apostalis super eorum fines." But spoons with London date-letters from 1478 to 1491 have been unearthed in a half dozen instances. St. Nicholas, while not one of the Apostles, was honored by a spoon, marked 1488, that sold for thirty-five hundred dollars at a London sale. Only five complete sets of the twelve Apostle spoons and the Master have been assembled in our day. One of those brought $24,500 at auction; another, $45,000. A single Apostle has been known to rocket to the astronomical heights of five thousand dollars.

The Apostles all wear the sacerdotal gown and the mortarboard cap, and would be indistinguishable one from the other, were it not for the insignia of their office or the sign of their martyrdom. St. James the Less has a fuller's bat; St. Bartholomew, a butcher's knife; St. Peter, a key, often a fish; St. Jude, a cross, a club, or a carpenter's square; St. James the Greater, a pilgrim's staff and gourd, bottle or script, often a hat with the scallop shell; St. Philip, a long staff, often with a cross in the T, in some cases a double cross or a basket of fish; the Savior or Master, an orb or cross; St. John, a cup (the cup of sorrow) with a serpent crawling out of it; St. Thomas, a spear or a builder's rule; St. Matthew, a wallet and script, often an axe or spear; St. Matthias, an axe or halberd; St. Simon Zelotes, a long saw; St. Andrew, a saltire cross and script.

In the Byzantine Manual, the figures of James the Less, Jude, and Matthias are replaced by Paul, Luke, and Mark. Paul, usually distinguished by a sword, or even two swords, was always a favored figure because his festival was the first Apostle's day on the calendar.

Apostle spoons are frequently referred to in Elizabethan literature. Thomas Middleton in his play, *The Chaste Maid of Cheapside,* has one Gossip inquiring of another, "What has he given her? What is it, Gossip?" Whereupon the other replies: "A faire high standing cup, and two great Apostle spoons—one of them gilt." The famous collaborators, Beaumont and Fletcher, in one of their plays, *The Noble Gentleman,* slyly satirize the custom of giving spoons: "I'll be a Gossip Bewford; I have an odd Apostle spoon." Ben Jonson likewise pokes fun at the "spoon chasers" in *Bartholomew Fair:* "And all this for the hope of a couple of Apostle spoons, and a cup to eat caudle in."

An interesting old Apostle spoon of Dutch make is that of Saint Paul shown on Plate X. It is the workmanship of Johannes Lelij, of Leeuwarden, in Friesland, the northernmost province of the Netherlands. As the date-letter indicates the year 1687, one would like to think that this spoon was brought over to England in 1688 by one of the Dutch courtiers in the train of William and Mary after the overthrow of James II. All the marks are on the reverse side of bowl. The year-letter A with the serif

18

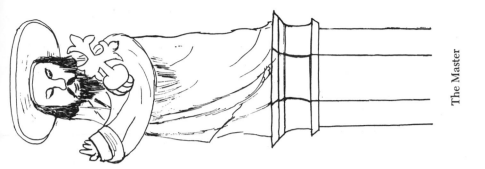

The Master

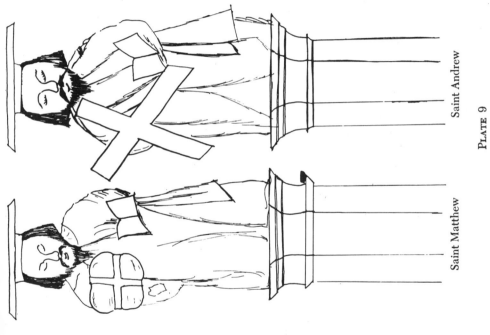

Saint Andrew

Saint Matthew

PLATE 9

APOSTLE SPOONS (from the Lambert set)

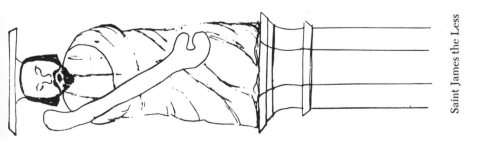

Saint James the Less

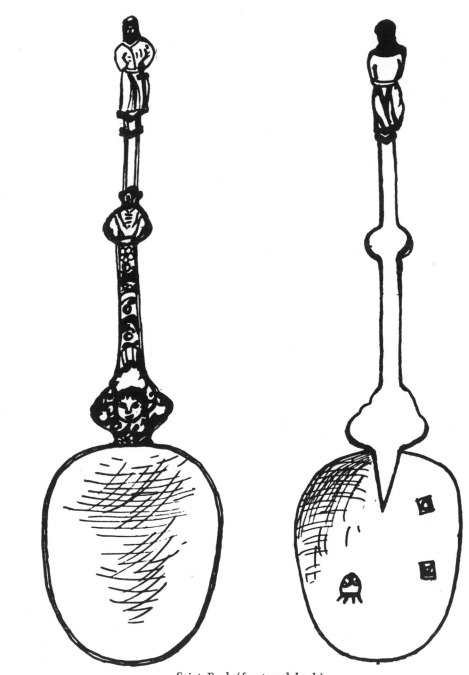

Saint Paul (front and back)

PLATE 10

DUTCH APOSTLE SPOON

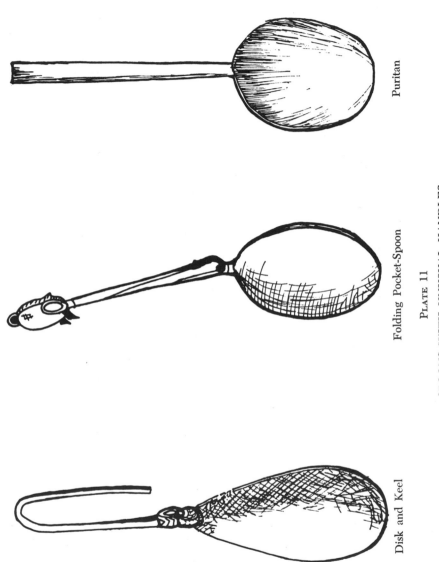

Disk and Keel   Folding Pocket-Spoon   Puritan

PLATE 11

SPOONS WITH UNUSUAL HANDLES

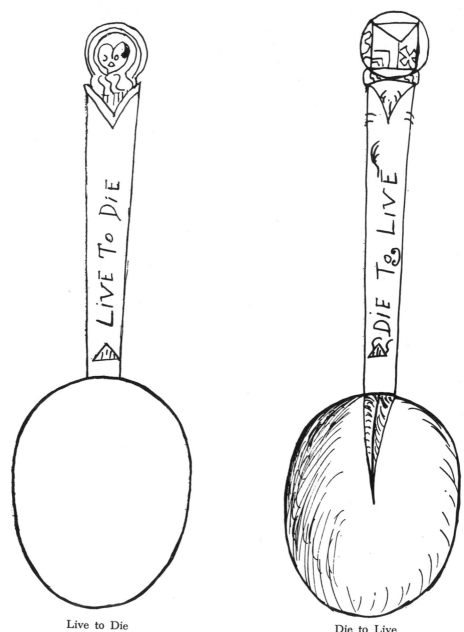

Live to Die   Die to Live

PLATE 12
YORKSHIRE FUNERAL SPOON (1670)

is across its top, while the containing box and even the lower part of the A are entirely worn away; the duty mark is stamped near the rat-tailed prolongation of the stem; the hallmark contains a lily or fleur-de-lis (after the maker's name, Lelij) and a Laubkranz (laurel wreath). The handle is unique in that it furnishes a combination of features: the figure of St. Paul with the characteristic sword in his left hand mounted on a quadrilateral capital and cornice placed at odds with the rectangular stem; the strange little figure of a squatting, pop-eyed beast resembling a monkey in the central plaque; and a cherub's head in the boss just above the bowl. Down the front of the handle runs a grooved channel of irregular ornamentation. The maker of this spoon, Johannes Lelij, and his son, Garbijnus van der Lelij (the son moved up a notch on the social scale by the additions to his name), worked industriously in Leeuwarden from 1680 to 1750, and pieces by them are highly prized by collectors of Dutch silver.

In the seventeenth century the custom of giving spoons to children led to the making of a special type, known as the christening spoon, which was quite prevalent during the early Stuart reigns. As with our American birth spoons, the bowls contained the record of a child's entrance into the world engraved with the specific data, for instance: "Margaret Austen born the 11 day of September 1610." Christening spoons drove the Apostle spoons out of fashion during the Commonwealth, when any saints or images were looked upon askance.

The middle of the seventeenth century witnessed the transformation of the spoon stem from the "six-squared Stele" to the flat handle, and the knop to all purposes disappeared. The flat, rectangular stem had been employed during the Middle Ages in the Near East; then during the Renaissance this style was taken up on the Continent, and even in Scotland as early as 1565, but in England the flat handle, as seen on the Puritan spoon, did not reach the peak of its popularity until the period between 1640 and 1675. The bowl likewise underwent a change in form, from the rounded fig to the somewhat lengthened or elliptical egg shape. Later Puritan spoons exhibit a limited amount of decoration in simple scroll work and foliage.

The Death's Head spoon, a forerunner of the Dutch-American monkey spoon, was a peculiar kind of souvenir that originated in Yorkshire, where at funerals it was the custom to present friends and mourners with such a keepsake to serve as reminders of the departed. These spoons were discarded or remelted by a younger generation that had no recollections of the persons commemorated. The sombre phrases LIVE TO DIE and DIE TO LIVE appear respectively on the front and back of the handle of the Yorkshire spoon, dated 1670-71, on Plate XII.

Some of the earliest Trifid spoons are known to have come from Dublin, Ireland, but they were made in many parts of the British Isles. The end of the stem handle is lobular and its form begins to assume a likeness to the caput so widely seen on our American souvenir spoons.

Two notches are cut, far up, on each side of the lobe, making two small ears below the disproportionately large, semicircular projection extending upward in the center. Sometimes this termination is known as the *pied de biche* or hind's foot. The bowl has a tongue-like plate or keel running into the handle, a precursor of the rat-tail spoon and a progression of the slipped-in-the-stalk. Many trifid spoons still exist, some cast as early as the reign of Charles II (1660-1685), others as late as Queen Anne's (1702-1714).

The Rat-Tail spoon, commonly associated with the House of Hanover, first made its appearance a few years previous to the accession of that family about 1705. The rat-tail is an extension of the rounded handle running evenly down the back of the egg-shaped bowl and tapering to a pointed end near the center of the bowl. The handle end is modified to form an upturned arch with a mid-rib while the trifid ears disappear altogether. Sometimes the rat-tail terminates in some sort of embellishment like a molded cockle-shell. The most frequent shape of the rat-tail, however, was an extended V, on each side of which were variegated scroll arabesques.

The double-drop on spoons was an outgrowth of the rat-tail principle. A shell, anthemion, or curl formed the second drop, while the stem became more circular in its general contours, except that a rib or channel often ran down the front side of the handle, which was evenly rounded in a concave curve at its end. It was undoubtedly of the rat-tail or double-drop spoons that Alexander Pope was thinking when he wrote, in *The Rape of the Lock*, about the delightful tea-drinking parties at Hampton Court Palace:

> For lo! the board with Cups and Spoons is crown'd;
> The Berries crackle and the Mill turns round.

The custom of placing spoons on the reverse side across the top of the cup when no more tea was desired may serve to explain the reason for the rat-tail or double-drop ornamentation. It is erroneous to believe that these features were added merely to strengthen the junction of bowl and handle.

After 1760 the rounded handle-head was turned down instead of up, and the bowl-tip became narrower. The Onslow spoon, named for the famous tea drinker, Arthur Onslow, a member of the House of Commons during the reigns of George II and George III, enjoyed a wide vogue for more than thirty years after 1748. The end of this spoon was not only turned down but also folded back, as Jackson explains, "in the manner of an Ionic volute, the upper side being moulded with a series of deeply-cut, curved members which converge to a point about halfway down the stem." A variation of the Onslow spoon was the Scroll Head, more curled than usual to simulate a scroll.

In the latter half of the eighteenth century the ornamentation on spoons became more florid. It was the age of Wedgwood and Spode, Chelsea and Worcester, in china; of Waterford, Bristol, and Nailsea in glass; and

24

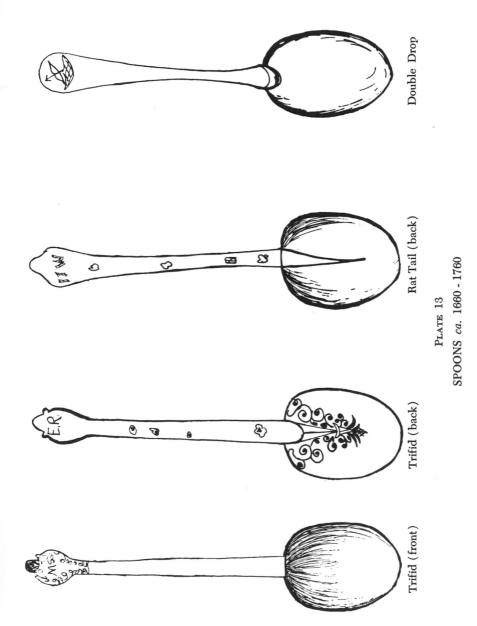

Double Drop

Rat Tail (back)

Trifid (back)

Trifid (front)

PLATE 13

SPOONS *ca.* 1660 - 1760

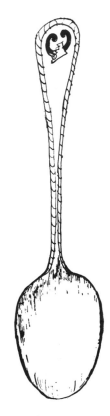

Onslow   Feather Edged   Fiddle Pattern

PLATE 14
SPOONS *ca.* 1748 - 1820

Persian   Spanish

PLATE 15

ORNAMENTAL SPOONS

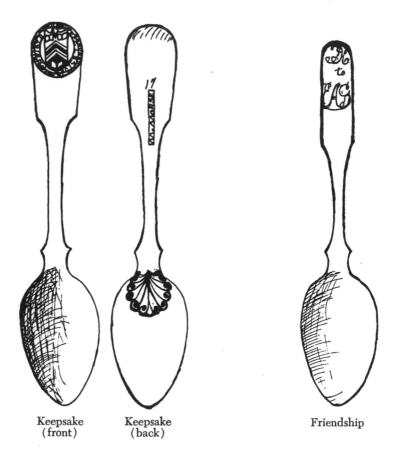

Keepsake   Keepsake   Friendship
(front)   (back)

PLATE 16

AMERICAN SPOONS *ca.* 1815 - 1830

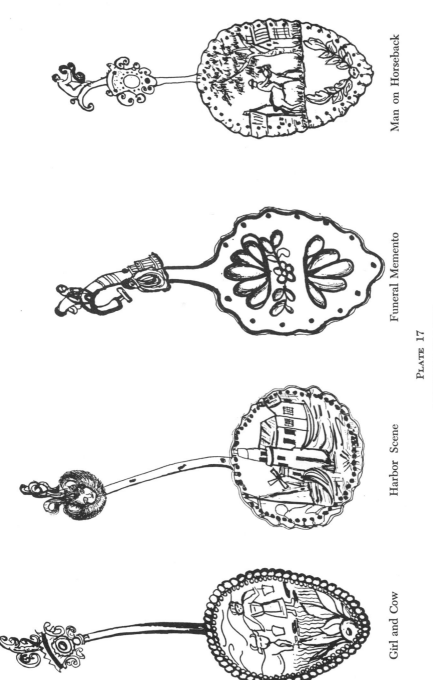

Girl and Cow   Harbor Scene   Funeral Memento   Man on Horseback

PLATE 17

MONKEY SPOONS

of Hepplewhite, Chippendale, Sheraton, and Adam in furniture—an age of superior production in all the arts. The prevailing styles in every branch of artistic production felt the influence of rococo, a term taken from the French word *rocaille,* meaning "a rockery" or a "richly bedight grotto." Rococo in silver was characterized preeminently by shell and scroll motifs; hence there is much evidence of shell and scroll work on spoons, the two appearing either together or singly on bowls, handles, and handle drops. Another manifestation of the rococo was the feather edge for a border decoration on all pieces of silverware. On spoons the feather edge assumed the shape of short lines weaving obliquely round the obverse margin of the handle—a style known as the gadroon. In the caput appeared family coats-of-arms embossed inside a rococo or cartouche ornamentation accompanied by the incuse initials of the master or mistress of the household. The feather edge has continued down to our own time so persistently that it may be called by natural right of preference the *Old English* pattern.

About 1810 there first appeared one of the most popular of our modern styles, the fiddle back, really the revival of a style that came to light in the excavation of old Roman villas. Sometimes the fiddle pattern was ornamented by a threaded or a thread-and-shell edge, but more often the handle margins were devoid of ornamentation.

Teaspoons did not come into being until after the introduction of tea in 1660. The size of teacups abbreviated the length of spoons to the point where both utensils conformed to equitable proportions. Caddy spoons, cream ladles, and salt and mustard spoons were developed toward the end of the seventeenth and the beginning of the eighteenth centuries to fit the need of well-stocked condiment and table sets. Snuff spoons were a natural development growing out of the introduction of snuff in the eighteenth century.

Two spoons among our illustrations, the Persian and Spanish, demand some explanation of the exquisite creations of those two highly artistic peoples. The Persians, or Iranians, are inherently poetic, with a natural love of beauty, decoration, lucidity, and poise, and an ingrained dislike of the clumsy, ugly, and banal. "We have to acknowledge," says Arthur Upham Pope, "that in the decorative arts it was Persia which must be credited with the highest achievements." The Persians have excelled in the molding of jugs, amphorae, and ewers, and in the weaving of carpets, rugs, and linens. The great value placed on their wares attests their skill in making pottery, bronzes, and woven goods, which are "not merely a delight to the eye or an entertainment to the mind" but which reveal to the initiate a far deeper significance in the symbolistic nature of their motifs. The spoon illustrated dates from the late sixteenth century, when the Safavid dynasty (1501-1734) was at the apogee of its power and glory. During the long reigns of three shahs, Ismael (1501-24), Tahmasp (1524-1576), and Abbas I (1576-1627), it is said that artists were placed on a par with the highest members of the nobility and the most powerful men of state. Oppressive rulers have come and gone, but they have not deterred the Persian people from making objects of superb craftsmanship, while maintaining visibly their refined decorum and unconquerable love of the beautiful in art.

The most striking characteristic of Spanish art is its uniqueness. More than any other Europeans, the Spanish people have evolved styles strictly their own, original and popular, with elaborate, decorative devices that are a blend of both Oriental and Occidental features, displayed in their architecture, iron grill work, furniture, wood carving (chests), embossed leather goods, ceramics, fans, laces, jewels, and costumes. The ornateness, intricacy, and delicacy of their work in filigree, so marked in all their artistic production, are manifest qualities in the spoon we have illustrated. It was carved from ivory, and has been ascribed to Francisco Saltillo (1707-1783), a Castilian from Salamanca, and an artist greatly moved by the Moorish traits and influences still lingering in Andalusia. The bird and flower motifs of this spoon are characteristic of Saltillo's style, displayed also in his carvings of rosaries, earrings, and necklaces.

Silversmithing in America had its beginnings in New England, where Boston, the most flourishing social and commercial center, led in the making of silver articles. New Amsterdam and Philadelphia also fashioned a considerable amount of plate for local consumption, the products of the former showing distinct Dutch influences. In the Southern colonies more silver was made locally than was formerly believed. One of the artisans arriving with Captain John Smith in 1607 at Jamestown was a silversmith. The rich planters of Virginia, Maryland, and South Carolina surprised travellers with the copious array of fine plate on their tables. Baltimore supplied some of this silver, but more of it was imported from England. Practically all this Colonial ware went into the melting pot during the Civil War.

The first American silversmith on record to wax fat on the trade was John Hull, who made so many pinetree shillings for the government of Massachusetts, receiving one out of every twenty for his just share, that he was able to give his son-in-law as a dowry his plump daughter's weight in silver shillings. There were soon many expert craftsmen making good things out of silver in the small towns of Massachusetts, Rhode Island, Connecticut, and New York. Of course, the most famous maker of fine teapots, tankards, and spoons was Paul Revere, familiarly known to every school child for his rousing midnight gallop.

The first silver goods made by the Colonial craftsmen were spoons, the patterns for which were found in the designs on articles imported from the Old Country, meaning in this case England or Holland. Consequently we find in America, from the latter part of the seventeenth century down into the nineteenth, the same trends of fashion as in Europe, such as the Puritan, the rat-tail, the double-drop, the scroll-headed, the feather-edged, the coffin-shaped, and the fiddle-back.

31

Until the Revolutionary War there were only three sizes of spoons made in America, the most artistic being the teaspoon, which approximated in size our postprandial coffee spoons of today. Another spoon, used for porridge, was often the only utensil placed on the table for breakfast in many homes. The tablespoon, somewhat shorter than in its modern form, had to do double duty—in the preparation as well as in the mastication of a meal. The teaspoon was always more ornamental and more expensively made than the other two types of spoons because it was seen and admired by tea-drinking guests.

By the time of the Revolution there were certain formalities that had already become unwritten laws of the social code to be honored at tea-time in the strictest observance of the letter. Those ignorant of the code suffered accordingly. Prince de Broglie, visiting at the home of Robert Morris in Philadelphia, had to drink twelve cups of tea poured by Mrs. Morris before he learned that he should place his spoon across the top of his cup to imply that he wished no more. To have openly blurted out that he would have no more of the delectable tea would most assuredly have offended the lady's sensibilities. This ceremony of the spoon impressed the Frenchman with the fact that Versailles had nothing on the American colonies when it came to the finer graces of civilization.

It is a moot question just when the first American souvenir spoons were made. Should the Apostle and monkey spoons be considered as such, or merely forerunners? Were not the early spoons bearing college crests incuse on handle-heads put out and kept as souvenirs by the alumni?

Americans have always been lovers and collectors of spoons—even in Colonial times. What Emerson remarked about the Englishman's love of old plate applies equally well to many an American of this day and of times past: "The Englishman is fond of his plate, and though he has no gathering of portraits of his ancestors, he has their porringers and punch bowls. Incredible amounts are found in good homes, and even the poorest have some spoons and sauce pans saved out of better times."

Spoons are priced at such moderate values that they are within the reach of one and all, yet nothing can be more highly prized than a collection of old spoons. In 1816 an impoverished young Boston minister, John Pierpont, grandfather of John Pierpont Morgan the financier, had to pawn a collection of valuable heirloom spoons to defray the expenses of printing his *Airs of Palestine*. Whether the story of the hocking of the Reverend Pierpont's spoons reached the ears of the general public or not, the *Airs* did, paying off to the tune of three editions. The redeeming of the spoons must have brought an upsurging demand for that article, because within the next few years Moses Morse of Boston, Jabez Gorham of Providence, Samuel Kirk of Baltimore, and others were making "keepsake spoons" in considerable numbers for graduates of Eastern and Southern colleges. For more than a generation, ever since the end of the Revolution, silversmiths had occasionally turned their hand to the making of this sort of spoon.

Johnny Fitch, the washed-up inventor of the steamboat, spent his last, unsobered days in Bardstown, Kentucky, in fashioning these spoons and other "trifling keepsakes" for his little friend, Eliza Rowan. There was no great attempt at ornamentation on most early keepsake spoons except for a simple flower, leaf, grape, scroll, or shell, sometimes nothing at all. On the college spoons, however, insignia and seals were placed incuse on handle heads. A number of these keepsake spoons still survive. The one illustrated is a Harvard seal spoon of conventional fiddle-back contours. It has the turned-up handle-end and the long, ovoidal-pointed bowl-tip. Made by Moses Morse in 1817, this spoon exhibits so much hard usage that the shell decor on the reverse of bowl just below the handle-drop has all but worn away.

Similar to the keepsake spoon is the friendship spoon, which usually exhibited the initials of both the giver and the recipient of the gift at the top of the handle. The one illustrated here was devised in the old handmade style in 1815 by Samuel Kirk (1793-1872), who founded the House which is considered today to be that of "America's Oldest Silversmiths." Kirk, of Pennsylvania Quaker descent, started his business career in 1815 in Baltimore, where the concern has always remained—in the hands of the same family. Working in nothing but solid silver, the firm of Samuel Kirk and Son has continued to turn out some notable patterns, of which the *Repoussé* is most highly prized by lovers of old and fine silver. In addition, the House of Kirk is represented by many exquisite museum pieces, such as the two goblets presented by Lafayette in 1824 to his Baltimore host, David Williamson; the silver spade employed by Marshal Foch in breaking ground for the War Memorial Building in 1921; and the dinner service made in 1906 and presented to the first cruiser *Maryland* by the citizens of the state. The friendship spoon in our illustration contains on the reverse of handle not only the mark of Kirk and Smith, as the firm was known from 1815 to 1820, but also the assay stamp of the city of Baltimore and the head of the Goddess of Liberty, the latter frequently seen on pieces of this period.

One of the strangest spoon-designs on record is the monkey spoon, which originated in Holland but found its way to the banks of the Hudson during the seventeenth and eighteenth centuries. The affluent Dutch patrons of early New York bestowed these spoons generously upon friends and relatives at funerals, betrothals, weddings, and christenings. Mary P. Ferris, the first person to delve into the history of this curious spoon, offers this explanation of its purpose and *modus operandi:* "Among the Dutch drinking is called 'zuiging de monkey' (sucking the monkey), and a drunkard is known as a 'sucker of the monkey' . . . When a worthy burgher was ready for his morning meal, he went to the old sideboard and took his morning tonic of Santa Cruz rum, following it with a pinch of salt. This morning dram was to serve only as an appetizer, and must be a small one, hence the use of the *monkey lepel* (monkey spoon) or liquor spoon with its shallow bowl. And as the flowing bowl played a prominent part in the weddings and funerals of our worthy Dutch ancestors, it will be readily seen that a monkey spoon was a most significant token of esteem, and hence an appropriate gift."

Genevieve Wimsatt in a recent and very illuminating article in *The American Home* on this particular spoon, displays an assortment of the varied types that she has collected. Most of them are of the curvicaudate variety, which makes it possible for them to be suspended from the rim of a punch bowl. Others, purposed simply for gifts or tokens of friendship, have straight or more often flexed handles without the caudate appendage. The knop in many instances exhibits, not a monkey, but a faun, crouching boy, skeleton, hippogryph, squirrel, lion, bird, or fowl. Most of them also have a boss, directly beneath the knop, exhibiting a cherub, heart, rosette, or a mourner standing by a cinerary urn.

There are no revealing clues, such as hallmarks, initials, or date-letters, to indicate the provenance of these spoons. We can, however, ascertain a general chronological period for their dissemination by the following account of the funeral of Philip Livingston, a descendant of Anneke Janse, in 1749: "As usual, there was the spiced wine, and each of the eight pallbearers was given a pair of gloves, a monkey spoon and mourning ring."

An elaborate mode of decoration is evident in nearly all the bowls which are either round or oval in shape. A betrothal spoon pictures two lovers plighting their vows by moonlight; a gift to an old friend displays a windmill, lighthouse, and homes near a landing pier, perhaps nostalgic reminders of childhood scenes; a friendship token to a young girl depicts a dairymaid ready to milk a cow, with tulip foliations in the foreground; a funeral favor represents St. Michael, assessor of souls, carrying a sword and scales.

Mrs. Ferris describes the most typical scene designed for tokens at a funeral: "The monkey spoon has a circular, very shallow bowl on which was represented a man on horseback, going from house to house to deliver invitations (to the funeral), with the church just behind him. This was hammered out in the bowl of the spoon, the silver of which was very thin. The handle of the spoon was of heavier weight, and on the end of the spoon was a monkey, half crouching, half charging, drinking from a goblet in solids." Surprisingly indeed, this very representative specimen turned up here in Kentucky when, after a discussion on spoons, an old lady went home and searched in the attic past midnight and into the wee hours of the morning, to disinter this very spoon from among her long-discarded belongings. It had passed through many hands on its migration from Holland via old New York, till it came into her possession— a curious substantiation of the fact that a spoon can have as many reincarnations as the proverbial nine-lived cat.

The great vogue of the modern souvenir spoon had its beginnings in the late eighties of the last century. The Leipzig Fair and the Paris

Exposition, in the same year, 1889, featured displays of this new mode of gifts in silverware. By 1891 sufficient interest was aroused for George P. James to bring out a small book on souvenir spoons. Many of the spoons listed in this book appeared in that volume. By 1893, when the Columbian Exposition was held in Chicago, the collecting of spoons had become not merely a hobby but a consuming rage. Throughout the Gay Nineties the avid interest continued, and well into the twentieth century. Everywhere that people went, on tours, excursions, vacations, or visits, by train or by boat, they brought back an assortment of spoons as memento-gifts for the folks and friends who had stayed at home. The fascination of spoon collecting at its apogee may best be seen in this observation by Helen Archibald Clarke in *Longfellow's Country*, written in 1909: "The only witchcraft exercised by Salem now is upon the pocketbook of the summer person who has a fad for souvenir spoons and a taste for the delectable confection made there and known as the Salem Gibraltar—a delicious compound of softness and peppermint. Coins large and small fly from their hiding places when coming into proximity with these luxuries."

Gradually, however, spoon interest waned about the time that the newfangled contraption, the horseless carriage, began to snort up and down our highways. Perhaps a reason for the subsidence of the fancy can be deduced from the changing modes of transportation employed by people in their travels. In the old days, not much space was left over for gifts in a tightly-packed, cumbersome grip that had to be "toted" considerable distances by hand from place to place. A half-dozen spoons could be packed away safely without danger of breakage or too much elbowing aside of necessary *articles de toilette*. Whether the automobile allowed travellers more room for the stowage of larger presents, or whether people were just tiring of the spoon-collecting fad, it is certain that the hobby had seen its better days by the outbreak of the First World War. A listing of *Trademarks of the Jewelry and Kindred Trades* in 1922 indicates that all those companies which had once existed prosperously by making only souvenir spoons had by then gone out of business. The larger companies dropped the production of souvenir spoons and continued with other lines of silverware. In the years from 1925 to 1930 a few companies attempted to revive the hobby by issuing sets imprinted with the busts of movie actors and actresses or specimens to attract the speculating tourists in the Florida boom-towns of that period. But the depression very effectively squelched that revival. Since then, only such events as the Century of Progress Exposition in Chicago, the World's Fair in New York, and the coronation of King George VI and Queen Elizabeth have impelled the silver tradesmen to turn out commemorative spoons. At present only the Robbins Company is actively engaged in this special branch of the industry.

An examination of trademarks leads one to the conclusion that more than fifty firms, at one time or another, made souvenir spoons. A brief mention of the more outstanding of these will be of interest to collectors. Answers to inquiries often revealed the fact that some of the companies had lost all record or knowledge of their former spoon-making activities. One company assured me that they had made only one souvenir spoon, while I had already seen more than twenty of them pictured on pages of their old catalogues.

The Watson Company, of Attleboro, Massachusetts, began operations as the Watson-Newell Company in 1879, and did the bulk of their business from the period of 1890 through 1914-15. The naval code flag or pennant, used from 1879 to 1905, is the most frequently seen trademark in any collection of souvenir spoons, and it appeared on spoons for every state in three or four sizes and also for every important city in the United States. In addition, the Watson Company put out many spoons featuring designs of fruits, flowers, birth months and signs of the Zodiac.

The Gorham Company, of Providence, Rhode Island, also made hundreds of souvenir spoons at one time. The founder of this firm, Jabez Gorham, was already, as a youth of fifteen in 1792, molding spoons in a blacksmith's forge. By 1831 Gorham, with two assistants, was making some dozen spoons a day, and his prosperity caused him to place a sign, "Silver Spoons and Jewelry" above the door of his modest shop. In 1842 John Gorham, son of Jabez, became head of the business. He had studied British methods of artistic production in Birmingham under the guidance of some of the most skillful English silversmiths. Under Gorham's third president, Edward Holbrook, the company witnessed a rapid growth after a complete overhauling and modernizing of the shop machinery. The Gorham sterling trademark is the lion, anchor, and G, the lion being the English hallmark for sterling, the anchor the sign of the State of Rhode Island and Providence Plantation, and the G indicating the company's name.

In *The Whitesmiths of Taunton,* by George Sweet Gibb, a complete and interesting account of Reed & Barton is presented from its humble beginnings in 1824, when two enterprising mechanics, Isaac Babbitt and William Crossman, having just finished their apprenticeship, established a partnership, out of which there eventually emerged the organization of Reed & Barton. Although the company changed hands and titles several times in earlier years, it has always remained true to the essential aims and purposes of its original founders. We have space here to refer to only one item in Mr. Gibb's book, since it concerns matter quite pertinent to our discussion, and I herewith quote: "In the late 1890's the line of sterling flatware was augmented to meet a great demand for souvenir spoons of all descriptions, and Mr. David Howe invented a process of etching upon metal which enabled both souvenir spoons and a new patented type of baby spoon to be inscribed with appropriate scenes and verses."

The Paye and Baker Manufacturing Company, of North Attleboro, Massachusetts, started business about 1900, and the first goods they made were souvenir spoons. By 1905 the firm had prospered to the extent that it was able to branch out in making all kinds of souvenir novelties that included (all of silver or in part) watch fobs and charms; hat, lace and belt pins; bookmarks, tie clasps, link buttons, thimbles, and ash trays; class and flag pins; manicure and desk novelties; card and cigarette cases; baby sets; food pushers; and every kind of souvenir spoon. On the back covers of their early catalogues appeared this statement in large letters: "We make a specialty of very unique souvenir spoons of special handle and bowl design, to be controlled by you exclusively." By 1912 this statement disappeared from the back covers; in a few more years the souvenir spoons themselves disappeared from between the covers. All their spoon dies were given for war material during the scrap drive. The trademark of this firm consists of three hearts enclosing P & B.

The Alvin Silver Company, now the Alvin Corporation, was organized in the late eighties of the last century at Irvington, New Jersey, but after a few years changed its general offices to Providence, Rhode Island. "In regard to our production of souvenir spoons," states a member of the firm, "a period of achievement was reached by the Alvin Silver Company at the time of the World's Columbian Exposition, held in Chicago, wherein the artistry, and skilled craftsmanship of the Alvin workmen were called upon to manufacture the official souvenir spoon. This spoon was made for the Exposition as its official memento for all visitors." The trademark of the Alvin Corporation is the letter A enclosed by an eagle on the left side and a quarter moon and cross on the right.

The Williams Bros. Silver Company, of Glastonbury, Connecticut, has been in business since 1880. It probably made more souvenir spoons of the nation's capitol over the years—mostly of the small coffee type—than any other firm. One of its especially fine spoons was put out for the Connecticut Tercentenary celebration in the early thirties. During the first part of the century this company supplied a souvenir spoon—made by the thousands—for Fairy Soap. The trademark of the Williams Bros. is a lion to the right and left of W, although several other marks of companies that have merged with this firm are occasionally encountered.

Shreve and Company was organized by George C. Shreve in San Francisco in 1852 during the height of the Gold Rush excitement. It is thus one of the oldest firms in the state of California, and also the only large silver company not located in the East. The Shreve spoons, not too numerous, deal exclusively with California scenes, and usually terminate in a bear finial. Shreve's trademark is composed of three figures: in the center is a quatrefoil or four-lobed figure inside of which is a pendent bell; on either side is a smaller, pentagonal figure containing an S.

The Robbins Company was started by Charles M. Robbins in 1892 as a jewelry business manufacturing school and college articles such as seals, pennants, badges, buttons, brooches, bar pins, and fobs. Mr. Robbins specialized from the very beginning in "French glass enamel—this being the application of vitreous enamel on precious or base-metal for decorative purposes." From the early years of the nineteenth century the Robbins Company has listed spoons among its souvenir items. In 1911 it started making seal spoons for all the states, the larger cities, and for many schools and colleges throughout the country. These designs included mountains, parks, lakes, and buildings near the various vacation spots and the famous tourist resorts; names and figures identified with various places; and college and fraternity crests. Another type of spoon shows various state flowers or special products including fruits and vegetables. In addition to its baby spoon, the company has made a special child's spoon with birth record in the bowl, which has spaces for the name, date, place, time of birth, and weight. An old catalog illustrates some special spoons made for Christmas and Thanksgiving and also those which were known as "Venetian spoons." These latter were very fine spoons on which pictures were reproduced in vivid enameled coloring.

Miss Catherine S. Thayer, speaking for the Robbins Company, explains the manufacturing process for their spoons thus: "In making spoons with a special design on the handle our hub cutter cuts the design in steel on a hub which is then forced into another piece of steel to produce the die for stamping in the metal. After this die is cleaned up and hardened, it is placed in a stamp and the spoon handle design is struck from it."

The Robbins Company resumed the making of souvenir spoons in 1946 after discontinuing their manufacture for many years. In the earliest catalogs of this firm the trademark was simply CMR in a horizontal lozenge. The second trademark combines the original design with two additional sections, the second of which is a shield showing the Massachusetts state crest, and the third is a round-cornered rectangle showing a robin as symbolic of the company's name. The present modernistic trademark carries the letter R in a stylized wing design.

A few of the companies which once made numerous souvenir spoons, but have long been out of business are: Shepard Mfg. Co.; George W. Shiebler & Co.; Silberstein, Hecht & Co.; Edward Todd & Co.; Howard Sterling Co.; Mount Vernon Co., Fessenden & Co.; Sterling Silver Mfg. Co.; Campbell-Metcalf Silver Co.; Codding & Heilbom Co.; and others. Only a very few trademarks have remained unidentified, and in some cases there have been no trademarks present to assist in their identification. Who the makers of these spoons were, must necessarily remain a mystery for the time being.

In concluding this introductory matter, the author can do no better than quote from an anonymous editorial on spoons in HOBBIES for September, 1947: "For the lover of silver, spoons are certainly of importance, there being few things that surpass them for historical and artistic interest."

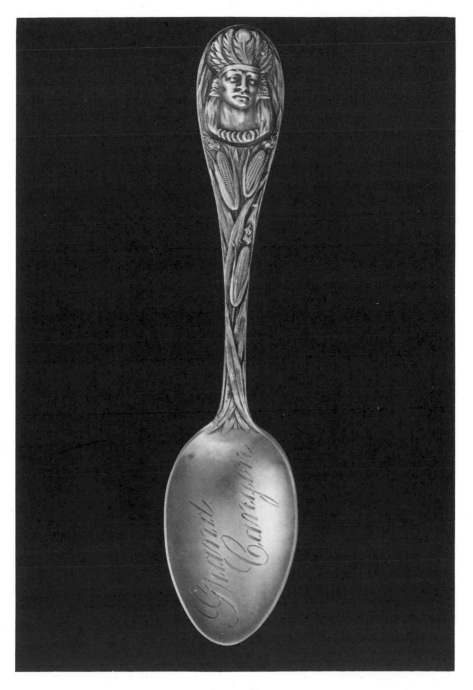

PLATE 18
1. GRAND CANYON

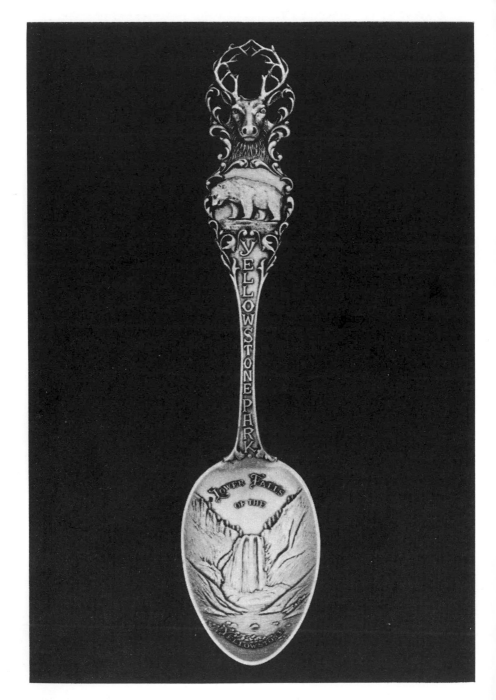

PLATE 19

2. YELLOWSTONE ELK-AND-BEAR

AMERICAN HISTORICAL SPOONS

No. 1 GRAND CANYON

How explain that magnetic spell which the Grand Canyon casts over its onlookers? Perhaps you can't do so in words. All you can do is to look in silence, and sense that here is something more like its prehistoric self than any other spot you have ever seen, and the restless, dominating white man, who is always wanting change, has not been able to master or mar it so easily as he has other less primordial and less enduring earth-surfaces.

Who first gazed upon those colored heights and depths, and felt their indescribable fascination? All we know is, that cliff dwellers dug into the walls and lived there for protection centuries ago. Shards of pottery, fire pits, and even grains of maize and pods of beans remain to attest their presence.

The three Indian tribes, the Navaho, Hopi, and Havasupai, now living in this region, are peaceful farmers, sheepherders, weavers, and potters. They have not warred on the palefaces who encroach on their boundaries, perhaps feeling there is plenty of room for all. They love this great colorful land and seem willing to welcome every one who comes and wants a share of its wild beauty.

White colonizers were slow in coming to live in this region. It was magnificent, but it was too remote, too inexplicable, too unlike anything known to them in their homelands.

In 1539 a Spanish friar, Marcos de Niza, back from an exploring expedition into the northern part of Arizona, created a flurry of get-rich-quick anticipations when he spoke of fabulous cities of gold which the Indians had told him existed there, but which he had not been allowed to see on his trip. At once a party of three hundred men led by Francisco de Coronado was dispatched to verify the report and possibly to bring back some of the precious metal. The expedition was a failure. About all the Spaniards encountered were villages of Hopi Indians eking out a miserable living by dint of hard scratching and primitive implements on parched, disfavored plateaus. A small scouting party under Luis Cardenas stumbled upon the brink of a "Grand Canyon" and attempted to cross it but had to give it up as an utter impossibility.

More than two centuries later, in 1776, two more Spanish friars followed the course of the Colorado River till they found a convenient fording place in Glen Canyon. Still the Spaniards made no efforts to establish a permanent settlement.

American trappers in the 1820's first began to pace the rims of the Canyon and to niche their names on its rocky walls. An occasional horse thief slipped into the shadows of the gigantic chasm for a refuge. Now and then trappers and fur traders would scramble up and down its bluffs, but only a few daring sheepherders thought of gaining a livelihood by settling in such a dry, barren region.

In 1886, when Benjamin Harrison was a senator from Indiana, he suggested the idea of making this region a national park. Not until 1908 did the dream become a reality when President Theodore Roosevelt signed the bill creating the park.

Superlatives cannot describe Grand Canyon. Its sublimity beggars words. Puny man can only stand and gawk in wonder. His eye can project itself over the panorama with one mighty sweep, but his brain can scarcely comprehend that the pages of geologic history for two thousand million years lie open before him. All the forces of erosion, the wind and the rain, the heat and the cold, the sunshine and the onsweeping water have been working here for ages, disintegrating, dissolving, and carrying off ton after ton of loosened rocks and sediments, leaving this upthrust labyrinth, two hundred and eighty miles in length and averaging twelve miles in width, showing shapes that resemble towers and turrets, cathedral domes and spires, flying buttresses and vaulted columns, truncated pyramids of terraces; shapes that are wrinkled, writhing, lacy, graceful, grotesque, fluted, flattened, peaked, measureless, motionless, massive. Prismatic colors rise, flash, fade, and die in an endless interweaving of rich, mysterious changes. The sight makes the thought of time senseless, of weeping and laughter a folly, of man irrelevant.

An artist who would attempt to portray any feature of Grand Canyon on a spoon would have to be something more than adroit. At most he could show only an infinitesimal segment. Therefore the maker of this spoon has discreetly refrained from any pictorial visualizations. In the bowl is engraved "Grand Canyon." An Indian's face rises high in a cameo-relief on the caput of the handle, a face at once impassive and impressive, symbolic in its rugged grandeur of the Grand Canyon itself, the grandest of all earth's natural wonders.

Made by Watson and Newell. Length, 5¾ inches.

No. 2   YELLOWSTONE ELK-AND-BEAR
No. 5   YELLOWSTONE BEAR RAMPANT
No. 135 OLD FAITHFUL

One of Nature's greatest wonderlands, easily accessible in the northwestern part of our country, remained comparatively unknown till late in our exploratory history. The first white man to see it was John Colter, who turned aside on his return from the Lewis and Clark Expedition in 1806 to roam through this picturesque region that promised good hunting, fishing, and trapping. Those who heard his Dantesque descriptions thought he had created an Inferno out of his own imagination, and listened incredulously.

In 1830 another explorer, Jim Bridger, brought back tall tales of the region. He had shot several times at an elk without fazing it before he realized he had been looking at the animal twenty-five miles distant through a glacier that served as a mammoth telescope. His tales were marked down as whoppers also.

The nation as a whole knew nothing about Yellowstone until two reporters in 1870, after visiting the scenic region, wrote an account of their travels for a Chicago paper. The public's attention was aroused, and in 1872 Congress passed a bill setting aside, before its natural beauty was marred, most of the virgin tract now contained in the Park. Additions have subsequently been made to include adjacent scenic features.

The tourist is amazed at the fantastic orgy of wonders in Yellowstone Park. Its wild, rugged beauty appalls, dazzles, and delights at the same time. The fauna and flora are rich beyond comparison. All the animals of the old Wild West live unmolested in these haunts: the bear, buffalo, moose, elk, deer, antelope, mountain sheep, and beaver. Birds of more than two hundred species, like the wild geese and ducks, the eagles and hawks, the pelicans and swans, may build their nests and eeries in the mountain crags or by the rippling lakesides of the valleys.

The flora of the region cannot be equaled for variety anywhere else in the northern hemisphere. Some of the most abundant of the seven hundred and fifty species of flowers found here are the Indian paintbrush (the Wyoming state flower), bitterroot, shooting star, aster, umbrella plant, phlox, lungwort, columbine, larkspur, monkshood, wild rose, primrose, violets, water lilies, wild geranium, magenta fireweed, and many others. A gorgeous phantasmagoria of shifting colors sweeping downward from the heights greets the eye of the spectator throughout the summer and fall.

The trees are mostly evergreens but include a few deciduous types. Evidences of warmer climate in prehistoric ages are seen in the petrified remains of oak, sycamore, rhododendron, and redwood.

But what attracts the tourist's attention most is the infinite variety of subterranean waters emerging to the surface in every conceivable guise: in shooting geysers; in muddy paint pots; in steaming fumaroles; in gurgling, growling gas vents; in placid springs and lakes and pools; in churning springs, frothing cascades, and turbulent falls. Merely to mention the most notable of these kinetic wonders presents a stupefying roll call of names. Of the geysers, the chief ones are the Vixen, Monarch, Rainbow, Giant, Giantess, Rocket, Artemisia, Steamboat, Beryl, Old Faithful, Castle, Riverside, Jewel, Whirligig, and Valentine; of the springs: Devil's Thumb, Mammoth, Hot, Emerald, Grand Prismatic, and Dragon's Mouth.

The mountains have an interesting number of peaks, cliffs, and lookouts. Sometimes there are placid lakes of vivid coloring nestled in the mountains, such as Swan, Sylvan, Lily Pad, Nymph, and Sunset; or pools, like Porcelain and Morning Glory. Again, from the laps of the mountains rushes a violent volume of waters like the Firehole and Kepler Cascades, or the Rustic, Crystal, Tower, and Lower Yellowstone Falls.

The latter fall, almost twice as high as Niagara, is shown in the bowl of the Elk-and-Bear spoon. A silvery cascade of water, like a bridal veil, drops 308 feet from heavily-wooded banks that slope steeply on either side. The timber crowds right up to the water's edge. A cloud of white mist hovers over the lower portion of the fall. Massive boulders close in on the foaming tide that rushes out of the narrowed chasm. Rock-heads are perceptible here and there, like irregular stepping-stones across the basin. Annealed at the crest of the bowl is the embossed inscription, "Lower Falls of the Yellowstone," the last word being separated, however, and placed below on the patte.

On the handle, the name of the park advances lengthwise through a constricted shaft, which widens out considerably into the nave. Here we perceive a grizzly bear standing on a cliff and looking quite pugnacious with his mouth opened in a displeased manner. The caput, or rather here, a knop, is that of an imposing elk head. The tines of his antlers are interlaced to form an overarching latticework closed together like an arbor with a pathway leading out and down across the animal's forehead. Four foliated scrolls, two below convexed and two above concave, on either side, rise from a level with the shaggy neck and make openings likewise till they touch the antlers directly above the ears.

The animal is a magnificent specimen. The nostrils are dilated, and the eyes appear to be alerted to a sense of approaching danger.

The devisal of this spoon is on a par, in its majestic beauty, with the natural wonders it represents. Made by Watson and Newell. Length, 6 inches.

Quite in contrast to the Gothic ornateness of this earlier spoon stands the classic simplicity of the Bear Rampant, a modern production, still obtainable, of the Robbins Company.

The bowl of this spoon is plain. On the shaft, "Yellowstone Nat'l. Park" runs in small, raised lettering. The nave is by far the most striking feature on the spoon. Bruin stands erect, forepaws dropped, ears cocked in a quizzical manner, as pacific in appearance as a gentle old housedog—quite the opposite of the bear on the previous spoon. A cluster of three western pine cones and needles rises beneath him and three more cones, disconnected, enclose his head.

The Gardner Entrance, on the north side of the park, is contained in the caput. This arch, resembling in general outlines a Roman or French victory arch, was erected in 1903, and President Theodore Roosevelt was present at the dedication. Although not shown on the spoon, the inscription above the entrance reads: "For the Benefit and Enjoyment of the People." A pine cone is aloft the arch for an appropriate adornment of the crown.

44

The general contours of this spoon are purely Greek, its beauty being in its modesty. Length, 5½ inches.

The third spoon in this group pictures, in the pierced caput and nave of the handle, Old Faithful Inn and Old Faithful Geyser, the latter being perhaps the best known and the most talked-of attraction in the whole park. The name of the famous geyser is a misnomer, and does not live up to its reputation in the claim that you can set your watch by it, that it goes off "every hour on the hour." According to a recently-devised gauge the intervals between eruptions vary from thirty-eight to eighty-eight minutes, with an overall average of sixty-three minutes and fifteen seconds between acts. In one sense, then, it does live up to its name, in that if the tourist waits long enough Old Faithful will sooner or later "kick up its heels." A rumbling, bass sound of swelling volume precedes each performance. The jet column soon emerges out of the crater in a cloud of powdery whiteness and ascends in a pillar of transparent clearness to a height of well over a hundred feet. Struck by the sunlight, the purling waters limn the varied hues and shapes of vast, kaleidoscopic spectra. Gradually the plumy jet subsides till it disappears altogether below the seamy surface of its built-up crater. It is estimated that 250,000 gallons of water are blown skywards daily by this geyser.

Old Faithful Inn, charming, comfortable, and hospitable, is located at a favorable vantage-point for those wishing to see the geyser in repeated action. It is built in the ever-fascinating, Swiss-chalet style, of native timber and stone, and six stories high in its main unit. The roof is steep, and broached with many dormer windows. Five hundred tons of rock went into the construction of the fireplace and chimney in the entrance lobby. Old Faithful Lodge, Old Faithful Museum, an herbarium, an amphitheater, and the "biggest geyser-water swimming pool in the world" are also found in the vicinity of Old Faithful Geyser.

Made by the Robbins Company, this spoon is 5½ inches long.

No. 3   FORT DEARBORN MASSACRE
No. 4   CENTURY OF PROGRESS
No. 6   BLACK PARTRIDGE
No. 34   FORT DEARBORN LIGHTHOUSE
No. 101 CHICAGO BLOCKHOUSE

Chicago had its beginnings around Fort Dearborn. It is true that French traders and trappers had been in this region more than a century before, but they made no enduring establishment. It remained for Captain John Whistler, grandfather of the famous painter, to build the first stockade on the south-bank bend of the Chicago River in 1803. He named the new fort in honor of Henry Dearborn, Secretary of War in Jefferson's cabinet. This Captain Whistler had served first with the British under Burgoyne; then, after being taken prisoner and freed, he switched his allegiance to the American side.

On the north bank of the river were the cabins of the Burns, Ouilmette, and Kenzie families. About a dozen more cabins had been built in the forests near the fort by the time the War of 1812 came along to furnish the Indians with sanguine hopes that they could successfully uproot the pioneer outposts on the western frontier. The redskins were becoming restive and apparently awaiting their chances. Some of the outlying cabins had already been attacked and the settlers killed or captured.

Captain Heald, in charge of the fort, received a message from General Hull, commander of the forces in the Northwest, that Fort Dearborn should be abandoned and the little garrison withdrawn to Fort Wayne. There was much discussion within the fort as to the propriety for such a removal. The controversy raged for a week. Kenzie, a friend of the Indians, advised against it. A small party of men under Captain William Wells were marching from Fort Wayne to strengthen the forces at Fort Dearborn. When Wells arrived, the decision to evacuate had already been made, and the stores of ammunition which could not be taken along were destroyed. All the provisions on hand were distributed among the Indians, who were dissatisfied that the barrels of whiskey were not also included. The liquor had been poured into the stockade well.

The day before the departure, a friendly chief of the Potawatomi tribe, Black Partrdige, entered the fort and handed back to Captain Heald a medal highly prized by the Indian because it had been given to him by the Americans as a token of their long mutual friendship. Black Partridge stated solemnly that "linden birds had been singing in his ears." It was a dire omen that the redskins were on the warpath.

Nevertheless, on the morning of August 15, 1812, the little pioneer band set forth resolutely on their journey to the cadence of the Dead March from Handel's *Saul*, played by the fife and bugle corps. They followed the shore line south along Lake Michigan, and had proceeded about a mile and a half when the Indians, appearing suddenly from behind the sand dunes, attacked in full fury.

The small party of whites, hopelessly outnumbered, defended themselves with the grim determination to survive in this deadly hand-to-hand fighting, but were as flickering candle flames in the wind. Captain Wells hewed to left and right, and brought down a number of the enemy before he succumbed in the fierce onslaught. The savages cut his heart out and devoured it before the very eyes of his widow, believing the courage, now deadened in that heart, would revive phoenix-like in their own.

Mrs. Helm, a daughter of the Kenzies, had ridden away from the fort on horseback, and during the battle became separated from the main part of the caravan. Dragged from her horse, she defended herself with

46

PLATE 20

3. FORT DEARBORN MASSACRE   4. CENTURY OF PROGRESS
5. YELLOWSTONE BEAR RAMPANT   6. BLACK PARTRIDGE.

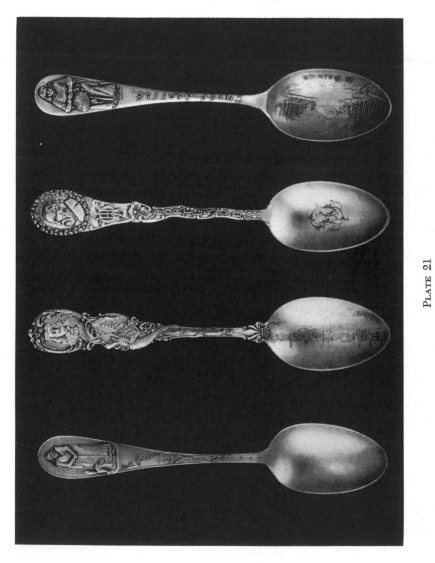

PLATE 21

7. MOLLY PITCHER   8. CADILLAC   9. LONGFELLOW   10. CHIEF SEATTLE

all the strength at her command against a warrior who was brandishing a tomahawk above her head. She had parried every blow until her assailant caught her by the hair and was making ready to scalp her alive. Just when she thought her last moment had come, another Indian came up, seized her, and bore her away quickly to the lakeside. There he carried her into the water till she was securely hidden from view behind a cluster of cattails and sedge, her head alone emerging from the water. Only then did she learn that her rescuer was a friend, Black Partridge, who meant her no harm. At various times in the past she had cooked venison steaks for this Indian, and he had thus repaid her kindness by saving her life at this critical moment.

The unequal contest did not last more than thirty minutes. Thirty-eight men, two women, and many of the children perished. More than half the party lay dead along the sand dunes. The rest surrendered, and were marched back to the fort so recently evacuated. They were held captives for several months till a ransom of one hundred dollars was paid for each of the survivors.

All the outlying cabins in the district were now attacked, and many settlers were killed. Black Partridge performed another deed of mercy by rescuing a Mrs. Lee, a farm wife, the sole survivor in a family of six.

The Fort Dearborn Massacre spoon, the official souvenir spoon of the World's Columbian Exposition in 1893, was cast by the Alvin Silver Company and controlled by C. D. Peacock. Seldom have so many figures been represented on a single spoon. The bowl contains a view of Chicago in 1832: two buildings in the foreground and one in the distance; two Indians in a canoe and one seated on a log along the shore. The handle in its entire length is an impressive panorama of the massacre at its bloody climax. About forty people can be distinguished, all in active combat except those lying dead or wounded on the ground. The covered wagons are surrounded by angry warriors, and the horses are rearing and plunging in the midst of the *melée*. Only around the abandoned fort, seen in the extreme right background, is everything peaceful. In the handle-drop is pictured the rescue of Mrs. Helm. Length of this spoon is 5¾ inches.

The Black Partridge spoon, put out by the Century Company for the Chicago World's Fair in 1933, portrays the friendly Indian chief in a side view on the caput. The Hall of Science appears in the nave, and along the shank are the words, "A Century of Progress." In the bowl is the Court of States building. The official guidebook of the fair says, concerning this structure: "The feeling in previous expositions has been that national participation could be shown only by a separate building for each state. This resulted in some useless expenditure, and participation on an elaborate scale by some, by a scanty representation by others, and by no participation at all in the case of many. Preferring to emphasize the solidarity of our Union, A Century of Progress determined that the States should be grouped under one roof, architecturally arranged with the

Federal building to indicate its support of, and united efforts with, the central government . . . It is a beautiful setting for reunion, overlooking the lagoon, with its broad and beautiful *Court of States,* opening by several entrances to the various state and territorial exhibits." This spoon has been used through the courtesy of its owner, Mrs. Annie Hahn, Louisville, Ky. Length, 6 inches.

Another spoon, designated as the Century of Progress, and included in this discussion because of its likeness of subject matter with the others in this group, was cast by the Watson Company for the Chicago Exposition in 1933. The bowl is plain, but the handle is implemented with many scenes. On the obverse side may be seen the Carillon Tower; a cornucopia in the nave, symbolical of Time's outpouring beneficence through the years, surmounted by the date "1933" above, and "A Century of Progress, Chicago," below the cornucopia; and the Hall of Science, symbolized by Laocoön struggling with the serpent appearing in a cameo inset. The shank is threaded by three lines along either edge. On the reverse side, "Fort Dearborn" and the date "1803" appear in the caput, and the Electrical Group of buildings along the shaft. Length of spoon, 5¾ inches.

The fourth spoon, the Fort Dearborn Lighthouse, varies the picture usually seen of the fort by a personal touch, in the bowl. Two Indians on sentry duty are standing at attention in front of the fort, one shouldering a gun, the other holding an arrow. "Chicago" in flourishing letters is the only ornamentation on the handle. A product of R. Wallace & Sons. Length, 5¾ inches.

The fifth spoon, the Chicago Blockhouse, a demi-tasse in size, was probably made also for the Chicago Exposition in 1933, because in general design it is modern and belongs to the period of the early thirties of this century.

In the gold-washed bowl are seen the watch tower and the fort, and behind both a brig with reefed sails lies at anchor close to shore. The lower half of the handle is plain, but the widening upper half contains, in swirled letters, the name of Chicago, surrounded and encroached upon from the borders by a tongues-of-flame ornamentation. Made by R. Wallace & Sons. Length, 4⅜ inches.

No. 7 MOLLY PITCHER

In the barn of one George Ludwig, a farmer near Mercer City, New Jersey, a fractious cow had just kicked over a pailful of milk. Molly, Farmer Ludwig's sturdy young daughter, her face turning as red as her hair, stood looking at the foamy white substance that spread in a widening circle through and underneath the straw litter of the cow-stall. The girl was exasperated. Such accidents had happened before. But this time she had almost finished milking, and wished to squirt the last—the richest and creamiest—drops of milk into the mouth of Toddy, her pet cat. It was then that saucy old Bossy had acted up.

As she stared at the total loss of the milk oozing into the ground, and pondered on the futility of her labors, Milkmaid Molly gave the placidly-munching animal a resounding slap on the rump, picked up her empty bucket, and walked defiantly toward the farmhouse. She was resolved to be a milkmaid no more.

Not long afterwards Molly was installed as a servant girl in the household of William Irvine, a doctor practicing in the village of Carlisle, Pennsylvania. In no time the girl had captured the fancy of the local barber, John Hays, a man of some means and almost twice the age of the fifteen-year-old Molly.

For six years she lived in the back of her husband's shop, through which she constantly passed to and fro, enlivening the place with her salty remarks. She had no children, but Toddy, the tomcat, remained with her as a faithful companion.

Come the Revolution, and Barber Hays enlisted at once in the forces being raised by Doctor, now General, Irvine. Hays's company was commanded by Captain Francis Proctor. Molly decided forthwith that she would not sit in the rear of a closed barbershop and twiddle her thumbs. Moreover, Toddy had just died of senility, so there was nothing to keep her at home.

For nearly three years Molly Hays stayed at the side of her husband, tramping, camping, cooking, sewing, mending, washing, and doing all sorts of odd jobs. Not the least of these odd jobs was a task that entailed more than a wonted display of bravado. During a skirmish Molly would go about fearlessly among the men, carrying an old broken-lipped earthenware ewer and a pewter cup, ready to pour a drink of cool spring water for any of the thirsty lads under Proctor's command. Grateful for these oblations, the men rechristened her Moll o' the Pitcher, a name subsequently changed to that by which history knows her.

On the twenty-eighth of June, 1778, at Monmouth, the Americans attacked the enemy who were retreating from Philadelphia to the sea across New Jersey. The day was extremely hot, and Molly moved back and forth among the troops with her pitcher. Sergeant Hays was manning an old muzzle-loading cannon. Just as he was getting ready to sight his charge, he was struck in the hip. His wife saw him fall, ran to his aid, and carried him back to a sheltered copse, where she helped a surgeon dress the wound. Then, when she returned to his cannon, she found some men already removing the piece from the field, as no one was available to fire it. Molly begged to take over, and during the rest of the battle she loaded or tamped the powder, set the charge on fire with the torch through the vent at the top, covered over, and blazed away. Occasionally she would return to her husband's side, and in transit fill her pitcher with water.

Word of her services came to the ears of General Washington, who declared that her heroism had so enflamed his men that a seeming defeat was turned into an outright victory.

After the battle Molly conveyed her husband back to their home in Carlisle, where he remained an invalid till his death shortly before the end of the war.

On the recommendation of Washington, the Continental Congress made Molly a sergeant and voted her a small pension for the rest of her life. She died fifty-four years after the battle, a very old woman. She lived alone during most of her widowhood, except for the companionship of her pet cats, all of whom were supposedly descendants of Toddy.

One of her husband's comrades, who knew her well, had this to say about her: "Big and boisterous she ever was, and ever ready with a merry quip, but she was never coarse or vulgar. Though brusque in manner, she was kindly, and always retained the respect and admiration of the soldiers with whom her husband's lot was cast."

Actually, the figure on the caput of this spoon, a crone-like old woman leaning on a cane, a cat with arched back and bushy, erect tail fawning close to her side, was meant originally to represent Moll Pitcher, a fortune-teller of local fame at Lynn, Massachusetts. She was called the "last of the witches," and was still living during the Revolution. It is said that a soldier acquainted with both women saw certain likenesses of temperament between the fortune-teller and the wife of Barber Hays, and thus dubbed the latter Moll Pitcher. Every one, however, has taken this spoon to commemorate the heroine of the Revolution.

The reverse of the handle carries the date, 1892, the imprint of W. H. Newhall, and the Durgin trademark. Length, 5¾ inches.

No. 8 CADILLAC

Antoine de la Motte-Cadillac is one of the most neglected heroes of American history. Outside Detroit, the name suggests only a well-known make of motor car. A couple of statues, a town, and a street in Detroit bear witness to his local fame. Even historians have been chary about placing Cadillac in the *Weltstrom* of American history. Yet he belongs there, even though he be a Frenchman who envisioned a New France extending over the whole of North America.

There is one very good reason why Cadillac has never received the accolade of biographers and historians, and that is, there are too many missing links in his story. The springtime of his life is obscured by the lack of authentic records, and his autumn was darkened by imprisonment and loss of fortune.

Even the date of his birth is uncertain. At the time of his marriage, his birth-year was recorded as 1661; at the time of his death, his birth was registered as 1657. One of the earliest historians of Detroit mentions 1658, while Cadillac himself states in 1703 that he was forty-seven years old, an age that would place his birth-date in 1656. Agnes Laut, author of the only book-size biography of Cadillac, declares that he was born in the heart of the Pyrenees on March 5, 1658. This last is perhaps the correct date.

Born of a noble family whose fortunes had dwindled successively with each generation, young La Motte set out from home in his sixteenth year, like his fellow-countryman, d'Artagnan, to seek his way by the metal of his sword and the mettle of his spirit. Miss Laut likens him to another Gascon, Cyrano de Bergerac, the points of analogy lying in the aquiline nose (that crag of prominence, the honor of which was so ably defended by Cyrano), the swarthy complexion, the wiry physique, the readiness to fight, the mastery of the foils, the abounding retort, their unquestioning devotion to friends, and the contemptuous insolence toward enemies.

How many duels La Motte fought while he was still a "Gascon cadet" in the French army we do not know, but he had not been long in Canada before he established a great respect for the skill of his sword-thrusts. He first came to Canada, in 1683, on a secret mission for the Crown: his business was to ferret out grafters in the colonial government. He shuttled about with such an observing eye and to such good purpose that his reports came directly to the King's notice. Too honest to be bought by chiselers, Cadillac reduced the size of the King's colonial budget materially. As a reward he was given a seigniory on the north coast of Maine, with a town house in Port Royal. In the last named settlement he met and married Thérèse Guyon, a choice he never regretted. Madame Cadillac seems to have been a woman in every way a worthy match to her husband in mental and physical powers, becoming in time the mother of thirteen children.

For five years, from 1689 to 1694, Cadillac was commissioned to make surveys of the settlements and forts of both New France and New England with the purpose in mind of laying plans for the eventual conquest of the British colonies. As yet the French were too few in numbers to look toward extirpating the heretical colonists along the seaboard. A greater emprise and vision were needed to consummate this grandiose scheme of empery.

Count Frontenac, the ablest governor that colonial Canada ever had, kept his perspicacious eye trained upon Cadillac for several years, and when the fur traders at Mackinac began to complain of British interlopers ruining their business, the Count knew of no better man than Cadillac to counteract this imminent threat to French suzerainty.

The post of which Cadillac was given charge was a trading center on the Straits of Mackinac between Lakes Michigan and Huron. Around the settlement at Fort Mackinac were clustered large numbers of Indians of the Huron, Iroquois, and Ottawa tribes. Once a flourishing mission, the place was now demoralized by the unlicensed sale of brandy, the excessive drinking of which by the natives caused endless disorders and all sorts of crimes.

Cadillac restricted the sale of brandy, but still allowed the Indians to buy a certain amount, believing on this score that if the French refused to sell them the liquor, the English would have no such scruples. And those Indians who resorted to the British for brandy would likewise offer their pelts in exchange. On this subject arose a vehement argument between Cadillac and the Jesuit, Father Carheil, who would sell no brandy to the Indians. When the commandant said that he was only obeying the royal orders in permitting the traffic in brandy, the Jesuit reproved him for obeying man, not God. This rejoinder rubbed the temperamental Gascon the wrong way. He reported on the incident: "I told him his talk smelt of sedition a hundred yards off, and begged him to amend his language. He told me that I gave myself airs that did not belong to me, holding his fist before my nose at the same time. I confess I almost forgot that he was a priest, and felt for a moment like knocking his jaw out of joint; but thank God I contented myself with taking him by the arm, pushing him out, and ordering him not to come back."

Cadillac was dissatisfied with his position at Mackinac. He clearly perceived that the site, while strategically important, lay too far north to be the pivotal keystone for trade between the Great Lakes and the Mississippi Valley. The Straits of Detroit, which lay at the northwestern end of Lake Erie and formed the connecting link between that waterway and Lake Huron, would be more feasible, not only as a trade emporium but also as a tightening screw against the growing pains of the British.

When Cadillac laid his plans for a settlement at Detroit before an assembly of officials at Quebec, Callières, the then governor, stoutly opposed the objectives outlined, which were in substance: first, that Detroit would become a hub of the fur trade; and, second, that the Indians around the new town would be civilized by teaching them French.

The intendant Champigny, a friend of the Jesuits, contended that the Indians should not learn French, that those young squaws and braves who had received some training at the Ursuline convent and the Boys' Seminary led looser lives than did the uneducated. "M. de Champigny does great honor to the Ursulines and the Seminary," twitted the mordacious Gascon.

Disgruntled over his stymied plans, Cadillac was determined to carry the matter straight to the King himself. In the fall of 1699 he set sail for France, armed with maps and reports, as well as letters written by Frontenac in his favor. Legend has it that he did not board the vessel in port, for fear lest his enemies might detain him, but galloped away in the dead of night and embarked from a canoe downstream.

At Versailles the king was busy with other matters and turned Cadillac's request and the weight of evidence over to Pontchartrain, advisor on colonial affairs. Either Cadillac was a persuasive talker or else the concession for a new fort was deemed feasible, since the commission was soon granted to the petitioner at one of the king's morning audiences. Cadillac, always noted for his severity toward any of his soldiers who were careless of dress, presented himself at court in a blaze of colorful regalia, received his commission, kissed his majesty's hand, and bowed out.

On June 5, 1701, began the journey from Montreal to the Straits of Detroit. Cadillac had assembled in his party fifty handpicked soldiers, fifty capable backwoodsmen, two Récollet friars, and a number of Algonquin Indians to serve as portage men and interpreters. Twenty-five canoes of birch and cedar were plentifully loaded with food, clothing, axes, garden implements, guns and ammunition. Their itinerary followed a northerly route through the Lachine Rapids, along the Ottawa River, around the Chaudière and the Rideau River Falls, up the Mattawa River, across Nipissing Lake, and out of French River into Georgian Bay and Lake Huron. He even cut across the latter lake to Mackinac ostensibly to pick up garrison supplies which he had hidden before his departure from there two years before. Skirting the west shore of Lake Huron southward, he sailed into Lake St. Clair, and thence into the blue waters at the northern end of Detroit River.

The history of the city of Detroit begins July 24, 1701, when Cadillac and his migrant party selected a site for their settlement on the north shore of the Straits, on a bluff below Belle Isle where the river perceptibly narrows as if from two bisected semi-circles. The journey of forty-nine days had been marked by only one untoward incident. Early in the trip several of the enlisted men, believing rumors they heard of dangers ahead from bushlopers during encampments, connived to take off with the provisions and ammunition. In the argument that followed, a buffet from the rear sent Cadillac's hat spinning off his head. Seizing his sword, he challenged the pork-heads to test their metal against his. No rapier except the commander's flashed in the sunlight. The mutiny was over, and no blood, good or bad, had been spilled.

Cadillac in his very unorthodox reports to the French court waxed as poetic as a Cyrano de Bergerac over the auspicious locality of this newly-established fort, named for his patron, Ponchartrain. Listen to him: "The climate is temperate and the air purified through the day and night by a gentle breeze. The skies are always serene, and spread a sweet and fresh influence which makes one enjoy a tranquil sleep . . . The grape-vine has not strength enough to support the weight of its fruit and it has not yet wept under the knife of the vine dresser . . . The shy stag, the timid fawn, the bounding bucks, the turkey hen with bulging crop and numerous broods, the golden pheasant, the quail, the partridge, the woodchuck, the turtle dove—all sweeten the melancholy of these solitudes . . . You can shoot thirty turkeys in an afternoon for food. Besides the game birds, there are tanagers, cardinals, cranes, blue birds, threshers, black birds, robins . . . The swans are like great lilies. The ducks are so thick they hardly move to let canoes pass amid their flocks." An idlyllic spot amid a wilderness plenitude was this site for a town which in time was to become the hub of our automotive civilization.

The woodchoppers and carpenters in the group set to work at once cutting down trees and building a stockade. Two days after their arrival, ground was broken for a chapel dedicated to St. Anne, patron saint of the voyagers. Fifty cabins were constructed before the cold weather set in. Small farms were laid off, wheat was sown, fruit trees were planted, and provisions stored away for the winter. In late September arrived Madam Cadillac and her five children. More women and children, as well as more settlers, continued to arrive through the winter.

At first the Indians looked askance at this intrusion of their territory. Cadillac soon dispelled their suspicions by inviting them to pitch their camps near the new port and barter their furs at his trading post. His friendly gestures brought more than six thousand Indians, members of the Huron, Miami, Ottawa, and Potawatomi tribes, to make their headquarters in the vicinity. Cadillac exulted over the report that only twenty-five Indians still traded off their furs at Fort Mackinac. He considered his success with the Indians as a personal triumph over his old Jesuit adversary, Father Carheil, and expressed a rather smug, chop-smacking satisfaction as he gloated: "I hope that in the autumn I shall pluck this last feather from his wing; and I am convinced that this obstinate priest will die in his parish without one parishioner to bury him."

Detroit prospered and grew during the years from 1701 to 1710 when Cadillac was commandant, but this very prosperity and growth brought a spate of charges from jealous onlookers. Most of these accusations had no basis in fact, but they were numerous enough. Cadillac was allowing Indians to join the royal regiments; he encouraged the savages to learn French, and granted them equal privileges with the whites in churches, hospitals, and schools; he sold goods cheaper than in Montreal and Quebec; he was making too much money from this fur monopoly; he spoke caustically of the Jesuits; he was detested by his troops and the settlers.

The malicious reports against Cadillac gradually had their effect. A new colonial minister, Vaudreuil, none too friendly toward the Detroit commandant, replaced Pontchartrain. Vaudreuil listened seriously to the accusations, and decided that the best means for removing Cadillac from his present post would be by promoting him to another one elsewhere. Hence this dispatch in September of 1710: "Having appointed you to the governorship of Louisiana . . . it is the will of His Majesty that you go at once to Louisiana . . . This is for the welfare of the service." The order was signed by Vaudreuil.

Vainly did Cadillac try to stave off the transfer, and delayed his departure to the southern colony for a year and a half. The worst feature about the transfer of the Detroit post to new hands was, that it carried all of Cadillac's property with it. These holdings were not large, but the loss involved everything that the commandant had managed to secure through initiative, thrift, and shrewd supervision on his part. He filed suit to retain his property and tarried eleven months in Quebec until he realized that the decrees of corrupt politicians at Versailles were inexorable.

Cadillac was still in Canada when the consequences of this removal made their effects felt. Dubuisson, the new commandant, sent a dispatch to Quebec for help in November, 1711, saying that all the Indian tribes were ablaze with insubordination. "By what miracle had Cadillac controlled them? . . . There was no obedience inside the fort, nor out." A Récollet gray friar records that it was terrible to see what was happening under the change. Detroit underwent a siege of nineteen days. There was a constant shifting of commandants for Detroit before peace once more descended on the harried settlement. The wonder is, that it survived.

Cadillac's exploits in Louisiana were far less brilliant than they had been at Detroit. Most historians of this part of his career seem to be biased against him and find little of commendation in his actions. A new clique of politicians, mostly strangers to him, had grasped the reins of government at Versailles. Cadillac had no intimate dealings with them. He sent them few reports, favorable or unfavorable. To tell the truth, his heart lay not in this semi-tropical country. Even though his recall, in 1717, came unexpectedly, and rudely worded to the effect that he had proved himself unfit to administer the King's affairs in Louisiana, he must not have grieved or wished to linger, for he immediately returned to France.

Just about the time that he set foot in the French capital, John Law's Mississippi Bubble was being blown to enormous dimensions. Cadillac, as always, more courageous than tactful, denounced the rash scheme with snorts of vehement condemnation. He boldly declared that no revenues could be derived from Louisiana for many years yet.

When he denounced Law as a fraud, Cadillac was clamped in the Bastille, where he might have rotted without further extenuation, if Law's scheme had not crashed so hard that the quake opened the prison doors for Cadillac to go free again.

But his life during his latter years sinks back into the same sort of obscurity out of which it rose. For a while he was the governor of a small department in southern France, a position which, since it was auctioned and sold to the highest bidder, cost him sixteen thousand five hundred livres. Here, at Castel-Sarrarin, he died on October 15, 1730.

Agnes Laut, in her colorful biography of Cadillac, speaks of him as "one of the few great early heroes in North American history whose life has never been written." Even Miss Laut, for all her painstaking research that carried her over most of the territory covered by Cadillac himself, still had to admit encountering many blind gaps.

Arthur Pound, historian of the "dynamic city," eulogizes Cadillac in these words: "On the whole, Detroit has reason to be proud of its dashing and dramatic founder, who stands out after a hundred and fifty years as one of the really great figures in America's colonial history. Cadillac is one of those leaders of destiny who grow in stature as the veils are drawn aside through historical research. A century ago he was almost forgotten; a century hence, when his daring record and enlightened opinions are better known, he may stand out as one of the trail-breakers of history."

The spoon honoring Cadillac purveys his portrait in the caput, his name being seen in the banderole beneath and the date, 1701, in smaller letters to the left side. A heraldic scaly-backed dragon, somewhat like a gargoyle, charges the left border of the nave, on which appears DETROIT. The dragon-tail, in its windings, divides the shaft into two sections, on each of which there is a fleur-de-lis. This distinctively French flower also forms the handle drop. A diorama of Detroit, viewed from a river-boat, appears in the bowl. The decor, being symmetrical, shows a definite rococo influence, late Louis XIV or early Louis XV. The spoon was cast by Dominick and Haff, a company later merged with Reed and Barton, for Wright, Kay & Co. The length of spoon is 6 inches.

No. 9 LONGFELLOW
No. 30 LONGFELLOW'S HOME
No. 137 LONGFELLOW'S BIRTHPLACE

Longfellow was literally born with a "souvenir spoon" in his mouth. Good fortune seemed to smile upon him all the days of his life. Seldom do we see a more favorable combination of happy chance and achievement in any man's career. Not a little of the disparagement voiced by his detractors springs from envy at the fortunate circumstances of his life and the uncritical adulation of his poetry. "When we see a person of moderate powers receive honors which should be reserved for the highest," says Margaret Fuller splenetically, "we feel like assailing him and taking from him the crown which should be reserved for grander brows."

Longfellow was born in Portland, Maine—then, still a part of Massachusetts—on February 27, 1807. The second of eight children, he was named after his mother's favorite brother, Henry Wadsworth, a naval officer who had lost his life three years before when his ship exploded during gunfire off the coast of Tripoli.

The father, Stephen Longfellow, of the sixth generation of the family in America, was a Harvard graduate like his father before him. He practiced law in Portland, and expected in the course of time to have his son follow in his footsteps. The mother was directly descended from John and Priscilla Alden, those two Mayflower voyagers who were to be so widely publicized and romanticized, much later, in *The Courtship of Miles Standish*. Stephen Longfellow and his wife were emancipated Puritans, still holding the same high standards of conduct and morality as their ancestors, but no longer having scruples about the enjoyment of beauty in the fine arts of painting, music, and literature. Indeed, Zilpah Wadsworth, in spite of her intellectual bent, had a streak of gayety in her nature: she loved dancing—though it cannot be said that she imparted any of her fondness for this amusement to her son, for he confessed that he cared only for an occasional waltz, and then his preference inclined toward the older women who appreciated such attentions more than did the younger girls.

Henry learned to read almost before he had cut all his teeth, that is, at the age of three, and thenceforward he progressed so rapidly that he was able to enter Bowdoin College at fourteen. By this time he had already published anonymously his first poem, "The Battle of Lovell's Pond," in the *Portland Gazette*. But a damper was put on the boy's poetic aspirations when at the dinner table the same day of its appearance, a judge picked up the *Gazette* and asked of Henry's father, "Did you read that poem in the morning paper? Very stiff, remarkably stiff. Moreover, it's borrowed, every word of it." From those remarks the youthful poet learned one valuable lesson: to get favorable reactions from your readers, you must write what they like to read.

At Bowdoin College, where Nathaniel Hawthorne was his classmate, he continued to write poems for the *Portland Gazette*. Most of these, if included at all among Longfellow's poems, are found among the "Juvenilia." An address which he delivered at his graduation deserves more than passing notice, however, as his theme was "Our Native Writers." To Thomas Wentworth Higginson this speech appears "to be one of the most interesting landmarks in the author's early career, and to point directly towards all that followed." A few excerpts will suffice to show its nature: "To an American there is something endearing in the very sound—Our Native Writers. Like the music of our native tongue, when heard in a foreign land, they have the power to kindle up within him the tender memory of his home and fireside . . . Is then our land to be indeed the land of song? Will it one day be rich in romantic associations? Will poetry, that hallows every scene—that renders every spot classical—and pours out on all things the soul of its enthusiasm, breathe over it that enchantment which lives in the isle of Greece? . . . Yes—and palms are to be won by our native writers!" He calls for a native literature emancipated from the English literary tradition. "We are a plain people, that have had nothing to do with the mere pleasures and luxuries of life; and, hence, there has sprung up within us a quick-sightedness to the failings of literary men and an aversion to everything that is not practical, operative, and thoroughgoing." He proceeds to say that "our poetry is not in books alone" but in those men whose hearts have been warmed by the beauty of our natural scenery. And he closes with that perfervid line from Scott to show his *amor patriae*—

This is my own, my native land.

Longfellow might have become a purely provincial poet, hymning the praises of his New England hills and hollows as jingoistically, if not so raucously, as Walt Whitman bellowed the beauties of Brooklyn, if one of those unexpected "lucky breaks" had not chanced his way. His alma mater offered him the chair of modern languages if he would go to Europe for the study that would equip him adequately for the position. He accepted the offer, glad to escape the bonds that would have made him a lawyer, like his father.

For three years he wandered over Europe, studying in France for eight months, in Spain also for eight months, in Italy for a full year, and in Germany for six months. He felt homesick for Spain when he went to Italy, but in the latter country he became so conversant with the language that hotel clerks mistook him for a native.

For six years Longfellow labored strenuously at Bowdoin, often writing or editing his own texts when none suited him or they were lacking. The college trustees granted him a professorship—when he stoutly refused a tutorship—at an annual salary of eight hundred dollars. He took over the duties of librarian also for an additional hundred dollars. In 1831 he married Mary Storer Potter, a native like himself of Portland. He saw her first in church, and was so attracted by her that he called upon her a few days later in the company of his sister. A whirlwind courtship terminated in marriage.

When the scholarly George Ticknor wished to retire as professor of modern languages at Harvard in 1835, he suggested Longfellow as his successor. Before assuming his duties, the young professor made a second trip to Europe to improve his knowledge of German, Dutch, and the Scandinavian languages. This journey was saddened by the unexpected death of Mrs. Longfellow in Holland.

For eighteen years he held the chair as "Smith Professor of the French and Spanish Languages and Literature, and Professor of Belles Lettres" at Harvard. He had a great deal of supervision to do, often acted as substitute-teacher, and was scheduled every term for a series of lectures. He complained once that seventy lectures were hanging over his head "like a dark curtain." "Six hours in the lecture-room," he exclaims, "like a schoolmaster!" As the emoluments from his literary labors increased, he found his academic duties becoming more and more distasteful. "My work here grows quite intolerable, and, unless they make some change, I will leave them, with or without anything to do," he wrote to his father. Somewhat later he questions himself, "Ought I to lead this life any longer? If I mean to be an author, should I not be one in earnest?"

60

Irritably he confides to his diary on December 31, 1853: "How barren of all poetic production this last year has been! I have absolutely nothing to show. Really there has been nothing but the college work." Finally, confident that his growing income would be sufficient for the needs of his family, he resigned his professorship at Harvard, to be succeeded by James Russell Lowell.

His family life was ideally happy during these years. In 1843 he had married, for his second wife, the daughter of a wealthy Boston merchant, Frances Elizabeth Appleton, a young lady whose portrait fully justifies all the laudatory epithets bestowed upon her for her "Junonian beauty," "kindest heart," "gentle face," "deep unutterable eyes." When, after her tragic death by fire in the summer of 1861, the poet bore his grief manfully and silently. Years later he tenderly wrote of her that—

> soul more white
> Never through martyrdom of fire was led
> To its repose.

There were two sons and three daughters born to this second marriage, and these children were always a source of happiness to the poet. He was especially fond of the little girls—

> Grave Alice and laughing Allegra,
> And Edith with golden hair.
>
> A whisper and then a silence;
> Yet I know by their merry eyes
> They are plotting and planning together
> To take me by surprise.
>
> A sudden rush from the stairway,
> A sudden raid from the hall,
> By three doors left unguarded,
> They enter my castle wall.
>
> They climb up into my turret
> O'er the arms and back of my chair;
> If I try to escape, they surround me;
> They seem to be everywhere.

Craigie House, where Longfellow lived first as a lodger, then as the master, from 1837 until his death, was a spacious three-story mansion overlooking the Charles River. The place was distinctive for its historical associations, even before Mr. Appleton bought and presented it to his son-in-law, the poet. George Washington made it his headquarters when he and Mrs. Washington spent the winter of 1776 in Cambridge. Talleyrand

and the Duke of Kent, Queen Victoria's father, had sojourned there as guests of General Craigie.

Longfellow's home became the focal point for an ever-widening circle of noted people. The poet was no introvert, like Hawthorne, to shy away from his fellowmen, nor did he even assume the pedestal-like posture which would cause people to shy away from him. Dickens, on his tour of America, made it a special point to visit Craigie House. Among his most intimate friends, who freely came and went, were Lowell, Emerson, Hawthorne, Howe, Howells, Ticknor, Bancroft, Parsons, Norton, Agassiz, Whittier, Sparks, and Prescott. His two favorite authors, Bryant and Washington Irving, although not frequenters of his home circle, were good friends whose acquaintance he had made in Europe.

Longfellow's study and adjoining library at Craigie House suggested to the visitor a pleasant sense of cozy *Gemütlichkeit,* as well as an atmosphere of expansive scholarship in the high, white-panelled walls, large open fireplace, comfortable armchair near the fire, and the informal piling of books on shelves and tables. Coleridge's inkstand and a statuette of Goethe stood on his desk. A gold-leaf Federal mirror hung over the mantel, and oil paintings, among them a Tintoretto, were spaced here and there along the walls. A lemon-tree in one window niche reminded him of Italy; an orange-tree in another brought back memories of Spain.

He was often interrupted in his musings by admirers, curiosity-mongers, and beggars, but he was never irritated by these unannounced visitors. One woman, among a group of English sightseers, offered this extenuation for an unheralded call. "As there are no ruins in this country, we thought we would come to see you." Penniless tramps and hungry beggars imposed on his soft-hearted generosity, and their sad tales, often fabricated, were a ready pledge for small sums of money and parcels of food before they departed. A steady stream of children trotted up the hallway to see the chair made from the "spreading chestnut tree" and presented to the poet as a gift from the children. The welcome mat was spread for all comers. Out of sheer compassion, he took an old friend, George W. Greene, to live out his last days as a pensioner at Craigie House. The poet even took much of his own time to wait upon this destitute, paralyzed old man.

Longfellow enjoyed a tremendous popularity both at home and abroad. For several years before his death in 1882, the children of America honored his birthday with special services in the schools. The simplicity, wide appeal, and moral purity of his writings endeared him to all young people. Typical of his influence is this incident told by a well-known bookseller when a stranger wished to buy a book of poetry as a Christmas gift for his daughter. "I don't want Byron or Shelley, or somebody like that," explained the stranger. "I want somebody like Longfellow—a good, safe, family poet."

In England he was more popular than Tennyson or Browning. Oxford University conferred the D.C.L. degree upon him, and Cambridge the LL.D.

When he visited London he was fêted by the most notable Englishmen of the time, among whom were Gladstone, Tennyson, Carlyle, Bulwer-Lytton, Aubrey de Vere, and Lord John Russell. The Queen herself invited him to visit Windsor, where the maids peeped from behind curtains to catch a glimpse of the royally-received American. At Newcastle his carriage was abruptly halted by a group of grime-coated miners, who opened the door and asked, "Are you Mr. Longfellow?" The poet, thinking he was about to be the victim of a robbery, rather hesitantly admitted his identity. "Well, sir," declared the spokesman, "we heard you were to pass by here at this time; so we got permission to come up out of the mines to see you. We just want to shake your hand and say, 'God bless the man that wrote "The Psalm of Life."'" This incident is not as surprising as it seems on the surface after this explanation by a British publisher: "A stranger can hardly have an idea of how familiar many of our working people, especially women, are with Longfellow. Thousands can repeat some of his poems who have never read a line of Tennyson and probably never heard of Browning." Two years after Longfellow's death, a bust of him was unveiled in Westminster Abbey. In our own Hall of Fame, the name of Longfellow was among the first selected for inscription on its walls. For his tomb in Mount Auburn the sole inscription, LONGFELLOW, suffices.

Singular as it may appear to us now, he began his career as a writer of travelogues. *Outre Mer,* exactly what its sub-title says it is, *A Pilgrimage Beyond the Sea,* describing his wanderings on his first trip to Europe, is written in a sentimental Irvingesque vein. His second work of prose, *Hyperion,* betrays the growing influence of Jean Paul Richter on his imaginative faculties. For several decades this book—now long out of print—was a sort of *vade mecum* for those wishing to familiarize themselves with the romantic associations of the Rhine Valley. "It opened up to Americans a new world," says Fred Lewis Pattee, "the splendid vista of continental beauty and it brought a new longing into a thousand American homes." His last prose work, *Kavanaugh,* the colorless romance of a New England village pastor, was less successful. The criticisms of it proving rather severe, he forewent any further ventures in prose fiction.

Voices of the Night, Longfellow's first volume of poems, was published in September 1839, two months after *Hyperion.* It contained such popular things as these: "A Psalm of Life," "The Reaper and the Flowers," "Footsteps of Angels," and "Hymn to the Night." Just how firm and permanent a hold some of these poems took on the public mind may best be shown by the fact that a century later, "A Psalm of Life" won, in a newspaper poll of sixty thousand readers, first place among the ten favorite poems of America. The criticasters may scoff at the didacticism of this poem as much as they please, yet the general public will continue to love it and feel as uplifted and encouraged by reading it as by any passage in the Bible. Harvey O'Higgins calls it the "paean of an ego facing reality courageously, disdaining the pleasure motive, and turning its back on the path of psychotic repression. It is a profoundly important psychological poem." To those critics who decry the sermonizing which Longfellow constantly injected into his work, Grant C. Knight says very pertinently that "no one has yet proved that a desire to instruct or improve is incompatible with the demands of art."

Ballads and Other Poems, issued in 1841, gave readers two straightforward narratives in "The Skeleton in Armor" and "The Wreck of the Hesperus," revealing for the first time the author's ability to tell a story in verse. "The Village Blacksmith," typical of the worst kind of Victorian poetry, yet presented at his best the most familiar character of village life in nineteenth-century America. Shoddy the poetry is, yes, but every American blacksmith, being a man of brawn rather than brain, could understand it, and I'll wager he appreciated the honor bestowed upon him. No one has done a similar service for the garage man of today.

The moralizing strain persisted in all those early poems, and yet it is this very characteristic feature that endeared him to the masses. The titles, though legion, are still familiar to us from our school days: "The Rainy Day," "Maidenhood," "Excelsior," "The Bridge," "The Day is Done," "The Old Clock on the Stairs," "The Arrow and the Song," "The Building of the Ship," "The Ladder of St. Augustine," "My Lost Youth," "Daybreak," "Seaweed," "Children," and "The Children's Hour." A glance at his later short poems reveals fewer and fewer familiar titles. Illogically enough, some of his best poetry is in these, especially in the sonnets, among which "The Cross of Snow," "Nature," "Venice," "On Translating the Divine Comedy," "Shakespeare," "Milton," and "Keats," are memorable achievements. *Tales of a Wayside Inn* is built up on the device employed by Boccaccio and Chaucer of having a group of people, thrown together for a certain length of time, relate stories for one another's mutual entertainment. A host of good narratives, derived from a variety of sources, abound in these pages, and each narrator tells his tale with right good zest. There is not a dull story among them, and especially fine are "The Birds of Killingworth," "The Legend of Rabbi Ben Ezra," "King Robert of Sicily," "The Saga of King Olaf," "Paul Revere's Ride," "The Monk of Casal-Maggiore," and "The Falcon of Ser Federigo."

His wings having grown strong on the short, swallow flights of song, Longfellow felt emboldened to make longer flights of passage. In three of these, *Evangeline* (1847), *The Song of Hiawatha* (1855), and *The Courtship of Miles Standish* (1858), he demonstrated his ability to write the sustained narrative form in verse with such success as to produce "best sellers." He also demonstrated his ability to discover the intrinsic, poetic beauty inherent in purely native themes. Let those who will carp about the rough spots in the hexametric measures of *Evangeline,* the sing-song iterations in *Hiawatha,* or the prosy lines in *The Courtship,* there will still be a host of people who will find pleasure in reading them in preference to the soul-wrenching eruptions of those "chaotic erotics" who give pleasure to nobody except themselves.

Another facet of Longfellow's talents that showed to good advantage was his expertness at translating. While he made translations from nine languages, his best work in this field may be narrowed to those four tongues from which he derived endless inspirations. From the Spanish he translated the *Coplas* of Jorge Manrique, a bit of work that compares favorably with Fitzgerald's *Rubaiyat;* sonnets from Lope de Vega; ballades from Góngora; and lines from St. Teresa of Avila. From the German there are perfect renditions from the songs and ballads of Uhland, Heine, Goethe, Arnim, and Brentano. Perhaps the most arduous task he ever set himself to do was the translation of Dante's *Divine Comedy* from the Italian, done in the years following the death of the second Mrs. Longfellow. From the Swedish he made translations of Tegner's *Children of the Lord's Supper* and *Frithiof's Saga.* Edmund Gosse says that there is such an affinity of taste and sentiment between Longfellow and the Scandinavians that a Swedish critic once placed Longfellow in an anthology among his native poets. Van Wyck Brooks speaks of a "secret kinship between the pastoral children of the Vikings and the child of Maine for whom the sea and the forest possessed an unfailing magic."

The belittlement of Longfellow's verse began with his contemporaries, those nearest in time and place, the Transcendentalists. His chief antagonist, Margaret Fuller, says bluntly that he is "artificial and imitative . . . mixes what he borrows so that it does not appear to the best advantage. The ethical part of his writing has a hollow second-hand sound." Poe, though sometimes laudatory, is on the whole much more condemnatory: "His conception of the aims of poetry is all wrong . . . His didactics are all out of place. He has written brilliant poems by accident; that is to say, when permitting his genius to get the better of his conventional habit of thinking, a habit deduced from German study." Some foreign critics, notably Swinburne, declare him banal and medieval in outlook. Coventry Patmore nicknamed him "Longwindedfellow."

To these endless animadversions that have continued down to our own day, the best rebuttal was made by George Saintsbury, most thoroughgoing of English scholars: "For my part, I made up my mind long ago that the critic who pooh-poohs Longfellow is a bad critic. If he cannot see the poetry of Longfellow because of the other things not quite so poetical which are there, he lacks the first qualifications of the critic."

Not the best poet that America has produced, Longfellow is still the best loved. Generations of our school children, after cutting their mental baby teeth on Mother Goose and other nursery pap, have cut their second permanent set on Longfellow's substantial diet of simples—always digestible. For the great mass of common people Longfellow has been and remains, so far as poetry goes, staple provender. Not only was his taste devoid of all objectionable faults, but his vision remained clear, unimpaired and far-reaching. It is said that the last words Goethe spoke were "More light." As typical of Longfellow were the last words he wrote—

It is daybreak everywhere.

All three spoons commemorating Longfellow show the poet's head in relief in medallion-form on the caput of the handle. The Longfellow spoon gives a profile view of the face from the left side, the entire oval encircled by a chaplet of laurel. The initials HWL appear in the nave, and PORTLAND on the shaft. The date, April 6, 1891, is still visible, though badly worn, on the reverse side of caput. This spoon, 6 inches in length, is a Durgin product, controlled by J. A. Merrill & Co.

The Longfellow's Home spoon presents a view of Craigie House, the poet's Cambridge residence, in the bowl. Diagonal reedings and tiny trefoils share equal portions on the shaft. The reedings traverse upwards, scroll-like, along the left margin of the nave, while acanthus foliage runs upwards on the right. Wild roses appear at the base of the caput, in which the author's face, guardant, is framed by an ogival arch. Made by Silberstein, Hecht & Co., this spoon measures 4¼ inches in length.

The Birthplace spoon pictures Longfellow's boyhood home in Portland, Maine, in the bowl. The stem carries the poet's name in engraved letters. Both at the top of the stem and at the bottom, running into the handle drop there are rosette bands, the rosettes being closely imbricated. The nave shows an open book-like scroll. The poet's face, identical in pose with that in the previous spoon, is encased in a caput influenced definitely by Renaissance design. Made by Watson and Newell Co., it is 5 inches long.

No. 10 CHIEF SEATTLE

In our history there are many Indian chieftains whose names are familiar to every schoolchild. Most of them are noted as redoubtable warriors who fought a truceless fight against the encroachment of the whites, and to all of them in the end came tragedy and inevitable defeat. To millions of Americans, Seattle is the name of a busy shipping port in the Northwest, a progressive municipality of which we speak with pride. But it is also the name of an Indian sachem, little known, whom we should really be proud to honor.

Chief Seattle, a man of integrity and always a friend to the white settlers, was born about 1786 on Bainbridge Island, located in Puget Sound midway between the present cities of Seattle and Bremerton. He belonged to the Duwamish tribe: peaceable, lazy Indians who ate plenty of salmon and wild berries, and who fled to the fir forests when hostile tribes took to the warpath and invaded their territory.

Seattle at the age of six shared in the universal excitement experienced by his elders when Captain George Vancouver, fresh from his voyage of explorations around South Sea Islands, dropped anchor in the Sound and came ashore on Alki Island. Little Seattle left off picking berries and ran to see the mammoth canoe, big as a sperm whale, and the achromatous creatures who had disembarked from Captain Vancouver's ship, the *Discovery*. At first the sailors were regarded as messengers of the gods. A little later, when they temporarily lost their senses through a potent liquid carried about on their persons, they were duly recognized as humans, some of them as inhumans.

White traders and trappers, pushing westward over the inland trails, soon became a familiar sight to the Indians around Puget Sound. Seattle, while yet a boy, learned to distinguish between those white adventurers actuated by good motives and, adversely, those actuated by bad ones. The young chieftain, a natural leader, became an imposing figure over six feet tall, with a voice strong and unmistakable in its meaning. His superior intelligence was recognized without dissent among his tribesmen.

Before his time the Duwamish were regarded almost in the light of pacifists by other Indians. Seattle was no more bellicose than his forefathers had been, but weary of the predatory raids made incessantly on his people by hostile bands slipping in from the south, he brought the marauders to a dead halt by an original method all his own.

The Muckleshoof Indians were planning a raid on the Duwamish, according to the report of scouts. Seattle abided his time till they were within striking distance. During the night, before the expected attack, he ordered his men to cut the tallest firs on both banks of a narrowed river just below a sharp bend, where a view for any considerable distance was obstructed by high bluffs. The Muckleshoof braves came gliding down the stream, twenty canoe-loads of them, cleared the bend at breakneck speed, and hit the rapids like racers rounding a bend. The night was too dark for them to perceive the watery pitfall awaiting them in the weir of fir-logs until their canoes were catapulted, capsized, or smashed to bits in the wildest confusion of a few seconds. The Duwamish leapt upon them with brandished clubs and tomahawks. The invaders, having lost their weapons in the débris, were stunned and defenseless. Most of their skulls were bashed in while they flipped and floundered about, that is, before they could figure out what had happened.

The clever ruse devised by Seattle, resulting in a top-heavy victory for the Duwamish, was hailed as a sensational masterstroke by the other tribes of the Northwest. Respect for the pacific Duwamish went up like heated mercury.

Within a few years Seattle had become the head-chief of a confederation consisting of six tribes. He created peace in the Northwest by being too formidable for active opposition. He made Bainbridge Island his headquarters—his capitol, if you will. And here he set up a capitol building, too, though it did not have a dome, so the white settlers could recognize it as such. It was more of a community house covering an acre and a quarter of land, nine hundred feet long and divided into forty apartments. Each apartment had a separate entrance, separate quarters, and a common hearth for kitchen and living-room. The six chiefs of Seattle's confederation lived together here under one roof. Harmony prevailed because the guiding spirit under that roof was a sagacious, wisely-tolerant leader.

The shell of this placid existence was broken by a Doctor David Maynard, who came into the region looking for possibilities to establish a salmon cannery. Chief Seattle received him amicably and even pointed out to him a location suitable for his undertaking. The Indians were to have a share in the enterprise. They were to catch the salmon that were to be salted down in barrels and shipped south to San Francisco.

The first buildings were set up in 1852. A small boatload of people landed during a heavy fall of rain. Doctor Maynard did not forget his Indian friend when the question of a name for the new settlement was broached. And thus a great Indian, honorable in all his dealings, scrupulously honest, simple in his ways but profound in his mental attributes, was signally memorialized in the name given to the borning metropolis.

In all his later transactions with the whites, Seattle pursued a policy of coöperation and good will. Even when the inevitable came to pass, and the Indians were herded off into reservations, Chief Seattle accepted the decision with resignation. He knew enough of history to be aware that war with the white men meant death and defeat for the redskins.

During the single subsequent period of trouble, known as the Siege of Seattle, in which about a dozen people were killed, Chief Seattle remained on good terms with the whites. One report has it that the Chief's daughter, the Princess Angeline, paddled a little dugout through a blinding storm to warn the town of an imminent attack by hostile warriors.

In 1854 the Territorial governor signed a treaty with Chief Seattle at Elliott Point. Three thousand Indians were present, and about three hundred whites. The speech made by the venerable Seattle, then nearing seventy years, showed no diminution in his powers of utterance. Here can be given only a few excerpts, but the entire discourse, recorded in full in Archie Binn's *Northwest Gateway*, reveals a poetic beauty even in translation, and all the more surprising, coming as it does from a "Siwash" (a corruption of "savage," the term applied by the whites to these Indians). It could well find its way into some of our collections of great orations: "Yonder sky that has wept tears of compassion upon my people for centuries untold, and which to us appears changeless and eternal, may change. Today is fair. Tomorrow it may be overcast with clouds. My words are like the stars that never change. Whatever Seattle says, the great Chief in Washington can rely upon with as much certainty as he can upon the return of the sun or the seasons. His people are many. They are like the grass that covers vast prairies. My people are few. They resemble the scattering trees of a storm-swept plain . . . I will not dwell on, nor mourn over, our untimely decay, nor reproach our paleface brothers with hastening it, as we too may have been somewhat to blame.

"Let us hope that the hostilities between us may never return. We would have everything to lose and nothing to gain. Revenge by young men is considered gain, even at the cost of their own lives, but old men who stay at home in times of war, and mothers who have sons to lose, know better.

"To us the ashes of our ancestors are sacred and their resting place is hallowed ground. You wander far from the graves of your ancestors and seemingly without regret. Your religion was written upon tables of stone by the iron finger of your God so that you could not forget. The Red Man could never comprehend nor remember it. Our religion is the traditions of our ancestors—the dreams of our old men, given them in solemn hours of night by the Great Spirit, and the visions of our sachems; and it is written in the hearts of our people.

"Day and night cannot dwell together. The Red Man has ever fled the approach of the White Man, as the morning mist flees before the morning sun. However, your proposition seems fair and I think that my people will accept it and will retire to the reservation you offer them. It matters little where we pass the remnant of our days. They will not be many.

"But should we accept it, I here and now make this condition that we will not be denied the privilege without molestation of visiting at any time the tombs of our ancestors, friends, and children. Every part of this soil is sacred in the estimation of my people. Every hillside, every valley, every plain and grove, has been hallowed by some sad or happy event in days long vanished . . . The very dust upon which you now stand responds more lovingly to their footsteps than to yours, because it is rich with the blood of our ancestors, and our bare feet are conscious of the sympathetic touch.

"And when the last Red Man shall have perished, and the memory of my tribe shall have become a myth among the White Men, these shores will swarm with the invisible dead of my tribe, and when your children's children think themselves alone in the field, the store, the shop, upon the highway, or in the silence of the pathless woods, they will not be alone. The White Man will never be alone.

"Let him be just and deal kindly with my people, for the dead are not powerless. Dead, did I say? There is no death, only a change of worlds."

Late in life, Chief Seattle accepted the Christian religion after giving it thoughtful study. During the Civil War, he suffered from lack of food and medicine, when the Government failed to make its promised payments. He lived to see the end of the War, and died in 1866, at the age of eighty. His grave was neglected till 1890, when some of his early pioneer friends raised a fund to mark his last resting place.

69

In 1912 an imposing monument was erected to his memory in the center of Denny Place in Seattle. The statue, molded in bronze by James G. Wehn, represents Chief Seattle with one hand extended in a gesture of welcome and friendship toward the arriving white settlers.

The embossed figure on the caput of this spoon shows the Indian Chief seated, his eyes closed, his hands folded in his lap, a braided, shell-shaped hat and a cane resting on one knee. This likeness is from a photograph taken by L. D. Lindsley in Chief Seattle's old age.

An image of Mt. Rainier is outlined in the bowl. The spoon, which is devoid of any identifying trademark, measures 6 inches in length.

No. 11 PINEHURST RETRIEVER

"Take an old-fashioned New England village, sprinkle it with pleasant homes and a handful of good hotels, add three magnificent golf courses and a hundred miles of bridle paths, garnish with a wealth of flowering trees and shrubs, serve with a clear, dry climate—and you have Pinehurst, North Carolina." So begins a booklet that describes this unique health and recreational center ensconced in the piney woodlands bordering on the Piedmont region.

In 1895 James W. Tufts visited this Sandhills area and was mightily impressed by the things he saw while wandering through the forests: an oxteam plodding along a picturesque pine trail; two young nimrods carrying a deer on a sling across a pinelog foot-bridge; mamma bruin and two playful cubs perched high on a pinetree lookout; rabbits, squirrels, foxes, possums, and coons scurrying about in amazing numbers; quail, grouse, doves, woodcocks, and wild turkeys courting an easy bag; soras, rails, and gallinules loitering around lakes in primeval abundance.

Mr. Tufts was enjoying his stroll immensely, when suddenly there came to him the dismaying thought that it was a pity so few people had a chance to enjoy, like him, a close acquaintance with all these denizens of the forest. At once he was struck by the altruistic idea of establishing a center to which people could come to derive the benefits of an outdoor life in this ideally mild climate through all twelve months of the year.

The original conception of Mr. Tufts was to make Pinehurst a health resort on the five thousand acres which he had bought from the family of Walter Hines Page. Gradually, however, the hotel he built was being patronized by so many huntsmen that he converted his place into a center for sports and recreation. From New England came most of the visitors, who liked especially the fall weather, which seemed to be one continuous Indian summer. December days here rivaled "October's bright blue weather" in the Northern states.

Unlike its twin resort, Southern Pines, Pinehurst has never been incorporated. It has preferred to remain a village, albeit an oversized one,

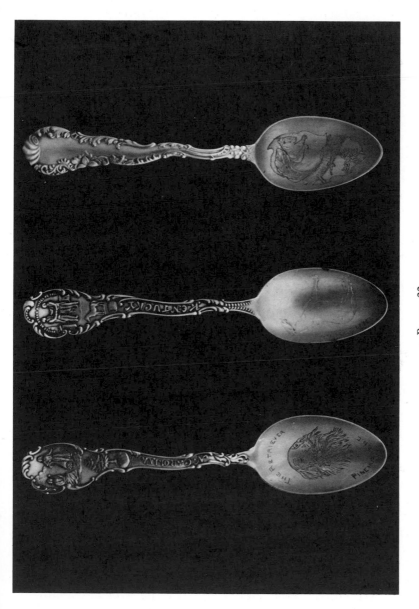

PLATE 22

11. PINEHURST RETRIEVER   12. KENTUCKY THOROUGHBRED
13. MAINE SQUIRREL

PLATE 23

14. WHAT CHEER ROCK   15a. ACTORS' FUND FAIR (obverse)
16. SARATOGA SPRINGS

with such rural regulations as those which prohibit dogs from prowling at night and roosters from crowing in the morning.

In addition to the mild climate, Pinehurst has another asset in its sandy soil. After a rain the soil is soon dry enough for sports. The humidity is low and the filtration of water through the sandy surface insures a fine, soft drinking water.

At one time the main sport at Pinehurst was hunting, for which the sandy hills and pine thickets offered excellent runs of quail, grouse, wild turkey, and deer. Today, however, the place is famous for its golf. In fact, it has become the "winter capital" of the game. Perhaps nowhere else are people so golf-conscious.

No small part of the credit for this addiction to golf is due to Donald J. Ross, whom Mr. Tufts engaged in 1901 to manage golfing activities. The Scottish-born Mr. Ross built more than six hundred courses, scattered from one end of North America to the other. Two tournaments were in progress at Pinehurst at the time of his death in 1948. Some felt that the contests should be cancelled or postponed. But others felt that, if Mr. Ross had had the decision to make, he would have told the golfers to proceed with the games. So the flag was lowered to half-mast on the clubhouse, and the tournaments continued without interruption.

The important role played by Pinehurst in the history of American golf may be stated in Mr. Ross's own words: "Pinehurst was absolutely the pioneer in American golf. While the game had been played in a few places in this country before Pinehurst was established, it was right here on these sandhills that the first great national movement in golf was started. Men came here, took lessons, and went away determined to organize clubs. Their influence gave golf the sort of start it needed."

And perhaps nowhere else is there such an atmosphere of pleasant indifference to the hectic passing of time in the outside world. Those who wish to wear the fashions of an earlier day may do so without being thought odd. Those who wish to ride in tallyhos or "surreys with the fringe on top" can gratify their wishes here. And there are plenty of lanes bordered by stately pines, soaring oaks and magnolias, dogwood, judas trees, and hollies shining with lustrous red berries, to lure one out of doors for delightful excursions. A horseback jaunt along any of the numerous meandering trails provides a haunting memory of never-to-be-forgotten scenes. Then there are occasional fox hunts, horse races, dog shows, turkey shoots, field trials, and gymkhanas on the list of entertainment.

The bowl of this Pinehurst spoon shows the engraved image of a retriever with a quail in his mouth. The handle shank bears the name of North Carolina, and in the nave appear a bale of cotton and a pine tree.

The North Carolina seal in the caput is represented by the two female figures of Liberty and Plenty. But contrary to the stances of the two women on the official seal, Liberty is sitting here and Plenty is standing, the end of the cornucopia touching her right hand instead of her left.

The reverse side of the handle reveals an eagle resting on an unfurled scroll-map of the United States, a drape and tasseled cords running down into the shank.

The Pinehurst Retriever spoon was made by the Shepard Company. Length is 5½ inches.

No. 12 KENTUCKY THOROUGHBRED
No. 124 HORSE-IN-HORSESHOE

To most people the casual mention of Louisville conjures up at once a vision of a half-dozen or so fleeting thoroughbreds dashing down the home stretch at Churchill Downs on Derby Day, and craning, straining necks— they don't all belong to the horses either—and the uninhibited crying of voices, some raucously stentorian, others trebly shrill. It's pandemonium broke loose for a couple of minutes. Then it subsides momentarily, till the great round of cheering indicates that another thoroughbred is being crowned king of the turf with a horseshoe of roses.

The term "thoroughbred" was not applied to horses till near the close of the eighteenth century. Before that they were "blooded" or "imported." Yet horse-racing was a well established sport in the British Isles already in the reign of James I, 1603-1625. This monarch, by his interest in creating lighter breeds of horses and by his regular attendance at the Newmarket Tracks, aroused the enthusiasm of the Scotch and English—and eventually the Irish—for this type of sport. He sponsored a law, however, which limited one's winnings to three hundred dollars; any surplus went to charity.

Blooded horses were imported into the Southern colonies by 1700. Racing clubs were formed in Charleston, South Carolina, and Annapolis, Maryland, by 1750. Daniel Boone and other Western pioneers rode horses into Kentucky through the Cumberland Gap, and one of the laws drawn up at the first legislative assembly in the new territory called for the improvement of equine strains. A four-mile race course was laid out at Lexington in 1789, part of it through the unpaved streets of the town. By 1850 the races at Lexington were drawing wildly-enthusiastic crowds of people, many of them from other states..

The Derby run was initiated at Louisville in 1875, and Aristides was the first winner to niche his name on the notable list of those "galloping ghosts." Most of the winners have been sired and trained on Bluegrass stock farms centering around Lexington, a city that holds its annual meet, the Lexington Trots, to display the finest showmanship there is of horses in harness. Another innovation, the steeplechase, has recently caught fire in the public imagination through the hurdle-jumping contests at the Oxmoor Steeplechase, held the last week in May at the famous old Oxmoor Plantation, near Louisville.

The education of a young colt (or filly) begins at the age of seven months. He is taught to respect the bit, trot or walk in circles, feel the presence of the saddle and human weight on his back, and know the commands of the rein. In trial heats he learns his business with competitors. By the time he is two years old, he is prepared for a series of races which culminate in the Futurity at Belmont. By the time he is three, he is entered—if he's among the lucky stars—for the great Derby event. The winnowing process narrows the competing field down to about a dozen, sometimes less.

The Derby is seventh of the eight races run on the first Saturday in May at Churchill Downs. The crowd starts filing through the gates early, often eating breakfasts, brought along, on the grounds. The grandstand seats are soon filled one by one until every single one is full. Thousands mill around on the infield. Entrance to the boxes is like a fashion parade— the Easter parade on Fifth Avenue has nothing on this one. Ticket sellers have more work than they can handle—handling other people's money. There is a matchless thrill in that moment when the Derby mounts march to the post to the strains of "My Old Kentucky Home."

The personal reactions of the individual spectator, the general over-all repercussions of the crowd, the climactic expectancy of "this is it!", and the anti-something-or-other aftermath of this classic showdown have been impounded by the present author in a none-too-poetic rondeau to give his own homespun version of the affair—

> "Oh, weep no more!" the brass band blares;
> And wildly every one prepares
>   To stand on tiptoe to adjust
>   Himself for that oncoming thrust
> Of lunging horseflesh-bombadiers.
>
> "They're off!" resounds. And unawares
> Each devotee repeats his prayers
>   Beneath his breath: to win—or bust!
>   Oh, weep no more!
>
> They round the curve, the goal post nears.
> Ye gods, a dark horse wins the cheers—
>   The favorite's bitten bitter dust!
>   The Derby's over. Ties are mussed.
> And my new straw hat's on my ears . . .
>   Oh, weep no more!

On the Horse-in-Horseshoe spoon the thoroughbred appears conspicuously in the knop, his head thrust through an inverted horseshoe, the latter surmounted by a jockey's cap. Two looping whips, one on either side of the horseshoe, form, as it were, small handles, beneath which are two large clovers. A bar bit (it is a gentle racer indeed that can be managed with such a bit) crosses both obverse and reverse sides of the handle to enclose the nave. Bridle reins cross twice in running vertically down the handle. An "old Kentucky home" is shown in the bowl, with a log cabin, windlass well, and chickens clearly denoted in the foreground. A product of the Watson Company. Length, 5¼ inches.

The bowl of the Kentucky Thoroughbred spoon contains the picture of a horse and "Louisville" cut out on the lower left side, above the animal's back. The serpentine handle contains "Kentucky" in embossed lettering, a keg, a horse, and the state seal—the latter having upon it the device of two friends embracing each other, and the state motto, "United We Stand, Divided We Fall." Made by the Shepard Mfg. Co. Length, 5½ inches.

No. 13 MAINE SQUIRREL

The squirrel, one of the most fascinating exhibitionists among animals, has always been popularly portrayed on glass, three well-known patterns being much prized by collectors. Lap robes in the horse-and-buggy days often bore the squirrel in some sort of antic pose, either on the ground, up a tree, or safe at the top of a high stump, being barked at mightily by a frustrated puppy. China makers have been less disposed to put squirrel designs on dishes.

The healthy and happy-looking little creature on the bowl of this spoon is sitting on the compact part of a limb close to the tree trunk, his paws empty of nuts and his thickly-bushed tail in a curlycue behind his back. His figure is incised in a gold-glint outline against a silver backdrop that closes in around him from the golden bordure of the bowl.

Under the tree limb, in backstroke flourishes, is written "Island, Me." Squirrel Island, here represented, has long been a favorite summer resort. Even before colonists settled on the mainland, the island had been frequented by voyagers, and Kidd's Cave, a grotto of considerable length on the east coast, testifies to a belief that the doughty freebooter cached some of his pickings in this area.

At one time the island belonged to a Squire Greenleaf, and when he sold the land to the resort corporation, he made a request that sand be brought from the farthest tip of the island as a covering for his grave on the mainland. In carrying out this stipulation, the crew-members commissioned on the errand decided it would necessitate less hauling to scoop up sand from the point closest to the mainland.

On the way back to shore, however, a furious squall arose and the boat was in imminent danger of sinking. And then something strange happened. The wraith of the old squire appeared, like a jinni out of an Arabian Nights story, and bobbed up and down over the heads of the terrified seamen, extending his claw-like hands in wrathful, menacing gestures. The crew, fearful of being swamped for their failure to carry out the squire's specific orders, cleared the decks of the accursed sand and went back to reload the lighter with the sand called for in the unwritten contract. The tempest moderated at once, and in peaceful waters the boat on its second journey returned safely to shore.

The handle of the spoon is sinuous, being plain except for a border of sea-lettuce leaves. The caput is crowned by a scroll of seashell. Length, 5½ inches.

No. 14 WHAT CHEER ROCK
No. 121 ROGER WILLIAMS

It took three centuries for America to realize that in Roger Williams she had been witness to the first of her major prophets. Even now, when he is beginning to be rightly appraised as one of the great fathers of our American democracy, we are surprised at the amazing modernity of his thought. He was so far ahead of his time that we are still searching for the right catoptrics with which to view more clearly the many mirrors of his faceted mind. Nor have we found for him any of those stereotyped labels which we like to use for bracketing conveniently our famous men. As yet, there is not much unanimity in these labels, and the epithets of his own day, such as "enemy of society," "incendiary," and "rebel" are still echoed in the chatter of the unwitting. True, he was a rebel against every sort of stick-tight, unthinking orthodoxy, and he did come "loosing wild foxes with firebrands" to burn out the dead brushwood of inherited narrownesses. But he was far more constructive than destructive in blazing new trails. Modern historians, being more tempered to Williams' way of thinking, qualify their judgments and speak of him, to employ Parrington's terms, as a forerunner of Jefferson, Emerson, Channing, and Paine; a social architect; an intellectual barometer; the incarnation of Protestant individualism; a bold innovator; the most generous, most open-minded, and most lovable of the breed known as "the Puritan saints."

Roger Williams was born in London of parents who had migrated from Hertfordshire in the Welsh border region. We do not know definitely what year it was, as the parish records that could have told us were swept away by the great fire of 1666, but it would be safe to say that he ventured into the world about the time Queen Elizabeth left it, that is, in 1603.

His father was a master tailor who on occasion made fine clothes for fine gentlemen, among whom was Sir Edward Coke, chief justice of the Star Chamber Court. Roger assisted his father at times, and from a workshop window he could look out across the way at Newgate Prison, from the doors of which there often issued sundry poor wretches being shuffled off a short distance to Smithfield Square to be hanged by the neck or roasted at the stake.

Witnessing the executions of these people who were dying because their religious beliefs were at variance with those of the church authorities created a deep impression on the boy. He expressed a great compassion for them to his father, but the old man disapproved of such chicken-hearted sentiments. Common sense expediency demanded that one should believe—his father declared—as the state church authorities believed. But the boy had been imbibing from various sources the new unsanctioned teachings flowing abroad through the land, and in spite of persecutions done upon him in his father's house, Roger already at the age of eleven believed it were better to obey conscience than the adventitious practice demanded by expediency.

When he was fourteen, a widow by the name of Margery Pate, being a communicant of the church Roger attended, left him a small legacy which enabled him to advance his education. He studied shorthand, becoming such an expert that Sir Edward Coke made him his personal secretary. Years later the daughter of the eminent jurist scribbled a note on the back of a letter that Williams wrote her, perhaps to freshen her memory: "This Roger Williams when he was a youth would, in shorthand, take sermons and speeches in the Star Chamber and present them to my dear father. He, seeing so hopeful a youth, took such a liking to him that he sent him to Charter House . . . Full little did he think that he would have proved such a rebel to God, the King, and his Country."

At Charter House he did so well that he won a scholarship to Pembroke College, Cambridge, where he possibly met John Milton, who was there at the same time. They were intimate friends in after years, for in 1654 he was teaching the Dutch language to Milton, then Cromwell's Secretary of Foreign Tongues. He left the university in 1627, and a year later was ordained to the ministry. Sir Edward Coke would have secured for him a good living in London, but preferring to be at a greater—and safer—distance from Bishop Laud, who was threatening to crop the ears of all nonconformists, Williams accepted the chaplaincy of a country estate in Essex.

The master of this lovely old manor house at Oates was Sir William Masham, a member of one of the most Puritanical-minded groups in England. Here the young chaplain moved in an atmosphere of intellectual revolt, mingling with men who were strenuous Parliamentarians pitted against King Charles and his arbitrary government.

The beauty of the moated grange, Italianate gardens, ivied walls, park with gamboling fawns, waterfall slipping over mossy rocks, and lilied pools, must have been conducive to the spirit of romance, for Roger fell in love. The object of his fervor was Jane Whalley, the niece of the aristocratic Lady Barrington, the mother of Lady Masham. The girl reciprocated his attentions, and all would have followed to the inevitable union of the two if the hawk-eyed aunt had not intercepted the match. A considerable correspondence was exchanged. In one letter the chaplain begged to visit her Ladyship at Broad Oaks, her country seat, but she graciously declined to see him. He admitted the inequalities of their social and financial status, saying it would be "some indecorum" for Jane to demean herself to his "low ebb." On a cheerful May morning he gloomily writes: "We hope to live together in the Heavens though the Lord have denied that union on earth!" He mentions a number of "thunderclaps of late" that the Lord had sent to "open the door of your Ladyship's heart . . . Certainly, Madame, the Lord has a quarrel against you."

The Mashams pleaded the cause of their chaplain with Lady Barrington, but she barred any further contact or communication between the young minister and the "passionate and hasty, rash and inconstant Jane." For his part, Roger took to bed with a "burning fever." The Mashams thought he was gasping his last breath and implored Lady Barrington to relent and proffer Mr. Williams the boon of her friendship again. She did so, but the match was definitely a thing of the past.

The hurt to his heart was not long in being assuaged. Lady Masham's daughter by a previous marriage, Jug Altham, had a maid named Mary Barnard. The chaplain often talked with the two young women as they strolled together over the countryside. The spirited Jug was too high-born for him ever to turn his eyes her way. But more and more he perceived the fine traits of character and housewifely virtue of the humble servant-girl. He began to search his own heart for the eradication of his most besetting sins. He had courted Jane Whalley partly out of a desire to advance himself socially. And while he was absorbed in this worldly pursuit he had been neglecting his spiritual duties. He humbled himself and prayed God to uproot the tares of self-seeking and self-exaltation planted in his mind by the devil. Early in December, 1629, Lady Masham added in a footnote to her mother: "Mr. Williams is to marry Mary Barnard, Jug's maid."

The next year Roger and Mary Williams sailed on the good ship *Lyon* for America, and after a sixty-seven-day trip, marked by dangerous storms, landed near Boston, on February 5, 1631. Immediately an offer was made him of the largest church in the colony, that of Boston, but when he heard that Bishop Laud was still its titular overlord, he refused the offer, and went to Salem instead as a religious teacher. From there he went to Plymouth, and then back to Salem. Everywhere he disclaimed the authority of Bishop Laud, proclaimed the right of the church to be free of domination by the State, and denied the right of the State to interfere with a man's religious beliefs.

In October, 1636, Roger Williams was brought to trial before the leading citizens of the Massachusetts Bay Company, meeting in general court at New Town, now Cambridge. He was spreading "divers new and dangerous opinions" from the pulpit. Cotton Mather expressed himself about the matter in his *Magnalia*: "There was a whole country in America like to be set on fire by the rapid motion of a windmill in the head of one particular man." One of the torches held by Williams that must be put out was that incendiary idea that the Indians should be paid for their lands. It was not likely that Williams would be acquitted. They knew his views and he acknowledged them.

The verdict was guilty, and the sentence, exile within six weeks. In the midst of winter it was certain that he would perish of the cold or from the claws of wild beasts. If he recanted his heretical opinions, the judges would be lenient and allow him to stay his banishment till spring.

The sentenced man had so many friends, and received so many expressions of sympathy that his home became a regular clearing house of ideas for his visitors. His enemies, jealous of these attentions, decided to capture Williams, carry him off under cover of darkness, and put him on board a ship about to sail for England. A friendly letter from former Governor Winthrop apprised him of the plot and suggested that he seek refuge among the Narragansett Indians. He was gone three days when his would-be captors from Boston arrived at his house in Salem.

Weak from a long illness, he was forced to plow through snow up to his knees and wade through half-frozen swamps. When he came upon the Indians he found the three sachems, Massasoit, Canonicus, and Maintonomo, engaged in a bitter quarrel that threatened to break into open warfare. Being considered a sachem and held in the highest respect by the bickering chiefs, Mr. Williams, quite familiar with the Indian language, set about to rig up a compromise that would avert hostilities, and his efforts were entirely successful.

In gratitude for his effective work as peacemaker, Massasoit gave Williams a strip of land along the Seekonk River where he could set up a "shelter for the poor and persecuted." Williams and several of his followers began to clear land and plant corn when an order arrived from Governor Winslow that he would have to move again, since he was still within the bounds of the Bay Colony.

Being advised by the governor to settle on the opposite side of the river where the land was not under the jurisdiction of the Bay government, Williams and his men pulled up stakes and sailed up the river till they came to a place where a large rock jutted out into the water. Hearing a familiar call, "What cheer, friend?" from some Indians fishing on the rock, Williams stopped and went ashore to talk with them. They walked together some distance from the river to a large fresh-water spring where a number of Indians were gathered, ready to eat. Inviting the white men to join them at their meal, the Indians hospitably served up bowls of succotash and platters of boiled bass.

This welcome in the wilderness from men who were supposedly savages was never forgotten. In an oral agreement with Canonicus and Maintonomo, he was given a grant of land embracing this very spring as well as What Cheer Rock, and his new settlement he called Providence, "from the freedom and vacancy of the place and many other providences of the most holy and only wise." The sachem Canonicus was not stirred to sell this land in return for money. Says Williams, "I declare to posterity that I never got anything out of Canonicus but by gift."

The new settlement grew rapidly, and soon Providence was a flourishing town, welcoming every one regardless of race or faith. Other settlements followed, all holding the same tolerant principles. Quakers were allowed to hold their meetings in peace. The first Jewish synagogue in America was established at Newport.

The Boston authorities cast a suspicious eye at the thriving new colony, calling the people of Rhode Island the "Lord's débris." The Puritans scoffed at this "Rogue's Island" with its "windy fancies." Unable to swallow up the new colony by means of peaceful persuasion at home, the Massachusetts people took their case to London. Roger Williams was aware of this intrigue, and in the spring of 1644 he journeyed to the British capital and, with the aid of influential friends, secured a charter for Rhode Island, whereby the plantations of Narragansett Bay could exercise the full power of sovereignty to rule themselves "by such laws as they should find most suitable to their estate and condition." The seal on the new charter bore this motto: "Love will conquer all things."

In contrast to the theocratic form of government prevailing in Massachusetts, the system established in Rhode Island was a democracy, the first in the New World. The merchants, farmers, fishermen, and hunters met at first in the open forest to discuss matters of general welfare. Laws were passed by a majority vote. The discussions often led into noisy altercations, but after a few sessions, the system was seen to be a most effectual one, staunchly upheld by men of all religious beliefs and shades of political opinion.

In the same year that he obtained a charter for Rhode Island, Roger Williams also wrote a treatise setting forth his views on religion and statecraft. In *The Bloody Tenet of Persecution* he argued for complete separation of Church and State, declaring that the church should be neither subsidized nor patronized by the government, but should "gird itself only with the breastplate of righteousness, the helmet of salvation, and the sword of the spirit."

In a famous controversy with John Cotton, the chief advocate of religious coercion, Roger Williams clarified his views still more fully. No one should be forced to worship according to governmental dictates, since the "Christian religion cannot be propagated by the civil sword." No one should be accused of harboring wrong beliefs, for a "false religion out of the church will not hurt the church no more than weeds in the wilderness hurt the enclosed garden, or poison hurt the body when it is not touched or taken." No one should be forced to attend a church if he chooses to absent himself. Even atheists should not be punished.

In the realm of political government, he advocated the right of everyone to vote and to be eligible for holding office. He also contended that the tenure of office should be limited to two or three years. These ideas, first put into practice in Rhode Island, gradually spread westward and southward till they conquered, as Gervinus, the German historian says, "the aristocratic tendencies in the Carolinas and New York, the High Church in Virginia, the theocracy of Massachusetts, and the monarchical persuasion in all America."

Among other things, Roger Williams advocated care by the state for widows and orphans, for the insane and the aged poor, for highways and transporting systems, as well as consideration for all those problems that arise from the social relationships of ordinary citizens. Whites, Indians, and Negroes should be looked upon with the same due regard for their civil rights.

And withal, Roger Williams was a very learned man. He knew Latin, Greek, Hebrew, French, and Dutch from his college days; in New England he lived with the Indians long enough to become conversant with their multiple dialects of speech. He enjoyed the best in literature and music, and thought the latter stimulating to religious worship. He was a shrewd business man, always fair and square in his dealings. He put all those who came into his presence fully at their ease, whether it were a lord of the London drawing room or a swart-brown savage of the American forests. He used wine abstemiously, and smoked tobacco with the Indians as a friendly gesture. Many men, even his political opponents, such as Governor Winthrop, felt the magnetic draw of his pleasing personality. He was devoted to his wife and six children, and provided well for them during their enforced separations. He was engaging in conversation and used apt figures of speech to illustrate a point. No one ever produced more telling effects than he in the placement of words. When Governor Endicott in the most conciliatory manner proposed a merger of the two colonies, Williams replied that he preferred to live among the "Christian savages" on Narragansett Bay rather than among the "savage Christians" on Massachusetts Bay.

Roger Williams died at the age of eighty, in 1683. He had lived long enough to see his colony of Rhode Island firmly established, and the liberal principles he stood for fairly well on their way toward becoming the ideals of the future American democracy. "The Puritans banished him to the wilderness to perish," says Charles Smull Longacre, "but Providence watched over him, protected and nurtured him, and gave him the courage of a hero and the spirit of a martyr . . . Persecuted in the Old World and banished in the New, he was led forth by Providence to a new and goodly land to found an asylum for the oppressed children of God, where the wicked should cease from troubling them."

The first spoon in our heading shows in the bowl, which is almost a perfect circle, the warm welcome being given by the four Indians on What Cheer Rock to the four men arriving at shore in the boat. Williams and one of the Indians are shaking hands. The words *What Cheer* and

1636 are printed in relief. The shaft of the handle rises gracefully in a slender fluted column of the Ionic order to a voluted capital, on the abacus of which rests the seal of Rhode Island showing an anchor placed diagonally and the State motto, *Hope,* above it. Made by Gorham & Co., the spoon measures 5¼ inches in length.

On the second spoon, of Colonial design, Roger Williams stands atop a "pillar of Hope." His figure showing him with a Bible in his left hand occupies the entire caput. On the shaft is embossed the name of Providence. The gold-washed bowl is plain. Manufactured by the Williams Bros. Silver Co., the spoon is only 4 inches long.

No. 15 ACTORS' FUND FAIR
No. 22 LOTTA'S FOUNTAIN
No. 25 RIP VAN WINKLE

An entire book, or even a series, could be written about the great actors and actresses whose faces appear on the Actors' Fund Fair spoon. They represent a period in the history of the American theatre that is long definitely closed, and few are the people, indeed, venerable enough to recall having seen them in person on the stage. How little they mean to the present generation of movie and television fans may be gathered from the fact that, when famous stars of that era have survived into our own, the newspapers make scant mention of their passing. To prove that my contention is correct, I quote a release item coming from New York as I write this: "Mrs. Alberta Gallatin Childe, 87, once acclaimed as one of America's greatest actresses, died yesterday in a city hospital. In her stage career of more than thirty years, Miss Gallatin was co-starred with such distinguished leading men as Edwin Booth, Maurice Barrymore, Otis Skinner, Richard Mansfield, and Jacob Adler." Certainly a grudging notice, tucked away on the inside of a newspaper under conspicuous advertisements, for some one who once enriched the lives of thousands by her superb acting. But that is the tragedy of extreme longevity in this topsy-turvy, cockeyed, forgetful world.

The Actors' Fund Fair here commemorated, May 2nd to May 7th, 1892, was the first of its kind ever held by that organization, which was founded in 1882. It took place in the old Madison Square Garden, at Madison and Fourth Avenue, 26th and 27th Streets, and was enormously successful under the direction of A. M. Palmer, the then president of the organization.

The five women who appear on the obverse side of the handle are Charlotte Cushman, Mary Anderson, Clara Morris, Agnes Ethel, and Lotta Crabtree. A San Francisco spoon showing Lotta's Fountain has been included in this sketch because of its intimate associations with Miss Crabtree. On the reverse side of the handle are the busts of the five men:

Edwin Forrest, Edwin Booth, E. L. Davenport, Joseph Jefferson, and William J. Florence. Both sides of this spoon are shown (on Plates 23 and 24). The Rip Van Winkle spoon naturally evokes memories of Joe Jefferson, who long played the lead role in the drama dealing with that notorious ne'er-do-well.

Charlotte Cushman, whom competent critics speak of as our greatest native-born tragedienne, stands almost alone on the heights, approached only by a chosen few, such as Mrs. Siddons, Eliza Rachel, Sarah Bernhardt, and Eleanora Duse. The gods did not grace her with beauty but they endowed her with a robust intellectuality that enabled her to vault all the crooked hurdles leading upward to the peaks of superlative art. Ironically enough she sprang from that Puritan stock which had looked with horror upon the stage since the days of the Cavaliers. One of her ancestors, Robert Cushman, was a Pilgrim minister who helped found Plymouth Colony. She was born in Boston in 1816, the oldest of five children—a wild hoyden who could not endure dolls and toys, considering them infantile distractions. Her father died young, leaving his family burdened with debts; the responsibility of supporting the family devolved largely upon Charlotte.

She took vocal lessons with the intention of being a teacher, but encouraged by several critics who heard her sing the role of the Countess in *The Marriage of Figaro* at the Tremont Theatre in Boston, she turned toward a singing career on the stage. Her teacher, James G. Maeder, secured an engagement for her in New Orleans. Whether it was caused by the climate or by an overstraining to reach the higher tones in her register, her vocal vigor failed her; the bright prospects of an operatic career went glimmering into darkness. The English actor Barton, who had witnessed her performances, advised her to switch from singing to acting, and coached her in the part of Lady Macbeth, for which he played the role of her husband. Her performances for a season in New Orleans were so cordially received that she went to New York, hoping to duplicate the same success. When she sought an engagement at the Park Theatre, the manager merely offered her a place on the waiting list. Indignant at this ice-box reception and being short of money, she accepted an opening at the run-down Bowery Theatre for twenty-five dollars a week. Here, while playing Lady Macbeth and Jane Shore creditably enough, she was harassed by a host of troubles. Rheumatism, which was to become her most redoubtable enemy, plagued her remorselessly, leaving her prostrate in bed for days on end. She had gone into debt for an extensive wardrobe, and while she was in bed, the Bowery Theatre burned completely, every one of her costumes going up in smoke.

For a short period she appeared at the National, where she first acted two of her favorite roles, Meg Merrilies and Romeo. The story is told that she took the role of the half-demented gypsy woman, Meg Merrilies, on a few hours' notice, the lady scheduled for that part having become

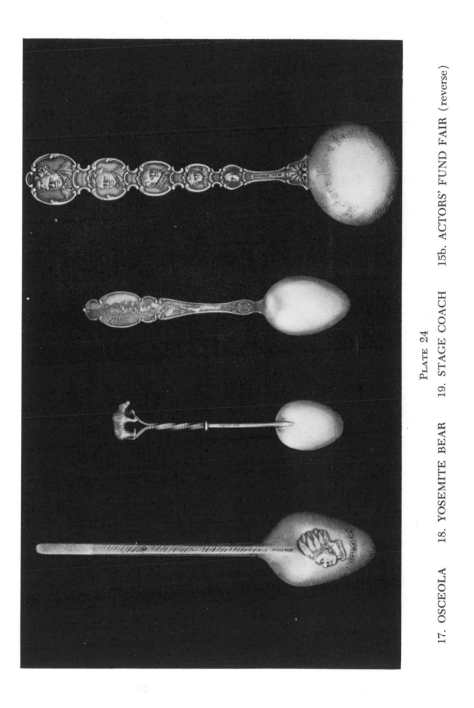

Plate 24

17. OSCEOLA   18. YOSEMITE BEAR   19. STAGE COACH   15b. ACTORS' FUND FAIR (reverse)

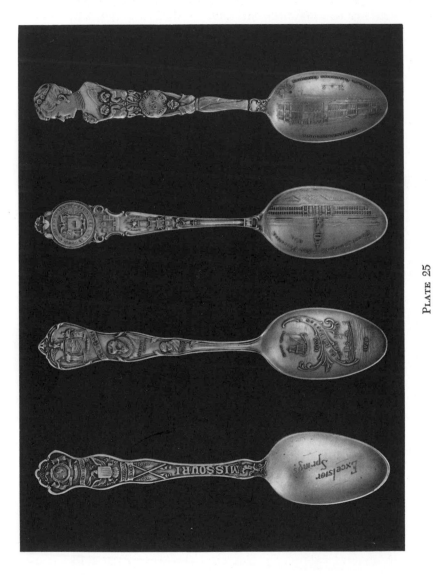

PLATE 25

20. EXCELSIOR SPRINGS   21. HUDSON AND FULTON
22. LOTTA'S FOUNTAIN   23. BERTHA PALMER STATUETTE

ill. She was told she might read the lines, but by the time the curtain rose she had learned all the forty speeches well enough to amaze the audience with her graphic interpretation.

A short engagement followed at Albany. Here the happiness of having her family with her was marred by the sudden death of a younger brother, who was thrown from a horse that Charlotte had just bought for him.

For three years, beginning in the fall of 1837, Miss Cushman played "general utility" parts at the Park Theatre. She was now willing to undergo the disciplinary training demanded by the more exacting traditions of this, the principal show-house in New York. She added the characters of Portia, Emilia, Joan of Arc, and many others to her repertoire. An apathetic English critic with slight esteem for American acting was electrified by her performance of Emilia and had to resort to the program to find out who had so shocked his slumbering sensibilities. "I knew that there was no ordinary artiste in this then comparatively unknown young woman. I saw her next in Lady Macbeth, and my conviction was only the more confirmed by this terrible test of any genius. I went away filled with admiration, resolved to see this powerful actress as often as I should have the opportunity. I then foresaw her fame, and time has justified my prophecy."

For two seasons Miss Cushman was the manager of the Walnut Hill Theatre in Philadelphia. At this time, she met and played opposite the English actor Macready, who was making a triumphal tour of the chief American cities. He recognized her abilities and suggested that she should try her luck in London—the plaudits of a British audience would add immeasurably to her prestige.

Charlotte Cushman landed in London unheralded and unhired. Even with letters of introduction from Macready and other people whose word should have borne weight, she encountered difficulties. To tell the truth, she was far from being a striking figure off the stage. She was tall, rawboned, and homely. Her deep contralto voice sounded mannish when not warmed by the passionate intensity of stirring lines. When Maddox, the manager of the Princess's Theatre, curtly refused to make any offers, she rose and walked to the door where she wheeled and burst out dramatically, "Yes, I know I have too many rivals here already (and she clinched her fists), but so help me God, I shall defeat them!" Maddox glimpsed her forensic powers in her sweeping gestures and called her back for an audition. Not long afterward she was playing the role of Lady Macbeth opposite Edwin Forrest.

At first she met with considerable opposition in London, not from her audiences but from members of her supporting cast. When she chose to act the part of Romeo to her sister Susan's Juliet, the actor who impersonated Mercutio declared, "There should be a law against such perversions. Romeo requires a man!"

The critics came, saw, and were conquered. Said one: "For a long time, Romeo has been a convention. Miss Cushman's Romeo is a creation; a living, breathing, animated human being." Said another: "I listened and gazed and held my breath, while my blood ran hot and cold." Lawrence Barrett, who was in the cast of *Oliver Twist*, for which she played Nancy, termed her acting magnificent and breath-taking: "Her voice, as she called for Bill (at her death) and begged him to kiss her sounded as if she spoke through blood."

At a benefit performance before Queen Victoria, she acted the part of Queen Catherine in *Henry VIII*. This vivid personation of a truly tragic character, so admirably adapted to the grand manner, aroused the critics to new heights of enthusiasm. It revealed new facets in Miss Cushman's nature by the sweetness and gentle womanliness of her portrayal.

Her engagements after her return to America in 1849 were like one long triumphal march. Everywhere she played to packed houses and co-starred with such noted actors as Edwin Forrest, Edwin Booth, E. L. Davenport, John Gilbert, and George Vandenhoff. But though she was now rich with honors and freed of financial worries, she was becoming more and more susceptible to rheumatic attacks, which caused her to take several official farewells. When finally cancer was added to her old ailment, it was necessary for her to forego all further work.

Her final appearance in New York took place at Booth's Theatre on November 9, 1874, before a vast assemblage of people. After her brilliant performance as Lady Macbeth, Miss Cushman was called back upon the stage crowded by such notables as Joseph Jefferson, John Gilbert, Dion Boucicault, Richard Henry Stoddard and William Cullen Bryant. A tremendous ovation greeted her, and homage was paid to her art in speeches and poems. At the end of the ceremony Bryant, then in his eightieth year, advanced and placed a laurel wreath on her head, with these words: "What came to your hand in the skeleton form you have clothed with sinews and flesh, and given it warm blood and a beating heart. Receive then the laurel crown as a token of what is conceded to you, as a symbol of the regal state in your profession to which you have risen and which you so illustriously hold."

She appeared for the last time in her native Boston May 15, 1875, as Lady Macbeth. Her death occurred early the next year.

William Winter, the eminent author and critic, has written several fine studies of Miss Cushman's art from which I shall quote briefly: "She was not a great actress merely, but she was a great woman . . . When she came upon the stage she filled it with the weirdness and the brilliant vitality of her presence . . . She diffused, as no other representative of the part (Lady Macbeth) in our time has done, the awe-inspiring, preternatural horror which is the spirit of that great tragedy—the most weird, portentous, sinister, afflicting work of poetic imagination that the brain of man has produced . . . When Meg Merrilies sprang forth in the moonlight and stood with towering figure and extended arms, tense, rigid, terrible, yet beautiful, glaring on the form of Henry Bertram, the spectator saw a creature of the ideal world and not of earth . . . She needed great moments on the stage and when they came she invariably filled them; whenever the occasion arrived for liberated power, passionate feeling, poetic significance, dramatic effect, she rose to that occasion and made it superb . . . She not only acted great parts but, in acting them, she gave something to her auditors. She imparted to them a conception of noble individuality, and an incentive to noble behavior. She told them that they also were of an immortal spirit; that it was their duty to live pure lives; to do right; to endure with fortitude; and to look onward with hope and trust. She did not fill their minds with images of decadence and prompt-ings to degeneracy, recklessness and failure. She was a minister of the beautiful; and therefore she was a benefactor to her time and to all times to follow . . . Many female actors have been distinguished in tragedy on the American stage, many beautiful women have appeared, and many displays have been made of genius and ability in various lines of dra-matic art; but of opulent power in acting, such as was manifested, at certain supreme moments, in the Othello of Forrest, the Lear of Booth, and the Lady Macbeth of Charlotte Cushman, the audience of the present day has seldom seen a superior example . . . Her best achievements were white marble suffused with fire."

Many poets were swayed to pay fealty to the consummate art of Miss Cushman. Sidney Lanier expressed this homage most aptly when he wrote:

> Full calm thine image in our love doth lie,
> A Motion glassed in a Tranquility.
> So triple-rayed, thou movst, yet stayst, serene—
> Art's artist, Love's dear woman, Fame's good queen!

* * * *

Mary Anderson, unlike Charlotte Cushman, did have the advantage of beauty. And it was no ordinary beauty. She was loveliest when she assumed a statuesque pose and allowed her audience to gaze upon the superior structure of her classic figure with its tall, stately form, and its radiantly charming face. Ranken Towse speaks of the noble, stag-like poise of her head, the gracious refinement of her manner, and the sweet, virginal innocence of her art, attributes which cast a potent, enduring spell over those who saw her. A product of the "provinces," she quickly became an ideal of the finest type of American womanhood.

Mary Anderson was born at Sacramento, California, on the 28th of July, 1859. Her mother's parents were Germans living in New York, strict Catholics, and much opposed to the theatre. Her father was an English-man who had spent most of his youth in the South. "With all his graces and accomplishments," says his actress-daughter, "he was, unfortunately, not religious, and his proposal for my mother's hand was met by a stern refusal from her parents." The pair corresponded in secret for several months, then eloped. They left New York immediately for California. When Mary was only a year old, her parents moved to Louisville, Kentucky, and from this time to the end of her stage career her name was always associated with that city. Her father enlisted in the Confederate army, rose to the rank of first lieutenant, and died of malarial fever at Mobile, Alabama, in 1863. It is said that the actress greatly resembled her father, who was known as the "gallant cavalier" by his Southern friends.

Her early training was supervised by a Franciscan priest, an uncle to her mother. After she graduated from the Ursuline Academy at the age of thirteen, she began to study elocution and literature under Professor Noble Butler, that distinguished teacher and textbook-author in whose widely-used grammar appeared that oft-quoted, self-violating rule: "A preposition is a word you should never end a sentence with." Professor Butler oozed an infectious enthusiasm for the classics, and he drilled "Mamie" in readings from Shakespeare. Most of the monologues she learned were from the male characters in *Hamlet, Richard the Third, Macbeth* and *Romeo and Juliet;* she was also coached to give long passages from Schiller's *Joan of Arc* in German, a language she had learned to speak rather fluently from her mother. The character influence of the Maid of Orleans cast a profound influence upon her entire after-life.

When she was fifteen years old, she made a special trip with her mother to see Miss Cushman, who was then staying in Cincinnati. They met in the lobby of a hotel, where the noted actress was seated, waiting for her carriage. Mary introduced herself, and Miss Cushman vigorously shook her hand, inviting her to come back early the next morning. When Miss Cushman had departed, Mary begged to be the first to occupy the seat just vacated by the famous woman, whom she reverenced. When Mary appeared and gave some of her readings, she made a very favorable impression. Miss Cushman told her that, although she had the three essentials required for the stage, voice, personality, and gesture, she still needed a year's hard study before venturing before the public. For a teacher, George Vandenhoff was recommended. And finally, the acknowledged queen of the stage admonished her to "start at the top" and "stick to the best"— an excellent piece of advice which she never forgot.

A few months later, George Vandenhoff came to Louisville to help stage a special performance of *Romeo and Juliet.* The cast consisted of purely local talent and the performance was not widely advertised, but Mary Anderson in the role of Juliet stirred the audience to their feet in wild volleys of applause by the dazzling lure of her presence and the freshness of her impersonation. As William Winter says: "The sweetness, sincerity, force, exceptional superiority, and singular charm of that nature could not be mistaken. The uncommon stature and sumptuous physical beauty of the girl were obvious. Above all, her magnificent voice—copious, melodious, penetrating, loud and clear, yet smooth and gentle—delighted every ear and touched every heart."

John McCullough, the noted Shakespeare authority, attended a repeat performance and waxed so enthusiastic over the acting of this "mere novice" that the girl was hired for a regular engagement at Macaulay's Theatre beginning January 20, 1876. Before the season was over, Miss Anderson was hailed affectionately by her native Louisvillians as "our Mary"—a name soon taken up by the rest of the country. For eight seasons she went on tour from one city to another, always as a star, and everywhere she played to packed houses, well sold out long before her appearance. Her fame increased, and the news of her coming was always heralded as an event of transcendent importance. She scored an unprecedented line of successes and her popularity suffered no diminishments in public esteem during repeated engagements.

Only once, when she attempted the impersonation of Meg Merrilies, did she verge on the borders of failure. Spectators, long familiar with Cushman's particularized version of this role, disparaged Miss Anderson's artistry, according to their preconceived notions, as inferior in conception. Certain detractors, having little else to criticize, found Miss Anderson lacking in voluble warmth. The criticism was justified only in the sense that she did not stoop to soppy displays of passion in melodramatic mush.

Many and diversified were the roles which she played, including Juliet, Galatea, Parthenia, Hermione, Perdita, Rosalind, and Desdemona. Juliet always remained the favorite with the public, though her crowning achievement was the doubling of the mother-and-daughter parts in *The Winter's Tale*. In the semblance of Hermione, Miss Anderson reached the full heights of her regal stature, the apogee of her art, in "not merely wearing royal attire but being invested with the royal authenticity of divine endowment and consecration." In contrast she endued her Perdita with the captivating charm of youth, the joyousness of life and lovely thoughts, and the embodiment of that beauty which is an ecstasy forever. Many people admired the charming childlike naturalness of her Galatea, so totally devoid of sophistication or semblance of artifice.

Three seasons in London, provincial tours, and appearances in Edinburgh and Dublin made her as much a favorite in the British Isles as at home. Then returning to this country, she appeared one more season before she announced her intention of retiring. In April, 1889, after thirteen years of unparalleled success on the stage, and still young and affluent of health, she played her last role, that of Hermione, in the national capital.

The next year she was married to Antonio de Navarro in London, and for the remainder of her long life she lived in the pleasant countryside once the haunts of her beloved Shakespeare. She made no public appearances except occasionally for charitable benefits.

George Arliss, who knew her intimately, relates in his memoirs: "When I look at Mamie now, she is so little changed that I cannot believe it is fifty odd years since I first saw her at the Lyceum Theatre—when I used to sit in front, night after night, because she was the greatest actress and the most magnificent creature I had ever seen. Just how great an actress she was I cannot say; but I do know that she took London by storm and was able to hold her own with all the English actresses then playing. The fact that she left the stage when she was thirty and yet is still vividly remembered by all old theatregoers seems to me to prove that she was an actress of great charm and ability."

Miss Anderson died in 1940. Although she left Louisville more than seventy years ago, her name is still quite familiar, for the Mary Anderson Theatre, like a guidepost on the main downtown street of the city is passed daily by thousands of pedestrians from whose lips you will frequently hear escaping the sounds: "Past the Mary Anderson? Near the Mary Anderson? Yes, at the Mary Anderson!"

❀   ❀   ❀   ❀

Some critics of the dramatic art have denied genius to Mary Anderson and even to Charlotte Cushman, stressing the physical force in the one and the intellectual stamina of the other to account for their phenomenal successes. Nobody ever gainsaid the divine gift of genius to Clara Morris, albeit that genius was an uneven one. The true test of an actor's forensic abilities lies not solely in his intellect, his gratifying physical appearance, his knowledge of stagecraft, or the mastery of many diversified roles, but in the presentment of great emotional crises to that degree where the actor and the part acted suffuse into a single entity in the sympathies of the audience. Clara Morris could do that. She did not become lost or submerged in so doing, for often she recreated a dull colorless part, animating it with her own personality. She resuscitated more lifeless plays than any other actress. No accusation was ever hurled against her as against Mary Anderson, that the part had to fit her like a glove before she was successful.

She was born on St. Patrick's Day, 1846, at Toronto, Canada. Her mother, a humble Irish-immigrant, working girl, had married a French-Canadian, only to find out after the birth of her third child that her husband was a bigamist with another wife and family. The poor, distracted woman fled to Cleveland, resumed her maiden name of Morrison, put her two smallest children in an orphans' home, but kept Clara, the oldest, with her. A soul-blighting childhood fell to the lot of Clara, who apparently shortened her name from Morrison to Morris in an effort to help forget her hard, unhappy past. Her formal schooling was scant. At fifteen she was dancing in ballets and operettas at the Academy of Music. Her early proclivities pointed toward music, but after entering stock companies, she underwent a long, grueling education in the practical school of dramatics, traveling about from one city to another, working chiefly in Chicago, St. Louis, and Indianapolis, which were then called Western towns.

Her first opportunity to take a leading role came to her unexpectedly, at an age when the average person has already given up all stellar aspirations. She had joined Daly's company just a few days before the first performance of *Man and Wife*. The play had already been advertised when Agnes Ethel, the leading lady, refused to act the part on account of certain objectionable lines, which she assumed to be immoral. The next lady in line was out of town and left no address. Daly then gave the role to Miss Morris, who changed the indelicate lines, and the play which only a short time before seemed headed for the rocks leapt into popular favor through Miss Morris's fervid portrayal of an unjustly-treated wife.

The New Magdalen, written, like *Man and Wife*, by Wilkie Collins, was revived by Miss Morris for her next production. She made several changes in the dialogue to suit her purposes, the plot remaining essentially the same, yet the play was something new. It was not only dramatic but also homiletic; it pled for tolerance toward those women who would lead virtuous lives after being shipwrecked by vice.

Miss Morris had few graces of voice or gesture; there was nothing clever, cunning, or skillful in her purpose; her artistry was amateurish; but for the presentation of painful, vivid reality and the startling poignancy of her emotional utterances, she was never surpassed. In *Miss Multon*, a variation of the "East Lynne" story, she plummeted the depths of despair in portraying the unrecognized mother. In *Alixe, Raymonde, Jane Shore* and *Madeleine Morel*, she revealed various aspects of that passionate love which can be hidden in a woman's heart. In *Article 47* she made beads of perspiration purl down the brows of her auditors by her graphic incarnation of a poor demented, heartbroken woman, sent forlornly to a lunatic asylum. In *The New Leah*, an adaptation of the German folkplay *Deborah*, she personated a Jewish maiden who has been cast off by her Christian lover. The scenes of the curse pronounced in the churchyard, of the lonely wanderings of the homeless girl, and of the forgiveness changing the curse to a blessing after many years, showed Miss Morris's abilities to portray the saint-like traits of patience, endurance, simple piety, and forgiveness as well as the climacteric emotions engendered by a frenzied love.

The great emotionalism in Miss Morris was regarded by many as a natural phenomenon, inexplicable in the ordinary terms of education or training. She was awkward in her movements and gestures; she blurred her r's, enunciated poorly, and stumbled over big words; in routine scenes she was as lifeless as a puppet. Then suddenly, in dramatic moments she rose to great heights of inspired passion. Louis James, who played opposite her in *Miss Multon*, said that "her acting had not only her audience but her fellow actors in a condition almost hysterical." He was so stunned in the scene where, as the heartbroken mother, she flung herself at the feet of her husband and, with tears coursing down her cheeks, exclaimed, "Maurice, for God's sake, let me see my children!" that he was incapable of uttering a word. "Yet in that moment of supreme agony he heard her whisper, "'I say, what ails you up there? Are you dumb?' The effect was like a shower bath."

She essayed several classical roles. *Camille* was definitely in line with her *métier*, but critics were curiously interested to see what she would make of Lady Macbeth. Every one was pleasingly surprised by the originality of her characterization, so different from the traditional ones made by Siddons, Cushman, and Terry. She humanized the lady, divested her of her conventional, regal imperiousness, and endowed her with all the attributes of a naive femininity. At times she was weak, nervous, and inconsistent, but always wholly woman. At odd moments she laughed or moaned, her sleep-walking scene was weirdly effective, and her "invocation to the spirits to unsex her was uttered with the concentrated intensity which she could always command." Her ideas of Lady Macbeth's appearance likewise differed fundamentally from those of her predecessors. A buoyant, petite figure, she wore gorgeous gowns that accentuated the curves of her wasp waist, and a diadem of sparkling stones that enhanced the luxuriance of her golden hair, making her an alluring Lorelei, who did not have to browbeat the king to win her points, but made his heart beat faster and in more obedient measures at sight of her charms. Mrs. Siddons believed that the blonde type was the true one, consistent with the Celtic origin of Lady Macbeth, but Mrs. Jameson disagrees, believing the Black Agnes of Douglas type more in accord with the character. This achievement with the blonde type was a triumph of original over hackneyed ideas.

In 1874, Miss Morris was married to F. C. Harriott. She continued her career as a great emotional actress until physical disabilities forced her retirement in 1894. For the next thirty years, till her death in 1925, she wrote numerous books and magazine articles on the varied vicissitudes of her stage career and about the many interesting people she had met during her long arduous climb to stardom.

Edmund Clarence Stedman, the banker-poet of Wall Street, paid her a well-deserved tribute on one of her few return engagements when he wrote:

> The secret given to her alone
> No frigid schoolman taught her—
> Once more returning, dearer grown,
> We greet thee, Passion's daughter!

❋ ❋ ❋ ❋

On the twenty-second of January, 1857, the curtain had just fallen upon *Camille,* the triumphant première of the season at Wallack's Theatre in New York, when a Mrs. McEthol and her six-year-old daughter Agnes pushed their way in an opposite direction through the great throngs of people streaming out the aisles and into the corridors. In spite of the difficulties encountered, they eventually managed to secure an *entrée* to the dressing room of Matilda Heron, the actress who had just scored such a success as Camille that she was forever afterwards to be identified with that role.

All the other admirers had to stand by when the actress learned that she and Mrs. McEthol had come from the same county of Londonderry in Ireland. But while the two women were conversing in the quaint brogue so sweet to their ears, the actress was attracted to the little girl at her mother's side. No spectator had been more struck by Miss Heron's recent impersonation than the actress, in her turn, now was by the strange, elfin beauty of the child.

"No fairies of the old sod are half so pretty," exclaimed Miss Heron. And addressing the winsome child, she asked, "Would you like to be an actress some day?"

"Yes, and I would like to act Camille just like you," declared the little girl confidently, affecting certain of Miss Heron's mannerisms in her bodily movements and voice.

"Oh, no, Agnes!" said her mother firmly, somewhat horrified at the thought that her only daughter should leave a comfortable home to share the unpredictable fortunes of a troupe of actors gallivanting around the country in all sorts of questionable situations and none too favorable circumstances.

The close friendship that began between the temperamental Miss Heron and the ethereally beautiful child in that dressing room was terminated only by the death of the older woman twenty years later. When Agnes was in her teens, she became a pupil of Miss Heron's and studied not only the part of Camille but also the Shakespearean roles of Ophelia in *Hamlet*, Viola and Olivia in *Twelfth Night*, Celia in *As You Like It*, and Hero in *Much Ado About Nothing*. These "sweet girl" parts were admirably adapted to her personality. They seemed to have been molded especially for her, or with some one exactly like her in mind.

On Saturday night, October 10, 1868, a select audience sat in Jerome's Theatre, then on the southeast corner of Madison Avenue and 26th Street, and watched the private debut of Agnes Ethel, sponsored by the solicitous Matilda Heron. She had fearlessly invited the most seasoned critics, who expected to see an ambitious but callow amateur cleverly coached by her preceptress go through the feint of playing Camille. Anything else would have been better because there were bound to be unfavorable comparisons, the popular role having been enacted by so many professionals in recent years. But the appearance of Agnes Ethel completely disarmed the most carping of critics. 'She is a blonde, delicate in frame, quite handsome, and thoroughly in earnest," stated the reporter for the *Times* the following Monday. "She had a graceful timidity in the early acts that was truly delightful." Her voice was none too strong and prevented a show of forcefulness in the first three acts. Thus far Miss Heron's guidance was obvious in the semblance of stance and gestures, and in the idiosyncrasy Miss Heron had of ignoring period pauses. In the fourth and fifth acts, however, where "quivering tones are all potent, the debutante exhibited clearest knowledge of what was required, and answered with an emotional power all her own."

On the merits of this initial appearance Agnes Ethel, the stage name assumed by Miss McEthol, was offered a place in a company that traveled through the season of 1868-69. She played not only her Camille and the Shakespearean roles but also several bits in dramatic efforts, mediocre and clumsy to say the least, written by Americans.

There is no evidence that the company played outside of New York state except for short visits to Philadelphia and Boston. And here it might be well to note that Agnes Ethel was exclusively a phenomenon of the New York stage, and never ventured far away from that big city.

In the autumn of 1869, Augustin Daly undertook the management of the Fifth Avenue Theatre, a showhouse that rarely drew large crowds, changed hands regularly, and had lately degenerated into a burial place for cheap variety shows. An announcement was forthcoming that "this superb house," closed for an overhauling, would reopen August 16, 1869, for the "production of whatever is novel, entertaining, and unobjectionable, and for whatever is rare and worthy in the legitimate drama."

Daly assembled a notable company of players, most of them "has-beens," who drew the largest salaries and did the least to earn their pay. There was also some young blood, untried, whose mettle was yet to be tested in the fires of experience. "Of course, the two most interesting among the fresher aspirants," says Odell, "were those wonderfully attractive young women, Agnes Ethel and Fanny Davenport, whose lauds and glories will soon be amply sung. I love to write their names, and wish I were a poet, to tag them in rhyme."

The Fifth Avenue Theatre opened as scheduled on August 16, 1869, with a pleasant but fantastic comedy called *Play* by Robertson, then the most popular of British playwrights. The inconsequential "Play" dealt with the life of guests idling away time in the fashionable watering place of Baden-Baden. Agnes Ethel took the part of the chipper Rosie Farquhere and aroused considerable interest by her performance, in which she exhibited a "succession of alternations between wildness and delicacy, grace, and the most abandoned rompish gaiety, and the tender sweetness of a wise and gentle womanhood." Every one was attracted by the rapt beauty of the gifted young woman. After a run of three weeks *Play* was succeded by *Dreams*, another comedy by Robertson, but the public had enough of this British humor which it could not relish. Ethel took the part of Lena in this piece.

To bolster his sagging office receipts, Daly had to change his program radically; he resorted to *Twelfth Night*, which, for the sheer beauty of its lyrical fancies, is unsurpassed by anything else which Shakespeare ever indited. Agnes Ethel portrayed Olivia the "virtuous maid" who "abjured the company and sight of men" until the proper man swam into her ken. Then the masterful countess was no longer "queen o'er herself." Ethel was eulogized for the "swan-like elegance" of her bearing in this comedy, which ran for two weeks.

Daly tried serving a different fare in *King Rene's Daughter*, a poetic drama translated from the Danish and successfully performed on occasion in London. Then he put a number of English and American plays on the bills, but these all wilted after the first or second performance. To meet expenses he had to turn again to Shakespeare. In *Much Ado About Nothing* Agnes Ethel played the role of Hero, a mild but colorless maid in juxtaposition to her wilful, quick-tongued cousin Beatrice. But Miss Ethel imparted a lustre and grace to the role seldom seen before. As Celia, the quiet but intelligent girl, in *As You Like It*, she received warm commendation from the press. In fact, she reversed the usual procedure and eclipsed the witty Rosalind.

From August 16th to January 11th eighteen different bills were presented —what an onerous grind! It kept the players constantly on their toes and there were few interims of rest for anybody. Agnes Ethel was on fourteen of the eighteen bills. After a day of rehearsing and a performance at night, the weary actors often had to work till after midnight on the alteration of their costumes, ripping a pleat here, snipping off frills there, and sewing on needed buttons. "Even the mechanics were worn out," writes Daly's son, "but health, hope, and buoyancy of heart carried them over all the disappointments. There was always some incident to laugh over, some trifling mishap, some misadventure turned to merriment; then the stage was cleared for another effort, and the feet of youth, which always tread upon air tripped lightly after their untiring leader, who as everyone knew, labored longer and harder than anyone else, and got no salary, not even his expenses. He came to the theatre in the morning before the watchman left, and he was the last at night upon whom the key turned. He spent nothing on himself. All that came in went upon the stage. The scenery was exquisite, the dresses costly, the furniture real. So far all had been struggle—now came reward."

The reward came with the tremendous success of a play translated from the French of Meilhac and Halevy. The very title *Frou Frou* suggests the gaiety, the frivolity, and the enchanting allure of the Paris boulevards. *Frou Frou,* one of the great emotional dramas of the nineteenth century, was different in type from the usual French comedy of manners because it ended in tragedy. Gilberte Brigard, the dainty little Parisian housewife popularly known in the sidewalk cafés as Frou Frou, meaning that soft sound of rustling silk so dear to the ears of French women, goes gaily on her flirtatious way for three merry acts, neglecting her home and her husband until she finds to her sorrow that she is supplanted in her husband's affections and then cast out. The reversal of situation is terrifyingly tragic.

Too late does the amusing little giddy-pate learn the terrible wages of her own levity.

Agnes Ethel absolutely stunned her audiences by her audacious playing of the title role. She became a sensation overnight. Her name was on the tongues of all theatregoers. Dithmar gives us a description of her at this time: "Her youth, fragility, delicacy, and elusive charm made her performance of one of the most difficult parts in the whole range of modern drama not merely acceptable, but, for the time being, thoroughly satisfying. With long crinkly waves of light brown hair shading her pale face, her graceful, almost fairy-like presence, her appealing eyes, she seemed the very embodiment of fascinating irresponsibility."

Frou Frou ran for one hundred and three nights. After the one hundredth performance, Daly entertained his company with a gala banquet at the St. James Hotel. His dreams had materialized with financial returns surpassing his fondest expectations. Everyone was happy except Fanny Davenport who, in a fit of jealousy at Agnes Ethel's popularity, had resigned her subordinate part in *Frou Frou* several days before.

The first season at the Fifth Avenue Theatre ended with the showing of Sardou's *Fernande,* Agnes Ethel again in the title role. The play ran for five weeks and the public, having learned to appreciate French emotional dramas, followed the fortunes and misfortunes of Fernande as eagerly as they had those of Gilberte Brigard.

The second season opened unpleasantly. There were strained relations between Mr. Daly and his leading lady. More than likely it was a matter of salaries. Some of the older figures, who should have been superannuated, were drawing the largest checks. Mrs. Jennings and E. L. Davenport were paid $200 a week and George Holland $150; while Agnes Ethel and Fanny Davenport, as mere novices, received only $50. After some bargaining, Miss Ethel's contract for her second year called for $125 weekly. Daly had already learned that it did not pay to hire "big-name" people. He was determined not to employ stars but to create them. He quietly rid his company of all barnacles.

Clara Morris, then practically unknown, entered Daly's company the second season. She soon learned, as she relates in her subsequent memoirs that there were two antagonistic factions in the group, the Ethelites and the anti-Ethelites, the latter spearheaded by Fanny Davenport. When Daly called the players together to assign them their parts, he handed Clara Morris the comic minor role of Blanche for Wilkie Collins' *Man and Wife.* The next morning he called Miss Morris to his office and reassigned her the leading role of Anne Sylvester, which, Daly said, Miss Ethel had refused to take "on moral grounds," and he would change no lines to suit any temperamental woman's fancy. "You will tell the people that you were to play Anne in the first place," Daly advised Miss Morris. Really, had Miss Ethel been asked to play the role? Was the shift in roles a slap to humiliate Miss Ethel, a move to placate Fanny Davenport, or a ruse to arouse publicity? All the newspapers heard from him was the statement that Ethel had sprained her ankle, although said cripple walked without a limp.

Clara Morris was really suited for the leading lady in *Man and Wife,* simply because Anne Sylvester was a screaming, hysterical woman at times, and Miss Ethel did not possess the voice for that type. After one of Morris's impetuous outbursts during rehearsal, this remark was overheard in the wings: "I ain't afraid to bet twenty good dollars that she makes pie out of Ethel's vogue!" Miss Morris was aghast at the manifest hostilities proceeding apace behind the scenes, and wisely held her peace when "the anti-Ethelites suddenly placed me on one of the sixty-four squares of their chessboard; but I knew not whether I was castle, knight, bishop, or pawn; I only knew that I had become a piece of value in their game, and they hoped to move me against Ethel."

Clara Morris, as we know, proved a great sensation in *Man and Wife* and temporarily overshadowed Agnes Ethel, whose dethronement was hailed with grim satisfaction by that faction led by the "full-blown, buxom Davenport." Obvious efforts were made to stir up enmity between the two leading ladies. But Miss Morris was too discerning to poison her mind with "the cruel jibes, the bitter sarcasms reported to me as coming from Miss Ethel." She confesses that she was cut to the quick by the "unpleasant stories" purportedly emanating from her rival during the run of *Man and Wife,* but she said nothing. "Then one night," says Miss Morris, "I met her—a slender, auburn-haired, appealing creature, with clinging fingers, sympathetic voice, and honest eyes—a woman whose charming and cordial manner not only won my admiration but convinced me she was incapable of the brutalities charged to her."

Meanwhile Miss Ethel continued to play, supported by Daniel H. Harkins, sometimes at the Fifth Avenue Theatre but generally on loan to other houses. Several times she performed in revivals of *Fernande,* as Julia in *The Hunchback,* and as Olivia in *The Twefth Night.* In the latter piece she shifted to the role of Viola, one of her finest Shakespearean interpretations. With George Vandenhoff she gave recitations for various charitable causes, and played in the *Lady of Lyons* and *Camille* opposite Walter Montgomery.

E. L. Davenport, a good soul who was perturbed at the unfortunate hostility existing between his daughter and Miss Ethel, enlisted the latter to play Ophelia for his Hamlet in an abridged version at a benefit for the enfeebled George Holland at the Brooklyn Academy of Music. Laurence Hutton writes of this performance: "Miss Ethel was a perfect picture of the most beautiful Ophelia. It was her first attempt at anything like a legitimate tragedy part, and was decidedly successful."

In the spring of 1872 Daly lent the services of Miss Ethel to the Olympic Theatre to play in *Horizon,* a drama of superior literary merits which Daly himself had written. In this play of pioneer life in the Far West,

Miss Ethel, as Med the "White Flower of the Plains," became a sort of Annie Oakley and created a mild sensation by her ability in handling a gun against the Indian attackers of a new settlement. The play, which had an excellent cast, ran for eight weeks.

At the end of the third season not only Miss Ethel, but several other players, including Kate Claxton, Ada Dyas, D. H. Harkins, George Parks, Fanny Morant, and Plessy Mordaunt, resentful of the dictatorial ways, strange inconsistencies, and the supercilious treatment accorded them, seceded from Daly's company.

In the summer of 1872, Albert M. Palmer, who had assumed the management of the Union Square Theatre, was feverishly casting about for experienced actors to entice patronage to his new enterprise when some one suggested Agnes Ethel, now out of a job and considered by her enemies as "washed up." Miss Ethel, who had been in contact with Victorien Sardou, brought with her a play *Andrea,* written especially for her by the famous French playwright.

Palmer rechristened the play *Agnes* and used it for his première, which opened September 17, 1872. Miss Ethel had an excellent supporting cast in D. H. Harkins, Walter Montgomery, Plessy Mordaunt, George Parks, Ed Lamb, Welsh Edwards, F. F. Mackay, Emily Mestayer, and Kate Holland. *Agnes,* one of the most epochal triumphs of the American theatre, ran for one hundred nights to such record-breaking audiences that it practically killed competition at other showhouses. Sardou, with his skillful technique and uncanny knowledge of stagecraft, knew how to create parts which would enable a large number of players to make the most of their lines. Not only was Miss Ethel superbly cast but her supporters also added lustre to their names. "I wonder," says Odell, "what Daly, whose autumn had been one of numerous changes of bill, thought of this new rival in his old field, especially with Miss Ethel, Harkins, and Parks, all secessionists from his corps, in the leading roles?"

For the first three months of 1873, Palmer tried various dramatic mediums, but failed to draw crowds. At his wits' end he revived *Agnes* (twice to cover up fiascos), *Fernande,* and *Frou Frou,* all of them sure-fire vehicles for box-office successes. After a run of nearly six weeks, *Frou Frou* was forced off the boards by the illness of Miss Ethel.

The brief but brilliant stage career of Agnes Ethel was over, contained within five years, at a period when the American theatre reached its most glorious heights. After 1873 we hear no more of her except for the readings of scenes from her plays at charity matinées. Among her many acts of generosity was the unstinted assistance she gave to her old coach, the improvident Miss Heron, who, although she had earned more than $100,-000, died penniless. Being none too robust, Miss Ethel decided to retire at the end of the 1872-73 season, and after her marriage the next year, she led a life of tranquil domesticity until her death in 1903. William Winter describes her at the height of her career: "Agnes Ethel's loveliness was of a peculiarly sweet, insinuating, enticing character. She actually was a woman of uncommonly strong will and great vital energy, but her apparent fragility was such that she seemed to be a sylph."

Two of her rivals, if they can be called that, Clara Morris and Fanny Davenport, went on to win laurels for many more years. Miss Davenport, pudgy, immature, but irrepressibly ambitious in the early years at the Fifth Avenue Theatre, was destined to develop into a great emotional actress, find unhappiness with two husbands, and die from the strain of too many undertakings.

Clara Morris, who experienced much the same difficulties with Daly as Miss Ethel had, soon transferred to Palmer's establishment where she occasionally had contacts with the well-known star. "While I never worked with her," says Miss Morris, "I received such gracious courtesies from her kindly hands that the name of Agnes Ethel must ever ring pleasantly in my ears." The fact is, both these women were great actresses in their own right. The essential difference between them and the primary distinction of each may be clarified by this animadversion on a certain actress: "She possessed all the freshness of Agnes Ethel without her fascination and all the energy of Clara Morris without her power."

Even though her career be the shortest perhaps in the annals of the stage, it founded securely the fortunes of the two most famous theatrical managers in our history, Daly and Palmer. She contributed no little part to the introduction and popularity of the French emotional drama which held sway in America for nearly two decades till the advent of Ibsenism. Then, too, her slight, buoyant, girlish figure with its fragrant essence of innocence and beauty, was wonderfully adapted for portraying those exquisitely tender girl-creations of Shakespeare . . . those marvelous conceptions which so few actresses are capable of rendering with a vivid reality. Miss Ethel's favorite role was that of Viola in *Twelfth Night,* that maid who "never told her love but let concealment, like a worm in the bud, feed on her damask cheek . . . pined in thought . . . [and] sat like Patience on a monument, smiling at Grief." The acme of femininity, epitomized in her very name, Agnes Ethel was a vision of delight, a cameo of supernal beauty, a joy forever to those who were once privileged to gaze upon her fascinating presence.

✿   ✿   ✿   ✿

In the old days it was customery for actors to establish a reputation in New York or one of the big Eastern cities before they went West on tours to enhance their growing fame. What the Eastern seaboard had seen and praised, the West wished to see and appraise also. But Lotta Crabtree reversed the usual procedure by acquiring such a reputation on the West Coast that the East was clamoring to know what this will-o'-the-wispish idol of the remote mining camps had to offer.

Lotta Mignon Crabtree was born in New York on the 7th of November, 1847. Her father ran a bookshop that did not provide a comfortable living; so the mother, an English-born woman, did upholstering to help meet family expenses. John Crabtree was an impractical visionary, a sort of Micawber, who saw a chance for escaping the confinements of a dreary bookstall and striking it rich when he joined the gold-rush trek to California in 1850. Mary Ann Crabtree lingered in New York three more years before she decided to go West also.

Mary Ann stayed in San Francisco with her small daughter long enough to become aware of the craze there for theatrical entertainment. There was drama in the air because there was drama in the making in the Golden Gate city of those days. When she learned the whereabouts of her husband, she departed with Lotta for Grass Valley, a mining camp high in the hills of the Sierras.

When John Crabtree had found a suitable boarding-house for his wife to keep, he set out again in search of gold. A few doors away lived Lola Montez, a very emancipated female who could never free herself from her own follies and mischances. Lola was attracted to the small Lotta and invited her in to see her two pet bear-cubs. Noticing the bewitching way in which the child skipped about in her garden, Lola offered to teach Lotta some Spanish dances, which had been the specialty of the notorious woman before she was kicked off the European stage. Mrs. Crabtree had no objections, and soon Lotta had learned not only how to do a few fancy steps, but also how to sing pretty ballads as well. Before a crowd assembled in a blacksmith's shop at Rough and Ready, Lotta was placed on an anvil, and while Lola beat out time with her hands and hummed, Lotta danced in such a spritely fashion that her mentor declared she should go to Paris for further study. At this idea the mother balked; she wanted to keep the child by her side.

There were numerous children playing small parts in the companies traveling up and down the Mother Lode country. Tiny mites often made the biggest hits with the mining element. As Mrs. Crabtree looked upon the performances of these infant prodigies, ideas began to creep into her mind. Although there were no theatrical antecedents in the family, Mary Ann thought that her daughter showed enough histrionic ability to stand comparison with any of the child-actresses she had seen. Her plans did not materialize, however, for another child, John Ashworth, was born to her at this time. Then Crabtree, spouting enthusiasm about the rich deposits of gold to be found farther up in the hills, moved his family to Rabbit Creek, where Mary Ann had to fall back on keeping another boarding house to eke out a living for herself and children. Crabtree went on prospecting but found nothing.

At Rabbit Creek, Lola Montez paid the Crabtrees a visit with the ostensible purpose of carrying Lotta along with her on her forthcoming trip to Australia. Again Mary Ann refused. She had run into Mart Taylor, an Italian, who owned a saloon and a log-cabin theatre. He was a versatile man with many interests, among them being dancing and music—he played the drum to perfection. On the guitar he could strum chords for a few plaintive ballads. But his finest gift was an ability to improvise words on the spur of the moment for any old tune.

At Mary Ann's connivance, Taylor rigged up a show featuring Lotta, for whom a dapper green outfit was made, consisting of stovepipe hat, swallowtail coat, tight-fitting breeches and a pair of brogan shoes. Plenty of instrumental music was provided. In addition to the guitar and drum on which Taylor doubled, and the triangle which Mary Ann had learned to beat, there was a violin, which supplied animation and verve to the ensemble.

The occasion was St. Patrick's Day, and when Lotta danced her Irish reels, wielded her shillalah, and exuded mirth with her rippling laughter between songs, she almost brought the roof down by the riotous enthusiasm she aroused especially when she was dancing, and her effervescing merriment became infectious. The other numbers on the program were simply side features to Lotta's act. The rude miners, starving for entertainment, coaxed the red-haired black-eyed Lotta back for encores by showering her with nondescript pieces of gold: slugs, nuggets, pesos, dollars, watches, rings, and even pokes of gold. Mary Ann watched carefully that none of this precious metal escaped her; she gathered most of it up in her apron and swept up the dusty scrapings later into one of Lotta's brogans.

The future of the eight-year-old child was now settled. Mary Ann determined to form a troupe with Taylor and travel up and down, playing in all the mining camps and heading eventually for the biggest game of all—San Francisco. Before she departed forever from Rabbit Creek, she left a note and a pot of cooked beans on the table for Crabtree, who occasionally blew in for something to eat.

They traveled in a covered wagon. Lotta often preferred to ride a burro, while Ashworth, barely able to walk, had to be kept in the wagon. They found few stages but always a ready audience wherever they tarried. More often than not they played in some barroom, where Lotta, if too crowded for space, danced and sang on the counter. Taylor would walk through the streets beforehand, beating his drum, to announce the time and place of a performance. The attendance was good but the gold drippings from Lotta's act were better. Everywhere the crowds became boisterous, once to such an extent that the Crabtrees had to lie behind a counter till a private feud was settled on the barroom floor. They crawled out only when the dead bodies were being carried out.

The company was a success but had to disband when it came time for Mary Ann to have another child. It looked as if maternal duties would wreck all the theatrical ambitions she had planned for her daughter. As soon as baby George was a few months old, however, she left the two boys with her sister Charlotte, then living in San Francisco, and set out with a new company of players from the mushrooming city by the Golden Gate for the Valley of the Moon.

Lotta now had a legitimate role as Gertrude in *A Loan of a Lover*. Her initial appearance was at Petaluma, a place that boasted a genuine theatre, even if it was upstairs, with boxes and a parquette. Mary Ann wove small comic bits into Lotta's part to enhance its importance till it stood out in a unique setting of its own. "She had, in fact," remarks Constance Rourke, "receded into the position which she was to occupy for years, that of Lotta's mother, Lotta's manager, the dragon who made the bargains and guarded the rewards." They met up with Mart Taylor once more, Mary Ann not only beating the triangle this time but also impersonating a Miss Arabella in one act. The roving troupe christened themselves the Metropolitan Company, and played to paying audiences in such towns as Oakland, Sacramento, Stockton, Fresno, Placerville, and Eureka.

Lotta added parts to her repertory, all of them being of the variety type. She became a blackface, a cockney sailor, a Highlander, a miner with pick and shovel. She remained as much of a hit as ever, and the gold nuggets were flung at her sometimes in such quantities as to frighten her off the stage. She mastered the banjo and struck responsive chords in the hearts of her listeners with *O Susanna* and *Old Dan Tucker*.

Their most profitable showings were in the smaller towns. In San Francisco there was too much competition, rivals parodied her songs and belittled her style. There were discouragements all along, but Mary Ann was always fortified with an indomitable will power against every rebuff of fate.

Lotta was growing up. One young fellow who admired her wanted to take her horseback riding, but Mary Ann declined the invitation in her daughter's name. The girl had no companions except her mother, certainly none of her own age. As soon as her part of the entertainment was over on the stage, Mary Ann whisked her daughter off to bed. She was suspicious of too friendly overtures. In San Francisco, Lotta occasionally met her old acquaintance, Lola Montez, who still thought she should go to Paris. Lotta also met another actress, Adah Isaacs Menken, and her latest husband, and in their company she frequently ate at the Cliff House. It was this pair who convinced Mary Ann that her daughter should try her luck in New York. Lotta's great popularity in Northern California and her recent successes in San Francisco stood to show that her dancing and singing in the East would also meet the acid test of approval.

In the spring of 1864, Mary Ann and Lotta, accompanied by Pa Crabtree, boarded the train for New York, the two boys being left behind. At first it was not easy because Mary Ann did not know how to make the proper contacts. Placed on a circuit that started in New York, Lotta played in Buffalo, Philadelphia, Pittsburgh, Cincinnati, Louisville, Nashville, New Orleans and Mobile. She was hailed as the California Favorite in a variety of acts that now included both Ma and Pa Crabtree, the latter usually appearing as a grandiose figure smoking a big cigar, ambling across the stage in leisurely fashion, and thinking himself a very significant addition in his very tiny bit. The homely Mary Ann seemed proud of her handsome but quite worthless mate puffing with importance on the stage, while the audience merely tolerated his presence because of its flitting briefness.

John Brougham, who first publicized her in New York, called her "the dramatic cocktail"—a title that horrified Mary Ann. She played before packed audiences at Niblo's, Wallack's, and the Broadway. Then she went on to Boston, Philadelphia, Chicago, St. Louis, and the Southern cities. Brougham wrote his own version of *Little Nell and the Marchioness*, so butchered that Dickens would not have recognized his own creations, but showing Lotta's jigs and reels, her banjo pickings, and her inimitable tricks to the best advantage. She played both title parts and kept her audience either laughing or crying most of the time.

San Francisco heard so much about her phenomenal successes in the East, that they wanted to see her again. In 1869 she made her reëntry on the California stage. Bret Harte read an informal note of welcome for the homecoming of its most famous daughter. The applause for each of her acts was overwhelming, and she gave generously of her encores. The old bonds of intimacy between the stage and its spectators, an art she had learned in the mining camps, were never so close as when she romped, kicked, skipped, and danced with the most hoydenish abandon before the "home folks" in San Francisco. Everybody was delirious with joy and showed it, that is, everybody except Mary Ann, who sat poker-faced in the wings, drinking in her daughter's triumph. Invitations to dinners poured in galore, but Mary Ann refused them all. The other actors might go out after the show and celebrate with caviar and cocktails or shrimp and champagne, but Lotta abstemiously dunked a few crackers in a glass of milk and went forthwith to bed. Mary Ann was truly indulgent when she allowed Lotta to buy her first silk dress in San Francisco. A thoroughgoing Puritan, Mary Ann's head was never turned by gauds or finery; hers was not the tradition of pomp and circumstance.

London was conquered next. "Lotta is the incarnation of drollery, mischief, and broad farce," said one Londoner. Another spoke of her youthfulness; she seemed to have bathed in the Fountain of Youth! "I expect every morning, looking over the newspapers, to find her name among the births."

The little strawberry blonde with the impish ways captivated the hearts of Englishmen in full measure. "Lotta's Marchioness is a performance *sui generis*," comments the London *Theatre Magazine*. "It is outside the domain of serious criticism. It is a thing to be seen and laughed at. It is the quaintest, oddest conception in the world, and though it may be heresy to say so, her breakdown is the funniest thing ever done in comic dancing. The scene between Swiveller and the Marchioness was the making of the play, which is, as all the Dickens plays must be, a procession of various well-known characters; Lotta's face, as she sits on the kitchen table eyeing that dreadful mutton-bone, haunts one."

When the American papers reported that the chill foggy atmosphere of London did not agree with Lotta, that she was dying perhaps, an outcry went up. She must come to America. And when she did come home, she played to jam-packed audiences everywhere. New Orleans held her for half a season before everyone had laughed enough. In the Midwest, where they never do things by halves, young men met her at the station, unhitched the horses, and themselves pulled her carriage to the hotel. And Lotta reciprocated by making pals with her audiences, but only across the footlights.

And what was Lotta's private life like in those days? It was accurately described by Teddy Marks, who said to James T. Powers one day: "There goes the great Lotta with her mother, her constant companion and chaperone. The old lady has mapped out Lotta's life for her, and marriage is barred. While Lotta is playing, she takes the greatest care of her; at four every afternoon Lotta is ordered to bed, and when safely tucked away, the mother takes a chair and like a sentinel sits outside the door. If any guests pass the room, they see the little figure with her finger to her lips as she whispers, 'Quiet please, my daughter is asleep.' She has all the guests, bell boys, and chambermaids walking on their toes."

And thus this idolized comedienne went on playing with undiminished popularity till her retirement in 1891. She bought a modest home on the shores of a lake in New Jersey and spent her leisure there in sketching and painting. Sometimes she would give entertainments in her barn-studio for the neighboring children, who loved and applauded her uproariously. She bought a few thoroughbred horses and rode around the countryside on horseback. Occasionally she was seen riding a bicycle.

After her parents and her two brothers died, she lived a very lonely life. In her old age she took an apartment in a hotel which she owned in Boston. When she died in 1924 it was discovered that her fortune amounted to four million dollars. All sorts of spurious claims were advanced immediately for this rich lode of gold. One woman claimed she was Lotta's daughter by a secret marriage but her fantastic story was quickly discredited by the too well-known facts of Lotta's life. The entire mass of this fabulous fortune, accumulated solely on the stage and hoarded religiously by Mary Ann Crabtree, went to charity, the disabled veterans of World War I being the main recipients.

To most people who saw her there "was only one Lotta and there will never be another like her." Yet it might be well to hear this animadversion on Lotta's acting by the dispassionate critic, J. Ranken Towse, who says: "Of no artistic importance in herself, a theatrical will-o'-the-wisp, she was a striking example of the slender capital with which popularity and fortune may be won before the footlights in a degenerate age. She attracted the attention of some theatrical agent on the lookout for a novelty, was diligently and successfully photographed, brought East, and introduced as a prodigy of humor and pathos. She was a bright and piquant morsel, prankish, audacious, with a pleasant aroma of girlish innocence about her, and she 'caught on.' For years the public adored her. She appeared in many parts and played them all in exactly the same way. She never developed or suggested any real dramatic force or adaptability . . . The so-called pathos of her Little Nell was the emptiest and dreariest of affectation. But she had splendid press notices, as if she were a luminary of purest ray serene. Modern press criticism has a good deal to answer for." What Towse seems to have overlooked is the strong personal element in Lotta's acting, which provided good, clean fun capable of making the world split its sides with healthful, harmless laughter. He misses the point entirely when he says her acting was of no artistic importance; it was not meant to be artistic but human, and truth expressed in terms of human values transcends artistic values. But you can't argue with some one who believes that all plays except Shakespeare's are trash.

Lotta's Fountain, on the spoon featuring San Francisco scenes, was given by the actress to the city in 1875. The fountain, originally a watering trough for horses but converted later into a drinking fountain for persons, stands on one of the main intersections of the city. It consists of four fluted bronze basins, adorned by lion heads, surrounding a cylindrical shaft of stone. It is one of the few landmarks that survived intact the catastrophic earthquake of 1906.

Lotta's Fountain is a favorite spot for carolers at Christmas. At other times during the year concerts are held here. Perhaps the largest crowd ever seen here, about one hundred thousand people, assembled to hear Luisa Tetrazzini sing on Christmas Eve in 1910. Speaking of these Christmas gatherings at Lotta's Fountain, Aubrey Drury says that they are "an eloquent tribute to the climate . . . Often the silvern notes of a prima donna hush to silence the mighty crowd; sometimes choir boys carol loud and clear; sometimes all the people together take up familiar hymns of praise and rejoicing, all creeds joining, and the singing of thousands of voices reverberates under the stars of a California Christmas."

❖   ❖   ❖   ❖

The chief tragedy in which Edwin Forrest played the major role was his own life. With not too much difficulty his story could be traced through its rising and falling actions, so necessary for good tragic drama, in steps that are ready made and rough hewn, though clearly discernible at all points. Shakespeare would have found him excellent bullion for his literary mint. Forrest himself recognized the tragic seam in his greatcoat during his latter days and, like a true Shakespearean character, only then did he somehow sense that the gaping rents had first been opened by his own scissors. To McCullough's compliment, "I never saw you play Lear so well as tonight," Forrest rejoined imperiously, "*Play* Lear? What do you mean, sir? I *play* Hamlet, Richard, Shylock, Virginius, if you please; but by God, sir, I *am* Lear!" His acting was cut like his character out of the web and woof of his own mammoth conceits. "His nature," says Winter, "fulfilled itself, and for that reason his life was a failure. It was this which made him a pathetic figure." In his temperament he may be compared, perhaps, to Andrew Jackson; like Benedict Arnold, he betrayed those nearest and dearest to him; as with Aaron Burr, his monstrous egotism and inordinate vainglory led him astray; but no one else is exactly like him; he is one of America's great tragedies.

He was born in Philadelphia, March 9, 1806, of immigrant parents, half Scotch and half German, yet no one was ever more chauvinistically American than he. Barely could he walk and talk well before he had decided definitely upon a stage career. He was molding candles for ships to help feed the family, his father having died early, when his first opportunity came to fill in a female part at the old South Theatre of his native city. Attired in dress and petticoats and displaying horse-hair ringlets from under a blazing turban, he advanced onto the stage as Rosalia de Borgia. The audience refused to take him seriously, and one youngster, sighting the heavy boy's boots under the dress, yelled out, "Look at his legs, would yuh?" The would-be-actress strode to the footlights and threatened to "lick the hell" out of the "hoodlum" after the show. The uproar that ensued brought the curtain down on the performance. The threat was successfully carried out, but under no circumstances would the manager rehire Forrest. The ambitious boy took matters into his own hands and slipped onto the stage, some time later, after the curtain had fallen, to recite Goldsmith's famous epilogue for Harlequin. He acquitted himself well, and when he left the stage with hand-springs and flip-flaps, the audience gave him enough applause to warrant an encore.

Having once tasted the sweets of applause, he craved more. The managers of the Walnut Street Theatre gave him a chance to play in *Douglas*, billing him as "A Young Gentleman of the City." A critic complimented him for the naturalness and careful articulation of his speech, and predicted a promising future for the fourteen-year-old boy. When Edmund Kean gave a series of performances at the Walnut, young Edwin studied his acting closely.

He now cast about for a permanent engagement. In 1822 he joined a company that traveled about, playing at Pittsburgh, Cincinnati, Newport, and Lexington. A salary of eight dollars a week was promised him but he did not always receive it. At Pittsburgh the roof leaked so badly that the audience had to hoist umbrellas to keep from being soaked. At Cincinnati a starving dog gnawed one of his boots to pieces and Edwin, unable to buy new footwear, substituted an old house slipper for his loss and limped on and off the stage, affecting a sore foot.

The rough-shod experiences of these difficult days gave Forrest a wonderfully diversified training. He adapted himself to step into any role almost at a moment's notice, being at one time a direful Richard III, at another a blackface comedian. Once he was so hungry he stole, between acts, some roas'n-ears, "hard as Pharaoh's heart," from a cornfield in back of the barn serving as a theatre. The company folded up at Lexington, and Edwin, at his wits' end for resources, found work with a circus at twelve dollars a week.

Soon he received an inducement that took him to New Orleans to play in James Caldwell's stock company at eighteen dollars a week. Forrest, then in the flush of youth, was extraordinarily handsome and attracted notice by his large, dark eyes, his black curly hair, and a fine figure as muscular as a Roman gladiator's. His voice, strong and clear as a clarion, could literally blow any man down. The fact that Forrest had caught the eye of the beautiful Jane Placide, the leading lady of the company, aroused Caldwell's jealousy, and he assigned the young actor to all the roles calling for old men. Forrest accepted his parts without resentment, and went about studying carefully the old men whom he met. He also visited the gaming tables and the race tracks, asked the famous Bowie for pointers on the use of his knife, and spent a month vacationing with Push-ma-ta-ha, living as primitively as the Indians.

Back in Albany, New York, the next season Forrest procured employment from Charles Gilfert, who let him play Iago for Edmund Kean's Othello. Kean gave him a copious meed of praise for saying two words in a whisper, a manner that struck the older actor as being the right one.

Forrest soon drifted down to New York and wondered what he would do next, when the chance came to play Othello at the Park in a benefit preformance for Woodhull, a destitute actor with an over-stocked family. Gilfert the phlegmatic Dutchman was down from Albany, dropped in to see the show, and was so delighted at the enthusiastic bravos given the young actor that he lost his pipe, specs, and snuff box in the rush backstage to congratulate Forrest.

When the Bowery opened the next season under the management of Gilfert, Edwin was drawing forty dollars a week. Envious theatres borrowed him from Gilfert for two hundred dollars a night! On the renewal of his contract, Forrest demanded that exorbitant price, and Gilfert willingly paid him that amount each night for eighty nights.

The success of Forrest wherever he went was unbelievable. People stood in line for hours to be sure that they would secure tickets. In New York choice seats were auctioned off, and a box of six chairs sold for one hundred and fifty dollars. One source of his popularity stemmed from his staunch advocacy of an American theatre free from British influences. He assumed all kinds of risks to introduce plays written by native dramatists.

The Gladiator, by Dr. Robert Bird of Philadelphia, was shown not only in America but was placed first on the list of those plays which Forrest earmarked for London, whither he repaired in 1836. Before this first English season was over, he had played Macbeth at seven performances, King Lear at eight, and Othello at nine.

Everywhere he was cordially hailed by the theatre-goers and the critics alike. William Macready, afterwards to be his bitterest enemy, entertained him at the Garrick Club. At the home of John Sinclair, the singer, he met the daughter of the house, the bewitching Caroline Norton Sinclair. Their hearts were soon singing in unison, and there being no objections, they were speedily married in St. Paul's Cathedral.

It would seem that the gods had led Forrest undeviatingly to the pinnacle of popularity with his eyes open, but at this perilous point they blindfolded him and gave him one nasty jab after another to send him careering headlong downwards.

It all started when Macready was making his first tour of this country. A great many people—not necessarily blue-blooded aristocrats with long genealogies and proud armorial bearings, though they were called that, and worse—favored the acting of the Englishman as being more genteel than that of the American, and possessing more finesse. The red-blooded patriots retorted that this "prissy pet of the Anglomaniacs" could draw applause from kid gloves, but that the virile American democrat could do better in drawing tears from strong men's eyes. The newspapers, opening their columns to this reprehensible sort of argument, hardly realized what seeds of folly they were sowing. Two wars fought with England had not been enough; this third, if fought only on a small stage, a tempest in a teapot, aroused much bad feeling and ill will that had lain dormant for a long time on both sides of the water. The two men directly involved were innocent bystanders of this petty warfare, that is, at first. But the old demon, professional jealousy, had reared his ugly head in their bosoms.

When Forrest made his second appearance in London, in 1845, he heard some hisses from the pit. He also learned now that he spoke with a "dreadful Yankee nasal twang" and grinned like a "wolf showing its fangs."

Forrest traveled about after he left London, and in Edinburgh he attended a performance of Hamlet by Macready. From a box seat Forrest sat leaning over the railing and was almost as conspicuously in view of the audience as the actors on the stage. At that point where Hamlet learns that the court will attend the play, he becomes merry and tells Mercutio; "I must be idle. Get you to a place." Macready, here acting like a sportive mad man, cavorted back and forth across the stage and fluttered a handkerchief above his head. As the proverbial red rag is to the bull, so was this handsheet to Forrest—a namby-pamby idea, so he thought, that could be conceived only by a foppish actor. At the third "gallopade" across the stage, Forrest, unable to stomach more of this "business," rose slightly and, with elbows still on the edge of his box, registered his disapproval by uttering a long, pronounced hiss. Coming from an ordinary lout, the contemptuous sound would have escaped comment. Coming from Forrest, it evoked strong condemnation from the press.

To add to the bad *pourri* in the pot, Forrest spewed forth more venom by a written defense of his action in the London *Times*: "Mr. Macready thought fit to introduce a fancy dance into his performance of Hamlet, which I thought, and still think, a desecration of the scene. That a man may manifest his pleasure or displeasure after the recognized mode, according to the best of his judgment, actuated by proper motives, and for justifiable ends, is a right which, until now, I have never once heard questioned; and I contend that that right extends equally to an actor, in his capacity of a spectator, as to any other man."

What a bad taste this acidulous subject leaves in the mouth, and one would fain drop the matter here and be done. But the climax had not yet been reached. The Amercian newspapers picked up their cudgels in defense of Forrest, now roundly attacked in the British press. Forrest's cause was the battle for independence from Britain on the artistic front. And no punches were pulled in that slugging match of acrid wits.

The democratic masses stood loyally by Forrest when Macready made a third tour of the United States. The "Forrestites" and "Macreadyites" lacerated one another's flesh and poured salt on the open wounds. What epithets were bandied about: Traitor, shoddy hero—high-brow, low-brow—pussyfoot, club foot—kidglove, rawhide—pusillanimous prig, blustering bull. It seemed that every sore, long scabbed over, broke open at once into a pussy stream of virulence.

The two protagonists in this off-stage drama did not stand idly by. Both were now writing "angry cards" to each other and to the newspapers. Macready defended himself and made remarks about Forrest before the footlights of a Philadelphia Theatre. He was showered with rotten eggs. The Boston *Mail* flashed in large headlines: MORE ABOUT MACREADY—HIS ABUSE OF FORREST—ENDEAVORS TO PUT HIM DOWN—HIS ABUSE OF AMERICANS. There were more headlines like that in other papers. Some of Macready's private opinions about Americans came to light, and they were not too favorable. He liked Americans in general but he disliked their crudities and discomforts. He condemned slavery in the presence of Southerners.

The climax of this stupid drama came when Macready began his farewell engagement by playing Macbeth at the Astor Opera House in New York, May 7, 1849. Bedlam broke loose when he stepped upon the stage. "Down with the English hog!" and "Down with the bigwig aristocrat!" were the cheers that greeted him along with flying eggs, onions, bricks, and an asafoetida bottle. When two chairs sailed down from the gallery onto the stage, the curtain dropped, and the play was over before it began.

Macready would have canceled his engagement if he had not been assured henceforth of police protection. On the night scheduled for his second appearance, the house was heavily posted with policemen. There were scornful hoots and shaking of fists; four men were arrested and locked in the basement under the theatre, to which they vainly tried to set fire.

Macready finished the stage-tragedy of Macbeth, but the real tragedy of that night occurred outside the theatre. An angry mob was gathering on the streets; bottles and stones came flying through windows. A third of the spectators left the theatre before the play was over.

As the police were leaving the building, the ugly mob attempted to crash the doors in search of Macready. The mounted militia rode up to halt their rush. Insults followed threats, and shots followed a disregard of both. The wildest pandemonium prevailed for half an hour, and when the smoke cleared, twenty-two people lay dead and thirty-six were wounded. Macready escaped through the riotous crowd unrecognized, boarded a train for Boston, and sailed immediately for England. He retired a year later from the profession which he had always despised, his chances for knighthood having vanished.

Forrest continued to play to packed houses for several years more. He was looked upon as a hero by some, but the beginning of his decline soon set in when he sued his wife for divorce on the grounds of infidelity. He could prove nothing, and testimonials showed the case to be a wreck-tangle—a four-sided rather than a three-sided affair, harmless indiscretions having been committed on both sides with no malice prepense. Forrest lost many supporters by his asinine outbursts of choler during the trial. His wife won many adherents by her quiet demeanor, and the jury decided in her favor. She was granted an alimony of three thousand a year—a sum which Forrest steadfastly refused to pay. Mrs. Forrest went into the show business herself and died a very rich woman, many years after her husband.

After the Civil War, Forrest gradually ebbed in popularity with the public. People were weary of him. New stars were burgeoning their points. New styles of acting were drawing the crowds. Forrest was getting old, irritable, and crotchety. His "puissant animal splendor and ground-swell of emotion" had worn thin. He was playing to empty houses and he saw the handwriting on the wall. Still, the lonely, deserted old man would not give up. His last performances were pathetic failures, and he tottered from the stage in time to die a few days before Christmas, 1872.

A kind word might be said for the better side of Forrest's nature. The first big amount of money he earned, four hundred dollars, he deposited in his mother's hands. Wherever he was, even in far-away New Orleans, he sent groceries and fresh fruits home. As soon as he was able, he bought a comfortable home for his mother and three sisters, provided well for them and buried them all. His only child, a son, died young, and the loss is said to have embittered him. But he always tenderly loved children and built a miniature theatre in the basement of his home for them, working for hours with them there. Once he was infuriated, and cast all manner of obloquy at a member of his cast who did not show up. When the miscreant appeared, to explain that one of his children had just died, Forrest was overwhelmed, spoke tenderly to the grief-stricken father, and gave him fifty dollars, all he had in his pockets at the time. One night, after a strenuous performance, he found a sick mother and a crying child next to his room at a boarding house. He paced the floor with the ailing child in his harms and nursed it till morning with milk he had sent for. The doctor declared that Forrest had saved the infant's life by the warmth, food, and care he had provided. In his will he stipulated that his luxurious home near Philadelphia be converted into a sanctuary for impoverished old actors, with generous provisions for their comfort.

A memorable man was Edwin Forrest, our first great actor, but unfortunately one who played too long and let his artistic powers run to seed. A sober lesson is entailed in his story, and that is, how closely bound is greatness to the littleness in human nature.

❀   ❀   ❀   ❀

Just as Miss Cushman was her most magnificent self as Lady Macbeth and Edwin Forrest the living reincarnation of King Lear, so did Edwin Booth become by the quality of his melancholy reflective nature the very embodiment of Hamlet. "Booth was Hamlet," says Edward Robins. "So long as the memory of his performance endures, no other Hamlet can take his place; to the American playgoer he seems the greatest exponent of the part, whether we think of the past with its long line of fine Hamlets, or of the future when tyros and accomplished actors alike will have their fling at the sabled fatalist."

How inseparably associated the characters of Booth and Hamlet were in the minds of theatregoers, old or young, may best be illustrated by an incident related by Mrs. Goodale, the former Kitty Malony who played in Booth's company in later years: "My little niece, scarcely more than a baby, came behind for the first time in her life, and to her mind Hamlet was Hamlet—not Mr. Booth. She gazed so yearningly at Hamlet that I overcame my timidity and presented the mite to him. But I need not have hesitated, for Mr. Booth's face became tender. He impulsively stooped and kissed her, saying, 'You *are* a beautiful little one.' She did not smile but gazed heavenward, murmuring, 'Hamlet kissed me!'" A quarter of a century after Booth's death, two days after the armistice for the First World War was signed, a statue of Edwin Booth was unveiled in Gramercy Park, New York. The figure on the pedestal shows Booth in the character of Hamlet—and to the school children, for whom Booth in person is not even a memory, it is Hamlet standing there and for them it will always remain Hamlet.

Junius Brutus Booth, the actor and father of three sons who were actors, left England for America because of a rivalry with, as well as an annoying similarity in appearance to, Edmund Kean. That similarity did not extend as far as his bandy legs, which were the subject of many a wise crack. Once, when he was playing in *Cymbeline* a joker from the gallery broke up the show when he yelled: "Ah, ha, you're a pretty fellow to stop a pig!"

This elder Booth was married twice. By his first wife he had one son, who eventually died in the Confederate service. His second wife bore him nine children, of whom Edwin, named for Edwin Forrest, was the sixth, born the 13th of November, 1833, on a night when the heavens were bright with shooting stars.

"The Farm," the home of the Booths not far from Baltimore, was a pleasant ménage when the father was there in the summer, or between engagements in the winter. Very early little Edwin was assigned the task of accompanying and caring for the father on his travels. The boy received scant formal education, but close association with his father, a graduate of Eton, and a well-read man, enriched his mind with a treasury of literary knowledge.

Junius Brutus Booth was an erratic man, prone to wander off and not keep his engagements on the stage. Edwin would often tag along and plead with his father to bring him back on time. Once, after a show the old man paced up and down a deserted market place till the farmers began to open their vegetable stalls at daybreak. In Boston, when the father wanted to stroll off after the show, Edwin earnestly begged him to remain at the hotel. Surprised at his son's unyielding attitude, the elder Booth disappeared into a dark closet and locked the door behind him. For two hours, Edwin did not hear a sound; he did not know if his father were dead or alive. When he was finally sure he had better call for help to remove his suffocated parent, the supposed victim marched out, undressed, and went to bed without a murmur of explanation.

Being the veritable guardian of his eccentric father made Edwin prematurely serious and thoughtful. The strain of sadness in his disposition was early evident, and it grew more pronounced with time. While he had an apt sense of humor, he seldom gave vent to an exuberance of mirth. The characteristic thing about his laughter, some one has said, was its soundlessness.

Junius Brutus Booth was resolutely opposed to any theatrical ambitions for his children. Seeing how facile Edwin was with saw and hammer in adjusting stage properties, he planned for him a career as cabinet-maker. But Edwin abided his time and, when less then sixteen, got his first chance, in Boston, to appear on the regular stage. His father was to act in *Richard III*, and the prompter for the show complained that he had enough to do besides taking the part of Tressel, the mounted messenger. Edwin volunteered to relieve him, and, already dressed for the part, announced the fact to his father, who forthwith drilled him on the character of Tressel. Edwin answered all the questions correctly, but was censured for forgetting the spurs, those accessories so necessary for a fast-riding courier.

114

A few months after this performance, Edwin and a friend got up a blackface show in their home town of Belair, Maryland. The posters advertising the event had been sent around with an elderly slave who, with the best of intentions, tacked the signs upside down, yet a big crowd attended this "Grand Dramatic Festival" and enjoyed the plantation songs played by Edwin on the violin and banjo.

In 1851 he played his first major role. His father had been billed at the National Theatre in New York to act Richard III, his most popular role. Just before he was to go on the stage, he felt a strange indisposition and cried out, "I can't go on!" When Edwin begged him to "pull himself together" and go through with the part, Junius Brutus retorted, "Go act Richard yourself!" And Edwin did, declaiming the lines as well as his father. The spectators felt at first they were being rooked and imposed upon by a mere stripling. As the play progressed, their sullen attitude shifted to one of appreciation, and before the end there were enthusiastic calls for encores. The father sat in the rear and quietly watched his son present the part of the humpbacked, bandy-legged monarch. He never tried thereafter to dissuade Edwin from entering upon a stage career.

The next year Junius Brutus Booth and two of his sons, Junius Junior and Edwin, traveled to California, taking the short cut across Panama by stagecoach. The West Coast was suffering just then from a slump, and the times were not propitious for actors. The income from their services was a mere pittance, and Edwin derived more money from his black-face offerings than from Shakespeare. The father pulled up stakes and set out for home, leaving the boys to fend for themselves. He died on a steamboat en route. The news reached Edwin when he was roughing it in the snowbound mining towns of Nevada.

Edwin and Junius Junior experienced a variety of vicissitudes. Many times they were on the verge of starvation. Once Edwin was wandering about the streets of San Francisco wondering where the money for his hotel bills would come from. A man to whom he had lent twenty dollars a few months before walked up and deposited two ten-dollar bills in his hand. Delighted at this windfall, Edwin figured that Dame Luck was his attendant that day; so he strolled into a gambling parlor, staked his money on a roulette wheel, and promptly lost it. His ill-fortune taught him a salutary lesson, for he never gambled again.

Leaving his brother in San Francisco, Edwin sailed for Australia, which was enjoying a prosperity boom. He played opposite Laura Keene on this tour. On the return trip, the company stopped in Honolulu and played before appreciative audiences. King Kamehameha IV sat behind the stage and watched a performance of *Richard III*. After the show the sovereign complimented Edwin on his acting, saying he was equally as good in the part as his father, whom the king had seen in New York some years before.

Back in California Edwin traveled about from town to town, adding one role after another to his repertoire but nothing to his bank roll. He returned East and played first in Boston, where his acting of Sir Giles Overreach was highly commended. His reputation preceded him to New York; there he was billed as the "Hope of the Living Drama." He was hailed as the "son of a great tragedian," but this appellation was soon shortened; the son was a great tragedian in his own right. In Philadelphia he played Macbeth in support of Charlotte Cushman's Lady Macbeth. The two differed radically in their conceptions of the ambitious king. To Miss Cushman, Macbeth was the "grandfather of all the Bowery villains." Booth interpreted Macbeth as an intellectual villain, a composite of good and bad motives struggling constantly for the upperhand.

Booth's long apprenticeship had made him a thorough master of his art. The press accorded him the highest praise wherever he appeared. A public fed up on the heavy, pompous style of Edwin Forrest forsook the trumpetings of a Stentor grown hoarse to hear the sweet "flute-like" tones of the sad-faced young idol, who secured his most telling effects seemingly in the kaleidoscopic nuances of expression emanating from a profound intellectuality. "His genius," remarks Edward Robins, "was a dramatic trinity of mind, poetic feeling, and power of expression. He was a deep and lucid thinker, to whom Shakespeare was an open book, not a mystery; he had keen sensibility, and a vivid imagination quick to grasp every subtlety and possibility of a part, and he could, by the magic of his look, tone, or gesture give theatrical form to every idea that was passing through his fertile brain."

Booth married twice. His first wife, Mary Devlin, was a native of Troy, New York; an accomplished musician and a very lovely woman, she was influential enough to cause her husband to give up his immoderate drinking, a weakness that had started and grown upon him during his Western travels. The three years of their wedded life were ideally happy and he was always passionately devoted to his daughter, Edwina, the one offspring of this marriage. His second wife, Mary McVicker, played the part of Juliet to his Romeo at the opening of Booth's Theatre in New York. This marriage, which lasted for twelve years, was harrowed by the tragedy of Mrs. Booth's insanity toward the end of her life. Those who knew what dark clouds were hovering over Booth's home marveled at his patience, endurance, and ability to play night after night in the theatre.

The season of 1864-65 saw Booth at the pinnacle of his career. The unprecedented run of his *Hamlet* for one hundred nights at the Winter Garden in New York set a record for Shakespearean performances in this country. On November 25, 1864, the three Booth brothers, Junius, Edwin and John Wilkes appeared together in *Julius Caesar* while their mother, from her proscenium box, proudly witnessed the tribute of cheers and curtain calls given her handsome sons.

But the happiness of that moment was dashed not long afterwards by the direful tragedy perpetrated by the youngest son at Ford's Theatre in Washington. The assassination of Lincoln—whom he had supported and voted for—by his brother struck Edwin Booth like an atom bomb. He cancelled all engagements and hurried to New York, where he stayed in the seclusion of his home, brooding over the sorrow which that "rattle-pated fellow, filled with Quixotic notions" had brought to his family as well as to the nation. He could find no words to comfort his distraught mother—who was to live for twenty years after the calamity.

He would have retired permanently from the stage if friends had not insistently declared that it would be foolish for him to do so. His re-appearance as Hamlet in 1866 at the Winter Garden was greeted with flowers, enthusiastic cheers, and a wild waving of hats.

Soon after, he planned and built a theatre to be a model of its kind. The expenditure ran above a million dollars, and the debt thus incurred he could never pay off. He ran the house for three seasons; then it passed out of his hands.

He made several tours of the continent. His appearances in England in 1861 were coldly received, partly because of an intense dislike of "Yankees" at that time. The unfriendly reviews of critics kept spectators away from theatres where he was playing. A pleasure jaunt to Paris afforded him relaxation, and several receptions were given in his honor. On his second visit to England in 1880, he was accorded a much better reception, although one critic stated peevishly that he was prone to "gobble like a turkey."

His tour of Germany was perhaps the happiest in Booth's life as an actor. He received tremendous ovations everywhere—in Berlin, Hamburg, Bremen, Hanover, Leipzig, and Vienna. Trophies were showered upon him, and once he was handed a laurel crown consisting of gold leaves. Kitty Malony in her memoirs, gives an account of Booth's contacts with the very formal stage manager in Berlin. In Mr. Booth's own words: "He embarrassed me. His punctiliousness was harder to endure than contempt or rudeness. His directing let me see at once he was a student of Shakes-speare and an authority on stagecraft. He knew his business . . . I had no fear of his working against me. I should have what I was entitled to; but not one jot more did he intend me to get out of him.

"The rehearsal ended and the performance began. I was busy and so was he! I had not given him a thought—the scenes ran too smoothly for that—but—when the final curtain fell, it occurred to me there might be something pleasanter in life than running against this hostile stage manager again, so I turned to leave the stage. Something solemn charged the atmosphere. It arrested me. The actors stood as statues—but—the stage manager came to me. He bent over my hand—he seemed to be kneeling—he kissed my hand and said, 'Herr Meister!' It was done so simply—with such sincerity—I wanted to cry."

Mr. Booth never did retire but his appearances were less frequent in his later years. He presented an infinite variety of roles and traveled far and wide over our country, stopping even in many small towns. In Cheyenne a brass band was out to greet him at the station with "Lo, the conquering hero comes!" Sometimes he was accused of being too cold and formal at his curtain calls but to this his usual reply was, "Why should I be worked up over the approval of unripe judgment?"

He always inspired a sense of loyalty in the other members of his cast. He referred to the young people affectionately as "my little chickens." He was never known to quarrel or lose his temper over minor details. One incident will reveal his easy-going manner. "Where do you stand?" he inquired of one young fellow, whose answer was: "Mr. Barrett had me over there." "I usually have him here," said Mr. Booth, pointing to the opposite side of the stage; "but never mind. Suit yourself. I'll find you wherever you are." Would that all people were as complacent and easy to please!

He suffered a stroke of paralysis in 1891, and his health gradually failed till his death on June 8, 1893. "I cannot grieve at death," he once wrote. "It seems to me the greatest boon the Almighty has granted us." Thomas Bailey Aldrich, in describing Booth's funeral, writes: "Just as Edwin was laid in the grave, among the fragrant pine-boughs which lined it, the sun went down. There in the tender afterglow two or three hundred men and women stood silent, with bowed heads. The soft June air, blowing across the upland, brought with it the scent of syringa blossoms from the slope below. Overhead, and among the trees, the twilight was gathering. 'Good night, sweet Prince,' I said under my breath. Then I thought of the years and years that had been made rich with his presence."

❀   ❀   ❀   ❀

While other actors are known preëminently as either tragedians or comedians, outstanding in a few distinctive roles, Edward Loomis Davenport is known simply as a stage star famous for his versatility. He could act, sing, or dance equally well. His repertoire included everything from the Shakespearean tragedies and comedies to the most preposterous farces; with his fine tenor voice he could sing the part of Thaddeus in *The Bohemian Girl,* the merry ballad of *Sally in our Alley,* a plaintive plantation ditty, or the lofty strains of the *Messiah;* he could trip the light fantastic in the stateliest measures, the tap-and-heel of a hoe-down jig, or the thumping clatter of a sailor's hornpipe. He could give an evening's readings from the poets, orate eloquently, or preach a funeral sermon. He was seldom miscast, and as a rule he could grasp any situation by forelock or fetlock and master it with unseeming effort.

Davenport was born November 15, 1815, the son of a Boston innkeeper. His parents were strait-laced people who "abhorred theatres." Yet the boy at an early age was already anxious to get into "other garments than his own" at school entertainments. Long afterwards, when a teacher of his, a Mr. Lovell, then an octogenarian, saw his former pupil perform, the old man wept the entire time.

For a while E. L.—as he was subsequently known—clerked in a hotel, then in a dry-goods store.

He was interested in amateur theatricals, and when Edwin Forrest saw him in one of these and gave him some encouragement, the disinterested clerk abandoned his dry goods for the more glamorous costumes of the stage. The minor parts he handled at a Providence theatre prepared him for a more seasoned role at Newport in Douglas Jerrold's nautical drama, *Black-Eyed Susan*. The character of William, which he personated, continued to be popular for years; an English sailor once declared that Davenport's insight into a seaman's life knocked the "very salt water out of his bloomin' top-light."

Not till he became associated with Mrs. Anna Cora Mowatt in 1845 did he advance to the position of a star. Under her management he began to play Sir Giles Overreach, the best of all his personations. In the fall of 1846, Mrs. Mowatt's company toured the South, stopping in Louisville, Nashville, Augusta, Macon, Columbus, Montgomery, Mobile, and New Orleans. The stages were often inadequate—sometimes there was none—but the vicissitudes encountered were valuable, and interesting. On a steamboat between Louisville and Vicksburg, Henry Clay was aboard and Davenport, determined to get acquainted with the famous statesman, rigged himself up in an odd assortment of clothes, clapped a red wig over his poll, strode on deck, and in a voice as twangy as a Yankee rustic's said loudly, "Wal, I hyear that thar feller Henry Clay's aboard; I guess I'll get acquainted." Of course, Clay overheard the remark; the two struck up an immediate friendship; and for the rest of the trip the entire company was regaled by the hilarious jokes and tall tales of the two expert funsters.

In 1847 Mrs. Mowatt's company sailed for England, where Davenport met and married the English actress, Fanny Vining. His sojourn abroad, quite agreeable in all its aspects, lasted for seven years. At one time Macready invited him to play in his support. But soon the Englishman became jealous of the attention that Davenport was attracting, and bellowed irritably, "I wish you wouldn't try to overact; your extreme earnestness detracts from the total result." Davenport obediently subordinated his efforts to such a degree that Macready now charged him with deadening the total effect of the show.

When he returned to Boston after his long absence, he was greeted by cheering crowds. A banner flung across a main thoroughfare, bore the words: "Welcome home, E. L. Davenport."

For ten years he handled an incredibly large number of roles, made several tours, and served as manager at numerous theatres. It was nothing for him to act two roles in the same play—in *For Branded* he actually personated five parts and came off amazingly well. He appeared alongside an imposing galaxy of stars: Charlotte Cushman, Edwin Forrest, Edwin Booth, Lawrence Barrett, John McCullough, Matilda Heron, Mr. and Mrs. W. J. Florence, George Vandenhoff, Agnes Ethel, Mary Devlin, Joseph Jefferson, J. W. Wallack, Kate Claxton, Adelaide Neilson, his daughter Fanny—in fact, with everybody of any importance.

He was an affable man who made few enemies. Although he fell out with the irascible Edwin Forrest over the rights of performance to a certain play, the two men eventually came to have a high regard for each other. Forrest, when he once heard Davenport spoken of as being "just above the average," offered this stout rebuttal, "They may say what they please, although Davenport and I haven't spoken for years, he is the best actor on the American stage." Davenport returned the compliment; in his opinion Forrest was "by far the most original and greatest actor America has ever produced."

As a manager Davenport was not too successful. He wished to hurt no one's feelings; he was not satisfied till all the members of a cast were satisfied with their parts. For him every one had possibilities and he was ever anxious to help develop the latent talent, however little it was, which he saw in the worst of amateurs. He was generous and thoughtful of others, and a spirit of kindliness emanated from his very presence, making life humanly pleasant for those around him. When he hung up a notice: "Boys don't smoke, and if you love your manager, turn down the gas," the boys were amused, but obeyed the behest.

The family life of the Davenports was singularly happy, and the doors were always swinging open to welcome visitors informally. A frequent guest for Sunday dinner was Edwin Booth, who was visibly brightened by the antics of the nine romping children. There was a side table at which any misbehaving youngster had to eat alone. One Sunday when Fanny, the eldest child, was thus humiliated, Booth moved his chair to her table and kept her company, much to the delight of the mischievous young lady.

Mr. Davenport is described in his later years by Goddard as "tall, not over-stout, but with a well-knit figure, mild blue eyes, florid face, prominent nose and thin light hair that revealed coming baldness. His voice, like his manner, was indescribably pleasant and winning."

The two outstanding roles which he presented were those of Brutus in *Julius Caesar* and Sir Giles Overreach. J. Ranken Towse says that he was a "splendidly dignified and magnanimous Brutus," and it was largely owing to his superb interpretation that the play was so popular, running for two hundred and twenty-two nights. One veteran devotee of the stage penned this tribute to his acting of Sir Giles:

While viewing each remembered scene,
  before my gaze appears
Each famed depictor of Sir Giles for
  almost fifty years.
The elder Kean and mighty Booth
  have held all hearts in thrall,
But, without overreaching truth, you
  overreach them all!

His Bill Sikes in *Oliver Twist* made people shudder at the vividness of his personation. His Hamlet and his Richelieu were likewise intrinsically good, worthy of mention with the best. Had he limited and identified himself more fully with fewer roles, he would have received the greater measure of recognition which he merited.

When he died September 1, 1877, he was followed to the grave by a large assembly of people from all walks of life, William Cullen Bryant and Judge Daly being among his ballbearers. The epitaph on his tomb begins with "Our Father who art in Heaven," and follows with a lament on the loss to the world by the passing of a noble, virtuous, Christian gentleman.

Seven of Mr. Davenport's children were actors at one time or another. We have already mentioned Fanny (1850-1898), who won spectacular successes in the emotional drama toward the end of the century. Like her father, she essayed every type of role from Shakespeare to ebullient froth. A remarkable actress, she overtaxed herself and died prematurely.

The youngest member of this histrionic family, Harry Davenport (1866-1949) could boast of the longest acting career in American stage history, stretching over seventy-eight years. He began at five, played later with Lotta Crabtree, Minnie Maddem Fiske, and his older sisters. At the age of seventy he switched to Hollywood, and was filmed in more than one hundred movies, among them being *Gone With the Wind*, (in the role of Dr. Meade) *Forsyte Saga, Meet Me in St. Louis,* and *The Farmer's Daughter.* For longevity of effort, he should become a legend with Louis XIV, Queen Victoria, George Bernard Shaw, and Methuselah.

✹　✹　✹　✹

There is no more striking contrast than that presented by the careers of E. I. Davenport and Joseph Jefferson. The one portrayed the most varied types of characters, totaling more than six hundred in all. Jefferson confined himself for the last forty years of his life almost exclusively to a single character. And yet, in spite of this particularity, Jefferson is still pleasantly regarded as the greatest comedian of our legitimate stage.

Some critics would refuse to grant Jefferson a place in the category of great actors. Lewis C. Strang remarks: "Should one resolve seriously to consider Mr. Jefferson as an interpreter of characters and of plays, what is there to say in his favour? The fact of the matter is, Mr. Jefferson never interpreted anything in his life; he knew too much to try." J. Ranken Towse takes a similar viewpoint: "None of the parts in which Jefferson delighted his audiences could by any stretch of the imagination he called great. None of them sounded the heights or depths of emotion, lofty flights of imagination or passion, or demanded the exhibition of uncommon intellectual, moral, or dramatic power. They all lay within the limits of the middle register. All of them were played, and often very well played, by actors of no extraordinary capacities." But Towse is willing to acknowledge that the "secret of Jefferson's popularity and fame" lay in his "consummate artistry and personal fascination."

On the other hand, William Winter is disposed to rank Jefferson with the best. "He was not only a great actor, he was a man of noble mind, original character, sympathetic temperament, and lovely spirit; he not only exercised a potential influence upon the dramatic profession, but by virtue of the sweetness and kindness that his genial nature diffused, through the medium of his acting, he deeply affected the lives of thousands who were personally strangers . . . No name throughout the teeming annals of art in the nineteenth century has shone with a more genuine lustre, or can be more proudly and confidently committed to the remembrance and esteem of posterity." Disregarding the disparagements of critics, a sympathetic public, from the very first presentment of his Rip Van Winkle, took Mr. Jefferson to their hearts and kept him there with no diminution of their attachment.

The Jeffersons were one of the "famous actor families of America."* Thomas, the first of these actors, was encouraged by David Garrick to go upon the stage. It is said that the comic vein in his descendants was inherited from his wife, who died from a ruptured blood vessel in the brain during a merry outburst of laughter. The impersonator of Rip declared that he always felt a sharp pain in his head if he laughed too heartily. The first Joseph Jefferson left England for America, not only because he was drawn instinctively toward our republic but also because he quarreled constantly with his step-mother. This Joseph I generally portrayed the parts of old men; once he did it so effectively that a sympathetic old lady started a subscription to retire him from the stage. His natural bent was entirely comic; a single attempt at tragedy swept him off the stage in a gale of laughter. John Pendleton Kennedy, the noted novelist, leaves a testimonial of the abilities of "Jefferson, the imp of ancient fame," to provoke uninhibited exhibitions of mirth when he came to Baltimore: "He played everything that was comic, and always made people laugh till tears ran from their eyes. Laugh? Why, I don't believe he ever saw the world doing anything else. Whomsoever he looked at laughed. Before he came through the side scenes when he was about to enter O. P. or P. S., he would pronounce the first words of his part to

---

* This term was used as the title of a book by Montrose J. Moses.

herald his appearance and instantly the whole audience set up a shout. It was only the sound of his voice. He had a patent right to shake the world's diaphragm which seemed to be infallible. No player comes to that perfection now."

Joseph Jefferson I had three sons, all of whom were actors. One of them injured his lungs when a high jump from a rocky ledge, called for by his part, landed him painfully hard, not on his feet but on his chest. A second son slipped on an orange peel, left on the stage from a previous act, and fractured his skull. Joseph II also played the parts of old men who were invariably reprobates, vagabonds, or aging buffoons. He married a widow ten years his senior, the daughter of French refugees from Haiti. Mrs. Jefferson had by her previous marriage a son, Thomas Burke, who became a close companion to the two Jefferson children, Joseph III and Cornelia.

The future Rip Van Winkle was born at Philadelphia, February 20, 1829. He was hardly able to walk and talk well when "Jim Crow" Rice carried him onto the stage in a sack and emptied him out head foremost, after which the two, both blackfaced, did a hotfoot jig and sang:

Ladies and gem'men, I'd have yuh for to know,
I'se got a little darky here, to jump Jim Crow.

The spectators laughed unroariously, and after the tall, angular Rice and the diminutive boy of four sang through a dialog consisting of crazy questions and crazier answers, they were pelted with a shower of pennies, sixpence, and shillings from the pit and the galleries.

During a large part of his boyhood we find young Joseph accompanying his family, now strolling actors, through the West and South, pushing their way from town to town, playing in make-shift theatres, fording the Mississippi on rafts, losing half their clothes and scenery overboard, following buffalo trails in covered wagons, sleeping in unheated hotels, and frequently speculating when they would eat next. Once they had to hire a homely-looking lawyer named Abraham Lincoln to override an act of sequestration on their stage properties. The father, worn out by the constant drain on his physical resources, caught the yellow fever and died in Mobile, Alabama.

The family continued its tours till the Mexican War broke out. Joseph followed the Army into Mexico, where his mother and sister assisted in selling coffee, eggs, ham, and hot cakes over an improvised bar.

Returning to this country he secured minor comic roles in companies that played in New York, Philadelphia, Baltimore, and several Southern cities. In 1850 he married Margaret Lockyer, an actress whom he played opposite in several comedies. His sister Cornelia, as capable a comedian as her brother, made a distinctive hit as Little Pickle in *The Spoiled Child*.

After a short trip to Europe in 1856, Jefferson entered Laura Keene's company and for the first time he attracted more than the usual attention by his Asa Trenchard, which, paired with E. A. Sothern's Lord Dundreary, made *Our American Cousin* one of the comic highlights of the season. Two other characterizations, Caleb Plummer in *The Cricket on the Hearth* and Bob Acres in *The Rivals,* brought him further affectionate notices from the public.

After his wife's death, Jefferson wandered off once more, spending almost four years in Australia. Then he returned to England and applied for engagements from several managers but was refused because he had nothing new to offer. He submitted a version of the *Rip Van Winkle* he and his half-brother, Charles Burke, had written, but it was rejected.

For several years Jefferson had been toying with the idea of playing this character. As early as 1859 the obsession began to take hold of him, and it derived from the reading of Washington Irving's life and letters. He was vacationing at the time with his family in an old Pennsylvania-Dutch farmhouse near the Pocono Mountains. It was a rainy day, and Jefferson had found a quiet sconce in the attic under the eaves to read. His eyes suddenly came across a passage in which Irving mentions his pleasure from a visit to the theatre where Jefferson was performing on September 30, 1858; the comedian was delightful, reminding him, in look, gesture, and size, of the elder Jefferson, who, in Irving's opinion, was the best actor he had ever seen.

This praise from his favorite author, the great Washington Irving, for the acting of the two Jeffersons thrilled him inordinately. And to think that he had no reputation beyond that of the common run of actors. Yes, he would repay that compliment. And how better than to represent Irving's most famous creation, Rip Van Winkle, a character which had always fascinated Jefferson.

One day the actor met Dion Boucicault, the playwright-author, and asked him to revise the rejected version. Boucicault read both Jefferson's play and Irving's story. To him Rip was a picturesque character but hopelessly undramatic. The old sot lacked interest and romance. He must be a happy-go-lucky blade, a curly-headed, good-humored scamp, with such mischief in his eye as to turn girls heads and excite children and dogs to scamper after him. "Oh, no," declared Jefferson, "that would never do." But Boucicault insisted on this more dramatic conception, and within a short time handed his version to Jefferson with the apology, "It is a poor thing, Joe."

Three weeks later, on September 5, 1865, *Rip Van Winkle* was presented at the Adelphi Theatre, and took the sophisticated London audience by storm. It ran continuously for one hundred and seventy nights. But that success was nothing in comparison to the one scored in America, where it was performed thousands of times and ran for years and years. L. Clarke Davis wrote in the *Atlantic Monthly* soon after the play came to America: "From the moment of Rip's entrance upon the scene—for it is Rip Van Winkle, and not Mr. Jefferson—the audience has assurance that a worthy descendant of the noblest of the old players is before them . . . There is no fustian, no sham passion, no tawdry sentiment, no untruth of any kind . . . From the rising of the curtain on the first scene, until its fall on the last, nothing is forced, sensational, or unseemly. The remarkable beauty of the performance arises from nothing so much as its entire repose and equality." Brander Matthews made this observation in *Scribner's Magazine*: "It is saturated with kindly and wholesome humor. Although Rip is an idle good-for-nothing and ne'er-do-well, we accept Mr. Jefferson's presentation of him as a personification of the beautiful and the good." And George William Curtis in *Harper's Monthly* adds that "people return again and again to see him as to see a lovely landscape or a favorite picture. Indeed, it is the test of high art that it does not pall in its impression."

People were quick to see that the play carried a moral import as well as its burden of pathos and humor. A minister asserted after he had witnessed a performance: "I never saw such power, I never remarked such nature in any Christian pulpit . . . So simple, so true, so beautiful, so moral! No sermon written in the world, except that of Christ when he stood with the adulterous woman, ever illustrated the power of love to conquer evil, and to win the wanderer, as that little part does, so perfectly embodied by this genius which God has given us, to show in the drama the power of love over the sins of the race."

And thus we can well understand how Joe Jefferson affectionately came to be called Rip Van Winkle simply because he was Rip Van Winkle, genial, generous, gentle, and warm-souled. Fame and fortune actually came Jefferson's way because he was spontaneously portraying the sterling qualities of his own amiable nature. Off-stage he was as willing to do a good turn for some one as Rip was on the stage. It was he who first gave publicity to the Little Church Around the Corner by taking an actor there for Christian burial after being refused at another church.

Mr. Jefferson married a second time in 1867. He had a numerous brood of children, six by his first wife and four by his second. Seven of these children were boys and Mr. Jefferson was once asked what he was teaching them. He meditated a moment and then replied in the slow, pausing voice so characteristic of Rip, "To fish and—to tell the truth." That his sons were truthful as well as humorous may be seen from the following incident. When Willie Jefferson was in Paris, he cabled his father: "Send me two hundred." The cable returned with a query: "For what?" And Willie answered, "For Willie!"

In his private life, Mr. Jefferson was as highly esteemed as he was on the stage. He was sociable to folks of all ranks and ages, high or low, young or old. His company was enjoyed on fishing trips as much by ex-president Cleveland as by many a small country urchin. Wherever he angled, at Buzzards Bay, on the Florida lakes, or by Louisiana streams, his whistle and halloo were heard with amusement when he landed a sea-bass, a snook, or a pompano. Often he occupied himself with painting, which he had learned from his father on tours, when the stage scenery, "runny" from frequent soakings, needed refurbishing. Harvard and Yale invited him to lecture on the art of acting, and granted him honorary degrees. He was active in raising money for the Actors' Fund and was president of The Players, succeeding Edwin Booth. When he died at Palm Beach, Florida, on April 23, 1905, which by the way, was the anniversary of Shakespeare's death, the country felt that it had suffered a distinct loss.

Once he was accused of lacking ambition: "Why, you can only play one part. You are the prince of dramatic carpet-baggers, and carry all your wardrobe in a gripsack. Look at that huge pile of trunks—mine, sir, mine! Examine my list of parts! Count them—half a hundred at the very least. You ought to be ashamed of yourself. Where is your versatility?"

"My dear Charlie," he replied, "you are confounding wardrobe with talent. You change your hat, and fancy you are playing another character. Believe me, it requires more skill to act one part fifty different ways than to act fifty parts all the same way."

And thus, by portraying the single character of Rip Van Winkle "fifty different ways" so that it never staled on him or his audience over a period of nearly forty years, Joe Jefferson became immortal, our greatest comedian.

* * * *

Yankee characters proved popular on the stage as early as 1799, when George H. Hill took to reading Yankee stories on the Boston stage between acts. Later "Yankee Hill" went to the Park Theatre in New York, and from there elsewhere over the country, showing the dramatic possibilities of this crude but shrewd old wiseacre. Even before this, Royall Tyler had introduced a Yankee servant into his play *The Contrast*, produced in 1787, in Jonathan, the prototype of all subsequent stage Yankees. James H. Hackett, the most famous impersonator of Falstaff in this country, utilized Yankee dialect in the characters of Solomon Swap, Jonathan Ploughboy, Lot Sap Sago, and Colonel Nimrod Wildfire, all of them endearing him to unsophisticated theatregoers. When he played the colonel in *A Kentuckian's Trip to New York* on the London stage in 1833, he scored a tremendous success. And the colonel's fiancée, Miss Patty Snap of Salt Licks, who had no "back-out in her breed, could whup her weight in wild cats, and had shot a bar at the age of nine," familiarized London with the species of indomitable female who had helped wrest the American forests from savagery for the refinements of civilization. Then came F. S. Chanfrau who, as Mose, the volunteer fire-boy, in *A Glance at New York*, dragged a hose back and forth across the stage, to the delight of his New York spectators. Joe Jefferson played Asa Trenchard the amiable Yankee as a foil for Sothern's Lord Dundreary in *Our American Cousin*. John Edmond Owens provoked belly-shaking laughter in that comical country teamster, Solon Shingle. John T. Raymond animated the part of Mulberry Sellers,

126

the Southern colonel rigged up by Mark Twain and Charles Dudley Warner, in *The Gilded Age*. A host of other plays of this type included *Davy Crockett, M'liss, The Old Homestead, Way Down East, Alabama, David Harum, Margaret Fleming,* and *Kit the Arkansas Traveller.*

American audiences had been well-trained to recognize Yankee characters when W. F. Florence introduced a new one, fascinating though unctuous, in the Honorable Bardwell Slote, the politician-hero of B. E. Woolf's *The Mighty Dollar*, first performed at the Park Theatre in New York, September 6, 1875. "It was an original character," says Lawrence Hutton, "fresh, quaint, and entirely possible to life, who is destined to walk down to posterity arm in arm with Rip Van Winkle, Solon Shingle, Davy Crockett, and Colonel Sellers, the typical stage American of the nineteenth century, Mr. Florence's most enduring character by a large majority."

Billy Florence, whose real name was Conlin, was born in Albany, New York, July 26, 1831, of parents who had migrated from Ireland a few years before. Always intensely interested in dramatics, he left Albany for the state metropolis in 1846, but had to plug along in amateur productions for three years, clerking in a shoe store to gain a livelihood by day and freedom for his theatrical activities at night.

He secured a small professional engagement in 1849 as Tobias in *The Stranger* at the Marshall Theatre in Richmond, Virginia. He soon made his way back to New York, joined a company at Niblo's Garden, and not long afterwards had an opportunity to play Macduff for Booth's Macbeth at Providence, Rhode Island.

He was then engaged by Brougham's Lyceum to do utility parts, in several of which it was seen that he was far above the average run, as audiences frequently called him back for encores. He married the dancer, Malvina Pray, on January 1, 1853, and in June of the same year they appeared at the National Theatre as the Irish Boy and the Yankee Gal in a feature that lifted them at once to stardom and a conspicuous success that was repeated everywhere on the tours they made around the country. Mrs. Florence astonished audiences by her versatility in acting, dancing, singing, and playing of musical instruments. The tunes she introduced were soon hummed and whistled, and sold by the thousands.

In 1856 they went to London, where they remained for five years. At Drury Lane the comedy, *Yankee Housekeeper*, featuring Mrs. Florence as the gawky but not so stupid servant-girl, played for fifty consecutive nights to sold-out houses. Mr. Florence's role of Captain Cuttle in *Dombey and Son* was such an excellent impersonation that Dickens asserted it "thoroughly realized his conception of the character."

In 1861, on their return to America, the couple not only repeated their British successes but also played together in *Ticket-of-Leave Man*, he as Bob Brierly and she as Emily St. Evremonde. The characterizations were far more serious than anything either had previously undertaken. They

127

were regarded as sensations, the play running at the Winter Garden for a hundred and twenty-five nights. Then followed two plays, *Caste* and *No Thoroughfare*, which provided Mr. Florence with two more original conceptions in George d' Alroy and Jules Obenreizer. It was now apparent that he had developed an extraordinary versatility, and could portray characters diametrically divergent in tastes, temperaments, and abilities, yet thoroughly convincing in minutiae of detail.

When he added Bardwell Slote of *The Mighty Dollar* to the list of his distinctive portraits, he was recognized as an unrivaled master, to quote Towse, "In the art of self-effacement, there is certainly no other actor of prominence in this country capable of presenting three characters so completely distinct as those of Obenreizer, Bardwell Slote, and Captain Cuttle, not to speak of other personages in his theatrical repertory." He could be a comedian, ridiculous, jovial, or fancifully poetic; he could endow serious parts with the dynamics of a fierce, explosive energy or languish, uncurably resigned, like one whose will power is completely broken; each successive part manifested subtle niceties like a new canvas, freshly painted. One Chicago critic says very pointedly: "To sum him up in a word, Mr. Florence is an actor—and how few actors we have today! We mean those actors who play one part well, but can never submerge that character or their own individuality in any other part."

The presentment of the Honorable Bardwell Slote, although a caricature, created a furore of comment because it was so true, and recognizable. The "smirking, grasping, greedy, shrewd, yet simple" member of Congress might be from the Cohosh district, but his counterpart was to be found obviously among the representatives from every state in the Union. Undeniably dishonorable in politics, which he used as a springboard for the most detestable practices, the M. C. from Cohosh had many fine qualities as a private citizen which endeared him to his friends and family. William Winter likens him to a character out of Dickens, "portly, grizzled, slightly bald, red-nosed, bright-eyed, addicted to black satin waistcoats and big bosom pins . . . A politician, resident in Washington, and engaged in trying to feather his nest by taking bribes for lobbying railroad bills through Congress." This rich caricature was played by Mr. Florence with such droll archness that audiences actually came to love the amiable but patently dishonest politician.

Mrs. Florence received a generous share of praise for her inimitable personation of Mrs. General Gilflory, the comely, vivacious widow who was always spouting forth, at the most inopportune moments, the most irrelevant French phrases—in a French so execrable that no Frenchman could understand her. "She is simply superb," exclaimed a London critic. "Mrs. General Gilflory is not an original character. She is a combination of Mrs. Ramsbottom, Mrs. Malaprop, and the Begum in *Pendennis;* but her wit, her humor, her good nature and her wonderful French are all Mrs. Florence's own."

128

It might be worth noting that, twenty years later, Alfred E. Smith won his first political laurels through his successful playing of the Honorable Bardwell Slote in *The Mighty Dollar*.

The occasional teaming of Billy Florence and Joe Jefferson was a felicitous combination that delighted theatregoers immensely. As early as 1881 they had played the two gravediggers in *Hamlet* together. The seasons of 1889-90 and 1890-91 saw them together again. In *The Rivals* a brilliant cast was assembled that included Jefferson as O'Trigger, and Mrs. John Drew as Mrs. Malaprop. In *The Heir at Law* Jefferson acted the part of Dr. Pangloss and Florence that of Zekiel Homespun. Mr. Florence was called "extremely delightful" in both these characterizations.

At various times during his life Mr. Florence acted in classic roles from Shakespeare, Goldsmith, and Sheridan, as well as in modern dramas, in the company of such players as Forrest, Cushman, Booth, Henry Irving, E. A. Sothern, Lotta Crabtree, Mrs. John Drew, McCullough, Barrett, Toole, Brougham, Burton, and Raymond.

Off the stage Mr. Florence was an excellent companion. He was fond of jokes and was always being reminded of some incident that was applicable to the circumstance of the moment. Once an actor complained that he had to stand on his feet too much during rehearsals while his feet, filled with corns and calluses, sorely pained him. "I wish I were a shoe clerk," said the distressed actor; "then I could try on all the shoes in the store till I found a pair that fitted."

Mr. Florence, recollecting his early job in a shoe store and his dislike for the work, then began to tell about his experiences with a colored barber. "Haircut!" said he tersely as he sat down in the chair. Putting both his hands on Mr. Florence's head, the barber proceeded to thump his cranium like some one getting ready to plug a watermelon. Amazed at this inexplicable action, he roared "What on earth are you doing? I said, *hair* cut!" "Yes, suh! Yes, suh! Scuse me, suh. But I reads bumps," declared the barber grandiloquently as if he were revealing the greatest secret in the world. "You know, suh, ah can read infallubly just what a man's business in by duh bumps on hees haid." "All right," snorted Florence, "tell me mine quickly and get to work on my hair." "Youse certainly got high bumps, dat is high-brow bumps—dey makes yuh an aristocrat—and dey are very ripe." Then after some hesitation, the barber blurted "Dare now Ise got it!" And walking triumphantly in front of the chair, he bowed ceremoniously and whispered "Shoe-store man!" Mr. Florence in no uncertain terms, enlightened him as to his real profession. "Den, suh," mourned the incorrect guesser, "Yuh sho' missed your calling."

Mr. Florence was a faithful communicant of the Catholic Church, while his wife was an Episcopalian. He was one of the two co-founders of the Mystic Shrine of Masons in America. He died November 19, 1891, and lies buried in Greenwood Cemetery, Brooklyn.

There is no finer instance in the annals of the American stage of a couple whose work was more integrated to serve the purposes of good, clean acting than that of Mr. and Mrs. Florence. Thomas E. Garrett paid them a deserving tribute when he wrote:

Lustrous beacons of the stage
In a fickle, feverish age;
Striving on with honest heart
For the claims and aims of Art.

Twin stars—circling year by year—
Radiant o'er a hemisphere;
Models of the good and pure,
May your influence long endure.

✿　✿　✿　✿

The figures on the Actors' Fund Fair spoon were quite representative for the period of the early nineties. The question arises: Twenty years later, or at the present time, what figures would have been chosen? If certain famous stage stars seem to have been omitted, it is, because their light had not yet become so effulgently bright in the early nineties as later. Everyone who is interested in theatrical stars probably has some favorites not represented on this list.

The Actors' Fund Fair spoon, a rare prize for any one who holds one, was cast by Gorhams in the form of a bouillon spoon or cream ladle. Length, 6 inches.

Lotta's Fountain spoon is replete with scenes from San Francisco; the Ferry Building, City Seal, Lotta's Fountain, Post Office, Mission Dolores, and the Callel Dome. No trademark is given. Length, 5¾ inches.

The Rip Van Winkle spoon, reminiscent of both Washington Irving and Joseph Jefferson, is a Durgin product, patented March 31, 1891. Length, 6 inches.

No. 16 SARATOGA SPRINGS

The Saratoga Springs spoon, intended for a chocolate muddler, portrays the earliest known visitors to this famous watering place in the central part of New York state. On the finial of the handle stands an Indian with an upright bow in his left hand and a quiver of arrows tucked into the waist-band at the rear and extending above the right shoulder to form part of a baldric that runs diagonally down across the Indian's bare breast to the waist-band in the front. Three arrows, showing the head, shaft, and butt-feathers in independent relief, form the shank and drop of the handle.

Embossed in the gold-washed circular bowl is a group of four Indians around High Rock Spring in the days of its primeval-forest setting. A squaw with papoose on back is kneeling beside the spring to cup water to her mouth with one hand. A husky child of three or four years is peering into the hollow crater of a cone-shaped mound, truncated at the top, the whole mineralized formation resembling a miniature volcano. A warrior similar to the one on the handle, stands behind the rock spring. To the right is visible a tree trunk from which a bare, gnarled limb is extended. A forest closes in from the background, and there a wigwam and another Indian may be seen.

Around High Rock Spring the Mohawk and Oneida Indians were wont to gather in early times to partake of the beneficent waters for their various ailments. Sir William Johnson, a powerful influence among the Indians, was brought here on a stretcher in 1767, and he returned several times after that to secure relief from his rheumatism.

Saraghoga, meaning the "place of running waters," was a favorite haunt of the Indians also for their hunting expeditions, as wild animals abounded in the heavily wooded forests nearby. In 1789 Gideon Putnam made the first clearing around the springs, and a few years later built Union Hall, the first hotel to make the place accessible to visitors. "Putnam's Folly," as this hotel was facetiously called, was soon too small to accommodate the increasing crowds of people who came during the summer season; so Putnam set about building an additional structure, Congress Hall, in 1811. Several other fine hotels were built before 1900, most of them now outmoded but splendid examples of ornate Victorian architecture and furnishings at their best.

The eighties and nineties of the last century witnessed the peak of popularity for this fashionable spa. All the élite of society, presidents and senators, big and little capitalists—in fact, everybody of any importance— came to Saratoga. Of the presidents whose eminent names were registered at its hotels at one time or another mention should be made of Millard Fillmore, Franklin Pierce, Buchanan, Johnson, Grant, Hayes, Garfield, Arthur, Cleveland, Benjamin Harrison, and Theodore Roosevelt. President Arthur was always a favorite at Saratoga, where he and his wife entertained informally a host of friends. When President Harrison appeared at a Charity Ball, given at the United States Hotel in 1891, every one rose to his feet, applauded, and fluttered handkerchiefs as the band struck up "Hail to the Chief." Among other guests in an early day were the statesmen, Clay, Webster, Sumner, and Seward; of generals listed were Winfield Scott, Winfield Scott Hancock, John Sherman, and Philip Sheridan. "Every governor that New York has had since 1800 has made the acquaintance of the spa," wrote Joseph Smith in 1897.

Mr. Smith who spent the four decades from the sixties through the nineties as usher or manager at the Union Hall, and the Clarendon and United States hotels, wrote a book of reminiscences on his experiences and the illustrious personalities with whom he came in contact. The pages of his record are an intimate revelation of life at Saratoga in the heyday of its popularity. Many people whose names once filled the front pages and the society columns of all newspapers are here revitalized creatures of flesh and spirit, as they stroll before our eyes along the spacious halls and piazzas of elegant hotels. "The charm of Saratoga to me," a guest once remarked to Mr. Smith, "is its cosmopolitan flavor. At Newport you find New Yorkers; at Cape May and Atlantic City, Philadelphians; Boston fills the Maine resorts; but here you get the cream of every city in the Union."

Sometimes a name looms up in these annals with added interest because of an important descendant. Such is the case of Leonard W. Jerome, the grandfather of the wartime prime minister of Great Britain, Winston Churchill. Mr. Jerome was one of the chief promoters of the Saratoga Association for the Improvement of the Breed of Horses, incorporated in 1865. He was noted for his skill in driving four-in-hands at Saratoga; likewise, for his good fellowship. Once he offered a medal for the best representative of a perfect gentleman in a graduating class at Princeton. When asked for his definition of a gentleman to be used as a guide in making the selection, he replied, "He who is the most thoughtful of others" —a dictum that is nothing more than a restatement of the Golden Rule. Mr. Jerome's daugher, Jennie, was married to Lord Randolph Churchill in 1874 and became the mother of the famous Winston Churchill.

A great pair of jokers often seen together with Mr. Jerome at Saratoga were the comedians, Ed Sothern and Billy Florence. There was hardly a day passed that they did not provide some sort of amusement for the Saratogans to laugh over. Once Florence expressed great concern over the poor health of the Duke of Beaufort within the Duke's hearing. Then he approached the peer and confidentially suggested that he try a certain exercise whereby, diverted of his outer garments, he would run back and forth in his room raising and lowering a chair with serpentine movements. Florence solemnly declared that he had been troubled the same way at one time, and had secured marvellous results with this exercise. Jerome and Sothern joined in persuading the Duke to make the experiment, and "it was contrived, too, that the ridiculous bit of calisthentics was to be tried on the very day when the Duke was to receive prominent visitors. And just when the noble victim was in the heat of his mad chase with the chair, Florence took the eminent visitors quietly up to the room, and through the key-hole showed them an apparent maniac in the person of their friend. Of course, they went about one to another echoing the lamentation of Florence: 'It's very sad about his Grace, the Duke!' "

A few days later the Duke's clothes were hidden and a cry of "Fire!" was made while he was taking his chair-lifting exercise. The Duke dashed down into the lobby in his night-gown, bathroom slippers, and a plug hat on his head! The Duke thus confirmed, to the satisfaction of all the loungers in the lobby, the whispered reports that they had heard about his insanity.

The first practitioner of homeopathy in America, Dr. John F. Gray, a familiar figure in Saratoga, was noted for his charity and kindness of heart. Typical of his many good deeds is the following story. To a poor ailing seamstress who came to him for treatment, he gave a bottle of medicine and prescribed several days of rest in bed. When she declared that she could not waste so much time in bed, that she would starve if she did so, the magnanimous doctor said promptly that he would have to change the prescription a little. Whereupon he took back the bottle, wrapped enough bills around the bottle to take care of all her wants for at least a week and handed it back, saying, "Now, go home and take the medicine, wrapper and all!"

Among other distinguished guests at Saratoga in the early days were: John Godfrey Saxe, the popular poet and wit whose "Six Blind Men of Hindustan" and other humorous tales in verse appeared regularly in the columns of many magazines and newspapers; August Belmont, one of the shrewdest financiers of his time; Robert Bonner who achieved a phenomenal success by his original advertising methods; W. W. Corcoran, who established the famous Corcoran Art Gallery in Washington, erected a monument to John Howard Payne, author of "Home Sweet Home," and gave so generously to the support of impoverished Confederate widows; Mr. and Mrs. William H. Vanderbilt, who sent many Thanksgiving dinners and Christmas gifts to orphan asylums and hospitals without mentioning themselves as the givers; John Graham, the authority on criminal law, and General Daniel E. Sickles, who were such inseparable companions that they came to be known as David and Jonathan—it was Graham who said that "God never made but one man in a century like the great Webster;" Mrs. Coventry Waddell, the acknowledged queen of New York society, a woman who counted among her close personal acquaintances such men as Washington Irving, Daniel Webster, Henry Clay, William Makepeace Thackeray, Judah Philip Benjamin, John Pendleton Kennedy, as well as the "charmed circle" of the Astors, Rhinelanders, Minturns, and Schermerhorns.

To Saratoga on their honeymoon came John Vinton Dahlgren and his wife, the former Elizabeth Drexel, from Philadelphia, the bride wearing a three-hundred-year-old ring, a ruby set in silver, once the engagement ring given by Martin Luther to Catherine von Bora, his bride.

There were 30,000 visitors to the spa during the season of 1890, says Mr. Smith, and of these, 17,000 stayed in boarding houses while the rest resided in the more pretentious hotels. The daily receipts for these visitors averaged about $90,000 for lodging and food alone; the amount spent on carriages and blooded horses, the races, and other forms of amusement must have been a much larger sum. Miss Giulia Morosini, beautiful daughter of Jay Gould's banking partner, created a sensation by driving three horses tandem through a crowd of vehicles, the spirited horses being guided by a set of snow-white lines, though seeming to be guided by magic rather than human intelligence.

A ruddy-faced Texan flashed three diamond rings on one hand that lifted a glass of Hathorn water to his lips. A stately dowager from Boston wore to one ball a dazzling string of great solitaires on her neck, a scintillating diamond star on the crown of her head, and an amazing array of rings set with all sorts of precious stones on her hands. The alluring blonde daughter of one millionaire displayed a set of ear-rings large as silver quarters, studded with bands of diamonds. On this spectacular show of great wealth, Mr. Smith merely comments, like a philosopher: "If there were no beauty to be adorned by diamonds, and no fortunes to buy them, to what would the seekers after precious stones turn their hand or the dealers in them?"

John Wanamaker, then Postmaster General and owner of the largest dry goods store in America, spent ten days with his wife and daughter in a simple cottage. Mr. Wanamaker was also known as the superintendent of the largest Sunday School in the world. Thomas Ochiltree, of Galveston, Texas, was also among the guests at Saratoga in 1890. The story was told of him that as soon as he graduated from law school, he was left in charge of his father's law office for a while. When his father returned, he saw a huge sign over the door of his office: "Thomas Ochiltree and Father."

In 1891 there was held in Saratoga the first Unitarian Convention, at which George William Curtis presided. Mr. Curtis was a scholarly gentleman, highly esteemed for his beautiful story, *Prue and I*. A few years later, the fifth General Convention of the Unitarian Church was held in Saratoga, of which gathering Edward Everett Hale was the master of ceremonies. Dr. Hale, the author of the *Man Without a Country*, proudly made mention of the fact that five of the leading poets of America were Unitarians, namely, Longfellow, Lowell, Bryant, Holmes and Emerson.

During the season of the early nineties, Mr. Smith mentions as some of the notable guests at Saratoga: Phillip Brooks, the leading minister of the Episcopal Church in America and author of many hymns, including that Christmas favorite, "O Little Town of Bethlehem;" Mrs. Julia Grant, widow of the late president; ex-President Hayes, whose wife had just died; Mrs. George McClellan, the attractive but unassuming widow of the Civil War general; John D. Rockefeller plainly dressed and scarcely looking his age; George Pullman, the palace car king, "cool as the centre seed of a cucumber" in business dealings, but easily moved to tears by a simple tale of hard times in the early West; Elihu Root, whose mother-in-law thought him a "big man, not in stature but in greatness;" the Princess Eulalie of Spain, who left four hundred dollars to be distributed as tips for those who had waited on her; Levi P. Morton and Roswell P. Flower, both worthy governors of New York; Jay Gould, John Jacob Astor, Henry Flagler, Joseph Pulitzer, Chauncey Depew, and an unending list of other people who might be singled out for special reference.

134

One of the most popular figures seen often at Saratoga was Ward McAllister, who coined that term the "Four Hundred," referring to the most exclusive persons in the upper circles of society. Mr. McAllister was a Southerner, born in Savannah, but a lawyer who had spent most of his life at Northern resorts, organizing picnics and parties that made him famous. He once made a pie costing one hundred dollars—we wonder what the ingredients were! As for wines, he knew their history, their philosophy and their values down to the last penny. He posed as a polished man of leisure, always wore clothes of the latest cut, trimmed his beard and mustache with courtly precision, walked down Fifth Avenue every afternoon at exactly the same time with a fresh flower in the lapel of his coat, loved a title, and was regarded as the prince of epicures. His wife being an invalid, he did the honors of society for both.

Saratoga Springs still attracts a gala throng of visitors through the summer months. The peak of the season comes in August during the races. The crowds that now come to Saratoga are somewhat less aristocratic than formerly; members of the "Four Hundred" are there, it is true, but they are lost among the hurly-burly throngs of little people. Yet they all have just as good times as they ever did in the "gay nineties."

The Saratoga Springs spoon which I have in my possession bears the date of its purchase, August 4, 1892, and the initials of its erstwhile owner, M. F. F., engraved on the back of the rounded bowl. Length of spoon, 5 inches.

No. 17 OSCEOLA (SEMINOLE SOFFKEE)

One of the most original of spoons, differing from all others in the contours of its bowl and handle, is the *soffkee* spoon. To the Seminoles it is known as the *cotaseechobee,* hand-carved usually from bald cyress wood, sometimes from custard apple or live oak, and is used to stir a pot of soffkee, a favorite Seminole food compounded of cornmeal, vegetables, and the meat of turtles or fish.

Osceola, the most famous figure in Seminole history, appears in a facial profile on the reverse of the bowl. This is not a true likeness of Osceola, if we are to judge by the portrait painted of the warrior by George Catlin when Osceola was a prisoner at Fort Moultrie, Georgia. Catlin's painting shows Osceola wearing three ostrich feathers thrust into a multi-colored tarboosh wound around the rear of the head. His dress consists of a vivid calico smock, bunched in closely above the waist by a wide, coiled sash of prismatic beads. A flowering baldric rests over the left shoulder, and three beaded necklaces circle in varying lengths around his neck. A rifle rests in his hands.

The face on the spoon reveals genuine Indian features. The head is decked full of short feathers, an annular earring hangs from the lobe of the left ear, and a choke necklace of coffee shells and shark's teeth encircles the throat.

The front view of Osceola painted by Catlin might lead one to think that the painter had hired a white man, attired in Indian habiliments, to pose for his picture. The fact it, there is not too much evidence of Indian blood in Osceola's features. The skin was slightly dark, but his hair shaded toward a reddish brown, and his eyes, set far apart, were light in color, an inheritance from his Scotch grandfather. Not the least of his Celtic characteristics were a volatile temper and a pride endued with the defiant haughtiness of a Marmion or a Roderick Dhu. He was born among the Creek tribes that hunted and fished over Alabama and Georgia. His stepfather was white, and he might have grown up as a peaceable American if the Creeks had not been forced to abandon their happy hunting grounds when Osceola was four years old. His mother carried the child with her into Florida, where he developed into a stalwart warrior, embittered by the injustices which the Indians had to endure at the hands of unctuous, land-grabbing white men.

A violent animus toward the whites was engendered in Osceola when Morning-Dew, his wife, and the mother of his four children, was carried off to be a slave on the flimsy pretense that she had a taint of negro blood in her veins. This unforgivable offense rankled in the soul of the young warrior like a virulent poison. He craved passionate vengeance. "Am I a slave? My skin is red, not black. I am an Indian—a Seminole. The white man shall not make me black. I will make the white man red with blood, and then blacken him in the sun and rain, where the buzzard shall feed upon his flesh and the wolf shall crush his bones to bits!"

Osceola was not the head chief of the Seminoles, but he soon became their acknowledged leader by his indomitable force of will, an amazing courage in the face of great odds, and the ability to organize and carry through intricate plans of action. When the Government set out to transfer the Seminoles to reservations in the West and thereafter open up Florida for white settlement, the Federal agents were unaware of the commanding personality of the Indian leader with whom they were dealing. General Thompson did not expect to encounter a "savage" with such a "manly, frank, and open countenance, remarkably keen, bright eye, and independent bearing." The American general sought to wheedle the Indian into signing a treaty which would send his people into an eternal exile from the moss-garlanded haunts of their homeland.

Osceola listened tautly to the blandishments of the white agents, his hands hidden in the folds of his red mantle. He said nothing until Thompson threatened to withdraw payment of certain small annuities if the emigration treaty were not signed. Osceola was striding backward and forward slowly, but he wheeled dramatically at the mention of a threat, dashed to the desk, and thrust his dagger into the treaty with a mighty slash. His voice was hoarse with rage as he cried contemptuously, "The only treaty I will ever make with the whites is with *this!*"

The war dragged on indeterminately for seven years. One after another the unsuccessful generals were recalled by the Government: Thompson, Clinch, Jesup, Gaines, Winfield Scott, Call, Hernández, and Worth. Colonel Zachary Taylor, leading a force of one thousand men, fought one of the bloodiest battles of the war in deadly hand-to-hand fighting against three hundred Seminoles near Lake Okeechobee on Christmas Day of 1837. The Americans lost one hundred and thirty-eight men; the Indians, fifteen. After this carnage the future president declared that Florida was not worth fighting for at such cost of human blood, and suggested the peninsula be turned over to the Indians for keeps.

The war became a series of ambush skirmishes. Guerrilla tactics were employed on both sides, but the Indians showed to better advantage in such warfare. Osceola was the master strategist planning and animating the unexpected assaults. Black-flag adventurers abetted the Indian cause by bringing in guns and ammunition from the West Indies, and even joining in many a strike-and-scatter encounter. Andy Jackson in the White House tore at his rebellious red locks and swore at the contumacious savages. Bloodhounds trained in Cuba were employed to ferret out the Indians hiding in hummocks deep within the mysterious swamp lands. But the bloodhounds, baffled by watery trails, did little more than track the few negroes attached to the American army-camps.

General Hernández, pitted against the shrewd intelligence of an intrepid savage leader, and sensing the futility of continued combat under such adverse conditions of terrain, revised his strategy and called for a peace conference.

Under a flag of true Osceola and several of his sub-chiefs assembled at the place designated for the meeting. At a given signal the Indians were surrounded, taken prisoners, and marched to Fort Marion in St. Augustine. Then Osceola, realizing how he had been tricked by obviously unfair means and incarcerated in a gloomy dungeon, became moody and refused to speak. When accosted by General Hernández, he turned to a subordinate and said, "I feel choked; you speak for me."

He occupied the same cell with Coacoochee and Talmus Hadjo. These two men starved themselves till they were slender enough to crawl through the iron bars of the small casement overhead, leap into the moat outside, and make their way to freedom.

Osceola languished for months in the prison at St. Augustine. He might have liberated himself like his two confederates, but he declared that he would not try to escape by the same sort of dishonorable tactics employed by the Americans; that justice demanded his restoration to liberty by every code of honorable warfare. He became emaciated, and the once strong body, starving for the sunshine and free air of the great outdoors, was an easy prey to sickness. His proud nature wilted as he saw the clouds of doom lowering over his race. Shadows of sadness flitted across his once imperious face. He accepted the defeat of all his purposes in a spirit of noble resignation.

Shortly before his death he was transferred to Fort Moultrie in South Carolina, where George Catlin painted his portrait. The soldiers stationed in this America Bastille compassionated his condition, favored his release, and looked upon him as a hero who deserved a more fitting close to a tragic career. Osceola's hatred for the whites softened under the sympathetic treatment accorded him. A large section of the American press, heeding the voice of an indignant public, called for an end to Osceola's imprisonment. But too late. An hour before he died, he attired himself in the clothing he had worn in time of war, girded on his war-belt, bullet-pouch, and powder-horn; painted his face, throat, wrists, and hands a vermilion red; and "with most benignant smiles" he shook hands with all the American officers and the members of his family; went to his bed, clasped his scalping-knife between both hands crossed over his breast, and lying thus, he passed into eternal peace in the thirty-third year of his age.

❋   ❋   ❋   ❋

Somehow the voice of the martyred Osceola, THE PRISONER OF FORT MARION, seems to be speaking to us across the vistas of time, and his words, if we understand them aright, run somewhat in the following fashion:

> My eyes turn upward toward that little vent
> They term a window (it has iron bars)—
> The only means in my imprisonment
> To prove there still are things as moon and stars,
> That there's a brighter world outside of this
> Small zone of dusk: a torture to the mind
> That thirsts for fountains of the sunlight's bliss
> O'er broad savannas, free and unconfined.
>
> I live as one that's dead, whom life recalls:
> I walk around and touch these four blank walls
> Which close me off from all that leaps and sings,
> Which shut me in with creeping, crawling things.
> I sit in man-made darkness like a stone—
> Impassive, helpless, useless, cold, alone.
> But I'm no passive stone! I have sharp eyes
> To guide me if my feet could freely rise.
> I have a beating heart that knows the pain
> From losing those I shall not see again.
> O curséd be forever that dark day
> That led my feet so blindly here astray!
> I cannot rest . . . I will not rest so long
> As my proud spirit knows that there still beams
> A sun beneficent and pouring strong
> Upon these walls its light in countless streams.

138

The serpent is less cunning than these men
Whose faces are so fair, whose minds so black
With thoughts that fain would grasp our lands and then
Would drive us out, a beaten, sniveling pack.
The serpent is more honest, for he wills
To give his foe fair warning ere he kills.

I was a leader once, and bound to see
That fight we must from sheer necessity.
I knew the right from wrong, and laws I set
For justice to be meted out and met;
And gave commands for cause so truly just.
And though my captors grind me into dust
Because they fear me, knowing I am right,
They cannot slay my spirit in fair fight.
In peace I was a hunter, free to roam
In happy sport throughout our forest home;
I ate the soffkee, berries, fruits, and maize;
I loved our tree-girt swamps, our streams and bays,
And all the pleasant wonders of our land;
And lived as did the birds that haunt our strand.

I heap derision on the very hint
That caused my fellow-prisoners to stint
Their bodies till they shrank as thin as nails,
And thus could squirm between those bars, as snails.
I too could have denied myself, and through
Those bars escaped, but that I would not do.
I came in honor, and I will maintain
That honor to depart. Their hope is vain
That I should stoop, forlornly, to betray
My people, or to sign their rights away.
The roaring of the sea I love to hear,
The starlight and the moonlight are most dear;
For me the constant sunshine is a balm,
A never-failing ointment, healing, calm.
But dearer far is the eternal light
Of justice shining in to break the night.
I will not sign, no, I will never yield!
Unto my purpose I will hold as sealed.
Though you may break my bones, O tyranny,
I, Osceola, still will victor be!

Our pale-faced foes will come to this fair realm
In droves onsurging till they overwhelm
Us by their throngs. Yet, without use of swords
The Great Red Spirit will defeat their hordes.
The Indian blood that's nurtured in this soil
Will rise from every grave. In plant and coil
Of every vine it will rise up once more.
That Spirit, knowing all of nature's lore,
Will teach the white men many things so rife
Among us, secrets of our health and life:

For they shall bathe in waters they now shun,
And leap upon our shores in sportive fun,
And eat the fruits that ripen in our sun,
And use the roots and herbs as remedies
Which we have known and used for centuries.

And then the Great Red Spirit with his beams
Will bronze the white man's face the while he dreams
Along our beaches. And his skin likewise
Will wear a golden brown like ours. Scant wealth
Of clothing for our clime he will devise—
But graceful, colorful, bestowing health;
And he will worship the great Sun as we.
Though all our lands be taken, still there'll be
Our spirit in the soil and in the air.
Though I be crushed, yet I cannot despair;
For some day in this land, when all this strife
Is gone forever, and *our* mode of life
Is called the right and true one, I foretell:
Red men will in the souls of white men dwell!

❖   ❖   ❖   ❖

On the obverse side of this spoon there is one feature worth noting. The Old Cape Florida Light, shown in the bowl, was built in 1826 and withstood an Indian attack during the Seminole wars.

The Osceola Soffkee spoon is a Gorham product, and is here used through the courtesy of its owner, Professor Reuben Y. Ellison, University of Miami, Miami, Florida. Length, 5¼ inches.

No. 18 YOSEMITE BEAR

The Yosemite Bear spoon is shown in this book on its reverse side because of the rat-tail handle, which is a rarity on souvenir spoons, not more than half a dozen of this stem-type having been made. The rat-tail is a triangular-shaped tongue extending down the back from the handle and applied to a small upper surface of the bowl. From 1675 to 1725, during the reigns of the later Stuarts and the early Hanoverians, rat-tails graced nearly all the spoons made for flat tableware.

The handle of this spoon is divided into two sections, separated by a horizontal ring. The lower section is smooth and cylindrical; the upper, fluted on the two folds that advance to a cleft top. This open lamination is a feature definitely indicating a late Restoration influence. California's familiar grizzly bear stands athwart the bifurcation. The shaggy animal occupies a place of prominence on both the seal and the flag of California. Only one other state, Missouri, delineates the grizzly for these purposes, two rampant bears being imaged there as supporters of the circular band containing the state motto.

140

On the concave side of the bowl is a cut-out of the Bridal Veil Fall in Yosemite. The height of this fall is six hundred and twenty feet, neither the highest nor the widest, but perhaps the loveliest among many. Thomas Starr King, who went West in 1861 to arouse and strengthen Union sentiment in California, was so deeply moved by the scenery in Yosemite Valley that he wrote to his friends back East: "But what words shall describe the beauty of one of the waterfalls, as we see it plunging from the brow of a cliff nearly three thousand feet high? It is comparatively narrow at the top of the precipice; but it widens as it descends, and curves a little as it widens, so that it shapes itself, before it reaches its first bowl of granite, into the charming figure of a comet. But more beautiful than a comet, you can see the substance of this watery loveliness ever renew itself, and ever pour itself away. And all over its white and swaying mistiness, which now and then swings along the mountainside, at the persuasion of the wind, like a pendulum of lace, and now and then is whirled round and round by some eddying breeze as though the gust meant to see if it could wring it dry—all over its surface, as it falls, are shooting rockets of water which spend themselves by the time they half reach the bottom, and then reform, for the remaining descent—thus fascinating the gazer so that he could lie for hours never tired, but ever hungry for more of the exquisite witchery of liquid motion and grace."

Thousands of other spectators, in visiting this region, have been held spellbound, as was Thomas Starr King, by the sheer loveliness of lacy waterfalls leaping like comets over rocky heights into the valley below. Yosemite, located in three counties of east-central California, was created a national park in 1890. Another attraction for the present-day tourist is an extensive area of giant sequoias, considered the oldest of living trees.

The maker's mark is not indicated on this dainty spoon, which measures 3½ inches in length.

No. 19 THE STAGE COACH

When a Hungarian magnate presented to a French king an extraordinarily fine carriage made in the village of Kocs, on the pusztas of Hungary, the new vehicle was named in honor of the obscure place where it had originated. The word slipped into universal parlance throughout Europe, being one of the very few words in English derived from the Hungarian. Then, later, the Anglo-Saxons, with their ingenuity for compounding words, placed a Gallicized Latin word before the coach to indicate a public conveyance that made stops at regular stations or "stages" for passengers.

For a hundred and fifty years after the first settlements, the American colonists generally traveled by saddle or in private coaches. Roads were rough and in many places too "stumpy" for any vehicle but an ox-cart.

141

There were some persons who preferred walking, especially on those roads where inns and ordinaries offered frequent liquid inducements to loiter.

As early as 1718 there were stage coaches running short distances in the colonies, usually making quick connections between boat-stops on the rivers. There were no regular schedules for such trips; and traveling by this means was mostly a matter of private arrangements. The first regular coach service between Boston and New York was established in 1772, and by 1786 a passenger could travel by schedule all the way from Maine and New Hampshire to St. Augustine, Florida, although he had to make numerous transfers.

The first coach line west of the Alleghenies began operations in 1803 between Lexington and Olympian Springs, one of the early watering places in the Bluegrass.

In the first part of the nineteenth century the coach underwent a series of improvements. The types known as the Cumberland, the Trenton, and the Troy were all superseded by the Concord coach, first built in Concord, New Hampshire, in 1813. Not only was this conveyance more commodious but it was also more luxurious than its predecessors. Painted in striking colors with gilt lines on the exterior, it was embellished on the inside with murals based on historic scenes, damask cushions with arabesque patterns, and tasseled cords for the passengers to hold onto when the road was jolty.

The coach-and-four, shown at a halt in the extension through the nave and caput on the reverse-handle of this spoon, appears to be of the Concord type. While it is possible to see only two persons on the inside, it must be well filled because all the space on the top is occupied and one person is seated beside the driver.

The front team for such a coach were called the leaders, and the team in the rear were the wheelers. The leaders were usually older horses noted for their intelligence, reliability, and long acquaintance with the road. The main burden of the haul devolved upon the back team, younger horses that did most of the ascending pull and served as brakes on a rapid downhill run. Fresh horses were installed about every fifty miles along the route. The shift was often effected before the coach springs could stop oscillating, according to one observant passenger.

As a rule, the driver, as expert with his whip as with the reins and supremely confident of his skill, was held in great respect by those whose safety lay in his hands. On the larger coaches, a guard was poised on the top rear-seat to keep an eye on the baggage and to blow the calls on his key-bugle: one to announce an approaching halt, two for the "All aboard!" signal, and three for a clear-the-road warning at tollgates and bridges. Guide-posts and watering troughs, the latter usually hollowed oak logs, were significant features of the turnpike along which the stage coach traveled.

142

Although a journey by stage had many inconveniences, such as the early hours for starting in the morning and long stop-overs at transfer points, it did provide many thrilling moments, pleasant contacts, and happy memories. One has only to read some of the Victorian novelists, especially Dickens, to realize what romance this mode of travel possessed. The invention of the steam locomotive marked the beginning of the end for the stage coach, which reached the peak of its performance in the 1850's. After the Civil War the decline in turnpike travel was rapid. In the Eastern states the stages were discontinued one after the other in the nineties; the last stage coach in Kentucky suspended operations in 1912.*

Like many of the first souvenir spoons made, this one does not bear the name of any town or state. The bowl is plain, but the obverse side of handle points to a region of mountains, evergreen trees, and hair-breadth waterfalls. According to all indications, the scenes depicted here are in the White Mountains of New Hampshire or the Green Mountains of Vermont. I might be mistaken, however, in my deductions about the locality.

A reel and pole, a creel, and a .22 rifle on the reverse-shaft might lead one to believe that this coach is staging a pleasure jaunt for vacationists.

This spoon was made by Edward Todd & Co. Length is 4½ inches.

No. 20 EXCELSIOR SPRINGS

Like many other mineral springs of the Midwest, Excelsior Springs in central Missouri has grown out of a local reputation, acquired solely in the neighborhood for its hydrotheropeutical values, into one of our national spas. When the health resort was first developed in the early eighties, there was only one spring, but others with a variety of mineral contents were gradually added. The iron manganese in the flow of two of these springs is found nowhere else in such abundant quantity.

Today Excelsior Springs, besides being a health resort, is popular also for its golf and bridge tournaments and for the mule fiesta, the latter an entertaining exhibition held here in the fall.

A few miles away from Excelsior Springs is the Robert James farm, which tourists turn aside out of curiosity to see because it was the birthplace of the notorious Jesse and Frank James. The older part of the house remains without alteration much the same as when it was built in 1822. Robert James, a Baptist minister, brought his convent-educated bride here from Kentucky in the early 1840's. After his death the widow married a Doctor Samuels.

The early life of the two boys was uneventful till the Civil War, when

* See Winston Coleman, Jr.: *Stage-Coach Days in the Bluegrass.*

Union soldiers hanged Dr. Samuels, a Southern sympathizer, maltreated his wife and daughter, and horsewhipped Jesse into unconsciousness.

The two brothers, infuriated at this procedure, joined a guerrilla band that harried the frontier towns of Missouri and Kansas. Outlawed by the state government after the war, they took to the road as highwaymen. Many are the tales of their exploits which ranged in area all the way from Minnesota in the north, west into Kansas, and south into Tennessee, Kentucky, and Arkansas. Doubtless many of the robberies attributed to them were staged by other "gentlemen of the road," since the turbulent Reconstruction Period offered easily-obtained loot and quick getaways in the holdup of stagecoaches and the cracking of bank locks.

On September 3, 1880, the stagecoach from Mammoth Cave to Cave City was held up, and the seven passengers were relieved of eight hundred dollars, their jewelry, rings, and watches. A valuable watch, worth two hundred dollars, was taken from the aged Judge Rountree.

Two years later Jesse James, living in St. Joseph under the alias of James Howard and running a livery stable, was shot in his home on April 5, 1882, by a former associate, who was induced to do the deed for the reward of $10,000 which had been offered for the capture, dead or alive, of Jesse James. On the lifeless body Judge Rountree's watch was still found ticking.

Frank James gave himself up to the authorities, served a term in the penitentiary, and spent the remainder of his eighty-two years peacefully on the old family farm, where he died in 1915.

The Excelsior Springs spoon belongs to the National Union series, with the name of Missouri, the national emblem, and the state seal on the handle. The United States shield shows on the reverse side of the handle.

The spoon was made by R. Wallace & Sons. Length, 6 inches.

No. 21 HUDSON AND FULTON
No. 29 STEAMER ROBERT FULTON
No. 133 HUDSON-FULTON CELEBRATION

In two enormous volumes containing 1,421 pages and weighing eleven pounds—slightly less with the dust removed—lie embalmed the minutest details of the Hudson-Fulton Celebration, 1909, prepared by a special commission appointed by the New York legislature. These two ponderous books would be terribly dull if it were not for the illustrations, which cover 388 pages. These alone redeem the vast piece of reporting of any further accusations on my part.

The more I looked at the pictures of the fifty floats in the carnival parade and the fifty-four in the historical pageant, the greater became

PLATE 26

24. YOSEMITE LOVERS   25. RIP VAN WINKLE
26. OLD IRONSIDES   27. GENERAL GRANT

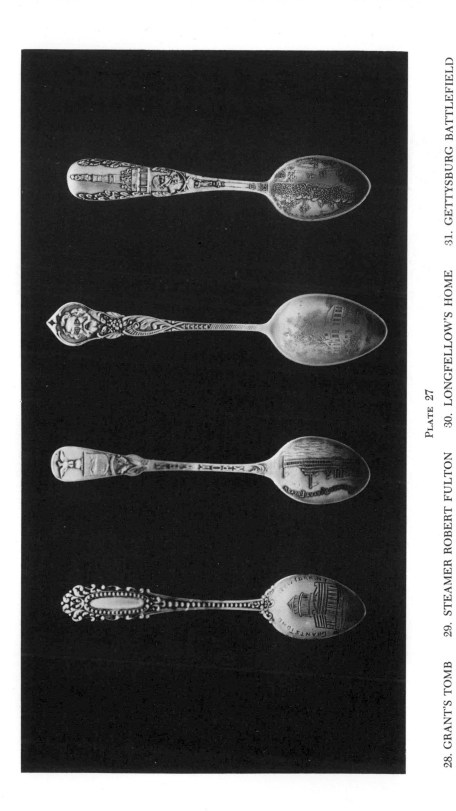

PLATE 27

28. GRANT'S TOMB   29. STEAMER ROBERT FULTON   30. LONGFELLOW'S HOME   31. GETTYSBURG BATTLEFIELD

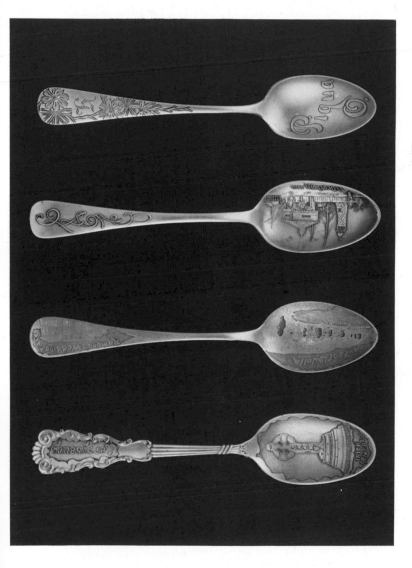

PLATE 28

32. IRISH BRIGADE   33. CAVES OF LA JOLLA
34. FORT DEARBORN LIGHTHOUSE   35. PIQUA

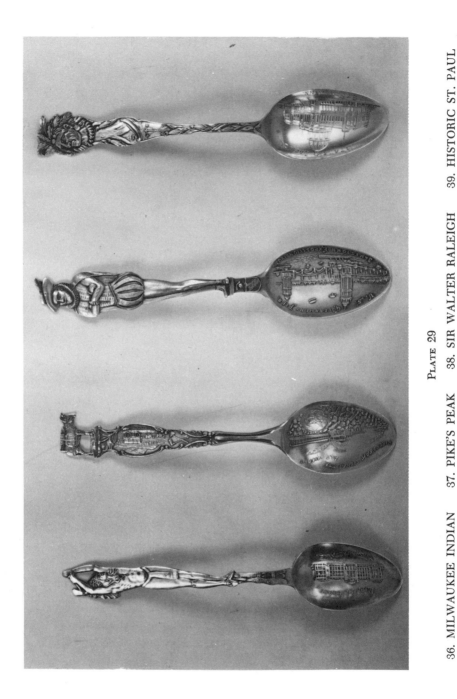

PLATE 29

36. MILWAUKEE INDIAN   37. PIKE'S PEAK   38. SIR WALTER RALEIGH   39. HISTORIC ST. PAUL

my amazement and admiration. The majority of floats in the average parade usually flaunt a spectacle of colorful novelties without any progressional sequence of any kind, but the floats in this instance present a development and continuity of ideas truly educational.

The historical parade was a panorama of New York history from its beginnings down into the twentieth century, covering the periods dominated by the Indians, Dutch, English, and finally, the independent Americans. Mention of a few floats will reveal the great amount of planning put into their construction: The Five Nations, First Sachem of the Iroquois, Fate of Henry Hudson, purchase of Manhattan Island, Bronck's Treaty with the Indians, Reception of Stuyvesant, Bowling on Bowling Green, Governor Leisler, New Amsterdam becomes New York, Trial of John Peter Zenger, The Stamp Act, Destruction of Statue of George III, Storming of Stony Point, Nathan Hale, Capture of André, Washington's Farewell to His Officers, Legend of Sleepy Hollow, Legend of Rip Van Winkle, the Clermont, Fulton's Ferry, Reception of Lafayette, Erie Canal Boat, Statue of Liberty, and Father Knickerbocker Receiving. These are all highlights in the history of New York.

The Carnival Parade exhibited floats devoted to music, art, and literature, including everything from Cinderella to the Queen of Sheba. The favorite operas at the Metropolitan were well represented, especially the Wagnerian music-dramas.

This celebration was held from September 25th to October 11th, 1909, to commemorate two closely-associated events, the three-hundredth anniversary of the discovery of the Hudson River in 1609 and the centennial of steam navigation on the Hudson in 1807. The primary motives behind the celebration were purely educational, not commercial, and any idea of an exposition tending to publicize modern industrial achievements was abandoned.

Of all the preparations for the occasion, none aroused greater interest than the reconstruction of Henry Hudson's vessel, the *Half Moon*. The Dutch government generously offered to do the work gratis. After much research, the Hollanders ran upon the original plans for the *Hope*, the sister ship of the *Half Moon*. The displacement of the vessel occupied 4,239 cubic feet and measured sixty-five feet in length. The *Half Moon* weighed anchor in the Brooklyn Navy Yard on September 25th and proceeded up the Hudson River at the head of a long naval parade. The *Clermont* offered more difficulties in the way of construction than the *Half Moon,* for no facsimile or blue print could be found for Fulton's steamboat. Finally the specifications were drawn from measurements mentioned in one of Fulton's letters. As built, the *Clermont* was one hundred fifty feet long and displaced 3,640 cubic feet of water. Beside the modern ocean liners, the vessel looked insignificant but quaint.

In addition to the parades, there were many dedications of parks and monuments along the Hudson. At the official reception of the foreign guests, Mrs. Julia Ward Howe, author of the "Battle Hymn of the Republic," arose and read a poem written especially for the occasion. The audience, out of respect for Mrs. Howe's ninety years, stood during the entire reading of this poem.

There were many ceremonies and social events in all the towns along the Hudson during the celebration. Many banquets were given in honor of the foreign envoys and distinguished American visitors.

Of the two men honored in the Hudson-Fulton Celebration, the first in point of time, Henry Hudson, explorer of the river which bears his name, is an obscure figure of whom absolutely nothing is known except during the last four years of his life, into which period are crowded the multiple vicissitudes of four voyages which have given him rank as a great discoverer, although he had no intention of making discoveries, his hope being only that of finding a passage to India.

"Our ignorance of Hudson's life is as complete as is our ignorance of his personal appearance," says his authoritative biographer, Edgar Mayhew Bacon. It was on a certain day in April, 1607, that he first emerged from the veil of obscurity and entered the pale of history. In the company of eleven sea-going companions he attended St. Ethelburga's Church in London, probably to pray for the success of their undertaking, which was to "discover a passage by the North Pole to Japan and China," according to the account given in the pages of *Purchas His Pilgrimes.*

His first two voyages for the Muscovy Company, undertaken to find the Northeast Passage to the Indies via the North Pole route, were failures. In both attempts he was turned back by the great fields of floe ice. On one occasion his vessel was being crushed by the jamming ice when a strong wind sprang up, and a changed current carried off the ice-floes which had hitherto been booming like thunder in their impacts.

Finding himself adjudged a bad risk in England, Hudson went to Amsterdam and found employment with the Dutch East India Company. His ship, the *Half Moon,* a vessel of eighty lasts displacement, a Dutch measurement corresponding to one hundred sixty tons, set sail from Holland April 4, 1609, and first sighted the American coast July 15th, the exact location not being known to us, as the description of pine forests ashore might characterize a long stretch of territory.

For two months Hudson skirted the coast, first heading south, then reversing his course to go northward. During the first week in September the crew landed about where Coney Island is now. On the 12th he began his trip up the river that now bears his name.

Wherever they stopped to fish, or waited for more favorable winds, the natives came out to greet them, bringing corn, pumpkins, grapes, tobacco, oysters, beaver and otter skins to barter for beads, knives, spoons, dishes, hatchets, saws, and trinkets.

At one point the natives came on board in such numbers that Hudson became suspicious of their good intentions, and to make them talk freely he gave them unstintedly of his brandy. One of them became so intoxi-cated that he fell into a deep slumber, from which his companions could not awaken him. Thinking the sleeper had been put under the spell of a magic potion, they fled precipitately. The next morning the intoxicated savage awoke, and feeling no ill effects, went ashore to apprise his friends of his well-being. The natives, grateful for his safety, returned to the boat with gifts of tobacco and a huge platter of steaming venison.

Hudson ascended the river for a distance of about a hundred and forty miles, probably reaching an area shortly above the site that Albany now occupies. The maps and the journal that he kept, although their value was not immediately recognized, soon proved to be the cornerstone on which the Dutch based their claims for colonizing the region around "Hudson's River."

Spurred on by the encouraging accounts given by Hudson, the London Company hired him to head another expedition, this time in search of a northwest passage to the Orient. Hudson assembled pretty much the same crew of men, to the number of tweny-three, whom he had used on his previous voyages. His son, John, aged twelve, was also included, as usual. Among the new men on this trip was a young fellow, Henry Greene, of good family, well educated, but of such depraved character that his own mother had cast him out. Hudson, hoping to reform the boy, even lodged him in his own home and privately promised him wages— the Company had refused to offer him anything.

The new vessel, the *Discovery*, weighed anchor April 17, 1610, from London, and sailed in a northwesterly direction till they reached the southern coast of Iceland. Here the crew disembarked and bathed in a spring hot enough to scald a chicken. At this place a quarrel broke out between the ship surgeon and the disreputable Greene, who in collusion with Robert Juet, the master's mate, began to talk with the other members of the crew in favor of an about-face to England.

Near Greenland they were disturbed by the presence of a great many whales, two of which passed under the ship without offering to capsize it, to everyone's relief. Mountains of ice floated by, and once a huge chunk turned somersault near enough to churn the vessel out of its set course. At one bay-landing the men ran upon freshly-made piles of stones. Peeping into these crude cellars, they discerned a large stock of dressed birds hung by their necks, as it were, in cold storage. Some of the men tried to persuade their commander to tarry here long enough for them to replenish their larder with this excellent supply of fresh meat, but he was too eager to press on for the western ocean, which he felt sure lay at no great distance.

All through September and October precious time was lost in exploring various streams that emptied into that great body of water, which thereafter always bore the name of Hudson Bay. The vessel had been stocked with provisions sufficient to last six months, and that period had now elapsed. Supplies of food were running low, and winter was coming on.

An untoward incident happened at this juncture. The head gunner died and instead of putting his clothes up for auction, as was customary, Hudson allowed his protégé Greene his choice of the clothing without a sale. This show of favoritism angered some of the men who were already in a mutinous disposition, since they were hungry and limping around with chilblains and frozen toes. Hudson unwisely ordered a search of all chests for remaining scraps of food, and when thirty cakes were discovered in a bag in his own cabin, the rebellious crewmen, among whom Juet and Greene were extremely active, plotted to make a definite move against their commander.

The mutineers waited for a chance to find him alone. The following morning, when Hudson emerged from his cabin, he was seized and his arms bound behind his back. When he asked for the meaning of this action, he was told to wait till they put him off in the shallop. The conspirators then set about seizing six men still faithful to Hudson, and these, along with the ship's master and his young son, were put aboard the shallop and lowered from the deck into the chill, fog-covered waters.

Pricket, the only friend of Hudson's still remaining aboard the *Discovery*, was kept because he alone was capable of piloting the vessel safely home. Pricket, on his knees, begged the mutineers, for the love of God, to be charitable and allow the eight men to stay aboard, but the conspirators would hear none of it. Hudson called to Pricket a last warning that Juet would yet be the death of them all. "Nay," replied Pricket, "It is that villain, Henry Greene."

Thus, Henry Hudson departed into the unknown just as mysteriously as he had stepped out of it. There is little doubt that he and his friends quickly succumbed to cold and hunger in such bleak, inhospitable surroundings. The following year another expedition, of which Pricket was a member, set out in search of Hudson—as well as of the northwest passage—but nothing further was ever heard of the lost commander.

❖   ❖   ❖   ❖

The question, "who invented the steamboat?" has not yet been answered to everybody's satisfaction. Quite a number of men did the spadework and cleared the way for Fulton's success. Among those who contributed a share in the development of the steamboat, mention should be made of William Henry, James Rumsey, John Fitch, William Symington, John and Robert Stevens, Edward West, and Robert Livingston.

William Henry (1729-1786), of Lancaster, Pennsylvania, was a pioneer in experimenting with vessels propelled by steam. Earlier in life he had served as a gunsmith with Braddock and later helped to equip the American forces with guns during the Revolutionary struggle. He eventually became an important manufacturer of the Kentucky rifle, invented the screw auger, and devised a method for controlling the heat escape from hot air furnaces.

In 1763 he constructed a steamboat with paddle wheels and launched it on the Conestoga River. Before he could make an effective demonstration of his invention, however, the engine by a curious accident slipped overboard and was never recovered. Some believe this story to be a hoax. Nevertheless, Henry did construct an improved model for such a boat and laid his plans before the American Philosophical Society in 1782, but nothing came of the matter beyond a speculative discussion.

James Rumsey (1741-1792) was a handsome, smooth-talking man, the proprietor of a hotel, "At the sign of the Liberty Pole and Flag," at Bath, an up-and-coming watering place in the western part of Virginia. Rumsey gained the ear of the unsuspecting George Washington, who, while a lodger at the Liberty Pole and Flag, listened to a very daring plan that Rumsey had in mind for making boats run upstream without the slightest aid of oar, sails, or any form of human exertion. Washington was so thoroughly convinced of Rumsey's abilities to construct boats "upon a model that will greatly facilitate navigation against the currents of rapid rivers," that he assisted the hotel keeper in gaining exclusive rights for any such navigation in the states of Virginia, Maryland, and South Carolina. Actually the device that Rumsey had in mind when he broached the subject to Washington was nothing more than a pole boat, though shortly after he had secured his monopoly, Rumsey began to think of the possibilities of using steam power on boats. After several years of experimenting, Rumsey made a trial run on the Potomac at Shepherdstown, December 3, 1787. When the boat moved upstream for half a mile and then turned back, the spectators became so enthusiastic they whooped, threw their hats into the air, and applauded "crazy Rumsey" as a hero. A second run was effected a week later, and the boat was then hauled ashore, never to operate again.

Although Rumsey had started experimenting on mechanically-propelled boats before Fitch, the latter actually demonstrated a steamboat in action three months before Rumsey's little exhibition on the Potomac. John Fitch (1743-1798), who was to become a bitter rival of James Rumsey for the honor of being acclaimed the inventor of the steamboat, was dogged all his days by a malevolent fortune that rendered him an unhappy, will-o'-the-wispish wanderer, so soured and disillusioned toward the end that he tried to drink himself to death. Failing to snuff out his existence by this means, he slipped into oblivion through an overdose of sleeping powders.

Fitch was as open about his plans for building a steamboat as Rumsey was secretive. He talked to everybody, and somebody advised him to approach George Washington for support in his enterprise. Fitch did so, his main purpose being to solicit from the general a letter of commendation to the Virginia legislature, but such a pat on the back was denied him.

Fitch's enthusiasm and eloquence found him enough supporters to supply his wherewithal to buy the essential equipment he needed. All through the spring of 1787 he worked in collaboration with Henry Voight, his right-hand man, to perfect his engine. In August of that year Fitch's steamboat ran its first trial heat on the Delaware River. A large number

153

of demonstrations followed, but the vessel traveled at too slow a speed to be of any value commercially.

Fitch improved on his boat till it could easily make seven or eight miles an hour. In June, 1790, his company placed this ad in the Philadelphia papers: "THE STEAMBOAT is now ready to take passengers and is intended to set off from Arch Street Ferry, in Philadelphia, every Monday, Wednesday and Friday for Burlington, Bristol, Bordentown, and Trenton, to return on Tuesdays, Thursdays, and Saturdays." For three months Fitch's steamboat plied back and forth between Philadelphia and Trenton, traveling more than a thousand miles till the line, not paying, was suspended. The increasing hostilities between Fitch and Rumsey played no little part in blighting the prospects of both. In all the colonies, now become states, there were struggles, quarrels, and litigations over the granting of rights to either contestant. In the end, the hopes of both were utterly ruined.

Edward West (1760-1827), a silversmith of Lexington, Kentucky, surprised everybody by announcing, along in the summer of 1793, that he would give a public demonstration, on South Elkhorn Creek, of a steamboat he had perfected. The performance was successful, but faith in steamboats had reached a low ebb by that time. No wealthy persons would risk money on a project the like of which had fallen flat so repeatedly. Twenty-three years later, in 1816, a steamboat company using West's demonstration boat for a model, built packets and started a commercial line with carriers that plied back and forth successfully from New Orleans for many years. West should be remembered as an inventor of sorts, ranging from the modern-type nail to an iron hobble for rheumatism.

It remained for Robert Fulton (1765-1815), an experienced engineer and a practical inventor, backed by such wealthy men as Chancellor Livingston, to put the steamboat on a commercial basis successfully. A poor widow's son, from Lancaster, Pennsylvania, he had been sent to Europe by charitable friends to study art under Benjamin West in London.

For twenty years Fulton resided in Europe. He turned aside from his art to invent such things as a derrick for use in canals, a rope-making machine, a device for spinning flax, a new method of tanning, a submarine, and the torpedoes to accompany it.

Fulton had already put one successful steamboat afloat on the Seine before he returned to America to build *The North River Steamboat of Clermont,* which Fulton himself always called *The Steamboat,* but which posterity has known merely as *The Clermont.*

For several months the boat was in process of building. It was a large vessel displacing a hundred and fifty tons, and using side wheels to secure propulsion through the water. The name *Clermont* was actually added as a happy afterthought by Fulton—Clermont being the pretentious country estate of Livingston, the backer of the enterprise.

Scant attention was paid to the sailing of the *Clermont* in New York on August 17, 1807. Only one newspaper announced the event beforehand

154

in its columns. People were too skeptical of new ventures in steamboats. A few spectators cheered when the *Clermont* chugged away from the wharf, but their approbation was silenced by the stopping of the boat a short distance out in midstream. Fulton went below, looked over the machinery, and discovered a "slight maladjustment." They were soon moving again, and after a brief period of nervous tension the crowd relaxed and assumed a gay holiday spirit. Some one burst into song; others joined in. Gawkers on the shore were awestruck, even terrified, by the "fire-belching monster" and the ferocious-sounding whistles that blew off steam near landings and bends.

Just before the steamboat reached Clermont, Chancellor Livingston addressed the crowd on deck on the momentousness of the occasion. Among other things, he announced the engagement of his cousin, Harriet Livingston, to Robert Fulton, whose name, he said, would descend into history as one of the world's great benefactors.

The boat anchored at Livingston's baronial estate, and the party went ashore to spend the night there. The next day the *Clermont* steamed into Albany, a distance of one hundred and forty-six miles in thirty-two hours. The return trip downstream required only thirty hours.

A granddaughter bestowed this note of praise upon the hero of that trip: "There were many distinguished and fine-looking men on board the *Clermont*, but my grandmother always described Robert Fulton as surpassing them all. 'That son of a Pennsylvania farmer,' she was wont to say, 'was really a prince among men. He was as modest as he was great, and as handsome as he was modest. His eyes were glorious with love and genius'."

Fulton was a busy man the remaining years of his life. When he died at the age of fifty, he had already built seventeen steamboats, in addition to launching the first steam warship. His death came unexpectedly, caused perhaps by overwork and harassments from an endless number of lawsuits over patent rights. He lies buried in an unmarked grave in Trinity churchyard.

✿   ✿   ✿   ✿

The Hudson and Fulton spoon portrays those two worthies in neat embossments on the handle, along with the state seal in the caput. The bowl is of splendid devisal, the *Half Moon*, 1609, being in the upper half and the *Robert Fulton*, 1909, in the lower. The two are separated by a foliated banderole, cornucopian in shape, along which is written, "On the Hudson."

The reverse side of the handle exhibits scenes on the banks of the Hudson; the state capitol at Albany, the Poughkeepsie Bridge, and the Statue of Liberty. Produced by Paye and Baker Co. Length, 5¾ inches.

The Steamer Robert Fulton spoon contains that gala vessel afloat, in the bowl of the spoon, while on the handle there appear the name of New

York on the shaft, some lilies-of-the-valley in the nave, and the state flag on the caput. An anthemion graces the reverse tip of the caput. Also a product of Paye and Baker, its length is 4 inches.

The Hudson-Fulton Celebration spoon, showing the *Clermont* in the bowl and *De Halve Maene* on the caput, bears the imprint of Tiffany and Co., the M after the imprint representing the surname initial of J. C. Moore, who was president of Tiffany & Co. from 1907 until 1940. The New York state seal and a laurel wreath also appear on the handle. The bowl is slenderer and longer than that usually found on souvenir spoons, and the handle-tip sways backwards to a lancet point, giving one the impression that the spoon was fashioned after the pattern of an old Dutch mold. Length is 5¾ inches.

No. 23 BERTHA PALMER STATUETTE
No. 90 BERTHA PALMER VIGNETTE

In 1902 Potter Palmer, one of the great real-estate magnates who had helped create a modern Chicago, lay dying in the palatial sandstone, Tudor-style mansion which for seventeen years had been his home on Michigan Boulevard. His will had already been drawn up, and his property, estimated at eight million dollars, was being left in a chunk to his wife, Bertha Honoré Palmer. When the lawyer broached the possibility that the still very vital Mrs. Palmer, a full generation younger than her husband, might remarry, the old realtor rejoined, "If she does, he'll need the money."

Potter Palmer, a simple Quaker lad, had descended upon Chicago a half century before and set up a dry-goods establishment that granted goods on approval and unstinting credit to female shoppers. During the Civil War he quietly bulged his warehouses with cotton and wool products before the inflationary spiral zoomed prices skywards. His foresight rewarded him with plush dividends. He paid the Federal government a million dollars in income taxes within three years. Then he sold out to Marshall Field and plunged into real estate.

He also plunged into matrimony about this time. The beauteous dark-eyed girl, not quite half his age, was Bertha Honoré, born in Louisville, Kentucky, in 1849. Her great-grandfather, a Frenchman, had settled at the Falls of the Ohio in 1806 and was the first navigator to operate a steamboat between Louisville and New Orleans.

The youthful bride seemed favored of the gods: not only beauty was hers, but smartness of several kinds—charm, wit, verve, and vivacity. She had an uncanny ability for saying and doing the right thing at the right time. An ideal hostess who invariably pleased, she became the acknowledged queen of Chicago's social élite. Majesty was to come later—when she established homes also in London and Paris, and hobnobbed with royalty.

Within two years of his marriage Potter Palmer was to suffer two huge financial reverses. First, the great Chicago fire in the fall of 1871 obliterated his booming business prospects. He would have decamped to greener pastures if his wife had not convinced him it was his bounden duty to stick gamely, if grimly, by the stricken city.

He gambled with chances for all he was worth to build new homes, new hotels, new stores. The Palmer House was an extravaganza in stone. People came from the wide open spaces all over the nation to stand in the main rotunda and gawk upward at the scintillating skylight.

But disaster was to overtake Palmer again in the panic of 1873. He was still burdened with debts from his recent speculative ventures. He had to beg, borrow, and juggle like a necromancer. His position was precarious, but he managed to weasel through this era of depression safely on top. He began to prosper abundantly after State Street, the main shopping mart of the city, had been fully reconstructed.

In the course of time Mr. Palmer retired more and more from active business and concerned himself solely with a close watch over his already numerous investments. When his wife entertained, he retired into the background and admired her from a distance. Sometimes he was not seen at all; then again he would descend from his secluded apartments in the tower of his house, sit for a while on a sofa in some sequestered alcove "just to rest his tired feet," and then withdraw as inconspicuously as he came.

In 1891 Mrs. Palmer was chosen president of the Board of Lady Managers for the Columbian Exposition in Chicago. This choice pleased her husband mightily. She made a trip to Europe to arouse foreign interest in the project. Her name appeared almost daily in the newspapers. Her strikingly handsome picture was featured on front pages throughout the country. It was on this occasion that the two spoons showing Mrs. Palmer were made.

But this lady continued to take an active part in all civic and charitable projects in Chicago for a good many years after the Exposition. In 1910 she entered upon another interesting phase of her career. Having read an ad in the Sunday Chicago Tribune about Sarasota in the "land of eternal sunshine," she decided to see for herself. For the next eight years she spent most of her time in Florida, built herself a beautiful mansion overlooking Little Sarasota Bay, developed "Meadow Sweet Pastures," a large cattle ranch in the Myakka River Section, and organized the Sarasota-Venice Realty Corporation. Under her guidance Sarasota was transformed from a somnolent fishing village into a bustling tourist town. When she died in 1918 the city flag was lowered at half mast as a mark of respect to the lady who has become in the retrospect of time the patron saint of Sarasota. She had tripled the fortune left her by her husband.

157

The bowl of the Statuette spoon contains a view of the Woman's Building at the World's Columbian Exposition. The shank shows a maiden flowingly clad, standing with arms aloft holding a globe or disk, on which is written, "World's Fair, 1893, Chicago." Two cherubs or cupids in the nave support the finial of Mrs. Palmer's bust—an armless bust comparable in its beauty to that of Venus de Milo. The cut-out head of this stately dowager is shown in profile. Around her neck are fine strands of pearls. A wreath of forget-me-nots forms a coronet in the upper coils of her hair. A pearl earring graces the lobe of her left ear and a spray of two roses adorns her right breast.

This spoon, occasionally surfaced with a gold wash, was imprinted by Dominick and Haff, now incorporated by Reed and Barton. Length 6 inches.

The Vignette, a demi-tasse spoon, shows the Children's Home, Chicago, in a gold bowl. The shaft, plain except for the name of Chicago, Illinois, is divided into three slightly differentiated sections. The nave bears a globe on which an eagle with outspread wings is perched. The two Americas are in evidence on this side. The profile figure of Mrs. Palmer, the same as on the previous spoon, is enclosed in a medallion-like caput.

On the reverse side of handle are the dates, 1492-1893; the Eastern hemisphere; the United States arms; and in the oval on the caput is a little girl holding a long-handled parasol over her head, superimposed by the words, "Going to the World's Fair."

This spoon is a product of the Alvin Corporation. Length, 4 inches.

No. 24 YOSEMITE LOVERS

Within the shadows of the great hills enclosing Yosemite there once dwelt two tribes, the Monos and the Ahwahneechees, who from time immemorial had smoked together the calumet, the pipe of peace. Together they celebrated the three chief feasts of the year, that of the manzanita berries, that of the acorns, and finally the late autumn feast at which choice venison steaks were served.

A strong bond of friendship had thus held the two tribes together for a long time in all their activities. When they played their ancient game of chance, the henowah, they pledged their best bearskins, wampum, and arrows on the outcome. When one tribe performed its tribal dances or recited the legends of its hero-ancestors, the members of the other tribe rendered a full tribute of applause. Likewise in their burial chants they clasped hands in common sorrow.

Now, at one of these venison feasts Tenaya, a chieftain of the Ahwahneechees, was attracted greatly by the strange, haunting beauty of Wahulah, a demure Mono maiden, whose voice was soft and low like that of a mourning dove.

Tenaya excelled himself in exhibitions of strength and skill during all the games solely to win the admiration of Wahulah. But in vain did he wait for a sparkle of love-light to dart in his direction. More eagerly than ever he sought to captivate her fancy by passing words of regard. But she did not reciprocate this affection at all.

The heart of Wahulah had not always been so recalcitrant. Two years before this, she had joined in the funeral wail for her true love, a handsome young Mono warrior whose frail canoe, caught in an eddying current, had carried him over the swift falls of Pyweack to an untimely death. Since then she had known no more happiness in this world.

The Ahwahneechee chief now felt deeply agitated in mind. All during the snows of winter his memory reverted warmly to the sweetly sorrowful face of Wahulah. He was able to endure the torment no longer. When spring began to melt the snowy trails, he journeyed across the greening hills to the lodge of the Mono chief, with whom he amicably smoked the peace pipe.

Yet ere dawn of the following day he had cut the bonds of tribal friendship in twain. Wahulah was gone. In the night Tenaya had abducted her from the elegant bower where she dwelt apart, and which had been built purposely for her high in a balcony of her favorite tree, the Wawona. A beautiful place was this balcony, graced by finely-wrought carvings obtained from the Spaniards. Tenaya had gained access to this lodge by the rope ladder which Wahulah inadvertently had failed to pull in after her when she retired. There, while resting on her couch of doeskins, she was rudely awakened out of her repose and borne forthwith down the ladder on the shoulders of the indomitable Tenaya. She made no outcries, knowing they would not be heard, since her father and other members of his tribe slept at a considerable distance away from this particular tree.

On through the forest and over the hills sped Tenaya, who did not tarry for rest till he had brought his prize to the camp of the Ahwahneechees. Then he placed her in a lodge of his own making, which he had carpeted and roofed with boughs of fragrant pine. She said nothing but sat there silent, with downcast eyes, while he went away to prepare for her a feast of appetizing bear meat, acorn bread, and the tender shoots of spring bracken.

While he was preparing this repast, delicious enough to please a goddess, Wahulah warily moved one moccasin slipper after the other over the pine-wood carpet, fearful lest a snapping twig would betray her meditated flight. Neither her hunger, increased by the smell of the savory stewing meat, nor the great physical weakness occasioned by the fear of failure deterred her from the course she was taking.

Onward she bounded along the trail bordered by tall swordferns, rhododendron, azalea, and dogwood. Fillets of moonlight streaked down through branches of the giant sequoias like ghostly fingers to clutch at her feet and stay her passage.

It was not long before her escape was discovered. A hue and cry rent the still night air, and she knew the Ahwahneechees were bounding through the forest like hounds hot on the trail. Her moccasined footprints were plainly visible on the soft, loamy soil in the moonlight. The Ahwahneechee braves knew every inch of ground that she traversed, every twining vine, root, rock, and crevice.

She sped close to the canyon trail where the Pyweack threw its spumy effervescence across her face. Out into the open, away from the mighty tree-giants, and straight toward the broad, calm, emerald breast of the river, ran the frightened Mono maiden. Close at her heels were her rabid pursuers, their exultant cries of triumph ringing in her ears and whiplashing her on to a mad desperation.

Down toward a cove of the placid stream she sprinted, sprang into a canoe there at haven, and pushed away from shore just as the Ahwahneechees clawed out to detain her. With deftly measured strokes Wahulah plied the shaven birch paddles, leaving behind her the demoniacal shouts of her tormentors. The current grew swifter and wilder and blacker. No need now for strokes from the paddles for guidance. Faster and faster she glided. Straight as a birch sapling she stood in the boat, the strands of her flowing black hair coruscating like will-o'-the-wisps in the moonlight.

Soon in a dizzying whirl the frail craft raced forward toward the falls of the Pyweack. Swift was the descent of Wahulah into the wild-churning caldron of waters. Into the murky, mysterious depths she went down, as went down her lover before her. And thus did the Great Spirit bring peace to the maiden . . . The waters rushed over her mourning.

The Yosemite Lovers spoon portrays on the handle the abduction of Wahulah by Tenaya from her elegant boudoir-bower in the niche of the Wawona tree.

In the bowl may be seen the Wawona Tree itself and the road leading up to the tunneled archway cut through the trunk, in 1881, to a height of ten feet, a width of eleven feet, and a length of twenty-five feet. While this is perhaps the most famous tree in the Mariposa Grove—often called the most famous tree in the world—there are other giant sequoias notable for their unique size and age. The Grizzly Giant, 209 feet high and 96.5 feet in circumference, is estimated to have reached the hoary age of 4,000 years—the oldest living thing in the world. The Fallen Monarch, another mighty tree, lies on its side to a length of nearly 300 feet. The Wawona, said to be the Indian word for "big tree," measures 231 feet in height. In all, the Mariposa Grove contains 545 trees.

This spoon was made by Rogers, Lunt and Bowlen Company, carrying an early trademark for their "Treasure" solid silverware. Length, 5¾ inches.

No. 26 OLD IRONSIDES

Without ships, what would our nation have been? A land not only without a past, but one also without a future! The *Nina, Pinta,* and *Santa Maria* carried Columbus and his men to the Great Discovery; the *Half Moon,* the *Mayflower,* the *Ark* and *Dove* brought famous explorers and pioneers to our shores; with the *Bon Homme Richard,* John Paul Jones captured more than three hundred British vessels during the Revolution; Robert Fulton proved the practicability of the steamboat when he plied the *Clermont* up the Hudson; the *Constitution* demonstrated the sea power of our infant republic against the Barbary pirates and the British man-of-war during the War of 1812; such clipper ships as the *Dreadnaught* carried the goods of Yankee merchants to the remotest corners of the globe; the Civil War produced those valorous fighters, the *Merrimac (Virginia)* and the *Monitor,* the *Alabama* and the *Kearsarge;* "Remember the *Maine"* became the hue and cry of the Spanish-American War, in which the battleships, the *Oregon* and *Olympia,* won distinction; during our two World Wars an innumerable host of ships performed their duties so quietly, effectively, and courageously that it is difficult to single out any one above the other, although the name of the "Mighty Mo" (the *Missouri)* somehow springs to the forefront in our minds.

Of all these ships none is so dear to the hearts of our people, young or old, for the long and glorious role she has played in our history, as the *Constitution,* affectionately known as "Old Ironsides." Louis J. Gulliver, formerly a commander of this frigate, has written: "The brave relic of brave days, *Old Ironsides* is not only a ship but a challenge. She represents the problems of a young, sparsely peopled country fighting for its life; we appreciate the idealism and strength that built her, manned her, and fought her. We realize our immense indebtedness to the past that lived and died that we might be as we are, free, powerful, a leader among nations. She is a part of what America has been, is, and will be . . . If one were to select a solitary symbol for America's adolescence, it would be this majestic Frigate that rides the seas today."

Early in March of 1794 several members of Congress, indignant over the humiliating fact that we were forced to pay tribute to the Barbary States in North Africa to keep their pirates from attacking our merchant vessels, demanded from Congress an appropriation for the beginning of an American navy. A measure for the authorization of six vessels was voted on and passed, March 27, 1794. Two weeks later Joshua Humphreys, a Quaker shipbuilder of Philadelphia, was commissioned by General Henry Knox, Secretary of War, to begin the construction of the *Constitution* according to models and measurements which he had already proposed. Work started immediately at Hartt's shipyard, Boston, under the general supervision of Colonel George Claghorn, assisted by Captain Samuel

161

Nicholson, the ship's first commander. General Knox sent an expert shipwright to St. Simon Island, Georgia, to select the best grades of longleaf pine, live oak, red cedar, cypress and white oak. To Paul Revere went the contract for the metallic parts—the heavy copper spikes, bolts, and braces. The spars, anchors, and sails were made near at hand. Skillings Brothers carved the figurehead, a likeness of Hercules, for the prow. Betsy Ross created all the bunting, including the flag with fifteen stripes and an equal number of stars. The ship measured 175 feet in length and 43½ feet in width at the center, providing a displacement of 2,200 tons.

Bad luck attended the launching of the *Constitution*. Scheduled originally for September 20, 1797, the launching did not actually take place till October 21st. Due to the settling of the runways, the ship could not clear itself into the water at the first two attempts, and considerable time was spent to give the ways a steeper descent. Most inauspicious occurrence of all was a round of fisticuffs between Colonel Claghorn and Captain Nicholson on the day before the frigate finally slid into the water. The Colonel granted an entry-pass to several spectators who had previously been denied this privilege by the Captain. A heated argument arose as to who held the rights of command at this juncture, the Colonel claiming they were his until the ship was launched. Nicholson raised his cane and Claghorn made a couple of thrusts at the Captain before neutral onlookers parted the combatants.

For three years the *Constitution* cruised in home waters along the Eastern coastline and around the islands of the Spanish Main, and then remained in port for two years before being sent as the flagship of the Mediterranean squadron to the Barbary Coast, where there were prospects of trouble. An American brig had been seized by a Moroccan cruiser, the *Meshboha*, belonging to the sultan, and in retaliation our frigate the *Philadelphia* promptly captured the *Meshboha*. Commodore Preble of the *Constitution* aroused the sultan from his slumbers, by a twenty-one gun salute, as the American squadron steamed into the Bay of Tangier. The sultan, frightened by this audacity, soon signed a treaty of peace granting the release of the American merchantman and promising to respect our ships in the future, while the *Meshboha* was returned to the sultan.

On the last day of October, 1803, the *Philadelphia* ran aground off Tripoli and was hauled into port as a great prize by the Tripolitan pirates. Knowing that the vessel would be reconditioned and used against their squadron, the Americans devised a plan for boarding and burning the captured vessel. A party led by Lieutenant Stephen Decatur, then only twenty-four, and Midshipman Charles Morris, only nineteen, in a small ketch crept up to the sides of the *Philadelphia* under cover of darkness, climbed on board, distributed combustibles, fired the ship, clambered back onto the ketch, and were gone before the pirate crewmen had time to realize what had happened.

162

Early in August of 1804 the American squadron began its bombardment of Tripoli, a city strongly protected by twenty-five thousand soldiers behind high walls mounting more than one hundred cannons at strategically-placed intervals. For two hours the *Constitution* withstood the bombardment from three batteries without receiving serious injuries, at the same time pouring "upwards of three hundred round shot, besides grape and cannister, into the town, the bashaw's castle and the batteries silencing the castle and two of its batteries. In all this unprecedented exposure to the deadly aim of a land battery, the frigate was only injured in her sails and rigging—her hull being but slightly peppered with grape shot."

Inside the city, during the worst part of the bombardment Captain Bainbridge and the Chaplain, "Schoolmaster" George Jones, both of whom had been captured with the *Philadelphia* by the pirates, were covered with a rubbish of mortar and stone when a cannon ball from the *Constitution* struck their prison walls. Both were speedily excavated from the débris.

During a close-in action on one of the gunboats, Lieutenant Decatur would have been cut down by an assailant from the rear if a seaman by the name of Jack Reuben James had not parried the blow, which side-swiped his own head. Afterwards, Decatur called seaman James before him on deck and asked him to mention whatever recompense he desired and it would be granted if it lay within the power of the donor. All his messmates whispered to seaman James to ask for such favors as these: "Double pay," "a pocketful of money and a swing on shore" or "a boatswain's berth." The bystanding chronicler relates: "Jack elbowed them all aside, and would have none of their counsel. After mature deliberation, he announced the reward to which he aspired; it was, *to be excused from rolling up the hammock cloths!* The whimsical request was of course granted; and from that time forward, whenever the sailors were piped to stow away their hammocks, Jack was to be seen loitering around and looking on, with the most gentlemanlike leisure."

A treaty was made the next year with the Tripolitans, who promised to respect the rights of American merchant ships on the high seas. A similar treaty was effected with Tunis somewhat later. Both these treaties were signed on board the *Constitution*.

On June 18, 1812, Congress declared war against England. The next day the *Constitution*, which had been lying in the Washington Navy Yard for repairs during the previous three months, slipped down the Potomac, took on extra stores of ammunition, and added a complement of crew members before working out into the open sea. On July 16th a squadron of the enemy fleet sighted the *Constitution* and gave chase. The British squadron consisted of four frigates, and a ship-of-the line, with two prize vessels, a U. S. brig and a schooner, in their midst. For three days the pursuit continued, but during a rainstorm on the early morning of the 19th the American ship managed to outdistance her stalkers so far that the chase was abandoned. Commented Captain Isaac Hull: "Now, we'll take a cruise by ourselves; but if I ever come across one of those chaps alone, depend on it he shall pay for this."

During the next month several barks flying the British colors were captured, or else fired and sunk. "But we always saved the crews, and living animals," noted Moses Smith in his seaman's diary. "I do not remember that a goat, dog, fowl, or cat was thus burnt up."

About 10 in the morning, August 19, 1812, an enormous vessel, so fully rigged with sails as to be awesome, made her appearance over the horizon. "Before all hands could be called, there was a general rush on deck"— I quote gun sponger Moses Smith, as I shall continue to do liberally, since he can tell this better than I can. "The word had passed like lightning from man to man; and all who could be spared, came flocking up like pigeons from a net bed. From the spar deck to the gun deck, from that to the berth deck, every man was roused and on his feet." Then the *Constitution,* that "noble frigate, fairly bounded over the billows, as we gave her a rap full, and spread her broad and tall wings to the gale."

It was soon apparent that the enemy vessel was the *Guerrière,* bearing thirty-nine guns, and she opened up with a fire that kicked up splinters but did no material damage. "Hull was now all animation. He saw that the decisive moment had come." He went about among his men exhorting them to do their duty. Hear him saying: "Sailing-master, lay her alongside! . . . No firing at random! . . . Let every man look well to his aim . . . Now close with them!"

At the firing of a broadside, the *Constitution* trembled in her timbers from stem to stern. Three huzzas rent the air at the charge, though some men went deaf for a while. "Amid the dying and the dead, the crash of timbers, the flying of splinters and falling of spars, the American heart poured out its patriotism with long and loud cheers. The effect was always electrical, throughout all the struggle for our rights. When the smoke cleared away after the first broadside, we saw that we had cut off the mizzen mast of the *Guerrière,* and that her main-yard had been shot from the slings. Her mast and rigging were hanging in great confusion over her sides, and dashing against her on the waves." At this discovery the cry went up: "Huzza, boys! We've made a brig of her! Next time we'll make her a sloop!"

At the sight of the American flag hanging downwards from the mast, a plucky little Irish lad, Dan Hogan, scrambled up the rigging, and clinging onto the topmast with one hand, fastened the flag upright again. "The smoke curled around him as he bent to the work; but those who could see him, kept cheering him through the sulphury clouds. He was soon down again, and at his station in the fight."

At this point a heavy ball from the enemy's guns struck the planking in the hull and bounded off into the brine. Immediately the cry resounded: 'Huzza! Her sides are made of iron!" And from that moment the ship was

164

re-christened OLD IRONSIDES, and known forever afterwards by that familiar title.

Soon the foremast of the *Guerrière* was toppled, the mainmast followed suit, and the mighty ship had indeed become a sloop. "As an added insult, the English had hoisted a puncheon of molasses on their main stay, and sent out word: 'Do give the Yankees some switchel. They will need it when they are our prisoners.' But we made a very different use of this molasses from what they intended. We soon tapped their sweet stuff for them, in a way which they little thought of. The Yankee shot tasted the English molasses, and not the Yankee lips. We made the decks of the *Guerrière* so slippery, that her men could hardly stand!"

The havoc had been wrought, and the *Guerrière* was a total wreck, helpless, barely afloat, and in a sinking condition. Quarter was asked and given; Captain Dacres pulled off in a small boat and surrendered his sword as soon as he stepped on deck *Old Ironsides*. When he asked what sort of men were fighting on this ship he received this reply from Captain Hull: "Only a parcel of green bush-whackers, Captain Dacres!" Whereupon the captured commander exclaimed, "Bush-whackers! They are more like tigers than men. I never saw men fight so. They fairly drove us from our quarters."

The victory of *Old Ironsides* over the *Guerrière* roused American spirits to the highest pitch of enthusiasm. The young republic of the West had demonstrated its ability to hold its own on the high seas. This jubilation mounted when, at the end of the year, *Old Ironsides,* now commanded by Commodore William Bainbridge, whose steps had been dogged with ill luck up until now, captured the *Java*, a British frigate of the East Indian fleet. *Old Ironsides* marched on from one glorious achievement to another. On February 20, 1815, under Captain Charles Stewart, she won a spirited contest by moonlight against the two light frigates, the *Cyane* and the *Levant*, off the coast of Portugal.

For several years after the war the *Constitution* was the flagship of our Mediterranean squadron; then she lay in idleness at the Boston Navy Yards till 1830, when John Branch, Secretary of the Navy under Jackson, signed the order to consign *Old Ironsides* to the scrap heap. It was the reading of this notice in the newspapers that aroused a young Harvard law student, Oliver Wendell Holmes, to write so feelingly:

> Ay, tear her tattered ensign down?
> Long has it waved on high,
> And many an eye has danced to see
> That banner in the sky;
> Beneath it rang the battle shout,
> And burst the cannon's roar;—
> The meteor of the ocean air
> Shall sweep the clouds no more.

Her deck, once red with heroes' blood,
Where knelt the vanquished foe,
When winds were hurrying o'er the flood,
And waves were white below,
No more shall feel the victor's tread,
Or know the conquered knee;
The harpies of the shore shall pluck
The eagle of the sea!

Oh, better that her shattered hulk
Should sink beneath the wave;
Her thunders shook the mighty deep,
And there should be her grave;
Nail to the mast her holy flag,
Set every threadbare sail,
And give her to the god of storms,
The lightning and the gale!

The ringing lines struck deep in the public soul, and reëchoed across the country. It was a challenge to action, and every newspaper took up the cry: "Save the *Constitution!*" Public indignation demanded that the famous old ship be saved. Secretary Branch rescinded the order for dismantlement. The Government now decreed that *Old Ironsides* should be "re-constituted." Recommendations for the reconditioning were made by Commodore Charles Morris, the naval officer who had participated in every one of the ship's notable engagements. Timbers from St. Simon Island, Georgia, were again used when the historic old vessel was refitted for active duty.

Through the years *Old Ironsides* served as the flagship for many squadrons on voyages to all parts of the world. Several times she has had to return to the naval yards for repairs. On her last foreign cruise, carrying American exhibits to the Paris Exposition in 1878, she arrived without mishap at le Havre, but on the way home she ran into the chalk cliffs off Ballard Head, England. It is one of those little ironies of history that *Old Ironsides,* victor over several of Britain's finest warships, had finally to be pulled off the rocks and saved from being battered to pieces—by English tugs.

In 1931 *Old Ironsides* became solely an exhibition piece, and since then she has been viewed with pride by thousands of Americans on her triumphal tours leisurely taken from one port to another around the country.

The *Old Ironsides* spoon, with its gold-washed fruit bowl, displays a rope-cable winding spirally upwards through the shank to its anchor-attachment. In the nave a banderole bears the inscription "Old Constitution, 1812." The caput, beautifully bordered in a décor suggestive of baroque, contains a fine embossment of the famous ship with sails unreefed, in quiet waters; to the fore is a small rowboat in which sit two men

166

handling the oars. "Old Ironsides" is seen in raised lettering on the reverse of handle.

This spoon was pressed by Durgin & Co., June 3, 1891, and controlled by J. Hutchinson. Length, 5¾ inches.

No. 27 GENERAL GRANT
No. 28 GRANT'S TOMB

Before recently reading four full-length biographies of Grant, two of them by Southerners, I had long held the notion that the general became a hero by a sort of "good-fortune trend" in military events. My opinion was based perhaps on his subsequent political career, for never have I heard a politically-wise person speak a word in his favor. Elected to the presidency as a military hero, he eventually lost his popularity in the fierce antagonisms of partisan tactics. His two terms in office were signalized by all kinds of troubles: devastating fires in Chicago and Boston; graft, crime, and corruption among high office-holders in the capital, New York City, and elsewhere; the crashing of stock values and the failure of banks, creating the panic of 1873; and the long, turbulent period of Reconstruction in the South. Looking back from our vantage point of time, we can see that Grant's tenure in the White House may be likened to that of Warren Harding or of Harry S. Truman—it came in the let-down period after a great war, when the profits of patriotism have degenerated into downright political loot.

But to Ulysses S. Grant must be given the credit of doing more, militarily speaking, than any other man has done, since Washington, to keep the *United* in front of the *States*. Had he not saved a united democracy for both North and South out of the welter of an uncivil war, there would today be within the borders of this nation a dozen or more peanut republics jumping to attention at the beck and call of every European strong man who came along.

He wrote finis to a war that had chalked up finis for seven previous commanders. Let his military glory remain unclouded. Only as a politician was he a failure. His great opponent, General Lee, once said: "Before you look for a man's bad points, first look for his good ones." So, let us "meet General Grant."[1]

He came of pioneer stock. In fact, his earliest American ancestors narrowly missed the Mayflower. His father named him after the wise Greek, Ulysses, his favorite character in legendary history. The boy disliked working in his father's tannery enough to prefer going to West Point. There he did not distinguish himself, but whatever he had to do, he set about doing, and did it to the best of his ability, which was not

---
[1] The title of a book on Grant by W. E. Woodward, a South Carolinian.

outstanding. Among the cadets he knew there, mention should be made of Buckner, Buell, Ewell, McClellan, and Longstreet, all of whom, on a later day, he would fight with or against.

He had a certain shoddiness of appearance that neutralized the attitude of the other cadets toward him—they neither liked nor disliked him. In only one respect did he stand out and that was as a horseman. Once, by reversing his sitting position and holding a mule by the tail, he mastered a brute that had thrown everybody else. After his graduation from West Point, he saw active service in the Mexican War, and was cited for gallant conduct.

At the age of thirty-two he resigned his commission and tried farming on sixty acres in Missouri—given him by his father-in-law. There was not even a cabin on the farm, and he still had to clear the land of its thickly-wooded white oaks. Finding the one slave he had a nuisance, he handed the negro his papers of manumission. Running into debt on his farm, he went to Galena, Illinois, to clerk in his father's hardware store. There he was when the war erupted. Thus, at forty, he was already considered a failure: a man of intemperate habits, lacking ambition, and working for less than a thousand a year.

His first request for a reappointment to a commission was pigeon-holed by McClellan, who did not bother to answer the letter. Then he offered to train the volunteers for a local guard. Back in uniform, he was given the command of a regiment recruited in southern Illinois. When he made his first appearance before his men, some one yelled for a speech. Others began cheering. Grant made himself master of the situation at once by his first command: "Men, go to your quarters."

The war had already gone into its second year before Grant attracted public attention. In quick succession he captured Forts Henry and Donelson, and won the battle of Shiloh. The story goes that after Buckner's surrender at Fort Donelson, Grant, knowing the defeated commander to be without money, offered him his purse. True or not, Buckner always held Grant in the highest esteem to the last, and followed him to the tomb as a pallbearer.

Successes and advancements in rank were rapid. His skillful maneuvers at Chattanooga were the most brilliant of the war. There were victories at Vicksburg and in the Wilderness; success in the siege of Petersburg; and finally, the forced surrender of the Confederacy at Richmond.

Grant's magnanimity in the terms tendered Lee for the final capitulation is classic. The soldiers of the defeated army were allowed their side-arms, baggage, and horses—the latter, said Grant, would be needed for the "spring plowing." He later admitted a sense of embarrassment in the presence of the immaculately-uniformed Lee. He remembered a rebuke once administered him in Mexico by Lee, then his superior, for his slovenly appearance.

Had Grant died after Appomattox or at least before he became president, he would today be venerated as our greatest military hero. His presidency was an anti-climax. He lived too long, surviving his usefulness and his country's gratitude. But his tomb on Riverside Drive in New York City is a fitting memorial to the military hero who was "ruthless in war and compassionate in peace"—the man who saved the Union from disunion.

The General Grant, which is a fruit spoon, has an unusual-shaped bowl. It is divided into two sections, the upper one being fluted into five scallops, like petals. "Defender of His Country" appears as an exergue high in the shank. Above it, in the nave, a sheathed sword and olive branch form a St. Andrew's cross. In the cut-out of the caput is the bust of the general, whose bearded face, uniform lapels, and insignia are showing, but not his arms.

Made by the Shepard Mfg. Co., this spoon, as evidenced by its style, was a product of the early Nineties. It could readily serve for a sugar shell. Length is 5¾ inches.

The little demi-tasse spoon showing Grant's tomb is simplicity itself. The mausoleum in the bowl is the only historical evidence telling us where the spoon was sold. The handle is beaded up the shaft, and in the caput around the empty medallion, which could well symbolize the cenotaph for a president who was "not there" when it came to the great game of politics.

Impressed by Watson and Newell. Length of spoon, 3¾ inches.

No. 31 GETTYSBURG BATTLEFIELD
No. 32 IRISH BRIGADE

At a time when the hopes of the Union were at their lowest ebb and the spirit of defeatism was rampant in the North, two events occurred which changed the whole course of the Civil War. One was the fall of Vicksburg, which opened the Mississippi; the other, the battle of Gettysburg.

Fresh from victories at Fredericksburg and Chancellorsville, Lee attempted to carry the war to the North by moving into Pennsylvania, there crush the Army of the Potomac, and clear the way for the capture of Philadelphia and Washington. If his plans carried through, the North would be compelled to recognize Southern independence. With this idea in mind, he began his march northward through the valleys of the Blue Ridge Mountains on June 3, 1863. By the end of the month Confederate forces were wheeling into position to take Harrisburg, the Pennsylvania capital.

General George Gordon Meade, who had been placed in command of the Northern armies only a few days before, occupied defensive positions at Gettysburg on Culp's Hill, Round Top, and Cemetery Ridge, from the crests of which he would have a natural advantage of terrain over the enemy.

For three days, July 1-2-3, the bitterest, deadliest fighting ever witnessed on this continent raged, much of it taking place in close, even hand-to-hand encounters. One third of the men in Meade's army were natives of Pennsylvania, and this invasion of their home soil steeled them to an unflinching resistance. Both armies were about equally matched. The numbers engaged have been estimated variously at from seventy to one hundred thousand on either side.

The lines fluctuated up and down the hills and back and forth across the plains for three days without decisive results. On the afternoon of July 3rd, during a temporary lull, when the Union troops momentarily ceased fire, Lee, assuming that the enemy's ammunition was running short, ordered General Pickett and his division of 18,000 men to charge across the open plains and up the rolling hills to occupy Cemetery Ridge. It was a desperate gamble, but in it lay the last chance for a Confederate victory. The lines of gray infantry surged forward steadily against a blistering fire from General Hancock's artillery. The ground was littered with dead and wounded. One company, under Armistead, clambered over the Federal breastworks and hoisted the "Bonnie Blue Flag" near the top of Cemetery Ridge. But the odds were too unequal for the Southern banner to remain there long. Their casualties, totaling about 25,000 men, were greater on the retreat than on the advance. The hopes for a Southern victory were shattered. Lee recrossed the Potomac successfully, but the Union victory at Gettysburg had definitely turned the tide of battle in favor of the North. It was the beginning that pointed toward the inevitable outcome of the war.

In 1938 the remnants of two once mighty armies assembled here for a Blue-and-Gray reunion. The two thousand aged survivors gathered in friendly converse, recounting the experiences that had befallen them when they met here in mortal combat seventy-five years before. Thousands of their old comrades had never left Gettysburg, but had been lying there peacefully all these years under the grassy sward.—

> By the flow of the inland river,
>   Whence the fleets of iron have fled,
> Where the blades of the grave grass quiver,
>   Asleep are the ranks of the dead:—
>   Under the sod and the dew,
>   Waiting the judgment day,
>   Under the one, the Blue;
>   Under the other, the Gray.

The bowl of the Gettysburg Battlefield spoon pictures the heights and ramparts of Cemetery Ridge after the carnage. The handle shows two monuments. The one in the shaft is a memorial to Father William Corby, chaplain for the Irish Brigade from New York City. The statuary image of the priest has the right hand lifted in the act of absolving and blessing the troops just before they marched off to wrest Round Top Knob from the enemy. In the caput is seen the Soldiers' National Monument, standing on that part of the battlefield where the dedicatory services were held on November 19, 1863, when Lincoln supplicated in terms too fraught with meaning for their full significance to be comprehended at the time, that "we here highly resolve that these dead shall not have died in vain; that this nation, under God, shall have a new birth of freedom; and that government of the people, by the people, for the people, shall not perish from the earth."

The bearded face of General Meade appears in the nave of this spoon. Although born in Cadiz, Spain, where his father was a naval attaché, he was always reckoned a native of Pennsylvania. He seems to have led a charmed life, for he narrowly escaped death several times. Once his hat was shot off his head and twice he had mounts killed under him. Philadelphia has always regarded him as one of her honored sons.

Made by the Alvin Corporation, the Gettysburg Battlefield spoon comes in several sizes and types. The length of this one is 3¾ inches.

The Irish Brigade spoon pictures, impressively needled in the bowl, the monument erected in the form of a Celtic cross to commemorate the courageous action of the Irish-born soldiers from New York City, most of whom perished and were buried on the battlefield. No unit of either Northern or Southern army suffered a more grievous loss of life at Gettysburg than the Irish Brigade. The edges of the bowl are unevenly scalloped, and the contours of the monument stand out slightly from the incised areas around them.

The shaft is reeded in widening ridges till it reaches the second section of the handle, the nave and caput being combined in one unit. *Gettysburg* appears here simply, surrounded by a foliate-scroll bordure, which is capped by two wave-scrolls and a shell crown. The maker of this spoon is not indicated. Length, 5¾ inches.

No. 33 CAVES OF LA JOLLA
No. 51 RAMONA'S WEDDING PLACE

Often coupled on postcards and scenic views because they are close together—both being tourist attractions near San Diego—are pictures of Ramona's wedding place along with the caves of La Jolla (pronounced *la hoya*).

La Jolla is a delightful little town, perched on sheer cliffs offering commanding views of the ocean and its beaches in front, with a backdrop of fine homes, gardens, and parks—all of which make this place an alluring rendezvous for artists, writers, and musicians. Walt Mason, the poet, once declared in the presence of Hildegarde Hawthorne that there was no better place in the world for a sensible man to live than in La Jolla. Whereupon she inquired if that went for a woman too. "It does," he answered with an equal conviction.

Underneath the precipitous cliffs the sea has bitten huge holes out of the soft stratification of sandstone rocks, leaving a strange configuration of many caverns, with openings that admit lights and shadows in such varying degrees that the rocks assume phantasmagoric forms and eerie aspects to the spectator on the inside looking out.

There are ten main caverns penetrating the cliffs along the La Jolla beach, some of them rising as high as two hundred feet in vaulted domes unlike anything ever constructed by man in his architectural imaginings. Old father Neptune, the sculptor of these seaside vagaries, rides in on every high tide with a bellowing roar to continue his labors on the water-hewn handiwork, and rides out again carrying away with him each time imperceptible particles from the vast subterranean walls.

Formerly the only entrance to the caves was by way of the sea, but since 1905 a flight of steps has been tunneled into the interior from the mesa above. This land approach has made it possible for tourists when they are on the stairs to see the evanescent chiaroscuros at different levels and from better vantage points. Most notable perhaps is the "phantom figure of the White Lady," about whom more than one story has been told.

The only piece of nature that in any way resembles the caves of La Jolla is the weird formation off the west coast of Scotland known as Fingal's Cave.

The bowl of the Caves of La Jolla spoon gives a view, taken at some distance, of the beach-side penetrations made into the cliffs by the recurrent poundings of the surf. At the top of the handle appears Ramona's Wedding Place. These two scenes have been made by stenciled etchings. This spoon, pressed by the Whiting Co., now a division of Gorham's, is 5¾ inches long, and bears on the reverse of its bowl the date, 1893.

❈   ❈   ❈   ❈

The sad but poignantly beautiful story of Ramona has always moved its readers so deeply that all the scenes connected with the unfortunate outcast maiden have become the most dearly beloved shrines in California: the Grapevine adobe house at San Gabriel, Ramona's birthplace; the Camulos Ranch, in Ventura County, faithfully pictured by the author, Helen Hunt Jackson, as the Moreno hacienda, Ramona's early home; the Estudillo adobe house at Old Town, San Diego, used for Ramona's wedding place; Temecula, where Ramona lived with her Indian husband amid his people till driven out by the greed of the land-hungry Americans; the Indian reservation near Soboba, where Ramona's grave is supposed to be. Annually in April and May a Ramona pageant, produced by the towns-people of Hemet and San Jacinto, reënacts the peaceful Arcadian folk-life of early Hispanic California. The Guajone Ranch is pointed out as the place where much of the novel was written.

Why have all these scenes become enshrined in the hearts of so many Americans? Only the readers of the romance can understand the secret. A town has been named after this heroine. Countless girls bear the name. It has been the inspiration for one of our most popular songs. The story has been filmed several times. Although such a character like Ramona may have never actually existed, is it not true that she steps out of the written pages as her misfortunes multiply, and that she becomes so real before our eyes that she can no longer be regarded as a figment of the imagination?

Loretta Young, when asked what role of hers she liked best, responded: "Of all my parts, from drawing-room comedy to period tragedy, Helen Hunt Jackson's classic *Ramona* is my favorite. Indeed, the book was my favorite when I was a little girl. I used to fancy myself as the persecuted Ramona; I'd wear a lace curtain for a mantilla and hang over the banister in lieu of a balcony. My affection for the half-Scotch, half-Indian girl never waned. When I was under contract to Fox, I talked so much about Ramona that the studio finally bought the book and cast me in the title role. That was a dream come true. The part had the magic of childhood make-believe as well as the inspiration of a character rich in courage, intelligence, and spirituality. I keenly felt the reality of Ramona as her beautiful and tragic story unfolded among the arrogant grandees, the kindly duennas, and the romantic caballeros—all that intriguing panoply of characters who moved through the history of early California."

Ramona's wedding place seen here on the bowl of this spoon, is a simple one-story structure, built in the form of an open quadrangle with the south side missing. The adobe walls are quite thick, and the tile roof on all sides slopes toward the street. While not visible on the spoon, the beams for the roof actually project from under the eaves, and cross pieces have their rounded ends extending a couple of inches beyond the cream-colored walls of the kitchen. Strips of rawhide take the place of nails in knitting the framework together.

Three trees, either palm or acacia—stand here on the northern and eastern exposures of the house. The windows of these two façades are barred with forbidding iron grilles, and the two recessed street doors are of heavy panelled oak.

There are many interesting features to this house not shown here: the beehive oven *(horno)* outside the kitchen, the arbor, the patio with a profusion of flowers from Old Spain, and somewhat apart the old chapel. A high two-wheeled oxcart from the early days stands along one of the patio walks.

This picturesque *casa de rancho* was built in 1825 by a Don José Estudillo, and was still in the possession of his descendants when Mrs. Jackson visited the place in the early 80's; she later used the chapel for the setting of Ramona's wedding. The house has since become a veritable mecca for "Ramonistas."

173

All the pictorial portions of this spoon are worked in relief. The handle belongs to the familiar motif of the Indian with a side view of the face, and corn husks along the shank. It is a product of Paye and Baker, its length being 5¼ inches.

No. 35 PIQUA

Piqua received its name, according to an old Shawnee legend, in a rather unusual way. The tribe was assembled around a campfire at its annual feast of thanksgiving. The fire had almost gone out when inexplicably out of the smoke a man's body rose in distinct contours above the smoldering embers and ascended toward the heavens. The spectators, awestruck at this mystifying apparition, exclaimed, "Otath-he-wagh-Pe-qua," meaning: he who has come out of the ashes. Ever since then the place has been called Piqua.

The town is situated on the Greater Miami River in the state of Ohio. Shawnee villages had long occupied the site until they were destroyed by George Rogers Clark in 1782. Clark, believing that the white settlers south of the Ohio would never be safe from sporadic attacks till the Indian strongholds north of the river were razed, assembled a thousand Kentucky riflemen, who marched so swiftly and quietly through the forests that they took the Shawnees by surprise. Swooping down upon Piqua unexpectedly, they killed most of the villagers; a few of them were able to escape with their lives but with none of their belongings. Their fighting power was broken.

For many years the Indians would return to visit the graves of their dead around Piqua, and to roam over the adjacent countryside which they had known and loved as children.

As a white settlement, Piqua grew slowly through the years, then stopped growing. It is still a small town with a reminiscent Victorian atmosphere—a good home-town. And moreover, it is interesting to note that the things made in Piqua largely pertain to the home, such as furniture, kitchen utensils, stoves and furnaces, carpets, rugs, and curtains. Like the Indians of yore, the native sons and daughters who have migrated from this spot to live elsewhere, still love to return to Piqua, which they think of as "home."

The Piqua spoon lacks any form of ostentation, yet it somehow engages our attention. Its shape, without a single angle in any of its lines, seems to possess practicability and beauty in equally mixed proportions.

The bowl contains "Piqua, O.", appliqued in a gentle descent from left to right, barely raised above the face of the bowl. On the stem are five flowers, forget-me-nots and cosmos, three of them ascending along the center and two appearing in the crown, all five attached together by a ribbon-like

174

vine. There is an open space left for an initial, and in this instance an H has been placed here.

On the reverse side of the handle is Gorham's trademark, and etched alongside of it "Addie," no doubt its erstwhile owner. The length is 5¾ inches.

No. 36 MILWAUKEE INDIAN

Few states have preserved so many Indian place-names like Wisconsin, itself an Indian word meaning a "meeting of the waters"—a description quite fitting to a state which counts over 8,000 lakes, 10,000 creeks, 4,000 miles of interior rivers, 500 miles of lake shoreline, and gushing springs on almost every farm. A glance at the list of lakes, rivers, counties, towns, and cities will reveal how universal is this survival of Indian nomenclature. Milwaukee, the great metropolis of the state, was once a "meeting-place by the waters" to the numerous Algonquin tribes who hunted and fished over the area. Even though the redskins are gone a hundred years, the abundance of fish and game still makes the hinterland region a sportsman's paradise. A delight in happy living naturally springs from an acquaintance with its woods and waters.

The territory was opened for development after the Black Hawk War ended in 1832. Three years later the land around Milwaukee was surveyed, and a county government organized. Two men, Solomon Juneau and Morgan Martin, platted a town, called it Milwaukee, and spent considerable money in promoting their project. Byron Kilbourn established a rival port, Kilbourntown, west of the Milwaukee River, and brought in settlers on a small boat from large vessels dropping anchor in Lake Michigan.

The year 1836 was a memorable one for Milwaukee. The town experienced growing pains from the rapid influx of settlers, most of them being backwoodsmen from farther east. The first small contingents of Germans and Irish were beginning to trickle in, later to swell into a floodtide for several decades.

The roads by which most of the travelers came were ribbon trails near the lakeshore, rounding the bend from Chicago. Rivers had to be forded or ferried, and sometimes in the process the main highway was lost. A simple expedient to mark the trail was to drag a tree back and forth between settlements. Logs were aligned across marshy terrain, making any kind of riding rough.

Often a traveler would thread his way through the forests alone. Only a few miles out of Milwaukee one such adventurer, a German musician, was attacked by wolves. Using presence of mind and his trumpet, he saved his life by blowing the musical instrument directly at the animals when they approached too near for safety. For two miles his progress was staged in a hurried walk, sudden stoppage, quick reversal of front, wild bugling, and then a forward march again. Several times the hungry beasts hurled themselves forward to despatch their hapless victim, but the loud, cacophonous notes of the blaring trumpet hurt their ears, and baffled by the strident pain in their heads, fell back howling in dismay. Not before the traveler sighted the lights of Milwaukee did the wolves slink away into the deep forests.

Two horsemen once met on the uncharted road. One admitted he was lost. "Why, you're in Wisconsin!" declared the other.

"Yeah, but whereabouts in Wisconsin?"

"Blamed if I know. I ony kim last week," was the honest reply of the second stranger.

Among the early taverns in the town were the Milwaukee House, the Green Tree, Veit's College Inn, Mirandeau House, and two German hostels, the Braunen Hirsch and the Bohnenviertel. At Mirandeau's, breakdowns were held in which the dancers were Indians, French-Canadians, half-breeds, and backwoodsmen, all mingling on the friendliest terms. The floor was crowded if more than two couples were dancing at the same time.

Caleb Wall started the Milwaukee House as a temperance hotel, and set the hour of ten as the time when all guests should be in bed. His thirsty patrons, however, sought amusement elsewhere, a fact which the host discovered when he bumped into a ladder leaning against an open window one dark night. The proprietor soon modified his stringent code, and eventually his hostel became the gayest place in town. His tables were always loaded with good food, his meats being deservedly famous for their savory tenderness. Once, when the house was short of meat after a heavy run of newcomers, Wall secured meat by a clever ruse. He paid a half-breed drover to drown "accidently" one of the government beeves being driven through to an army supply camp, the sale of such meat being prohibited to private individuals.

Prices on all commodities were high till the panic of 1837. Fortunes in real estate vanished into thin air overnight. But the panic in the pioneer town was only a momentary freeze-out, far less catastrophic than was the case back East.

In 1840 the Bridge War broke out between Milwaukee and Kilbourntown. The quarrel hinged over the payment for a new bridge spanning the Milwaukee River. The controversy raged for five years before the legislature declared the costs of bridges thereafter would be equally apportioned.

When Harrison was elected in 1840 the Whigs celebrated the occasion with a barbecue at the Milwaukee House. But during some long-winded orations to which the Whigs listened attentively, the Democrats stole the spitted ox from off the outdoor grill and whisked it off for a feast at Kilbourntown. When Mr. Pettibone, who had furnished the fatted ox heard of the outrageous theft, he dashed off to Kilbourntown, jumped upon the banquet table there, and strode its entire length, stamping and kicking every plate and platter, like the veritable bull in a china shop, while the would-be feasters jumped in every direction to avoid the flying débris of "goose and gravy gang agley."

By 1846, when Solomon Juneau was elected the first mayor of an incorporated city with a new charter, Milwaukee was well on the way toward becoming the "German Athens" of the West. Many liberal-minded Germans, frustrated in their attempts to democratize their country in the unsuccessful revolution of 1848, sought refuge here. The most famous of these refugees was Carl Schurz, who subsequently played an important role as a staunch advocate of the Union, clean politics, and anti-imperialism. The transplanted Germans, forming as high as 75 per cent of the city's population at one time, naturalized their Sauerkraut, Limburger, Pumpernickel, Apfulkuchen, Bratwurst, Wieners, Frankfurters, and Hamburgers. They introduced their lager beer, organized singing societies and Turnvereins, and founded theaters for serious drama and the opera. They laid out parks with beautiful tree-lined walks, ornate fountains, statuary, and bandstands. Their *Gemütlichkeit*—means actually, "good company with good beer"—led to the establishment of the four famous breweries of Schlitz, Pabst, Blatz, and Miller. Many advanced political ideas, once regarded as visionary, socialistic, or radical, first put into practice here, have gradually been adopted by the rest of the country.

This German atmosphere flourished down into the twentieth century. At the outbreak of the first World War there was a strong revulsion against the excessive German influence. "German spoken here" signs were hauled down and Sauerkraut became Liberty Cabbage—only for a while.

About 1900 another tide of immigration brought in the Poles, who introduced new festivities in the swiecoupa, wesele, and the smigus. Other nationalities introduced their customs to modify but not to alter the predominantly German characteristics of the city. Still, there exist survivals of Indian and French influences from an earlier day blending with the German and Polish in sufficient form to impart a peculiar charm to this interesting American city on the banks of Lake Michigan.

Opened in 1898, the public library, shown in the bowl of the Milwaukee Indian spoon, is one of the very few libraries in the country housing more than a million volumes, with an annual circulation thrice that number, figures giving Milwaukee the highest percentage of readers in America. Special attention should be called to the fact that one of the completest collections of juvenile books is contained in this library.

In front of the museum entrance to the building stands a totem pole, an interesting reminder of Indian influences in the early history of both the city and state.

A warrior with more covering on his head than elsewhere about him stands on an arrow-shaft pedestal, his hands bearing a poised battle hatchet. No name of maker is discernible on the spoon. Length, 5 inches.

No. 37   PIKE'S PEAK
No. 142 DYNAMITE (SPOKANE BURRO)

One of the ironies of history is the fact that the man after whom the celebrated Pike's Peak is named never scaled the heights, while thousands of motorists easily reach the top today by means of a smoothly surfaced highway. Leaving Pueblo on November 23, 1806, Lieutenant Zebulon M. Pike set out with a half-dozen adventurers, inadequately supplied with food and dressed in light fall clothing, to reach the summit of the peak, but turned back when overtaken by a heavy snowfall, and declared the crest was unsurmountable.

The first ascent of this mountain was made under more favorable conditions in 1820. Following the gold rush of the late fifties, the peak became a guidepost for prospectors who crossed the prairies in covered wagons bearing the sign, "Pike's Peak or Bust." Gold not being as plenteous as first reported, many of the would-be millionaires changed the signs on their conveyances to read, "Pike's Peak and Busted!"

The bowl of the Pike's Peak spoon contains two interesting pictures, symbols of two stages in our transportational progress. In the lower right-hand corner is the medallion inset of a saddled burro marked "The Old Way." The remainder of the surface shows a railroad track on which two cars, smoke puffing from their chimneys, are ascending the inclined rails. Beyond the railroad there is a signal tower and below, supporting the tracks, is a great mass of boulders. The words, "Pikes Peak Signal Sta. Alt. 14147 Ft.," run near the rim of the bowl. Beneath the boulder-pile and tracks we are told that this is "The New Way." No thought then of a newer way—the motor highway.

The miner's badge appears in the shaft of the handle, and a prairie schooner in the nave. The wagon is drawn by four mules, and the driver sits in full view, with whip in hand, and feet directly on the double-tree and tongue. A mountain sierra looms in the background.

The caput, consisting of one large columbine stalk (the Colorado state flower), supports a knop which, in this instance, is a passive-looking burro. On the back of the burro is a pack-kit of miner's implements, secured by a girth running the circumference of the animal's belly.

The metal of this spoon is thin and of rather light weight. Maker not indicated. Length, 5 inches.

❧   ❧   ❧   ❧

At first glance the two spoons placed together in this sketch might appear to be different sizes of the same spoon. But even a casual examination will reveal to the observer that the burros are headed in opposite directions, and the space is open beneath the Pike's Peak burro while not fully cleared beneath Dynamite, who apparently is a miner's mule from Spokane, Washington, if the picture in the bowl is any indication. The name of Dynamite, imprinted in front of the saddle-girth, belies the appearance of this grizzled, lack-lustre creature, but it is a common appellation ironically bestowed, throughout the West, on such woe-begone beasts of burden after years of hard and faithful service in the mines. Some of them, however, have a latent vitality in their old bones. The author well remembers holding on for dear life to the tail of such a dead-headed burro as he galloped down a dizzy trail in Colorado after a wounded mountain lion began to give evidence of his carnivorous instincts.

A mine wheel and tools are slung over the back of this Dynamite. In the earlier catalogs of Paye and Baker, the creators of Dynamite, the handle was beaded the entire length from the caput to the drop. But in subsequent catalogs the handle shows a pick and mallet in the nave, and a bucket suspended by a rope through the shaft into the handle drop.

The bowl of this spoon pictures the falls at Spokane, Washington. At one time this city bore the name of Spokane Falls, but the last word was dropped in 1890, although the prosperity and growth of Spokane can be attributed directly to the falls for its great industrial expansion. In its early days the town had a spirited struggle with Cheney to retain its position as the county seat. For a while the contest was fairly even, and the privilege of being the county hub teeter-tottered in favor of one, then the other. Finally, when Spokane forged ahead in population and business, Cheney gracefully relinquished its claims. Even a devastating fire in 1889 could not retard the growth of Spokane; the setback was only temporary.

The length of the Dynamite spoon is 3¾ inches. Used through the courtesy of its owner, Mrs. Gordon Scheimer, Hayward, California.

No. 38 SIR WALTER RALEIGH

England got off to a slow start in the New World. It is true that she made claims, as early as 1497, to the lands from Labrador to Cape Hatteras on the basis of discoveries made by John and Sebastian Cabot, Venetians in the employ of Henry VII. But following their two voyages none others were undertaken for a period of eighty years. The English freebooter, Sir Francis Drake, derived great personal profits from his expeditions preying upon Spanish vessels laden with treasure. This redoubtable fellow "singed the King of Spain's beard" by plundering ports in the West Indies, scuttling Spanish ships, and carrying off tons of unminted doubloons and pieces-of-eight. Drake incidentally was the first Englishman to circumnavigate the globe. Martin Frobisher sought to find a northwest passage to India in 1576 by sailing around the northern rim of the North American continent, but the great masses of ice blocked his way. On a second trip he brought home a cargo of cheap pyrite, thinking it was gold. On a third expedition he built a stone fort in Greenland, which was soon abandoned. Another navigator, John Davys, tried to find a northern route to India, but had to turn back when he had gone as far as the strait, off Canada, which bears his name.

As yet no real attempts were made to establish permanent colonies. It remained for Sir Humphrey Gilbert and his half-brother Sir Walter Raleigh to lay the foundation stones of English colonization in America.

Raleigh is one of the brightest stars in the imposing galaxy of sixteenth-century Englishmen, a compeer of the whole company and the nonpareil, if versatility be taken as the criterion, of any single one of them. He can be placed with the discoverers; he can shine with the courtiers; he holds his own as a soldier; he is worthy of a nook in that "nest of singing birds," which enhanced the glory of England's literary renaissance; and withal, he is such a man, such a gentleman, as to cause us to doff our hats to him down through the centuries—with pleasure.

The sixteenth century brought decades of internal peace to England after the ugly War of the Roses. And peace brought prosperity to the rising group of middle-class merchants. Elizabeth, reigning in the second half of that century, seemed to transmit to her people a more heightened and enlightened visibility clearing up the bad headaches occasioned by the dictatorial littlenesses of Henry VIII and his daughter Mary. It is in this latter period, when England burst the bonds of her insularity, that Raleigh finds a place among such universal figures as Sidney, Spenser, Marlowe, Bacon, Ben Jonson, and Shakespeare.

Born in 1552 at Budleigh-Salterton on the south coast of Devonshire, Walter Raleigh was the youngest son of Walter Raleigh, a country squire, and his wife Katherine, daughter of Sir Philip Champernoun. It so happened that Squire Raleigh had entered into two previous marriages, to which three sons had been born, but of this brood we hear little. Mistress Raleigh had likewise married before, and was the mother of three sons, John, Humphrey, and Adrian Gilbert, all of whom had distinguished careers. Carew, Walter, and Margaret were the three children born of this last marriage.

Young Walter grew up amid pleasant rural surroundings within sound of the sea, and he drank in eagerly the tales of seafaring ships told him by old seadogs, many of them blood-relations through the Champernouns, Gilberts, Carews, and Raleighs, of whom there was no better stock in all Devonshire. His education was supervised by his mother, a "woman of noble wit, and of good and godly opinions." His father, more of the active, out-of-door type, taught the boy how to ride expertly in the chase after the fox and the deer, and many was the time they went galloping over the hills, accompanied by the music of bellowing hounds. He was a handsome lad, with bright brown eyes and fair complexion, tall, graceful, and lithe of limb. He held himself proudly erect, with such an aristocratic poise that "ostentation became him, which, on a meaner man, would have passed into vulgarity." His parents were strict, church-going people, and from them he imbibed that straightforward faith—scorning falsity, meanness, and vice—that stuck with him to the end of his days.

At sixteen he entered Oriel College, Oxford, where he became the "ornament of the juniors, and was worthily esteemed a proficient in Oratory and Philosophy." S. F. Bacon, Baron of Ferulam, one of the many friends he made at the university, recalled that a fellow-student, an expert in Archery, once approached Raleigh with the lament that a big bully had roundly abused him, and he knew of no way in which he could square off matters with the bruiser. "Why, challenge him," spoke up Raleigh, "to a shooting match." The incident, trivial enough in itself, does show the youthful Raleigh's quick powers of simple deduction: If you can't beat a fellow with his own weapons, use other means at which you are more adept than he.

Only two terms were spent at Oxford, and Raleigh was off to France in a company of volunteers raised by his cousin, Henry Champernoun, to help the Huguenots in the desperate defense of their religious rights. Little is known of his adventures in that country, although he spent five or six years there. Then, for a short while he soldiered in the Netherlands before he returned to England, where we have no definite knowledge of his whereabouts until he turned up at Court. It is possible that he spent some of this time at his Devonshire home, to be near his mother in her declining years, for he was devotedly fond of her. A contemporary relates a gossipy little tale about this period of his life: "In his youthful time was one Charles Chester, that often kept company in his acquaintance; he was a bold, impertinent fellow, and they could never be at quiet for him; a perpetual talker and made a noise like a drumme in a roome. So one time at a taverne Sir W. R. beates him and seales up his mouthe (i.e. his upper and neather beard) with hard wax." This same contemporary must have admired this strong-arm bit of daring, for he comments crisply that Raleigh was no slug.

In June, 1578, Sir Humphrey Gilbert, after years of higgling over plans to find the northwest passage, obtained a royal charter "to discover, finde, searche out and view such remote heathen and barbarous landes, countries and territories, not actually possessed of any Christian prince or people, as to him his heires and assignes and to every or anie of them shall seem good." The idea of planting an English colony in the New World suited Raleigh exactly, and he participated enthusiastically in the preparations for the voyage. In September the eleven ships set sail, on one of which, the *Falcon,* Raleigh was in command. All kinds of trouble seemed to spring up. The crew of one ship mutinied, and turned the course of their vessel homeward. An autumnal storm drove the other ten ships right into the path of a Spanish squadron; a fight occurred, and the English ships were too battered to go any farther on their ventures. The enterprise was given up.

The American dream had to lie dormant for a while, for Raleigh was now commissioned a captain in Ireland, where a rebellion had broken out. He did not relish the idea of squelching freedom anywhere, saying, "I disdain it as much as to keep sheep." Of his exploits in Ireland we hear sufficient to know that he was brave, chivalrous, and diplomatic. Twice he pulled from a bog a certain Henry Moyle, who, unhorsed, was holding twenty men at bay with a pistol in one hand and a cane in the other. On another occasion he seized the castle of Lord Roche through a ruse and aided by only six musketeers. So persuasive was he that he won the disaffected lord, seated at the banquet table in his own castle, over to be a staunch supporter of the Queen.

Upon his return from Ireland he was just as persuasive in winning the Queen's favor. The story goes that Elizabeth was figuratively swept off her feet by his chivalrous manners, and once "Her Majesty, meeting with a plashy place, made some scruple to go on; when Raleigh, dressed in the gay and genteel habit of those times, presently cast off and spread his new plush cloak on the ground, whereupon the Queen trod gently over, rewarding him afterwards with many suits for his so free and seasonable tender of so fair a footcloth." Not long afterwards, in the Queen's presence chamber, he etched this line with a diamond ring on the windowpane: "Fain would I climb, but that I fear to fall." The Queen graciously smiling completed the couplet: "If thy heart fail thee, climb not at all."

Elizabeth knighted Raleigh in 1584 and heaped riches and titles upon him. She gave him the confiscated estates of Lord Desmond in Ireland and Anthony Babington in England, and the emoluments accruing from many commercial concerns in London. Such unlimited beneficences naturally aroused envy, speculation, and idle gossip among other courtiers, some of whom, winning no such favors after much striving, became backbiting enemies to this man who had risen out of comparatively humble circumstances to the pinnacle of good fortune.

Meanwhile, Raleigh was putting his newly-acquired wealth to good use. He could now consummate his ambitions for planting colonies in the New World. He fitted out an expedition under his half-brother, Sir Humphrey Gilbert, to establish a settlement in Newfoundland. Acquiescing in the Queen's wishes, Raleigh remained in England. Sir Humphrey reached Newfoundland, but the settlers, disliking intensely such frigid weather in a wild, unknown region, sailed home with the returning fleet. On the way Sir Humphrey's ship was lost between the Azores and England.

182

Nothing daunted by this grievous misfortune, Raleigh outfitted two more ships under Philip Amadas and Arthur Barlow to make an exploratory voyage farther South. The reports which his deputies brought back this time were far more satisfactory. Skirting the coast from Florida north to Virginia, they found the climate pleasant and the land so rich of vegetation that they felt as if they were "in the midst of some delicate garden, abounding with all kinds of odoriferous flowers." And the natives, two of whom had returned with them, were affably disposed, having lived all their lives "after the manner of the golden age." This land, "luxuriant to the water's edge," was henceforth to be known as Virginia in honor of Elizabeth, the virgin queen, and Raleigh assumed the title of its governor.

He immediately equipped a squadron of seven vessels and sent it forth, with a hundred and eight colonists under the command of Sir Richard Grenville, who, being more of a freebooter than a colonizer, waylaid two Spanish vessels and extracted good ransoms from the captured captains, sacked and burned an Indian town, literally dropped ashore the colonists, in charge of Ralph Lane, on the island of Roanoke, off the coast of North Carolina, and sailed back to England to exhibit proudly his chests bulging with looted treasure.

Lane, left to his own devices, explored the countryside, looking for gold mines, good harbors, and possibly some passage leading through to the Pacific Ocean. His men learned from the Indians the use of tobacco, potatoes, and corn. "It is the goodliest soil under the cope of heaven, the most pleasing territory of the world," wrote Lane. "The climate is so wholesome that we have not been sick since we touched the land. If Virginia had but horses and kine and were inhabited with English, no realm of Christendom were comparable to it." The settlers grew impatient, however, waiting for the supplies that were not forthcoming. When Sir Francis Drake put into port, freighted with spoils of his successful attacks on St. Augustine and towns in the West Indies, the colonists joyfully boarded his ships and departed with him for home. Grenville shortly afterwards arrived and found the island of Roanoke deserted. Unwilling to abandon English rights to the land, he left fifteen men, with a good supply of food, on the island.

Not to be discouraged, Raleigh elaborated more plans to put the colony on a firmer footing. In 1587 he organized a company of one hundred fifty settlers and sent them out with instructions to build the fortified "City of Raleigh." These colonists, in charge of John White and an able staff of assistants, found no trace of the fifteen men left by Grenville. The palisades of the fort had been destroyed but the houses were undamaged. Melon vines were already clambering up the walls of the cabins, and deer stalked in and out of the open doors and windows cropping the melons. From Manteo, one of the two Indians previously taken to England but now living in the native village of Croatan, it was learned that the fifteen missing men had been massacred.

On the eighteenth of August, 1587, a granddaughter was born to Governor White, and "because this child was the first Christian born in Virginia, she was named Virginia." Not long after this event the governor took ship for England to replenish the supplies of needed food and goods. His return was delayed by the feverish preparations then taking place in the homeland to ward off an impending Spanish invasion. White wasted precious time begging in all quarters for help, but in vain. Only Raleigh gave heed, though up to his neck in grave matters concerning the defense of his native soil. He secretly bought the provisions and supplied the money that White was sorely crying for. Even then the voyage was held up until the vaunted Spanish Armada had gone down to an ignominious defeat.

Governor White's homecoming to Roanoke was as rueful as that of the Spaniards to their native land, even yet more tragic. The Spaniards did find the solace of family and friends surviving. The governor found his colony uprooted, his colonists vanished, and no key to unlock the doors of his bafflement in regard to their mysterious taking-off. It was a sad journey's end indeed.

What had happened to his daughter Eleanor and the tiny baby, Virginia Dare, the first English child born on American soil? Who had despoiled the five chests of his belongings, which he had so carefully buried? Several bars of iron, two pigs of lead, and a few garden implements lay strewn about in the weeds and grass. On a tree, five feet from the ground, the bark had been stripped off and the letters C R O carved in capitals. This certainly was meant to be CROATAN, the friendly Indian village presided over by Manteo. But it solved nothing. The fate of the colonists to this day is not definitely known. Did they meet their end through Indians, Spaniards, animals, sickness, or departure into the wilds? There are many unraveled threads in the loom of history.

Raleigh was dismayed by his successive failures. He had lost upwards of forty thousand pounds in the five attempts to plant a permanent colony in Virginia. He busied himself with other experimental concerns. He introduced the potato as a staple crop on his estates in Ireland; likewise, tobacco was no less successful. He gave employment to a hundred and fifty men in a factory making staves for barrels, winecasks, and hogsheads. He engaged in commercial ventures abroad. Having met Edmund Spenser in Ireland and read his *Faerie Queene*, Raleigh arranged for a great fanfare of broadside commendations from notable patrons long before the publication of this allegorical poem, in reality a magnificat to the Queen. Raleigh, the English counterpart of the French Cyrano de Bergerac, also knew how to pipe gallant love ditties. He piped them not only to the Queen, but likewise to the Queen's goddaughter, Elizabeth Throckmorton. When Raleigh secretly married this young woman, the Queen waxed extremely wroth, and banished the couple for a while to the Tower. She forgave them, however, and Raleigh was soon off with a fleet of vessels seeking a gold mine in Guiana. He brought back no gold, but he did secure a foothold for England that she has held ever since in this northern part of South America.

With the death of the Queen in 1603 Raleigh's star began rapidly to wane. With the ascent of the pusillanimous James to the throne, Raleigh's fate was sealed by a sequence of misfortunes. The King, who harbored an innate dislike for anyone who shared the former queen's confidence, was determined to humble this proud favorite. At their very first meeting on the English border, where Raleigh had gone with the welcoming committee, James was icily chilled when Sir Walter refused to laugh at this puerile pun: "Rawly! Rawly! True enough. For I think of thee very rawly, man."

Before the year was over, Raleigh was hauled into court for treason, accused of accepting Spanish gold in a plot to overthrow James and put Arabella Stuart on the throne. Never was there a greater travesty of justice. The details on the trial are disgusting. The Lord Chief (In) Justice addressed Raleigh only as a "viper." His guilt was preordained. Twelve years he spent in prison, but they were no idle interval. He experimented with chemicals, inquired into the nature of drugs for reducing fever, discovered how to convert salt water into fresh, and devised ways for best curing tobacco grown in Britain. His *History of the World* won him a host of new friends, as well as a popularity so widely favorable that his Most Unmajesic Majesty was somewhat nonplussed, if not a little frightened at this intelligent exhibition of the public temper. The captive did not lack for visitors. His wife and two sons were constantly at his side. The Queen and the Prince of Wales were his devoted admirers. "Who but my father would keep such a bird in a cage?" once exclaimed the young prince.

Raleigh left his prison in 1616 to lead another expedition in search of the much-talked-of gold mines in Guiana. Since much of his wealth had been forfeited through his imprisonment, he had to appeal to others for financial support. Contributions poured in. The great man, now sixty-five, was deeply moved by the affection and implicit faith shown him by all classes of the people. But the king premeditated mischief to the expedition. The Spaniards, duly apprised of Raleigh's coming by letters from King James himself, awaited in force and crippled the English fleet.

Raleigh was condemned even before he returned to London. James had solemnly promised the Spanish ambassador that Raleigh's head would roll. The flimsy charge of treacherous action against Spain was brought up—this, unbelievably enough, from the craven king who had commissioned the voyage! The dying queen was only one of the many who pled vainly for the life of the hero. "This is a sharp medicine, but it is a cure for all diseases," said Raleigh, as he stood on the block and fingered the edge of the axe that was to take his life. He died as bravely as he had lived. "England had not such another head to cut off," muttered a witness to the execution. The man who had the vision of planting a greater England in America was mourned by a sorrowing nation that looked upon him as the last of the Elizabethan titans—as a man who was "every inch a king."

At Budleigh-Salterton in the center aisle of the village church there is a quaintly-lettered slab under which lies buried Mistress Katharine Raleigh, Sir Walter's mother. An old legend has it that the head of the great hero, after the decapitation, was whisked away and brought here to rest in his mother's arms. At least it inspired Miss Mulock to write:

> His tale is told and ended, the little Devon boy,
> The courtier-youth, gay sailing adown the stream of joy;
> The twelve years captive, breasting hard fortune like a rock—
> The old man calmly laying his head upon the block.
> And there you may believe it or believe it not,
> Still, the very legend sanctifies the spot—
> Some kind hand, nobly fearless, did play Fate's mis-played part,
> And placed the tired head, child-like, upon the mother's heart.

The handle of the Sir Walter Raleigh spoon is distinctive. The bowl runs two inches into the shaft and forms a shelving pedestal with armorial bearings directly under the cornice on which Sir Walter stands in the resplendent regalia of an Elizabethan cavalier, his arms crossed over his chest. The reverse side of handle pictures the feathered cap, flaring ruff, and the graceful folds of the slack cape in fine detail. On the cornice of the pedestal here we read "Official," and under it, "Pat. Applied For."

The scene in the bowl shows a scene at the Jamestown Exposition in 1907—the U. S. Government pier, with a fleet of small river craft and steamers sailing around in the waters below the pier. Two quadrilateral towers, slender but stately, rise at either end of a bridge. In the background a vast array of buildings, erected by the various states, offers a panorama of steepled flags and pennons. Two balloons are poised midway between the tall towers.

It is well they saw fit, on a spoon, to honor Sir Walter Raleigh at the Jamestown Exposition, for, through his many endeavors, the spadework was done that finally led to the successful colonization of Virginia, beginning with Jamestown.

The length of this spoon is 5¼ inches.

No. 39   HISTORIC ST. PAUL
No. 144   MINNESOTA PIONEER

There was never any Indian settlement on the land now embraced by the city of St. Paul, although the site was often used as a camping station by the Assenipoil tribe on their hunting expeditions. French-Canadian fur dealers, as soon as they entered this region near the source of the Mississippi, quickly saw the advantages of the site for a trading mart and erected a fort near here, in 1688, at the Falls of St. Anthony. A few British traders, likewise anxious to derive profits from the plenitude of peltries, drifted in occasionally to strike up bargains with the Indians. But neither the French nor the English struck taproots in the area, since the Spaniards held control, through somewhat tenuous claims, of all the land west of the Mississippi.

Shortly after the French were dispossessed of Canada by the British, a New Englander, Jonathan Carver, wandered through this western territory and subsequently published an account of his "Travels," a book which became immensely popular reading in London. Carver had a very lively imagination, and described a cave of huge proportions located in what is now the eastern section of St. Paul. Within the cave was a large lake extending to an "unsearchable distance," and Carver proceeds to say: "I threw a small pebble towards the interior part of it with my utmost strength; I could hear that it fell into the water, and notwithstanding it was of so small a size, it caused an astonishing and horrible noise that reverberated through all those gloomy regions." Carver roamed about, during the winter of 1766-67, with the Sioux Indians through the northern part of Minnesota, and in the spring he once again entered the cave in the company of the Sioux warriors who had come to bury their dead there. He reports this lament pronounced over the body of one of their deceased comrades: "You still sit among us, brother; your person retains its usual remembrance, and continues similar to ours, without any visible deficiency except that it has lost the power of action. But whither is that breath flown which a few hours ago sent up smoke to the Great Spirit? Why are those feet motionless that a short time ago were fleeter than the deer on yonder mountains? Why useless hang those arms that could climb the tallest tree or draw the toughest bow? Alas! every part of that frame which we lately beheld with admiration and wonder is now become inanimate. We will not, however, bemoan thee as if thou wert forever lost to us, or that thy name would be buried in oblivion; thy soul yet lives in the great country of spirits with those who are gone before thee, and though we are left behind to perpetuate thy fame we shall one day join thee, actuated by the respect we bore thee while living, we come now to tender to thee the last act of kindness it is in our power to bestow that thy body might not lie neglected on the plain and become a prey to the beasts of the field; we will take care to lay it with those of thy predecessors who are gone before thee, hoping at the same time that thy spirit will feed with their spirits, and be ready to receive ours when we also shall arrive at the great country of souls."

Whether this epicedium was ever actually given by an Indian dignitary or purely devised by the romantic Carver, it did possess sufficient merits

187

to inspire the famous German author Schiller to write a poem of twelve stanzas based on the subject. In a way, Schiller was well rewarded for his inspiration, for many years later the citizens of St. Paul erected a statue in his honor in one of their parks.

The history of St. Paul as a town began in 1820 with the establishment of a United States garrison at Camp Cold Water near the junction of the Minnesota River with the Mississippi. Lewis Cass, governor of Michigan and the whole northwest territory, paid the encampment an unexpected visit late in July, and some two hundred Sioux Indians, who happened to be in the neighborhood, took advantage of the occasion to present their green corn dance before the governor. General Andrews describes this tribal ceremony thus: "Large iron kettles filled with green corn cut from the cob were suspended over a fire. The Indians, both men and women, were seated in a large circle around them, who sang a slow chant, with solemn faces, accompanied by drums and rattles. When the music ceased, there were mysterious ejaculations, and then a young man and woman, joining hands, came forward to be received into the green corn society. After various questions they were admitted. At the termination of the ceremonies an elderly Indian advanced and ladled the corn out of the kettle into separate wooden bowls for the families present. As these dishes were taken, the persons retired from the lodge, keeping their faces toward the kettles."

Adventurers, few of whom were of native American stock, were attracted by the Army camp to build shacks in the vicinity. There was no semblance of an orderly planning, among these squatters, to set up even a village. Some of them merely pitched tent on grounds reserved for Indians or the future military range, and moved as they saw fit, watching always for chances to prey upon the easy money of the soldiers. They were a lawless element at most.

The first settler in the locality where St. Paul now stands was a French-Canadian, Pierre Parrant, better known because of his oafish appearance as Pig's Eye. Evicted from one place after another for selling whiskey illegally, Pig's Eye moved a few miles away, entirely out of the clutches of the military government, and established his groggery this time in that very cave-hideout visited years before by Jonathan Carver. Here, on the high bluffs overlooking the Mississippi River, came other people who were likewise driven off the reservation lands. This locality soon assumed the name of Pig's Eye. With the gradual accretion of French-Canadians, a church—a simple log structure—dedicated to St. Paul was built, and the better element among the people, preferring to call their village aften an apostle rather than after a bootlegger, named the settlement St. Paul, which, strangely enough, sounded very much like the name of the Assenipoil Indians who in former times frequently camped on this spot. The incoming settlers, who had little liking for Pig's Eye's rendezvous, induced

188

him to sell out his holdings for ten dollars. Today this land is probably worth the same integer in millions, since the bluffs containing his cavern have practically disappeared to make way for the many railroads, which eventually made the city a great center for that means of communication.

After St. Paul became the territorial capital in 1849, it grew rapidly. Contrary to the opinion held by strangers, it is not across the river from its twin, Minneapolis. Both cities are on both sides of the Mississippi River, which at this point still has 1,600 miles to flow before it disembogues into the Gulf of Mexico.

There has always been a spirited rivalry between the twin cities. In 1857 the territorial legislature aimed to change the capital from St. Paul to St. Peter, in Nicollet County. On the day set for the enactment of the bill which would make the change legally effective, Joe Rolette, the chairman of the committee on Enrolled Bills, did not appear. For five days the legislators waited, while the Minneapolis lawmakers scouted the premises of every building in St. Paul, rope in hand, declaring they would bring Joe Rolette back to the Council halls "dead or alive." At the end of the fifth day, Mr. Rolette was released from his confinement "for an unknown ailment" in an isolated hospital outside of town. His doctor and nurses—all male, and heavily armed—deemed his health sufficiently improved for him to go about freely without more personal attention. The legislature had then adjourned.

Many soldiers, as soon as they were mustered out of the Civil War ranks, came here from New England and elsewhere in the East. Irish and German immigrants poured in like a flood after the famine and revolutionary years of 1845-50. In contrast to Minneapolis, St. Paul received only a trickle of Scandinavians.

The people of St. Paul are noted for their love of music, art and sport. Orchestral and choral organizations have always been well supported. In various parts of the city stand statues of Nathan Hale, Henrik Ibsen, Friedrich Schiller and St. Francis of Assisi. The Peace Memorial commemorates the dead of the First World War.

The two main festive events of the year are the Winter Carnival and the Festival of Nations. The Carnival, which takes place in February, capitalizes on the inevitable abundance of snow. It is a week of good-natured merriment, and thousands of colorful costumes are worn by people at all times of the day, both at work and at play. An ice palace, presided over by Boreas Rex, King of the Snows, and his Queen, is an impressive place compounded of color and magic, until King Vulcan and his fiery cohorts scale its bastions on the last night of the festivities and overthrow this world of ice.

Assuming greater importance in recent years is the Festival of Nations, nurtured by the International Institute of St. Paul for the promotion of good will among the many nationalities from which the city's population is derived. Costumes characteristic of the old country are worn, old

189

familiar foods are served, and quaint foreign customs, so often looked down upon in many places, are here distinctly encouraged

The Historic St. Paul spoon, a Paye and Baker product, displays, incised in the bowl, a good example of the city's architecture, the State Capitol. Today this edifice has a familiar look, being more or less typical of other state capitols we have often seen. When it was built in 1898, however, it was entirely original. Cass Gilbert, the architect, drew his designs from Italian Renaissance models and included such features as the columned dome frontal arcade, central rotunda, lunette, and pendentive murals. A score of capitol buildings in other states are virtual replicas of this one.

On the handle are ears of Indian corn in orderly arrangement. Three arrows are crossed to form four acute and two obtuse angles. Other features, all Indian, are a canoe, a log campfire from which smoke arises, two wigwams, and an Indian adorned with shell necklace, metal earrings, and a plumy headdress of feathers. On the reverse side are leaves and ears of corn also. Length, 5¼ inches.

The Minnesota Pioneer spoon might well be picturing, on the finial, a typical settler of frontier days. The shoulder-length hair, steer-horn mustache, and flapping *chapeau* would seem to indicate a breezy, independent character of the backwoods type. The face stands out in unusually high relief as the caput-finial atop the slender, auger-like shaft. In the bowl appears the Minnesota State Capitol building. Made by the Baker-Manchester Mfg. Co., this spoon measures 5¼ inches in length.

No. 40 SERGEANT JASPER

In some inexplicable way our wars have bequeathed to us an imposing array of "little-folk" heroes who, washed up out of the common mass, have become in many instances more near and dear to our hearts than have their superiors, the stand-offish statesmen and generals. There are soldiers like Alan Seeger, Joyce Kilmer and John McCrae, prematurely cut off in battle, who have become a precious historical vintage to us through the legacy of their spirited lives. There is Little Giffen, who has been known and loved by thousands of school children ever since a country doctor in Georgia made him, the unknown soldier of the Civil War, the subject of a pulsating poem a few years after the war was over.

Sometimes a single act of daring or self-sacrifice has catapulted a name into the ranks of our hero-immortals. That happened in the case of Paul Revere, Molly Pitcher, Nathan Hale, Barbara Frietchie, Alvin York, and Colin Kelly. Time wings their fame to all posterity.

One such hero, Sergeant William Jasper, the Bayard of the backwoods, stands in a class apart because on three separate occasions he won renown by distinguished acts of unflinching courage. And stranger yet, every

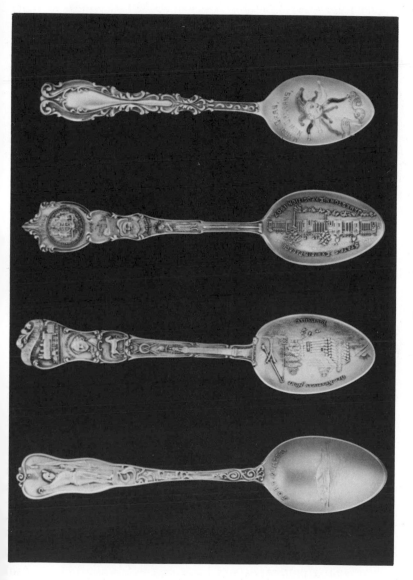

PLATE 30

40. SERGEANT JASPER   41. GEORGE D. PRENTICE
42. SMITH AND POCAHONTAS   43. MARDI GRAS

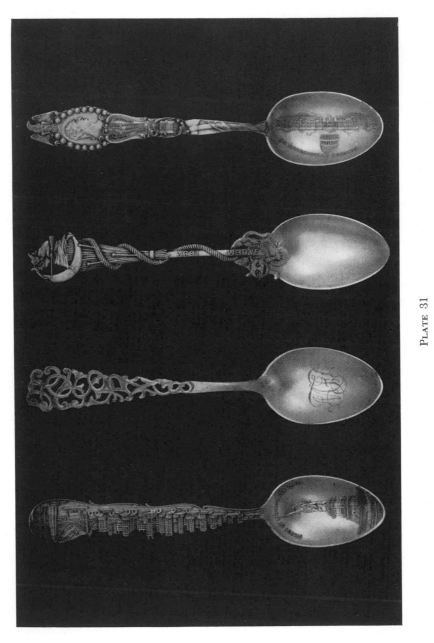

PLATE 31

44. STATUE OF LIBERTY   45. HOT SPRINGS   46. SALEM WITCH   47. WASHINGTON'S HATCHET

feat that he performed came about chiefly as the fulfillment of a vow or promise that had been made to a member of the gentler sex.

Born in the pine-hills country of South Carolina, of Scotch-Irish pioneer stock, he lost his mother before he had emerged from childhood. From that time on his father left him to fend largely for himself. There were days on end when he would have perished from starvation if he had not learned how to handle a gun expertly enough to replenish the family larder. Much of his boyhood was spent tramping alone through the forest uplands, clad in buckskin, a muzzle-loader in his hands. He could drive a nail, snuff a candle, or bark a squirrel as unerringly as any. He did not attend school, simply because there was none near or far for him to attend. He did learn, however, how to box and wrestle, and his powerful frame compelled the worst rowdy to act circumspectly in his presence.

At the outbreak of the Revolution he volunteered immediately for service in the partisan or patriot forces, and in September, 1775, he was assigned to regular duty with a company that was being drilled at Fort Johnson. He chafed under military restrictions and yearned for the old free, adventurous life of the forests. Yet, to take up the slack time on his hands, he learned from one of his comrades how to scrawl his name and spell out a few words feebly on paper.

In the spring of 1776 he was transferred to a camp at Corchester, South Carolina. Shortly afterwards he was sent to Sullivan's Island, off Charleston Harbor, to aid in the construction of a fort improvised out of rough palmetto logs and buttressed with sand bags, in a hurried effort to stave off an impending attack of the British fleet under Sir Peter Parker.

During the weeks of his sojourn at Fort Sullivan (later, Fort Moultrie) he found time to make the acquaintance of an attractive servant-girl in one of the taverns in Charleston. She was as fully devoted to the American cause as he, and during one of his visits he gallantly promised this sixteen-year-old girl who was waiting upon him that he would never allow the enemy's flag to fly over the city in which she resided.

The British fleet of ten vessels, sailing from Halifax, bore on board a large number of land troops, commanded by General Clinton, prepared to garrison the city as soon as it was taken. Major-General Charles Lee, in charge of the American operations, considered resistance futile and would have allowed the enemy to disembark peacefully without the discharge of a single gun. Colonel Moultrie, under whom Jasper served, resolutely opposed surrender, and steadfastly ignored Lee's orders to beat a hasty retreat. His dauntless courage whipped up a frenzied enthusiasm in the men under him to fight without any show of compromise.

Sir Peter Parker began his bombardment of the palmetto fortress early on the morning of the 28th of June, 1776. The batteries of Colonel Moultrie returned the fire, and for ten hours, all through the hot summer day, the roar of the heavy guns resounded, while the citizens of Charleston waited with bated breath for the fateful outcome of the battle.

At one of the most critical periods of the furious assault, a cannonball shattered the flagstaff of the fort, and the white crescent flag of South Carolina fell into the moat outside the ramparts. A cheer went up from the British squadron, believing the ensign had been hauled down and a white flag would be hoisted as a token of surrender.

"Colonel," cried the sharp-eyed Jasper to his commander, "don't let us fight without a flag!"

"What can be done?" inquired Colonel Moultrie. "The staff is cut in splinters."

Jasper shook his head with a determined nod of dissent and replied, "Then, I'll tie it to a sword's point and plant it on the merlon of the ramparts." And without more ado, he leapt through an embrasure, slid down into the ditch, grasped the fallen colors, and, regardless of the shot and shell pounding the bastion around him, scrambled deftly as a squirrel up and over the parapet. Mounting the banner on top of the merlon, he held it there resolutely till a new staff could be provided.

By sunset the cannonading was over. What was left of the British fleet limped out of the harbor. Their flagship was lapping water through a dozen holes in her sides. One vessel lying helplessly grounded on her starboard was abandoned after being set afire. It should be mentioned that Sir Peter Parker's pants had caught fire during the bombardment and he was badly burnt. The loss to the enemy in killed and wounded was two hundred and five; to the defending garrison, thirty-seven.

A few days later Jasper was called into the presence of Governor Rutledge, who magnanimously unsheathed his own sword and presented it to the sergeant. At the same time the governor tendered him a lieutenant's commission, but this offer was declined by the modest sergeant, who explained that his lack of education would embarrass him before a platoon. "I ain't fit to keep officers' company," he said.

Then for several years Jasper held a scouting commission, the type of military work for which he was best suited. His roving disposition made him restless if he had to stay in one place too long. He served at various times under Moultrie, Marion, and Lincoln, and his exploits read like sheerest romance. On three occasions he slipped inside the British lines in Georgia and brought back trustworthy reports on all the enemy's present maneuvers and future intentions. He was described as "a perfect Proteus in the ability to alter his appearance." His cunning and ingenuity grew apace with his activities.

The second act of daring by which Jasper is known transpired near a woodland spring not far from Savannah, close to the highway leading from Augusta. The previous day the distracted mother of five children had appealed to the sergeant to rescue her husband, who was being led, handcuffed with several other Americans, to a British prison in Savannah. The wife wept copiously when she stated her fears for the impending fate of her husband, who would surely be executed because, after a previous capture, he had taken the oath of allegiance to the Crown, then straightway deserted, and now had been captured again. The sergeant's heart was touched by the woman's sorrow, and he vowed that, come what may, her husband would be liberated before the inevitable happened.

With Sergeant James Newton, his favorite scouting companion, he hastened along the hot dusty highway, waiting for the first opportunity that presented itself to free all the prisoners. Knowing the countryside thoroughly, they concocted a plan to trap the escorting party at the aforementioned spring—which has ever since been called Jasper's Spring. To make sure that their plans would not miss fire, they enlisted the aid of a pretty girl to turn the escort aside and have them tarry at the spring for a while. The ruse worked.

The unsuspecting guard of ten men were happily drawn aside from their march. Stacking their muskets around a tree and leaving only two of their number to keep watch over the prisoners, they hastened to slake their thirst and refill their empty canteens with the cool refreshing water bubbling out of the large spring basin. In a trice Jasper and Newton sprang from the underbrush, brought down the sentinels, seized the muskets and freed the prisoners. The whole British escort, bereft of their firearms, were helpless. They surrendered without a struggle, and were clamped into the handcuffs still pulsing with the warmth of their late prisoners. Then, in reversed positions of command, they all marched back along the road in the direction from which they had started, joined by a jubilant group of wives, children, and well-wishers of the liberated patriots. The next morning they reached the camp of the American army at Purysburgh.

Before departing from Charleston, Jasper's regiment had been presented with a finely embroidered stand of colors by Mrs. Susanna Elliott, a staunch supporter of the American cause. In accepting this hand-wrought gift of honor in behalf of his comrades, the sergeant chivalrously gave her the following pledge: "The colors you have presented to my regiment, the Second South Carolina, I'll keep from dishonor with my life's blood." That pledge was consummated to the letter at the siege of Savannah.

Preparations were secretly under way for several months to recapture Savannah from the British by a strong concerted action on the part of the Americans by land and the French by sea. In September, 1779, a squadron of twenty vessels, under the command of Count d' Estaing, appeared off the Georgia coast. Even then the British leader, General Prevost, ill prepared as his troops were to withstand a siege, did not suspect that Savannah would be the target for this naval maneuvering. The Americans under General Lincoln were mustering all the forces available to help storm the city from the shoreward side. Unfortunately the Allies were blinded by over-confidence and delayed action, hoping for a negotiated surrender. The British within the city took advantage of an armistice to strengthen the batteries along the river and to build up the Springhill redoubt blocking any approach from Musgrove creek and the Augusta highway. These feverish preparations led D'Estaing to switch from a concerted assault to a constricting siege. For two weeks the cannonading poured shot and shell into the fortifications; people inside the town crouched in terror in their cellars. The besiegers tightened their vise-like grip on the beleaguered city by an outflanking movement. The morning of October the ninth at the break of day, the redoubts and batteries were to be stormed in a fire-raking onslaught. During the night, however, an informer carried details of the impending action to the British. Dawn found them ready for the main concentrated attacks. At the Springhill redoubt the heaviest fighting took place, and the carnage was frightful. Pulaski, leading the charge on his black stallion, was hit by a grapeshot and fell, bleeding profusely, from his mount.

Four times was the attempt made to hoist the colors of the Second South Carolina regiment aloft the ramparts of the Springhill redoubt. The last time Sergeant Jasper seized the flag from the falling hands of Lieutenant Gray and planted it once more on the parapet. The enemy's fire was too devastating for such an exposed position. The Americans were thrown back, Jasper bearing the standard with him. He was struck in the side, and fell dying, crumpled in the flag which was reddened by the flow of his life blood. The American casualties amounted to eight hundred and fifty men, the bloodiest engagement of the whole Revolutionary War for our forces.

Sergeant Jasper lies buried in an unknown grave, but his memory is prepetuated by the Jasper Spring monument in Savannah, unveiled in a three-day celebration, beginning February 22, 1888, with President Cleveland attending; by the "Jasper Battery," one of the redoubts at Fort Moultrie, in Charleston harbor; and by a county and town in Georgia and also a town in Florida named in his honor. Colonel Moultrie, later a general, and twice governor of South Carolina, esteemed him highly, saying that the unlettered hero was a "brave, active, stout, enterprising man, and a very great patriot."

The Sergeant Jasper spoon pictures Fort Sumter in Charleston Harbor, where the first blows of the Civil War were struck, in a gold-washed bowl. Running into the handle-drop are two scrolls with a swag-like appendage. The name of Jasper in a flourishing script extends perpendicularly through the shaft. The sergeant occupies both nave and caput; standing aloft on a parapet, he holds the flag in his left hand, and has his right arm upflung in a gesture of triumph. The design of the handle is typically Colonial, with a broken pediment or bonnet top.

On the reverse side appears the name of Charleston in the same type of flourishing script as on the front. Patented in 1891 by Dominick and Haff for James Allan and Company. Length, 6 inches.

No. 41 GEORGE PRENTICE

Of the thousands who constantly pass by the tall, erect figure of Lincoln on the lawn of the Main Public Library in Louisville, Kentucky, there could hardly be one who is not acquainted to some extent with the story of the Great Emancipator. But among those same hurrying pedestrians, how many might there be who know aught of the meditative figure who sits looking down from his pedestal before the main entrance of the library? The single word "Prentice" at the base of the Carrara-hewn statue suggests no legend.

It is true that some of the more historical-minded might know that George Dennison Prentice was the founder, and long the editor, of the *Louisville Journal,* predecessor of the famous present-day *Courier-Journal.* Fewer yet would know him as the man whose political support elected hundreds to office; whose editorial stand did more than anything else to save Kentucky for the Union in the Civil War; and whose collected poems after his death ran to a dozen editions. The merit of Prentice's work may be gathered from this opinion expressed by a New York reporter in antebellum years: "Louisville is situated on the south bank of the Ohio River, at the falls, but it is significant for nothing, except as the place where the *Louisville Journal* is published." But how few people today know anything of the man who promoted that noted journal. So, let us take a personal look at this transplanted Yankee who claims a statue close to that of the world-famous Abe.

Mr. Prentice was once conversing with Fortunatus Cosby, one of his reporters, when there entered an unkempt human derelict, a bilious back-biter, who, a few years previous, had set afloat some vilifying rumors concerning the editor. Mr. Cosby left the room during this interview, and when the latter returned, he inquired what business could have brought in such a washed-up specimen of humanity.

"That was my old friend, Thomas Jefferson - - -," said Mr. Prentice. "He told me he was depressed financially, and needed two dollars and a half to enable him to visit his sick mother."

"And I suppose," continued Mr. Cosby cynically, "you were silly enough to fall for that bait and hand him the money?"

Mr. Prentice hesitated for a moment as if a cloud had crossed his vision. Then he answered simply: "No. I recollected that I had a mother, and asked myself the question, what she would have thought of me, had I appeared before her in such woe-begone apparel. So I gave him twenty-five dollars, and told him to go and see his mother in the dress of a gentleman."

One of Mr. Prentice's great virtues was his charitableness. He was never able to say "No" to any hard-luck plea calling for financial help.

This farm boy turned editor was born in Connecticut in 1802. His mother taught him to read when he was hardly out of the cradle. At the age of four, during an eclipse that seemingly threatened to end creation, he proceeded to read some reassuring passages from the Bible to the other members of his family. His precocity was amazing.

His early education was irregular. From a Presbyterian minister acting as tutor he learned to read Latin and Greek. In six months he had familiarized himself with Cicero, Sallust, Horace, Virgil, Xenophon, the New Testament, and the first six books of the Iliad—all in the original, mind you. At a single recitation he translated the whole twelfth book of the AEneid. His teacher tried to keep him within the groove of his regular assignments. But remonstrance was useless: he flipped hand-springs over the other students. He memorized all the rules in an English grammar in five days.

For two winter terms he taught in a rural school, and saved enough to defray most of his subsequent expenses at Brown University. In three years he had a degree in law. But he soon gravitated toward a journalistic career. His influence made itself felt immediately when he became editor of the *New England Review,* and when the Whig party nominated six Congressional candidates whom he did not like, he nominated and supported through the columns of his paper six men whom he thought to be more capable, and in a hotly-contested campaign bagged victory for his candidates.

In 1830 he made a journey to Kentucky to secure material for a biography of Henry Clay, leaving John Greenleaf Whittier as his successor in the editor's chair of the *New England Review.* Once in Kentucky he was induced to stay and found a daily in Louisville to oppose the *Public Advertiser,* a staunch prop of Old Hickory. The *Louisville Journal* soon became the ablest exponent of Whig principles in the nation, certainly in the South and to the west of New England.

Mr. Prentice's editorials were freighted with sharply incised epigrams, flashes of satire, and quixotic witticisms. They were quoted everywhere, even in the European newspapers. They were discussed, imitated, and admired. Let us scan through a few of them:

"Messrs. Bell and Topp, of the N. C. Gazette, say that 'Prentices are made to serve masters.' Well, Bells were made to be hung, and Topps to be whipped."

"Men are deserters in adversity; when the sun sets, and all is dark, our very shadows refuse to follow us."

"Mr. William Hood was robbed near Corinth, Alabama, on the 13th inst. The Corinth paper says that the name of the highwayman is unknown. But there is no doubt that he was Robbin' Hood."

"Mr. John Love, of Alabama, was recently lost during a passage from Texas to Mexico. We had supposed that no Love would ever be lost between those countries."

"The man who lives only for this world is a fool here, and there is danger that he will be (we speak it not profanely) a d--d fool hereafter."

"When a young man complains that a young lady has no heart, it's pretty certain that she has his."

For a while in the fifties Mr. Prentice gave support to the short-lived American or Know-Nothing party, which was opposed to the unrestricted immigration laws allowing a flood of foreigners to pour into the country in such unlimited numbers, but after the discreditable "Bloody Monday" riots on election day in 1855, he washed his hands of the party in a strong condemnation of its tactics.

Although he had become a part and parcel of the South, Mr. Prentice vehemently opposed the secession movement. He backed Bell and Everett, of the Constitutional Union party, in 1860, but after the election, when the die was cast, he threw his support behind the Union cause in the war that followed. For his stand he was taunted and derided, losing both friends and substantial offers of emolument. President Lincoln considered Prentice the unwavering rudder holding the Border states in line. On one occasion a special dinner was given in Washington to honor the Louisville editor.

But sadness dogged his latter days. His two sons, Courtland and Clarence, joined the Confederate forces. Courtland, the older and favorite son, was killed in a skirmish three weeks after he left home. "I feel very, very desolate," wrote the grieving father. "The wind of death has swept over my life and left it a desert, but in my sadness I will try to do my duty as I see it." In 1868 Mrs. Prentice died. In the same year he handed over the active editorship of the *Journal* (soon consolidated with other papers to form the *Courier-Journal*) to Henry Watterson, a man destined to become equally as influential as Prentice ever was in the political affairs of Kentucky and the South.

During the severe Christmas weather of 1869, when he drove to the country home of his son Clarence, he caught a bad cold that developed into pneumonia. He died early in 1870, in an upper room at his son's house, at a moment when the angry flood-waters of the Ohio were licking their way across the lower floor beneath him.

We may very aptly repeat, almost as a dirge over this man who was such a power in his day but now well nigh forgotten, a few lines from "The Closing Year," his finest poem—

> Remorseless Time!—
> Fierce spirit of the glass and scythe!—What power
> Can stay him in his silent course, or melt
> His iron heart to pity? On, still on
> He presses, and forever. The proud bird,
> The condor of the Andes, that can soar
> Through heaven's unfathomable depths, or brave
> The fury of the northern hurricane

And bathe his plumage in the thunder's home,
Furls his broad wings at nightfall, and sinks down
To rest upon his mountain crag—but Time
Knows not the weight of sleep or weariness,
And night's deep darkness has no chain to bind
His rushing pinion. Revolutions sweep
O'er earth, like troubled visions o'er the breast
Of dreaming sorrow; cities rise and sink,
Like bubbles on the water; fiery isles
Spring, blazing, from the ocean, and go back
To their mysterious caverns; mountains rear
To heaven their bald and blackened cliffs, and bow
Their tall heads to the plain; new empires rise,
Gathering the strength of hoary centuries,
And rush down like the Alpine avalanche,
Startling the nations; and the very stars,
Yon bright and burning blazonry of God,
Glitter a while in their eternal depths,
And, like the Pleiad, loveliest of their train,
Shoot from their glorious spheres, and pass away,
To darkle in the trackless void: yet Time,
Time, the tomb-builder, holds his fierce career,
Dark, stern, all-pitiless, and pauses not
Amid the mighty wrecks that strew his path,
To sit and muse, like other conquerors,
Upon the fearful ruin he has wrought.

The George D. Prentice spoon is crowded with historic features. The log cabin, once representative of an "Old Kentucky Home" before it was superseded by the more stately museum-piece at Bardstown, appears in the bowl. Along the obverse side of handle may be seen the Confederate Monument in Louisville, a thoroughbred, cross-whips and horseshoe, Mr. Prentice (in conspicuous relief), a locomotive (as a sign of "Progress"), and LOUISVILLE on a banderole surmounted by a plumy foliation.

On the reverse of handle appear the old state capitol building at Frankfort, a barrel of whiskey, and a stalk of tobacco.

The makers of this spoon were Watson and Newell. Length, 5¾ inches.

No. 42 SMITH AND POCAHONTAS

In the pages of the *Southern Literary Messenger* for the summer issue of 1857 there appeared a poem by the editor, John R. Thompson, called "The Jamestown Celebration," giving an informal account of the first commemorative services to be held in honor of the first permanent English-speaking settlement in the New World.

A signal gun was fired when the sun came up over the ripening wheat fields on that May-day of 1857.

Five times fifty years had glided
Over earthy states and kingdoms
Since the keel of Smith and Gosnold
   There had grated on the sand,
When the sons of Old Virginia
Came with pomp and martial music
To commemorate the virtues
   Of that little pilgrim band.

The river that morning bore a tawny color like the copperish skin of an Indian. Yachts and steamers, bearing the stars and stripes as well as the *Sic semper* banner of Virginia gaily aloft, landed the crowds of passengers, some of whom straightway hammered on the gravestones or pulled bricks out of the ivied ruins of the church tower as souvenirs—no spoons available as mementos in those days.

After a two-mile tramp through dust and weeds, with collars wilting from the heat, the crowd assembled around the platform, where the band played "Hail Columbia." After the invocation by the aged George Washington Parke Custis, ex-president John Tyler stepped forward and read a long oration accompanied by eloquent gestures. James Barren Pope did better with his poem for the occasion—

So our gifted Jamestown minstrel
Sang of Smith the stalwart Captain,
Sang the strange and sad adventures
   Of the beauteous Indian bride.
Mingling his historic story
With our own romantic legends
In the song of Pocahontas
   Early lost and sanctified.

The governor also spoke a few appropriate words; then the militia and band paraded before the reviewing stand. There was neither dancing, nor drinking, only a display of fireworks, after which the hungry, thirsty, and tired crowd straggled back toward the distant steamers. Thus ended the first gala commemoration at Jamestown, and the poet concluded:

'Twas a highly patriotic,
Picturesque, auspicious, happy,
Hot and dusty celebration
   As was ever sketched or seen.

How different was the occasion "five times fifty years" before this, when the "Susan Constant," a vessel of one hundred tons commanded by Captain Christopher Newport, the "God Speed," of forty tons, in charge of Captain Bartholomew Gosnold, and the "Discovery," a pinnace of twenty tons, under Captain John Ratcliffe, anchored in the James River on May 14, 1607, and the passengers, about one hundred and fifty weary souls, went ashore at Jamestown.

This expedition, financed by the London or Royal Virginia Company had departed from the port of Blackwall, December 9, 1606. In addition to the three commanding officers, there were other important personages, effective for good or bad purposes, on board: Gabriel Archer, an imperious know-it-all, who gave himself a superior rating from having been on an earlier exploratory trip to America; John Martin, an honest man but weakened by illness; Edward Maria Wingfield, a typical aristocrat of the old school, who believed no one soiling his hands by honest work could ever be a gentleman; Master Robert Hunt, the clergyman, who by much patience and godly exhortations cooled the fires in many a factious dispute; George Kendall, so disloyal and disgruntled from the fact that he could not play a larger part in the colony's affairs that he was finally beheaded; George Percy, the eighth son of a nobleman, without practical experience, but a sincere advocate of whatever seemed best to make the enterprise a success; and Captain John Smith, a soldier of fortune and a man with good common sense and much worldly wisdom bolstered by a forceful personality. Among the other passengers were listed a barber, a blacksmith, a doctor, a tailor, four carpenters, twelve manual laborers, and a drummer. The rest were mainly gentlemen, well versed in dining, wining, dicing, and swearing. There were far too many of this type, "ten times more fit to spoyle a commonwealth than maintaine one . . . unruly gallants, packed thither by their friends to escape ill destinies." A sealed box containing the names of those seven men who would compose the membership of the colonial council was placed on board with the explicit instructions that it was to be opened within a day after the landing of the colonists in their new home.

The voyage of five months is one of the longest on record. Instead of crossing more in a straight line from England to Virginia, the little squadron sailed south to the Canaries following the old course set by Columbus. By the time they reached the Canaries, Smith had already been cast into irons for intentions to "usurpe the government, murder the councell, and make himself king." It was a skillful fabrication by some one jealous of Smith's manifest capabilities, and the spleen against him must have continued in full strength, for at Nevis in the West Indies a resolution was actually passed to hang him. Only by a last-minute commutation of that sentence did he escape the gallows.

Perhaps the balmy atmosphere of the West Indian islands put the voyagers in a better frame of mind, and made them more forbearing toward Smith. They were struck with the wonders they saw. At Monaca they picked nearly two hogsheads of birds from the bushes; at Guadaloupe they encountered "a bath so hot, as in it we boyled Porck as well as over the fire." They marveled at the abundance of living things: pelicans, parrots, flying fish, tortoises, alligators, wild boars. There was no lack of wild fowl, and catching a drove of sea-turtles on shore, they feasted for three days. On the island of Mona, where they disembarked to search for fresh water, they hunted wild boars over such precipitous ground that a gentleman of excessive avoirdupois—"whose fat melted within him, by the great heate and drought of the country"—expired, presumably from a sunstroke.

Sailing up the coast of Florida they encountered four days of continuous storm and were driven far out of their course. The supply of food was running short (some of it had become unedible from the mold), the drinking water was vile, and to add to the discouragement, they had lost sight of land and for three days tried in vain to touch bottom with a lead line reaching to a depth of a hundred fathoms. Captain Ratcliffe proposed that they relinquish their search and head for home.

On the morning of April 26th the weather cleared and the coast of Virginia in its fresh verdancy loomed alluringly before their eyes. They entered Chesapeake Bay between two promontories, one of which, on the north, they called Cape Henry after the Crown prince, the other, Cape Charles after the king's second son. "There wee landed and discovered a little way," George Percy later records, "but we could find nothing worth the speaking of, but faire meddowes and goodly tall trees; with such fresh-waters running through the woods, as I was almost ravished at the first sight thereof." They found the large oysters abounding there delicious, and the strawberries, covering large areas, four times as large as any they had ever seen in England.

The thirty men, after this short exploratory tour, were making ready toward nightfall to go aboard again, when they were assailed by savages lurking in ambush. Gabriel Archer was struck by arrows in both hands, and a sailor wounded seriously in the body. A discharge of muskets quickly routed the savages and sent them yelping back to the bushes.

While the ships were anchored that night near a spit of land, which they called Point Comfort, the box containing the names of the council members was opened. The men who had been selected were: Wingfield, Gosnold, Smith, Newport, Ratcliffe, Martin, and Kendall. It was a surprise to some that John Smith should have been among those chosen by the company, and still being suspect, he was denied a seat in the council.

For several days they sailed along the banks of the river which they called the James, reconnoitering the terrain to find the best possible spot for a settlement that could be easily defended from shore and within close distance to good anchorage. Gosnold and Archer selected a site on high ground, which eventually did become the permanent location, but at this time their preference was overruled by Wingfield, who had been chosen president of the council. The matter aroused lively debate and some bitterness of feeling, but the choice of a low, marshy spot prevailed because there the ships could be brought so near to shore that they could be "moored to the trees in six fathom water."

On the fourteenth of May everybody disembarked and set to work constructing a fort, which received the name of Jamestown. Smith, with a knowledge gained from practical experience, did not like the type of brushwood fort planned by President Wingfield, in the shape of a triangle with half-moons at each corner. Gosnold and Archer were dissatisfied, and quickly took an I-told-you-so attitude when it was discovered the available drinking water was brackish at flood tide and slimy during the ebb.

Newport set out soon to explore the country. Taking Smith, Percy, Archer, and several others with him, he sailed up the river as far as the hills and the falls where the city of Richmond is now located. On the twenty-fourth of May, during Newport's absence, the fort was attacked, when the settlers least expected it, in the middle of the day, by a screaming horde of two hundred redskins. The assault lasted an hour; a dozen men were wounded, and one killed. An arrow churred through Wingfield's beard.

A cloud of discontent hovered over the fort, but the atmosphere cleared when Newport returned; his conciliatory manner kept the colonists from deposing Wingfield and moving to another locality. He overruled the president, had the brushwood thrown aside, and ordered new walls of strong timber for the stockade. Smith now was given his rightful place at the council table in spite of protests from Wingfield, who deemed it an insult to his dignity to have to sit in company with a common vagrant— Smith had just shortly before the voyage gone on a walking tour through Ireland.

Captain Newport, thinking he had conciliated all factions within the fort, made haste to depart for England the twenty-second of June with a cargo of timber and specimens of various fruits and minerals garnered from vines, trees, and rocks of the forests. The hundred and five souls left behind were already worn out by the intense heat, the pestiferous mosquitoes, and the obligation of being on guard duty every third or fourth night. "Being thus left to our fortunes, it fortuned that within ten days scarce ten amongst us could either go, or well stand, such extreme weakness and sickness oppressed us" writes Smith in his *General Historie*. "Had we beene as free from all sinnes as gluttony, and drunkennesse, we might have been canonized for saints." From the common kettle each man received an equal share, "and that was half a pint of wheat, and as much barley boyled with water . . . and this being fryed some twenty-six weeks in the ship's hold, contained as many worms as graines; so that we might truly call it rather so much bran than corne, our drinke was water, our lodgings castles in the ayre; with this lodging and dyet, our extreme toile in bearing and planting Pallisadoes, so strained and bruised us, and our continual labour in the extremitie of the heat had so weakened us, as were cause sufficient to have made us miserable in our native country, or any other place in the world."

In July the majority of the settlers were struck down with sickness, in the form of "swelling fluxes, burning-fevers, and by wars, and some

204

departed suddenly, but for the most part they died of mere famine . . . Thus we lived for the space of five months in this miserable distress, but having five able men to man our bulwarks upon any occasion. If it had not pleased God to put a terrour in the savage hearts, we had all perished by those wild and cruel Pagans, being in that weak state as we were: our men night and day groaning in every corner of the fort, most pitiful to hear. If there were any conscience in men, it would make their hearts to bleed to hear the pitiful murmurings and outcries of our sick men, without relief, every night and day, for the space of six weeks: some departing out of the world; many times three or four in a night; in the morning their bodies trailed out of their cabins, like dogs, to be buried."

Forty to fifty of the pioneers perished—the estimates differ. Captain Gosnold died the twenty-second of August. The plethora of deaths brought a flood of complaints against Wingfield. In September he was deposed as president, and brought to trial in which among other things he was accused of libel on Smith's character. The jury awarded Smith a compensation of two hundred pounds for this defamation.

Ratcliffe was chosen the new president, but he soon proved to be less practical than Wingfield and far more tyrannical. A revolt against his administration led Kendall before a firing squad. Smith, too, was condemned to die, immediately after his return from captivity among the Indians on the outlandish charge that he had been responsible for the death of Robinson and Emry, his two companions, at the hands of the Indians. Archer was the promoter of this infamous cabal, and Smith would have come to a prompt demise if Newport had not returned from England in time to scotch the execution.

It was during an exploratory voyage up the Chickahominy River that Smith was taken captive; his two companions were slain; and as a consequence of his captivity, he first made the acquaintance of Pocahontas, the Indian princess with whom his name is invariably associated. He had become separated from the main party of his men, leaving only Robinson and Emry with him as a bodyguard. The Indians offered to show him the nature of the soil and they went ashore. It was shortly thereafter that his two companions were murdered and he was set upon without warning. Seizing the nearest Indian, Smith used him as a barricade against the others. He might have shielded himself from injury or capture, if he had not stepped into a quagmire. Seeing escape was hopeless, he surrendered, and was led before Chief Opechancanough, to whom he presented a compass and described as best he could its use. He was treated well: "Though eight ordinarily guarded me, I wanted not what they could devise to content me: and still our longer acquaintance increased our better affection."

After being taken from one place to another for several weeks, he was escorted before an assemblage of more than two hundred warriors in the midst of whom sat the Emperor Powhatan, covered with a robe of raccoon skins, on a seat like a bedstead. Two Indian maidens sat on either side of him, and before him two rows of men, with as many women behind them, painted a bright red, their heads adorned with the white down of birds and long chains of white beads circling their necks. "A long consultation was held, but the conclusion was two great stones were brought before Powhatan; then as many as could laid hands on him, dragged him to them, and thereon laid his head, and being ready with their clubs to beate out his brains. Pocahontas, the King's dearest daughter, when no entreaty could prevail, got his head in her armes, and laid her owne upon his to save him from death: whereat the Emperour was contented he should live to make him hatchets, and her bells, for they thought him as well of all occupations as themselves." Two days later, Smith was released from his captivity and escorted back to Jamestown by twelve of Powhatan's warriors.

There is nothing about this story of Smith's being snatched from sudden death by an Indian princess that should cause us to be incredulous or it to be incredible. The story is indeed melodramatic, with aspects of the epic in its composition, a tale to be told to wide-eyed children, but it must be remembered that the Indians demonstrated themselves to be a child-like people in most of their actions, and the motivations for those actions were always prompted by a far greater spontaneity and impetuosity of feeling than in ours. Long centuries of training have imposed ironclad restraints on excessive displays of emotionalism in the Anglo-Saxon ethos. Imagine an English princess rushing upon the scaffold to interpose in the execution of a Sir Walter Raleigh, one of her own countrymen—much less of some foreigner, the acknowledged enemy of her race! There—we would all be doubting Thomases!

In September, 1608, Smith was unanimously chosen to replace the inept Ratcliffe as the president of the none-too-thriving colony. Thus, within a year and a half after his arrival in chains and disgrace, Smith had climbed to the highest rung on the ladder of leadership, and now towered above that jostling, jealous crowd of dog-eat-dog adventurers. He possessed those essential qualities that they lacked: industry, resourcefulness, courage to think and act, and that hard-gained, hard-headed, first-hand, sink-or-swim experience without which no pioneer can expect to survive and thrive. It is the proper place to pause here and retrace briefly the early career of this colorful leader.

Plain John Smith was born in 1579 at Willoughby, England, of tenant-farming parents. He never received enough schooling to master the art of spelling, nor did he take kindly to schooling, for he sold his books and satchel, "intending secretly to get to Sea, but his father's death stayed him." He served a short apprenticeship with a merchant at Lynn, but the yearning for adventures being too strong upon his mind, he ran away and joined an army fighting in the Low Countries. Then he came back to England for a while, and immured himself in what he called a "Pavillion of boughes" to study the finer points of soldiery. He practiced faithfully to acquire adroitness with sword and pistol, and rode a horse at full speed while tilting his lance at rings in the trees. His main reading pap consisted of Machiavelli's *Art of Warre* and Marcus Aurelius' *Meditations.*

On his second trip to the continent he fell in with "four French gallants" who absconded with his trunk leaving him so penniless that he had to sell his heavy cloak, though in midwinter, to pay for food and lodging. He traveled toward the south of France and accidentally encountering one of the four thieves who had so impoverished him, alone on a forest highway, he dealt with him so that the thief "no more, from that time forward, cozened honest men." At Marseilles he embarked for Italy on a ship loaded with pilgrims bound for Rome. A storm arose and continued without abatement till the passengers, discovering there was a single heretic aboard in the person of Smith, voted to rid themselves of this Jonah by casting him to the angry waves. He reached the island of St. Marguerite safely, where he was picked up the next day by a ship from Brittany. This merchantman soon engaged in battle with a richly laden ship bound for Venice, and the French ship coming off the victor, Smith was rewarded by a thousand sequins for his services.

After rambling about from one city to another in Italy, Smith joined a Hungarian army fighting the Turks in Transylvania. Serving under Prince Sigismund Batory in an army that was besieging the walled city of Regall, Smith found occasion to exhibit his powers and skill at arms in three notable bouts that put him, in the eyes of onlookers, in the same category with the superman Beowulf. A certain Lord Turbashaw, hoping "to delight the ladies, who did long to see some court-like pastime," sent a challenge to fight "any captain that had the command of a company, who durst combat with him for his head." The besiegers accepted the challenge and drew lots to decide which cavalier should oppose him. The choice fell on Smith, who rode forth in full view of the spectators from both camps. The city walls swarmed with "veiled dames and turbaned warriors." The Lord Turbashaw, "all bedecked in bright and dazzling armoure, shining with gold and silver and precious stones, and on his shoulders the semblance of rich and glittering winges, came stately forth upon the field; the voice of hoboyes and other martial musicke governed the order of his step." After courtly salutes, the two combatants rushed at each other with raised lances. At the very first charge the Turk was wounded and knocked from his horse by a deadly thrust through the bars of his helmet. Smith quickly dismounted and cleft the Turk's head from his body.

Grualgo, a friend of the vanquished Turbashaw, defied Smith to meet him in the lists the next day. There was the same panoplied array to witness the combat. The two adversaries, after shattering their lances, employed pistols. At the second shot the Turk's left arm was so disabled he could not manage his horse. As a result he was thrown to the ground and dazed to such a degree that he speedily lost his head.

These deadly duels between the two opposing religious camps did not end till a third contest had taken place. The Moslem challenger this time was a Bonny Mulgro, noted for his great size, strength, and ferocity. The battle began with pistols; then the clash came to closer quarters with a charge of battle axes. Smith effectually parried his enemy's thrusts by adroitly wheeling his horse and "so featly bending his body as thereby to avoid the blows aimed at him." He waited his chances for an opening, and presently finding one, he pierced his opponent "clean through to the back."

These exploits, which read very much like something out of Don Quixote's library, would readily give rise to doubts in the minds of most readers if their veracity were not fully substantiated by the parchment copy sworn and attested to, in the Heralds College of London, of a transmission from Hungary to this effect (the original is in Latin): "Sigismundus Bathor, by the Grace of God, Duke of Transylvania, Wallachia, and Moldavia; to whom this writing may come or appeare. Know that we have given leave and license to John Smith an English Gentleman, Captaine of 250 Souldiers . . . in the warres, of Hungary and in the provinces aforesaid under our authority; whose service doth deserve all praise and perpetuall memory towards us, as a man that did for God and his country overcome his enemies: Wherefore out of our love and favour, according to the law of Armes, We have ordained and given him in his shield of Armes, the figure and description of three Turks heads, which with his sword, before the towne of Regall, in single combat he did overcome, kill, and cut off, in the province of Transylvania."

This patent of "three Turkes heads in a Shield for his Armes" was presented to Smith in 1602 by the Transylvanian prince. In 1625 it was entered in the registry of heraldry by William Segar, Garter King of Arms, after an official examination of all the evidence. Francisco Farnese, secretary of Sigismund Bathory, in his history of the wars against the Turks in Hungary, tends to corroborate all the exploits given in Smith's own accounts. There must be some grains of truth among the chaff of disbelief blown out by subsequent historians.

Smith had a great many other adventures while he was soldiering against the Turks. He had the misfortune once to fall into the hands of the enemy, who sold him to a rich pasha in the slave-market of Axiopolis. An iron collar was now riveted about Smith's neck and he was put to work tending the flowers and orange trees in the garden of a fine lady, the Charatza Tragabizanda, at Constantinople. Before long the Turkish lady cast caressing glances in Smith's direction, and sent him a clove, a rose, and a piece of cloth, the three objects denoting, respectively, in plain language: "I have long loved you though you do not know it;" "I condole with your misfortunes, and would render you more fortunate:" and "you are surpassing fair to me, and priceless." The iron-throttled Smith, none dismayed at the thought of further bonds, played the gallant and reciprocated the amorous honor by sending the lady a wheat-straw with this missive slyly attached: "Accept me as your slave." A rendezvous was held in the rose garden by moonlight, attended by the singing of nightingales. The impetuous slave begged the lady to fly to England with him—he would strangle her guards to effect a safe getaway. But a member of the guard detail—no other than the Lady Tragabizanda's own mother—inadvertently overheard the sweet dalliance of the lovers and burst upon them in full fury from her fig-tree covert.

The upshot was, that Smith was packed off summarily for service on the estate of Timour, the Tartar, on the shores of the Black Sea in north Crimea. Here he was meanly dressed in sheepskins, and placed among other slaves threshing out wheat in a granary. The Tartar was a harsh taskmaster, and applied his rawhide whip to the backs of his menials at the least sign of malingering. Smith soon decided that he would endure this cruelty no longer than he could help. One day, finding himself alone in an isolated barn with his abusive master, he flung his flail with animated strength against the cranium of Timour the Tartar and left him lying senseless on the threshing floor. Robing himself in the dead tyrant's fine clothes, he jumped on the Arabian steed champing outside the stable door and galloped away to the Russian border. Here he had the iron yoke struck from his neck and pursued his way back to Hungary, where Prince Sigismund presented him with fifteen hundred ducats. With this windfall he was able to travel at ease through Germany, France, Spain, and Morocco before turning up again in England.

Hearing so much talk about the expedition that would presently take off for the New World, he flamed with ardor to participate in the wonderful enterprise. "Who can desire," he rationalizes, "more content that hath small meanes, or but only his merit to advance his fortunes, than to tread and plant that ground he has purchased by the hazard of his life? If he hath any graine of Faith or Zeale in Religion, what can he do less hurtful to any, or more agreeable to God, than to seeke to convert those poor Savages to know Christ and humanity? What so truly squares with honour and honesty, as the discovering things unknowne, erecting Townes, peopling countries, informing the ignorant, reforming things unjust, teaching vertue and gaine to our native Mother Country?"

Here we may resume the thread of Smith's existence where we previously left him, at the head of the Virginian government. He was still a comparatively young man, only twenty-eight, but his wide experience made him appear like a much more seasoned personage. During his administration the number of colonists increased, and he discouraged any attempts to abandon the colony with the severest measures. He kept the friendship of the Indians, sometimes at the point of the rifle, in order to secure the heaping bushels of corn so vital to the well-being of the settlement.

Some one found a clay bank filled with dirt and pebbles of a very yellow sheen. Whereupon there was great excitement, for "there was no thought, no discourse, no hope, and no work but to dig gold, wash gold, refine gold, and load gold." Newport on his next voyage took home a load of this pyrite, or fool's gold, and made a laughing-stock of himself for his credulity. Not wanting to be gulled again, he brought back with him two refiners, two goldsmiths, and a jeweler. Smith was disgusted at this lust for gold. "When you send again," he wrote the London Company, "I entreat you send but 30 carpenters, husbandmen, gardeners, fishermen, blacksmiths, masons, and diggers up of trees' roots, well provided rather than 1,000 of such as we have; for except we be able both to lodge and feed them, the most will consume with want of necessaries before they can be made good for anything."

Smith strove to make workingmen out of the many "proper gentlemen" idling around the fort. He did succeed with some of them; the axes blistered their fingers when they were cutting down trees to make clapboards, but soon they toughened to the task, and delighted to hear the tall trees crashing down like a roll of thunder. The captain disliked profanity, and he employed a good method for abolishing it: all oaths were counted through the day, and at night each offender had a can of water poured down his sleeve for every oath he had uttered. Within a week all swearing had stopped.

Smith continued exploring the country and made fairly accurate maps of the territory around Chesapeake Bay. He commanded the respect of the native redskins, wherever he traveled, and bought a tract of land from them with the intention of removing the colony at Jamestown to higher ground. His little friend Pocahontas and her playmates visited the settlement every few days, and once during a period of privation, "brought him so much provision, that saved many of ther lives, that els for all this had starved with hunger."

In October, 1609, when Captain Smith was returning in a canoe after a visit to the future site of Jamestown, a gun that discharged by accident detonated a keg of gunpowder. Smith was asleep at the time, but was so badly burnt, that he had to roll over the side of the boat into the water to extinguish the flames from his clothing. There being few medical comforts in the colony, he sailed for home on the next ship and spent several months in a hospital before his wounded thigh was healed. He never again visited Virginia.

Five years later he was called upon by the Plymouth Company to chart the American coast farther to the north, in expectations of founding another colony. He explored the country from Maine south to Cape Cod, and gave the name of New England to this region. For his services he was honored with the title, "Admiral of New England." In 1616 he visited his friend Pocahontas, now the wife of John Rolfe and renamed, since her conversion to Christianity, the "Lady Rebecca." With her husband, a tobacco planter in Virginia, she had come to England and was being royally fêted in London. She burst into tears at her first meeting with Captain Smith after all these years, saying, "They had always told me you were dead, and I knew not otherwise till I came here."

Pocahontas died in March, 1617, just when she was preparing to return to her native country. She left a little son from whom many prominent Virginians have claimed descent. Smith always referred to her as "my blessed Pocahontas." He remained quiety at home, unmarried, the rest of his life, writing the story of his adventures and publishing maps of the New World, till his death in 1631. He had lived long enough to see a rising tide of eager immigrants flowing into a great, brave New World.

George Piercie, one of those who lived through all the early struggles of Jamestown for its very existence, paid this tribute, in after years, to the courageous leader: "What shall I say of him but this, that in all his proceedings he made justice his first guide, and experience his second; ever hating baseness, sloath, pride and indignitie more than any dangers; that never allowed more for himselfe than his souldiers with him; that upon no danger would send them where he would not lead them himselfe; that would never see us want what he either had or could by any meanes get us; that would rather want than borrow, or starve than not pay; that loved action more than words, and hated falsehood and covetousness worse than death; whose adventures were our lives, and whose losse our deaths."

The present spoon was put out in 1907 for the Jamestown Exposition, and the bowl shows the States Exhibit Palace. Pocahontas appears in the shank, below her the type of club used by the Indians to crush the skull of some one, like Smith, doomed to die. Captain Smith, with his characteristically bushy beard, and an old sailing ship, which could be the "Susan Constant," "God Speed," or "Discovery," occupy the nave. The first seal of Virginia is found in the caput.

On the reverse side are seen the present seal of Virginia, the U. S. battleship Virginia, and the signature of H. G. Tucker, president of the Jamestown Exposition Company. This was the official spoon for the exposition, and has been used through the courtesy of its owner, Professor O. J. Anderson, University of West Virginia, Morgantown, W. Va. Length of spoon is 5¾ inches.

No. 43 MARDI GRAS

In the early weeks of 1872 New Orleans was titillating with excitement. Royalty was coming. The Grand Duke Alexis of the imperial Romanoffs, the ancient royal dynasty of Russia, had accepted an invitation to be present at the Mardi Gras festivities.

The Carnival had been languishing for a decade or more. During the Civil War it had been discontinued altogether. Its revival was actually a fight for survival. Carpetbaggers were controlling the city, but opposition to their rule was strong-willed and bitter. On many sides there was apprehension lest the affair be an incitement for mob rule to take over. Mud, flour, lime, oranges, and tomatoes had been thrown promiscuously during the two previous celebrations, and the same kind of disorder could be expected again.

The idea then to invite the Grand Duke was considered an efficacious means to divert the minds of the spectators away from political animosities and to bring the Carnival back into a true focal perspective of its original purpose—an extravaganza for good-natured fun-making.

Alexis Romanoff Alexandrovitch, tall, fair, handsome, aged twenty-two, lieutenant in the Russian navy, and next to his brother, the Czarevitch, in line for the throne, had landed in New York late in November, 1871, from a special escort of Russian vessels. Royalty had been seen so seldom on these democratic shores that even the most undemonstrative acted like hobbledehoys falling over each other in doing the Duke honors.

New York greeted him with rhapsodic speeches, fired its cannons—souvenirs from the late war—and roared its collective hoarse rasp. The Trinity chimes peeled out the Russian national anthem. Everybody turned out to see him at his public appearance. Maidens swooned from the intensity of his glances. The Duke had a flair for pretty girls anyway, and he declared he had never seen so many of them as in this country. But the one who struck his fancy most was a peach-plump blonde, Lydia Thompson, starring just then in the Broadway burlesque, *Bluebeard*. One sentimental ditty in the show, "If Ever I Cease to Love," appealed inordinately to the Duke, and soon Lydia was singing the endless refrains of this song for him at tête-à-tête dinners. Presently he ordered a gorgeous bracelet for Lydia from Tiffany's, bade her a fond farewell, and set about on his sight-seeing tour of the provinces.

The high-caste pandits of the Boston environs, Longfellow, Lowell, Holmes, Eliot, Bancroft, and many other lights toasted him with bad odes and worse homilies. President Grant regaled him with champagne and vodka at the White House. His receptions in Buffalo, Cleveland, and Chicago were memorable events. Niagara Falls made him shiver as if with an ague. The "Michiganderesses" thought him the incarnation of Apollo when he visited Detroit. Buffalo Bill met him in St. Louis and accompanied him west to Denver. On a buffalo hunt he became acquainted with the sister of Chief Spotted Tail, and rode beside her on the way back to Topeka. Heading South, the Duke made stopovers in Jefferson City, Louisville, and Memphis. In these towns he heard that Lydia had been playing here but had left just before his arrival. To all appearances it looked as if he were pursuing her and she were eluding him.

Naturally all the fanfare attendant on this royal progress dovetailed neatly with the schemes elaborated by the New Orleans receiving committee. A bigger Carnival was planned. A new krewe, including both federal appointees and indigenous elements, was organized, and a new King Rex, Lord of Misrule, was to preside over a new parade of floats. To gloss over the antagonism of the two political factions in the city, Louis Salamon, a Jew, and considered a neutral, was chosen to be the first King Rex. No queen was selected on this occasion.

The *James Howard,* a Mississippi River luxury steamboat, brought the Duke to the city piers, docking shortly after nightfall on February 11th. A large crowd waited tensely to catch the first glimpse of the Duke as he descended the gang plank. A band was ready to strike up "God Save the Czar" whenever he passed with his entourage. The mayor held in his hand a hearty-welcoming speech to read before His Highness. But the speech was never read nor the Russian anthem played. The Duke preferred to remain on board the river steamer overnight. Everybody, especially the ladies, uttered a murmur of disappointment. They consoled themselves, however, with the thought that they would see him the next day.

That night the Duke danced waltzes and quadrilles in the salon of the steamer. Some thought that Lydia Thompson was present. Anyway, it was known that she had sent him an invitation to witness her performance of the stellar role in *Kenilworth* at a local theatre.

The next morning a larger crowd than that of the night before assembled to view the disembarcation of the Duke. Accompanying him was an admiral who began to speak in French to the surging throng of spectators. The mayor promptly interrupted him and informed him that his audience did not understand, since New Orleans had become a thoroughly English-speaking city. The Creoles did not like that; nevertheless, the admiral proceeded to say a few garbled sentences in halting English.

Several hours later the Krewe of King Rex initiated the first parade in its long-triumphal history. In front of the City Hall a throne was constructed for the Duke on a perch conspicuously high, so that he could see everything without obstruction, and every one could see him too, without too great a craning of necks. Ambitious maidens practiced making curtsies in the event they had a momentary chance to march before the throne.

The Duke Alexis had a mind of his own, with decided opinions, to which he stuck without reservations. He would not mount the improvised throne; he preferred to stand with the other onlookers. The governor, the mayor, and the members of the city council importuned him, implored him to accept this seat of honor. No, he was in a democratic country that officially recognized no royal titles, and he would abide by the laws of the country in which he was a guest. His persistent stand disconcerted not a little the young girls, who had thus practiced their curtsies in vain.

The procession began to file by. As soon as the first band drew near the City Hall, the strains of Lydia Thompson's familiar song reverberated in the Duke's ears:

> If ever I cease to love,
> If ever I cease to love,
> May the fish get legs
> And the cows lay eggs,
> If ever I cease to love.

The next band took up the tune, and the next. Some people hummed, then they burst into singing. Everyone seemed to enjoy the music except Alexis. He stood poker-faced, and stared straight ahead. Refrain after refrain was tossed off.

> May sheepheads grow on apple trees,
> If ever I cease to love.
> May the dogs all wag their tails in front,
> If ever I cease to love.

Some of the parodies might have irritated the Duke but he was careful to show no evidence of it. A great deal of laughter was provoked at the bluff democracy in these lines:

> May the Grand Duke ride a buffalo
> In a Texas rodeo,
> If ever I cease to love.

That night Alexis witnessed the other great parade of Mardi Gras, the pageant of Comus. Later he attended a ball, but refused to dance a single time. A bevy of beaming belles milled about before his eyes. Everybody was stepping to the strains of "If Ever I Cease to Love"—except the Duke.

The next evening, instead of seeing Lydia Thompson in the dull tragedy of *Kenilworth*, Alexis went to look at the inimitable comedienne, Lotta Crabtree, in *The Little Detective*. And the Grand Duke's heart was speedily lassoed by the impish, Titian-haired hoyden who could *ad lib* so effectively and set an audience on their ears with her booby songs, crazy gigs, and droll mannerisms. Night after night the Duke witnessed Lotta's performances, asked her out to dinner, and gave her a priceless bracelet of diamonds and pearls. Ma Crabtree, the vigilant bodyguard of the popular actress, refused the Duke's invitation to dinner for her daughter, but accepted the bracelet with gracious thanks. Nonplussed, his Imperial Highness the Grand Duke Alexis made ready to go aboard his ship in the Russian squadron that had just steamed into the Gulf port, and now lay waiting to transport him back to Europe.

The Duke had served New Orleans well by his visit. There ever after, the official theme song of Mardi Gras was to be that inconsequential but amusing bagatelle, with its catchy campmeeting-revival tune, "If Ever I Cease to Love." The occasion was henceforth to be a public holiday for schools, banks, and affairs of state. Two new parades were inaugurated;

214

in addition to the Krewe of Rex, the Knights of Momus also organized a Krewe. The hatred of Reconstruction factions was submerged by the more important task of welcoming a member of the real, and not the make-believe, kind of royalty.

The Carnival period in New Orleans opens on Epiphany of Twelfth Night, which falls on the 6th of January. The season is short or long, depending on the time that Lent begins. The earliest date for Mardi Gras or Shrove Tuesday is February 7th; the latest date possible is March 7th.

The early French explorer, Sieur Pierre le Moyne d'Iberville and his companions are said to have initiated the Mardi Gras festivities in simple fashion while sailing up the Mississippi Delta in the year 1699. Antonio de Ulloa, sent to be the governor of Spanish Louisiana in 1766, sternly forbade the celebration of Mardi Gras because he feared a masked rebellion of the French inhabitants, irate at the imposition of Spanish rule. The Creoles continued to observe the custom quietly under the Spanish, however, and made merry when Louisiana was turned back to the French. For several years after the Louisiana Purchase in 1803, the Americans looked askance at the masking of costumed figures. For a while the Carnival was suppressed, but the continued petitions of the Creoles led, in 1826, to the reëstablishment of the pageant with masks. By 1857 Mardi Gras had degenerated into an occasion, like Hallowe'en, for a great deal of hoodlumism. Its demise was freely predicted. But happily, in that year, something occurred to save the day and revive the good standing of the celebration. An organization, calling itself "The Mystick Krewe of Comus," was formed to build floats for a street parade. In two years this colorful pageant had become so successful that thousands of persons, instead of hundreds, witnessed the procession.

Gradually through the years the festival has gained in popularity, and the parades have grown to a staggering number. The most notable ones are held during the climactic week preceding Mardi Gras: On the Tuesday before, the Krewe of Cynthius parades; on Wednesday, Babylon; on Thursday, Momus; on Friday, Hermes; on Saturday, Nor (the children's organization, standing for New Orleans Romance); on Sunday, Venus (the only Krewe of women); and on Monday, Proteus.

Of course the big day is Mardi Gras, the Tuesday before Ash Wednesday, which ushers in Lent. From early till late there are resplendent parades. In the morning the Krewe of Crescent City forms a pleasing display of children in unusual costumes. A colorful pageant is that afforded by the Zulu king and his court. The king wears a leopard skin, voodoo charms along with strings of copper coins, a tin can or some other grotesque headgear, and an ermine robe. The negroes who participate in the Zulu parade usually dress as Indians or Baby Dolls. The main parade of the day, that of Rex and his Krewe, begins at noon. The Twelfth Night Revelers, the Atlanteans, and the Orleaneans follow. All masks come off at 6 p. m. About dusk the pageant of Comus brings the carnival spirit to its highest pitch of enthusiasm. Most of the floats are drawn by mules, haulers of garbage during the rest of the year but glorified figures garbed in white for this occasion.

The all-out merrymaking, mummery, buffoonery, dancing, and gayety exhibited by the native Orleaneans in the street make a spectacle, the enthusiasm of which is difficult for an outsider to comprehend. But to the insider, one who has lived in the city all his life, Mardi Gras has become an all-powerful tradition, a heritage in which he takes the greatest pride. There are dens where men are kept busy for months ahead of the Carnival, using their ingenuity and skill to devise themes for floats that will provide a bigger and better pageant for the every-increasing number of spectators hailing from every state in the Union. New Orleaneans claim that Mardi Gras is the greatest show on earth. Who will dare argue that they are wrong?[1]

The Mardi Gras spoon is a beautiful, ornately decorated piece of workmanship, washed entirely with gold on both sides. In the bowl is a hand holding a staff on which is mounted a clown's head with cap and bells in green and purple enamel, typifying the favorite colors of Mardi Gras. Two scroll or shell-like rosettes are seen in the base end of the bowl. The handle, richly embellished with sinuous foliations, terminates in a garlanded bonnet showing Louis XV influence.

Patented November 17, 1896, this spoon was made by the Frank M. Whiting Co. Length, 5½ inches.

No. 44 STATUE OF LIBERTY (NEW YORK SKYLINE)

Izaak Bedloo, a native of that very small Dutch-speaking area which juts down along the North Sea into France, set sail from Calais in 1642 for New Amsterdam. Instead of settling on the mainland among other Dutch colonists, he chose to live, undisturbed by neighbors, on a twelve-acre island southwest of what is now Manhattan. This farm was Izaak Bedloo's idea of true freedom.

Thirty-five years later his widow sold the island, which eventually became the property of the city. Convicts under sentence of death were brought here to be hanged. During the War of 1812 a fort was built here to protect the harbor. For a while the fort served as a military prison, then finally as a garbage disposal point.

Today, Bedloe's Island harbors the most famous of American monuments, the Statue of Liberty Enlightening the World. On a 142-foot granite pedestal stands the 151-foot figure of a woman, holding in her right hand a lighted torch high above her head, and in her left, a tablet on which is

---

[1] Two most thorough (and excellent) accounts of the celebration are Eleanor Early's *New Orleans Holiday* and Robert Tallant's *Mardi Gras*.

engraved *July 4, 1776.* The statue is composed of copper plates, held together by 300,000 rivets, covering an inner network of iron weighing 225 tons. There is a staircase of 168 treads inside the figure, winding from the pedestal landing to the crown.

For the inception of this monument we are indebted to Eduard de Laboulaye, a French historian who had studied and greatly admired our American democratic institutions. A young sculptor from Alsace, Auguste Bartholdi, after he had heard Laboulaye speak on the subject, was fired with enthusiasm for the practical accomplishment of the idea. He spent some time on this side of the Atlantic and made the acquaintance of many prominent Americans. Back in Paris, Bartholdi set to work, using the face and figure of his mother, Charlotte Beysser Bartholdi, as his model for the statue.

The first appeal for funds to defray the expenses of building the statue was made in France shortly after the Franco-Prussian War. The government proffered no official contribution; all the donations were given by private citizens. By 1880 the amount collected was sufficient to finance the total costs. But public opinion in this country was apathetic toward raising money for the proper installation of the statue. The *New York World,* under the inspiration of Joseph Pulitzer, began a campaign for arousing public interest in the project. Editorials appeared every day in the newspaper calling upon all citizens, rich and poor alike, to support the campaign by some sort of contribution. The results were extremely gratifying. Many, many small sums, including a great number of penny-collections from piggy-banks, were sent in by school children. The fund was soon oversubscribed.

Major General Charles P. Stone supervised the erection of the pedestal. Bartholdi was on hand when the French steamer *Isère* sailed into New York harbor on June 19, 1885, bearing the statue. The formal dedication did not take place till October 28, 1886, when a special holiday was proclaimed for the occasion. President Cleveland delivered a welcoming address, and more than a million people witnessed the parade leading up to the official ceremonies. The close bond of friendship that had existed between the French and American nations for over a century was significantly stressed.

The years have passed, and still the Statue of Liberty remains a beacon light of hope and inspiration for all the peoples who have come to set up a new way of life on our shores, where all are equal before the law and every native-born citizen may reach the highest seat in the land. From dusk to dawn the torch in the uplifted hand of the statue, set with ninety-two 1,000-watt bulbs, casts its light far out over the darkness of the deep, symbolizing the welcoming hand of the New World, whose ideals of freedom have been conceived in a government of, by, and for the people.

Emma Lazarus, the invalid poetess, whose parents had come to America as penniless refugees, caught the spirit of the symbolic figure perhaps more fully than any other when, at the time of the dedication, she wrote, personifying the voice of the statue, these words, later engraved on the monument:—

> "Keep, ancient lands, your storied pomp!" cries she
> With silent lips. "Give me your tired, your poor,
> Your huddled masses yearning to breathe free,
> The wretched refuse of your teeming shore.
> Send these, the homeless, tempest-tossed to me;
> I lift my lamp beside the golden door."

The Statue of Liberty is portrayed twice on this spoon, once in the bowl and again on the reverse side of handle in the caput. The New York skyline along the entire front shaft is strikingly well done; a magnifying glass is indeed needed to bring out the minute detail of window-lines in the tall buildings.

The three sections on the handle-back are distinctly separated by squarish stretches of grass and structural foundations. In addition to the Statue of Liberty, Grant's Tomb and the Singer Building are embossed in the nave and shank respectively. It is interesting to note that the Singer Building dates this spoon, for that skyscraper held the record, during only a few months back in 1907-08, of being the tallest of such ugly mammoth-monstrosities—or, such lovely cathedrals of finance, if you prefer.

The maker of this finely-conceived spoon is not revealed by any trademark. Length 5¾ inches.

No. 45 HOT SPRINGS
No. 50 HOT SPRINGS HOSTELRY

The tune, "The Arkansaw Traveler," and the book, "A Slow Train Through Arkansaw," have done much toward creating the legend for this Southern and/or Western state of being the natural habitat of jig-tune fiddlers and hepcat corn-drill dancers; patched-overalls-clad, bewhiskered hillbillies and tobacco-spitting, circuit-riding preachers; razorback hogs and hard-kicking, hard-headed mules—a legend that the natives of this state find difficult to contradict or counteract. Anyway, the Arkansans have acquired that sort of rusticated reputation nationally, and they have never been able to live it down . . . not that they wanted to . . . or didn't.

The fact is, the natives of Arkansas do not belong to just one type any more than do people of other states. The Arkansan is, by and large, a composite of four main types, made up of the influences that enter, like the wind, from all four points of the compass. In the east, just across the Mississippi, he may approximate somewhat to the national notion of a gun-totin' Ozark hillbilly, but on traveling southward you encounter Creoles who have drifted in from Louisiana to live among the southern pines and gnarled live-oaks coated with soft gray moss, and among these

218

people the romantic atmosphere is considerably heightened. If you are looking for a typical Arkansan in the north, you will find him much like his Missouri kinsman, the cotton planter across the border. In the west, he is indistinguishable from the breezy, spit-bouncing Texan who sports a ten-gallon hat, chaps, and spurs, and lives on horseback among his grazing cattle. And in Arkansas you will run upon that unique specimen, a diamond miner, for this is the only place in the Western Hemisphere where diamonds are found in the rough.

In Hot Springs you encounter all these figures as often as you do in Little Rock, the capital, because both towns are in the central part of the state. But in Hot Springs you can point out other people who do not fit into any of these type-revealing categories, for here you run into "foreigners" of every description—people who have come to straighten out the kinks in their rheumatic bones or to recuperate from an overdosage of sloe gin and aspirins.

The first owner of the land around Hot Springs was a Louisiana Creole, Jean Emanuel Prudhomme, guided to the springs by Indians who found relief from their ailments in the thermal baths. Later, the government set up a reservation covering the area. The place remained a mere village, however, till a railroad, in 1875, connected the town with points farther north. A disastrous fire in 1913 paved the way for the erection of modern hotels and better equipped bath-houses. The focal thoroughfare is Central Avenue, and the bath-houses, hospitals, and residences sprawl up and down hill on either side of this avenue.

The forty-seven springs in the Hot Springs National Park are owned and operated by the government. The water, issuing from the mountainside at the rate of 180,000 gallons a day, varies from 95 to 147 degrees Fahrenheit, although the average temperature is nearer 140 degrees. The water is piped in some places for a considerable distance through insulated aqueducts to preserve the original heat, supposedly derived from passing over igneous rocks far below the earth's surface.

Hot Springs is a leisurely town, as well befits a health resort, where people taking the thermal baths have all the time in the world to loiter and make their way slowly. The town neither increases nor decreases in population; like the temperature of the water, the population seldom varies. It remains static in numbers, with about twenty-five thousand all-year-round residents.

The Hot Springs spoon is absolutely unique. The manner in which the name appears on the upper portion of the handle is very suggestive of a thermal-bath resort, for the letters of HOT SPRINGS intertwine one with the other to form an open lattice-work design, resembling the misty steam rising from the hot waters of the bath, or even the vapors emanating from a volcanic fumarole. Unless the words are spelled out for him, the average person will overlook the letters hidden in the arabesque design altogether.

Made by Myrick, Roller & Holbrook, a firm formerly established in Philadelphia, but out of business by 1915. Length is 6 inches.

The Hot Springs Hostelry spoon is practically the same in design as those of the Union Station and Ramona's Wedding Place, except for the variations pictured in their respective bowls. This pattern with its Indian motif on the handle is represented thus three times in this book, mainly to indicate the possibility to the collector that he can acquire a whole set of this one pattern portraying a wide variety of scenes in the bowls, to be used for practical purposes, if so desired. A product of the Paye and Baker Company, it measures 5¼ inches in length.

No. 46 SALEM WITCH

Unusual things were happening in the household of the Reverend Samuel Parris in the village of Salem. The time was shortly after New Year of 1692. The daughter and niece of the minister were crawling into holes, under beds, and up the stairs on all fours; contorting their arms, legs, and faces into queer shapes; uttering shrieks, grunts, groans, and gibberish; in short, acting in a manner completely unintelligible to their elders. There were four neighbor girls also plagued by the same antic malady.

The minister, alarmed, sent out a call for all the wiseacres from the surrounding villages and towns to come and see for themselves the strange manifestations of the girls under observation.

It took very little observing for the visitors to be convinced that the girls were bewitched. A doctor declared they were beyond the aid of medicine. Upon being questioned, the girls accused three women of bringing on their anguished condition.

Sarah Good, aged seventy, the first woman to be examined, had been in depressed spirits—really, in poor health—for several years. She was unpopular, being suspected by two witnesses of bewitching a great many cattle, hogs, and sheep which had died under peculiar conditions for said witnesses lately. Sarah Good strenuously denied all accusations brought against her, saying that she had made no compact with the devil, harmed no children, and muttered nothing under her breath except psalms. The afflicted girls writhed in torment at these denials. One witness testified that, having refused shelter to Sarah Good for the night, she saw the old woman ride out of the house on a broomstick.

One girl cried out piteously during the trial that Dame Good had stabbed her, leaving the broken knife-point sticking in her flesh. She produced the knife-point as evidence, whereupon a young man arose and exhibited a knife with its blade broken and the point missing. He had thrown away the broken part only yesterday. Evidently the girl had picked up the blade-end to carry along with her to strengthen her fabricated story in court. The auditors were somewhat jarred at the girl's mendacious testimonial. Nevertheless, the old woman was convicted. She was hanged on Gallows Hill, protesting over and over her innocence and warning old Judge Hathorne at the very last that some day he would choke to death on blood.

Sarah Osburn, the second woman accused, got up from a sick bed to attend her trial, but death intervened while she was lying in jail and thus cut short the proceedings against her.

The third woman accused was a West Indian negress, called Tituba, a slave in the Parris household. More than any other she was instrumental in creating this witchcraft delusion. She had told the girls so many lurid tales of voodoo practices, black magic, ghosts, and witches—brought with her from her native West Indies—that the impressionable girls could not sleep, and cried out in their dreams, the creatures in Tituba's wild imagination having become vivid realities in theirs.

The slave girl vigorously denied being a witch, but said she had once been compelled to accompany Good and Osburn when they went sailing through the air on a broomstick seated fore and aft of two cats, one black and one red. But Tituba eventually broke down and confessed her master beat her and forced her to tell the stories she did. No further action was taken against her, but she languished thirteen months in prison, whence she was sold again into slavery to pay for her upkeep while a public charge.

Other well known trials were those of Bridget Bishop, Rebecca Nurse, Martha and Giles Cory, John Alden (son of the famous John and Priscilla), and the Reverend George Burroughs. Nineteen persons who stoutly denied being witches were sentenced to death. Fifty-five who admitted they were, escaped with their lives but suffered incarceration for a while. No one could feel safe. Even the wife of Governor Phipps was accused.

Then the governor, having become disgusted by this senseless blood-letting, stepped in and demanded that the executions be stopped. He suspended sentence on those condemned to die, opened the prison doors for those awaiting trial, forbade any more arrests, and removed the judges conducting the trials.

The witchcraft excitement was over in New England. Most of the judges and jurors were repentant, and admitted that the whole thing was a nasty, frightful error. When we consider the fact that three hundred thousand people were executed or burned as witches in Europe, the figures for America look quite insignificant. The tragic delusion had been dispelled once and for all in this country, but it was well over a century before the last witch had been dispatched in Europe. It is good to note that the first thorough-going condemnations of the evil practice were written by New Englanders.

The bowl of the Salem Witch spoon is long and plain. The handle is an inverted broom, and around its drop a hideous-looking cat arches her back, thrusts forward her pointed ears, opens her mouth unusually wide to display her serrated teeth, and extends her paws long and sharp as an eagle's talons. A rope serpentines its course around the entire length of the broom handle, even projecting into the bowl a short way.

An inverted crescent moon in the caput is surmounted by a foul hag, who is grasping a broom in one hand and the moon in the other. A peaked hat sits rakishly to one side of her head. Her garments seem to be blown by a strong breeze, and her feet are far apart, to give her either a surer balance or a better toe-hold. ~

Impressed in 1892 by Gorham's for Daniel Low of Salem. Length, 6 inches.

No. 47 WASHINGTON'S HATCHET
No. 63 WASHINGTON'S TOMB
No. 64 WASHINGTON'S BUST

The man who created the "Washington Legend" and called himself Parson Weems, formerly rector of Mount Vernon parish, was, properly speaking, only an ex-parson, and it is doubtful whether he ever attended a service in the Mount Vernon church. But apparently he did pay at least one visit to the Washington manor, for he was no hesitant introvert, but a fellow who enjoyed life immensely and visited everybody of importance in the furtherance of his book-hawking trade. At Mount Vernon he was, without doubt, favorably received—perhaps regaled with a good meal at the plenteous board and allowed a swig of Jamaica ginger at the general's sideboard-bar.

Van Wyck Brooks describes this book-vender of the highroads so inimitably that I can do no better than repeat what he says about this forerunner of our modern, high-powered salesman: "With his ruddy visage and the locks that flowed over his clerical coat, one saw him bumping along in his Jersey wagon, a portable bookcase behind and a fiddle beside him. A little ink-horn hung from one of his lapels, and he carried a quill pen stuck in his hat; and he stopped now and then at a pond or stream to wash his shirt and take a bath, suspending his linen to dry on the frame of the wagon. He was abroad in all weathers and all over the country . . . 'Roads horrid and suns torrid' were all the same to Parson Weems."

Even the most impassable roads did not deter the Parson from plying his trade, and many of these highways were in the sunny South, where he found the most pliable clientele. He did a good business, and kept his ear to the ground to discover what books his customers wanted. If he did not have in stock the volume desired, he always had something better on hand to recommend.

222

Soon after Washington's death Weems became aware of a demand for a biography of the deceased hero. There being none, he set about to fill the vacuum. He wrote it in transit—you can sense the ruts of the road in the rhythm of the sentences, hear the jog-trotting of the old bay mare on good, gravelly stretches, or feel yourself holding onto the dashboard when a wheel drops into a squashy mud-puddle.

No biography was ever less documented, less taken from other printed sources. It was sublimely original, struck off at white heat, all emphasis—dashes, underscored words galore, misquotes, absurd figures of speech, trivial incidents transmogrified into lustrous events, and "unblushing fabrications."

The first edition of *A History of the Life and Death, Virtues and Exploits of General George Washington*, by Mason Locke Weems, was published in 1800. It took the country by storm, and it continued to be a best seller through more than seventy-five editions. Long before its sales had shriveled, its purpose was accomplished: Washington had been lifted to the heights of a deified hero and Parson Weems, with the dividends from the book, had paid off the mortgage of his modest farm at Bel Air, Maryland. What did it matter if the story of the famous hatchet and the cherry tree were invented—it could be true, or it should be. The ex-parson of Pohick had discovered an inherent psychological weakness characteristic of his fellow-countrymen; they believed what they liked to believe, especially if it is that sort of fiction which is interlarded between two buttered truths.

The biography begins with an anecdote, which sets the tenor for the rest that follows. Napolean Bonaparte is conversing with some young Americans and at the mention of Washington's name, the Frenchman sighs, "Posterity will talk of him with reverence as the founder of a great empire, when my name shall be lost in the vortex of Revolutions!"

The author tells us in all honesty that he is dealing specifically with the *private* life and deeds of his protaganist. "Of these private deeds of Washington," he declares, "very little has been said. In most of the elegant orations pronounced to his praise, you see nothing of Washington below *the clouds*—nothing of Washington the *dutiful* son—the affectionate brother—the cheerful schoolboy—the diligent surveyor—the neat draftsman—the laborious farmer—the Widow's husband—the orphan's father—the poor man's friend. No! this is not the Washington you see; 'tis only Washington, the HERO, and the Demigod—Washington the *sun beam* in council, or the *storm* in war." What the Parson actually proceeds to do is to erase the "demi" from "demigod," and to place before us a man in whom the world has found no equal. And the method he employs for this purpose is very effective. "Those *over delicate* folk, who are ready to faint at thought of a second marriage, might do well to remember, that the greatest man that ever lived was the son of a second marriage."

We cannot help wondering if the Parson did not intend to add another book to the Scriptures: his tones are so purely Biblical in sound and intent, and his iterated paraphrases too obvious to be mistaken: "Parents that are *wise*, will listen, well pleased, while I relate how moved the steps of the youthful Washington, whose single worth far outweighs all the oaks of Bashan and the red spicy cedars of Lebanon. Yes, they will listen delighted while I tell of their Washington in the days of his youth, when his little feet were swift towards the nests of birds; or when, wearied in the chase of the butterfly, he laid him down on his grassy couch and slept, while ministering spirits, with their roseate wings, fanned his glowing cheeks, and kissed his lips of innocence with that fervent love which makes *the Heaven!*"

Early did the father seek to instill in George's mind the merits of truthfulness. The youthful prevaricator is regarded with apprehension wherever he goes, and parents loathe his presence among their children. "Oh, George, my son!" warns the affectionate father, "rather than see you come to this pass, dear as you are to my heart, gladly would I assist to nail you up in your little coffin and follow you to your grave." Stern stuff, this father, a guardian angel of the same mold as the inexorable Mateo Falcone.

Of course, this preachment is necessary for its sequent, the most famous of all the Parson's fabrications, told him by a most excellent lady, undeniably true, for any gentleman who doubts a lady's word is not a *true* gentleman.

Six-year-old George had just become the "wealthy master of a hatchet!" And like all children, born savage with destructive proclivities, little George ran out to hack and hew at the object of his father's tenderest care, an imported cherry tree. The father at once espied the gaping wound on the tree and the chips knee-deep round about it. In an agonized anger, he went from one to another, inquiring who had done this ghastly deed. No one knows anything about it till George comes on the stage. He is confronted point-blank with the *tough question*: "George, do you know who killed that beautiful little cherry tree yonder in the garden?" The rest of the story is such precious Weemsiana that it must be given verbatim, or its savory essence will be lost: "George staggered under it [the question] for a moment; but quickly recovered himself; and looking at his father, with the sweet face of youth brightened with the inexpressible charm of all conquering truth, he bravely cried out, 'I can't tell a lie, Pa; you know I can't tell a lie. I did cut it with my hatchet!'—'Run to my arms, you dearest boy,' cried his father in transports, 'run to my arms; glad am I, George, that you killed my tree, for you have paid me for it a thousand fold. Such an act of heroism in my son is more worth than a thousand trees, though blossomed with silver, and their fruits of purest gold'."

The moral of this tale is that if a child is taught *to think* as well as *to feel*, he can be led easily and pleasurably "along the happy paths of virtue."

George was a manly little fellow who despised "such trifling play as marbles and tops." At school, during the recreation period, he divided his small comrades into two armies, took charge of one himself, and, with cornstalks for muskets and calabashes for drums, promoted furious sham battles. At running, jumping, wrestling, and boxing, he was unexcelled. His cousin, Colonel Lewis Willis, vouched for his ability to throw a stone across the Rappahannock at Fredericksburg, a feat not easily duplicated by the pygmies of aftertimes. His fowling-piece was of such a ponderous weight that others needed a steadying support to fire it; yet he could hold it at arms-length and blaze away at the swans on the Potomac, of which birds he "has been known to kill, rank and file, seven or eight at a shot."

George had not been born with "a silver spoon in his mouth," but he was luckier yet. An Indian fighter who took a sizable part of the credit for Braddock's defeat voiced this, for him, disconcerting revelation: "Washington was never born to be killed by a bullet, for I had seventeen fair fires at him with my rifle, and after all could not bring him to the ground."

Henceforth, Washington was to lead a charmed life. Bullets might ring circles around his neck, yet a protecting providence would frame his body within a blind coat of impenetrable steel. His mother recalled a puzzling dream she had when George was a child. Flames were bursting through the roof of their home when George came to the rescue, climbed a ladder as agilely as a squirrel, and threw water from a gourd on the fire. The conflagration was getting the better of him when a "venerable old man, with a tall cap and an iron rod in his hand, like a lightning rod, reached out to him a curious little trough, like a *wooden shoe!* On receiving this, he redoubled his exertions, and soon extinguished the fire." The symbolized figures are easily interpreted: the fire is the Revolution; the gourd, the Continental army; the old man, Franklin; the wooden shoe, assistance from France, the peasants of which nation are shod in sabots. Thus, various devices of the old Greek epics are pressed into service, and, in general, add to rather than detract from the substance of this grandiloquent work. Now and then, especially as the book travels along, we are surprised at Parson Weems's ability to handle antithesis as consistently well as he does, for example: "On hearing in Congress the fall of Cornwallis, the doorkeeper swooned with joy—on hearing the same news announced in Parliament, Lord North fell back in his chair, in the deepest distress." Sometimes we feel, too, that he could say things very adroitly, even felicitously: "Then full leafed and green the olive branch of peace was held out to the nations; and the eyes of millions, on both sides of the water, were lifted in transport to the lovely sign . . . Long accustomed unerringly to predict what Britain would do, from what he knew she had power to do, he had nothing to hope, but everything to fear."

There are many excellences strewn along through the tangled passageways in Parson Weems's garden of thoughts, and had he done more pruning and weeding out, avoided too thick a planting, and sowed a greater variety of smaller blooms, there would not be in evidence so much of that rank growth of sunflowers—those hero-worshippers forever gawking at their god, the sun. Well, Parson Weems was such a growth, a sunflower with his gaze transfixed upon the chief luminary in his heavens, George Washington. And had he tried to assume the role of a more modest flower, he would never have been "Parson" Weems, nor the "rector of Mount Vernon parish" either.

The first of the three spoons we have in this group, the Washington's Hatchet spoon, is replete with historic scenes. The Capitol building in Washington is shown in the bowl; on the handle-shank is that famous hatchet; the nave contains small views of the family burial vault and mansion at Mount Vernon; a profile view of the first president appears in an oval medallion in the caput, bordered by cannon balls, at the top of which an eagle sits, wings outspread and arrows gripped in his talons.

On the reverse side, little George is seen chopping away at the cherry tree, in the caput. The Washington monument and a Revolutionary War cannon appear running down through the narrower part of the handle.

This spoon was pressed and stamped by the Campbell-Metcalf Silver Co., of Providence, out of business now for more than thirty years. The length is 5¾ inches.

In the bowl of the Washington's Tomb spoon we see a path leading to the entrance of a mausoleum, the door of which is barred by an iron gate beneath a Tudor arch. The two pilasters on either side are flanked by buttressed walls half the height of the entrance and extending toward the newel posts capping both ends of the façade.

Bordering the path before the tomb is an obelisk-type monument surrounded by an iron-picket fence. Several trees of indeterminate species rise behind the obelisks.

The shank contains the name of Washington written in a wavering slant. The caput embodies a close-up view of Mount Vernon in heavy embossment, very distinct, and superbly embellished by a foliated border of bay and magnolia leaves, with the bright berries of the former clearly in evidence.

On the reverse side the caput, enwreathed by the same ornamental border, bears the felicitous encomium bestowed upon Washington, "First in war, first in peace, first in the hearts of his countrymen"—worthy of Parson Weems at his best.

Made by R. Wallace & Co. Length, 5½ inches. Used through the courtesy of its own, Mrs. Alyse D. Westbrook, Hayward, California.

The Washington's Bust spoon is a fine example of the workmanship done in the early Nineties, before craftsmen began to exercise their ingenuity to achieve a sharp angularity of lines that has rendered so many later patterns grotesque and displeasing to the eye. The lines here are Colonial in effect, soft, chaste, and dignified, with gently-shaped roundings throughout the length of the handle that flattens out from a cylindrical shaft into a slight, smoothly-arched caput. There is no sign of division anywhere to denote the usual sections found on most handles.

All the work is embossed on this spoon. The Capitol building appears in the bowl. The shank contains the name of Washington in repoussé chasing, and in the caput is the cut-out of the first president, presumably copied after Gilbert Stuart's portrait.

Made by Codding and Heilbom, a company that went out of business in May 1918. Length, 5½ inches. This spoon has been used through the courtesy of Mrs. Alyse D. Westbrook, Hayward, California.

No. 48 ROYAL GORGE

The sources of two great river systems lie close to each other on the roof of our continent in Colorado. The Colorado, fed by small tributaries from Wyoming, rises and flows on the western side of the Continental Divide, through the Grand Canyon and past Hoover Dam, into the Gulf of California. Not more than forty miles away from the origins of the Colorado, the Arkansas River has its beginnings on the snowbeds high above Leadville, pushes turbulently through its own "grand canyon," the Royal Gorge, between Canon City and Gunnison, and then leisurely peregrinates through the placid plains of Kansas, Oklahoma, and Arkansas to embrace the Mississippi.

The history of the Royal Gorge was once as troubled as the swirling, booming, battling current itself. Two railroads fought for possession of the right to lay tracks through the almost impassable cleft in the red granite rocks. The two doughty personalities behind this internecine conflict were General William J. Palmer, representative of the Denver and Rio Grande Railroad, and William B. Strong, manager for the Atchison, Topeka and the Santa Fe.

Palmer had built his railroad as far as Canon City and rested there, balked by the difficulties of the Royal Gorge. He thought, since he held the charter from the government for sole rights of passage through the canyon, that he could extend the line whenever he pleased. Disgruntled by the delay, the citizens of Canon City began to prod the Santa Fe into action. Both parties moved in with working crews. When the Rio Grande pick-and-shovel men arrived, they were greeted by armed Santa Fe guards. Thwarted at gaining an entrance, the Rio Grande crew marched to the precipices directly above the chasm, lowered themselves by ropes, and began to blast off some of the sidewalls to secure a foothold in the narrow slit of the canyon below.

Meanwhile Palmer pressed the courts for an injunction against the rival company, which was forbidding him access to the canyon and thus impeding his progress. A court decree made matters worse by granting the right of way through the gorge to both companies. That was impossible. There was not even enough room for the laying of one track until one of the canyon walls had been hewn down considerably.

Tracks laid by one crew were torn up by the other. Spies prowled about both camps. Kidnappings were common occurrences. Shots were frequently exchanged, and some blood ran. One reconnoiterer, resisting capture in a hot pursuit, jumped out of a window, cut the bridle reins on the sheriff's horse, and dashed away, amid a loud hallooing for help to overtake the fugitive.

General Palmer strengthened his claims financially by a ten million dollar loan floated in Wall Street. With this lucrative persuasion, the Rio Grande was able to arbitrate successfully. The Santa Fe was paid a generous sum for the tracks it had already constructed, and in return for this green-bill salve applied to its hurt pride, forewent all claims henceforth to the gorge.

The puffing of the first train into Leadville was an event of national importance. Two generals, William J. Palmer and Ulysses S. Grant, stepped off onto the platform to receive the rousing plaudits of a madly cheering, wildly celebrating swarm of spectators.

Today a suspension bridge, the highest of its kind in the world, spans the Royal Gorge, 1023 feet above the river bed. An inclined railway lowers and lifts sight-seers who wish to inspect the gorge close at hand.

The Royal Gorge spoon pictures, in the bowl, an excellent view of the precipitous mountain walls of the canyon, the railroad tracks hugging the narrow path between the massy rock above on one side and the swirling waters of the river below on the other. A train is puffing along the tracks, and the suspension bridge can be descried in the distance.

On the obverse side of handle are many objects typical of Colorado: two columbines (the state flower) in bloom, a team pulling a covered wagon, a burro, a miner panning gold, and an Indian face in profile, in the caput. On the handle back may be seen a mine and shaft, a team and plow, a drove of cattle, and a cowboy on his bucking bronco.

This spoon contains the initials of Eugene L. Deacon, a jewelry company, of Los Angeles, California. Length is 5 inches.

No. 49 UNION STATION

Among the many structures appearing on old souvenir spoons, the heaviest casualties of time have been hotels and post offices, most of them having been replaced through the years by more pretentious edifices. Courthouses and other public buildings follow next on the list. Railroad stations have been more fortunate—or, more unfortunate—in that respect, and remain unperturbed, though frequently very outmoded, as virtual museum-pieces.

Some of these old depots, especially in small towns, can be pleasant, restful places, but all too often they are not, being a little run-down at the heels and showing visibly the ravages of time. In spite of their impres-

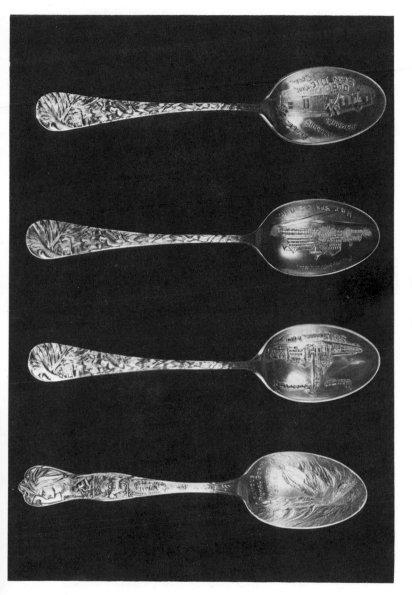

PLATE 32

48. ROYAL GORGE   49. UNION STATION   50. HOT SPRINGS HOSTELRY
51. RAMONA'S WEDDING PLACE

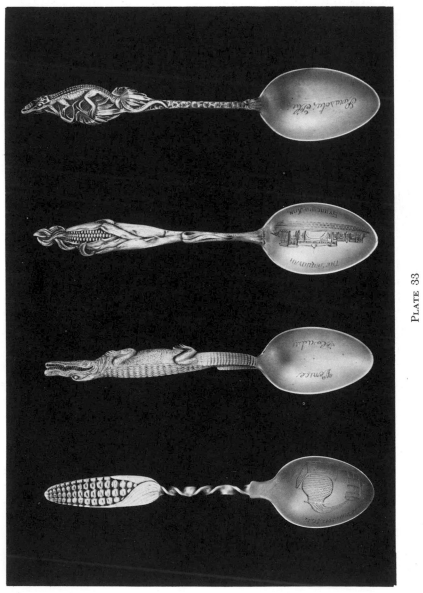

Plate 33

52. PEORIA CORN-AND-JUICE   53. VENICE ALLIGATOR   54. SEQUOYAH
55. SARASOTA ALLIGATOR

sive size and modernity in the larger cities, these stations are anything but pleasant and restful, and seem rather, at times, to be centers of bedlam-breaking-loose for jumpy, jangling traveler's nerves. Who does not remember the unsettling noises and commotions, the hurrying and scurrying of passengers in transit? Who has not noted the anxiety registered on the faces of those seated, motionless, waiting, in stations of such cities as New York, Philadelphia, Boston, Chicago, Cincinnati, St. Louis, Detroit, Washington, Jacksonville, or Atlanta? The minds of travelers amid the throngs in such places seem distracted, absent, elsewhere.

Many years ago, when I was much more callow and much less calloused than I am now, I was standing in a crowd of people in Union Station, St. Louis, waiting my turn to get through the gate onto the platform, where I might board the train for Denver. I was, I confess it, excited from the newness of being away from home, alone, for the first time going my own way. As I stood there, my hands encumbered with luggage, a man walked up to me and handed me my wallet, which contained my ticket and all my money except for a small amount of change in my pockets. I had left it lying on the lunch counter. The man had sat near me, and he remembered me well enough to identify my face among a crowd of waiting passengers. "You might need this before you get back," he said with a smile, and hurried off. I thanked him incoherently—too astounded to say much before he was gone. And with what a bland humor did this self-possessed man assure me that I might need that billfold before I got back—when the need was pressing right then and there, just that minute, before my leaving!

Ever since that little occurrence, inconsequential now, it is true, but of considerable import to me at the time, I have been led to have more faith in the goodness of mankind in the mass; and I have been firmly convinced since then, likewise, that most people are, after all, inherently honest and amicably disposed toward others in this, the best of all possible worlds—even in the hurly-burly, maddening rush of a big railroad station.

Union Station, St. Louis, which is embossed in this spoon bowl, covers nearly twenty acres. Designed by Theodore Link, it was completed in 1896. Built of Indiana limestone in an over-all Romanesque style, it has several added Gothic features. To the right of the main entrance a bell tower, showing clocks on two of its façades, rises to a height of two hundred and thirty feet. To the side of the peaked belfry-roof is a stanchion surmounted by a waving flag. A pointed hexagonal tower of larger dimensions flanks the front right wing of the building. The main-front façade is four stories high, three dormer windows piercing the roof at its base in the center. The approach to the main entrance is by two ramps leading to an esplanade. Toward the rear is seen a long extension under a low, straight roof, where the train platforms are located. Two offset, round towers soften the architectural lines at the corners.

The waiting room on the interior leads into an impressive Grand Hall open to the top of the highest tower. The lighting is enhanced by stained-glass windows.

The shaft contains a single stalk of corn with several unsheathed ears. Near the bottom a banderole encircles the stalk in three folds. An Indian in war bonnet faces toward the left in the nave.

On the reverse are a wigwam, an arrow, a tomahawk, and a pipe—features not found on the other spoons of the same set pictured in this book. Pressed by Paye and Baker, this spoon measures 5¼ inches in length.

No. 52 PEORIA CORN-AND JUICE
No. 118 PEORIA COURTHOUSE

From time immemorial there have been people living on the shores of the Illinois River where it empties into Lake Peoria and again where it empties out. Indians set up lodges here as often as they were destroyed by their enemies, and whatever tribe possessed it for the moment fought to retain it henceforward. When the French explorers, Father Marquette and Louis Joliet, turned aside from their Mississippi voyage and came upon the scene in 1673, they found, living along the shores of what is now the Illinois River, a confederacy of tribes of which the main branches were the Peoria, Cahokia, Kaskaskia, and Michigamea. The general name given to the members of this loosely formed union by the Indians themselves was "Illini," an apple-polishing term meaning something like "perfect specimens of masculinity." Some of the specimens whom Marquette met on his ascent of the river belonged to the "Peourea" tribe, well-built men, tall, and with shiny white teeth.

Marquette died of consumption before he could return, but his report on the region impressed Count Frontenac, governor of New France, favorably enough to encourage Robert Cavalier, Sieur de La Salle, in his ambitions to win the Illinois region over to the arts of civilization. In January, 1680, La Salle and his men built a fort at the lower end of Peoria, on a bluff overlooking the river and not far from the present site of Peoria. La Salle left his newly-built fort in the hands of a lieutenant, but when he returned to the spot three months later, he found it had been despoiled by his own forces, discontented with life among savages in the wilderness.

In 1691, the first permanent white settlement in Illinois was established with the removal of Fort St. Louis from Starved Rock to Lake Peoria. Fur traders and merchants gradually clustered around the fortress for safety, while at the same time doing a flourishing barter business with the Indians.

Various names were given to the settlement—Au Pe, De Pe, Le Pe, Au Pay, Opa—according to the preference or ignorance of the speller.

232

Not until a century later did Piorias (the s silent), and then Peoria, become a fixed designation.

The French, mingling on more or less friendly terms with the Indians, almost lost contact with the outside world till the French and Indian War placed them under the British flag. Not long afterwards the Revolutionary War shunted them into the American corral, but this change of sovereignty was accepted with the utmost indifference by the settlers, who were quite used to managing their own affairs, in a local fashion, as they best saw fit.

The same sort of domestic conflict occurred here too, as it does everywhere. One diverting story has it that the heart of Captain Maillet, the French commandant, was being besieged by a Madame La Voissière, whose husband was so insanely jealous that he hatched a plot for making an end to the insufferable situation. He invited the suave Captain Maillet to dinner, at which he aroused the suspicions of his guest as well as of his wife by his peculiar actions in leaving the table several times without any plausible excuses. Suddenly Captain Maillet felt such a premonition that something was going wrong, that he jumped up from the table and dashed out, followed by Mme. La Voissière and two servants. While they stood on the outside trying to figure out why they had left so unceremoniously, a terrific explosion sent the house flying heavenward in shattered pieces. The husband had evidently ignited a keg of gunpowder as a means of ending, in a high-flown style, this improper romance. While he perished thus by his own doing, he foolishly cleared the way for his widow and the captain to march happily to the altar without any qualms of conscience.

During the War of 1812 the French-speaking inhabitants of Peoria were accused of disloyalty to the American government, under which they had been living now for three decades. The mischief-making rumors began with a tramp who had been hustled out of town for pilfering. He declared the Peorians were supplying the Indians with ammunition and rifles, stealing cattle from farmers farther east, and driving out American settlers. Governor Ninian Edwards, mistakenly believing these propaganda stories were true, dispatched soldiers to the town in the dead of winter. Thomas Forsyth, an American agent, was the only person who could speak English in Peoria, and he tried to convince Captain Craig, commander of the soldiers, that he should withdraw, as the French were loyal citizens. Not satisfied to leave without seeing action, the soldiers looted houses, broke into stores, and made themselves obnoxiously drunk. The next morning, the soldiers awoke with a start when they heard a farmer outside the town shooting several beeves. They jumped up in alarm and marched around town, pulling people out of their beds, setting houses on fire, destroying a full granary, and despoiling the church. The men, mostly in their underclothing or naked, were chucked on board ship as prisoners; the women and children were allowed to flee into the forests;

the torch was put to the town. Not until spring were the scattered members of families allowed to return to their devastated village.

The next year the Americans constructed Fort Clark on the site of the old fort. In spite of Indian raids and the hardships of frontier life, land-seekers began to push into the new territory. For several years the town was designated by the Americans as Fort Clark, but in 1825, when the English-speaking people had already come to embrace a majority, the original Indian-French name of Peoria was officially reinstated, and the town was made the seat of a county government which placed Chicago and a large section of Illinois under its jurisdiction for a while. Being the center of a widely expanding agricultural area, Peoria set about devising ways and means to supply the growing demands for farm implements. From her factories poured out a constant stream of plows, threshers, reapers, planters, and cultivators. Corn and rye from the rich alluvial lands and the pure, cool under-surface water made a perfect combination unsurpassed for the manufacture of spirituous liquors. Accordingly, a large number of distilleries were located there already before the Civil War.

In 1857 a young lawyer, Bob Ingersoll, set up his shingle in Peoria, and for the next quarter of a century he was to be one of the most commanding figures in the political picture of Illinois. One of the great orators of all times, he was either cordially loved or cordially hated, and would have gone far in politics if it had not been for his outspoken views on religion. Though the son of a Presbyterian minister, he was always hostile to Christianity and all other forms of organized religion. On the lecture platform he proclaimed his agnosticism, and large crowds went to hear, not so much what he said, as how he said it. He rebelled wholeheartedly against the Christian concept of Hell—eternal pain and prison, everlasting helplessness and hopelessness. "All that the human race has suffered in war and want, in pestilence and famine, in fire and flood," he said; "all the pangs and pains of every disease and every death—all this is nothing compared with the agonies to be endured by one lost soul . . . This frightful dogma, this infinite lie, made me the implacable enemy of Christianity . . . It makes man an eternal victim and God an eternal fiend. It is the infinite horror. Every church in which it is taught is a public curse . . . Below this Christian dogma, savagery cannot go . . . It gives me joy to know that Christians are becoming merciful, so merciful that the fires of Hell are burning low—flickering, choked with ashes, destined in a few years to die out forever."

Ingersoll's oratory, like William Jennings Bryan's, may look as if it were too richly spiced with rolling rhetoric on the written page, but the sound of it, as it fell on the waiting ear of the listener, struck home with the melodious magic of a "poet hidden in the light of thought." His apotheosis of love was the sort of thing that won the rapt attention of his audiences for him. Imagine a voice attuned to the proper pitch and vibrant with overtones caressing our ear with such liquid language as

234

this: "Love is the only bow on life's dark cloud. It is the morning and the evening star. It shines upon the babe and sheds its radiance on the quiet tomb. It is the Mother of Art, inspirer of poet, patriot, and philosopher. It is the air and light to tired souls—builder of every home, kindler of every fire on every hearth. It was the first dream of immortality. It fills the world with melody—for music is the voice of love. Love is the magician, the enchanter that changes worthless things to joy, and makes right royal kings and queens of common clay. It is the perfume of that wondrous flower, the heart, and without that sacred passion, that divine swoon, we are less than beasts; but with it, earth is heaven and we are gods."

Ingersoll could dramatize a situation and hypnotize an audience better than could any other man of his time. His first legal case gained him the reputation of a spellbinder. He was called upon to defend a Peoria County pig-raiser charged with murder. The farmer had returned from town to find a fence deliberately torn down and his pigs gone. Certain that some dirty thief had made off with his stock, he buckled a six-shooter, Colt's latest, in his belt and proceeded to scour the locality in hopes that he might overtake the rascal and recover his pigs.

The search led eventually to the local pound. The farmer recognized his pigs, and began to tear enough boards off the fence to open a passageway. The pound master commanded him to stop till he paid for the damages wrought by the pigs in neighboring gardens. The irate farmer refused to listen and the pound master came towards him with a pick-axe. The pig master opened fire and felled his attacker. Then he drove his pigs home.

Feeling ran so high in the neighborhood that the trial was transferred to the adjacent town of Groveland to secure an unprejudiced jury. Until the moment that Bob Ingersoll rose to speak, it was the concurrent opinion of all the bystanders packed into that courtroom that the accused man would be convicted of first-degree murder and hanged. But the young defense lawyer, twenty-seven years old, caught the jury off their guard by approaching the case from a new angle, a purely domestic one: he pictured the man's family, his wife and children, the struggle to keep body and soul together, the earnest defense of his sole livelihood, his pigs. It was sheer sentiment that Ingersoll was using, but no other soap was better. It brought the blubber out. He described the desolation and destitution of a fatherless home. Then he pointed to a brighter alternative: the homecoming of a father to his family, the inexpressible happiness of the wife and mother, the laughter of children around the fireside.

Red bandanna handerchiefs were mopping tears thicker than hayseeds out of many a rural Reuben's eyes. The prosecuting attorney was—he admitted it afterwards—bawling like a calf. The jury sent in a vote of acquittal.

Ingersoll's reputation as a speaker grew by leaps and bounds. He steadfastly refused to offer himself for office, being well aware that some people believed him the devil incarnate, with hoofs and horns concealed under a polished exterior. At first a Dougles Democrat, he switched to the support of Lincoln for his second term. The speech he made nominating James G. Blaine for the presidency was considered a masterpiece of its kind, equalled only by Bryan's "Cross of Gold" oration.

When Ingersoll moved to Washington, D. C., in 1877, the people of Peoria first realized how great a figure he had become nationally, and his departure from their midst sincerely saddened them. The mayor of Peoria expressed the sentiments of his fellow townsmen when he said: "During his twenty-five years of life in this city as a neighbor, I can truthfully say that no citizen was more esteemed, none whose views were more sought for, and none who received, whenever he addressed our people, such tokens of public approval . . . Colonel Ingersoll has never spoken in this city without disappointing hundreds who desired to hear him on account of the want of space in the building he spoke in, even when he lectured for charity at a dollar a ticket. The religious views of the colonel I care nothing about; his politics I dislike. But the man himself I admire, honour, and esteem; and such I believe to be the sentiments of nine-tenths of the people of his old home, Peoria. Our great regret is that he has left us."

A bronze monument was erected to Ingersoll at the entrance to one of Peoria's best known parks, in 1911.

Another personality whose actions often created news items for the front page, Carrie Nation, was once invited to be the guest editor of a leading Peoria newspaper for a day, and she was given free rein to voice her strong crusading sentiments against the red demon, whiskey, which was distilled and bottled so extensively in the city. Mrs. Nation accepted the challenge, expressed her viewpoint in pungent editorials, and lectured to a full house at the largest theatre in town. After that she was invited to speak in Pete Wiese's barroom. Her auditors listened attentively between sips. Before she left she expressed disapproval of a picture on the wall exhibiting nude women gamboling among trees. Mr. Wiese promised he would board it up. Later he sent her fifty dollars to help "forward her good work."

The Peoria Corn-and Juice spoon pictures accurately the city's chief industry, the manufacture of corn and rye whiskey. A primitive kind of still is etched in the bowl. The shaft of the handle is formed like a corkscrew, extending from a rather high handle-drop to the caput, which exhibits an unusually large ear of corn, the kind that grows in abundance on the Illinois prairies. Made by Graff, Washbourne & Dunn, this spoon measures 5¾ inches in length.

The second spoon contains, in the bowl, the Peoria County courthouse, a high-domed, cross-shaped structure showing an amalgam of both

Romanesque and Gothic features of late Renaissance styles. The Soldiers and Sailors Monument, erected shortly after the Spanish-American War, appears here in the foreground of the courthouse square.

The caput embodies the state seal of Illinois, a design showing an eagle resting one foot on the national emblem, the other on a boulder; in his beak is a scroll inscribed with "State Sovereignty" and "National Union." The sun is rising beyond the distant prairie horizon. Two ears and a tassel of corn rise above the waist belt in the nave. A cluster of fruit, presumably apples, and a pine tree are shown on the shank.

A product of the Watson Company. Length, 5¼ inches.

No. 53 VENICE ALLIGATOR

The history of Venice, Florida, is a study in antithesis. The witches who visited Macbeth might well have hovered above Venice also at one time or another, and muttered over it their incantation, "Fair is foul, and foul is fair." Seldom has a town presented a more dramatic alternating series of high hopes and grandiose failures than Venice. But more of that later.

The earliest settler in this section of Florida was Jesse Knight, a farmer and part-time Methodist preacher, who brought his bride south from Georgia in 1852, located first near Tampa, and toward the end of the Civil War pushed southward into the wilderness along the West Coast, intent on removing his livestock from the clutches of marauding guerrilla bands. With his family he set out in a numerous caravan of ox-drawn covered wagons, mule-drawn buggies, and a large herd of cattle. Progress through the roadless jungles proceeded at snail's pace. Axes and hacksaws were kept burnished in clearing aside the matted growth of trees and shrubs in many places. When the party neared what is now Shakett Creek, the mules balked at fording the stream. One of the Knight youngsters concocted an ingenious device to change the minds of the "obstropulous critters." Taking two dry deer skins and making wind bags out of them, he popped them together with all the force at his command. The repercussion was louder and much more terrifying than expected. The whole cavalcade of mules and oxen, frightened by this inexplicable charivari, dashed out into the stream beyond their depths at a mad stampeding gallop. Everything behind them was thrown helter-skelter into the water. Some of the wagons capsized, and many of the most precious family possessions were lost.

The journey, thus by accident, had to come to a halt on a spot near what is now Venice Bay. Jesse Knight looked the land over, thought it good, and decided to stay. Before very long, his herd of cattle multiplied from the hundreds into the thousands. Other families, forced by the hardships of Reconstruction days, abandoned the upper Gulf states, and trekking southward, pitched their tents near the Knights.

The little community was long called Horse and Shay, a name acquired from the striking likeness of two palm copses along the coast to this mode of conveyance when seen from vessels sailing on the Gulf. The name stuck in the vernacular of the region, even though the earliest maps designated the settlement as Eyrie. In the eighties, when the first post office was established here, the quaint name of Horse and Shay had to give way to Venice, certainly more reminiscently appropriate to a town surrounded by bayous, bays, and inlets.

The numerous Knights intermarried into almost all the families that entered the locality. Northerners were sprinkled occasionally among the newcomers. One of these, Frank Higel, a Pennsylvanian with a flair for building air castles, interested Hamilton Disston, a Philadelphia tycoon, in a new method for extracting starch from the roots of the cassava, a West Indian plant of the tapioca family. Higel persuaded Disston to devise a machine for the new process and to bring it south with him from Philadelphia for experimental purposes. Higel wrote glowingly of the wonderful climate and fertile soil around Venice: a natural for every kind of tropical plant. He drove north to Tampa, then the southern railroad terminal on the West Coast, to meet Disston and bring him on to Venice for an authentication of the praises hymned by Higel in his epistolary report.

The two men took lodgings for the night in Tampa's best, though unheated, hotel. Higel spoke enthusiastically of south Florida and the vast possibilities of Venice as the hub of an expanding metropolitan area, to be industrialized by Disston's mildewing millions. But the weather on that night of January 10, 1888, acted like a bad, spiteful goddess to sidetrack the well-laid plans of both men. It grew colder by the minute, and flurries of snow whisked through the air. The temperature set an all-time low of 19 degrees for Tampa. Disston was a thin, elderly man, and the cold penetrated to his very marrow-bone. He had no heavy clothing in his grips; so he pulled the carpet off the floor and rolled himself up in it. After a sleepless night, he arose and looked out of his window. The ground was white; a rain barrel was frozen over; and icicles hung glistening from the eaves in the sickly morning sunlight. Disston was miserable—and thoroughly convinced that, if he wanted to get warm again, he would have to return to Philadelphia. And he did, taking his "starch-making machinery" with him. The dream of Venice as a manufacturing center had frozen, melted, and vanished with the icicles.

In the nineties, a New Englander, Joseph H. Lord, attempted to draw fruit growers and retired middle-class people as permanent settlers to the Venice area, but the panic of 1893 and its subsequent depression foiled plans he had blueprinted for making Venice the south Florida citrus center.

238

In 1911 the Seaboard rail lines were extended to Venice—and beyond. In fact they went so far beyond that the irate citizens changed the name of their town to Nokomis. Venice station was a mile away—away down in the jungle and across another bay. That explains the existence of the two towns facing each other across the bay, and the frequent hyphenation of Venice-Nokomis in the matter of schools, churches, banks, and business concerns.

In 1915 Mrs. Potter Palmer announced her intention of building a million-dollar hotel near the Venice shores, but the First World War came along and delayed the immediate construction of the sumptuous edifice. This dream vanished in thin air, for Mrs. Palmer passed away early in 1918.

The first genuine promoters of Venice were Doctor and Mrs. Fred H. Albee, who in 1916 came from Maine for a stay of only eight days, yet within that brief period of time they were so completely enthralled by the wonderful climate and the wild jungle beauty of the area that they decided to buy a bit of property here. Strangely enough, they were given the option of buying all the land within the "cities of Venice and Nokomis." They took it. Mrs. Albee, in her book *The Doctor and I,* offers an interesting account of their pioneering days. "How well I recall our first visit to Nokomis!" she says. "We found nothing there but palmetto land, cabbage palms and beautiful pine trees, and the remnants of an old stockade. The same old well which was in use at the stockade is still furnishing water to our first venture in building—an inn we named 'Pollyanna Inn.' . . . A short distance away was an old shelter, called the *Nokomis Railroad Station.* At Venice, the railroad station was an old freight car at the end of the railroad where the train turned at the Y, ready for the return trip. There was but one small store and the post-office which was across the street from the 'station,' serving about forty families scattered here and there, in Nokomis—and conditions were somewhat the same in Venice." The Albees put up several other buildings in the locality. Gradually other people moved in, many of them with grandiose ideas for placing Venice on the map.

But the most breath-taking scheme for making Venice live up to its name and be the West Coast counterpart of Miami got under way in 1925. The development was financed by the Brotherhood of Locomotive Engineers of America. Three sumptuous hotels were built, not to mention those costing under a million; many beautiful private villas—all in the authentic Venetian style—were erected amid spacious landscaped surroundings; a commercial emporium sprang up; avenues lined with acacias or palms were projected far out into the wilds; a Gulf beach was widened, and a bathhouse casino was "almost finished." Several thousand workmen were on the payrolls of the developing company. Some of the highest-priced orchestras in America were playing nightly in the dining rooms and dance halls of Venice. Truly, Venice was to be—in Byron's words—

> . . . as a fairy city of the heart;
> Rising like water-columns from the sea,
> Of joy the sojourn, and of wealth the mart.

The picture which Byron also painted of Brussels on the eve of the battle of Waterloo might be transferred corporeally to the canvas that was Venice in those days:

> There was a sound of revelry by night . . .
> And all went merry as a marriage bell . . .
> On with the dance! let joy be unconfined . . .

Suddenly the time-clock stopped ticking at Venice. The Brotherhood had run out of funds, and any further development was out of the question. All the millions had been spent, and no more were forthcoming. Venice was like a floundering, pestilence-ridden ship from which all the rats that had lately been gnawing holes in her sides scurried as fast as their legs could carry them.

Then for years Venice lay there: a derelict vessel, a ghost town, a deserted village, the biggest boom-time flop in the annals of American real-estate history.

But she still retained the spark of life in her vitals. She lay gasping a long time before catching a second wind. Slowly she began to revive

Like a phoenix Venice has risen anew, And is growing again. There is a lively tourist trade. Many a wayfarer, coming for a transient stay of two or three weeks, has been fascinated by the historical associations of the place, and decided to stay the remainder of a lifetime. The Kentucky Military Institute has made Venice its winter headquarters since 1933. The scars of the "Great Fiasco" have healed. The foul has become permanently fair for the outlook of Venice, and perhaps, after all, the aperçu on the Old-World city may ring equally true for its New-World namesake: "Men built Rome—the gods, Venice."

The spoon representing this town is one that has been used occasionally by other places along the lower Gulf, especially by New Orleans. But of no place is the alligator more symbolic than of Venice. The Myakka River, not ten miles away, is a natural haunt of this creature. At one time the Myakka, offering scenery that might be mistaken for the Amazon or the Congo jungles, was literally swarming with alligators, many of them mammoth in size.

The entire handle of this spoon shows, on both obverse and reverse sides, an old 'gator crawling along, with jaws half-open as if ready to tear into some succulent morsel of meat.

The trademark of the maker does not appear on the spoon. Length is 5½ inches.

No. 54 SEQUOYAH

In 1876 Fred Harvey, the man who "made the desert blossom with a beefsteak," established his first Eating House on the Atchison, Topeka and Santa Fe Railroad at Topeka, Kansas. His dollar dinner, which included an appetizingly broiled steak and all the accessories necessary for a good meal, was so successful that a series of Harvey Houses soon flanked the railroad line at regular intervals throughout the West. Cold, greasy box lunches fell into the limbo of gladly-forgotten things.

In addition to the first-class eating service rendered by his hostelries, Mr. Harvey planned these stopping-places architecturally so that they would have some historical significance in keeping with the region in which they were located. Near the Grand Canyon he built the Hopi and El Tovar; in Albuquerque, the Alvarado, represented in this book by a spoon; La Fonda, in Santa Fe; El Navajo, at Gallup. Spanish conquistadores such as Cárdenas and Castañeda, missionaries like Fray Marcos, and Indians like Sequoyah are everywhere commemorated in concrete, stucco, and stone structures of imposing dimensions.

Near the western confines of Kansas, in the high-plains country where trees are esteemed for their rarity, lies Syracuse, a town which has become, according to the Kansas American State Guide Book, a "cool, green oasis" to the people of the surrounding country because of its systematic planting and careful nurturing of parks and streets graced by a variety of tall, shady trees. The Harvey Eating House and Depot of the Atchison, Topeka and Santa Fe Railroad, erected out of concrete at a cost of $75,000, was called the Sequoyah, in memory of the Cherokee Cadmus who sojourned here a while with some Indians camping in the area.

Sequoyah, who devised a written language for the Cherokee Indians by a method entirely of his own invention, is perhaps best remembered by the fact that his name was given to the giant redwood trees that grow to such immense heights in the forests of the Pacific Coast.

One of the really great figures produced by the North American Indians, Sequoyah, or Sikwayi, known sometimes by the name of George Gist, was the son of a Cherokee squaw and a Pennsylvania-Dutch father. He was born about 1770 in that mountain-forest section of east Tennessee not far from the North Carolina border.

At an early age he began to exhibit an unusual talent for painting and carving. On stones, trees, and ceremonial robes he depicted the great events of Cherokee history as he heard them related around the campfires. He ornamented silver arm bands, gorgets, earrings, and brooches with exquisite designs. He inlaid tomahawks, wampums, moccasins, and belts with such consummate skill of execution that some members of his tribe attributed his ingenuity to magical sources. Begging a white man to write

"Gist" for him, he etched his autograph together with a rhododendron blossom on each piece of work that he did.

During the War of 1812 Sequoyah served as a private for two years in a company of mounted Cherokees and participated in the Battle of the Horseshoe, which dealt a crushing blow to the fractious Creeks. It is thought that the lameness he suffered in after-life resulted from this battle. Not long after his discharge from the army he married Sally, a woman described as "affable, pleasant, talkative, who spoke the English language fluently . . . was a good housekeeper, and had a loom." Nevertheless, she had little sympathy for, or any understanding of, her husband's artistic nature, considering his creative efforts a waste of time.

One day Sequoyah heard some warriors speak of the white man's system of communication by means of the "talking leaves" as sorcery, a gift from the Great Spirit that gave the whites superiority over the redskins. Sequoyah claimed that the Cherokees could likewise transmit their thoughts on paper if some one only invented the right system, and he asserted a belief in his own ability to figure out such a system. His listeners jeered at his pretensions, saying he had lost his reason.

But Sequoyah was never disheartened by ridicule. Over and over he said to himself, "I know I can make characters which may be understood. The white man is no magician. A white man named Moses made marks upon stones and for many generations his marks have been understood."

So Sequoyah set to work making scratches on stones. Soon he found out it would be easier to experiment on pieces of birch bark. He made a list of two thousand characters, each representing a distinct word, and still there remained a large vocabulary for which he had designed no characters. Now he realized he was on the wrong track, that his system was too rudimentary and cumbersome. He was forgetting some of his earlier signs already. His process would tax the memory beyond the bounds of reasonable perseverance.

He discarded this method and started on a new one. He traded a silver brooch, simulating an ear of corn, for an English speller and examined the strange letters in the book very carefully. He used wrapping paper this time instead of bark for his writing. He had no idea what those distinctive figures meant but he appropriated all of them, and still many sounds were unrecorded. So he turned some of them upside down, reversed others, and combined several in slight variations. What labor, but also what zest, this Indian who had never gone to school a day in his life put into his task!

The result was a syllabary rather than an alphabet, as each figure stood for a definite sound rather than a single letter. His auditory sense was not too keenly developed, and certain sibilant sounds gave him trouble. His wife, having no patience for his nonsensical obsession, would not assist him; so he called upon Eye-o-kah, his six-year-old daughter, for aid. The child exhibited an eager interest, and even suggested changes that would

242

simplify the system. He reduced the number of his figures from two hundred to eighty-six.

After two years of experimentation he had just about finished his work when his wife, becoming angered at his apparent waste of time with such tomfoolery, burnt all his papers. His enthusiasm was not dampened by her wanton act of destruction. "It must be done over," he said. Within a year he had rewritten all his symbols and even made some improvements.

A glance at the chart of his alphabet shows his complete ignorance of English. The A stood for the sound *go*, the H for *mi*, the W for *la*, the K for *tso*, the T for *i*, the R for an *e*, and the D for an *a*.

All during the time that he was so deeply engrossed in his work, his friends remonstrated with him that he was wasting his time and being looked upon as a fool. But Sequoyah replied to each adverse criticism by tersely saying: "If our people think I am making a fool of myself, you may tell our people that what I am doing will not make fools of them. They did not cause me to begin, and they shall not cause me to stop. Even though I am less respected, what I am doing will make our people more respected by others. So I shall go on, and you may tell our people."

Carefully he taught each letter to little Eye-o-kah till she could pronounce even those words of which she did not know the meanings. She learned to write any dictation which was given to her and could read anything her father wrote. The system, devised strictly according to sound, was actually superior to the white man's alphabet!

Now came the great trial before an assembly of Sequoyah's tribesmen. Eye-o-kah was placed at a distance from the meeting while Sequoyah wrote down whatever words or sentences he was bidden to write. Then the girl was called back to read what had been written.

After three days of this testing the tribe was fully convinced there was no trickery in Sequoyah's method. The young people became frenzied with excitement, and the forest reverberated with the echoes of their applause.

Everyone, young and old, wanted to learn. Enthusiasm waxed high for the "talking leaves." Gone were the jeers of ridicule, and forgotten the incredulity. The "Great Master" was besieged by a flock of students, and other pursuits were neglected by them for this thrilling preoccupation. Nearly every Cherokee in the reservation became literate in a short while. Paper being scarce, the fascinating art of writing was practiced on trees and rocks.

A Moravian missionary who witnessed the reception given to Sequoyah's syllabary describes it thus: "The alphabet was instantly recognized as an invaluable invention for the elevation of the tribe, and in a little over a year, thousands of hitherto illiterate Cherokees were to read and write their own language, teaching each other in cabins or by the roadside. The whole nation became an academy for the study of the system. Letters were written back and forth between the Cherokees in the east and those who had emigrated to the lands in Arkansas." The language was set for type, textbooks were written, large portions of the Bible were translated and printed, and a national newspaper, the *Cherokee Phoenix*, started publication. A code of laws, modeled after the United States constitution, was drawn up for governing the tribes of the Cherokee nation.

Honors were heaped upon Sequoyah. The Government granted him an annual stipend to further the work of education among his people. He was invited to Washington, where he was received by President John Quincy Adams, and his portrait painted by Charles Bird King. On the streets of the capital he was scrutinized closely by the curious, and much discussed. When he was signally honored with the presentation of a medal by a formal convocation of his own people, he was moved to shed unrestrained tears.

In 1828 Sequoyah left Georgia and moved to Arkansas to teach the Cherokees there his system of writing. Everywhere he was acclaimed, admired, and revered. John Howard Payne, the author of "Home Sweet Home," went to Arkansas to secure a history of the Cherokees from Sequoyah. He describes an interview: "We were all in the cockloft of a story-and-a-half log house where the light and wind entered through a thousand chinks. Guess (Sequoyah) sat in one corner of the fireplace and I on the opposite side at a desk; the other two between. Guess had a turban of roses and posies upon a white ground girding his venerable gray hairs; a long, dark blue robe, bordered around the lower edge and the cuffs with black; a blue and minutely checked calico tunic under it—the tunic open at the breast and its collar apart with a twisted handkerchief flung around his neck. He wore plain buckskin leggings. One of his legs is lame and shrunken. His moccasins were unornamented buckskin. He had a long dusky bag of sumac with him and a long Indian pipe, which he smoked incessantly, replenishing his pipe from his bag. His air was altogether what we picture to ourselves of an old Greek philosopher. He talked and gesticulated very gracefully, his voice alternately swelling and then sinking to a whisper, and his eye firing up and then subsiding into a gentle and most benignant smile. Before long, poor I seemed entirely forgotten by the rest of the audience. First, one quarter of an hour, then another; and then another went by, and no translation came." Payne never did get a rendering of this story, which had spellbound his interpreter.

Samuel Knapp, who prepared a lecture on Sequoyah, says: "His disposition is more lively than that of any Indian I ever saw . . . I have seldom met a man of more shrewdness than See-quah-yah . . . he passes from metaphysical and philosophical investigation to mechanical occupations with the greatest ease." Knapp tells how Sequoyah also created a set of numerals, along with fractions, up to a million, whereas the Cherokees hitherto had numbers only up to a hundred.

Sequoyah died in Mexico in 1843, while he was on one of his frequent trips in search of Cherokees who had wandered off to distant parts and consequently lost all connection with the main body of the tribe. The Cherokee nation, in consideration of Sequoyah's eminent cultural services to the tribe, granted a pension to his widow. "This," says Grant Foreman, "was probably the first literary pension in American history."

Scholarly research ascribes the paternity of Sequoyah to Nathaniel Gist, who lived for years among the Cherokees till he entered the Revolutionary Army. The high esteem in which he was held might be gathered from this remark by an old chief that Colonel Gist "might sit down on Great Island (Tennessee) where he pleased, as it belonged to him and them to hold good talks upon." Gist married a white woman after the War. One of his daughters married a U. S. senator from Kentucky; another, the editor of a Washington newspaper; and a third, one of the leading citizens of Lexington. Of Gist's grandchildren, one sat in Lincoln's cabinet; another was a brigadier-general in the Civil War. Two other grandsons were candidates for vice-president. John Mason Brown, Louisville lawyer and descendant of Gist, states that Sequoyah visited his Kentucky relatives on his return from Washington in 1828.

In 1905 the people of Indian Territory voted by a 47,000 majority for statehood in the Union, the new state to be named Sequoyah. But this proposal was rejected in Washington and the Territory was joined to Oklahoma shortly afterwards. The memory of Sequoyah has been perpetuated, however, in other ways. The Sequoyah Shrine in Oklahoma preserves his old home. A statue of him stands in the National Capitol at Washington, and two others near his old home in Georgia.

It is altogether fitting that one of the Harvey Houses should bear his name in tribute. The façade of the Sequoyah building in Syracuse is rather delicately engraved on the bowl of this particular spoon. The tracks of the Atchison, Topeka and Santa Fe are visible in front of the depot.

The handle pictures realistically a big ear of Kansas corn bursting out of its shuck.

The Sequoyah spoon was pressed by Watson and Newell. Length, 6 inches.

No. 55 SARASOTA ALLIGATOR

The Indians must have loved the land of Sarasota if the numerous burial mounds they left may be taken as a testimonial of their affection. Some of these mounds upon excavation have yielded as many as three hundred skeletons. The early inhabitants of the area belonged either to the Timucuan or Caloosa tribes, the two being closely enough related to understand each other's speech. They lived in simple palm-thatched huts of wood, raised fields of corn, made excellent pottery, and traded extensively with other Indians as remote as the Mayas of Mexico.

The early Spanish explorers tended to by-pass this region because they could find nothing but brackish water hereabouts. Hernando de Soto, whose name is thought to have some garbled connection with Sarasota, skirted the Gulf coast in 1539, came ashore, harried the Indians to find out where their gold was hidden, pilfered and burned their villages, and left a wide wake of ill will behind him. Legend gives him a daughter, Sara de Soto, passionately loved by Chichi-Okobee, an Indian warrior of princely rank. When the maiden sickened and died, the prince conveyed her body in a funeral cortege escorted by one hundred warriors in as many canoes to the center of Sarasota Bay. There, after the body had been lowered to the waves, Chichi-Okobee gave a signal, the warriors slashed holes in the canoes with their tomahawks, and, with a solemn requiem chant on their lips, vanished beneath the brine, to be henceforth a bodyguard for the lovely Sara de Soto, now transformed into a mermaid-princess in the lucent depths of the sun-kissed sapphire bay.

Some say that De Soto has no bearing on the genesis of Sarasota's name. Certainly he deserves no credit, and it was two full centuries after his death before Porte Sarasote appeared on a Spanish map, in 1768. On an English map appearing in 1794 the area is designated as Sara Zota.

By the time young Bill Whitaker and his half-brother, H. V. Snell, pushed into Sarasota Bay in 1842 in the *Lovinia,* a sailboat named in honor of their mother, the area had long been called Sarasota by the Cuban fishermen who came and went at will as transient squatters.

Snell went back to his family in Tallahassee after this exploratory trip, but Whitaker like the region and stayed on. In the course of time he acquired nearly two hundred acres of land fronting on the bay, weathered the terrific hurricane of '48, planted an orange grove, built himself a comfortable cabin, and fetched himself a very pretty wife from up the coast near Manatee. His marriage to Mary Jane Wyatt was no hap-hazard, rough-and-ready pioneer match. He had had his eye set on Mary Jane even before she was sent North to a finishing school for young ladies near Louisville, Kentucky. When she came back, she knew what the refinements of civilization meant. The offspring from this marriage reached eleven in number. The oldest of these, Nancy Catherine Stuart Whitaker, born in 1852, was the first white child born in Sarasota County. The other ten children following rapidly were apportioned only one name each.

Numerous homesteaders moved in after the Civil War, and formed settlements at Osprey, Laurel, Venice, Bee Ridge, Fruitville, and Myakka. One family, the Webbs, built an addition onto their house for the express purpose of taking in "winter boarders," who they hoped might come South in response to an ad which they placed in Northern papers modestly extrolling the   climate.

This gradual colonization was proceeding pleasantly until 1883, when something happened that threw the whole section into a turmoil. Shady dealings in the Florida legislature led to the sale of millions of acres of land to big capitalists, the reason being given ostensibly to pay off the state debt. Hamilton Disston alone bought four million acres of land at twenty-five cents an acre. Other huge chunks went for as little to other land corporations. About ninety per cent of the area in Sarasota County was swallowed up in these mysterious transactions.

Many of the homesteaders did not hold papers for their land grants. Some were squatters who had settled on unoccupied land and later filed claims that had not yet come through. No actual surveys had ever been made, and no blue prints existed to show where the exact boundaries lay. Now it seemed as if many would be dispossessed of their holdings. Land agents of the big speculators appeared in the vicinity of Sarasota and made it clear they wished to oust the small fry from their tenure.

Early in 1884 one of the homesteaders, Jason Alford, was arrested on a trumped-up charge of stealing a cow. In reality, his farm was obstructing an outlet to the bay for the speculators. At his trial Alford not only proved his innocence in the theft but also showed papers for the ownership of his coveted tract of land. He was acquitted, but the situation did not clear up. Instead, the pressure to evict the settlers became more intense.

Then in June there occurred a murder. Tip Riley was shot and his throat cut after he fell from the pony he was riding. Suspicions were rife, but nobody was arrested. Two days after Christmas the postmaster, Charles E. Abbé, was shot while coming from his orange grove near the bayshore. The gunman was seen this time, and it was not long until he and nineteen other men were apprehended. They all belonged to a secret society of Vigilantes.

The trial of the Vigilantes at the backwoods courthouse of Pine Level aroused sufficient interest to draw reporters from the big-city newspapers, which carried accounts of the trial in front-page columns. Three men were sentenced to be hanged. A second trial changed the punishment to life imprisonment. At a third trial four more men were given sentences of life imprisonment. Eventually they were all pardoned or escaped from prison through the connivance of friends.

The real reason for the two murders was never brought out during the trials. But it was evident that Riley and Abbé had both been acting in the interests of the "land grabbers." They had been quietly surveying the property of the homesteaders with "stepping-off" measurements. When this fact became known to their neighbors, the two men were doomed to die.

Out of this unhealthy speculation in Florida land did come, however, some tangible good. The Florida Mortgage and Investment Company, a British corporation, sent out a shipload of Scotchmen to found a town on Sarasota Bay. The new immigrants soon became disgusted with the proposition. Nothing had been prepared before their arrival, and when they were crowded into a ramshackle fish-shed, their dismay knew no bounds. Some slept on the ground under canvas awnings. Cooking was done in the open over campfires. To add to the discontent a severe cold spell set in. Even a little snow fell. At a Sunday service, when the passage "All we like sheep have gone astray" was read, the congregation involuntarily groaned out of utter misery.

The unseasonably cold weather, then mosquitoes, snakes, and the isolation from the common comforts of life all sufficed to make the Scots pull up stakes and embark on the first boats they could catch heading North. This first attempt to establish a town proved to be a dismal fiasco.

The Florida Mortgage and Investment Company soon sent out another Scotchman to promote their interests in laying out a town site. Their agent was John Hamilton Gillespie, a man who looked on life with such a rose-colored optimism that he succeeded in his own estimation even when his failures were most apparent to others. He built a hotel—on the company's money, of course—that was closed most of the time for lack of clientele. He measured off streets and cleared paths for sidewalks— which straightway grew up in weeds. He brought in construction crews that boomed the building of houses and stores. An artesian well was drilled at the convergence of five streets, the hub of the town, and a makeshift pier projected out over the bay. Gillespie started an experimental farm on the poorest land in the county—the experiments were fantastic, the results ludicrous. He interested a railroad company in building tracks from Bradentown (now Bradenton) to Sarasota. The one train that operated, called the "Slow and Wobbly," was an utter flop from the first. It seldom started on time and never reached its destination on time. The engineer and conductor followed no set schedule, and pulled out only when they had sufficient freight to pay for the costs of the trip. When the railroad company fell into arrears on tax bills, a court injunction chained the wheels of the engine to the tracks till the delinquent taxes were paid. After three years the anemic railroad gave up the ghost without benefit of tears.

J. Hamilton Gillespie, son of the high-born Sir John Gillespie, brought with him from Scotland a wife whose behavior was most unorthodox. She became famous for her ability to down more liquor than any man in town. One Sunday when Gillespie was preaching in the community hall, Mrs. Gillespie, more obfuscated than usual, staggered into a front pew, opened a scarlet sunshade, and wagged it rakishly over her head. When the service was over, she folded her sunshade, rose, fluttered a green handkerchief in congratulations (or farewell, perhaps) to her husband in the pulpit, burped, and oscillated toward the exit.

The pious Gillespie sought to establish an Episcopal church in Sarasota. He invited the bishop to come from Jacksonville and look the situation over. At a dinner, matters were proceeding decorously, when Mrs. Gillespie entered and stumbled into the waiter who was carrying a tureen of soup to the table. The contents of the bowl splashed into the lap of the bishop, who hastily left the table—and Sarasota. Soon Gillespie and wife also vanished from the scene. Several years later he returned, minus wife.

To Gillespie goes the credit for introducing the game of golf to Florida. He began by building first a four-hole, then a nine-hole course. The Scotch game grew so greatly in popularity that other Florida cities called upon him to lay out courses for them. Eventually golf became one of the main drawing attractions for tourists, and in this particular realm of sport Gillespie was an outstanding success. He died of a heart attack, in 1923, while playing golf.

The coming of Mrs. Potter Palmer to Sarasota in 1911 was a big event. She bought 26,000 acres and developed it under expert supervision into the flourishing Palmer Farms, from which large quantities of winter celery are now being shipped annually to all points of the nation.

During the Florida boom of 1924-26 Sarasota developed into a favorite winter resort for the increasing number of tourists. Many modern hotels were built, beautiful homes sprang up around the bay, and recreational centers were created, most of them aimed to draw and hold a well-to-do, middle-class clientele.

The Ringlings, of circus fame, began coming to Sarasota as early as 1912 for the winter One after the other, the five brothers built pretentious mansions, which eventually became their permanent, all-the-year-round homes. In 1927, just after the big boom had burst, the winter headquarters for the Ringling Circus were moved to Sarasota. In 1931 the John and Mable Ringling Museum of Art was opened to the public. This, the "little Louvre of America," contains the finest collection of Rubens paintings in the world. Other painters represented are Rembrandt, Frans Hals, Van Dyke, Lucas Cranach, Raphael, Titian, Filippo Lippi, El Greco, Goya, and Murillo—seven hundred priceless paintings, all originals, by the greatest masters in the world. In 1946 the Ca de Zan, home of the John Ringlings and a replica of the Doge's palace in Venice, Italy, was made accessible to visitors as a museum.

A jungle-gardens, a reptile farm, Lido Beach, famed for its white sand, and the Myakka State Park are other notable allurements for tourists. The Sara de Soto Fiesta is the crowning highlight of the winter season, drawing annually about a hundred thousand spectators.

Few places in the world are as colorfully enticing as Sarasota, especially when blizzardy blasts are sweeping over a cold, barren North. Is it surprising that poets are constrained to rhapsodize over the witchery of its wonders?

> Sarasota! Something magic
>   Forms a compact with the name,
> Banishing the trite and tragic,
>   Setting fantasy aflame.

All the myriad scenes of story
Favored by a fervid sun
Somehow find their gilded glory
Here star-mirrored all in one!
Dreaming, charming, smiling, gay . . .
Sarasota by the Sapphire Bay.

The Sarasota Alligator spoon has a plain bowl, except for the simple engraving of the town's designation through its center. The shank of the handle represents the slender trunk of a palmetto, the tufted crown of which is clutched rather closely by a sinuous alligator.

The reverse of handle is unadorned except for the trademark of the manufacturers, Watson and Newell. The length of spoon is 6¼ inches.

No. 56 ORANGE-O'-TEXAS

The story of Orange runs true to the form that characterizes most of the up-and-coming cities of Texas, a state that has gathered unto itself the finest blend of intrepid pioneer spirits ever to come larruping into one bailiwick from all the crossroad-junctions of the nation.

When Jean Laffitte, the pirate, sailed up the Sabine River, on the banks of which the city of Orange now stands, he saw that it was just the place for his headquarters, because it could easily be defended by means of a few accessible approaches. Some of the French seamen in Lafitte's outfit, attracted by the possibilities of trade with the Indians, stayed on and began to bargain profitably with members of the Attacapas tribe for the furs furnished by the mink, muskrat, weasel, raccoon, and fox that abounded here. The aristocratic ladies of the French court at Versailles attended many a gala ball adorned in capes dangling with the tails of foxes that once ran at liberty in this region.

For half a century the French plied this lucrative trade, until the Spaniards, casting envious eyes at French prosperity, moved in and attempted to gobble up the fur monopoly. But they could not digest their ill-gotten advantage. The Indians, feeling themselves looked down upon as a slave-race, were not amenable to the looting tactics of the Spaniards, and the profitable fur industry soon died an unnatural death.

In the early part of the nineteenth century long-shanked, rifle-toting American pioneers, realizing the states along the Eastern seaboard were becoming too thickly populated for good hunting and trapping, began to drift in and beyond this bayou country. Most of them passed on through, but one of them, John Harmon, needing fresh meat, roped his barge to a cypress stump, disembarked, and in no time secured for himself a savory diet of venison and wild turkey. Instead of proceeding toward the Western plains, he anchored himself to a twelve-thousand-acre land grant bordering on the banks of the Sabine River. He prospered until the Civil War came

250

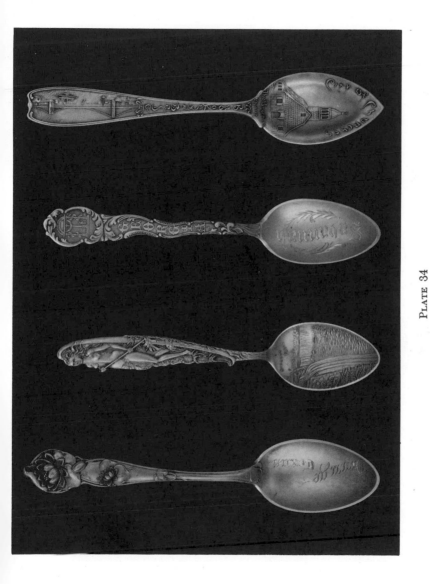

Plate 34

56. ORANGE-O'-TEXAS   57. MAID AND CANOE   58. HISTORIC SAVANNAH
59. BROOKLYN BRIDGE

PLATE 35

60. LEWIS CASS   61. ALVARADO   62. LAST SACRIFICE   63. WASHINGTON'S TOMB

along, when, just at the wrong time, he sold his entire tract for fifty cents an acre—payable in Confederate bills. Shortly after, he consigned the bundle of worthless bills to the muddy current of the river, and departed belatedly for the Western plains. His holdings had covered some of the most valuable industrial sections of present-day Orange.

It was not enough that the expanding prosperity of Orange should have been blighted by the holocaust of fire during the War. In 1865, just at the end of the conflict, a terrific hurricane swept in from the Gulf and demolished the very few houses still standing unscorched. There was nothing to salvage. Guerrillas were rampant. All signs of community life had vanished.

Slowly and painfully a new village built itself on the site of the old. By 1881 there were enough people in Orange to justify reincorporation. Lumber mills were beginning to spew sawdust again. Cotton, rice, and cattle raising were bringing life back to war-shorn plantations.

The great era of expanding activities was not to come till after World War I, at which time the river approaches to Orange were deepened, so that ocean-going vessels could dock at the very threshold of the city.

The transformation of Orange from a small town to a booming industrial city is one of the miracles of American ingenuity. The census of 1940 listed 7,500 people in Orange. But the impact of newly-born industries sent the population up like heated mercury. By 1945 more than 50,000 people were living within the city limits, and the housing problems were disposed of successfully and in short shrift by adroit planning and a firm grasp of the situation.

A few of Orange's industries antedate the war. The Weaver Shipyards have been constructing tugs, dredges, barges, scows, and cabin boats since 1898. Weaver dredges have cleared the inland waterways along most of the Gulf-State coasts. Of the more recent industries, the most important are those engaged in shipbuilding. Others are connected with the manufacturing of steel; the production of nylon, pulp, kraft paper, and creosote; the making of oxygen and acetylene gases; rice milling; and the canning of many truck-garden vegetables. About 30,000 head of cattle, mostly Brahman and Shorthorn, find pasturage on 93,000 acres of farm land in Orange County. Sixty gas fields are close enough to supply all the needs for the homes and commercial plants of Orange. Certainly a city of the future, and one to watch!

The Orange-O'-Texas spoon is heavily made, but stately in appearance. The entire spoon, on both obverse and reverse sides, is gold-washed; few are so richly bedight with that coloring. The name of the town is carved in Gothic script in the bowl.

The handle contains three waterlilies in three successive stages of growth. Toward the end of the shank is a bud with a long, oniony stem running downward to the handle-drop, which displays only a single leaf-pad without flower but with curlecue attached. In the nave the blossom has become more expansive, while the specimen in the caput, in unusually high relief, flaunts a full-blown efflorescence. A leaf-pad is folded over to form a hood in the finial. The waterlily, so typical of bayou country, is quite appropriate for this city, although orange blossoms might have been more in keeping with the name. It should be mentioned here that John Harmon interested himself in the raising of oranges, and groves of that fruit once flourished where large industrial plants now stand.

The reverse of handle has lily petioles gracefully thumbing their way along the entire periphery. The trademark of Watson and Newell, the naval code flag, would place the manufacture of this spoon prior to 1909. Length is 6 inches.

No. 57 MAID AND CANOE
No. 62 LAST SACRIFICE

Many years before the sound of woodman's ax broke the solitude of the forests, the ceaseless roar of the cataract at Niagara boomed through the woodlands to warn the Indians that a mighty spirit dwelt within those charging convolutions calling hoarsely, tumultuously, for propitiation and sacrifice. And whenever the children of the forest listened intently, they understood clearly that the choicest treasure desired, indeed demanded, by the Spirit's loudly intoned mutterings was the tribe's most peerless specimen of maidenhood.

Among the Senecas the nonpareil of maidens was Wenolah, the laughing, bright-eyed daughter of the stalwart sachem, Kwasind. Her cheeks had the healthy glow of leaves when first tinged by the scarlet brush of autumn; her lips were of a "tempting ruddy hue like mountain berries gleaming fair;" and her laughter, which scattered the sunshine of gladness around her, was like the purling cadence of brooks at play in leafy dells. But there was a more serious side to Wenolah's nature. As the only child of a widowed father, she found her greatest happiness in tending to his daily wants, and avoided all prospective suitors who would entice her from his side.

A council of warriors had gathered around the campfire. From their pipe bowls rose clouds of circling smoke, and they sat hunched up there for a long while, silent, smoking contentedly.

Then the tranquil hush was broken by the voice of Meda, the medicine man. He noted the need of food by every one in the tribe, and compared this present dearth with the full measure of former days. What had become of the fish and the deer? What had caused the maize to mildew in the ear? Why had the berries and wild grapes withered ere they ripened?

Slowly he spoke that his words might redound to their greatest effect. With deliberate cunning had he devised this oration, ever since the merry Wenolah had spurned him and his canting profession of love when they were alone together in the forest.

254

A vengeful spleen entered his soul as he spoke, though it was not apparent on the surface of his words: "Seneca warriors! Are you aware that the autumn has rolled around twice and left you nothing but blighted corn? And it threatens to happen again! The red deer are vanishing before your eyes! The wild geese no longer call from the fenlands! The trout yield becomes scantier day by day! Why hesitate longer to speak your minds when the food is being snatched from your mouths! Why, I ask you, is this so? Listen, and I will tell you. While I lay in troubled slumber, the Spirit of the Waters cloaked in his mantle of cloudy mist visited me, asking: 'Why do my children wish to avoid me? Once they brought me the best offerings to be found among their maidens, even the rarest sacrifice of a sachem's daughter! Hath prosperity undermined that faith? Yea, the bony claws of Famine shall reach out over the Senecas— and, I duly warn, the tribal race shall perish! Tarry not!' Thus I saw it. I have spoken."

When the speaker ended, there was a silence. A chill foreboding ran through the whole crowd huddled around the campfire. The old beliefs that had lain smouldering in ashes for so many years were relighted in their breasts by Meda's revealing dream.

Instinctively all eyes were fixed upon the visage of Kwasind, the strong, proud and courageous sachem who had never faltered on the battlefield or failed to make the final decision at a council meeting. For a while he sat mute, impassive, his features like "carved lines of chiselled stone." Then slowly rising, he crossed his arms across his breast, lifted his face toward the stars, and uttered his fateful decision. His pride had conquered his disbelief.

When Kwasind left the assembly, his heart was beating wildly. He was angry and bitter, but he suppressed his true feelings and went forthwith to apprise Wenolah of the tragic doom that awaited her. He advised her to look with courage and resignation upon her sacrifice as a noble act that would benefit her people and cast everlasting lustre upon her name—and his!

But in the quietude of night he could not sleep. His thoughts waxed rebellious; again and again he found himself uttering imprecations at the man who had conjured up this frightful vision; stronger and fiercer grew the conviction that this artificer of dreams must die. When his thoughts reverted to his daughter, the beauty and innocence of her person recalled the gentle mother who had been so ruthlessly murdered by a sneaking, sniveling band of marauders almost at the same age her daughter had now attained. He would have retreated from his decision and fled with this child of his bosom if his sense of pride had not impelled him to stay. He could not permit the branding stigma of cowardice to rest upon his fair name.

The time passed gloomily for Kwasind. But Wenolah deported herself in a cheerful and dignified manner. She did not seem to be grieving nor steeling her mind for the coming ordeal. The village was stirred momentarily by the death of the villainous Meda, whose lifeless body was discovered one morning, a knife-blade planted in his heart. The finding of his murderer was quickly thrust into the background by the urgent preparations for the momentous pilgrimage to the Falls.

It was a panorama of wild, incomparable beauty that lay before the expectant watchers ranged on the cliffs above the cataract. A harvest moon cast its golden effulgence over the foaming waves that scampered along, crisscrossing and tumbling over each other, riotously singing. Nearer, the Falls boomed and bellowed like a juggernaut, blind, blatant, and belligerent.

Hark, there is a shout! Then a hush. All eyes are strained toward a will-o'-the-wispish point of white. A slender birch canoe dartles about among the waves. On closer approach Wenolah is seen standing steadily in that frail bark, her hands clasped, her hair streaming in the winds behind her.

But lo! a startling surprise greets the eyes of the gaping spectators. A second canoe leaps and lurches in the onrushing cascade of waters. A cry bursts from all throats, "It is Kwasind!" It was indeed the heroic father who could not endure the thought that his daughter must go to her death alone. Together the two passed into the bourne of that mystic world from which no traveler has ever returned to tell us about.

This legend, retold here from William Trumbull's poem, "The White Canoe," has also inspired painters and musicians. J. F. Brown has painted two pictures, one depicting the final scene as reproduced in the bowl of the Last Sacrifice spoon. Here, the maid is seen on the verge of the falls and her father's shallop appears at a slight distance in the background.

The Falls are limned in the caput, which is surmounted by a border beaded at the apex and gadrooned farther down. In the shank are delineated the Whirlpool Rapids and alongside it, a short extension of railway. On the reverse of handle stands an Indian in full-feathered head-dress, with bow and arrows in his left hand. He is shading his eyes with his right hand. The provenience of this spoon is not known, no trademark being evident. Length is 5¾ inches. Used through the kind permission of its owner, Mrs. Alyse D. Westbrook, Hayward, California.

Wenolah and her white birch canoe form almost the entire picture on the Maid and Canoe spoon. The Falls are etched in the bowl. On the back of the handle the waves are more visible than on the front side. A product controlled by the Deacon Jewelry Co. of Los Angeles, California. Length, 5¼ inches.

No. 58 HISTORIC SAVANNAH

The colonial history of Georgia started at Savannah, and the founding of Savannah may well be called the first social welfare project started in the New World. The promoter of this humanitarian enterprise, James

Edward Oglethorpe, member of Parliament and officer in the British army, was moved to try his social experiment in America after learning of the mistreatment of prisoners in England: a friend of his had been thrown into a debtor's prison and, because he would not pay his jailer a bribe, was forced to live among some convicts suffering from smallpox. The unfortunate man contracted the disease and died, leaving a wife and three children without means of subsistence.

Oglethorpe, as chairman of the investigating committee, found conditions deplorable in these debtors' prisons. And he also found out that many of the incarcerated people were there for debts amounting to only a few dollars. Once impounded, they remained often for uncounted years, neglected and forgotten. After a great deal of discussion, Oglethorpe and his fellow-philanthropists conceived what they thought to be the wisest plan for bettering the lot of these helpless wretches. England at this time was not on very friendly terms with Spain, both countries striving to attain the dominant position in the New World. To the south of the English colonies lay Florida, a Spanish stronghold. When Oglethorpe petitioned George II for a charter to lands north of Florida, he met with no objection in any quarters. The proprietors of the Carolinas welcomed the idea of a buffer state to their rear under the guidance of a competent military man like Oglethorpe. The confines of the new colony were to lie between the Savannah and the Altamaha Rivers.

The good ship *Anne* cast loose from Gravesend on November 17, 1732, with thirty-five families aboard, most of whom had been released from prison after Oglethorpe had charitably cleared their debts. The ship reached Charleston in January, and after a site along the Savannah had been selected for settlement, the people disembarked the first day of February, 1733, on the Yamacraw Bluff and set up four tents for a temporary shelter.

The town of Savannah was laid out according to specific plans drawn up in *Villas of the Ancients,* a book by Robert Castell, an architect, who had died in a debtors' prison. It took a month to mark off the streets, lots, and public squares, all done so systematically that the city of Savannah still evinces the good effects of its initial well-ordered grooming. Small tracts of fifty acres were allotted to each family, but entailed to prevent speculation in land and to secure a large body of freeholders. Waldensian farmers from Piedmont, Italy, were brought in to plant mulberry trees and grow the worms from which it was hoped a silk culture might be evolved.

The colony also became a haven for those fleeing religious persecution, indeed, a veritable melting-pot, for within a few years three-fourths of the population consisted of a heterogeneous stock, including Scotch Covenanters, Austrian Lutherans (called Salzburgers), Moravian Brethren, and Swiss Presbyterians. Among the merchant class were not a few Jews. A little later Catholics, mostly aristocrats driven out of the French West Indies by revolution, and Irish, escaping after unsuccessful rebellions in their native country, sought refuge in Savannah. A treaty of friendship was signed with Tomochichi, the ninety-year-old mico, or chief, of neighboring Indian tribes, thus allowing the colonists the freedom to move about without fear of danger from the natives.

Oglethorpe imposed two restrictions on the new colony: he forbade the sale of rum and he prohibited the importation of slaves. Some of the farmers complained that they were placed at a disadvantage in competition with the Carolina planters who owned large numbers of slaves, but Oglethorpe stoutly refused to abide slavery in his altruistic enterprise. And he claimed that distilled liquors had been the downfall of most of the settlers in the Old World.

John and Charles Wesley, the founders of Methodism, spent a year, 1736-37, in the colony, and established the first Sunday School on our shores. George Whitefield, a follower of John Wesley, visited America seven times, and was so popular that he attracted crowds, up and down the colonies, said to have numbered as high as ten thousand persons on frequent occasions. The memory of Whitefield is well perpetuated by a famous institution, Bethesda, the oldest existing American orphans' home, which he founded in 1740, at Savannah.._

The great bellwether, Oglethorpe, departed for England—never to return —after ten years of gratuitous service to the "baby of the thirteen colonies," but he stayed long enough to trounce soundly the Spanish forces marching up from St. Augustine to obliterate this thorny obstruction growing so lustily to the north of his Spanish majesty's peninsular possessions. The battle took place in 1742 at Bloody Marsh on St. Simon's Island, the upshot of the encounter being that the few surviving Spaniards ran home faster than they came.

As soon as Oglethorpe left, considerable changes were made. The ban on the sale of rum was lifted, and the importation of slaves was legalized. The Georgia farmers grumbled that, without slave labor, they could not compete with the Carolina landed proprietors. It was soon made possible, too, for the shiftless to sell out their possessions to the more ambitious among the settlers and thus the large plantation system began to spread westward over Georgia. Rice and indigo became the staple export crops, supplanting the silk and vine cultures fostered so sedulously by Oglethorpe. In 1752 the trustees of the colony, disappointed at the miscarriage of their altruistic plans for Georgia's development, gave up their rights of proprietorship, and the colony became a royal province.

The approaching conflict with the mother country found a large contingent of loyalists in Georgia. Sir James Wright, the royal governor, was highly esteemed, and the colonists had been extraordinarily well treated in a flourishing back-and-forth trade with England. Still the younger generation began to feel the tug of insurgency so prevalent in the older colonies. Events marched apace to inflame the spirits of that small but sturdy band of patriots: the Stamp Act, the Boston Tea Party, the battles of Lexington and Bunker Hill, the siege of Charleston, and finally the Declaration of Independence. A Liberty Pole was set up outside Tondee's Tavern; inside, patriotic speeches were the order of the day. A convention was called, and members drew up a constitution for the State of Georgia. Archibald Bulloch, a great-grandfather of Theodore Roosevelt and great-great-grandfather of Mrs. Franklin D. Roosevelt, was chosen the first president of the New State.

The staunchest advocates of independence in Georgia were centered in Midway, a village in present-day Liberty County, a few miles south of Savannah. The community, consisting of about fifty well-to-do Puritan planters and their families, attended divine services in a picturesque old church where the worship of God and Liberty were inextricable. Two members of this congregation, Dr. Lyman Hall and Button Gwinnett, signed the Declaration of Independence.

Button Gwinnett, a native of Bristol, England, migrated first to Charleston, South Carolina, and then to Savannah in 1765. He abandoned his mercantile business there after three years and became a rice planter on St. Catherine Island, not far from Midway on the mainland, and Sunbury, a prosperous port that was soon to be wiped out by the British during the Revolution.

Although English by birth, Gwinnett was strongly in favor of independence for his adopted country. He was a delegate to the numerous local and intercolonial conventions, and attended the Congress at Philadelphia, where he was one of the three Georgia signers of the Declaration of Independence. Soon after, he assisted in setting up the state government at Savannah, and did more than any one else in writing the state constitution. When Archibald Bulloch died, Gwinnett was elected president and commander-in-chief of Georgia. "In two years," says the historian Thomas Gamble, "he had come from the position of a private planter to the highest command in the new commonwealth."

Now there occurred in swift succession a series of unfortunate events that culminated in the untimely demise of Gwinnett. On the very day of his election he was requested by his executive council to raise a force of militia and volunteers to be dispatched southward to free Florida from the incumbent British rule. It was supposed that the Floridians would throw themselves into the arms of their Georgian liberators.

Meanwhile the General Assembly had raised Lachlan McIntosh to the position of a brigadier-general. This appointment dashed the hopes of Gwinnett, who, having served formerly in the British army, now craved military distinction in the Continental lines. He brushed aside the new brigadier-general, and personally took command of the expedition against Florida. The welcome that awaited the Georgians was the opposite of their expectations. "It was conceived in ambition," writes a local historian caustically, "planned without due caution, and sadly marred in execution."

A strong force of British, Tories, and Indians dispersed the ranks of the liberators.

When the next General Assembly met, the members elected John Adam Treutlen as Gwinnett's successor to the presidency. During the meeting Lachlan McIntosh publicly called Gwinnett "a Scoundrell and lying Rascal." The vilifying epithets quickly reached the ears of Gwinnett, who, feeling insult added to injury, challenged McIntosh to a duel. These two political adversaries, both ardent patriots of the same cause but with a fierce animosity toward each other growing out of purely personal motives, met on the "field of honor" the morning of May 16, 1777. Stepping four paces apart, they about-faced and fired. Both fell with bullet wounds in the thigh. In trying to rise, Gwinnett fell and broke his wounded thigh-bone. Mortification set in and, although faithfully attended by his wife and daughter, he died three days later. Dr. Lyman Hall, his devoted partisan, sighed in apostrophe: "O Liberty, why do you suffer so many of your faithful sons, your warmest votaries, to fall at your shrine? Alas, my friend, my friend . . . Excuse me, sir, the man was *valuable,* so attached to the liberty of this state and continent that his whole attention, influence, and interest were centered in it, and seemed riveted to it. He left a mournful widow and daughter and, I may say, the friends of liberty on a whole continent to deplore his fall."

General McIntosh was practically ostracized in Savannah after the death of the popular Button Gwinnett, and he was soon transferred to the Northern theatre of the war. Colonial records contain the prevalent attitude toward him in this contemporary letter: "General McIntosh is called to the northward, which I am very glad of, both for his own and the State's sake. 'Twas impossible for him to have or to give any satisfaction here, prejudice was so strong here."

No section suffered more than Savannah and its environs during the Revolution. It was a disheartening record of repeated defeats for the patriots, who put up a spirited resistance against overwhelming odds. A sharp skirmish took place at Midway in which the British forces from St. Augustine were victorious. The road to Savannah lay open, and the city was soon compassed about by thirty-five hundred soldiers of the enemy under Colonel Campbell, while the defense under Howe could muster only one-fourth as many men. The inevitable defeat of the Americans occurred December 29, 1778. For three years and a half the British occupied Savannah, and kept most of the outlying territory in subjection. There was plenty of guerrilla fighting, and both sides resorted to the bad practices of plunder, theft, arson, sequestration, horsewhipping, tar-and-feathering, and even petty killing for personal grudges. In October, 1779, the patriots made a determined, coördinated effort to dislodge the invaders. Count d'Estaing brought in a French fleet of thirty-five ships; General McIntosh brought a small army down from the Carolinas; Count Pulaski led a brave contingent of foreign volunteers. In a fiercely contested battle more than one thousand patriots lost their lives, among them Count Pulaski and Sergeant Jasper, hero of the battle of Charleston two years before. The French fleet, badly battered, sailed away, and Savannah remained in British hands till General Anthony Wayne pounced down upon it in his madcap style and captured it in the summer of 1782.

Savannah enjoyed a growing prosperity in the period between the two great internal wars. In the Civil War the city was the final objective of Grant's March through Georgia; the Northern armies made their entry into the port on December 26, 1864.

But Savannahians have always felt they have had more distinguished visitors than these invading forces. General Washington was heartily welcomed on his "Southern progress" in 1791; the reception for Lafayette in 1825 was made a gala event; among other illustrious visitors more or less officially received may be numbered Presidents Monroe, Arthur, Cleveland, McKinley and Taft; Admirals Dewey and Schley; Daniel Webster and William Makepeace Thackeray.

Monuments have been erected to Oglethorpe, Pulaski, Jasper, General Greene, the Moravians, Bartow, the Confederate and the Spanish-American War veterans. John C. Fremont was born in Savannah in 1813, but this first candidate of the Republican party for president has never been favored with a monument. Tomochichi Boulder on one of the main public squares commemorates the Indian Chief who welcomed General Oglethorpe and his band when they first arrived.

Tourists in increasing numbers are visiting some of the notable old plantations around Savannah. It was at Mulberry Grove that Eli Whitney invented the cotton gin while he was a tutor for General Greene's children. At Grove Hill the first tobacco crop in Georga was planted; Bonaventure, the fine estate confiscated from its Tory proprietor and later recovered by a young son who joined the patriot forces under General Greene, is now a cemetery. Hall's Knoll holds interest for being once the home of Dr. Lyman Hall, signer of the Declaration of Independence. At Brampton Plantation the first Negro Baptist Church had its origin. The most enduring of all the noted old plantations is Wormsloe, an estate that has continued in the same family since the original founder. The camellia bushes have grown into glorious trees here. The best collection of Georgiana to be found anywhere was housed here till its recent sale to the University of Georgia. Other plantations of interest are Waverley, Greenwich, and the Hermitage. It should be mentioned that the cemetery at Midway reveals on its tombstones many famous Colonial names, such as those of General Daniel Stewart, a great-grandfather of Teddy Roosevelt, and General James Screven, who was killed at the battle of Midway in 1779.

Hymns of praise have been sung by every one who has ever felt the seductive charm of Savannah. Says the late Colonel O. C. Lightner, editor of Hobbies: "I think Savannah, Georgia, is one of the most interesting old cities in the United States. It is less spoiled by the march of progress than

New Orleans or Charleston, or the old cities of the east. The beautiful plans of Oglethorpe remain just as they were two hundred years ago." . . . "Yes," says the Savannahian solemnly, "every spot is hallowed here." And as a matter of fact, every visitor solemnly believes it.

The Historic Savannah spoon has engraved in the bowl the name of the city, surrounded at top and bottom by a chaplet, let us say, of Spanish moss. Throughout the length of the shank and nave runs the name of Georgia enclosed by a gracefully sinuous border of alternate beading and fluting. A generous amount of floral garniture is present. The caput contains the obverse side of the state seal showing three pillars and a crescent moon inscribed with *Wisdom, Justice,* and *Moderation* on encircling banderoles, the three words being symbolical of the legislative, judicial, and executive branches of the government. An arch with *Constitution* written upon it crowns the entablature. A man with drawn sword stands beween two of the pillars.

A product of the Towle Manufacturing Company. Length, 5½ inches.

No. 59 BROOKLYN BRIDGE

Along in the eighteen-sixties Walt Whitman was inspired to write a poem while he was crossing the Brooklyn Ferry at sunset. He watched the reflection of the summer sky in the water . . . the wide wake left by the passage, the quick tremulous whirl of the wheels . . . the thick-stemmed pipes of steamboats . . . the pilots in their pilot-houses . . . the barges, the hay-boat, the belated lighter . . . the sea gulls, high in the air, floating with motionless wings, oscillating their bodies. But he was inspired more by the scene close at hand—

> Crowds of men and women attired in the usual costumes, how curious you are to me!
> On the ferry-boats the hundreds and hundreds that cross, returning home, are more curious to me than you suppose,
> And you that shall cross from shore to shore years hence are more to me, and more in my meditations, than you might suppose.
>
> Others will enter the gates of the ferry and cross from shore to shore,
> Others will watch the run of the flood-tide,
> Others will see the shipping of Manhattan north and west, and the heights of Brooklyn to the south and east,
> Others will see the islands large and small;
> A hundred years hence, or ever so many hundred years hence, others will see them,
> Will enjoy the sunset, the pouring-in of the flood-tide, the falling back of the ebb-tide.

There was no hint of bridges or tunnels across to the mainland from Long Island when Walt Whitman penned this poem on the ferry. It was

262

still as free of steel spiderwebs as on the day when the Dutch farmers landed on the island in 1636 and began clearing the soil for planting around Gouwanus Bay. Some ten years later the first ferry service was started.

Breuckelen, with half a dozen variant spellings till it settled down to its present form about 1800, was first cleared of its trees in 1645. It signified "marshy ground," and stemmed from the Dutch town of the same name in the province of Utrecht, Holland. Rural it was intended to be and rural it remained for nearly two centuries. In 1816 it was incorporated as a village, in 1834 as a city, and in 1898 it was swallowed up as a borough of New York City.

The battle of Long Island on August 27, 1776, left the island sequestered in the hands of the British for the remainder of the Revolutionary War. But information got through to Washington of enemy troop movements and naval maneuvers. Abraham Woodhull and James Jay, brother of the more famous John, sent dispatches in invisible ink to Washington and thereby saved the French fleet from capture. When the letters could not get through, the washlines rendered yeoman's service. Clothes and accessories were hung out in such a way as to form cryptographic messages for all to see, but which only the initiated could read. Handkerchiefs and dydees did double duty in thus divulging military scerets also. By this means André was caught and the plot against West Point foiled. Caleb Brewster and Austin Roe crossed the Fulton Ferry regularly to peddle poultry, eggs, butter—and military intelligence. Nearly 12,000 Long Islanders died on the foul prison ship Jersey, martyrs for their patriotic convictions.

In the curious bowl of this spoon, which has a broad taffrail around its rim and ends in a lanceolate arch- tip, there is a splendid graph of "The Brooklyn Church, 1776," a wooden structure of the Dutch type with mansard roof, high belfry, and steeple like a weathervane. Around the pointed tip of the bowl is written "The City of Churches." At one time Brooklynites felt justly that such a title was not an overweening conceit. More than that, it has been a city of famous preachers, to speak only of Henry Ward Beecher, Eleazer Williams (thought to have been the lost Dauphin of France), De Witt Talmadge, and S. Parkes Cadman. In those days the ferries were packed on Sundays, bringing worshippers over from Manhattan to Brooklyn churches.

Spanning the nave and caput of the handle is the famous Brooklyn Bridge, the building of which was considered an incredible folly till it became an accomplished feat. It was finished after thirteen years of stops and starts, backaches and headaches and heartaches. Twenty workmen were killed from accidents; the original engineer, John A. Roebling, died of lockjaw from a fractured foot; his son, Washington Roebling, supervised the building plans from a sickbed for eleven years. When it was finally opened in 1883, President Arthur and all his cabinet—as well as Walt Whitman—were there to witness the fireworks and hear the booming cannon-salutes. For many years Brooklyn Bridge, 1595 feet in length, was the longest and mightiest, and yet the most artistic, bridge ever built. Since then, Brooklyn has been connected with the mainland by four other bridges and two tunnels.

Need I mention Coney Island or the Dodgers in connection with this old Dutch *dorp?*

The Brooklyn spoon is a Gorham product, bearing the imprint of C. A. Adams & Co. Length, 6 inches.

No. 60 LEWIS CASS

Time has not dealt too well with the fame of Lewis Cass, who is listed among the "also Rans" for president. Our history texts often refer to him as a "Doughface," and he has found few defenders and many detractors among superficial students of our history. Yet, in his day he played a significant role as soldier and citizen, patriot and statesman; was called the "Father of the Northwest" and the "Founder of Detroit;" his latest biographer, Frank B. Woodford, gives him a most apposite title, though it has something of the somber ring familiar to Greek tragedies about it— "the last Jeffersonian." Above all, it is well to remember him as one who loved and defended the Constitution as few others ever did.

Born in Exeter, New Hampshire, in 1782, he was the eldest of six children in a distinguished family of early New England forbears. One of his most vivid childhood recollections was the jubilation held in his native town when New Hampshire became the ninth state to ratify the Constitution and thus make it effective. His mother lifted him out of bed and carried him to a window, so that he could see the blazing bonfires.

For seven years he attended Exeter, and upon his graduation in 1800 his "excellent moral character" was rated superior to all his academic achievements. He proceeded at once to Ohio, whither his family had already moved, took up the study of law, and was admitted to the bar in his twentieth year. In 1806 he married, and thereafter led a domestically happy life. About the same time he was elected to the Ohio state legislature, and won high commendation from Jefferson for his maiden speech, a stirring denunciation of the Burr conspiracy.

Cass played a creditable part in the War of 1812. Breveted a colonel, he delivered a eulogium on the flag that was received with the wildest acclamation by his battalion when he wound up with this peroration: "You have rallied around it to defend her rights and to avenge her injuries. May it wave protection to our friends and defiance to our foes! And should we ever meet them in the hostile field, I doubt not but that the eagle of America will be found more than a match for the British lion!"

When General Hull surrendered Detroit, Cass shed bitter tears at what he thought was a base betrayal of American honor. In 1813 he was named governor of the Northwest Territory, and a year later the president designated him the governor of Michigan Territory, a post he kept for sixteen years.

In 1820, when the British were bribing the Indians to stir up trouble in the Northwest, Cass met with the redskins for a parley at Sault Sainte Marie. When he saw some of them raise a British flag on a hill opposite from that where the deliberations were being held, Cass arose, and without a weapon of any sort on his person walked alone into the middle of the camp, seized the foreign flag from its standard, and ripped it to pieces under his feet. Then turning to the awed beholders, he declared there would be no two flags flying over the same territory. The Indians admired this rare display of courage and agreed to terms of friendship with the redoubtable governor.

In 1831 Cass entered Jackson's cabinet as Secretary of War. Although the two men differed occasionally on matters of internal policy, Jackson always held the highest regard for the personal integrity of Cass, and when the threat of South Carolina's secession arose, Cass accompanied the president over the country and made many speeches in behalf of the stern measures taken to prevent disruption of the Union.

In 1836 he was appointed our minister to France. Immediately upon his return in 1842 he entered the Senate from Michigan. Two years later his name was placed before the Democratic convention as a candidate for president. He kept receiving additional votes on each ballot, and by the fifth he held a slight majority. It seemed, when the convention adjourned after the seventh ballot, that Cass would be nominated the next day. But during the night the back-room boodlers began to do a little horse trading. On the eighth ballot the name of James Knox Polk was placed before the convention. On the ninth Van Buren withdrew. A rousing rally stampeded the delegates to Polk—a "dark horse" hitherto considered too mediocre for "presidential timber." The "dark horse" won the nomination and also the presidency.

Cass kept his seat in the Senate. In the Democratic convention of 1848 it was almost a foregone conclusion that he would be the nominee. The opposition, headed by James Buchanan, melted, and Cass was nominated on the fourth ballot. But the Abolitionist forces were dissatisfied with Cass's conciliatory attitude toward the South. A group of Free-Soilers put up a ticket headed by former president Van Buren, the main plank in the platform being a declaration against the admission of any more slave territory.

Cass waged an aggressive campaign against General Taylor, the Whig candidate. The election was close, the two main candidates carrying fifteen states each. The Free-Soilers gave enough votes to Van Buren in New York to throw that state into the Whig column, and Taylor was elected. The country was not yet divided sectionally. Cass carried eight free and seven slave states; Taylor carried eight slave and seven free states.

Following his defeat, Cass was as active as ever in the Senate. In 1852 it was apparent that he would be the leading candidate again for the Democratic nomination. Although he led in the balloting for five days, a heated deadlock with James Buchanan brought a surprise nomination to another dark horse, Franklin Pierce.

After the election of Buchanan in 1856 Cass became Secretary of State. He was now seventy-five years old, and still an advocate of compromise. The epithet "doughface" was hurled at him now more than ever, since the doctrine of abolition was gaining ground and winning triumphs in the North. He was fast approaching the position once held by his Whig opponents, Webster and Clay. He wished by all possible means to preserve the Union through peaceful efforts, if that could be done. If not, force must be used. He was adamant against yielding. It was the same stand taken by Jackson against nullification nearly thirty years before.

After the election of Lincoln in 1860 Cass felt that his hands were tied in the crisis that was rapidly reaching the climax of its first act. He was a helpless minority against the President and most of his Cabinet, who wished to do nothing. He repeatedly advised Buchanan to act at once to ward off secession. On the thirteenth of December he called on the President to send reënforcmeents to bolster Fort Sumter—off Charleston. "These forts must be strengthened. I demand it," he declared. But the President replied, "I am sorry to differ with the Secretary of State." The following day Cass resigned from the Cabinet. His stand was widely hailed throughout the North. Said one editor: "It is tragic that a man has to break his sword twice in a lifetime, at the beginning and at the end of his eventful career. At the surrender of Hull at Detroit, Cass was so disgusted at the conduct of his commander and at not having to fight, that he broke his sword. Now again he breaks it because the chief won't fight."

At a Union rally in Detroit, Cass was cheered wildly when he exclaimed: "He who is not *for* his country is *against* her. I have loved the Union ever since the light of that bonfire [when New Hampshire celebrated the formation of the republic] greeted my eyes. I have given fifty-five years of my life to its preservation."

Happily he lived long enough to see the Union victorious. His last years were spent among his books, which he loved, in his home in Detroit. He had always been an abstemious man with strictly regular habits that lengthened his life to the age of four score and four, unimpaired by any ailments of body or mind. He was a large man, with a poise and dignity that commanded respect; the high caliber of his intellect won him the admiration if not the adulation of those who heard him speak. His fellow-senators remembered him for the palm-leaf fan which he always kept handy on warm days, and for the blue bandanna handkerchief which he used for mopping the profuse perspiration from his brow during his speeches. He lacked brilliance, a ready humor, and the art of repartee, but he thought an issue through with painstaking thoroughness and logic.

266

He loved liberty but he would not countenance lawlessness. Rugged, upright, sincere, he belongs in that category of misappraised statesmen alongside John Adams, William H. Crawford, Horace Greeley, and Herbert Hoover. His political career of sixty years is perhaps the longest in our history.

The spoon with the bust of Lewis Cass on its nave also contains the state seal of Michigan and the date of its admission, 1837, on its caput; the figure of Marquette, who established the first settlement in Michigan; and 1610, the date when the early French fur-hunters first entered the state.

On the reverse of handle are represented the state capitol, a university building, and Fort Michila on Mackinac Island. Sprays of apple blossom, the state flower, and a wolverine, which gives the state its nickname, are also represented on the handle.

This spoon was manufactured by R. Wallace and Sons. Length, 5¼ inches. Used through the courtesy of its owner, Mrs. Alyse D. Westbrook, Hayward, California.

No. 61 ALVARADO
No. 145 NEW MEXICO INDIANS

There are four Alvarados more or less prominent in the history of the New World. Two of them, Alonso and Pedro, assisted Cortes in the conquest of Mexico and Guatemala. Juan Bautista Alvarado was the first native governor of California under Mexican rule. Hernando de Alvarado, the figure with whom we are concerned on this spoon, was the leader of a small detachment from Coronado's expedition sent to explore the Rio Grande Valley, and in 1540 camped on the site where Albuquerque is located today.

Thirteen years before this, an expedition under Don Pámfilo Narváez had set sail from Spain for the conquest of Florida, which then embraced practically all of North America, according to the Spaniards. From the time they landed in Tampa Bay in 1528, these conquistadores fell heirs to a host of troubles, in malarial swamps and on barren plains, from hunger, sickness, and the slings of hostile redskins. Plodding westward across the plains of Texas to the Gulf of California, they reached Mexico City seven years later. Only four survivors lived to tell the tale of their odyssey. Cabeza de Vaca (meaning, the Cow's Head), the leader of the surviving band, related his adventures to Diego Mendoza, Viceroy of Mexico. De Vaca also relayed the tales he had heard from the Indians about the marvelous "Seven Cities of Cibola" to the north, incredibly rich in precious stones and metals, doorways being of turquoise, floors of silver, and walls of gold.

Mendoza needed no prodding to expedite a group of men to verify these reports. De Vaca could not go himself, as he longed to see Spain again, but he lent the services of his Moorish slave Esteban, who had been a keen observer on these recent long wanderings. Coronado was appointed commander of the expedition.

Now Coronado was a cautious man. He delayed the journey, and first sent out a scouting party under Friar Marcos, with Esteban as guide, to report on the country and its natives, and to ascertain what provisions and how many men would be necessary for the conquest of this rich empire.

The vainglorious Esteban was thrilled by his exalted importance in the undertaking. The former slave decked himself out as an Oriental potentate in brilliant robes and plumed helmet, and verily as full of bells as Poe's poem on the subject. An enchanted gourd also tinkling with bells and ornamented with one red and one white feather was sent ahead to announce the oncoming army and thereby to awe the native into submission.

The natives did not take kindly to Esteban's progress. When he would not leave the villages after being warned, he was put to death outside the walls of a Zuñi pueblo that he mistook for Cibola. Friar Marcos stood upon a mesa and gazed at this so-called city of Cibola from a distance. The adobe walls of the pueblo gleamed deceptively golden in the afterglow of a desert sunset. Erecting a cross and proclaiming the land henceforth a possession of the Spanish crown, he hurried back to Mexico. Marcos minimized nothing in an account bristling with superlatives.

Enthusiasm waxed to a fever pitch. The name of Cibola ran from tongue to tongue. Every young blade with a dash of adventure in his blood was itching to behold this golden paradise to the north.

Coronado made thoroughgoing preparations for the conquest. Three hundred cavaliers quickly enlisted. Eight hundred Indians went along on foot to drive the cattle and sheep needed for provisions. Coronado himself was arrayed in an impressive suit of armor flecked with golden scales. Friar Marcos wore as usual his simple garb of gray.

The procession advanced for a month over the hot, arid sands of the intervening desert. When they crossed the Gila River and caught their first glance of the Zuñi pueblo of Hawikuh, described by Marcos as an outlying city of Cibola, there were expressions of dismay on all sides. Vile imprecations were hurled at the all-too-imaginative friar.

Hawikuh was a village crowded with dirty, mud-walled hovels. The Indians defied the invaders, and the pueblo was not taken without a fight. Coronado was knocked from his horse and would have perished except for the timely assistance of Cárdenas, one of his officers. No gold was found, but provisions were plentiful. The much-abused Marcos deemed it advisable to return to Mexico with the messengers carrying reports to Mendoza.

Coronado made Hawikuh his headquarters while small parties were formed to explore the surrounding country. One detachment under Cárdenas ran upon the Grand Canyon in northwestern Arizona. Another band returned with reports of a region to the east teeming with hump-backed cows— the first mention made by Europeans of buffaloes. Hernando de Alvarado was dispatched with twenty men to explore this territory to the east. He was given three months to complete the mission.

Alvarado had only journeyed fifty miles when he came upon Ácoma, a pueblo situated on a sandstone mesa rising steeply to a height of three hundred fifty-seven feet and comprising seventy acres of level area on its crest. At the foot of this plateau began a stairway of two hundred steps with spacious treads. Then followed a hundred steps with contracting dimensions. From there on a tortuous escalade, mounted in some places by ladders and in others by toe and finger holds, was the sole means of final ascent to the top. It was impossible for a musket ball to be fired upward into this inaccessible sanctum. From their eerie perch the Indians could roll boulders down upon any invaders who attempted to penetrate their fortress.

Seeing Alvarado and his men moving about on the plains below, the "People of the Sky" came down to give fight, but desisted when they understood the Spaniards were only "sight-seers."

Continuing on his way, Alvarado came upon Indian villages extending along the banks of the Rio Grande River near the present location of Albuquerque. At some places on his journey, Alvarado was welcomed into camps by Indians playing on drums, rattles, and flutes.

In the fall of 1540 Coronado moved to a spot near Albuquerque, where he bivouacked for the winter. When Alvarado came back from his expedition, he brought with him a talkative Indian whom they called the Turk because he reminded them of one.

The Turk spoke glowingly of Quivira, a famous city of gold far to the East, bordering a river two leagues wide. Fish big as horses abounded in the river, and galleys with twenty oarsmen glided like water lilies up and down the stream. The Lord of this land fell asleep to the lullaby of golden bells swaying from the branches of a tall tree. The bowls and dishes, even of the poor folk, were of gold substance.

The Turk said he would be willing to go along to show them his country of Quivira if he could recover a gold bracelet which had been stolen from him by the Pecos, a tribe that had welcomed Alvarado with an extraordinary display of good will. Coronado believed the Turk implicitly and ordered Alvarado to go with the Turk and demand the surrender of the bracelet. Big Whiskers, chief of the Pecos, called the Turk an outright liar. Alvarado, having grown rather fond of the Turk, felt that this was an insult to his friend. So he clapped chains on Big Whiskers and another chief, a venerable old man highly respected by his tribe. The Indians, enraged at this indignity, drove Alvarado and his companions away from their village.

During the rest of the winter there were many skirmishes between Coronado's followers and the Indians. In the spring of 1541, when the expedition broke camp and marched off to find Quivira, the Spaniards left a trail of enmity behind them.

When Coronado, after months of hard marching, found that he had purposely been led astray by the Turk, he garroted the lying Indian, and headed south for Mexico. His mission had been a failure. Cibola had proved to be a deceptive mirage. He was soon relieved of his position with the viceroy's government, and he departed for Spain. The ill-smelling reports emanating from those in Coronado's retinue instilled no desire in any one to follow in his wake.

More than a century passed before a few daring souls ventured again into this region. In 1706 Francisco Valdez founded the town of Albuquerque, which was named in honor of the duke then viceroy of New Spain.

The Alvarado spoon contains a picture of the Hotel Alvarado in the bowl. This structure, housing a combination of depot, hotel, restaurant, curio shop, and museum, is one of the prize pieces of Moorish Revival architecture in the United States, with its enclosed porticos, arched windows, and rounded towers. It was built by Fred Harvey, of the famed Harvey Houses, and he spared no money or effort to make it authentic in all its details.

On the handle, in addition to the explorer's name, may be seen a Pueblo woman with a water pitcher on her head, a cavalier on horseback, and the crest of the Alvarado family.

On the reverse of the handle the name of Albuquerque appears on the shank. A swastika, a papoose, and the church of San Felipe, one of the first buildings erected in Albuquerque, are represented in the nave and caput. "F. Harvey" is embossed at the foot of the handle next to the bowl.

Length of spoon is 5½ inches. Used through the courteous permission of the owner, Mr. Gerald Irving, Hayward, California.

There are more Indians in New Mexico than in any other state with the exception of Oklahoma and Arizona, and their numbers are increasing. The Navaho, once decimated almost to the point of extinction, now constitute the largest single tribe in the United States; about one-half of them live in New Mexico, where they make up more than two-thirds of the entire Indian population. Though classified with the nomadic or wandering tribes, the Navaho Indians are rapidly become sedentary, conforming to the modern style of stone or adobe houses, prevalent in this area, for their homes.

There are two main divisions of the nomadic Indians in New Mexico, the Athapascan (or Apache) and the Shoshonean. Among the nomads, in addition to the preponderant Navaho, may be counted the Jicarillas, Mescaleros, Mogollones, Gilas, Utes, and Comanches.

The Pueblo or stationary Indians live in eighteen settlements. They are divided linguistically into three groups, but gradually, through education, most of them are coming to speak either Spanish or English. The Pueblo Indians are primarily farmers, and long before the advent of white men they were irrigating their crops of corn, beans, and squash.

270

The gold-washed bowl of the New Mexico Indians spoon also contains an incised picture of the Alvarado Hotel at Albuquerque. The handle is replete with Indian features: in the caput, the head of a warrior wearing the feathered head-dress and tooth-strung necklace; in the nave, a papoose in his sheltered doe-skin cradle, with tomahawk, hatchet, and arrows around him; in the shank, an ala of feathers and the dot-and-latticework of moccasin-leather. On the reverse, throughout the caput and nave, is the figure of a warrior poised on one foot in the act of shooting an arrow perpendicularly into the air—a good tablature. In the shank is a quiver of arrows.

Made by the Shepard Manufacturing Company. Length, 5 inches.

No. 65 SOAPY SMITH

Whether the physiognomy on the caput of this hand-wrought spoon represents a bear, an eagle, a human being, or a heathen god, matters little: we shall give it the sobriquet of Soapy Smith because Jefferson Randolph Smith, alias Soapy, who called himself a "gentleman from Virginia," though he was not, is the most notorious bad man of Alaska's gold-rush, mush-and-plush days, and his history was most intimately bound up with the history of Skagway at that time.

This benign-mannered, soft-voiced character actually hailed from St. Louis—this fact revealed itself when his wife put in a claim for his estate, after his death—but he had traveled (faster than the police or his record) from one Western town to the next, selling soap wrapped in a five-dollar bill for one dollar. Eye-witnesses were not fast enough to detect the legerdemain which substituted a phony for the real bill. He worked his way westward, preferably through the larger towns of Colorado, Nevada, California, and Washington, to Alaska. His duplicity was too quickly scented for a prolonged dalliance in the smaller settlements.

Skagway was most ideally adapted for his devious, underhanded devices, and when he looked in upon the scene in '97, he decided it was an excellent place for him to pitch camp, pull up his sleeves, and go to work.

He did not literally pull up his sleeves—he was too svelte and immaculate a dresser to look like a menial doing common chores. His black beard was trimmed as neatly as if he were sitting for a Velazquez portrait. And when he rode forth in a white silk shirt on a milk-white charger, his black tie and detachable cuffs were adorned with diamond studs and links that flashed, along with his watch charm and diamond rings, like streaks of lightning in an ebony sky. Not dapper enough yet, he had to sport spats and don a broad-brimmed felt hat worthy of a Southern colonel. Incidentally he carried a six-shooter on his hip and iron knuckles in his pockets.

When he walked off the gangplank at Skagway, he sensed that this was the milieu where his special brand of business would thrive best. He set up modest establishments where flourished roulette, faro, blackjack, bunco, and the three-shell game. Lucky birds back from Klondike and the Yukon with pokes of gold dangling about their person were decoyed into his snares and methodically plucked to the marrow bone. Just in case the birds were shy on games of chance, there were real estate and information offices ready to help handle fluid bonanzas and give advice for profitable investments. But somehow, always during such conferences, the lights were doused, feathers were roughed, and the luckless birds, bereft of their golden plumage, went flying out into the gutters. To no avail did the victims seek redress of grievances. Restitution of fly-by-night fortunes was wishful thinking. No one would reach out a hand to a penniless pot.

When the Spanish-American War broke out, Soapy secured an appointment as recruiting officer. He carefully screened the volunteers, accepting those who were ready to do his bidding and rejecting those who might prove intractable. He even offered the services of Smith's Guard to the government in a voucher to President McKinley. The President declined the proffered assistance in a letter which was framed and conspicuously hung in Soapy's office.

Smith's Guard marched in a patriotic demonstration on the fourth of July. Soapy was now a local judge with a considerable group of henchmen always available and willing to carry out his injunctions. Nor did he lack support from certain well-meaning citizens of Skagway. He put cold cash on the spot for whatever he bought, and generously threw in something for interest. To any one who waited on him he tossed tips with a magnanimous gesture.

But even in the turbulent mushroom-town there were still many people who had a wholesome respect for the law, and when Marshal Rowan was shot, and his duties taken over by one of Soapy's gang, the honest citizens of Skagway were aroused to the fact that their town was being run by a bunch of silky-gloved mush workers with gunning ways. A few weeks later a miner by the name of Bean was murdered in Smith's gambling parlor, and the new marshal did nothing about it. Then J. D. Stewart, a miner in from the North was relieved of his gold-dust nuggets and swept out of Soapy's parlor, half dead.

Stewart lived to tell the tale. A meeting of law-abiding citizens was called. One hundred and one persons attended, and formed a citizens' committee. The poke coppers were invited to leave town. The desperadoes responded to this tender by calling a convocation of their own and forming a "Society of Law and Order, composed of 317 Members." The two opposing organizations held further meetings.

On July 8, 1898, the better element assembled on the newly-improvised docks, and stationed Frank H. Reid at the entrance to the long gangplank

PLATE 36

64. WASHINGTON'S BUST   65. SOAPY SMITH   66. BALANCED ROCK   67. LOG CABIN

PLATE 37

68. WHITE SULPHUR SPRINGS   69. CALVERT AND KEY
70. GARDEN OF THE GODS   71. RED WING

to intercept any unwelcome snoopers. Reid, a Minnesotan who had experienced many hazards as a soldier, civil engineer, and miner, was not a man to be buffaloed or bribed. A New York reporter, in the pay of the racketeers, tried to wangle his way into the meeting and was turned back. When Soapy was informed of this indignity, he swore and drank himself into a frenzy of desperation. He knew that Reid was a courageous man not to be intimidated by threats. With a Winchester repeater by his side and followed at a distance by several of his cohorts, Soapy headed for the docks. Reid sought to intercept his passage, and he swung at the guardsman with his rifle, aiming to knock him down. Reid caught the muzzle of the gun and held it till he could grab his own revolver. The first shot went wild. Reid wrenched the rifle free from Soapy's grasp and fired. A mutual exchange of two more shots each was enough to send both the combatants reeling to the ground.

Soapy was dead. One bullet had penetrated his thigh, the other had entered his heart. Reid was carried to the hospital, mortally wounded. On his tomb his fellow citizens paid him grateful tribute with this inscription: "He gave his life for the honor of Skagway." A waterfall that forms a backdrop to the panorama of Skagway's mountain scenery was named in honor of Reid.

The cortège that bore Soapy Smith to his last earthly abode was composed of the faithful little men whom he had befriended. They remembered his genteel manners, his generous loans when they were in debt, and his gifts of candy to their children. His tombstone, with no inscriptions of gratitude, was long ago chipped to pieces for souvenirs.

Soapy's chief followers were soon shipped into exile. A few of his underdogs, becoming ostracized, left of their own will. His gambling parlor was eventually converted into a museum.

On entering Skagway today, the visitor is greeted by the sight of a man's head painted on a cliff overlooking the harbor. This is called Soapy Smith's Skull.

Skagway is now a quiet, law-abiding town, with a population far smaller than that in the boom days. It has acquired a considerable reputation as a museum piece, a sightseeing resort, and the hub of a wide area unsurpassed for its good hunting, fishing, and mountain climbing.

The Soapy Smith spoon, with Skagway needled in its bowl and the queer caricature cut in the caput, is in the best sense a souvenir spoon, original and different. It is an example of Indian workmanship, handmade, without an indication of its maker, and without exact duplications, although there are hundreds of its counterparts in the hands of collectors. The length varies slightly on these spoons; this one measures 4¾ inches in length. Used through the courtesy of its owner, Mrs. Alyse D. Westbrook, Hayward, California.

No. 66 BALANCED ROCK
No. 70 GARDEN OF THE GODS

The Garden of the Gods, three miles from Manitou Springs, Colorado, has borne its picturesque appellation since 1859, when two visitors were commenting on its scenic value. When one suggested it would make an ideal beer garden, the other rejoined that, far from being a beer garden, it was more like an assembly in Valhalla, a garden of the gods.

In her travel notes Helen Hunt Jackson, who loved this part of Colorado so much that she requested her body be brought back here from California for burial, described the smaller red rocks as "queer little monstrosities looking like seals, fishes, cats, and masks," and the larger ones as "colossal monstrosities looking like elephants, like gargoyles, like giants . . . all motionless and silent, with a strange look of having been stopped and held back in the very climax of some supernatural catastrophe."

Of all the strange formations of rocks hewn out by the cataclysmic upheavals of nature in the Garden of the Gods, none arouses more interest than Balanced Rock at the southwestern entrance to the park. It is a Gargantuan sandstone mass resting on an axis so slight that one might easily be led into thinking it could be set rotating or pushed off balance by a good shove. Although the sloping sides at the base seem to offer excellent vantage points for, even a wagering invitation to, a strong shoulder, few people would venture to risk their lives under the menacing rock to bring about its downfall. Nevertheless, it has always stood there, looking ready to topple, yet undeviating on its base, impervious to wind and storm, inspiring its beholders with a sense of apprehensive wonder or an unpleasant feeling of claustrophobia. More than one person under the shadow of this inverted pyramid has been moved to utter in awe, "Let us get away from it quickly—before it falls!"

The semblance of a wry face can be discerned on the rock from certain points of view. Eyes, ears, nose, mouth, and chin may be descried, but these features might be taken for the mask of a sleeping satyr rather than the profile of a human being.

The image of this rock is embossed in the bowl of the Balanced Rock spoon (the name here reading Balance, without the d). A man with an alpenstock in his hand stands beneath one crag, his size being Lilliputian compared to the Brobdingnagian counterpoise above him.

The handle is divided into four sections. On the shank, enfolded twice by a banderole, appear two sheaves of wheat, a plow, and some columbines. A miner thrusting his pick against the hillside and a burro are represented in the two sections of the nave. In the caput is the state seal. On the reverse side of handle a silver refinery and a feathered Indian with club, spear, and tom-tom may be seen.

The Balanced Rock spoon was manufactured by the Edward Todd Company. Length, 4¼ inches. Used through the courtesy of its owner, Mrs. Alyse D. Westbrook.

As far as the scenic view on the second spoon is concerned, postcards may give us a brighter picture heightened thus by a coloring like that of the red Morrison sandstone, but the impression produced by the sculpture-like imbrications of simulated rock-strata and ridges in the bowl of this spoon is more realistic, and leaves us with the feeling that we are back in the Paleozoic Age, in the morning of time. We are in the presence of the primitive, of something the child-gods were set by the Norns to hew and shape, but which they, in preferring more sportive tasks, neglected to finish. Rodin's "Thinker" would have felt at home here. It might have made a good immolation scene in the heroics of the old Norse gods.

The vivid impression we get in this cameo-picture derives from a fine use of contrast. In the foreground is a roughly-beaten, appliquéd mass of silver portraying a grotesque configuration of seamy ridges, jagged rocks, grottos, and creviced bird-haunts in the "gateway" to the Garden of the Gods. Far to the rear looms a mountain peak. The silver workmanship is smoothly done, the perspective convincing.

The handle shaft pictures the columbine, Colorado's state flower, and a lone prospector with pick on shoulder. The banderole at the waist bears the word "Colorado." In the nave a loaded burro shambles along in a curious posture; one ear forward, one backward; his four legs in four different stances.

The caput contains the state seal. On the upper part of a shield are three snow-capped peaks surrounded by clouds; on the lower part, a miner's implements. Above the shield there is a Roman fasces, which, on the official state seal, has the words, "Union and Constitution," but these are missing here. At the top of the shield in a triangle is God's eye with its rays, symbolic of divine guidance, emanating from the two upper sides of the figure. Below the shield is the state motto, NIL SINE NUMINE (Nothing without God).

On the reverse side are the customary objects of this Wigwam state seal series: wigwam, canoe, oar, tomahawk, peace pipe, and calabash. Made by Watson and Newell. Length, 5½ inches.

No. 67 LOG CABIN

Moqua, the industrious squaw, sat in front of her tepee beading a pair of doeskin moccasins she had just made. So anxious was she to finish her task before the daylight faded that she forgot to fetch water from the distant spring for her evening meal. Noticing a trickle of sap from a maple tree nearby, she caught barely enough in a pan to use for boiling her victuals of samp and moose meat.

When Woksis, the brave, returned for his supper, a strange, new, delightful odor radiating from the steaming kettles greeted his nostrils. A sweetish, viscous liquid was adhering to the chunk of moose roast, and the sugary taste imparted to the samp by the maple sap was truly delectable. With increased gustatory vigor Woksis and Moqua fell to eating, and devoured their savory repast with exclamations of grateful surprise and praise.

At once Woksis assembled his tribe and explained how Kosekusbeh, the great spirit-teacher to man among the redskin deities, had revealed to his squaw a new method of sweetening food. It was not long until maple syrup was tickling the palates of all the Algonquin and Iroquois tribes.

The colonists, as early at 1634, had already learned the use of maple syrup from the Indians. Many a household depended solely on this source for their sweetening. With two buckets suspended from a shoulder-yoke, the pioneers made many an excursion into the forests in late March or early April to gather the sap which was piped into hand-hewn log troughs and boiled out of doors in caldrons swung over a bonfire.

Today the making of maple syrup is done scientifically, and is pursued seriously for its commercial value, upwards of 800,000 gallons being put on the market annually. Most of the sap gathered for this purpose comes from the hills of New England, especially Vermont, the Northwest woods, and the St. Lawrence region of Canada, although this pursuit is widely cultivated, as the sugar maple area extends as far south as Kentucky and as far west as Missouri.

The alternating spring weather of freezing nights and thawing days sets the sap running. The sugarhouse must be tidied, the evaporator burnished, the buckets scoured, and a goodly supply of firewood stacked in the shed to the rear of the evaporator. Out in the forest, holes are bored two or three inches deep in a tree and a spile driven in to channel the sap. One bucket is usually enough for a tree, though as many as three or four may be hung onto very large trees.

Wooden barrels or tin vats are placed on sleds drawn by two horses or, in some areas, four oxen. The farmer goes from tree to tree and keeps emptying the sap buckets into the big containers till the load becomes an arduous pull back to the sugar shanty. When the run is heavy, the workers must form a double shift and carry on through the night. A cold snap will check the free flow of sap, and the amount caught tapers off considerably. The sap-gathering season lasts from three to four weeks, till the sun, having melted all the snow, proclaims with warmth that the "year's at the spring." Then the sap soars on upward, to burst forth into tender buds, winged seeds, and a myriad of cloven leaves.

In 1887 Mr. P. J. Towle, a grocer in St. Paul, Minnesota, dissatisfied with the corn syrup and the sugar cane molasses ladled out of sticky barrels by the gallon to customers in grocery stores, decided to manufacture and sell a syrup which was the best, according to his taste. To him maple was the most delicious of all flavors, but the price of syrup extracted from pure maple was too exorbitant for the general consumer's pocketbook. So he experimented with blends of Vermont and Canadian syrups mixed with those from Louisiana sugar cane until the resultant combination was exactly what he wanted.

Mr. Towle realized that a good trade name will help sell a good product. And this gave him an opportunity to honor Abe Lincoln, his boyhood ideal, with the "Log Cabin" label. Furthermore, he sealed the ingredients of his syrup formula in convenient-sized tin containers made in the likeness of log cabins. The buying public took to the felicitous combination of Towle's Maple Syrup enclosed in log-cabin tins. Any one who once sampled the syrup repeated the purchase. In the course of time Log Cabin Maple Syrup became another American institution. In 1927 Mr. Towle's company was incorporated into General Foods Corporation.

About 1910 the Log Cabin spoons, in both demi-tasse and teaspoon sizes, were offered to the public as premiums in return for coupons or for coupons with a nominal sum of money. The spoons were turned out by the William Rogers Manufacturing Company, and were eagerly sought. Thousands of them found their way into homes all over the country.

The demi-tasse spoon shown in the illustration has a plain bowl, but the handle exhibits a shank simulating a thick, gnarled vine or a tree branch, from which numerous smaller limbs have been lopped, leaving their annular rings exposed throughout the extension of the handle.

A log cabin rests as a finial in the perch formed by the bifurcation of the viny branch at the shank terminal. The cabin shows an outside chimney, one door, and the name of "Towle's Log Cabin" on the roof. A single window appears on the reverse side.

This spoon was given as a premium to Mrs. Alyse D. Westbrook, Hayward, California, in 1910. Its length is 4½ inches.

No. 68 WHITE SULPHUR SPRINGS

The Indians had a pretty legend concerning the origin of White Sulphur Springs. According to this story a brave who had once been the most invincible fighter of his tribe lost all interest in combat when he met up with a gentle Indian maiden in this valley at the crest of the Allegheny Mountains. Heedless of all remonstrances, the warrior dallied in the glades near his beloved. The god of battle, angered at this disobedience and seeming cowardice, bolted two arrows from the clouds, in a streak of lightning, at the courting pair while they were walking together. One of the darts pierced the warrior's heart, killing him instantly. The other, aimed at the maiden, missed its mark and rooted itself in the ground close by her feet. The grief-stricken girl grasped the embedded arrow to pull it from the earth and consummate its intended mission. But the arrow, on being drawn from the soil, released a gushing body of water, which in time came to be known as the White Sulphur Springs. The warrior was buried on the ridge to the west of the valley, now "The Sleeping Giant," behind which the sun sinks to rest. The god then inflicted a punishment of mental torture on the maiden by compelling her to wander alone through this valley as long as the waters gushed from the spring. Not until the spring dried up would she be reunited with her lover. Her mourning voice may still be heard far up and down through the valley in the soughing of the winds and the sighing of leaves.

Herds of buffalo once roamed near the spot to drink of its refreshing waters. Indians resorted to the spring for its therapeutical values in curing many ailments. The first white patient, a woman helpless and crippled with rheumatism, was borne hither in 1778 on a litter. After two months of treatment she was able to walk away with her limbs restored to their normal uses.

James Caldwell, owner of the property from 1816 to 1851, publicized the Springs and devised every means possible for the comfort and relaxation of visitors. An old record tells us that the following famous people were all registered at the same time at the hotel—an unbelievable assembly of notables: Andrew Jackson, Henry Clay, Daniel Webster, Millard Fillmore, John Tyler and his second wife on their honeymoon, John James Audubon, and Rufus Choate. Other presidents who occasionally came here were Martin Van Buren, William Henry Harrison, and James Buchanan. Many lesser lights are also mentioned.

Charles Dudley Warner, editor and essayist, gives us the day's routine at the spa in the eighties of the last century. It is a realistic, though not an exciting picture: "The business at the White Sulphur is pleasure. And this is about the order of proceedings: A few conscientious people take an early glass at the spring, and later patronize the baths, and there is a crowd at the post office; a late breakfast; lounging and gossip on the galleries and in the parlor; politics and old-fogy talk in the reading-room and in the piazza corners; flirtation on the lawn; wine parties under the trees; morning calls at the cottages; servants running hither and thither with cooling drinks; the barroom not absolutely deserted and cheerless at any hour, day or night; occasionally a riding party; strolls in Lovers' Walk and in the pretty hill paths; dinner from two to four; supper at eight, and then the full-dress assembly in the drawing-room; the nightly dance, witnessed by a crowd on the veranda, followed frequently by a private german and a supper given by some lover of his kind, lasting till all hours of the morning. And lest their life should become monotonous, the enterprising young men are continually organizing entertainments, mock races, comical games. The idea seems to prevail that a summer resort should be a place of enjoyment."

Like other watering places of this sort, White Sulphur Springs has enjoyed its "ups" and endured its "downs." Its proximity to the national capital and other big centers in the East has helped to make it a favored spot with vacationers, especially when sojourns must be short. The beautiful mountain views, high altitude, and salubrious climate are factors tending also to bring people here when the weather elsewhere is sweltering hot.

The name of this well-known resort is engraved in the gold-washed bowl of the spoon we have in hand. The shaft is adorned perpendicularly with a series of conifer crests, diaper fashion, and a stalk of corn, or Indian maize, with the ear bursting from the shuck. The banderole at the waist carries the inscription, "W. Virginia." The nave contains focally a sheep, facing left, grass and stubble below, and heads of grain above, more likely those of barley than of wheat because of the long beards.

The caput pictures the state seal, in general outline more like the disc on the state flag. The motto, *Montani semper liberi* (Mountaineers are always free), is inserted at the top, contrariwise to its official place at the base. On the left a farmer, clothed in the hunting outfit of a pioneer, places his right hand on a plow handle, and with his left balances an axe over his left shoulder. A rock, waist high, showing 1863, the date for the formation of West Virginia as a separate state, is intertwined with ivy around its base, and the sun with flaring rays peers from behind the rock. This latter feature is absent from both state flag and seal.

On the right is a miner, right arm akimbo, his left supporting a miner's pick on his shoulder. To his rear may be seen an anvil and sledge hammer.

At the base of the seal are two cross-rifles, surmounted by a Phrygian cap at the point of contact.

The reverse of the handle is ornamented by a bundle of faggots tied together by ribands crossed diagonally; cross-flags; an eagle with disproportionately high outspread wings; a wreath, supposedly of mountain laurel and cereal leaves; and minor decorations of one sort or another.

Made by the Watson Company after 1905, when the crown W and lion, used here, replaced the old naval code flag trademark of Watson and Newell. Length of spoon, 5½ inches.

This spoon has been used through the courtesy of its owner, Mr. Frank Hanshaw, Jr., Huntington, West Virginia.

No. 69 CALVERT AND KEY

The title of Lord Baltimore was held by six members of the Calvert family, all in direct lineal descent. Of these, the first, third, and fifth lived in or, at least, visited the New World; the second, fourth, and sixth did not do so. As proprietors they usually sent out governors to administer their domains; only the third and the fifth Lords remained for any considerable time in Maryland and attempted to serve personally as its governors. Other members of the family also served as governors. This long, dominating influence of the Calverts—on the whole, wise, tolerant, and beneficial—set its seal permanently upon the social, political and religious attitudes characteristic of Maryland's history.

George Calvert, subsequently the first Lord Baltimore, was born in Yorkshire in 1580, of a family partly Flemish by descent, with some Irish connections, and inclined toward the Catholic faith, but conforming outwardly, owing to the rigid laws against their religion, to the Established Church. The father, who belonged to the educated class of landed gentry, wished to give his son as good an education as possible and accordingly sent him to Oxford, where he displayed a special aptitude for languages, acquiring a thorough mastery of Latin, Greek, French, Italian, and Spanish. After his graduation he traveled extensively on the Continent before returning to Oxford for his master's degree, after which, gaining favor with Lord Cecil, he held several governmental positions and became a member of Parliament from a constituency in Cornwall. Appointed to a royal clerkship in Ireland, he lived for four years in that country and eventually acquired large holdings there.

In 1604 he married the daughter of a Hertfordshire gentleman, and in the eighteen years of their wedded life eleven children were born to them. In 1617 he was knighted by King James, who made him his principal secretary of state and a member of his privy council. His missions to several European countries were eminently succesful.

For years King James hankered after an alliance with the Spanish royal family. Calvert naturally favored a marriage between the young Prince Charles and the Infanta Maria, and much of the correspondence promoting the match devolved upon his hands. Charles was sent, in company of the Duke of Buckingham, to Madrid to press his suit in person at the Spanish court. Charles stopped over in Paris and met the French princess, Henrietta Maria, and evidently found the French demoiselle more to his liking than the Spanish señorita, for he returned to England without the Infanta Maria, and all further negotiations in that direction were dropped.

The failure to consummate this alliance between the English and Spanish royal families was a bitter blow to Calvert, who had hoped thereby that he would be insuring good will between the two countries, with the avoidance of many needless wars henceforth, to the detriment of both nations. He therefore retired from all offices, and publicly announced his adherence to the Roman Catholic Church. The King, in recognition of the many years of Calvert's faithful service to the Crown, bestowed upon his favorite minister the title of Lord Baltimore among the Irish peers of his realm.

In the course of his duties Calvert had found ample opportunity to observe the progress of colonizing efforts in Virginia and New England,

and seeing the restrictions constantly hedging his fellow-Catholics round about, he sought means for establishing a colony in the New World where all men, including more particularly those of his own faith, could profess whatever religion they chose, publicly proclaimed, without fear of persecution.

From an old Oxford classmate, Sir William Vaughan, who held the patent, Calvert procured rights for a settlement on the southeastern tip of Newfoundland. The young King Charles showed his generosity by extending the rights to include the whole of Newfoundland when he granted Calvert a charter, which in substance permitted the introduction of a palatine form of government. The palatinate, a survival of a feudal type of suzerainty, gave to its rulers almost complete powers of control over the lives, lands, and liberties of their subjects, providing they vowed absolute allegiance and loyalty to the king.

The new colony was to receive the name of Avalon, the idea for such deriving probably from the mythical island of that designation lying off the shores of Paradise, according to old medieval romances. "A Relation of the New-found-land," by Captain Richard Whitbourne, was circulated among prospective emigrants, and no doubt the latter were greatly influenced by the marvelous descriptions of "filladies, nightingales, and such like that sing most pleasantly;" of fruited bowers and benign sunshine, even in winter. The seas round about swarmed with strange fishes of all sorts, possibly mermaids among them. The animals of the forest were "gentle and humane." Scant mention was made of the natives, who were harmless and helpful.

For seven years the colonists of Avalon struggled to survive. They did not find the songbirds, the wild strawberries, and the fish, except during the summer, and that was all too short. The land was locked in sheets of ice, as impenetrable as coats of mail, from seven to nine months of the year. The "Harbor of Heartsease" became one of "heartache," the "Bay of Flowers," a bed of fleecy icecaps.

Worse than the wintry weather were the constant plagues of sickness. The small cabins served not as homes but as hospitals all winter long. On his second trip out in 1628, Lord Baltimore brought his second wife and several of his children with him. Shortly after, a French fleet appeared in the Harbor of Heartsease, and a severe fight took place; the French were driven off, but in spite of this victorious encounter, the morale of the colony was shattered. "I came to build, and settle, and sow, and I am fallen to fighting Frenchmen," he lamented in a letter home.

Disillusioned, Calvert and his little band hoisted sail with their few belongings on board ship, and headed south for Virginia. Not finding too warm a welcome among these Church of England people, and not wishing to take the oath of supremacy, which would compel him to recognize the King as head of the Church, he set out for England to seek a grant for settlement to the south of Virgina, somewhere in the territory adjacent to Raleigh's lost colony of Roanoke.

Hearing of this, the Virginia council sent to London a commission, which effectually blocked the disposition of any land in the Carolinas to Lord Baltimore. Undaunted in his purpose, the latter continued his efforts till he had secured the approval of King Charles for a settlement in the uninhabited parts of the Virginia territory, that is, to the north as far as the fortieth parallel and as far south as the Potomac River.

Before affixing his signature to the charter, the King asked his Lordship what he intended naming the new colony. Calvert replied diplomatically that, since the sovereign's name had been preëmpted in the term *Carolina*, he expected to use "Crescentia," signifying the Land of Increase. "Why not call it *Terra Mariae* in honor of the Queen?" suggested the King. It was accordingly named Maryland after the royal consort, Henrietta Maria.

The provisions of this charter were similar to those in the Avalon grant, and the sole compensation required of the colony in return for His Majesty's beneficence was "Two Indian Arrows of those parts, to be delivered at the Said Castle of Windsor, every year, on Tuesday in Easter week; and also the fifth part of all Gold and Silver Ore which shall happen from time to time to be found within the aforesaid limits." The stipulation about the arrows may sound to our ears like a piece of tomfoolery; also, like the cover-up of a most magnanimous gift—especially from a monarch always hard pressed for money. It must be remembered, however, that the Virginia enterprise had bankrupted the London Company, and the New England colonizing experiments had paid no dividends. The King, then, very naturally did not want any strings of responsibility attached to the agreement which might pull open the drains to the royal exchequer, nor could he foresee, on the other hand, any sources of emolument in the future unless gold and silver mines were discovered in the area—hopes for such a streak of luck were not to be entirely dismissed . . . there was always the remote possibility.

Before the Great Seal had been affixed to the charter, Lord Baltimore passed away in April of 1632, having reached his fifty-second year, worn out prematurely by a train of troubles and trials. He had spent most of a large fortune in support of the Avalon and Maryland ventures; the rigorous climate at Avalon had sapped his vitality, and left him an invalid; he had suffered a grievous blow in the loss of Lady Baltimore, his second wife, and several of his children, who were drowned at sea on their return from Virginia. Moreover, he had sorrowed deeply at the adverse lot of his co-religionists. Still, by his "patience, constancy, and a clear practical view of the needs and risks of colonization in America," and, in spite of the failure of his first attempt, "that failure," observes the Maryland historian, William Hand Browne, "showed him how to lay the foundation of the first English colony that was successful from the start." J. Moss

Ives likens him to Moses, for "although he had beheld the promised land, he was never to set his foot thereon."

Cecil Calvert, the second Lord Baltimore, then twenty-six years old, proceeded rapidly with the enterprise. The two vessels, the *Ark*, a ship of four hundred ton burden, and the *Dove*, a pinnace of only forty ton, departed November 22, 1633, from Cowes in the Isle of Wight. About three hundred people were on board; the estimates as to the proportion of Catholics to Protestants among them have always varied widely, but they must have been about equally divided.

Lord Baltimore himself felt it advisable to stay in England to protect the interests of his charter, his two younger brothers, Leonard and George, being in charge of the expedition. On the way the little *Dove* could not keep pace with the more stalwart *Ark*, so that the latter had to reef a portion of its sails to slacken its speed. Before their arrival at the Canaries, a violent tempest separated the two vessels. The distress signal-lights went up on the tiny *Dove*, which tossed about like a cork on the writhing waves. "We thought it was all over with her," narrates Father Andrew White, one of the priests aboard, "and that she had been swallowed up in the deep whirlpools, for in a moment she had passed out of sight." For six weeks the *Ark* continued along on its way toward the West Indies, everyone on board believing disconsolately that the *Dove* had gone to the bottom of the briny deeps. Imagine, then, the joy of the voyagers on the *Ark*, when, on January 3, 1634, the brave little pinnace hove into sight at Barbados.

Their first landing was at Point Comfort on February 24th. Several weeks were spent in exploring possibilities for a good town site. On March 25th they landed on St. Clement's Island where the Catholics celebrated the feast of the Annunciation, and the entire group participated in a ceremonial of thanksgiving for their safe arrival. All of them were greatly impressed by the vernal beauty of the virgin forests in these early days of spring.

The site selected for their first settlement was a high bluff on the St. Mary's River. They had brought along with them from Virginia a captain, Henry Fleet, who, from having lived five years among the Indians, acted as an interpreter and guide. The Indians, a branch of the Algonquins, willingly sold their village to the settlers for hatchets, axes, and cloth, since they wished to move away from this territory, out of reach of the hostile and more powerful Susquehannas and their allies, the Iroquois.

The new town was named St. Mary's in honor of the Virgin Mary. As the Indians continued to occupy their wigwams till the corn crop was harvested early in the fall, they taught the colonists the secrets of making good corn pone, samp, and other palatable dishes out of corn. There was an unlimited abundance of wild game and fowl in the forests; hence, the settlers did not lack for meat of a great variety, such as that derived from the deer, wild duck, goose, turkey, and ruffled grouse. The waters of the river and bay teemed with fish, oysters, diamondback terrapin, crabs, and clams. The first corn crop of the colonists was so successful that several tons were shipped off for sale in New England.

Attractive inducements were offered to secure more settlers. Every person paying his own passage was given a hundred acres of land; his wife and every child over sixteen were entitled to the same allotment; every child under sixteen received fifty acres. Servants unable to pay their way were indentured, that is, they hired themselves out for a specified period, after which they became freemen and could claim their proper share of land. A quitrent consisting at first of wheat, later, of tobacco, to the value of four shillings, was paid annually on every hundred acres of land, to the lord proprietor.

There were now three types of government found in America. In Virginia, after the London or Royal Virginia Company became insolvent in 1624, the colony was governed directly by the King, who appointed the governor and council members. The assembly, called the House of Burgesses, was elected by the various groups of landholders. The charter type of government, which prevailed in New England, allowed the people to elect their own governor, council, and assembly, and to make their own laws. In Maryland the proprietary government or palatinate gave the lord proprietor the right to select his own governor and to adjust all relations between the colony and the Crown. A group of freemen, however, soon set up an assembly chosen by popular representation, with powers to establish courts of justice and to enact laws to promote the best interests of their commercial and agricultural pursuits. At first Lord Baltimore vetoed several laws, but seeing that serious conflicts would be inevitable if he continued such a policy, wisely decided it would be far better to refrain from interference in the internal affairs of the colonists and to allow them, by and large, to govern themselves.

The keystone in the foundation of Maryland's historical structure was tolerance of all religions. The primary purpose of Lord Baltimore in establishing the colony was to effect a sanctuary for Roman Catholics, who were undergoing severe disabilities in the public profession of their religion in England. But from the very beginning, the doors of immigration were opened to Puritans and Anglicans as freely and as widely as to Catholics. So rapidly did Protestants of all degrees swarm in, that by 1649 they composed three-fourths of the population. In that year the assembly passed the famous Act concerning Religion that contained this clause: "No person or persons whatsoever within this province, professing to believe in Jesus Christ, shall from henceforth be in any way troubled, molested, or discountenanced for, or in respect of his, or her religion in the free exercise thereof, nor in any way compelled to the belief or exercise of any other religion, against his or her consent."

This law was scrupulously observed to the last letter for many years. The Baltimores occasionally appointed Protestant governors, members of

286

the assembly represented various faiths, and all worked together in harmony for their mutual good. As one of the isolated instances of intolerance and its rebuke may be taken the case of Thomas Gerrard, a Catholic member of the assembly, and owner of St. Clement's Manor, an estate of nearly twelve thousand acres. Gerrard removed the hymnals and hid the keys of the small chapel used for services by both Protestants and Catholics at St. Mary's; he was tried by a jury composed exclusively of members of his own faith and fined five hundred pounds of tobacco, the fine going toward the upkeep of the Protestant minister. It is obvious the various religious groups were bending over backwards to maintain good will one toward the other. And it paid dividends throughout the years.

During the Puritan ascendancy in England, however, the Puritans likewise gained control of the Maryland assembly and intolerantly passed a law disfranchising both Catholics and Anglicans. This law endured briefly, and was soon revoked. Then, in 1692, following the overthrow of James II and the accession of William and Mary, the Calverts lost their proprietary rights, and the Anglican church became the sole recognized church by the royal government.

Maryland was fortunate, in its early days of colonization, in not being plagued, as Virginia or Plymouth had been, by serious sieges of illness; tortured by insufficient protection from the cold or by actual starvation from the lack of proper food; nor yet massacred wholesale in their beds by hostile Indian attackers. Still there was one fly in the ointment, and that was the long, seemingly endless quarrel with Virginia about over-lapping boundaries. The Virginians had always looked askance at the proprietary to the north, and questioned the right of the Calverts to the disposal of unoccupied lands claimed by the Cavalier commonwealth. The sharpest thorn in the side of the Maryland proprietors was one William Clayborne, settled already in 1631, before the arrival of the *Ark* and the *Dove,* on Kent's Island far up Chesapeake Bay. Clayborne refused to acknowledge the authority of Maryland over his trading post, being intensely proud of the fact that he was a member of the House of Burgesses, and formerly secretary of state, within the Old Dominion. Pitched battles took place between the two factions of Clayborne and Calvert, and a few lives were lost. Clayborne was ousted from Kent's Island, but he never accepted this forced eviction with equanimity. He always felt a grave injustice had been done him, and even as late as 1677, at the age of ninety, he sought restitution of his island home in a petition to Charles II, but nothing came of it.

Cecil Calvert, the second Lord Baltimore, died in 1675. He had seen his proprietary colony grow from a population of a scant three hundred to twenty thousand. Charles Calvert, the third Lord Baltimore, lived until 1715, but he had been deprived of his political powers since 1692, although he continued to enjoy the emoluments accruing to him as a landlord. To his son, Benedict Leonard Calvert, who had become a Protestant, the proprietary title and prerogatives were restored, but he survived his father only a few months. The fifth Lord Baltimore, Charles Calvert, was considered by Walpole as the "best and honestest man in the world with a good deal of jumbled knowledge." It was during his time that the city of Baltimore was founded, in 1729. The last proprietor, Frederick Calvert, was a bad poet and not a very good man. His natural son, Harry Harford, did not inherit the lordship's title but received the rights of the proprietorship. The whole antiquated structure of the palatinate, a political anachronism already when it was set up, toppled with the outbreak of the Revolutionary War. But the live-and-let-live policy toward all religions in the beginnings of Maryland was something new, a salutary lesson for the other colonies—one that should not be lightly forgotten.

❖   ❖   ❖   ❖

The other figure with whom we are concerned in this sketch is Francis Scott Key, author of "The Star Spangled Banner." Three monuments have been erected to honor Key. One of them overlooks the West Coast in Golden Gate Park in San Francisco. The other two are in Baltimore. One of these, erected in 1911 in the northwestern part of the city, pictures Key in the act of handing over a copy of the national anthem to Columbia. The monument in the bowl of the Calvert and Key spoon shows Orpheus, the entrancing poet-musician of ancient Greece, holding a banner aloft in his hands. This legendary figure, constructed of bronze, stands on a granite pedestal supported by four fluted Doric columns forming an open space in which there is an Olympic fire basin.

At the foot and out in front of the monument is a skiff, in which the bronze figure of Key is standing erect, face turned upward, one foot on the gunwale, and his right hand extended as if hailing the supreme votary of song. There is also in the skiff a boatman, seated, his oars at rest in his hands. At the base of the bowl, all of which is in relief, is the date "1814" and around the feet of Orpheus is inscribed the name of the monument.

Francis Scott Key was born in Frederick County, Maryland, in 1779, while his father was serving in the ranks of the Continental army. An uncle was fighting on the Tory side.

After Key's graduation from St. John's in Annapolis, he studied and practiced law with his brother-in-law, Roger Brooke Taney, who later became Chief Justice of the Supreme Court.

During the War of 1812 Key rowed out to the British fleet anchored in Chesapeake Bay as an emissary, carrying a letter from President Madison in behalf of a Doctor Beanes who had been abused and imprisoned aboard an English transport for his allegedly insulting remarks about the British soldiery. Key delivered his missive but was detained on board pending the enemy's attack on Fort McHenry. During the bombardment, which took place the night of September 13-14, 1814, Key could see through his porthole the "rockets' red glare, the bombs bursting in air"—a new kind of illuminating rocket.

Key worked out the entire poem in his mind, and did not put it to paper till the next morning when he was being conveyed to shore. Then he used the inside of an envelope for a manuscript, now preserved in the Walters Art Gallery in Baltimore. Printed first in the *Baltimore American*, it was reprinted as a broadside and hawked through the streets. Key had written the words to a tune running through his mind, an old English drinking song, "Anacreon in Heaven."

Key died in 1843. His brother-in-law, Justice Taney, published in 1857 a collection of Key's poems, none of them memorable except for his one inspired effort. Would that Key had had a more singable tune coursing through his head when he wrote our national anthem!

The Calvert and Key is an extremely interesting spoon, embracing a wealth of native matter in its outlines, so much so that it could aptly be dubbed "Maryland, my Maryland"—it is relieved, really, with enough suggestive details to suffice for half a dozen spoons.

"The City of Baltimore" runs lengthwise inscribed on the shaft. In the nave is the Battle Monument. The caput is superbly treated, shaped like a Hepplewhite chairback, in showing the bust of Lord Baltimore. This is definitely George Calvert, the first of the proprietors, since he is the only one of the six Calverts to wear a hirsute adornment on his face. All the others were clean shaven.

The reverse side of handle bears on the caput the state seal of Maryland, representing the arms of the Calvert and Crossland families; in the nave is the Battle Monument; along the shank are seen a wild duck, a diamondback terrapin, a crab, and two oysters.

Made by the Watson Company. Length is 5½ inches.

No. 71 RED WING

Many of us who have passed the midway span of life can clearly remember when the whole nation was singing or humming sentimentalized Indian ditties like "Red Wing," "Silver Bell," or "Rainbow." Every one then thought of a graceful Indian belle when he sang—

> Oh, the moon shines bright tonight on Red Wing,
> My pretty Red Wing.

Not every one knew, however, that Red Wing was the name of a whole line of Indian chieftains who camped along the serene bluffs overlooking the Mississippi River where the town of Red Wing is situated today in Minnesota.

One of these Dakota leaders seized Father Hennepin when he was exploring the upper reaches of the Mississippi in 1680. The Indian word was Koo-poo-hoo-sha, *Koopuha* meaning wing, *sha* red, from the feathers of the swan which had been dyed red and worn as a headdress by the chief.   The Dakotas then resided in the Thousand Lakes region.

Nearly a hundred years later another Red Wing cleared the forests for an encampment on the present site of this town.   Zebulon Pike, of Pike's Peak fame, passed by the village in 1805 on his journey westward.

Swiss missionaries were the first white people to come among these Indians, about 1835, to convert them to Christianity.   The amalgamation of whites and redskins was peaceful, and descendants of Dakotas and Sioux still live in Red Wing.

The turreted structure cut out in the bowl of this particular spoon should have double significance for the antiquarian because it no longer exists.   The "L.L.Seminary" engraved on the left side of the bowl stands for the Ladies' Lutheran Seminary, which was built by the Norwegian Lutheran Church in 1893 on a picturesque eminence with a commanding view of the town and the meandering river banks.   The structure was built of pressed brick surmounted on a foundation of hewn stone.   The concept of the school stressed the value of Christian training in education, and while all the academic courses were pursued, music took precedence over any other, and the glee club and choir were widely known throughout the rest of the state and elsewhere in the Northwest.   The seminary burned in 1920.

The handle contains the name of Minnesota on the shaft.   In the nave are a gopher and a moccasin flower, the latter being the state flower.

The seal of Minnesota stands in the caput.   A white settler is seen at the handles of a plow, plodding eastward but with his face turned backward toward an Indian galloping by on horseback.   The setting sun, noted on the official seal, is not visible here.   In the right background the Falls of St. Anthony appear indistinctly, somewhat like a cloud of mist.

The state motto in French, "L'Etoile du Nord" (Star of the North) is placed at the collar of the stem.   On the reverse side may be seen the state capitol building and a lumber camp.

Made by the Sterling Silver Manufacturing Company, now out of business.   Length is 5¼ inches.

No. 72 TAMPA STRAWBERRIES

The soapbox rabble-rouser who cried out, "Come the Revolution, and you will all git strawberries and cream," was making no mistake in his efforts to influence his auditors when he mentioned America's favorite berry crowned with cream for a prize-winning dessert.   The strawberry appeals not only to the palate but equally as well to the eye and the nostrils. Perhaps it was this extraordinary appeal that caused Doctor William Butler

PLATE 38

72. TAMPA STRAWBERRIES   73. LOS ANGELES GRAPES
74. JACKSONVILLE ORANGES   75. ROCKY FORD MELONS

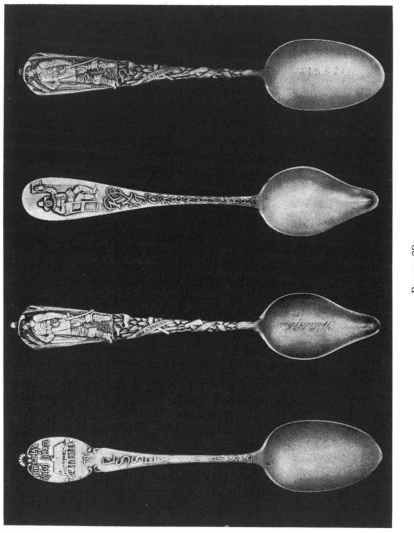

PLATE 39

76. BIRTHPLACE OF RUFUS CHOATE   77a. MILES STANDISH (fruit bowl)
78. KNICKERBOCKER   77b. MILES STANDISH (oval bowl)

to exclaim, "Doubtless God could have made a better berry, but doubtless He never did."

That the strawberry, known in some Northern countries of Europe by the lowly name of "earth-berry," has always been highly regarded, is attested by the fact that in the British peerage the coronet of a duke bears eight gold strawberry leaves gracefully surmounting the golden head-band. The coronet of a marquess alternates four golden strawberry leaves with four silver balls on a circlet of silver. An earl's coronet carries eight small gold strawberry leaves alternating between elevated silver balls, all topping the circlet of silver. In Scandinavia numerous members of the nobility employ the strawberry or its leaves on robes, coronets, and heraldic devices.

When the early colonists arrived in this country, they found large areas of land covered with the wild scarlet, or Virginia, strawberry. To a lesser extent other species of the fruit were seen in colors of white, yellow, green, and purple, and in shapes varying from oval to conical. In their reports Roger Williams and Captain John Smith mention a wide distribution of the strawberry growing along streams, on hillsides, and in open woodlands of the Atlantic coastline. The Indians considered the fruit a delicacy, and crushed the berries for a flavoring syrup over cornbread, thus anticipating our modern type of shortcake.

For more than two centuries the raising of strawberries was restricted almost wholly to the home gardens of farmers and of small-town dwellers. During the 1860's many gardeners living near the big Eastern cities began to cultivate the strawberry more intensively, seeing there was a constantly increasing demand for this table delicacy. Today the sales of this small-fruit crop reach a total amount of about fifty million dollars annually. No other fruit is so widely grown under the most varying climatic conditions and during every season of the year. There are early berries and late berries; some are produced for their richness of flavor, some for their large size; others are noted for the hardiness of their flower buds in cold weather, their firmness in packing, or their resistance to scorch, mildew, virus, red stele, and leaf spots.

The South is the chief strawberry-growing section of the country. In the production of quarts, the states lead in this order: Louisiana, Tennessee, Arkansas, Florida, Virginia, Kentucky, and North Carolina. The earliest shipments from Florida begin during the first weeks of December, and from then until the first of March that state is the sole supplier of our midwinter berries.

Hillsborough County, in which Tampa is located, raises more than three-fourths of the strawberries grown in Florida and tops the list of strawberry-growing counties in the United States. The focal point for the production of this crop, however, is Plant City, several miles east of Tampa. Officially named after Henry B. Plant, the railroad magnate, when the town was incorporated in 1885, the site was originally known as

Ichpucksassa, meaning "tobacco fields." In early times the Seminoles prized this area for its rich yields of tobacco. The first white settlers raised cotton here until the returns from that crop became unprofitable in competition with other sections of the South. Toward the end of the nineteenth century experiments proved that strawberries could be grown successfully in a semi-tropical climate.

The Klondike and Blakemore were the first varieties planted in Hillsborough County. Gradually, however, the Missionary has supplanted all other varieties. This species bears a dark crimson, cone-shaped berry, somewhat below the average in size, firm in texture, slightly acidulous, strongly resistant to scorch and leaf spots, and robust enough for any shipping purposes. It ripens quickly in the alternation of sunny days and cool nights, and can withstand considerable cold. Sometimes, indeed, it is necessary to nail pecky cypress boards in the form of V-shaped troughs over the plants, to ward off the frost during cold snaps. Pine needles or a straw mulch are then strewn over the plants, but such a covering must be quickly removed with the return of warm weather.

The strawberry business has been truthfully called a "year-around job." Preparation of the soil begins ten days or two weeks before the plants are set. Furrows are spaced, and fertilizer evenly distributed. Shovel-toothed cultivators are run through the furrows to prevent an excess of fertilizing deposit in any one spot near the plant roots. The beds are hilled up directly above the furrows. Nursery plants are set out on these hill rows during January and February, but the running tendrils are not allowed to spread till fall. This enables the parent plant to conserve its strength and build up a thick tuft of roots and leaves. Throughout the summer the flowering stems must be removed, the plants thinned and cultivated, weeds killed, and the ground properly mulched. The healthiest runner plants are reset in permanent fields from August to November.

The picking and marketing season, which lasts from early December to late March, is an exciting time in the vicinity of Plant City. Modern refrigerating methods and rapid express cars transport huge consignments of berries within two days from the Florida fields to the Northern markets. Lively auctions are held in the warehouses, and buyers bid heatedly against each other after a couple of pint-boxes laden with luscious berries have been passed around for sampling. Consignments are loaded daily into refrigerated cars and headed North. About 700,000 crates are sold annually, and this amount yields about $1,500,000.

All hands are kept busy during the rush season. Special arrangements have been made whereby the school term is extended into the summer for those children who drop out to help during the berry harvest. At this season on the highway, which runs through a thriving truck-gardening section between Plant City and Tampa, there may be seen many roadside stands selling boxes of strawberries, jars of strawberry preserves, cans of strawberry juice, and even strawberry shortcake.

At the height of the greatest activity comes the gala Strawberry Festival at Plant City in February, and the magnificent floats coming from all parts of Florida make a spectacular parade that vies with the best seen in a state noted for its parades.

The Tampa Strawberry spoon is a beautiful piece of silver with a fruit-type bowl shaped like a strawberry. The name of Tampa is engraved in the bowl. Three lovely, ripe strawberries in high relief, surrounded so realistically by clusters of leaves, vines, and tendrils on the handle make such a strong appeal to the gustatory senses that one, on seeing them, can hardly refrain from watering at the mouth.

On the reverse of handle appears another strawberry with a décor of leaves and tendrils. This spoon was pressed by the Watson Company. The length is 6 inches.

No. 73 LOS ANGELES GRAPES

Grapes or the leaves and tendrils of the grapevine have always been used for decorative purposes by the various arts. In ancient Greece and Rome the grape was a feature on many architectural designs. It has been used occasionally on furniture for ornamentation of chairbacks and dresser-pulls. On china, clusters of grapes have been extensively used, especially on cake plates and trays, to adorn borders or as centerpieces. On glass no patterns have ever been so popular as those featuring grapes. More than thirty well known patterns of this fruit, in one form or another, exist on glass. The demand for the Heavy Panelled Grape, with its exquisite details so prominently clear in relief, has surpassed that of all other patterns in glass, and its popularity is unceasing.

On silver, however, the grape has appeared less frequently than it has on glass. But it has a natural right, appearing as it does here on this souvenir spoon, to be connected geographically with some section of California, for about nine-tenths of the nation's commercial grapes are grown in that state.

In the Eastern and North Central states most of the grapes are those developed from the native wild varieties and, as often as not, do not find their way to market but are planted on a small scale for local or home consumption. Chief among the varieties from the North Atlantic westward across the Great Plains are the Catawba, Concord, Delaware, Fredonia, Golden Muscat, Niagara, Portland, Seneca, and Worden. In the South and along the Gulf Coast the Scuppernong, the Beacon, and the Muscadine or Southern Fox Grape have been cultivated from high-climbing wild species.

In California the European-type grape has been introduced and developed intensively by the best scientific methods, and being less perishable in shipment and storage, has many commercial advantages over the native stocks grown elsewhere in the country.

At San Gabriel, eight miles northeast of Los Angeles, Franciscan friars planted one of the earliest vineyards in California. An enormous grapevine, about one hundred feet in length and covering a wide area, is contained in the patio adjoining the mission and clambers over trellises, walls, and into the embrasures of the belfry. It is said to have been planted in 1771. From San Gabriel, ten years later, a small expedition of soldiers, local-store merchants, and vine-growers set out under the Spanish governor to establish a new pueblo on the site of what eventually became the thriving city of Los Angeles.

Vineyards graced the area around all the early missions. San Diego Mission claims the earliest planting, in 1770. At Jolon an old tavern boasts a vine that has passed the century mark. The great vine that once existed at Carpenteria east of Santa Barbara measured nine feet in circumference arounds its base and bore an average of eight tons of grapes annually for many years before it died in 1916. All these large grape stocks, more like twisted tree-trunks, are of the Mission variety.

In 1852 the Hungarian expert on viticulture, Augustin Haraszthy, began to import and experiment with the European type of grape with low, thickset stock, eventually setting out more than 200,000 plants. As a result, there are grapes produced for every use in California today. For the table are grown the Malaga, Castiza, Sultana, and Tokay; for raisins, the Muscat Alexandria and the Sultanina; and for wines, both in black and white varieties, the Zinfandel, Alexandria, Barbara, Burger, Green Hungarian, and Palomino. Around Sacramento originated the Thompson seedless grape, the growing of which has spread to other regions. The areas north and south of San Francisco near the coast produce most of the dry wines. The sweet-wine grapes are grown in the central valley around Fresno, Stockton, and Lodi. The great Guasti vineyards are located in San Bernardino County, east of Los Angeles, in a territory which would be absolutely arid and valueless without irrigation.

This spoon shows a delicious cluster of grapes in a gold-washed bowl that sparkles with an oxidized flare. The incised finger-carving is done with a deft craftsmanship, the name of Los Angeles appearing along the right side of the bowl. The handle-shaft is threaded as far as the nave, along the sides of which and around the caput runs a dainty floral trim, fastened back like a curtain on either side by four doubly-wound fillets, the tied ends of which curl like tendrils. The lines of this handle are very graceful, showing a Louis XV influence in its rococo design.

The spoon was cast by R. Wallace and Sons, and was patented in 1899. The length is 5⅜ inches.

No. 74 JACKSONVILLE ORANGES

Jacksonville is not a land of oranges so much as it is the gateway to that land. Many a tourist has seen the first oranges growing on trees around Jacksonville and eaten the first golden-yellow fruit plucked by his own hands in this vicinity. Jacksonville is moreover the gateway through which the boxed fruit and canned juice roll north by rail, truck, and water.

Directly to the south and southwest of the city begins the area where grows the best citrus fruit. The Satsuma orange, imported from Japan, is grown profitably throughout north Florida because it withstands a lower temperature than any other variety. Its smallness of size and thinness of peeling are compensated by the earliness of its maturity. The Parson Brown and Hamlin, thin-skinned and sweet-fleshed, are likewise early bearers, being gathered before there is a need for protection from frost.

Midseason varieties include the Pineapple, Homosassa, Enterprise, and Nonpareil, oranges which have originated in Florida from native permutations of seed plantings. While sweet and juicy, they tend to be medium in size and seedy.

Of late varieties are the Valencia, Boone, Ruby, St. Michael, Temple, and Lue Gim Gong. These, with the exception of the last named, are importations from Mediterranean coasts. The Valencia, popular both in Florida and California, is a large, almost seedless fruit that keeps well in shipment. The Ruby and St. Michael, oblong and red-pulped, bear prolifically.

The Temple is a late-comer among Florida oranges. Beautiful to the eye and most delicious to the taste, it is bound to supersede many of the older varieties. To the connoisseur its flavor, which lacks tartness, and its brimming succulence are unequaled. Many recent groves in south and central Florida are Temple plantings.

Navel oranges, though originating in Florida, do better in California. The two main varieties of this seedless orange are the Washington and the Surprise. Sour-orange trees serve for grafting purposes. Low-lying areas, subject to excessive moisture, are planted with these trees, which are strongly resistant to root and bark diseases. Variations of the orange have developed into distinct fruits like the tangerine, tangelo, and calamondin.

The orange tree matures slowly, and does not grant a full yield till its seventh or eighth year. A well-tended tree will bear four to five hundred pounds of fruit annually for many years.

Spanish missionaries brought the orange along with other tropical fruits to Florida in the sixteenth century. Many groves, once thriving, were abandoned, after the main period of their productivity, to the native jungles. The trees, becoming acclimatized, survived and flourished on their own amid the wild native growth.

Citrus did not become king in Florida till the eighties of the last century, when Flagler and Plant began the building of railroads, which provided an outlet in northern markets for oranges and grapefruit. Shipments of these fruits begin in September and rise steadily in volume till January; then the market gradually tapers off till June. At the height of the season, around Christmas, more than three hundred carloads travel north-bound daily.

For many years tourists traveled no farther south than Jacksonville or St. Augustine. In the early seventies luxurious steamboats offered excursions down the St. Johns River from Jacksonville, and tourists caught glimpses of picturesque orange groves bordering the broad, placid stream.

Long before Jacksonville was founded and named in honor of Andrew Jackson, who incidentally never graced the town with his presence, there were orange groves along the St. Johns River. In 1765, during the British occupation of Florida, Denys Rolle, a wealthy member of Parliament, acquired a land grant of 80,000 acres some fifty miles south of Jacksonville and brought in a group of ne'er-do-wells from the London slums to work on his enormous plantation. Finding these settlers shiftless and unprofitable, he imported slaves, who were more adaptable to work in the tropics. Rolle did a great deal of experimentation with oranges. Among the items which we find in his shipments to England in one season were a thousand gallons of orange wine.

In 1767, Dr. Andrew Turnbull, a Scotchman, settled 1,500 foreigners, mostly Minorcans, on a grant of 100,000 acres near New Smyrna. It was a grandiose scheme, fostered by the British Government, which hoped for extensive shipments of indigo, sugar, and fruit from the colony to the mother country. After a hectic existence of nine years the rebellious colonists destroyed the buildings and scattered to other parts while Dr. Turnbull was in England, trying to stabilize the finances of the wobbly enterprise. Several thousand acres of newly planted orange trees reverted to the jungle. The ruins of an old sugar mill, recently reclaimed, attest the impermanency of this lost colony.

The site on the St. Johns River, where Jacksonville now stands, was known to the Indians as Wacca Palatka, meaning a "ford for cows." The Spaniards in 1740 built a fort on the south bank of the river to hold control of this passageway. During the English occupation the place was simply known as Cowford.

While the region was still under Spanish rule Americans were already acquiring grants of land for plantations. Immediately after the United States' purchase of Florida in 1821, a town at Cowford was plotted out and renamed Jacksonville. For thirty years the settlement remained isolated except for transportation by water. Union forces burned the town in 1863.

The Reconstruction period witnessed the real beginning of Jacksonville's growth. Northerners came to spend the winter as tourists, the most notable among them perhaps being Harriet Beecher Stowe. The channel of the St. Johns River was dredged deep enough for steamships to traverse the twenty-six miles from the Atlantic as far as the city docks. The rapid rise of industries began in the eighties when Jacksonville was made the hub of a network of railroads running north, south, and west to connect with the ocean traffic fanning out into the Atlantic.

Jacksonville long maintained its position as the largest city in Florida. Although it has recently lost that preëminence to Miami, it still boasts the largest number of industries in the state. No small part of the credit for this industrial development is due to the Negroes, who comprise one-third of the city's population. While the majority of them are manual laborers, many own and operate prospering businesses, participate in varied religious, musical, and literary activities, and contribute their share to the progress and well-being of the city.

Few tourists pay Jacksonville more than a fleeting visit: to them, in going north, it is the last outpost of Florida; in going south, they regard it as the gateway to the glamorous, golden land of sunshine and oranges.

This spoon, engraved for Jacksonville in the bowl, bears the leaves and fruit of the orange on both the reverse and obverse sides of a handle that terminates in an ogival arch. Impressed by the Shepard Manufacturing Company, it measures 6 inches in length.

No. 75 ROCKY FORD MELONS

Emerson once expressed himself to the effect that a man who could surpass every one else in the excellence with which he did a thing, even were it a mouse trap, would have a path beaten to his door by the rest of the world. The small rural community of Rocky Ford, on the plains of eastern Colorado, did just what Emerson had in mind when the farmers in that section began to experiment with the idea of raising a melon which would excel all others in quantity, quality, and size.

There are three general types of muskmelons grown in this country, namely, the nutmeg melon, the cantaloupe, and the winter melon. The first type has a thin netted rind with a green fleshy pulp that extends from the outer surface to a depth of about half an inch. The meat of this melon is very sweet. The winter melon is a variety that can be stored away for winter use. It has a pastel-green coating rind that lacks the delicate aroma emanating from other types.

The Rocky Ford melon is in reality a cantaloupe, large and savory, with well-indented lines that are spaced far enough apart to afford cuttings of thick, crescent-shaped slices. This deep-ribbed melon sometimes rivals a pumpkin in size.

Rocky Ford derived its name from the bed of stones found in the shallow waters of the Arkansas River at this point. In many places elsewhere in the river, quicksand bottoms made treacherous crossings.

The development of the Rocky Ford melon began along in the 1890's, and in a few years the Eastern seaboard was calling for more carloads than could be supplied by the Colorado growers. Epicurean appetites once whetted by the taste of Rocky Ford melons wanted no other kind.

The man who deserves the credit for the development of this melon, prized by gourmets, was George Washington Swink, a grizzled adventurer who came West to pan gold but went no farther than Rocky Ford. He saw the possibilities for making the desert bloom here through irrigation. He accordingly dug ditches and planted melons on his irrigated acres. He harvested a bumper crop. Other settlers took the clue and did likewise. Swink mapped out a town, planted an abundance of trees along the streets, and sold real estate. He struck a bonanza but the rich yield of golden nuggets was disguised in the shape of big succulent melons.

In addition to its melons, Rocky Ford grows thousands of tons of sugar beets. It also furnishes the seed for many flowers and vegetables, sent in a wide distribution over the country.

The name of Rocky Ford is engraved in the bowl of this spoon. The shaft of the handle contains a melon leaf and tendril at either end. The nave displays a smaller melon and a large five-pointed leaf, while the caput shows a handsome big melon with huge wedges, capped by a leaf looking somewhat like the star at the top of a Christmas tree. There are vines and leaves on the reverse of the handle also. Made by Watson and Newell, this spoon is 5½ inches long.

No. 76 BIRTHPLACE OF RUFUS CHOATE

High on the roster of those famous men who have most ably expounded the law in America stands Rufus Choate, a person who in many respects resembles Doctor Samuel Johnson, but who unfortunately had no Boswell trailing around after him to put down the sparks of wit and the flashes of light emanating from the vast storehouse of erudition in his brain. Great lawyers, unless they happen to be prominent politicians as well, are usually relegated to the limbo of forgotten men after they depart from the arena of the courtroom known to their own generation. Rufus Choate, however, is one lawyer whom posterity does not will to forget.

Rufus, the fourth child and the second son of David Choate, a veteran of the Revolution, and his second wife, Mariam Foster, was born "Tuesday, Oct. 1, 1799, at 3 P.M.," according to the family Bible, on Hog Island, in the district of Essex, off the coast of Massachusetts. The house stands on a prominence high enough to offer a commanding view of the Atlantic Ocean as well as of the numerous villages dotting the mainland. The

300

picturesque old homestead had already cradled four generations of the Choates by the time Rufus came along, and still belongs to members of the family. During the Revolution, while all the menfolk were away in the army, the mother and sisters of David Choate had zealously kept the cattle and sheep pasturing in the wooded uplands, out of sight from passing British ships which might have been tempted to land forces to carry off this valuable source of the Choate livelihood. After dark the womenfolk would drive the cows down to the barn near the house to be milked.

When Rufus was six months old, his parents moved to the mainland but still managed the island farm, to and from which they navigated daily by means of a substantial boat hollowed out of a big log. The boy's earliest memories were those of the sea, and to the end of his days he was always fascinated by the white foam of the breakers and the white sails of seafaring ships.

He was extraordinarily precocious in his reading. By the time he was six, he had memorized long passages from the Bible and *Pilgrim's Progress*, and had digested Plutarch's *Lives* and Josephus' *History of the Jews* before his tenth year. He was robust enough in the work out-of-doors to cause a stone mason whom he was helping lay a wall express pity that such a stout-constitutioned boy should be sent to college. But Rufus quickly spoke up in defense of the college education and the profession he intended to have in his future, "Mr. N. (this to the mason), if ever I'm a lawyer, I'll plead all your cases for nothing." On the farm he acquired an intimacy with inanimate nature somewhat akin to Wordsworth's in its human warmth, as illustrated by the fact that when he cut a switch to drive the cows home, he invariably returned and threw the swich down under the tree from which he had cut it, saying, "Perhaps there is after all, some yearning of nature between them still."

Rufus was only nine years old when his father died, and it was thereafter difficult at times for him to proceed with plans for a higher education, but his mother, a remarkable woman who remained a widow for upwards of half a century, managed the monetary affairs of the family surprisingly well, although the budget oftentimes had to be pretty skimpy.

He entered Dartmouth College in 1815 on borrowed money. In all his studies he strove for perfection; so thorough was the preparation of his exercises that he could rarely be tripped up. He was especially strong in Latin, Greek, history, and literature, but in every subject he betrayed his scholarly aptitudes to such an extent that he was looked upon with a certain amount of awe by his less diligent classmates. One of them afterwards stated that Choate was "the ideal scholar and pride of the college," and had "completely won the admiration of the faculty, of his fellow-students, and of the people of Hanover." Unfortunately, he overtaxed his strength, and when at his graduation he emerged as the valedictorian, it was thought that he would be unable to deliver the valedictory address. He surprised everybody, however, by rising from a sick bed, and the ringing tones of his voice "moved his hearers as they were seldom or never moved before on any similar academic occasion."

After tutoring for a year at his Alma Mater, he began his studies for the law at Cambridge, then entered the office of William Wirt in Washington, returned to Massachusetts for continued study at Ipswich and Salem, was admitted to the bar in 1823, and then opened an office in Danvers. He had so little practice the first few years that he was tempted to venture into other fields. He seems to have resigned himself to a slow growth of clientèle, for he wrote to a friend: "But, after all, all situations are very much alike. The first years of a professional life—spend them where you will—must be years of hard labor and scanty revenue; so at least I shall find it, and then the money and the applause of one community are worth just about as much as those of another."

In 1825 he married Helen Olcott, a girl who lived in Hanover, New Hampshire, and with whom he had got acquainted while there in college. The marriage was a happy one, and to the union were born seven children. In 1828 he moved to Salem, and a few years later to Boston.

As his friends and clients swelled in numbers, his reputation as a lawyer likewise increased, and much against his will he was drawn into the political arena. At first as a National Republican and then as a Whig he served two terms in the Lower House of Congress. He was opposed to Jackson in most matters, but supported the President in his stand against nullification in South Carolina. In 1841 he entered the Senate, replacing Webster, and remained there for four years. At the expiration of this term he resolutely refused to run for any other political office. In 1851 Webster tried to persuade him to accept a seat in the Supreme Court, but without success. The courtroom was his natural milieu and he was never satisfied away from it.

He always took a great interest in political affairs, but preferred a ringside seat in the front row. He campaigned vigorously for Harrison in 1840, for Clay in 1844, and for Taylor in 1848. An editor who accompanied Choate on a speaking engagement to Brookline in the interests of the Taylor candidacy describes the great lawyer immediately after the delivery of a brilliant address that had required a week of preparation: "He got into the coach, his locks dripping with dissolved camphor, and complained of a raging headache. He clutched his temple with his hand and leaned his head on my shoulder to see if he could not, by reclining, find ease Just as we touched the Mill Dam, the evening moon poured her level rays over the beautiful waters of the Back Bay, and filled the coach and atmosphere with dreamy light. The scene instantly revived him. He put his head out of the coach window, and was absorbed with the sweetness of the view. The sight of the still waters, moonlighted, seemed to drive away his pain, and he struck into his old rapture . . . He amazed me with his vast power of thought. I have seen men stirred with passion; men eloquent; men profound and brilliant in conversation; but in the whole

302

course of my life I never saw a man more roused than was he. He poured out, without stopping, a torrent of conversation upon history, constitutional law, philosophy, poetry; upon Burke, Plato, Hamilton, the future of the Union. No other word would explain his style but 'torrent' or 'cataract:' for what he spoke in that hour would have made a small volume—brilliant, and full of philosophy and learning. And I think that I never realized as much as then the power and unapproachableness of genius."

Having overtaxed himself by speaking engagements and in the conscientiously hard preparation for every legal case with which he was connected, he began to suffer from nervous exhaustion, and took an extended vacation by going to Europe. He was back, refreshed and strengthened, in time to be a delegate at the Whig nominating convention of 1852 in Baltimore. He made an eloquent plea for the nomination of Daniel Webster, but in spite of his efforts, General Scott was nominated. Not long afterwards he had occasion to show the great esteem he held for Webster, who died a few weeks before the fall election of 1852, by an address before the United States Circuit Court for Massachusetts and a commemorative discourse before the faculty, students, and alumni at Dartmouth, both of which eulogies occupy more than a hundred pages in the collection of Choate's addresses and orations.

The rise of the Republican party he viewed with alarm, and he strongly decried its appeal to sectionalism. In the election of 1856 he supported Buchanan, saying that the Republicans had set up "a new geographical party . . . a sectional, anti-Union party, and nothing should be left undone to defeat them." As the controversy over slavery waxed in intensity, he defended the Constitutional rights of Southerners to manage their own affairs. He clearly stated the position of the nonplussed Whigs, whose party was rapidly being squeezed out of existence, when he declared, "We join ourselves to no party that does not carry the flag and keep step to the music of the Union." He advocated a policy of give-and-take and condemned the attitude of fanatics on both sides. "Extremists denounce all compromises, ever. Alas! do they remember that such is the condition of humanity that the noblest politics are but a compromise—an approximation—a type—a shadow of good things—the buying of great blessings at great prices? Do they forget that the Union is a compromise; the Constitution—social life—that the harmony of the universe is but the music of compromise, by which the antagonisms of the infinite Nature are composed and reconciled?" Choate's stand lost him many friends in the North. It struck the *coup de grâce* to the Whig party. He did not survive to see the triumph of the Republican party in national politics or the head-on collision of sections in the Civil War. In June, 1859, he prepared for another voyage to Europe, but proceeded no farther than Halifax, Nova Scotia, where he disembarked from ship and took up quarters in a quiet boarding-house. From his window he had a commanding view of the sea, which he had always so dearly loved. At his bedside were his favorite

303

books, the Bible, Shakespeare's *Tempest,* Macaulay's *History,* and Luther's discourses on the Psalms. "If a schooner or sloop goes by," he advised his son who was accompanying him, as he dozed one day, "don't disturb me, but if there is a square-rigged vessel, wake me up." A victim of Bright's disease, he passed away on the morning of July 13, 1859.

The great personality of Choate etched itself too deeply on every one who knew him ever to be lightly forgotten. Some months after his death, a young lawyer who had been frequently associated with him made this confession, a beautiful expression of homage to the older man: "How often I think of Choate! You do not know what a hold he had on me, or rather what a *necessity of life* he had become to me. When I have seen anything peculiar in the development of human nature, of social or political systems, I have thought, 'I will tell that to Choate'—and then—Is he indeed dead? Gone—never to be seen, or heard, or conversed with again? All that wisdom and wit, that kindness to me, as of a father or elder brother? Is it possible? I tell you, my dear friend, if I pass the rest of my life at the Boston bar,—life will be a different thing to me without Choate."

Rufus Choate was, like Doctor Johnson, a conversation-piece among his acquaintances. They were constantly repeating to one another little anecdotes about him as the following: One morning his attenion was diverted by a group of those little earth-worms which turn over on their backs when the sun strikes them. Mr. Choate stopped and patiently put all of them in an upright position again with his cane. "But what good will it do for you to help them over with your cane, when you know they will become supine again?" asked his walking companion, whose curiosity was aroused. "I give them a fair start in life," he replied, "and my responsibility is at an end."

Things which would have angered most people left him without a show of irritation. Once, while he was making an impassioned address to the jury, one woman arose with a great swishing of silk garments and loud tapping of high-heeled shoes, and marched like an ostentatious peacock out of the courtroom. Choate never batted an eye in her direction but continued talking without evidence of being disturbed. Later, when some one asked him if he had noticed the noisy departure, he replied, "Noticed it? Why I thought forty battalions were moving!"

His humor was of that kind "seldom provoking loud laughter, but perpetually feeding the mind with delight." Once, on attending the opera he was at a loss to know what the story was about. Turning to his daughter, he inquired with mock gravity, "Helen, interpret to me this libretto, lest I dilate with the wrong emotion!"

He summed up the qualifications of a certain candidate for office, under discussion, in these laconic terms: "Self-sufficient, all-sufficient and *in*sufficient."

He read omnivorously. He read while he was getting up or going to bed; while dressing or undressing; while snatching a bite of lunch. He bought books daily. His library was filled to overflowing with the choicest works of antiquity as well as with the latest publications. If something were inadvertently covered up by the piles of accumulating books and papers, it was seldom resurrected. His most famous lecture, "The Romance of the Sea," disappeared in an unaccountable way. He thought it was perhaps stolen from his handbag in New York City. More than likely it perished in one of the periodical onslaughts he made on his stacks of old papers.

He especially loved to browse around in second-hand bookstores, and usually he emerged with a burden of musty books to carry home. A dealer in old books wrote in the reader's column of the *New York Times*, after Mr. Choate's death, that, the distinguished jurist had once spent nine hours at a stretch, without food or drink, in his shop, and left only when compelled to do so at closing time. "He had been greatly interested as well as excited, at what he had seen; 'for,' said he, 'I have discovered many books that I have never seen before, and seen those I had never heard of; but, above all, I have been more than overjoyed at discovering, in your collection, a copy of the Greek bishop's [Eustathius's] famous commentary on the writings of Homer in seven volumes, quarto, a work that I have long had an intense desire to possess.'" You may be sure that he purchased the "precious volumes."

Choate's physical features and movements fascinated people as much as did his utterances. His appearance at court, when he had done without a wink of sleep the night before, presented the haunting aspects of a Zombi, with his wild profusion of hair flying in all four directions, his cavernous eyes dull or flashing intermittently, his hands gesticulating with perfervid abandon, and his whole body surcharged with restless energy like that of the sea at high tide.

His writing was done at a furious speed. Nobody could read it. Webster facetiously likened it to the tracks of antediluvian birds. Whipple said it resembled the "tracks of wildcats with their claws dipped in ink, madly dashing over the surface of a folio sheet of paper."

The style of his literary essays and orations, approximating that of Bunyan, Milton, and Swift, was actually modeled after that of the ancients. He was influenced most by Cicero and Demosthenes, and his vocabulary leaned heavily on words of Latin derivation. When read, his style seems ponderous, but it was admirably adapted for producing the best dramatic effects when spoken. None of his auditors noticed that one sentence in his eulogy of Daniel Webster ran on for four pages before reaching its first period. His meaning was always clear and his thought easily followed. His voice, on the platform and in the courtroom, was modulated constantly to induce the most telling effects. George F. Hoar said that he held a jury with the same hypnotic powers as those exercised by a snake over a helpless bird. The magnetism of his melodious voice and the "unearthly glance of his deep, spectral eyes" won a panel of twelve men entirely over to his way of thinking. The unerring logic of his thought, enveloped in a fiery blaze of oratory, devastated one by one the points of his opponent's position. A shorthand expert trying to follow Choate's argument at one trial gave up in despair saying, "Who can report chained lightning?"

Mr. Choate never became a rich man because he was totally indifferent to money matters. As often as not he forgot to send bills to his clients, who then had to nag him to dun them. Sometimes he refused to accept remuneration from a poor client, especially if that person were a widow, or a man with a large family of children. His receipts varied from thirteen to twenty-two thousand a year for an average of seventy cases, and the largest fee he ever charged was $2,500. After he had entered into a partnership with his son-in-law, his records were more systematically kept.

His home life was ideally happy. Nothing pleased him more than to have his children diverting themselves in his presence. On Sunday evenings they would cluster around the piano in the parlor for a songfest, and he gave them plenty of vocal exercise by his repeated requests for favorite hymns or popular ballads of the day. One of his daughters, in jotting down a few reminiscences of her father for her children, said: "We children used to have very fierce wordy warfare with our playmates as to the merits of our respective parents; and I well remember that one little girl (whom I'm afraid I quite hated for it) convincingly showed her father to be taller and stronger, and that he had more hair, and longer whiskers, and more of all the other virtues, than your grandpapa, when I brought the dispute to a triumphant conclusion by declaring that my father could repeat the story of *The House that Jack Built* quicker than her father could, which she was unable to deny, because her father had never told it to her at all, and so all comparison being out of the question—since my father could do something well which her father never had done in any way—I remained the victor."

There are several good biographies of Rufus Choate, all replete with anecdotal reminiscences, but for lack of a faithful dog like Boswell to attend him, it is doubtful whether more than a part of his complete story has ever been told. His fame survives today, not so much as that of a great lawyer or a great orator, but as that of a great personality.

The spoon picturing the birthplace of Rufus Choate and giving the date of his birth, 1799, on the caput, bears also the name of Essex, Massachusetts, along the shaft of the handle. Imprinted by the Durgin Company for E. S. Burnham. Length, 6 inches.

No. 77   MILES STANDISH
No. 85   PRISCILLA
No. 91   JOHN ALDEN AND PRISCILLA
No. 92   PLYMOUTH COURTSHIP
No. 130 PLYMOUTH ROCK

Longfellow had already written two long narrative poems on American themes successfully, when he was urged by his friends to turn his attention to the Puritans or Quakers for his next topic. "An excellent subject for a tragedy," he reflected. Only a short time before, Hawthorne had gained name and fame in two highly successful, though quite gloomy, novels having an early Puritan background.

For several months Longfellow labored over the beginnings of what was ultimately to be *The New England Tragedies*. At times he was repelled by the joyless atmosphere of the subject, and felt constrained to put it aside. As an antidote for his mental depression, he turned to a more cheerful theme, a story that was not much more than a yarn handed down, in effect, as a family tradition through several generations. He first called it *Priscilla*.

Work on this new poem was a psychological escape. Longfellow was graced with a happy, optimistic temperament, and in his contacts with other people he always presented the most pleasant aspects of his nature. In addition to this benignity of disposition, he often exhibited moods that were sprightly, sportive, lightsome, slyly humorous, or downright funny by sudden turns from more serious trends of thought. There was nothing of saucy quip or mordant satire in this type of humor which merely sought to throw rays of sunlight over situations that needed brighter relief. But he had too much good sense, good taste, refinement, and chivalry in his being ever to be disrespectful or hurtful of other people's feelings by saying things merely for the sake of being clever.

Very little of this sunny humor, which animated his personal presence, manifested itself in his poetry. Occasionally he confided to his journal mild bits of waggery like the following: "What is *auto*biography? What biography *ought to* be." And, when alone with boon male companions, he is known to have been a good raconteur of jokes with a Boccaccian flavor, circumspectly told.

It was with a great deal of pleasure, then, that he worked upon this story which showed the lighter, brighter, more pleasing side of Puritan life. In slightly less than two months, from January into March, 1858, he completed the first draft of his poem. Somewhere toward the middle of the work he changed the title to the one we all know, and it was a felicitous move, because in so doing, he definitely enriched its humorous connotations and provided the keys for the general interpretation of the poem in terms of its comic, ironic, and paradoxical aspects. It is not the courtship of the irascible, swashbuckling warrior at all, as the title implies, but that of his undemonstrative, non-warrior-like friend, John Alden. The philosophy of the doughty Miles, that you must do a thing yourself if you would have it done well, is ludicrously ironical in its practical applitions, which reveal so clearly the philosopher's failure to put his own preaching into practice. The heights of paradox are reached at that moment when the elaborate arguments of the Captain's proxy are bowled over by one single puff from Priscilla, that modernistic, direct-hit miss of the true-blue, non-swooning American go-getter type.

We have a varied assortment of spoons on the characters and scenes of this early American love-triangle, made famous by Longfellow's romance. The two spoons showing Miles Standish full length in the caput of handle are, of course, one and the same, but are given here simply for the sake of exhibiting the two types of bowls customarily put on souvenir spoons of the early nineties. The fruit bowl, sometimes called the orange bowl, in shape resembles a pear.

The figure of Standish that crowns this spoon poses him in his very characteristic stance, a swaggering stride. We wonder for what particular occasion he is making his present stage appearance. In the poem we first see him striding

> To and fro in a room of his simple and primitive dwelling,
> Clad in doublet and hose, and boots of Cordovan leather.

At this time he is not wearing the high-topped, broad-brimmed Puritan hat which appears on the spoon. But he is eyeing his cutlass, steel corselet, and sword of Damascus hanging along the walls.

> Short of stature he was, but strongly built and athletic,
> Broad in the shoulders, deep-chested with muscles and
>   sinews of iron;
> Brown as a nut was his face, but his russet beard was already
> Flaked with patches of snow, as hedges sometimes in November.

He boasts of his feats of arms in times past, and of his prodigious memory, being able to recall the names of every man in his army—there were twelve in all!

On the second advent of Standish he reveals the testy mettle so characteristic of his composition. Priscilla's reply to his proposal has just been delivered:

> Up leaped the Captain of Plymouth,
>   and stamped on the floor, till his armor
> Clanged on the wall . . .

Then we see him striding about in his chamber sputtering and spewing till his rage fairly chokes him—always a "little chimney and heated hot in a moment!" But the exacerbations of nettled pride pass quickly when he is imformed of Indian raids being made upon the settlement. Here we note that he—

> Took from the nail on the wall his sword from its
>   scabbard of iron,
> Buckled his belt round his waist, and frowning
>   fiercely, departed.

The choleric Captain blusters, and thrasonically strides up and down before the Indians, from whose savage attack he defends the fort. Sometime later he is reported dead. On the wedding day of John Alden and Priscilla Mullins, however, an apparition in armor appears on the threshold.

> Into the room it strode, and the people beheld
>   with amazement
> Bodily there in his armor Miles Standish, the
> Captain of Plymouth!

Possibly, then, this ever-striding figure is the Standish visible on our spoon, for he seems framed in a background of stockade posts, from which all the branches have not yet been closely lopped.

This spoon, six inches in length, was pressed by Durgin and Company in 1891, the patent date appearing on the reverse of shaft.

The early story of Miles Standish is shrouded in mystery. Except for the last half of his life, the forty-year period of association with the Pilgrims, we know practically nothing certain about his origins, his youth, his early manhood, or his reasons for coming to the New World. He was born either in 1584 or 1585 in the county of Lancastershire, England, of a wealthy, aristocratic family that was sorely divided by the political and religious quarrels of the period. Some have thought that he was unjustly mulcted of his inheritance, for investigations made by his American descendants indicate all the pages on the old parish registers that might furnish data have been destroyed or rendered undecipherable by the rubbing of pumice stone over certain entries. It cannot be verified that Miles was ever born, although for years before and after 1584 the records show that there were many members of the Standish family born both at Standish Hall and at Duxbury Hall, the two seats of the rival branches of the family.

Disgusted perhaps by the eternal wrangling and feuding of his kith and kin, Miles, who had been educated for a military career, secured a commission to enter the Queen's forces then fighting in the Low Countries. His combat experiences against the armies led by the fierce Duke of Alva provided excellent training for his subsequent leadership in the New World. A treaty of peace left the Captain without occupation, and presently having met the little group of Puritans in Leyden, he threw in his fortunes with them when they embarked for America on the Mayflower.

His military capabilities were not recognized by the leaders in the administrative councils of Plymouth until, with his iron-guard host of eight men, he had saved the infant settlement from destruction at the hands of treacherous Indians. He may have boasted like a Cyrano de Bergerac but he could likewise wield his weapons as dexterously as did that Gascon braggadocio. He had no hesitant scruples about attacking and killing a Goliath-sized Indian who taunted him on his abbreviated stature—and that done in the very wigwam of the enemy. By his very boldness he instilled a dread, even a healthy admiration, in the bosoms of savages who shortly before were plotting the extermination of the entire colony.

Some accounts, such as Mrs. Cheney's A Peep at the Pilgrims, picture Standish as an affable man in his personal relations. Although no churchman himself, he lived on the closest terms of friendship with Elder Brewster, the spiritual leader of the Pilgrim flock. Governors Carver, Bradford, Winthrop, and Winslow came to have an increasingly high regard for his common-sense opinions in political matters. He was chosen treasurer of the colony in recognition of his spirited public services. Hobomok, the magnanimous Indian who gave up his white wife when her lost husband returned, became a devoted friend to Standish and wound up his days as a faithful servant in the home of the Captain.

It can be said also that Standish was a good family man. Jane G. Austen in the authenticated novel, Standish of Standish, stresses the disconsolate feelings of Miles on the death of his wife Rose a month after the landing. It becomes obvious that, manly and courageous as he is, he yet needs the womanly support and comfort of a helpmate. When Priscilla Molines (a variant spelling here) rejected him, he sought solace in marriage with Rose's younger sister Barbara, who came over from England after the Captain had proposed to her by letter.

In 1625 Standish moved across the bay a few miles from Plymouth to a place which he named Duxbury after his ancestral seat in England. Here he cleared an area of one hundred and fifty acres, enough as he thought to be sufficient pasturage for his growing herd of livestock. For more than thirty years he lived in a modest cottage that he built on an eminence still known as the Captain's Hill, a site affording a magnificent panorama of all Plymouth Bay and as far east as the sickle-end of Cape Cod. The original house is gone, but another called the Standish House stands nearby, with the date of its erection, 1653, above the lintel, and it is said to contain timber from the earlier construction.

Standish lived long enough to see Plymouth rise from a decimated flock of fifty souls barely surviving the ravages of disease and the rigors of a cold winter without sufficient shelter, to a thriving colony of eight thousand people. And there were eight towns doing a lively trade in the colony now. Elsewhere along the coast other settlements were coming into existence in ever increasing numbers. He expressed a wish before his death in 1656 that his grave might be located next to those of his only daughter Lora and his daughter-in-law, Mary Standish, both girls

310

whom he loved tenderly. His second wife survived him. In 1872 a monument was erected to the memory of this illustrious hero who possessed an "all-daring contempt for peril" and a "power of breathing his own fiery heart into a handful of followers till he made them an army able to withstand a host in the narrow gates of death." Thus, he forged one of the first strong links in that chain which has made our nation a "Union indivisible, now and forever."

Priscilla Mullins, the most vividly realistic character that Longfellow ever drew, appears on three spoons in our present grouping. The dainty demi-tasse size, which bears her name alone, shows her figure on the caput in the Puritan garb of cape and Phrygian-like hood, knocking at a rough-hewn door, above which on the lintel is inscribed, "Lord, have mercy on us." She carries a basket partially concealed by her cape, and evidently is on an errand of mercy. The shank bears the name of Priscilla on a banderole that weaves around the thorny twigs of the sea-thistle. A beading runs narrowly around the caput enclosing the figure of the Puritan Maiden. Patented by Durgins in 1891. Length, 4½ inches.

The John Alden and Priscilla spoon is of a strikingly fine design. On the caput, the couple, showing perhaps a few years of maturity after their marriage, are apparently on their way to or from church, because she is carrying a Bible and he is shouldering a gun—a practice then necessary on frequent occasions. There is no marked distinction between nave and shank, for the names of the pair run the entire length of the two sections. In the bowl, people are disembarking on Plymouth Rock from the ship's boat. A pine tree is visible to the left of this scene. While the maker's trademark does not appear, the name of H. E. Washburn indicates the jeweler for whose business the spoon was imprinted. Length, 5½ inches. Used through the courtesy of Mr. Howard Heffron, Adrian, Michigan.

The Plymouth Courtship spoon is likewise of a richly ornate pattern, and contains all three characters of the love-triangle. Miles stands in his most characteristic pose, in the caput; John and Priscilla in the nave, are also standing, and, as the spinning wheel is before them, we may conjecture that they have just heard the false report of the Captain's death. On a banderole spirally descending the shaft are the famous words: "Speak for yourself, John." There is nothing in the bowl except the name of Plymouth.

The reverse caput contains the Standish coat of arms, three annulets on an azure field, two on the sinister and one on the dexter side of the bendlet. A beavered helmet in profile rests on the arms. The old spelling, "Myles Standish," is found in the nave. This spoon, 5½ inches long, is a product of Codding and Heilbom Co., and has also been used through the courtesy of Mr. Howard Heffron, Adrian, Michigan.

Priscilla Mullins, featured on the three spoons just described, belonged to a family of aristocratic, French forebears. Originally Molines or Molyneux, the family left the old feudal castle in Normandy, journeyed to

England, then to Holland, and finally to America in search of religious freedom.

Priscilla was a spirited girl of eighteen, with a piquant daring in her manner and speech, when along with the other members of her family she boarded the Mayflower. She was among the gayest of those who went ashore near what is now Provincetown on November 24, 1620, to wash the great pile of dirty clothes that had accumulated on the two months' voyage, soft water being scarce on board ship.

On this laundrying excursion, many of the women caught colds, which led eventually into pneumonia and influenza. Priscilla must undoubtedly have possessed a robust constitution, for, notwithstanding her full share of duties as nurse, she survived the malignant illness which swept away both her parents, her brother, and the hired man, leaving her an orphan to fend for herself in a strange, new world.

The general facts in Longfellow's poem of which she is the heroine are pretty well authenticated, although the poet embroidered the story considerably. He accepted the version told by Priscilla's great-great-granddaughter who died at the ripe old age of one hundred in 1845. The story had already found its way into the popular ballads and legends of New England by that time.

Priscilla was married to John Alden in 1622. Within five years they had three children, and William Bradford in his *History of Plymouth Plantation* states that by 1647 the couple had eleven children and four grandchildren. At their deaths, in the same year, 1686, they were survived by one hundred and forty-four descendants. Thus, it is not to be wondered at that thousands of people today claim that their ancestors came over in the Mayflower, for the progenies from this one couple alone have literally "multiplied like the stars in the heavens."

The longevity of this strain is likewise remarkable. John Alden lived to be eighty-eight, Priscilla eighty-six, all their children passed the three quarter-century mark. A grandson died a patriarch of one hundred and two. Longfellow and Bryant were both descendants; one lived to be a septuagenarian, the other an octogenarian. Five presidents—John Adams, John Quincy Adams, Zachary Taylor, Ulysses Grant, and William Howard Taft—claim descent from the Aldens. It may be noted that John Adams lived to be ninety-one, the oldest of our presidents. Among other prominent people of this genetic connection there have been signers of the Declaration of Independence, generals, governors, congressmen, presidents of colleges, ministers, writers, and actors.

Only by a lucky coincidence was John Alden, the cooper, aboard the Mayflower: A stipulation in the chartering of the ship called for the inclusion of a cooper. Though not a Puritan originally, he became favorably disposed toward that mode of worship on shipboard. He was fortunate too in his marriage with Priscilla, for she was "well dowered financially, physically, and mentally," according to the account of her in Green's *Pioneer Mothers of America.*

A tall, strikingly handsome man, "fair-haired, azure-eyed, with delicate Saxon complexion," the quiet, unassuming John Alden, of no importance at first in the eyes of the Puritan elders and practically unknown to them almost till the day of their sailing, gradually came to fill a very honorable position in the affairs of the struggling colony. For several years he was one of the eight signers of the note pledging payment to the London bankers for all the money that had been borrowed for the establishment of the New World enterprise. This debt was a burden weighing sorely on the backs of the Pilgrims for more than a quarter of a century, till it was paid off in 1646. At one time or another Alden was a farmer, a surveyor, an overseer on the highway commission, an aide on the governor's staff, deputy for the town of Duxbury, and member of various trade and administrative councils. He was also the last survivor of those who signed the Mayflower Compact on the passage over in 1620.

It might be thought that Miles Standish, having been bested in his suit for Priscilla's hand, harbored a jealous grudge against the Aldens. One old tradition has it that "the captain never forgave them to the day of his death." On the contrary, according to the best of contemporary accounts, the two men remained the best of friends. At one time Alden was held prisoner by the Massachusetts Bay authorities on charges that he was implicated in the murder of two sailors at a trading post which he had recently visited. When the news reached Plymouth, the governor appointed Standish to make an investigation, whereupon the latter journeyed to Boston, gathered all the known facts, and established proofs for a case of mistaken identity. Alden was set free, and the homecoming of the two men was a joyous one, although the Plymouth people were irked by the unjust accusation.

Later, Standish and Alden were on the same committee that settled boundary disputes for the local farmsteads. This business naturally threw them frequently into close association with one another. So, any animus that Standish may have held toward his successful rival must have certainly become an incidental matter, to be forgotten in their later lives. And it should be stated that Alexander, a son of Miles Standish and a chip off the old block in that he too was swarthy, peppery, and short of stature, married Sarah, daughter of the Aldens, a beautiful fair-haired, azure-eyed, undemonstrative girl who towered in height at least a head above her husband. Thus, the two families were united in their descendants.

The last spoon in this group pictures Plymouth Rock, which has often been called the "cornerstone of the nation." In addition to being the spot where the Pilgrims disembarked, it plays an important part in Longfellow's narrative poem, which, says William J. Long, the literary historian, "has led more people to Plymouth Rock than have all the histories of the period." Mention of the famous landing place is made several times in the poem, and the scene for the return-sailing of the Mayflower occurs here. As preparations are under way for boarding the ship's boat, Alden stands with "one foot placed on the gunwale, one still firm on the rock." He is ready to embark till he sees Priscilla among the assembled crowd. With a sudden, swift change of mind, he springs back. He will remain!

> Yes! as my foot was the first that
> stepped on this rock at the landing,
> So, with the blessing of God, shall it
> be the last at the leaving!

After the vessel had departed over the horizon, carrying not one of the surviving Pilgrim band with it, the Elder called his flock to prayer.

> Mournfully sobbed the waves at the base
> of the rock, and above them
> Bowed and whispered the wheat on the
> hill of death, and their kindred
> Seemed to awake in their graves, and to
> join in the prayer that they uttered.

The crowd slowly disperses, each going his own way homeward, but Alden tarries—

> Musing alone on the shore, and watching
> the wash of the billows
> Round the base of the rock, and the sparkle
> and flash of the sunshine,
> Like the spirit of God, moving visibly over
> the waters.

The Plymouth Rock spoon contains a rather slight etching of the Mayflower in the gold-washed bowl, a slender corkscrew handle, and an excellent verisimilitude of the Rock perched finially at the top of the handle. On the Rock is embossed 1620, the date of the Pilgrims' landing. Designed by Codding and Heilbom Company, this spoon is an interesting specimen of the rat-tail type, rarely seen on souvenir spoons. Length, 4 inches.

No. 78 KNICKERBOCKER

Through the summer and fall months of the year 1809 there had been appearing in the New York papers such factual items as these: "A small, elderly man dressed in an old black coat and a cocked hat," by the name of Diedrich Knickerbocker, had disappeared from the house where he had been staying without leaving any knowledge of his destination; he owed his landlord a tidy sum for food and lodging; he had last been seen boarding a stage coach headed for Albany; he had left in his room the completed manuscript of an early history of New York; said manuscript would be duly published and sold to cover sundry debts incurred by the errant author.

Many honest citizens took these notices seriously. One city official wished to post an offer of reward for knowledge of the missing gentleman's whereabouts. Soon after the publication of the aforementioned manuscript, which began with the creation of the world and ended with the downfall of Dutch rule in New Amsterdam in 1664, the real perpetrator of the hoax was learned to be one Washington Irving, a petty clerk in the import-trade office.

The book had a remarkable success. Readers were chuckling over its fantastic humor—even in England. Sir Walter Scott, who read it aloud to his wife and some friends, said, "Our sides are absolutely sore with laughing." Everybody enjoyed it except certain descendants of those Dutch worthies with whose actual history Irving had taken a great many liberties. One Albany *vrouw* declared that if she were a man she would horsewhip the author. Irving bearded the irate lady in her own den. After an hour of assuaging amenities on Irving's part, the lady's lacerated pride had been pretty well healed, and they parted as friends. In fact, the popular young historian was soon eating more good roast-goose or basted-duck dinners in the homes of his erstwhile critics than had ever previously been his privilege.

There was no spleen, patent or latent, in Irving's humor. He tended to convert sober historic facts into comic ones by interlarding them between broad sketches of drollery coined out of his own fancy. Just listen to this stirring depiction of Governor Stuyvesant—better known as Peter the Headstrong—as he was about to marshal his hosts to march against New Sweden: "There came on the intrepid Peter—his brows knit, his teeth set, his fists clenched, almost breathing forth volumes of smoke, so fierce was the fire that raged within his bosom . . . Then came waddling on the sturdy chivalry of the Hudson." There was a long roll call of names preceded nearly always by Van and Vander. "Brimful of wrath and cabbage," he mounted a stump and harangued his followers long and eloquently in Low Dutch. "Then lugging out his trusty sabre, he brandished it three times over his head, ordered Van Corlear to sound the charge, and shouting 'Saint Nicholas and the Manhattoes!' courageously dashed forward. His warlike followers who had employed the interval in lighting their pipes, instantly stuck them into their mouths, gave a furious puff, and charged gallantly under cover of the smoke."

The description of another Dutch governor, Wouter Van Twiller, is a masterpiece of caricature vouched for as solemn truth: "He was exactly five feet six inches in height and six feet five inches in circumference. His head was a perfect sphere, and of such stupendous dimensions that Dame Nature, with all her sex's ingenuity, would have been puzzled to construct a neck capable of supporting it; wherefore she wisely declined the attempt, and settled it firmly on the top of his backbone, just between the shoulders.

. . . His legs were short, but sturdy in proportion to the weight they had to sustain, so that when erect he had not a little the appearance of a beer-barrel on skids. His face, that infallible index of the mind, presented a vast expanse, unfurrowed by any of those lines and angles which disfigure the human countenance with what is termed expression. Two small gray eyes twinkled feebly in the midst, like two stars of lesser magnitude in a hazy firmament, and his full-fed cheeks, which seemed to have taken toll of everything that went into his mouth, were curiously mottled and streaked with dusky red, like a spitzenberg apple. His habits were as regular as his person. He daily took his four stated meals, appropriating exactly an hour to each; he smoked and doubted eight hours, and he slept the remaining twelve of the four-and-twenty."

Irving's *Knickerbocker's History of New York* is regarded as our first genuine piece of literature—at least, it was so accepted by the Europeans, who relished its effervescent, tangy humor as avidly as did American readers. In time, Diedrich Knickerbocker came to be the personification of the jovial New Yorker, and the very people whom he burlesqued had bestowed upon them the "patent of an unofficial ancient nobility" by those who were mere newcomers in the expanding metropolis. Public enterprises and commercial concerns resorted to the use of his name; elite social clubs were honored by his patronymic. Knickerbockers, more recently metamorphosed into knickers, are visible reminders of him. Diedrich Knickerbocker was never so well known as after his flight into the unknown. He is of all ages in life and appeals to all ages. He belongs to the legendary, Homeric springtime of our history. Few people are so real.

The spoon representing Knickerbocker was made by Durgin's. There are two versions described in *Souvenir Spoons of America*, published by the Jewelers' Circular Publishing Co. in New York in 1891. In one illustration, Knickerbocker is seated sideways in a chair, holding a pipe in his right hand at rest on the chair back, and lifting a tankard, top drawn open, in the left. The other illustration shows Knickerbocker at a desk writing his history. The article concludes: "The first mentioned design seems to be the more popular. The demand has been very heavy and is increasing. The Knickerbocker is made in tea, orange, and miscellaneous sizes. J. H. Johnston & Co., New York, control this spoon."

The spoon shown here follows the first description given above, and has the fruit-type bowl. "Knickerbocker" runs along the handle-shaft in raised letters, and the Johnston cut is on the reverse of handle. Length is 5¾ inches.

No. 79 GOVERNOR ALTGELD

Sometimes it is a perplexing problem to identify some one whose face appears on an old souvenir spoon if the name is not also given. Occa-

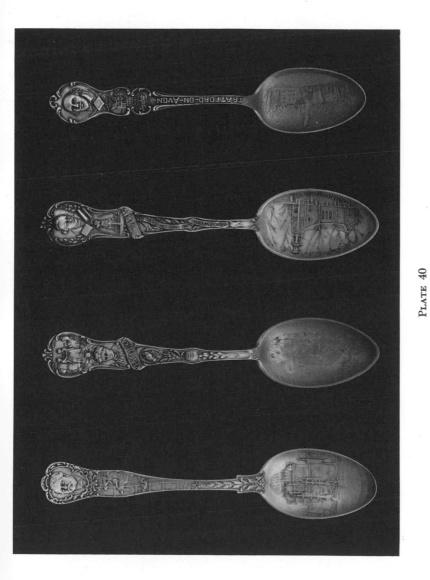

PLATE 40

79. GOVERNOR ALTGELD   80. DANIEL BOONE

81. PATRICK HENRY   82. SHAKESPEARE

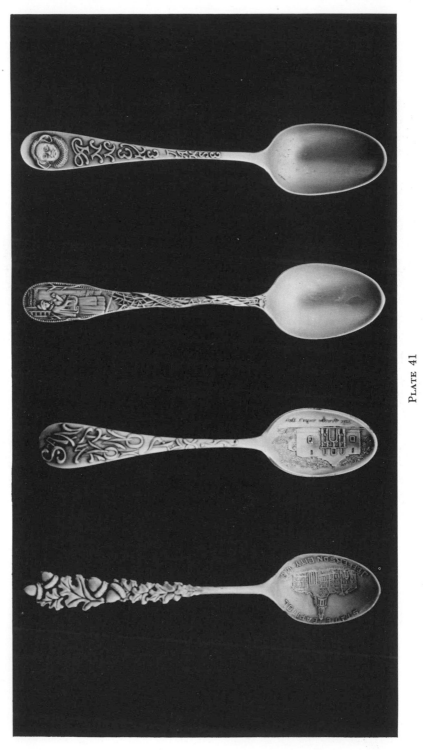

PLATE 41

83. HEARTS OF OAK   84. ALAMO   85. PRISCILLA   86. ANNEKE JANSE

sionally a name will accompany a face or bust having no approximation to the actual likeness of the character in question. Such was true in the case of Osceola. The present spoon is an instance of this disagreement in regard to the person shown in the caput. Governor Altgeld, like Lincoln, is most often seen with a bearded face. His earlier portraits picture him with a wild growth over most of his visage. Later in life, while he was governor of Illinois, he shaved off all his hirsute stubble except the mustache, which, it is said, he preserved in order to conceal his harelip.

One of the most controversial figures in our entire political history, John Peter Altgeld is unique in several respects: he was Illinois' first governor of foreign extraction; the first Democrat to win the gubernatorial election since before the Civil War; and the first Chicagoan to be governor.

Born of humble peasant parents in 1847, he was brought to this country from Germany when scarcely a year old. He lived in Ohio, working on a farm, till he joined the Union army in 1864. After the war he traveled in the West, taught in a rural school, and studied law. Even while he was teaching school, he still had to look in the dictionary for one word out of every five, according to his own confession.

He moved to Chicago in 1875. There his advancement in public office was rapid, until in 1892 he was elected to the governorship, which position he held from 1893 to 1897. Almost his first act in office was to pardon four men who had been sentenced to prison for complicity in the Haymarket riots of 1886. A storm of abuse was hurled at his head by the press everywhere in the nation. He was accused of being an anarchist and an abettor to crime. In an eighteen-thousand-word pamphlet he answered every charge: the jury had been hand-picked for the trial, the judge swayed by an excited press, and the defendants convicted on weak circumstantial evidence.

During his tenure of office the World's Fair or Columbian Exposition was held in Chicago. He advocated and pushed through the legislature a measure stopping the lease of convicts to private individuals, and the construction of a reformatory for women and an industrial school for the blind. He sponsored the first legislation for the protection of the working man, whose hand he was not afraid to shake, and appointed women to public office for the first time in his state.

Perhaps the most admirable act in Altgeld's whole career came after his failure to win reëlection to the governorship. His wealth, which had been acquired through real estate, was gone. But he could have quickly recouped his fortune if he had listened to Charles T. Yerkes, who was pushing a bill through the state legislature giving him a fifty-year streetcar monopoly in Chicago without restrictions or any payment whatsoever for the privilege. Yerkes offered Altgeld five hundred thousand dollars to allow the bill to pass without a veto, and gave him the key to the bank box where the money was deposited. Altgeld went to the bank, opened the box, and counted the money. It was all there, enough to make him a rich man for the rest of his days. But it was not enough to make him a dishonest man for the rest of his days. He left the money untouched, handed back the key to Yerkes, vetoed the bill, and returned to his home with seven dollars in his pocket.

When Altgeld died in 1902 he was practically penniless. Yet he was held in greater respect by the masses of people than ever before. Had it not been for the constitutional clause disqualifying any person of alien birth from the presidency, it is probable that Altgeld would have received the Democratic nomination in 1896, although his name was anathema to many in both parties.

On the other hand, there were people who thought that Altgeld was a much maligned person. Across the street from the governor's mansion in Springfield, Illinois, lived a fourteen-year-old boy, Vachel Landsay, to whom the governor appeared as a kind of demigod in his heroic defense of the rights of the common people. After Altgeld's death Lindsay wrote one of his most moving poems, "The Eagle That is Forgotten," to commemorate his boyhood idol—a poem that has done as much as anything to keep Altgeld's name alive as a legend of national interest.

In the bowl of the Altgeld spoon is pictured the administrative building of the World's Fair, a structure as ornate as a rajah's palace. A plant with leaves like chicory proceeds from the upper edges of the bowl, through the handle drop into the nave. In the latter section we perceive Columbus and two monks, presumably in a cloister, where they are engaged in an animated discussion over a globe. The Altgeld bust appears in the caput.

On the reverse of handle is Gorham's trademark and the imprint of Spaulding and Company. This firm was established in 1888 by Henry A. Spaulding, who was previously associated with the Tiffany Company of Paris. The business flourished, and soon Spaulding meant to Chicago much the same as Tiffany did to New York. The firm carried the very best in "jewelry, diamonds, silverware, gold and silver mounted leather goods, stationery and a full line of English hall and mantle clocks."

The length of this spoon is 5¾ inches.

No. 80 DANIEL BOONE

Who were the first Europeans to penetrate into the Indians' happy hunting grounds of Kentucky? Who was the first white man to wander over this region, explore its magical forests, and attempt to build a home here? But before we proceed on the trail of these questions, let us go back in time to hear what some of the earliest Kentucky settlers known to our recorded history had to say about the matter.

Shortly after his return, in the winter of 1782-83, from his campaign against the Indians on the Little Miami, General George Rogers Clark passed the word around that there would be a meeting of all "historical-minded persons" on a certain night at his cabin quarters in the fort of Louisville. A schoolmaster, John Filson, then engaged in writing a history of Kentucky, would be present to hear whatever matters worthy of preservation to posterity might be discussed.

At this meeting, held around a cheerful log fire, the discussion seems to have centered solely on the idea that Welsh voyagers, coming to the American continent under the aegis of a Prince Madoc in the year 1171 A.D., forged their way upward from the Gulf of Mexico, through the latter-day states of Alabama, Georgia, and Tennessee, and eventually made settlements within the confines of Kentucky and adjacent territories.

Colonel Reuben T. Durrett, in his *Traditions of the Earliest Visits of Foreigners,* a Filson Club Publication for 1908, gives this condensed version of the meeting then held in the pioneer fort:

"General Clark spoke first, and confined himself to what he had learned from a chief of the Kaskaskia Indians concerning a large and curiously shaped earthwork on the Kaskaskia River, which the chief, who was of lighter complexion than most Indians, said was the house of his ancestors. Colonel Moore spoke next, and related what he had learned from an old Indian about a long war of extermination between the Red Indians and the White Indians. The final battle, he said, between them was fought at the Falls of the Ohio [Louisville] where nearly the whole of the White Indians were driven upon an island and slaughtered. General Clark, on hearing this statement by Colonel Moore, confirmed it by stating that he had heard the same thing from Tobacco, a chief of the Painkeshaws. Major Harrison next spoke, and told about an extensive graveyard on the north side of the Ohio, opposite the Falls, where thousands of human bones were buried in such confusion as to indicate that the dead were left there after a battle, and that the silt from inundations of the Ohio had covered them as the battle had left them. Sanders spoke next and said that in his intercourse with different tribes of Indians he had met several of light complexion, gray eyes, and sandy hair, but had never talked with them in the Welsh language, if they spoke it, because he did not understand it himself. The last White Indian he ever saw was in a hunt on the Wabash River. A White Indian had joined a party of Red Indians, as Sanders had, for a hunt. While separated from the rest of the party the White Indian had come upon a panther and wounded it. The infuriated animal turned upon him and literally tore him to pieces before any assistance could reach him."

There were further testimonials from others in the group to the effect that they had seen White Indians at one time or another. John Filson, the last to speak, went into such detail relative to the Welsh legends of

Prince Madoc's voyages that the auditors fell asleep before he had reached the point of the Prince's departure from Wales for the New World.

In the same year that John Filson was gleaning this information in Louisville, John Sevier, later governor of Tennessee, ran upon "traces of very ancient, though regular, fortifications" while engaged in a campaign against the Cherokee Indians. Later on, Sevier inquired of Oconostata, the aged chieftain of the Cherokee Nation, the origin of these remains. The venerable old leader divulged this information: "It was handed down by the Forefathers that the marks had been made by the White people who had formerly inhabited the country now called Carolina [which then included eastern Tennessee]; that a war had existed between the two nations for several years." These white Indians, said Oconostata, migrated north along the Tennessee River to the Ohio, and thence onward to the Big River (the Mississippi) and westward for a considerable distance up the Muddy River (the Missouri). But, he continued, there are now "no more white people; they are all become Indians, and look like other red people of the country." He had heard his forefathers say these white people were "a people called Welsh, and that they had crossed the Great Water and landed first near the mouth of the Alabama River near Mobile . . ."

Evidences continued to crop up through the years tending to substantiate the validity of these Indian declarations that Welshmen once roamed over a wide area of our south-central states. In 1799, six "skeletons in armor" were dug out of the sand on Corn Island in the Ohio, adjacent to Louisville. The armor consisted of a brass breast-plate upon which appeared the Welsh coat-of-arms, the Mermaid and Harp, together with the Latin inscription, "Virtuous deeds meet their just rewards." A few years later, a stone purportedly marking a grave with initials and the date 1186 on it was unearthed in southern Indiana.

In the issue of the Louisville *Public Advertiser* for May 15, 1818, there appeared this story, the results of an interview with a Lieutenant Joseph Roberts:

"In the year 1801 being in the City of Washington in America, I happened to be at a hotel, smoking a cigar according to the custom of the country, and there was a young lad, a native of Wales, a waiter in the house, and because he had displeased me by bringing me a glass of brandy and water warm instead of cold, I said to him jocosely in Welsh, 'I'll give thee a good beating.'

"There happened to be in the room at the time one of the secondary Indian chiefs who, on my pronouncing these words, rose in a great hurry, stretching forth his hand, at the same time asking me in the ancient British tongue, 'Is that thy language?' I answered him in the affirmative, shaking hands at the same time, and the chief said it was likewise his language and the language of his father and mother and of his nation. I said to him, 'It is also the language of my father and my nation.' Upon this the Indian began to inquire from whence I came and I replied, 'from Wales,' but he had never heard of such a place.

"I asked him if there were any traditions amongst them whence their ancestors had come. He said that there were, and they had come from a far distant country, very far in the east and from over great waters. I conversed with him in Welsh and English, but he knew better Welsh than I did, and I asked him how they had come to retain their language so well from mixing with other Indians. He answered that they had a law or established custom in their nation forbidding any to teach their children another language until they had attained the age of twelve years, and after that they were at liberty to learn any language they pleased. I asked him if he would like to go to England or Wales; he replied that he had not the least inclination to leave his native country and that he would sooner live in a wigwam than a palace. He had ornamented his naked arms with bracelets and on his head were ostrich feathers.

"I was greatly astonished and greatly amazed when I heard such a man who had painted his face yellowish red and of such an appearance speaking the ancient British tongue as fluently as if he had been born and brought up in the vicinity of Snowden. His head was shaved except around the crown and there the hair was very long and plaited, and it was on the crown of his head he had placed the ostrich feathers, which I mentioned before, to ornament himself.

"The situation of these Indians is about eight hundred miles southwest of Philadelphia, according to his statement, and they are called the Asguawa, or Asguaw nation.

"The chief courted my society astonishingly, seeing that we were descended from the same people. He used to call upon me almost every day and take me to the woods to show me the virtues of various herbs which grew there, for neither he nor his people were acquainted with compounded medicine."

This account might be laughed off as purely fictional if there were not too many material evidences to furnish proof that, centuries ago, Europeans or their descendants did inhabit a wide area eight hundred miles more or less, to the southwest of Philadelphia. Zella Armstrong, Judge John Haywood, Albert James Pickett, Lucian Lamar Knight, and others have pointed out likenesses and made comparisons between the ancient British or Welsh type of fortification and those three great forts of pre-Columbian origin at Fort Mountain in Georgia, DeSoto Falls in Alabama, and the Old Stone Fort in Tennessee. Colonel Bennett H. Young studied the archaeological remains of nearly a hundred mounds, earth-works, stone fortifications, and enclosures throughout Kentucky, but he did not ascribe them to Welsh origins. He simply uttered this plaintive "coronach" over the great mystery: "One cannot resist the temptation to call the dead from their sleep of ages, clothe them with flesh and blood, and have them revisit the scenes of their contests for this land now so beautiful to those who possess it, and which to them if such things were possible, would be ever dearer and more to be desired."

Even after the "official discovery" of America by Columbus, more than two centuries were to pass before Europeans began to cross the Alleghany Mountains and penetrate the Kentucky wilderness. It is believed that the Frenchman, La Salle, about 1669, navigated the waters of the Ohio as far as the falls at Louisville in his search for a passage to the Pacific. In the same year a young Virginian, John Lederer, rambled westward over the Alleghanies and in all probability saw a portion of Kentucky. Two years later Governor Berkeley of Virginia commissioned a party headed by Captain Thomas Batts to explore the possibilities of a river route to the Pacific. Captain Batts hoisted the British flag and took possession of the lands lying between the Kanawha and the Big Sandy Rivers in the name of Charles II. Colonel Abraham Wood, Gabriel Arthur, John Howard, John Peter Salling, Christopher Gist, John Finley, James McBride, James Smith, John McCullough, and numerous members of that roving band, the Long Hunters, may be credited with cursory visits, before the time of Boone, to the Happy Hunting Grounds of Kentucky. Doctor Thomas Walker and five associates, sent out in 1750 by the Loyal Company to set up claims to land in the Western country, passed through a mountain gap to which they gave the name of Cumberland Gap, and entered the state of Kentucky for a distance of some forty miles. They chose a site near what is now Barbourville for a settlement, and there set up the first house known to have been built by white men in the state. Within a few months the uncomfortable presence of prowling savages sent these settlers scurrying back to the pales of civilization.

The explorations of all these earlier rovers can, in no wise, dim the fame that has accrued to the everlasting credit of Daniel Boone, that apotheosis of the true pioneer type. Others may have done their bit of spadework, but it was Boone who laid the broad foundations which led to the successful settlement of Kentucky and its organization as the first state west of the mountains in 1792—exactly three hundred years after Columbus discovered America. Boone, like Columbus, appeared at the historically right moment. As Emerson Hough said, Daniel Boone did not discover Kentucky; it was Kentucky that discovered Daniel Boone.

Born October 22, 1734, Old Style, Daniel Boone was the sixth of the eleven children of Squire and Sarah Morgan Boone, worthy members of the Quaker faith, residing at the time in Berks County, Pennsylvania. The schooling that Daniel received was so scant that he was wont to say afterwards to his children that he had never been to school a day in his life. In one sense that was true, for the boy received only enough tutoring at the hands of a great-uncle to give him a smattering of the three R's. Always a notoriously bad speller, he is known in later life to have spelled the same word in one document three different ways, none of them right.

Young Dan got into as much mischief as did other boys of the frontier. One moonlit night he and his good friend, Henry Miller, an apprentice in his father's blacksmith shop, slipped away on Squire Boone's best saddle-nag. Seeing the family cow lying down in the pasture placidly ruminating, the two boys decided to do a little steeplechasing. They headed the horse in a gallop toward the cow, but just as the hurdle was being made, old Bossy rose on her haunches, and the horse, tripping, came down squarely on his neck to a speedy demise. Luckily the boys fared better, for they landed on the soft grass without serious injuries. Daniel never confessed the role he played in this piece of "night-errantry" to his father, who long wondered at the manner of his nag's untimely taking-off.

Daniel was a scrapper from his earliest days and, belying his Quaker heritage, believed in returning blow for blow. Hence, two giggling little neighbor girls, who thought it fun to splatter a piggin of fish offal over the sleeping Daniel, went home bawling with faces none the prettier after a few well-laid-on upper cuts from Daniel's fists. Mrs. Boone defended her son's action by declaring it was high time the girls were taught good manners.

When Daniel was ten years old, his father acquired twenty-five acres of woodland pasture for his growing herd of cattle, and it devolved upon the boy to take the cows back and forth to graze on the new land. This gave him a wonderful opportunity to roam through the woods during the long hours of the day, and he took full advantage of his time to acquaint himself with all the intimate phases of forest, stream, and hillside lore. His father presented him with a rifle when he had reached the age of twelve or thirteen, and from there on he worked assiduously to improve his marksmanship in daily rounds of target practice. He became far more expert at driving the nail, barking off squirrels, and snuffing the candle than he ever was at spelling or adding correctly.

When Daniel was in his sixteenth year, his parents decided to seek greener pastures. The first move took them to the Shenandoah Valley in Virginia and two years later they went on southward to still more sparsely settled country, along the Yadkin River in North Carolina. Here a plenitude of wild game stalked like troupers in a colorful pageant through the canebrakes of the valleys and the traces of the tree-girt hills— buffalo, deer, wild turkey, bear, beaver, otter, fox, wolf, and wildcat— affording an earthly paradise to such an eager, Nimrod-minded young fellow like Daniel.

The Boones were hardly settled in their new home when news broke of bitter conflict already in progress between the French and English for mastery of the North American continent. North Carolina was far away from the actual scenes of combat, and sent relatively few men, but among the one hundred or more mustered for service under the command of Captain Arthur Dobbs to join General Braddock in his effort to send the French reeling back into Canada was Daniel Boone, who as a teamster, blacksmith, and wagon-mechanic had to follow in the rear, ready to mend harness, repair broken axles, or tend any mishaps to the horses. Although this was not the sort of service Boone wanted, it did grant him an unexpected pleasure in the companionship of John Finley, a great lover of the hunt and, more than that, one who had actually ventured into that "second Garden of Eden"—called Kentucky by the Indians—"blessed with the richest of soils and the balmiest of climates, with noble forests and luxuriant expanses, where thousands of buffalo and other big game browsed." The enjoyment of listening to Finley's soul-stirring tales over a campfire was peremptorily cut short by the sudden, fierce attack of the French and Indians in the ravine at Turtle Creek. Braddock's forces were put to utter rout. Boone, seeing that disaster was inevitable, disengaged the horses from the baggage-wagons by cutting the traces, leapt bareback on one of the fastest mounts, and galloped away, showing no desire to tarry till he was back home in the Carolinas.

This unsoldierly retreat, prompted primarily by discretion, was hastened in all likelihood by reasons known only to Daniel himself. A few months before his departure he had become acquainted with a comely, black-eyed girl of sixteen, by the name of Rebecca Bryan, living near the Boones in the Yadkin Valley. Before he left with the Braddock expedition they had plighted their troth, and it was not long after his return that they were married, on August 14, 1756. Rebecca Boone proved to be a wonderful woman and wife, quite worthy of her husband, and she bore the hardships of the frontier with such a high degree of fortitude that Daniel was wont to say, in after years, that all a man required for complete satisfaction in this life was "a good gun, a good horse, and a good wife." Rebecca Boone met all the requirements for "a good wife." The children born of this marriage were nine in number: James, Israel, Susannah, Jemima, Lavinia, Rebecca, Daniel, Morgan, John B., and Nathan, scattered in their arrivals over a period of the next quarter-century.

At first the young couple lived in a cabin in the yard of Squire Boone's home, but soon they moved onto a tract of wild, wooded land, 640 acres in extent, which Daniel had bought from his father for fifty pounds. But this home lay in the path of dangerous Indian marauders, and soon Daniel had to take his family toward the East for safety.

During the next few years he fought Indians, did a little farming and a great deal of hunting. He also found time to cross over the Blue Ridge Mountains, do a bit of exploring in eastern Tennessee, and carve his name on a host of beech trees whenever he happened to kill a bear in the vicinity.

In 1765 Boone and his younger brother, Squire, induced by offers of large land grants to English-speaking settlers in the recent British acquisition of Florida, set out in October for St. Augustine. They traversed the state from east to west in the long northern part, and Daniel actually took out papers for a homestead near Pensacola. He arrived home in time to enjoy a Christmas dinner of wild turkey which Mrs. Boone had herself secured from the forest for the occasion. She welcomed her husband joyously, but balked at the idea of settling in the land of swamps and alligators. So the matter was dropped.

In the fall of 1767, accompanied by his brother Squire and a friend, William Hill, Boone set out at last to visit Kenutcky, that mysterious mecca toward which all his hunter's thoughts were directed. They pushed northwest through the Holston and Clinch Valleys, intending to strike the Big Sandy, follow it to the Ohio, and thence continue on to the Falls. But they had started too late in the season, and a blizzard held them snowbound at a salt spring near what is now Prestonsburg, Kentucky. They were in no danger of starving, for droves of animals approached the salt spring, and here Boone brought down his first buffalo. The explorers returned home in the early spring, loaded heavily with a rich harvest of pelts.

Back on the farm, Daniel still kept dreaming of Kentucky with its teeming stores of wild game. And who should turn up in the Valley of the Yadkin, just at this indeterminate moment, but John Finley, the man who had sown the seeds of this gravid yearning in the heart and soul of Boone? It had been fourteen years since the two men had sat together around the blazing logs, during that fateful Braddock expedition, and Boone had first heard Finley's wondrous tales. Bakeless graphically describes the spell which Finley cast over his auditor thus: "Kaintuck— there was a land for you, game in such abundance as no man dreamed of. A deer at every lick. Buffalo thick upon the traces. Herds so huge that a man had to be careful lest he be crushed to death in their mad stampedes. The ground rumbling with their hoofs. At the Falls of the Ohio, wild geese and ducks so plentiful there was no need even to kill them. All a man could eat were drawn by the current over the falls and thrown up freshly killed on the banks below. One might pick up enough fresh fowl for dinner any day. And land—land such as a man might dream of. Well watered, lush and green, with fertile soil in all directions. A settler's paradise. A hunter's paradise too, with deerskins at a dollar each."

It was not long, therefore, before a grandiose idea was hatched. Already there were men on the Eastern Seaboard who had visions of opening up land for settlement west of the mountains. Among these was a Colonel Richard Henderson who thought to emulate the example set by the great landed proprietors in the coastal colonies by securing title to large holdings in the western country. The proprietary rights to this fertile region once legally obtained, Henderson and several of his associates felt certain that immense profits would accrue permanently to them from their investments. It now seems certain this group quietly financed the exploring expedition which set out from Boone's abode early in May of 1769. The little party included, in addition to Boone and Finley, four other men: John Stewart, Joseph Holden, James Mooney, and William Cooley, the last three being taken mainly as hired help to tend camp, care for the provisions, and cook the meals.

The six men rode forth on horses that carried each an additional load of camp utensils. Passing through Cumberland Gap, they proceeded north along the warrior's path until they had reached, on the seventh of June, the Red River, a tributary of the Kentucky, at a point about ten miles south of the present town of Winchester. Shortly after, from the prominence of a high bluff, they beheld stretching far away below them the soft, billowing meadows of the beautiful Bluegrass Region in the velvety sunlight. We can well imagine, on that lovely day in June, that Boone and "all his men looked at each other with a wild surmise" when that expansive panorama swam like some new planet into their ken.

For six months Boone and Stewart remained in Kentucky, hunting, fishing, exploring, roaming from place to place, changing camps frequently, and fully enjoying the scenery and weather in this blissful solitude. The three camp followers were soon frightened by signs of Indians, and Finley agreed to take them back where they could go to sleep in peace without the haunting fear of waking up minus scalps.

Boone and Stewart were now left alone. Twice they were captured by Indians, and both times they quickly effected an escape. One of the most unusual rencontres in history occurred in January of 1770 when Daniel ran upon his brother Squire and his companion, Alexander Neeley, in the heart of the Kentucky wilderness. Squire Boone arrived in the nick of time with a fresh stock of ammunition, which enabled Daniel to continue his hunting and explorations without abatement for another six months.

Not long afterwards, Stewart and Boone separated, promising to come together again two weeks later. Boone appeared at the appointed time, but Stewart never did. He had vanished completely, a casualty of the mysterious forest. Then Squire Boone and his companion left for the Carolina settlements, and Daniel remained alone once more, feeling as never before the great need of "exercising philosophy and fortitude"—as he afterwards confessed to John Filson. He wandered far and wide, up and down the Kentucky River Valley, east to west along the Ohio as far as the Falls, as far east as the Big Sandy, and as far west as the Green and Cumberland Rivers. He became conversant with all the hills and streams, the confluence of watercourses, the buffalo licks, the haunts of richest game, the Indian trails, and the caves where camps were safest. Once standing on the high cliffs above the Kentucky River, he found his escape cut off by Indians. Boldly plummeting himself into the summit of a giant maple, he seized hold of the treetops to break the impact of his fall, slithered down through the limbs like an eel, and was sprinting away to safety while the surprised Indians grunted admiration at his reckless daring.

Wolves were such constant pilferers of his meat supplies that he had to kill one wolf dam more troublesome than usual, but he promptly adopted her cubs and tried to "civilize" them—to no avail. The varmints wouldn't be tamed and remained savage still. Boone's deep tenderness of heart was again evidenced when he ran upon a feeble old Indian abandoned by his fellow tribesmen along the roadside. Turning in his tracks, Boone· brought the old man fried venison he had left uneaten a mile or so back.

On the 27th of July, 1770, Daniel and Squire met again as John Filson words it for Daniel, "according to appointment, at our old camp—to my great felicity." After selecting a location on the Kentucky River suitable for future settlement, the brothers headed for home. On the way they encountered the Long Hunters, a group of forty men who had spent nearly a year already in southern Kentucky, engaged mainly in hunting and sporadic explorations. Daniel Boone reached home, after an absence of two years, in May, 1771.

For the next two years no move was made to establish a definite settlement in Kentucky, although Boone, as well as others, constantly talked up such a project. Richard Henderson seemed reluctant to back the undertaking or else was unable just then to furnish the necessary amount of money. Finally, becoming impatient at Henderson's delay, Boone sold his farm and all his belongings and set about persuading a few brave souls to follow him westward into the wilderness. Five families, including his in-laws, the Bryans, joined the little caravan that got under way in September, 1773. A number of adventurers, falling in along the way, had increased their ranks to more than fifty by the time they reached the confines of Kentucky. But misfortune soon dogged their steps. An unexpected Indian attack caught them completely unawares, and several men were killed, among them, James Boone, Daniel's eldest son. Their horses and cows had fled to the woods. Their most essential supplies were lost or stolen. Thoroughly disheartened, the majority would venture no farther, but retraced their steps as fast as they could to the homes they had so recently abandoned.

Still, Daniel was undaunted by this dismal failure. In fact, he was more determined than ever to open up Kentucky for settlement. When Governor Dunmore of Virginia accordingly wished to send scouts the next year to warn the few adventurers, hunters, and surveyors roaming about in Kentucky of pending Indian hostilities, Boone was˙ willing to undertake the journey. Accompanying him was Michael Stoner, an experienced backwoodsman from Pennsylvania. The two traveled more than eight hundred miles, stopped at the new settlement of Harrodsburg halfway between the Salt and Kentucky Rivers, reached the stockades of Louisville overlooking the Falls of the Ohio, and warned the unwary everywhere of Indians on the warpath.

The full fury of the gathering storm reached its climax in the Battle of Point Pleasant. Eleven hundred frontiersmen and volunteers from the coastal colonies clashed headlong with the strong confederation of Shawnees and their allies, led by the vigorous Chief Cornstalk. Although the whites lost nearly a hundred dead and as many more wounded, they broke the organized power of the Redskins to harry the frontier indiscriminately at their will.

Colonel Henderson was now ready to carry out his ambitious plans for a great proprietary domain in the heart of the wilderness. The Indians would be more amenable to the idea of swapping land for money. The land that Henderson desired was a sizable chunk of about twenty million acres—all that part of Kentucky and Tennessee lying south of the Ohio and between the Kentucky and Cumberland Rivers. The negotiations at Sycamore Shoals on the Watauga proceeded slowly because the shrewd old Chief Oconostata foresaw the danger of allowing the whites to settle west of the mountains. There was much feasting and more oratory till the treaty was finally signed on March 17, 1775. The Transylvania Company, headed by Henderson, agreed to pay the Indians fifty thousand dollars for the cession of their land. The payment was made chiefly in the form of goods, and ten wagons stocked with merchandise stood at hand in full view of the redskins. It looked, in bulk, like an enormous amount of clothing, trinkets, firearms, and spirituous liquors, but when distributed among twelve hundred braves, it amounted to very little. A shirt or two was the sole share of many a disappointed warrior. And the liquor did not even go halfway around.

Boone was off to make a saddle-path through the wilderness a week before the treaty was signed, the final acquiescence of the Indians being a foregone conclusion. Along with Boone were twenty-nine men bearing axes and rifles, the latter being needed several times to drive off small bands of roving Indians who had not yet heard of the recent treaty. Within two weeks the roadmakers had reached the present town of Richmond. By April the first they were camping on the Kentucky River.

No time was lost in starting a fort, because many of the men were discouraged by the sporadic Indian attacks, the constant straying of horses and cattle, and the general lack of shelter, comforts, and security. The new fort was called Boonesborough in honor of the indomitable pioneer who had brought about its realization.

Word was sent to Henderson to make haste in coming out with more men, that the new settlement might thus be strengthened sufficiently to withstand any Indian onslaught. Henderson's party arrived April 20, 1775, and Daniel Trabue, one of the newcomers, noted in his diary: "We were saluted by a running fire of about 25 Guns, all that was then in the Fort—The men appeared in high spirits and much rejoiced at our arrival."

Quarrels soon arose between the Transylvania Company and the adjacent settlements around Harrodsburg, all of which lay within the territory purchased by Henderson from the Indians. In a gesture of good will the new proprietor called for a legislative assembly to meet during the week of May 20-28, 1775. Eighteen delegates representing Harrodsburg, Boiling

Springs, Logan's Station, and Boonesborough convened under the wide-spreading branches of a towering elm that stood in "a beautiful plain surrounded by a turf of fine white clover, forming a green to its very stock to which there is scarcely anything to be likened." Henderson spoke in a conciliatory manner, and several laws were soon voted upon, effecting the establishment of courts and a band of militia for the civil and military defense of the new domain. Among the various bills proposed was one by Boone for the improvement of all breeds of horses. This was the first and last meeting of the Transylvania legislature, for the state governments of Virginia and North Carolina were resolutely opposed to the actions of the proprietary land company. Eventually Henderson and his friends came to terms with these older colonial governments, and relinquished their far-reaching claims, receiving in compensation a mere two hundred thousand acres. Daniel Boone, who was to have received a generous allotment of the company's land, found all his claims were null and void. He received nothing.

At its best, life at Boonesborough was none too good. Less than six hundred people were found in the new territory, and of these only twenty were women. Daniel brought his wife and family out to the wilderness settlement in September. Bitterness over rival claims to land created endless legal frictions and prevented a rapid increase of the better type of home-makers, many of whom left in disgust over the constant wrangling of get-rich-quick adventurers.

Another grave matter presently reared its ugly head. The rebellion in the coastal colonies against English rule was having its repercussions in the border lands. The Indians, hoping to profit by this internecine struggle between the two hostile factions of white men, were becoming restive. This was their opportunity to wrest control of the lost, but still coveted, hunting grounds away from the interlopers on the border. And they were now wise enough to see that only by concerted action of the previously warring tribes could they drive the encroaching settlers back east across the mountains.

The situation grew more critical as the redskins grew bolder. Whole families were dragged out of their beds and murdered in the dark of night. Cabins were looted and burned, and cattle killed or driven off as the spoils of war. Boonesborough, riddled by the dissension of claim-jumpers and the dubious titles held by proprietary grants, dwindled to a scant fifty souls. The other fortified stations were crowded by a multitude of isolated settlers fleeing for their lives. Some advocated the wholesale abandonment of Kentucky to the Indians. Patrick Henry, then governor of Virginia, gave timely heed to the multiplying pleas for help by despatching George Rogers Clark to the Ohio Valley with five hundred pounds of powder.

Boonesborough, hitherto undisturbed by the gravity of the situation, was suddenly aroused to swift action by the kidnapping of three girls on the Sunday afternoon of July 7, 1776. Jemima Boone and the two Callaway sisters, Betsy and Fanny, went out to pick flowers and paddle about in the river. Five Shawnee warriors, hidden in the canebrakes, were intently watching to see which direction they would take. As it happened, the canoe bearing the three girls stuck on a sandbar so close to their hiding place that all the Indians had to do was to reach out and pull the boat with its occupants to shore. The young women displayed the metal from which they were molded. They struggled desperately to defend themselves: little Fanny Callaway cracked a paddle over the head of one Indian; the other two screamed and fought until threatened into silence by upraised tomahawks. Jemima Boone had a sore foot and could not walk fast enough; she was therefore placed on a pony by her captors. As they were moved along, all three left traces of their trail behind them: twigs were broken, bits of their skirts were easily snagged and torn off by briers and bushes obstructing their path, and toes were dug into muddy spots as deeply as they dared without positive detection.

There was a great flurry of excitement inside the fort when the kidnapping was discovered. Daniel Boone arose from his Sunday afternoon nap, grabbed his gun, and hurried away, shod only in socks. Sam Henderson, the fiancé of Betsy Callaway, dashed out with only one side of his face shaved—the other bristled with a week's growth of whiskers. Flanders Callaway, to whom Jemima Boone was engaged, mounted his horse and accompanied by several men galloped off toward the ford of the Licking River. John Holder, the betrothed of the fourteen-year-old Fanny, joined the party led by Daniel Boone and John Floyd.

The pursuers followed the captors for three days, traveling from dawn till dark, guided always by the unmistakable clues left by the clever girls. Noticing a faint curl of smoke rising from a campfire of the Indians on the morning of the third day, Boone's men at a given signal rushed forward upon the unsuspecting Indians and killed four of them before they had time to offer any resistance. Only one Indian escaped, and he decamped without benefit of moccasins, knife, or tomahawk.

There was much rejoicing when the rescuers, the three happy girls and their sweethearts returned to Boonesborough. Three weeks later the first marriage in Kentucky took place when Squire Boone performed the marriage ceremony of Samuel Henderson and Betsy Callaway. The first watermelons raised in Kentucky formed an important part of the menu at the wedding banquet, and the festivities wound up at night with a lively number of square dances, jigs, and reels, accompanied by the music of Squire Boone's fiddle. The other two pairs of lovers were married a few months later.

Early in 1778 Boone set out with a party of thirty men to replenish the settlers' supply of salt, which was running low. They had been drying out salt for several days at the Blue Licks on the Licking River, when quite by surprise they were surrounded by a hundred Shawnee warriors who, the prisoners learned, were marching southward to attack Boonesborough. The bagging of so many prisoners without a fight was such a signal accomplishment that the elated Indians changed their plans for attacking the fort at once, to herd their large batch of prisoners quickly back to Detroit without the attendant risks of delay.

Boone immediately made himself a great favorite with the Indians by participating wholeheartedly in their games, and allowed himself to be always beaten, however by the narrowest margins, in target matches just to gratify the vanity of the Indians in their belief that they were superior marksmen. He became the adopted son of Chief Blackfish, had his hair plucked, his body scrubbed to wash out his white blood, and his face and arms painted a coppery-red. On his head he wore an array of turkey feathers.

For four months he remained on the best of terms with the Indians as the son of Blackfish and his squaw, but he was abiding his time. When he learned fully the plans of the savages for attacking, he quietly disappeared overnight and traveled the distance of one hundred and sixty miles, scarcely stopping to sleep or eat, till he had reached Boonesborough.

The backwoodsmen set to work at once to strengthen their woefully inadequate defenses. The news of Boone's return and the imminent danger to the fort spread rapidly. Harrodsburg and Logan's Station sent all the men they could safely spare. A second well was sunk to make sure of sufficient water supplies, more corn, meat, and ammunition brought in, and the blockhouses heightened at each corner of the palisades.

Finally, on September 7, 1778, the investing army arrived—more than four hundred Indians, led by Blackfish, and a dozen French-Canadians under a Captain De Quindre. The attack was not immediately begun, because the Indians hoped by negotiations to bring about a peaceful surrender of the stockade's defenders. During the delay the walls of the fort were strengthened, the cows and horses brought inside, and all preparations made to withstand the oncoming siege.

Angered at the obstinate refusal of the settlers to surrender, the Indians now tried a ruse. Inviting Boone and eight of his men to a parley for making peace without recourse to arms, Blackfish asked each of the white negotiators to shake hands with two of his braves as a proof of good intentions on both sides. Boone's men, although skeptical of this friendly gesture, went through the formality of shaking hands, but when they found themselves being gripped tightly by the savages trying to take them prisoners, broke loose and fled toward the fort. Onlooking sharpshooters protected their speedy retreat to the stockade.

The Indians now began the siege in full fury. The fifty men inside the fort were ably aided by the ten women who donned buckskin breeches and coonskin caps, to make it appear the palisades were fully manned. For ten days the siege lasted. Time and again the Indians tried to set fire to the fort by hurling torches and arrows lit with pitch onto the cabin roofs, but drizzling rains helped as much as the active fire-fighters, armed with squirt guns, to extinguish every incipient blaze. Each onrush of the attackers to scale the timbered walls was repelled by a suicidal burst of bullets. Captain De Quindre attempted to engineer a tunnel from the river bank to a spot directly beneath the fort, hoping to blast an opening through its defenses, but the wet surface grounds kept tumbling into the excavations. Failure to make headway was wearing Indian patience thin. The collapse of their subterranean passage was the last straw. Gathering up their dead, they departed during the night of September the eighteenth. Those in the fort counted as their casualties two dead and four wounded. The most prolonged contest in the whole history of western border warfare was over; the defenders had withstood the concentrated fire from an enemy eight times as large. The attack on Boonesborough was never repeated, although other forts passed through similar ordeals during the next few years.

With the coming of more and more settlers the forces protecting Kentucky were greatly strengthened. The Indians, even if they made flying raids in small bands, were gradually being driven farther north and west.

In 1786 Boone moved away from the Kentucky River to Maysville on the Ohio. Two years later he moved upstream to Point Pleasant, still on the Ohio, but out of Kentucky territory. In the spring of 1799 he crossed the Mississippi and settled in Missouri, then entirely outside the United States. It seems during these years that Fortune was always playing tricks on Boone by dangling before him baited promises, which he could never grasp and hold onto permanently. All his claims to land in Kentucky slipped through his fingers one after the other. Once, on the way to Richmond, Virginia, from the Yadkin, he was robbed of twenty thousand dollars which he intended to use for buying land warrants. Worse still, a considerable sum belonging to others was also taken. Boone always believed himself the victim of an avaricious innkeeper who managed to conceal an old woman in his bedroom before he entered, as he had carefully bolted the door before he went to bed, yet found it unbolted when he awoke, and the money gone. He was utterly crushed for a while by this blow, but no one, not even among those who were likewise losers by the theft, impugned his honesty or doubted his story.

Boone tried various ventures: surveying, horse-trading, tavern-keeping, ginseng-peddling. He dabbled in real estate, and lost five thousand dollars at the hands of Gilbert Imlay, an unctuous-scoundrel of the soft-soap type. When he heard that the Wilderness Road was to be widened for general traffic, Boone applied to Governor Shelby for the job but the governor did not bother to answer his letter.

Anyway, Kentucky was getting too full of people, many of them fast becoming wealthy on land over which he had once freely roamed. Hunting was no longer a profitable occupation. Boone needed elbow-room;

so he moved to Missouri to be near his younger sons who had already preceded him there. In his latter years his limbs were so stiffened by rheumatism that his good wife, Rebecca, had to go with him when he hunted, to steady for him the long rifle barrel whenever he took aim. When his wife died in 1813, fifty-six years after their marriage, the old man moved into the spacious home of his youngest son, Nathan. In 1820 he passed away at the age of eighty-six. In 1845 the bones of the hero and his wife were brought back to Kentucky soil, where they now repose on the high hills at Frankfort overlooking the beautiful Kentucky River Valley.

Long before his death, Boone had become an immortal legend in the pages of our history. In Europe his name was a familiar one. Let Lord Byron bespeak the fame that was his in England—

> Of the great names which in our faces stare,
>   The General Boon, backwoodsman of Kentucky,
> Was happiest among mortals anywhere;
>   For killing nothing but a bear or buck, he
> Enjoy'd the lonely, vigorous, harmless days
> Of his old age in wilds of deepest maze.
>
> And what's still stranger, left behind a name
>   For which men vainly decimate the throng,
> Not only famous, but of that good fame
>   Without which glory's but a tavern song—
>
>   ❁   ❁   ❁   ❁
>
> 'Tis true he shrank from men even of his nation,
>   When they built up unto his darling trees—
> He moved some hundred miles off, for a station
>   Where there were fewer houses and more ease;
> The inconvenience of civilization
>   Is, that you neither can be pleased nor please;
> But where he met the individual man,
> He show'd himself as kind as mortal can.

Truly he was, as J. Donald Adams rightly calls him, the American Ulysses, a wanderer, wise, courageous, and resourceful, yet dogged all his life by will-o'-the-wisps beckoning close but forever beyond his arm's length.

The Daniel Boone spoon contains, in the bowl, a cut-out of the pioneer type of log cabin with "Old Kentucky Home" and "Louisville" appearing around the rim. Along the front of the handle may be seen the state seal, Boone himself, a horse-in-horseshoe, a keg, and a stalk of corn. The reverse side of handle is crowded with embossments: the former state capitol, the same cabin as in the bowl, the Daniel Boone monument at Frankfort, and a branch, presumably of the elderberry of sumac, with two clusters of three drupes each. Made by Watson and Newell before 1909. Length, 5¾ inches.

No. 81 PATRICK HENRY

Like Christ and Socrates, Patrick Henry wrote practically nothing. In the case of all three it remained for their followers to record their words and transmit the secret of their power to posterity. While other Revolutionary orators, like James Otis and Samuel Adams, are only distant echoes to us now, Patrick Henry still commands the attention and admiration of every schoolboy. Axelrad calls him the "voice of freedom." He, more than any other, sired the American Revolution.

The beginnings of Patrick Henry were not auspicious. The second of nine children, he had one brother older and seven sisters younger than himself. His mother had also had a son by a previous marriage. His education was none too thorough. Under the guidance of his uncle and godfather, the Reverend Patrick Henry, rector of St. Paul's Church in Hanover, Virginia, he learned to read Latin and Greek. But the boy was averse to books. He preferred to handle shotguns and fishing-rods, and to tramp through the woods, swapping yarns with trappers and backwoodsmen. And, too, he was adept at playing practical jokes. He could adroitly tilt or swerve a canoe when a companion had just snagged a fish, so that the line entangled in the tree branches above; then, later, he would have a good story to tell and the unsuccessful fisherman would become the butt of his pleasantries.

At seventeen he went into partnership with his older brother to start a crossroads store, but he allowed his customers too much credit, and the business folded up after a few months. Then, at eighteen, without a penny's promise on his future, he married and began to raise a family. He also tried to raise tobacco on a farm owned by his father-in-law. A forest fire razed his house and barns. Once more he set up as a storekeeper, but too frequent absences from behind the counter to hunt foxes, possums, and coons scuttled this venture also.

Casting about for a livelihood, he hit upon the law. After six weeks' study, he was admitted to the bar, but only after considerable reluctance on the part of two out of the four examiners to sign the licensing papers. One of these was persuaded to sign on Henry's promise to continue his legal studies. The other categorically refused his signature. At this time Thomas Jefferson, who had come in contact with the young lawyer at certain Christmas festivities, looked down upon him with supercilious contempt. "His manners had something of coarseness in them. His passion was music, dancing, and pleasantry. He excelled in the last, and it attached every one to him." Henry's pronunciation of "yearth," "naiteral," and "larnin'" jarred on Jefferson's sensitive ear. The latter erred, however, when he spoke of Henry as an unread man with no specific knowledge of any one subject. Patrick Henry read only what he liked to read. He was fond of history and he was a sincere student of the Bible. There was a deeply religious strain in his nature.

The first realization that Henry had great forensic abilities came during the celebrated Parsons' Case. About twenty ministers had "struck" for higher wages. The House of Burgesses had passed a law in 1758 making 16,000 pounds of tobacco the maximum sum, payable in paper currency, for a preacher's annual salary. The clergy protested, tobacco prices being sorely depressed at that time, and the king in London refused to sign the bill. The little courtroom at Hanover was packed when Henry rose to defend the law. His father, always a staunch supporter of the royal authority, sat in the seat of the presiding judge. His uncle, the Reverend Patrick Henry, had been implored not to be there.

Things did not go too well for the ungainly young lawyer at first. It was always hard to spark his eloquence. When he began to question the right of a sovereign, three thousand miles away, to reject arbitrarily those statutes duly weighed and passed by the representative law-making body of Virginia, a shout of treason was heard—the first but not the last one aroused by Henry's numerous utterances.

The farther along the speaker went, the more interested became the audience. They had never heard such magnificent oratory, nor their rights as free men so ably expounded before. Their king was a tyrant who would not listen to reason. The ministers were "harpies" who would greedily "snatch from the hearth of the honest parishioner his last hoe-cake, from the widow and her orphan children her last milch-cow, the last bed—nay, the last blanket from the lying-in woman!"

The twenty ministers rose in a body and rushed out, unwilling to hear more of this blistering castigation. Tears of pride flowed from the eyes of the presiding judge when he heard his son declare that Virginians must fight to defend their liberties. The jury was convinced and the state of Virginia had won its case. The young orator had suddenly become a hero. He was carried from the courtroom on the shoulders of his jubilating admirers.

The rest of Patrick Henry's life is common history. His speech in the House of Burgesses in 1765 when, at the cries of treason, he ended dramatically: "And George the Third may profit by their example. If this be treason, make the most of it!" His address before the Continental Congress in 1774, when he electrified his auditors by asking: "Where are your landmarks, your boundaries of colonies? The distinctions between Virginians, New Yorkers, and New Englanders are no more. I am not a Virginian, but an American." His masterpiece delivered in old St. John's Church, when he swept the members of the dissolved legislature meeting there off their feet by his clarion call to the inevitable struggle for liberty— or death. His two terms as wartime governor of Virginia. His backing of George Rogers Clark with a loan to push the conquest of the Northwest

Territory. His retirement and refusal to accept any further political honors in his old age.

An amiable man, he was greatly beloved by his family and a host of close personal friends. The deaths of Henry and Washington were only a few months apart in 1799, and the two greatest heroes of the Revolution were gone. A crop of legends has sprung up around both men. Whether they are truth or fiction doesn't greatly matter. The pen and the sword . . . the voice and the instrument of our freedom . . . Patrick Henry and George Washington: their place in the hearts of their countrymen is irrevocably fixed.

✻   ✻   ✻   ✻

Briefly now for the spoon, in the bowl of which, in a cut-out design, is old St. John's Church in Richmond. In front of the church are several leafless trees, and grouped rather methodically in the churchyard is a crop of tombstones.

Inscribed on a banderole running plumb with the shaft are Patrick Henry's most undying words, which we need not repeat. His name traverses the waist below the nave, on which stands the Washington Monument. Then Henry's bust appears in the caput, looking pretty much as we are used to seeing it in the history texts, his specs resting familiarly on his head just back from his high brow.

The obverse side of the handle contains cut-outs of the State Capitol, the Jefferson Davis Mansion, and the equestrian statue of General Lee. The shaft is enhanced with a spray of bayberries.

The spoon was made by Watson and Newell. Length, 5¾ inches.

No. 82 SHAKESPEARE

Some authors have crossed the confines of their own nation and, literarily speaking, been adopted by readers in other countries like native sons. Dumas has never been taken seriously by the French, but his public is world-wide. Byron is still considered the greatest of English writers by some continental Europeans. Cervantes was accepted wholeheartedly beyond the Spanish pales before his countrymen realized his surpassing worth. Ibsen's great reputation was earned largely outside of Norway. The high esteem held for Poe in France brought home to our minds an increasing respect for that sombre genius. A Swedish anthologist included Longfellow among the poets of his own country. To Persians, Omar Khayyam is known as an astronomer and mathematician; to the English-speaking world he is a great poet. The thoughts of Homer, Dante, Goethe, and Tolstoy have leapt the barriers of language to reach a world audience, while Shakespeare's works have been read and revered more than any other writings, except the Bible, in all the corners of the globe.

No apologies need be extended for including Shakespeare in a book that is devoted chiefly to matters concerning our American heritage. He has been with us almost from the beginning, and has grown upon our consciousness, there being no barriers of language, to such a degree that even the most illiterate of our people often quote him without being aware of it. Who has not repeated some of these expressions?—What's in a name? . . . As merry as the day is long. . . . Every inch a King. . . . The milk of human kindness. . . . Brevity is the soul of wit. . . . Something rotten in Denmark. . . . The very pink of courtesy. . . . Comparisons are odorous. . . . It was Greek to me. . . . There's a divinity that shapes our ends. . . . Ill blows the wind that profits nobody. . . . The devil can cite Scripture for his purpose. . . . The course of true love never did run smooth. . . . There's small choice in rotten apples. . . . The wish was father to the thought. . . . With bag and baggage. . . . Without rhyme or reason. . . . As good luck would have it. . . . A dish fit for the gods. . . . There is nothing either good or bad but thinking makes it so.

Naturally a large number of these utterances were not original with Shakespeare, but the fact that he first recorded and applied them to the most apposite situations has tended to clinch them, in his particular way of phrasing them, for all aftertimes. They are part and parcel of our American speech.

For three centuries Shakespeare has been a mighty factor in the thinking habits of America. We have become increasingly aware of his influence, and in recent years several fine studies have called this influence to our attention, among these being Esther Cloudman Dunn's *Shakespeare in America*, A. V. R. Westfall's *American Shakespearean Criticism*, and H. W. Simon's *The Reading of Shakespeare in American Schools and Colleges*.

Only four editions of Shakespeare's writings were put out in England during the seventeenth century, and these were edited in expensive folios. The copies sold were not numerous, as the great poet was still not appraised at his full value. Yet there was one copy of the first folio, printed in 1623, said to have been in the library of Cotton Mather; at least the book was in the hands of his descendants as late as 1874. We do know, however, that Seaborn Mather, son of the famous parson, copied in a notebook while he was an under-graduate student that lyrical passage from *Measure for Measure* beginning, "Take, O take those lips away." Seaborn Mather graduated from Harvard in 1651. "Today the only copy of a Shakespearean play apparently recorded in America in the seventeenth century," according to E. E. Willoughby of the Folger Shakespearean Library in Washington, was a copy of *Macbeth* listed by a Virginian gentleman, Captain Arthur Spicer, in 1699. Since the plays were first published separately in 1673, followed by a bowdlerized edition the next year, the Spicer *Macbeth* may have been dated from either one of those editions.

As early as 1716 plans were drawn up for a theatre in Williamsburg, then the capital of colonial Virginia, but details concerning the outcome of this enterprise are totally lacking. A permanent theatre was established here in 1751, when the Hallam Company from London opened the season with a performance of *Richard III*. The second season began with *The Merchant of Venice*. Lewis, the twelve-year-old son of the Hallams, was so frightened when he played the part of Portia's servant that he broke into tears, an incident which furnished the highlight of the performance for the spectators. Another interesting feature of this season was reported in the Virginia Gazette. The "Emperor of the Cherokee Nation," the "Empress," their son and several chieftains, having come to town to renew a treaty of friendship with the whites, were taken to see a showing of *Othello*. A sword-duel on the stage caused such apprehension in the tender-hearted "Empress" that she ordered her attendants to rush forward and halt the combat before any blood were shed. Washington attended a show at Williamsburg during this season, but it is not recorded what play he witnessed. This theatre functioned regularly for twenty-five years, till interrupted by the Revolutionary struggle. The chief Shakespearean productions during this time were *Richard III, The Merchant of Venice, Henry IV, King Lear,* and *Romeo and Juliet*.

Interest in theatricals was sporadic in New York during the early part of the eighteenth century, the performers beings local amateurs. Such a group gave an adapted version of *Romeo and Juliet* in 1730. A warehouse belonging to the Honorable Rip Van Dam, deceased, was converted into a makeshift theatre in 1746. Three years later something like a regular season began, and three performances of *Richard III* were listed, the only dramatic morsel from Shakespeare. A second feature was added twice to tempt patronage. What these added features were like may be easily deduced from their farcial titles, *The Beau in the Sudds and The Mock Doctor*. "Such a double bill," remarks Miss Dunn, "offers something heavy and something light. It caters to a taste none too subtle which asks for excitement tending both toward chills of horror and toward titters of mirth."

During a performance of *Romeo and Juliet*, the theatre in New York was so cramped for space that a number óf gentlemen had to sit on the stage. They had to rise and move their chairs off the stage to make way for Juliet's funeral procession. Odell describes the place facetiously as "sans ventilation, sans space, sans everything."

David Douglass, at one time connected with the Hallams, built the John Street Theatre in New York in 1767, with space enough in two rows of boxes, a pit, and a gallery, to prevent the overcrowding so frequent in previous structures. Douglass had the temerity to offer new Shakespearean attractions in *Cymbeline, Taming of the Shrew,* and *Antony and Cleopatra*, though these were in adapted versions. A group of Cherokee Indians from South Carolina, visiting in New York, announced their intention of seeing a play; the John Street Company accordingly pulled out their bloodiest stops for the delectation of the savages in a special performance of *Richard III.*

Philadelphia had to buck a strong tide of opposition to theatricals from several religious groups in the first half of the eighteenth century, yet we find a disregard of legal prohibitions growing to such an extent that private performances were given in the late 1740's without arousing comment from the Press. Again, it was Douglass, that inveterate promoter, who shrewdly circumvented legal restrictions by building his Society Hill Theatre in 1759 before a petition opposing its construction could be brought up and voted into a prohibiting law. The advocates of the theatre had to step gingerly; on the opening night Francis Hopkinson read a prologue before the curtain, stressing the "heavenly influence" and the "bright example" that would be kindled in each bosom by the "celestial fire" emanating from the stage. And lest the uplifting impact of the theatre might not yet be clearly divined, Hopkinson prayerfully concludes:

> So may each scene some useful moral show;
> From each performance sweet instruction flow.

Douglass was so greatly gratified by the patronage of this first theatre that he built a second in 1766, and actually a third in 1769. On his theatrical menus he judiciously sprinkled as much Shakespeare as his clients could digest, and he added a savor of distinction in bringing out a wider choice of plays, namely, *Hamlet, Julius Caesar, The Merry Wives of Windsor, The Tempest, Henry IV* (Part I), and *Othello.* There is some justification in the claim made by T. C. Pollock, in his study of the colonial stage in Philadelphia, that the dignity and circumspection of its Shakespearean performances have never been surpassed by later presentments of the same plays.

Charleston, Baltimore, and Newport, Rhode Island, had established play houses before the Revolution, but the oncoming conflict frostbit all these burgeoning stages in the bud.

Miss Dunn's research has led her to discover a goodly number of Shakespearean readers among our Revolutionary leaders. John Adams likens England as a mother to Lady Macbeth. Under a Sabbath entry for 1772 in his diary, Adams extracts this assertion made by Mrs. Ford to Mrs. Page, in the *Merry Wives of Windsor,* "If I would but go to hell for an eternal moment or so, I could be knighted," to express the seductive blandishments by which he might rise momentarily, through the betrayal of his finer instincts, to the dizzy heights of an ignoble importance.

Abigail Adams, surely one of the elect among all the Puritan intelligentsia, was an astute student of Shakespeare all her life. When the inevitable conflict was fast approaching its crisis, we find her exclaiming, "The time is hastening when George, like Richard, may cry 'My kingdom for a horse!' and want even that wealth to make the purchase." She issues a timely reminder in that warning, "There is a tide in the affairs of men," to guard against "supineness." She signed herself "Portia," thinking perhaps there was an analogy between herself and that "true and honorable wife" of Brutus, who was the "noblest Roman of them all."

John Adams and Thomas Jefferson were both in London in the spring of 1786, and together the two men made a pilgrimage out to Stratford-on-Avon, Shakespeare's birthplace. Would it not be interesting to know what they talked about on their journey? All we have in Jefferson's journal is a very dry record, which carefully lists each item of the expenditures for the day.

As a young man Jefferson had access to Shakespeare's works in his father's library. Frequently he transferred passages from the plays to his notebook. He included six from *Julius Caesar*, four from *Coriolanus*, and several spoken by Falstaff, including that highly original peroration on honor, at once both famous and infamous:

"Can honor set to a leg? No. Or an arm? No. Or take away the grief of a wound? What is honor? A word. What is that word? Air. Who hath it? He that died o' Wednesday. Doth he feel it? No. Doth he hear it? No. 'Tis insensible, then. Yea, to the dead. Therefore I'll none of it. Honor is a mere scutcheon: and so ends my catechism."

A friend once asked Jefferson for a list of the best books that could be bought within the value of fifty pounds sterling. Jefferson not only jotted down all of Shakespeare but also added some running commentaries on the efficacy of such fictions as the murder of Banquo by Macbeth to arouse a "horror of villainy" and the ill-treatment of Lear by his daughters to instill a "lively and lasting sense of filial duty." Jefferson fully lives up to the title bestowed on him, the Sage of Monticello, when he solemnly asserts that the lessons learned from such fictions teach us more than "all the dry volumes of ethics and divinity that were ever written."

In the early nineteenth century, handsome theatres sprang up in many cities of the Eastern Seaboard. The Chestnut Street Theatre in Philadelphia, a pretentious structure that went up in 1791, vied in splendor with "Old Drury" in London. Three years later the Federal Street Theatre was opened in Boston. Park Street was built in New York in 1798, to be replaced in 1821 by a more sumptuous edifice, over the entrance of which a bust of Shakespeare was installed. Theatres of lesser dimensions were gradually built in all the cities of New England, New York, and the other Eastern states.

The reign of Shakespeare had begun on the American stage. English actors came to our shores, just as American actors went to London, and the ultimate criterion, the acid test, by which every one had to pass muster was his skill in personating the characters of Shakespeare. Almost in every instance our great actors and actresses have come to be identified solely with one or two Shakespearean roles: Charlotte Cushman (Lady Macbeth); Edwin Forrest (King Lear); Edwin Booth (Hamlet); James H. Hackett (Falstaff), Lawrence Barret (Brutus); Mary Anderson (Juliet);

Henry Irving (Hamlet); E. L. Davenport (Brutus); John McCullough (Othello); Junius Brutus Booth (Richard III); Agnes Ethel (Viola); Fanny Davenport (Rosalind); Ellen Terry (Portia); and Adelaide Neilson (Imogen). The list could be far more extended.

Maurice Morgann, a Welshman who wrote a famous study of the character of Falstaff, prophesied in 1777 that the "hand of time," after it has swept aside all the editors and commentators, and even the French tongue, in which Voltaire once presumed to call Shakespeare a barbarian, "shall be no more, the Appalachian Mountains and the banks of the Ohio shall resound with the accents of this barbarian." Not many years after the Welshman made his prophecy, the "barbarian" had passed the Eastern mountains and the Ohio, crossed the Mississippi, and traveled on to embrace the Pacific.

In 1816 Noah Ludlow and his troupers were playing *The Merchant of Venice, Othello*, and *The Taming of the Shrew* in Lexington, Kentucky. Incidentally, Ludlow had to draft the son of a local Methodist minister for a minor role. Between lines the boy rotated his quid of tobacco from one cheek to the other, and once, when he mispronounced a word, he was corrected so loudly backstage that the audience broke into gales of laughter. The play halted ten minutes till the merriment subsided.

Ludlow, Joseph Jefferson II, and other troupers traveled over the South and West, stopping in Chicago, St. Louis, Cincinnati, Louisville, Pittsburgh, Nashville, Natchez, Mobile, and New Orleans. Nor were the smaller towns overlooked, for even in the most rugged settlements there could always be found an audience receptive to Shakespeare. Sol Smith found two local characters able to play Cassius and Brutus—though somewhat spottily—when he visited Greenville, North Carolina, in 1832. The next year Smith and his troupe, just over Cumberland Gap, put up for the night at Tazewell, Tennessee. On a small platform in the hotel dining-room one of the actors held a crowd of twenty people enthralled by his rendition of "All the world's a stage," from *As You Like It*, interrupted by a "Set down that julep!" from the adjoining bar. At Columbus, Georgia, Smith paid twenty-four Creek Indians fifty cents and a glass of whiskey each to play as extras in *Pizarro*. The next night the redskins were back, proffering their services for *Macbeth*. At Houston, Smith hired a saloon keeper and professional gambler by the name of Stanley to play the ubiquitous Richard III. When the humpbacked king was courting the Lady Anne, one old-timer yelled out to Stanley that he couldn't do that, he already had two Mexican wives back home.

The Chapman family plied a beautiful showboat up and down the Mississippi and on the Ohio, from Cincinnati to New Orleans, stopping at every town and landing-place that provided a paying audience. The Chapmans were partial to Shakespeare, and they usually managed to sandwich him in as the *pièce de resistance* between numbers of their blackface minstrelsy.

The Chapmans followed the gold craze to California and played Shakespeare, along with the Booths *père* and *fils,* Laura Keene, and lesser lights in San Francisco.

For most of us an acquaintance with Shakespeare began with Lamb s *Tales.* A few oldsters may still recall learning the famous soliloquys and Antony's speech from the *McGuffey Readers.* High school courses in English extend the knowledge of the Bard through a half-dozen plays, still selected according to Victorian standards. Most colleges offer complete courses of these dramas, while special students are opening up new vistas to our view in such scholarly studies as those by Caroline Spurgeon, Cleanth Brooks, Robert B. Heilman, Roy Walker, T. S. Eliot, George Bernard Shaw, A. C. Bradley, John Drinkwater, Clutton-Brock, Granville-Barker, Tucker Brooke, J. M. Robertson, L. C. Knight, Charlton, Hapgood, Palmer, Wilson, Warde, Furness, Folger, and no end of others. The output of Shakespeareana is increasing in quantity and quality. Nor must we forget the fine work advanced in an earlier day by Coleridge, Hazlitt, and Mrs. Jameson.

Shakespeare is English, American, universal—all in one. And the timeless devotion, amounting in some cases to obsession and idolatry, held by so many Americans, is all the more amazing when we realize that the man himself, living in the age of Drake, Raleigh, Drayton, and Hakluyt, reveals no interest either in exploratory voyages to or descriptive accounts of the New World. He makes one wee mention of America and none of Virginia. *The Tempest,* his only play that deals with the discovery of new lands, leads to a mysterious island in the Mediterranean. He must have loathed the sea and its ships. All his seafaring voyages lead inevitably to shipwrecks. His knowledge of geography may have even been faulty; he speaks of the seacoast of Bohemia, when there is none. We are aware of no trips that he ever took abroad, not even of a Channel crossing. The only journeys he ever made were those back and forth from Stratford to London. He grew up a country boy and he remained that to the day of his death, being always the Bard of the Avon, never of the Thames. The London that impressed him was that of an earlier day, when Yorkists and Lancastrians fought gory battles for the wearing of a crown. Historically speaking, he dwelt in the Feudal Age. He was an isolationist pure and simple; he took pride in his insular fastness—

> . . . this little world,
> This precious stone set in the silver sea,
> Which serves it in the purpose of a wall,
> Or as a moat defensive to a house.

He scorned the shopkeepers and the mobs of London. The main characters in his plays belonged to the titled ranks, and his interests were subservient to the upper classes. He remains: a mass of contradictions

344

the great enigma and eternal paradox. And because he dwelt so truly in the only real world—that of the mind—he is

> . . . not of an age, but for all time!

The Shakespeare spoon pictures in its bowl Holy Trinity Church, where the poet is buried. On the obverse of handle appear Ann Hathaway's college, the Shakespeare house, a book above cross-quills, and a bust, all in clear relief. On the reverse of handle are the Shakespeare arms, the grammar school, the signature, and the Stratford coat of arms.

Apparently this spoon was brought back by some American pilgrims who went, as Adams and Jefferson, to repay many favors that the Master Skylark had made them in the past—along the wingèd avenues of the spirit. Length of spoon, 5½ inches.

No. 83 HEARTS OF OAK

That the oak with its fruit, the acorn, has always been a favorite for designers is testified by the fact that the oak-leaf and the acorn appear on a score or more glass patterns, many pieces of china and silver, numerous buttons, visiting cards, and decorative designs for household furnishings and architectural detail. Thirty-eight states have post offices listed under some compound form or derivative of "Oak."

The uses of oak are manifold, the most common being for building materials, naval construction, farm implements, railroad ties, kegs and cooperage, furniture, fuel, medicines, food, and park shade—a diversified list. Squirrels, rabbits, mice, and pigs have always found acorns delectable tidbits. Indians prepared savory oils from acorns as a relish for their meats.

There are more species of oak than of almost any other tree. The white oak was the most plentiful in the early American forests, and extended over a wide area, from Maine to Florida, and west to Missouri, Texas, and Minnesota. Among the other important varieties, distinguished generally according to their leaves, are the mossy cup, red, black, scarlet, yellow, iron, cow, turkey, bear and willow. This list is far from complete.

An object of affection in the South is the live-oak, which grows in the sandy regions from Virginia south to Florida, and west to Texas and California. The leathery leaves of the live-oak are not scalloped as with other species, but have even margins. They hang on tenaciously until the new shoots dislodge them in the spring. The sweet-kerneled acorns grow in clustered groups. The festoons of Spanish moss hanging like pendulated tails from the limbs of a live-oak in the deep South form felicitous pictures not easily disframed from the memory.

The oak has played an important role in the lives of men from the earliest times. To the Greeks, oaks were considered the symbolic cup-bearers of the gods. Among the ancient worshippers of Thor, the storm-resistant oak was a sacred tree. The Celtic druids invested the oak with magic charms, believing the spot beneath its branches was a favorite haunt for the dance-loving fairies.

In England those "green-robed senators of mighty woods, tall oaks," to use Keats's expression, long possessed supernatural powers, and to cut down an old oak was to invite "calamities unshorn." The Royal Oak, amid whose branches Prince Charles hid from his pursuers, long held the homage of many Englishmen, and fragments from it are still preserved in the Bodleian Library. The Charter Oak at Hartford, Connecticut, was venerated by both the whites and Indians for its historic associations. When a storm toppled it over in 1856, a solemn funeral service was held over its remains. When Samuel Woodworth penned his immortal lines—

> The old oaken bucket, the ironbound bucket,
> The moss-covered bucket that hung in the well—

he selected the wood which appealed most to the hearts of his listeners.

As the lion is considered the king among beasts, so the oak is looked upon as the king among trees. Maud Going, in her splendid book, *With the Trees,* tells us why this tree has always been held in the highest esteem: "The oak alone seems master of its fate. Its branches do not evade the main issue with gravity by inclining upwards, like those of the Lombardy poplar, nor yet by arching, like those of the elm. Nor do they bow before the blast, like the branches of the willow. They meet the gale like a boxer who strikes straight from the shoulder at his adversary, and with their massive weight held horizontally they seem to defy gravity to drag them earthward if it can. Two or three trees, native to temperate climates, can attain to greater size than the oak. Others can equal or even excel it in longevity. But its uncompromising attitude belongs to itself alone, and this is perhaps why the oak has always been reverenced as the tree of the gods who ruled the fates of men."

The handle for this tiny demi-tasse spoon, displaying four acorns surrounded by a half-dozen oak leaves, brings forcefully to mind the old adage that "great oaks from little acorns grow."

The name for the spoon is found in Charles Kingsley's *Ode to the North-east Wind:*

> What's the soft South-wester?
> 'Tis the ladies' breeze,
> Bringing home their true-loves
> Out of all the seas;
> But the black North-easter,
> Through the snowstorm hurled,
> Drives our English hearts of oak
> Seaward round the world.

The gold bowl of this spoon contains the picture of the state capitol in Jefferson City, Missouri, and it is most appropriate to associate the oak tree with the state of Missouri, which was hewn out of the primeval white-oak forests in the heart and center of the American continent.

A Paye and Baker product. Length, 4¼ inches.

No. 84 ALAMO
No. 131 ALAMO FACADE

The first European definitely known to have set foot in the locality of San Antonio was Father Damian Massenet. Turning aside from a group of explorers, he paused long enough among the friendly Indians to lay out a plaza lined with cottonwood trees (*álamos* in Spanish) and to designate the place on the map as San Antonio de Bexar.

Nearly thirty years later, in 1718, another priest, Father Olivares, established a mission here, encouraged horticulture, and taught the natives how to irrigate their land.

Not until the first decade of the nineteenth century did the Americans from the North begin to wander into the region, just about the time that Mexico, alongside the other Spanish-American colonies, was fighting to win its freedom from Spain. A brutal massacre of Mexicans and their Yankee allies occurred on August 20, 1813, when a Spanish general incarcerated the remnants of a defeated army in a poorly ventilated building till eighteen of them had suffocated; then he despatched the remaining two hundred and fifty before firing squads. That was the first time Americans shed blood for liberty and independence in Texas—but it was not to be the last.

Then, after Mexico had won its freedom from Spanish rule, there were Texans who began immediately to think of gaining their freedom from Mexican rule. Some would have been satisfied to settle for a provincial government granting them control of their local affairs. But in 1824 Texas was joined to the state of Coahuila "south of the border," that is, below the Rio Grande, and the capital of the new state removed from San Antonio (or Bexar) to Saltillo. Colonists, mostly of the agricultural type, kept drifting into Texas, and a few of them were bold enough to think of a declaration of independence and even raised the flag of Fredonia at Nacogdoches, but Stephen Austin and most of the older settlers were still loyal to Mexico and threw cold water on the movement.

By 1830 there were three times as many Americans as Mexicans in Texas. The national government in Mexico City began to look uneasily at this rapid influx of "foreigners," whose droves of cattle and sheep were waxing fat on the grassy, open-weather ranges of Texas. Stricter immigration laws were accordingly decreed: colonists could still enter Texas provided they did not come from bordering territories of the United States. Taxes were upped, and high tariffs placed on goods imported from the northern republic. Garrisons were set up in the small towns, and civilians were governed by decrees issued from military courts. There was discrimination against Anglo-Americans before the law. Slavery was abolished in Texas but not in the rest of Mexico; this was done to give those south of the Rio Grande the advantages of cheaper labor in competition with the Texans.

In 1832 Colonel Juan Bradburn, officer in charge of the Anahuac Harbor, on Galveston Bay, imprisoned some colonists who were found to be smuggling in American goods on which heavy import duties had been placed. A minor revolt flared up, and the port commander was compelled to release his captives.

In 1833 Stephen Austin was delegated to carry a petition for statehood to Mexico City. General Santa Anna, who had just overthrown the Mexican republic and made himself a dictator, clapped Austin in jail, where he languished for eighteen months. Santa Anna not only reënforced the military garrisons, thus excluding any further hope for civilian rule, but also imposed higher levies on American manufactures brought into Texas. When Austin was finally released from his confinement, he returned a confirmed advocate of the idea that if Texans wanted their freedom they would have to fight for it.

In the fall of 1835 the Mexican commander of the garrison at the Alamo demanded the return of a cannon granted to the town of Gonzales by the government. This border settlement, composed mostly of Americans, refused to obey the order and raised a banner bearing the inscription, "Come and Take It." The Mexican commander came but he did not take it.

The Texans proceeded to set up a state government, with the provisional capital at San Felipe de Austin. General Sam Houston was chosen commander-in-chief of an army yet to be raised. A volunteer army, independent of Houston's orders, scored several surprisingly quick victories, captured the Alamo, and cleared the state of Mexican troops before the end of the year.

This walk-over victory held its pitfalls for the victors. The Texas riflemen went back to their ranches, lulled into thinking that Santa Anna would now be amenable to the idea of making terms that would grant them, if not independence, at least the choice of home rule. Most of them, too, felt safe behind the barriers of long intervening desert-stretches, over which it would be well nigh impossible to drag any massive pieces of artillery.

At this juncture the new government practically fell to pieces. General Houston was unable to raise any regular army, while the volunteers who had defeated the Mexicans were loosely organized and did not feel constrained to obey any orders from Houston. Unknown to the commander-in-chief, several officers were so confident of themselves that they contemplated raising an army to invade Mexico.

Santa Anna was a very capable general, and he determined to squelch the rebellion by marching swiftly and directly against the strongest unit of resistance, which was centered at Bexar. "The enemy came in sight, marching in regular order, and displaying their strength to the greatest advantage, in order to strike us with terror," wrote David Crockett on February 23, 1836, in his record of the forthcoming siege.

A short council of war was held, and Colonel William Travis, in charge of the motley group of soldiery at Bexar, decided the most practical means of defense would be a withdrawal into the fortress at the Alamo. The Mexicans had an army of five thousand men, while the American defenders could muster but a meager one hundred and seventy-four, most of these being of that heterogeneous, adventurous type found commonly along the fringes of Western civilization. The Southern states furnished the largest quota with ninety-six, one third of these from the border slave states of Virginia, Kentucky, Missouri, and Maryland; twenty-five came from the Northern states; forty-four were European-born, including seventeen from England; and nine were Mexicans. Tennesseeans composed by far the largest group, with twenty-nine.

Among the more notable characters included in this contingent, besides Colonel Travis, commander of the garrison, were James Bonham, who borrowed money that he might come West to fight for Texan independence; James Bowie, inventor of the hunting knife that bears his name; and David Crockett, famed frontiersman, whose motto was, "Be sure you are right, then go ahead."

Colonel Bonham was not there at the beginning of the siege, but slipped in a few days later with his detachment of thirty men from Gonzales, "just in the nick of time to reap a harvest of glory." Bonham had been away on a mission to enlist the help of the four hundred men, the so-called "Volunteers," preparing to embark on an expedition for the conquest of Mexico, but failing to interest their commander, he had gone on to Gonzales and succeeded in getting the help of the thirty recruits he had just brought back with him.

Crockett's journal gives a good day-by-day account of the siege until the beginning of the final assault. A crony of his, whom he called Thimblerig, was struck in the breast by a bullet which Crockett extracted and handed over to its intended victim with the suggestion that he carry it on his person as a watch charm. But Thimblerig refused to do so, saying that lead was too precious to be wasted, and should therefore be returned to its senders with compounded interest.

By the morning of February 27th food was becoming scarce, and what there was, lacked variety, consisting solely of corn-beef hash, meal after meal. The enemy's attempt to cut off the fort's water supply from the river proved a failure. Ten bombs hurled into the fort exploded without damage.

On the 28th a little variety was added to the menu when hunters went foraging and, under cover of darkness, slipped in several hundred pounds of pork and bacon. The hunters brought back word, too, that Santa Anna was desolating the country round about, burning homes and barns, destroying crops, and driving women and children off without so much as a nightgown on their backs. "For just one crack at that rascal," declares Crockett, "I would bargain to break my Betsey, and never pull trigger again."

On the morning of the 29th—it was leap year, mind you—the Mexicans had drawn up a cannon close enough to make direct hits against the fort. Crockett polished off five men who made ready to discharge the piece before they discreetly threw up the attempt as a bad bargain.

A great boost was given to the morale of the besieged when a second contingent of men from Gonzales, thirty-two this time, arrived and successfully entered the fort after nightfall on the first of March. Two couriers, Sutherland and Smith, were riding hard and fast over the sparsely-settled areas beseeching aid. Although apprised of the desperate plight of the gallant defenders within the fort, the officers stationed at Goliad, intent on their preparations for the Mexican invasion, did not lift a finger to help the beleaguered men at the Alamo. By March 3rd Colonel Travis had given up hope that any assistance would be forthcoming from the four hundred "volunteers" idling away their time at Goliad. He therefore made a rousing speech before the whole garrison, exhorting every man to stick to his guns and make the victory as costly as possible for the enemy. It is said that he offered to allow any man who so desired to depart peacefully by dropping down over the walls, but that every soldier who was willing to fight to the death should step over a line marked by his sword in the dust. Crockett leapt across immediately after Travis. Bowie who had been sick with pneumonia since the beginning of the siege was carried across in his cot. Every one stepped across the line except a certain soldier of fortune, a former mercenary in the armies of Napoleon. Deciding he would not fight for a hopeless cause, he disappeared over the walls and lived to tell the story of his desertion.

By March 4th Santa Anna had the fort ringed about on all sides with a heavy investment of artillery. The siege was bearing down on the war-torn, sleep-weary defenders. The batteries poised within close range of the crumbling walls were sending pound after pound of explosive shells ripping into the beleaguered bastion.

On the fifth of March Crockett made the last entry in his journal: "Pop, pop, pop! Bom, bom, bom! throughout the day. No time for memorandums now. Go ahead. Liberty and independence forever!"

An ominous hush prevailed on the morning of the sixth just before the bugle call for battle was heard in Santa Anna's camp, to be followed by the more blood-curdling sound of the *degüello*, a call formerly used by the Spaniards in their deadly combats with the Moors, a call meaning

350

that no quarter would be given and none asked. The Mexicans charged in a madly furious onslaught, and tried to plant their scaling ladders against the south wall. General Duque, leading the charge on the north side, was wounded and crushed to death underfoot by the wild, disorderly retreat of his own men stampeding to safety.

On the second assault the Mexicans actually made their way up the ladders to the brink of the south wall, but were toppled off or forced to back down in a scatter-and-run withdrawal.

Again the cut-throat call, the *degüello*, was sounded, and the assailants sprang forward from all sides at once. The north wall was breached, and soon the defenders found themselves fighting behind them and before. The carnage was frightful. The enemy kept pouring in. Against overwhelming numbers the garrison fought with unequaled fury, "muzzle to muzzle, hand to hand, musket and riffle, bayonet and bowie knife."

In their dogged defense of the hospital, the Americans left forty-two enemy dead piled up in front of a single door. In the courtyard, around Crockett and two of his fellow-Tennesseeans lay the blood-stained corpses of seventeen of their assailants. Bowie was slashed to pieces on his bed and his body pitched from the point of one bayonet to another around the hospital floor.

Reuben Marmaduke Potter, the first to gather a complete and authenticated record of the tragic happenings at the Alamo, recapitulated the final scene in a stirring poem which was once declaimed by every Texan schoolboy. The last stanza runs as follows:

> They come—like autumn's leaves they fall,
>   Yet hordes on hordes they onward rush;
> With gory tramp they mount the wall,
>   Till numbers the defenders crush—
> Till falls their flag, when none remain!
>   Well may the ruffians quake to tell
>   How Travis and his hundred fell
> Amid a thousand foemen slain!
>   They died the Spartan's death,
> But not in hopeless strife:
>   Like brothers died—and their expiring breath
> Was Freedom's breath of life.

Greece had its Thermopylae, Rome its bridge defended by Horatius, Finland its one-man defense in Sven Duva; our nation had its Alamo, with no survivor to tell of its defeat.

"Remember the Alamo!" became the battle cry that aroused every Texan to a fighting frenzy and made him vow to avenge the defenders of the Alamo. With that shibboleth on the lips of every soldier, the independence of Texas was won.

From the bright gold bowl of the Alamo spoon gleams the walls of the historic old fortress—or rather, what was left of it. Whether the roughened background is meant to represent cottonwood trees or utilized to heighten the perspective is not clear. At the bottom of the bowl we read, "The Alamo Built in 1718."

The handle, without any partition into sections, terete halfway up the shaft, widens imperceptibly and sways backward slightly at the crown, closing in to form an even arc. The reverse flattens out as it approaches the crown. "San Antonio, Tex." runs from the top midway down the handle in flourishing script. There is no trademark, but the imprint of the sales-control merchant, E. Herzberg, appears on the reverse side of handle. Length, 4 inches.

The Alamo Façade spoon belongs to the well known state series having the wave-handle. The outlines of the old mission are clearly defined in the bowl, with the inscription of the date of its construction above it, and "San Antonio, Texas," below.

The handle pictures a bale of cotton, a leaping steer, and the lone star of Texas almost encircled by a wreath of alamo or cottonwood leaves. Made by the Shepard Manufacturing Company, the spoon is 6 inches long.

No. 86 ANNEKE JANSE

Perhaps not one in a million persons knows the story of the *goed vrouw* whose bust appears on this spoon. Even though any one had read of her, he would have seen her name spelled in the correct Dutch fashion, Annetje Jans. In no wise was she particularly outstanding—only quite representative of the sturdy Dutch stock that settled in and around New Amsterdam in the early days, and prospered.

Her mother—a nurse and doctor—gave her an excellent education. Anneke was already herself the mother of three daughters before she left the old country. Her husband, Roelof Janse, stayed as superintendent of a patroonship up the Hudson long enough to provide himself with the wherewithal for a farm of his own on Manhattan Island. He had hardly erected a house for his family when he died in 1635.

Three years later Anneke remarried, her second husband, Everhardus Bogardus, being a minister of the Dutch Reformed Church. Dominie Bogardus had some property of his own called the Bouwerie, and this farm now merged with his wife's was leased out to tenants who paid their rental through the clearance of trees and the making of various small improvements. In 1642 the minister perished at sea, and Anneke was again left a widow with four small sons in her second ménage.

Anneke survived this husband by twenty-one years. She was described at this time of her life as still an attractive woman with fine features, sparkling dark eyes, cheerful disposition, and much kindliness in her nature. She spoke both English and Dutch, and learned the Algonquin language in order to deal forthrightly with the Indians who visited her farm.

352

She took good care that no one impugned her reputation as a virtuous matron and mother. She once sued a former sister-in-law who commented on her skill in showing her ankles in public. In court the backbiting relative was forced to admit that she had seen Anneke lift her skirts only when walking over puddles left by the rain in the streets.

Many of her descendants attained prominence of one kind or another. Her great-great-grandson, Philip Livingston, was a signer of the Declaration of Independence.

Within a year of Anneke's death New Amsterdam became New York, and the English governor, Colonel Lovelace, bought the Bogardus property. The Colonel, notorious for his failure to pay his debts, decamped. The Duke of York seized the Colonel's property and added it to his own. In this process of consolidation all boundary lines were erased on the deed. In 1705 Queen Anne, now owner of the Bogardus estate long swallowed up in the larger domains of her father, the former Duke of York, deeded all of her farm to Trinity Church forever.

Anneke Janse's name has been perpetuated to history in an unusual way. Had it not been for a series of famous lawsuits, she would not have had her bust pictured on this spoon. In 1738 was filed the first suit contesting the legality of the Bogardus and Janse holdings by the Trinity Church Corporation. For nearly two hundred years these claims were presented from time to time by a new crop of contenders. After such a great lapse of time, the courts decided at every hearing that the descendants of Anneke Janse no longer had any more valid claims on this property than did the original Indian owners. But, granted that a court decision had upheld their contention of being the defrauded rightful owners, Anneke Janse's heirs would today be among the richest persons on earth. It was worth a stone's throw at an imaginary Goliath that could have converted an impossible dream into a possible reality. The God of Fortuity is fickle.

On the caput of the spoon appears the head of Anneke Janse covered with a kerchief, and with a ruched collar about her neck. Below the bust her name runs vertically almost the entire length of the shaft.

Length of spoon is 4¼ inches. On the reverse side of the handle is the Durgin trademark and the sales-control imprint of J. H. Johnston & Co.

No. 87 ALABAMA BLUE SEAL

Kaiser Wilhelm II suggested repeatedly to his admirals that they read Raphael Semmes's *Memoirs of Service Afloat*, for, he declared, "I reverence the name of Semmes. In my opinion, he was the greatest admiral of the nineteenth century." German U-boat commanders may have tried to emulate the exploits of this Southern seaman, but none equaled his achievements.

This maritime hero of the Confederate navy was born in 1809 in Maryland, of early French stock with a generous admixture of English and Irish blood. His mother was a descendant of that Arthur Middleton who signed the Declaration of Independence for South Carolina.

Semmes obtained his training as midshipman on the *Lexington,* and on his maiden voyage the vessel went to Trinidad to bring home the body of Commodore Oliver Perry. Later he had assignments on the *Erie* and the *Brandywine,* traveling between the Dutch West Indies and our Eastern ports. After he passed the midshipman examinations at the head of his class, he studied law for two years, becoming the "lawyer of the Navy."

He saw service both on land and sea during the Mexican War, being attached for a while to the staff of General Worth at Puebla. He practiced law at Cincinnati and Mobile, making the latter city his home after 1849. In 1856 he was appointed an inspector of lighthouse stations on the Gulf of Mexico. For three years, until the outbreak of secession, he was a member of the Lighthouse Board in Washington. Then he resigned his commission in the United States Navy and proceeded to go South. When the train on which he was a passenger plowed through the smoke of a pine-forest fire in northern Alabama, it seemed like a symbolic curtain cutting him off from all ties with his past career.

In April of '61 Semmes was appointed commander of the *Sumter,* a passenger liner transformed into the first warship of the Confederate navy. He gathered about him an able personnel in Lieutenants Kell, Chapman, Stribling, Evans, and Howell; the crew was made up of a heterogeneous assortment of nationalities. For two months he waited rather impatiently till the makeshift cruiser was readied. Then, on Sunday, the last day of June, he headed the vessel out of one of the lower passes of the Mississippi into the open Gulf.

The *Brooklyn,* a Union man-of-war, sighted the *Sumter* and gave chase. A desperate race ensued. The Northern ship was gaining on its adversary until a heavy rainfall obscured the horizon. When the atmosphere cleared, the pursuer, making twelve knots an hour by steam, was closer than ever to the *Sumter,* which could make only ten knots. Semmes was preparing to heave his money box and papers overboard in case of an enforced surrender, when a stiff wind blew up, and the *Sumter,* under a full rigging of sails, gradually left the baffled pursuer far astern. The chase had lasted four hours.

The cruise of the *Sumter* was only a work-out, an earnest of the superior abilities of Semmes as a navigator. In the six months before it was shelved permanently at Gibraltar, the raider had made a haul of eighteen northern merchantmen. One of these was captured on July 3rd, two on the 4th, two on the 5th, and three on the 6th. There were as many prisoners as crew members on board at one time, and Semmes had to keep half of

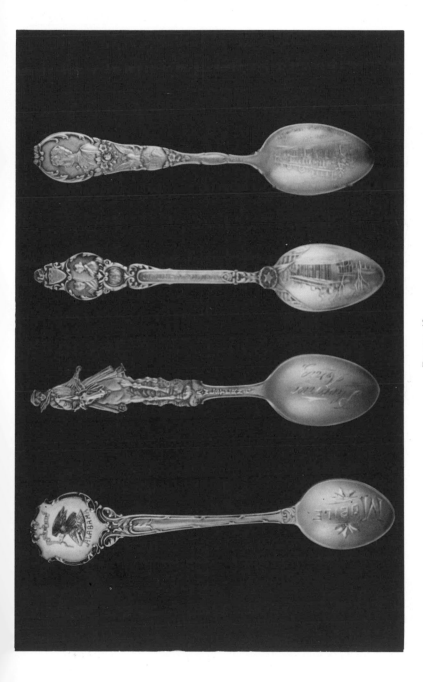

PLATE 42

87. ALABAMA BLUE SEAL   88. PHOENIX GIRL
89. GEORGE AND MARTHA   90. BERTHA PALMER VIGNETTE

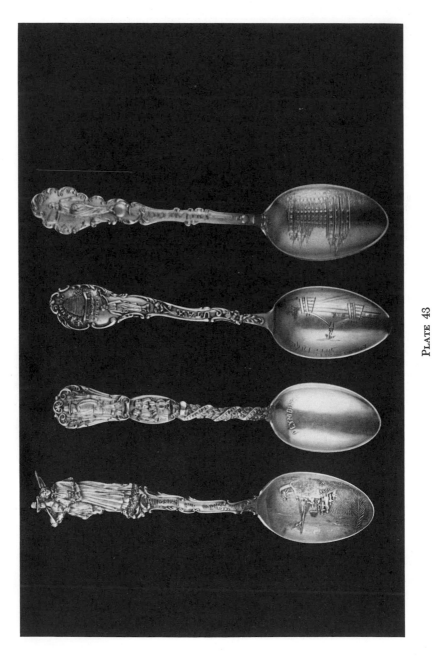

Plate 43

91. JOHN ALDEN AND PRISCILLA   92. PLYMOUTH COURTSHIP
93. BEEHIVE   94. ANGEL MORONI

them in chains to prevent a mutiny. The work of the *Sumter* was done when the vessel put in at Gibraltar for repairs. She had destroyed a million dollars' worth of shipping for the North.

Meanwhile a new ship had quietly been commissioned by the Confederacy from a shipbuilding firm in Birkenhead, England. Known only as *290*, it was popularly supposed to be the number of the English well-wishers who had contributed to the building fund. Semmes was in the Bahamas when he received word to repair to the Azores.

On Sunday, August 24, 1862, Semmes, his officers, and the eighty-five enlisted men of the crew boarded the new vessel in dashing gray uniforms. On quarter-deck, as four bells sounded, Captain Semmes read to the assembled crew his commission as commander of the Confederate steam sloop *Alabama*. Two black balls wriggled upward to the mastheads, a forecastle gun boomed out, and the black balls were broken, revealing the Stars and Bars, which replaced the English banner, and the Southern Cross, battle flag of the future ship-of-war. The band struck up the soul-stirring strains of Dixie, and a deafening round of cheers brought the formal ceremonies to an end. "Thus," reports Captain Semmes, "amid this peaceful scene of beauty, with all nature smiling upon the ceremony, was the *Alabama* christened; the name *290* disappearing with the English flag."

The *Alabama* measured 235 feet in length and 32 in width, displaced 20 feet of water, carried twin engines, and could negotiate at her best between 12 and 14 knots an hour. Her batteries consisted of 7 broadsides. On the steering wheel was inscribed the motto, *Aide-toi et Dieu t'aidera*, which words were put into practical application most effectually during the next twenty months.

Yankee schooners in great numbers were fishing for whales around the Azores at this season, and the first of these boats to be sighted was the *Ocmulgee*, busily engaged in denuding a fine sperm of its blubber. The Yankee skipper, oblivious to the fact that a war was in progress, was flabbergasted to learn he was actually a prisoner of war. He bemoaned the loss of his rich strike of whale blubber. The crew of thirty-seven men was transferred to small boats which were towed close to the Azores and unloosed. The whaler was burned the next morning.

Prize after prize fell into the net of the Confederate raider. Almost the entire whaling fleet was rounded up and destroyed. Semmes was amused at the large amount of goods packed onto the small boats taking the men ashore. When he saw one of the frail barks loaded with barrels of beef and pork, seamen's chests, and even the pet cat and parrot, he asked the skipper if the craft were not too heavily laden to be seaworthy. "Oh, no!" was the reply; "they are as buoyant as ducks, and we shall not ship a drop of water."

Semmes stood on the horseblock and watched the boats pull for the shore line. "That night landing of the whaler's crew," he says, "was a beautiful spectacle. The moon was shining brightly, though there were some passing clouds sailing lazily in the upper air and fleckering the sea. Flores, which was sending off to us, even at this distance, her perfumes of shrub and flower, lay sleeping in the moonlight, with a few fleecy, white clouds wound around the mountain top like a turban. The rocky islets that rise like so many shafts out of the sea, devoid of all vegetation and at different distances from the shore, looked weird and unearthly, like sheeted ghosts. The boats moving swiftly and mysteriously toward the shore might have been mistaken, when they had gotten a little distance from us, for Venetian gondolas, with their peaked bows and sterns, especially when we heard coming over the sea a song, sung by a powerful and musical voice, and chorussed by all the boats. Those merry fellows were thus making light of misfortunes, and proving that the sailor, after all, is the true philosopher."

As soon as the Northern papers got wind of the *Alabama's* successes, Semmes was called a rebel ruffian, a pirate, a fit companion for Lafitte and Kidd, a conceited coxcomb ("Old Beeswax" sporting a waxed mustache in imitation of Victor Emmanuel), a terrorizing monster who tortured his victims by chaining and mistreating them, a drink-crazed incendiarist.

When the whaling season had ended, the *Alabama* sped north to the trade routes between the Yankee ports and Europe. Here, many of the merchantmen were carrying wheat and corn to the value of fifty thousand dollars in their hulls. A Negro boy, David H. White, the slave of a Delaware citizen, was captured on one ship. Semmes freed the boy, gave him a job in the messhall, and placed him on equal pay with the white mess stewards. Any livestock taken was transferred carefully to the *Alabama*, providing a welcome addition to the supplies of fresh meat.

One packet captured, the *Ariel*, belonging to that "bitter enemy of the South, a Mr. Vanderbilt of New York," contained five hundred passengers on board, bound for California. Many of the passengers were women who, having "read the accounts which a malicious, mendacious Northern press had been giving us," were fearful of the "plunderers and robbers" into whose hands they had fallen. Some wept, and a few were in hysterics. Semmes sent for a handsome young lieutenant, ordered him to array himself in his best uniform and buckle on his sword, placed him in a gig newly painted and outfitted with scarlet cushions, and bade him go on board the *Ariel* to coax the ladies out of their tears and fears. "Oh! I'll be sure to do that, sir," boasted the dapper young blade. "I never knew a fair creature who could resist me more than fifteen minutes." It didn't take that long in this case before the young ladies were snipping buttons off his coat for souvenirs. Says Semmes: "When I got my handsome lieutenant back, he was like a plucked peacock. And there were no more Hebes drowned in tears on board the *Ariel*."

In all, sixty-eight Northern merchant vessels were burned or bonded— what a record was the *Alabama's!* One Union cruiser, the *Hatteras*, was despatched off Galveston in a fight that lasted thirteen minutes. And the elusive *Alabama* went everywhere: to the tropic isles of the Spanish Main, south across the equator to Brazil, off to the sea lanes rounding the Cape of Good Hope, pushing in and out of Cape Town, Mozambique, Borneo, Condore, Singapore, and a rendezvous at Angra Pequena with the *Tuscaloosa*, a recent addition to the small list of Confederate warships. This last was a heart-warming meeting.

But the *Alabama* was growing weary, she was aching in all her joints, she needed repairs, a good overhauling. On June 11, 1864, she steamed into the harbor of Cherbourg. The U. S. S. *Kearsarge* soon moved about before the entrance of the harbor. She was a foe of long standing, ever alerted for an engagement with the famous Southern seahawk. Her captain was John A. Winslow, a North Carolinian who had once bunked with Semmes when both were midshipmen. The crews and guns of the two ships were rather evenly matched. But Semmes was unaware that around the hull of the *Kearsarge* was a heavy coating of sheet-chains cleverly concealed by boards that gave her the appearance of a wood-bound warship with sides as vulnerable as those of the *Alabama*.

The Southern man-of-war need never have departed from the harbor. She might have stayed in the French port for the duration, the end of the war now being a matter of months. But Semmes saw his men were enthusiastic for a tussle with the enemy. When he spoke his willingness to Kell, the faithful lieutenant pointed out the defects of the *Alabama* and the bad condition of the gunpowder, which had lost much of its explosive power during its long stay in the musty holds. But Semmes was not to be swayed from his purpose by Kell's objections. He sent a challenge to the *Kearsarge*.

On Sunday, June 19, 1864, the fateful battle was fought six or seven miles off shore from Cherbourg. The encounter began at a range of five hundred yards, the *Alabama* opening with three broadsides before the fire was returned. When Semmes saw his projectiles failing in effectiveness, and rebounding into the water before exploding, he ordered the use of solid shot. Too late he learned the real nature of the enemy craft and sought to swing in close for a hand-to-hand combat, but Captain Winslow was too astute to accept this outmoded form of naval conflict, and with his superior steam power avoided any closing-in tactics. The Southern Cross was shot down once but promptly replaced. For an hour and ten minutes the *Alabama* remained afloat till a shell ripped into the engine room and spun her around. When she began to list, the white flag went up, and the gunners ceased their firing. When the vessel started settling at her stern, small boats were lowered and preparations were quickly made to leave. Semmes and Kell stood together as they threw their swords into the sea. An English boat which had been witnessing the spectacle soon picked them up, and thus they escaped becoming prisoners of war.

The news that the "scourge of the sea" had been destroyed was received with rejoicing in the North. Doctor Francis O. Ticknor best expressed the noble sentiments of regret in the South:

> The billows plunge like steeds that bear
> The knights with snow-white crests.
> The sea winds blare like bugles where
> The Alabama rests.
>
> Old glories from their splendor-mists
> Salute with trump and hail,
> The sword that held the ocean lists
> Against the world in mail.
>
> For here was Glory's tourney field,
> The tilt-yard of the sea,
> The battle path of kingly wrath,
> And kinglier courtesy.
>
> And here they rest, the princeliest
> Of earth's regalia gems,
> The starlight of our Southern Cross,
> The sword of Raphael Semmes.

Promotions to the rank of rear admiral and brigadier general were given to Semmes after he returned home in the closing days of the war. He spent his last years in Mobile practicing law and enjoying the companionship of his wife and family. Roberts in his biography of the naval hero says: "Mobile was the true home of Raphael Semmes, and he assuredly would not have been happy if he had deserted it. The people of his city venerated him. They presented him with the house on Government Street, shaded by magnolia trees, where he passed the rest of his days, a dignified and beloved figure."

He was given a military funeral when he died August 30, 1877, in his sixthy-eighth year. Just before the funeral there had been a heavy rainfall, and his grave was half-filled with water, a circumstance certainly symbolical of his career on the sea. He had lived and died a cultured, chivalrous, Christian gentleman.

The Alabama Blue Seal spoon bears the name of Mobile engraved in its bowl. The caput contains the seal of Alabama on a blue and white enameled background. In the center of the seal is the representation of a shield and eagle. From the mouth of the bird rises a banderole carrying the motto of Alabama: "Here we rest."

The spoon is a product of Paye and Baker Company. Length, 4½ inches.

360

No. 88 PHOENIX GIRL

Seven hundred years ago the Hohokam, a peaceful people engaged in agricultural pursuits in Salt River Valley of Arizona, held a great convocation. A serious problem vitally affecting their lives stared them in the face. The Valley was drying up. A long series of drouths, unrelieved by a single rainy season, made it impossible for them to grow any more of their precious corn or vegetables. Their live stock had become so emaciated and so weakened that they were dying by dozens of hunger, thirst, and disease. The provisions wisely hoarded from the fat years had all been consumed. The canals held no more reserves of the cool mountain water to turn into the long, deep ditches and thereby to slake the thirst of the desiccated fields. The fruitful Valley had truly become a barren desert. What had they done, they asked each other, to offend the Great Spirit and cause Him to send them no more rains?

The Hohokam agreed at their council that Fate hardly offered them an alternative. They must migrate to greener fields—or starve. Even though they loved this land of perpetual sunshine, and had never wandered far beyond the rim of its mountain-bowl, they must surely leave it. Many of the older ones remembered long dry spells before, but the waters always came sooner or later to give relief. This time they had waited in vain, and the duration of drouth doubled, tripled in length over any previous period of waiting.

The birds were already gone; that fierce little dweller of the desert sands, the pink-and-white Gila monster had disappeared. The Hohokam, too, must go. There was some kind of mysterious curse hovering over their beloved habitation. And so they quit the Valley.

For centuries it remained a desolate region. The earliest Americans thought of it as a dreary waste and considered themselves lucky when they did not die of thirst in crossing it. Speaking of the Arizona deserts in general, a traveler of the sixties says: "Everything dries; wagons dry; chickens dry; there is no juice left in anything living or dead, by the close of summer. I have even heard complaint made that the thermometer failed to show the true heat because the mercury dried up." Many whoppers were told of the excessive dryness. Mules brayed only at nights, their throats being too parched in the daytime. When cows switched their tails against their backs, the sound resembled the crack of a rawhide quirt. When snakes crawled along, they creaked like wooden imitations of themselves. Spit hardened into small BB-like pellets and often boomeranged.

Jack Swilling, one of the first farmers in the Salt River Valley, was observant enough to notice more than the fertility of the soil. His sharp eyes discerned traces of the extensive irrigation system which had been utilized and then left by some unknown, ancient agriculturists. After a little scraping, leveling, and calking, he made these prehistoric ditches resume their time-honored functions with amazing success. Other farmers moving in followed suit and irrigated from old ditches or dug new ones.

Charles Trumbull Hayden, the storekeeper of the Valley, did enough business alone in flour to warrant setting up a mill run by this ditch water. He also set up a blacksmith shop, a dairy, and a doctor's office; and soon the village consisted in large part of his multifarious structures.

A genteel character with a cockney accent and a red nose, Darrell Duppa, was hired by Hayden to serve as paymaster for the newly organized canal company. Struck by the evidence of an ancient civilization on all sides—mounds, bones, pottery, artifacts, canals, primitive farm implements—the literarily-inclined Duppa suggested for the rising settlement the name of Phoenix, which according to the old Egyptian religion was the symbol of the sungod, a marvelous bird that perished every five hundred years from its own heat and was immediately resurrected with a more splendid vitality than ever.

And out of the ashes of a sunburnt desert-valley a new life blossomed in Phoenix, made fruitful again by its impounded waters. To mention all the diversified crops, amazing in their multiplicity, that are being produced in Salt River Valley would be wearisome. It must suffice to speak of alfalfa, Egyptian cotton, sugar beets, oranges, strawberries, mulberries, dates, persimmons, watermelons, olives, apples, and onions as being but the main crops. Everything from the four points of the compass grows here prolifically. The great Roosevelt Dam, begun in 1903 and completed in 1911, has a capacity for holding 456 billion gallons, and serves the threefold purpose of irrigation, power production, and flood control. Other more recent dams above the Salt River Valley are the Horse Mesa, Mormon Flat, and Stewart Mountain.

Canalizing the water over the Valley has not only banished drouth; it has also taken the dryness out of the air. George Wharton James speaks of Phoenix as the "real, modern, western Garden of Allah. It sings to us, whistles to us, cheers, encourages, stimulates, strengthens us . . . in a climate that begs us to come out into the open."

The "Western Girl" on the handle of this spoon is enjoying an exhilarating ride in the wonderful atmosphere that Mr. James speaks so enthusiastically about. Perhaps she is repeating these lines from *Cadences*, by Samuel T. Clover, a reporter who, coming West to write up Indian uprisings for Eastern newspapers, soon learned to love just such country as this in California and Arizona—

> I am riding, riding, riding, on the hard dirt road,
> And my horse's ears are pointed, and my horse's neck is bowed.
> For in his veins pulsating is the ichor of the spring,
> And I catch the lilt of music his dancing hoofbeats ring:

It's "Good-to-be-alive! Good-to-be-alive! Good-to-be-alive today!
What-fun-it-is! What-fun-it-is!" they seem to me to say;
And in the saddle, marking time, I fervently repeat,
"I love-it-too! I love-it-too!" with every rhythmic beat.

Clippity-clip! Clippity-clip! the hoofbeats strike the ground,
But more than that the message I gather from the sound;
I get from it the thrill of joy so bounteously bestowed,
When I am in the saddle on the hard dirt road.

The Phoenix Girl spoon was pressed by Jos. Mayer, Inc., for which firm the Northern Stamping and Manufacturing Company is the successor. Length of spoon is 4¼ inches.

No. 89 GEORGE AND MARTHA

In the early part of March, 1758, while Colonel George Washington and Bishop, his attendant, were waiting for a ferry to transport them across the Pamunkey River, they were accosted by a Major Chamberlayne, who importuned them to come to his house not far away for dinner. At first Colonel George declined, saying it was urgent for him to get to Williamsburg, the Virginia capital, to consult a doctor about his stomach complaint, which had been troubling him since the previous fall. So serious did he consider the nature of his ailment that he feared his life far gone in the process of decay. He had even heard that a report of his demise was gone abroad.

The major then added an extra inducement to his invitation. A charming young widow, a Mrs. Martha Custis, was to be a guest in his home that day for dinner. The colonel quickly reversed his refusal into an acceptance. The doctor could wait; the stomach complaint was not so serious after all.

The young widow proved to be such attractive company that the colonel tarried well into the next day. Bishop chafed impatiently at this delay and led the horses around in repeated circles before the door until Washington appeared.

On the journey back from Williamsburg the colonel must needs pause for refreshments at the White House, the home of the widow Custis. A month later business for the King's army drew the colonel to Williamsburg, and again he saw the widow. In May he ordered an engagement ring for two pounds and sixteen shillings from Philadelphia. A few months of correspondence while he was soldiering on the frontier, and then, in January of 1759, the two were married.

Born eight months before this second husband, Martha Dandridge Custis Washington had been brought up to learn how to sew, cook, and keep house better than to spell, write, play the spinet or charm by the higher social graces. When she was sixteen her father took her for the winter to Williamsburg, where she drew admiration, not for her studied elegance but for the artless simplicity and domesticity of her tastes.

When Daniel Parke Custis met Martha Dandridge he must have been struck by her homely virtues. Fifteen years before this he had proposed to the beautiful and brilliant Evelyn Byrd. When she rebuffed his suit, he put away thoughts of marriage and decided to remain henceforth a bachelor. At the age of thirty-eight he married the eighteen-year-old Martha, by whom he had four children. Two of these, Jack and Martha, survived out of infancy, and were six and four years old respectively at the time of their mother's second marriage.

Mrs. Washington brought to her husband the considerable estate of fifteen thousand acres, several houses in Williamsburg, and some ten thousand pounds in bond, all entailed from her first husband. Upon Washington devolved the administration of her affairs, as she seemed unable to do it herself. In addition, he had to perform the same offices for his two stepchildren, whose fortunes almost equalled their mother's in amount. In this onerous task of tending to the affairs of his family, Washington acquitted himself honorably and unselfishly.

He loved his stepchildren and they loved him in return. He was never severe with them, and they invariably went to him rather than to their mother for advice, something which they did not always heed. He spent money on them lavishly for their clothes, and ordered only the best and most expensive for them. He put no limit on prices for goods shipped to them from England. His orders usually read like this: "1 very good Spinet."

Little Martha, or Patsy as she was called in the household, was a dainty, demure little lady, who suffered from bad health. Her stepfather took her across the mountains to "Warm Springs" in hopes that the baths would improve her condition. When she died at the age of seventeen, Washington wept at the loss of a "sweet, innocent girl."

The handling of Jack Custis required "greater circumspection." The boy was expelled or had to be withdrawn from three schools. Private tutors gave him up in despair. His books were opened more by the throwing than the studying of them. All his interests lay in dogs, horses, and guns. He was an eager companion of his stepfather at foxhunts or the racing of horses. When he became engaged at the age of eighteen to Eleanor Calvert without parental knowledge or assent, there were few objections from either his or her family. Martha had just died and the sixteen-year-old bride was welcomed by the Washingtons as another daughter, although Mrs. Washington was still too grief-stricken to attend the wedding. Four children, three girls and a boy, were born to this union before Jack Custis died at the age of twenty-eight shortly after the victory at Yorktown. Washington threw himself on a couch and wept again—he was thinking of the great sorrow this would occasion his wife. The tenderness in Washington's soul has generally been overlooked. He knew the deeply affectionate nature of his wife, and every grief she had to endure made him suffer for her sake. Dobbin was never more loyal and devoted to Emmy Sedley than George to Martha Washington.

Eleanor Calvert Custis remarried and went on having progeny to her "twentieth confinement." After the War the old couple at Mount Vernon were very lonely, and as Mrs. Washington's daughter-in-law had an infinitude of offspring to spare, the two youngest children of Jack Custis, Nelly and Washington, came to enliven the hearth of the old plantation on the Potomac. Mrs. Washington idolized and verily spoiled these two grandchildren. Nelly was a lively little elf, not at all like the quiet, dignified maiden little Martha had been. She was the constant companion of the General and took long rides and walks with him over the countryside. He bought her a beautiful harpsichord but she preferred the out-of-door tramps to practicing on this very fine instrument. When she married Washington's favorite nephew, the General's joy knew no bounds.

Through the forty years of their wedded life, George and Martha Washington were seldom separated. Only six months after their marriage George said that he was settled down for life on his plantation with an agreeable consort, and expected the routine of his placid existence would be little disturbed by outward events. The bounteous hospitality at Mount Vernon became proverbial. So great a burden did this entertainment become that George was once compelled to exclaim, "Would any one believe that with a hundred cows I should still be obliged to buy butter for my family?"

During the War Mrs. Washington spent every winter in headquarters with her husband. The first season in camp the General had refused when she begged permission to come to be with him. Two months later he changed his mind and gave his assent, realizing the great comfort of her society. Her presence with him at the Craigie House in Cambridge greatly improved the morale of the entire personnel. She met with and entertained the officers and their wives. She organized bands of women to sew and patch for the soldiers.

At Morristown, New Jersey, a delegation of women called upon Mrs. Washington to pay their respects. "We dressed ourselves," said one of the delegates later, "in our most elegant ruffles and silks, and when we were introduced to her ladyship, we found her knitting with a specked apron on! There we were sitting in State without a stitch of work while General Washington's lady was knitting stockings." She went among the common soldiers, listened to their needs, and helped nurse them when they were sick. She relit the flame of faith in many a discouraged soldier's soul when the spark had all but gone out. As soon as she was back in Mount Vernon she set the looms weaving and the wheels spinning to provide clothes for an army that was almost in a state of unadorned nature.

When the War was over, after eight years, and the treaty of peace signed, the Washingtons returned to Mount Vernon, hoping to spend the rest of their days in retirement. But the world sought them out. Not only Americans but foreign admirers came to visit them. All were welcomed, and all dined regally at the General's well-filled board. It was aptly described by Washington himself, in one of his facetious moments, as a "well resorted tavern." One wintry day he recorded this unusual entry in his diary: "Dined with only Mrs. Washington which I believe is the first instance of it since my retirement from public life two years ago."

But when Washington was called from his retirement to spend eight more years in the service of his country as president, Mrs. Washington was at his side. She presided over formal receptions and the informal weekly levees with "great dignity of manner and most pleasing affability."

Two more years together at Mount Vernon were granted the Washingtons before his death brought to an end their happy union. The man who was "first in war, first in peace, first in the hearts of his countrymen" was laid to rest in the tomb at Mount Vernon. Three years later Martha Washington followed her husband to that tomb. A pure-minded, loving pair, simple yet noble hearted, each was the complement of the other.

John Adams once petulantly asked, probably thinking of his astute but penniless Abigail, "Would Washington have ever been commander of the revolutionary army or president of the United States if he had not married the rich widow of Mr. Custis?" Strike out the adjective "rich" and I believe the historical answer would still be materially unchanged. Strike out the conditional proviso or change it to read, "If he had married some one else," and the answer would become a subject for debate.

The spoon shows the busts of George and Martha in scroll-bordered medallions in the caput, surmounted by the Washington crest in the knop. The nave bears the dates "1759-1799," the forty years of the couple's wedded life. In the bowl appears Mount Vernon shrouded apparently in a wintry landscape.

This spoon was handled by Moore and Leding. Length, 4 inches. Used through the courtesy of its owner, Miss Evalyn Rogers, Hayward, California.

No. 93   BEEHIVE
No. 94   ANGEL MORONI
No. 95   TEMPLE AND TABERNACLE
No. 108 SALT LAKE DAISIES

The decade of 1820-1830 was a period of religious upheavals and revivals in our country. Into the pioneer villages and frontier towns came men inspired to preach; meetings were held and enormous crowds attended; thousands who had previously taken no interest in religion were converted; and belief in the millennium was universal. A great deal of emotionalism

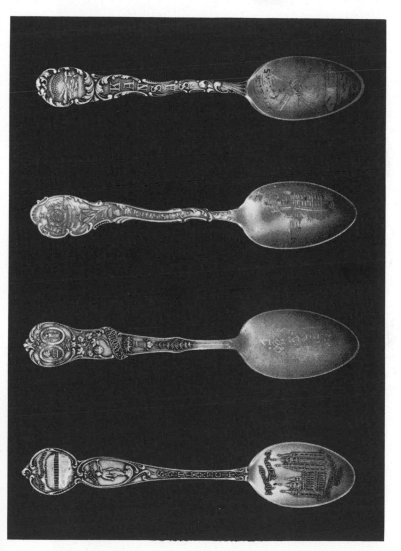

PLATE 44

95. TEMPLE AND TABERNACLE   96. NINETY SIX
97. JEFFERSON CITY   98. LAWRENCE WINDMILL

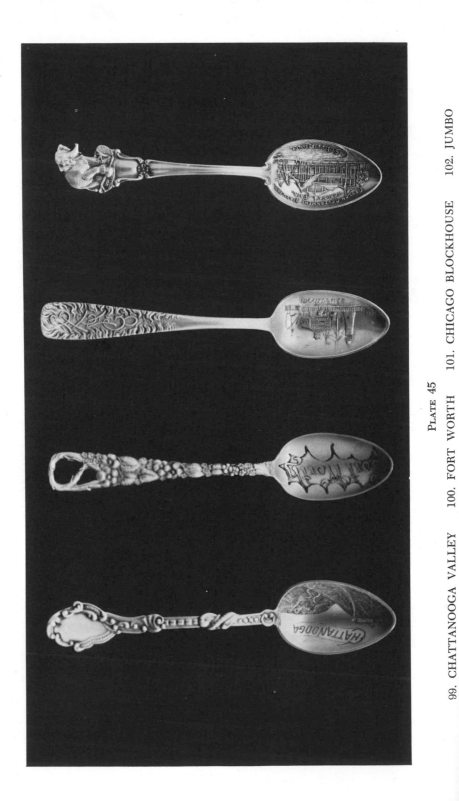

PLATE 45

99. CHATTANOOGA VALLEY   100. FORT WORTH   101. CHICAGO BLOCKHOUSE   102. JUMBO

accompanied these sectarian camp-meetings. People fell upon their faces, saw the Lord, writhed in convulsions, and gave vent to all sorts of articulate —as well as inarticulate—utterances.

Joseph Smith, a lad of fifteen, near Manchester, New York, was very much agitated by the religious manifestations that he saw on every hand. To him it seemed as if the people were confused by the multiplicity of sects, and were wandering blindly in search of a faith whereby they could be saved from eternal damnation. In this distracted state of mind he retired to a quiet woodland near his home, and in prayer and meditation sought to hear the "wee small voice" which would tell him just which church he should affiliate himself with. "And now something strange happened," explains Brigham H. Roberts, historian of Mormonism. "The youth had just begun timidly to express the desire of his heart in words, when he was seized upon by an invisible power that overcame him; his tongue was bound so that he could not speak. Darkness gathered about him and it seemed for a time that he was doomed to sudden destruction. He exerted all his powers to call upon God for deliverance from this enemy, . . . who possessed such strength as the youth had never before encountered. Despair seized upon him and he felt that he must abandon himself to destruction. At this moment of dreadful alarm he saw a pillar of light exactly over his head which shone out above the brightness of the sun, and began gradually descending towards him until he was enveloped within it. . . . As the light rested upon him, he beheld within it two personages, exactly resembling each other in form and features, standing above him in the air, one of these, calling Joseph by name, and pointing to the other, said: 'This is my Beloved Son, hear Him'."

In further communications from this illuminating Presence, young Smith learned that he must align himself with none of the existing denominations, the leaders of which were all speaking with the tongues of Babel to steer men astray; that he should found an entirely new church, but must wait until a complete and final interpretation of the right way to salvation were revealed unto him.

Ten years later, on April 6, 1830, the church of Jesus Christ of Latter-Day Saints, or the Mormon Church, came into existence in Fayette, Seneca County, New York. In the interim since he was first approached, Joseph Smith had lived for three years without any further converse with the Divine Presence; then the angel Moroni appeared to him in another vision and told him to repair to the hill of Cumorah, where he would find the *Book of Mormon* engraved on plates of gold in a stone box. For four years he visited this hill, but was not allowed to remove the plates until 1827, after which he took and translated them into English. *The Book of Mormon* was first published at Palmyra, New York, in 1830.

From then until the great trek in 1847 into Utah, or Deseret as it was originally called, the history of the Mormons is a story of persecution, rapine, despoliation, murder, rapid prosperity and growth, followed by sudden uprooting and ruthless dispersal—in short, a hectic, harrowing period of trouble, travail, and martyrdom for the faithful. From his native village in New York the prophet moved to Kirtland, Ohio; from there to various counties in Missouri; thence to Quincy and Nauvoo in Illinois; and finally, westward to the desert country of Utah.

The enterprising spirit and the religious zeal of the Mormons aroused jealousy and animosity toward them wherever they settled in preponderantly "Gentile" communities. Smith, like Moses, was never to see the Promised Land. He was tarred and feathered in one place, but still continued to preach there. Then, at Carthage, Illinois, he and his brother Hyrum were dragged out of jail and shot to death by a lawless mob of some five hundred men.

The new leader, Brigham Young, who followed Smith as the head of the Mormon church, was a remarkable statesman with unusual abilities in organizing and keeping his people together during times of great tribulation. He saw that the Mormons must leave the East, travel westward, and establish an entirely new state of their own if they were to survive. Early in 1846 a courageous group of seventeen hundred souls, known as the Pioneer Band, left Nauvoo, Illinois, passed through the state of Iowa, then remained for the winter at "Camp Israel," set up on both sides of the Missouri River in Iowa and Nebraska.

In the spring of 1847 they took up their journey again, their numbers being increased along the way by fellow church-members and converts who had come from various places to join them. It seems that their original intention was to proceed to the very shores of the Pacific Ocean. In fact, one group, the Mormon Battalion, marched through New Mexico and Arizona as far as San Diego, Los Angeles, and San Francisco. The party under Brigham Young, however, turned at Santa Fe, went north into Colorado and Wyoming, then west, before they reached the Great Salt Lake Valley. It is now thought that this was the original destination of the party from the start, that Young had been influenced by conferences with such explorers as Jim Bridger to select this desert country, practically uninhabited except for Indians, as the logical stopping-point, the promised land at the end of all their rainbow-wanderings. Jim Bridger had said that "nothing will grow in that God-forsaken place." Hearing this, one of Young's own followers strongly objected to the location in Utah, crying out, "Why nobody on earth wants that God-forsaken land!" Whereupon Brigham rejoined, "If there is a place on this earth that nobody else wants, that's the place that I am looking for."

Indeed, this was the place. A monument now stands on the spot where Brigham Young stood, overlooking the sagebrush desert, and made the momentous decision. The plowing of land began on July 23, 1847—it would be only a few months till winter, and they needed food.

For thirty years after 1847, till his death in 1877, Brigham Young guided the destinies of the Mormon people through a heroic struggle that made the barren wilderness-valleys blossom with rich harvests of grain, flourishing towns, and a progressive people—one of the miracles of our many-sided civilization.

It is always a matter of curiosity with many persons who have had no contact with the Mormons, to know just what they are like. I confess, personally, that when I began my teaching experience in a Western school, and encountered Mormon children for the first time, I somehow expected to see all sorts of colorful idiosyncrasies cropping out, which would differentiate these youngsters sharply from their classmates. I had never known a Mormon before. Only a short time served to eradicate my preconceived notions: in all activities they were indistinguishable from the other students, being just as intelligent, industrious, and pleasant to know. At an occasional attendance of their religious services, I found nothing esoteric, cabalistic, or fanatical in their worship, but much that was fine, spiritually and culturally.

Salt Lake City, the seat of the Mormon Church, is like a large, beautiful park with spacious streets and flower-bordered drives irradiating from it, chiefly north and south. The city actually occupies an oasis, watered and highly productive, and three-fourths of the Utahans live north or south of it within a perimeter comprising about one-tenth of the state's area. To the west lies a great stretch of arid land thirsting for water. The southern part of the state, once considered a valueless waste of inaccessible mountains, was visited by the Spanish explorers as early as 1540 but never colonized anywhere by them. Today this country, with its stupendous canyons and spectacular natural bridges, is being opened up for tourists who view with amazement its rugged grandeur and kaleidoscopic colorings.

Salt Lake City is girt on all sides by mountains. The town was charted squarely according to the points of the compass in straight, wide streets which visibly impress upon the stranger the conviction that here is a well-planned metropolis.

The focal point of the city is the Mormon Temple, seen embossed in the bowl of two spoons and engraved on a third. Over a period of forty years, from 1853 to 1893, the Temple was in process of construction, the architectural outlines dovetailing in detail with the historical and religious aspects of the Mormon faith. There are six peaked towers, on one of which in the east center stands the hand-wrought copper figure of the Angel Moroni blowing a trumpet. It was this angel that appeared to Joseph Smith and interpreted for him the gold-lettered pages in the *Book of Mormon*. It is imaged on three spoons: in the nave of two of them, and on the third the Angel occupies both caput and nave.

The Tabernacle is a behemoth-like structure of ovoidal contours, once unique but now more familiar to our eyes through its resemblance to the ubiquitous Quonset huts of World War II. The acoustics are such that the slightest sound can be heard from one end to the other of the auditorium, a distance of two hundred feet. The choir and organ music of the Tabernacle is well known to radio listeners all over the country.

The reverse side of the handle on the Temple and Tabernacle spoon contains pictures of the pavilion at Saltair Beach, Eagle Gate, a beehive, and several grains of wheat. The Eagle Gate, erected as an entrance to City Creek Canyon in 1859, was removed once as a hazard to traffic but later replaced at a higher level because it had always served as one of the city's oldest landmarks. It appears also in the bowl of the Beehive spoon.

There are several unusual symbols closely associated with and much venerated by the Mormon people. The Angel Moroni has already been mentioned. Another is the seagull, to which bird a monument has been erected, although Salt Lake City is eight hundred miles distant from the nearest ocean, the natural habitat of the seagull. During the first summer in their new home, the struggling pioneers were faced with the threat of starvation by grasshoppers which had descended upon the ripening crops in such hordes that every blade of the new green growth was being stripped bare. Just when the situation seemed most hopeless, swarms of seagulls swooped down like a miracle out of the skies and devoured the devourers. Ever since, the seagull has been regarded as a symbol of the Hand of Providence in times of distress.

But more than anything else, the beehive has been used as a characteristic Mormon symbol. Many business concerns employ it as a designation. The Beehive House was once used by church officials for their committee meetings. The Utah seal and the state flag both embody a beehive. It is seen on three of these spoons. On the Temple and Tabernacle, it appears on the reverse nave, lower half. The word "Industry" is written above it, and below, in the exergue is the date "1847." It is in the obverse caput on the spoon bearing the Beehive name, along with the date for the establishment of Utah as territory, September 9, 1850. On the Angel Moroni spoon the beehive is surrounded by two parallel circles, between which is again written: "Territory of Utah, 1850."

The Salt Lake Daisies spoon is a dainty little demi-tasse type, distinctively different from the other three listed here. While the state flower of Utah is the sego lily, the flowers appearing here on the caput approximate most closely the daisy, with certain likenesses to the pink or carnation. The four daisies are enameled in colors of red, white, blue, and yellow. The shank simulates the leafy stalk of a daisy.

These spoons are richly representative of the allegorical significance arising in the history of Utah and Salt Lake City. The Temple and Tabernacle spoon was pressed by Paye and Baker, and the Beehive by Shepard Manufacturing Company, the length of both being 5¾ inches. The Angel Moroni, 6 inches in length, was made by Gorham's. The Salt Lake Daisies, measuring 3¾ inches, is a product of R. Wallace and Sons. The latter is used through the courtesy of its owner, Mrs. Gordon Scheimer, Hayward, California.

No. 96 NINETY SIX

On a spring-like day in January, 1819, a young man of twenty-three, John Pendleton Kennedy, was proceeding on horseback through the hill country of western South Carolina. He had already traveled from Augusta, through Edgefield and Abbeville. He was now in the district of Ninety Six, the oldest settlement in the Up-Country section of South Carolina, having been founded about 1720.

The traveler had been enjoying the picturesque beauty of the Southern highlands as he pushed along through the evergreen forests of rhododendron and laurel. For five or six miles he had gone without meeting a single person, and was beginning to think he would have to spend the night in the wilderness, with his horse as his sole companion.

While he paused at a road forks, pondering on which path he should take, a boy on horseback, emerging from the thickets, galloped past him. Kennedy, happy at seeing any semblance of human life and knowing that there was some sort of habitation near, followed closely after the rider.

It was obvious that the little fellow had lost control over his mount, and when he rounded a curve, he was bounced out of his seat, and lay at the side of the road when Kennedy came up.

The boy was about ten years old, and Kennedy, lifting him easily, carried him to the nearest farmhouse, which happened to be the boy's home. The mother of the family was away, but the child's father and an older brother entered into a consultation at once about what they should do for the boy, who apparently was suffering a great deal from a dislocation in one of his shoulders. The doctor not being found in the vicinity, some one suggested that Horse-Shoe Robinson, the handy man of the village, be sent for.

Shortly afterwards, while Kennedy and his host were seated in front of a hearth lit up by a crackling blaze of pine faggots, a tall, sinewy man of striking appearance entered, and very soon the dislocated bones in the boy's shoulder had been reset.

Horse-Shoe Robinson, the substitute doctor—an old soldier of the Revolution—is described by Kennedy thus: "What a man I saw! With nearly seventy years upon his poll, time seemed to have broken its billows over his front only as the ocean breaks over a rock. The sharp light gilded his massive frame and weather-beaten face with a pictorial effect that would have rejoiced an artist. His homely dress, his free stride, as he advanced to the fire; his face radiant with kindness; the natural gracefulness of his motion—all afforded an index to his character."

At the host's request, Horse-Shoe began to narrate for Kennedy's benefit a "rich stock of adventure, of which his life was full." Until the small hours of the morning the men sat by the firelight. Kennedy was held spell-bound by the old soldier's straightforward way of recounting his wartime experiences. "A more truthful man than he, I am convinced, did not survive the war to tell its story. He seemed to set no value upon his own exploits, but to relate them as items of personal history, with as little comment or emphasis as if they concerned any one more than himself."

Kennedy made entries in his notebooks on Horse-Shoe's adventures while the stories were still fresh in his memory. Sixteen years later he repaired to these notes for the elaboration of *Horse-Shoe Robinson*, which appeared in 1835, and which Ernest E. Leisy in *The American Historical Novel* calls the "best ante-bellum novel produced in the South." When a copy was sent to Horse-Shoe, then nearing his ninetieth year, the story was read to him—he was illiterate himself—and it brought this comment from the old fellow: "It is all true and right—in its right place—excepting about them women, which I disremember. That mought be true too; but my memory is treacherous—I disremember."

Many of the scenes limned in the novel, one of the best first-hand accounts of the Revolution, are centered in the district around Ninety Six, the earliest trading post in the uplands of South Carolina. Opinions have varied as to the origin of that name, which might suggest merely the altitude or perhaps the date for the founding of the town, in 1696 or 1796. Legend has it that Cateeche, an Indian maiden, once rode ninety-six miles to the trading post to inform her white lover of an impending massacre planned against the whites by her tribesmen. Arriving too late and finding her sweetheart already murdered, she despairingly leapt from a cliff nearby to her death. The most logical reason for the name, Ninety Six, is undoubtedly that given by Edward McCrady, author of a monumental five-volume history of South Carolina, who says the place "derived its name from the circumstance that it was ninety-six miles distant from the principal town of the Cherokee Indians, called Keowee."

McCrady also claims that there was a greater number of encounters fought during the Revolution in South Carolina than in any other colony. And of the hundred and thirty-seven battles, large and small, which he enumerates, more of them were fought in the district of Ninety Six than elsewhere. "Ninety Six was the scene of the first bloodshed of the Revolution in South Carolina," he explains, "that of the siege of the 19th to the 21st of November, 1775—a struggle between the Whigs and the Loyalists of the state, which resulted in a treaty between the parties, scarcely made before broken." From then on until 1781 there were endless battles in the vicinity. The severest fighting took place, however, when the Americans under General Greene besieged the site from May the 12th to the 19th, 1781, resulting in American casualties alone of one hundred and eighty-five men. While this siege was unsuccessful, it did render the Tory positions around Ninety Six untenable, and the fort was soon abandoned to the patriots.

Naturally so much activity, prolonged for seven years, between two hostile forces has made the history of Ninety Six a rich field for the exploiter of tales with the smell of powder in them. After the publication of Kennedy's popular novel, other fiction writers were quick to avail themselves of this teeming material. William Gilmore Simms spun several of his adventurous romances around the actions at Ninety Six, the chief of these perhaps being *The Scout*. With the revival of interest in historical fiction during the last quarter-century, we have seen the siege of Ninety Six, from the Tory viewpoint, presented to readers by Kenneth Roberts in his remarkable novel, *Oliver Wiswell*. And if any one doubts that there is an abundance of material still lying fallow in the colorful history of this region, let him turn to the "breath-taking" tale of *Ninety Six* by Elliott C. McCants. A recent volume by Julien and Watson presents a good history, with splendid photographs, of landmarks in this "last frontier region of South Carolina."

"From Paris to Ninety Six"—a recent headline—is an apt phrase to denote a wide stretch of Aladdin's magic carpet. No wonder Bill Voiselle, pinch-pitcher for the Boston Braves, has always insisted that a big "96" be sewn on the back of his shirt. Not every pitcher's home town can be mentioned in the same breath with Paris.

The Ninety Six spoon, made by Watson and Company, belongs to the Wigwam series of state seal spoons. In addition to the South Carolina seal, a tall pine, a sheaf of wheat, and a stalk of cotton appear on the handle. "Ninety Six" is engraved on the gold-washed bowl in Gothic lettering. Length is 5¾ inches.

No. 97 JEFFERSON CITY

Missouri has had, through peculiar circumstances, more capitol buildings than any other state. Three of them were only makeshift till Jefferson City, named after Thomas Jefferson, was selected as the permanent location for the capital site. The fourth capitol, built here in 1823, was destroyed by fire in 1837, all the state archives and the first state seal being lost.

The structure depicted on the bowl of this spoon was built on a high bluff overlooking the Missouri River in 1840, and burned February 5, 1911, when a terrific bolt of lightning struck the dome and quickly enveloped the whole interior in a mass of flames. The present capitol, the sixth, was completed in 1918 at a cost of four million dollars, and stands on the same eminence held by its predecessor.

It was long uncertain whether Jefferson City would—or could—retain its seat as the state capital. Its growth was apathetic. At the time of its selection as the site for the state government there were only two public buildings in the town, a grog shop and a mission. Four years later it had added four more to the list: a blacksmith shop, a grocery store, a hotel, and a distillery. Cows, goats, and pigs were seen on the streets in greater numbers than persons.

Gradually, however, Jefferson City, aided by its central location in the state, began to show signs of an expanding prosperity, as small businesses were established and steamboat facilities increased. The first train service into the capital in 1855 was marked by a major catastrophe. A festive crowd was awaiting the arrival of the train, expecting to make it a gala event, but the train did not arrive. It crashed through the trestles over Gascoigne River; more than a score of the passengers were killed and many others injured.

During the Civil War the town was torn by rival factions. Governor Jackson, a Southern sympathizer, called for a referendum on the issue of secession, but the Unionists polled a majority of eighty thousand votes. Nevertheless, troops were enlisted on both sides, and two state governments fought for control of the capital. Skirmishes were frequent, and the wanton pillaging by lawless bands of guerrillas left the town badly crippled at the end of the war. The battle scars healed slowly, but since 1910 the population of the city has more than doubled in numbers.

The handle of this spoon is of the wave-stem type in a state seal series. The embossed name of the state curves in an arch along the shaft. A garb of wheat and two ears of corn occupy the nave.

The seal displays two grizzly bears rampant on both dexter and sinister sides. Within the circle of the armorial device there is another bear, white this time, in the passant guardant stance on the base. A crescent is engrailed on the chief, and the United States eagle to the right of the pale. A full-faced helmet is lodged in the crest. Below, on the scroll is inscribed the state motto, *Salus populi suprema lex esto* (May the welfare of the people be the supreme law). The date of Missouri's admission into the Union, 1820, is given in Latin notation.

The bowl of the spoon is gold washed, and the image of the old capitol incised on the silver face produces a diffusive glint that simulates a brilliant interior lighting. Made by the Shepard Manufacturing Company, the length is 5½ inches.

No. 98 LAWRENCE WINDMILL

Thirty-five miles from Kansas City, as the crow flies, at the confluence of the Kansas and Wakarusa Rivers, stands Lawrence, partly on the bottomlands that divide the streams and partly on the slopes of the gently rising hills forming the hinterland. The history of Lawrence is intimately bound up with the beginnings of Kansas, a tale of trials and tribulations, harrowing experiences, murder, loot, and the bitterest fighting between the pro-slavery and free-state factions locked in lethal enmity for the mastery of the state. For eleven years the struggle continued, mounting in intensity and ferocity till the issue was decided without question by the outcome of the Civil War in 1865. The subsequent story of Lawrence has been a quiet one, and the windmill seen in the bowl of the Lawrence spoon is symbolic of the peaceful, agricultural pursuits of the major portion of the population during the many years since the war.

The Kansas-Nebraska Bill, promoted by Stephen A. Douglas, became a law on May 25, 1854. By this bill the Nebraska Territory was regarded as free-soil, while Kansas, according to the "popular sovereignty" doctrine, was left open for the people themselves of the territory to decide. A storm of protest arose in the North; Douglas was burned in effigy by the irate inhabitants in hundreds of small Northern towns.

Since it was evident that the people of Kansas would have to decide the issue for themselves, there was a rapid influx of emigrants from both North and South, each faction determined to attain a majority that would impose its will over the entire territory.

Under the momentum of these circumstances, a party of twenty-nine people departed from Boston, July 17, 1854, traveled westward across Lake Erie, through Chicago, St. Louis, and Kansas City, past encampments of Shawnee Indians, till they reached the hills between the Kansas and Wakarusa Rivers on the first of August.

A second group of thirty-seven persons left Boston the latter part of August. There were several musicians with instruments in this party, and frequently along the way they broke into the strains of Whittier's *Song of the Kansas Emigrant:*

> We cross the prairie, as of old
> The fathers crossed the sea,
> To make the West, as they the East,
> The homestead of the free.
>
> We go to rear a wall of men
> On Freedom's southern line,
> And plant beside the cotton tree
> The rugged northern pine.
>
> Upbearing like the ark of God
> The Bible in our van,
> We go to test the truth of God
> Against the fraud of man.

This contingent, led by Doctor Charles Robinson, joined the earlier arrivals on September 9th. Two weeks later a town site was laid out and fifty-six lots were sold to the sum of $5,040. A considerable amount of land was reserved for a post office, courthouse, public schools, and a college. A meeting was held to select a name for the town, which had hitherto been called variously Yankee Town, New Boston, and Wakarusa. After some discussion the new settlement was given the name of Lawrence in honor of Amos A. Lawrence, treasurer of the "New England Emigrant Aid Company." Mr. Lawrence, wealthy member of a prominent Boston family, had practically financed the whole undertaking out of his own pocket, and had laid aside a sum of twelve thousand dollars for a college to be built eventually in the new town.

For several weeks the settlers lived in tents, timber being rather scarce. They set their tables in the open, and made seats out of kegs, wash-tubs, and blocks of logs. A cabin, fourteen feet square built out of slender cottonwood logs, served as the first community house. Then a boarding house, fifty by twenty feet, was constructed in the form of a "hay tent." This was a peculiar type of building made by covering two rows of poles joined together at the top with a heavy thatch of prairie hay. "This house," says Reverend Cordley, historian of the pioneer settlement, "was all roof and gable." Windows and doors were placed on either end where sod was piled up to form the walls. The first sermon was preached in this house, the pulpit consisting of two trunks of clothes. By Christmas about twenty houses were erected, "shakes" being substituted for clapboards, as there was no sawmill at their disposal to furnish boards or other kinds of lumber. Shakes were made by splitting log blocks into slender sheets of wood resembling rude shingles. They were at best merely a make-shift, for they allowed too much wind to whistle in during the cold weather.

The population was augmented to nearly eight hundred persons by spring. There were almost daily arrivals, some coming singly, others in parties. Many made Lawrence a stop-over point before hurrying on westward. A great deal of the land had been preëmpted by Southern sympathizers from Missouri, who, bent on keeping the abolitionists out of Kansas, rode over the prairies, drove stakes, and claimed title to large areas of land which they did not occupy. "Two thousand slaves in Kansas will make it a slave state," they said. But conditions were such that they feared to bring in more than a "token number."

The first dispute started over an improved quarter section which had been bought for five hundred dollars by the Emigrant Aid Company from a Mr. Stearns. Several claimants immediately appeared to contest the purchase. Two tents were now pitched on the land, and that meant trouble. A covered wagon drove up on the fifth of October, a woman jumped out, and while guarded by several armed men, packed the New England tent into the van. Several Northerners in the neighborhood, armed with revolvers, hurried to the scene and forced the surrender of the stolen property. The next day a band of eighteen Missourians appeared and threatened to remove the same tent again, but they were met by thirty armed men from Lawrence. The invaders milled around for three quarters of an hour, undecided what to do. Some one asked Dr. Robinson if they should shoot to hit or shoot wild. Robinson replied in a voice loud enough to be overheard by a member of the opposing party that he would be "ashamed to shoot at a man and not hit him." The Missourians soon dispersed, although a few of their band, sensing the absurdity of the situation, came over and entered into friendly conversation with their late enemies.

The election of members for the first territorial legislature, announced for the 30th of March, 1855, created a great stir of excitement on both sides, as they were mindful of the important issues that would come up before that legislative body. The first laws entered on the statute books would be passed by that legislature. The contest became a spirited one; the canvas by the free-staters was carried on in Kansas, while the pro-slavery people made their chief campaign in the border areas of Missouri. Oratorical fireworks blazed forth in a mass of meetings, secret societies were formed, and a call went forth that Missourians should enter Kansas in such preponderance of numbers that the free-state people would be hopelessly outvoted in every district. A typical excerpt from one of these inflammatory tirades ran like this: "I tell you to mark every scoundrel among you that is the least tainted with free-soilism or abolitionism, and exterminate him. I advise you one and all to enter every election district in Kansas, in defiance of Reeder and his vile myrmidons, and vote at the point of the bowie knife and revolver. Never give or take quarter from the rascals."

Governor Reeder endeavored to secure a fair election by having a census taken of the entire population as well as a separate one for those of voting age. The census for Kansas listed 8,601 people, of whom 2,905 were registered as qualified voters. The district including Lawrence recorded 369 voters.

The day before the election a thousand Missourians were camping outside the town of Lawrence. They brought their own printed tickets with them, and identified themselves by wearing white ribbons on their coat lapels. They cowed the election officials by threats and force of numbers, voted, and departed for home. The result was an overwhelming victory for the Missourians. Almost three times as many votes were cast as there were qualified voters, 6,307 for the whole territory and 1,034 for the district of Lawrence. Of the latter figure, 802 were cast by the interlopers. Only one free-state candidate squeezed through by a narrow margin. "The news of the outrage," says Cordley, "spread over the country on the wings of the lightning, and stirred the wildest excitement and indignation throughout the entire North. It was something that had no parallel in the history of the country. A body of invaders from another state had stolen a legislature, and there seemed to be no appeal."

As soon as the "bogus legislature" convened, steps were taken to remove Governor Reeder, who was only lukewarm to the pro-slavery program. The constitution was copied almost verbatim after the one in effect in Missouri. Sharper teeth were put into the slavery statutes, however. A person who abetted the escape of a slave was subject to the death penalty. Anyone who expressed sentiments against slavery was guilty of a felony and would be punished by a stiff prison sentence of at least five years at hard labor.

The people of Lawrence set about quietly to repudiate the laws of the phony legislature. At a Fourth of July celebration Dr. Robinson made a stirring speech in which he said that "tyrants are tyrants and tyranny is tyranny, whether under the garb of law or in opposition to it. So thought and acted our ancestors, and so let us think and act." His words were circulated and discussed everywhere throughout Kansas. George Deitzler was commissioned to return East and inform people there of the state of affairs in Kansas. An hour after his arrival in Boston, a consignment of one hundred Sharpe's rifles was despatched to Lawrence under the guise of "books." More boxes of "books" followed, including a howitzer, which Horace Greeley secured in New York for Deitzler.

There now existed two definite factions in the state, deadly hostile to each other. Through the summer and early fall months of 1855, all was peaceful on the surface, but both sides were stocking ammunition and making preparations for the time when the dam of hostile feelings would burst into open fury. Companies of men were being drilled in Lawrence and embankments built at strategic points around the town.

Then a series of events took place that brought the two groups into open warfare. A man by the name of Kelly was severely beaten in Atchison for expressing opinions against slavery. A minister who protested this use of violence was twice seized, his face smeared with black on the first occasion and his body tarred and feathered the second time. A quarrel between Charles W. Dow, a free-state man, and Franklin Coleman, a pro-slavery man, over rival claims culminated in the shooting of Dow in the back, as he was walking out of Coleman's yard. The murderer fled to Missouri, where he was concealed by the pro-slavery group to prevent his arrest. Jacob Branson, a friend of Dow's, expressed his indignation at the cold-blooded murder before a man named Buckley, who had a warrant sworn out for Branson's arrest. Samuel J. Jones, the sheriff of Douglas County, accompanied by fifteen men, went to Branson's home at midnight, broke the door down, and dragged their victim out of bed. Fifteen men of the neighborhood, apprised of the arrest, quickly armed themselves and hastened in the direction of Branson's house. They had not proceeded along the road very far when they encountered the sheriff's party with Branson in their midst. For an hour the case was argued, and when it was discovered that the sheriff had no warrant of arrest on Branson, he was forced to release the prisoner.

Jones appealed to the new governor, Wilson Shannon, to help put down the "rebellion" in Lawrence. The free-state men had defied an officer of the law by force of arms. The militia, consisting chiefly of men from Missouri, moved in, eager to "wipe out that nest of vipers" in the abolitionist stronghold of Lawrence. They hesitated to make an open attack, having heard "many big yarns afloat" about those dreadful Sharpe rifles which could discharge ten shots a minute and "kill a man a mile away."

380

About five hundred men sprang to the defense of Lawrence while the besiegers numbered some fifteen hundred in their camp. Circular earthworks were thrown up around the town, and two underground cellars were built for the protection of the women and children in case of actual combat. For a week the besieged city waited for the attack that never came. Meanwhile their numbers were augmented by several hundred men who slipped in at nights from the farms of the surrounding countryside. Dr. Robinson went about the streets among his men exhorting them to "suffer and be strong." Word was received that twelve more howitzers had arrived in Kansas City on consignment for Lawrence. A group of teamsters was dispatched to bring in this material assistance. When they neared Lawrence a strong detachment of men was sent out to escort the cannon safely into town. Free-state men everywhere rallied to the cause of Lawrence, which was considered the common cause of the whole state. Companies were organized in Osawatomie, Ottawa Creek, Bloomington, Palmyra, and Topeka. The news of a large contingent, well trained and well equipped, marching in from Topeka, created consternation in the ranks of the besiegers. Governor Shannon, alarmed over the serious aspect of the situation, appealed to the President for regular troops. The attackers, now outnumbered, were growing restive and wanted to go home.

Governor Shannon came to Lawrence himself and forthwith saw the situation in its true light. It was nothing more than a ridiculous show of mock-heroics, a much ado about nothing. He immediately went into a conference with both factions and soon drew up a peace treaty, the signing of which was effectively hastened by a severe blizzard that sent the thermometer scooting down to ten below zero. While the forces of physical nature were freezing up, the forces of Sheriff Jones's militia were melting away. The governor stayed over for a banquet given in his honor, and he declared that it was the "happiest day of his life."

Two other events should be recorded for this day. One was the killing of Thomas Barber, shot from his horse while riding from Bloomington to aid in the defense of Lawrence. The other was the unannounced arrival of a singular figure, a self-appointed angel of the Lord, who protested the signing of the peace treaty. "After the treaty and its stipulations had become known," says Professor L. W. Springer, "after the speeches of felicitation on the happy subsidence of troubles which threatened to engulf the settlement, had been made, an unknown man—tall, slender, angular; his face clean shaved, sombre, strongly lined, of Puritan tone and configuration; his blue-gray eyes honest, inexorable; strange unworldly intensities enveloping him like an atmosphere—mounted a dry goods box and began to denounce the treaty as an attempt to gain by foolish uncomprehending make-shift what could be compassed only by shedding of blood. Since that day the name of this unknown man plucked down from the dry goods box with his speech mostly unspoken, has filled the post horns of the world—Old John Brown."

On the 26th of May, 1856, Sheriff Jones, postmaster of Westport, Missouri, rode into Lawrence, protected by a posse of two hundred men, and served several writs of arrest. Seeing that the citizens offered no resistance, the sheriff and his mob took matters boldly in their hands to wreak vengeance on the town for all their past humiliations. The Free-State Hotel and Dr. Robinson's house were burned, the newspaper offices were sacked, and all the printing presses they could locate were carried off and dumped into the Wakarusa River. "The work of pillage spread through the whole town. Every house and store which could be entered was ransacked, trunks broken open, and money and property taken at will. In one house over two thousand dollars in money were carried away . . . Towards evening the forces were drawn off to their camp and the sack of Lawrence was concluded."

Again tempers rose to the boiling point. In Leavenworth one braggart, vowing he would bring in the scalp of an abolitionist in less than two hours, rode out, shot a Lawrence man in his carriage, scalped him and carried his gruesome trophy back to Leavenworth on a pole. Major S. D. Hoyt, who went from Lawrence to Fort Saunders on August 12th to negotiate terms that would end the wanton raids on the homes of innocent people, was shot by the two men who served as his escorts on the return trip.

Governor Shannon, dismayed at the general prevalence of lawlessness, resigned and his place was taken by John W. Geary of Pennsylvania. The new governor was hardly seated before new troubles broke out. The free-staters had just cleaned out several nests of marauders around Lawrence, and in reprisal the pro-slavery supporters raised an army of twenty-eight hundred men, most of them from Missouri, and began another march on Lawrence, aiming to finish what they had left unfinished in the spring. But Geary acted swiftly; he sent United States troops to prevent the Missouri men from wiping Lawrence off the map. On September 15th the governor entered the town along with the regular army. The infuriated mob of invaders, realizing that an attack now would be foolhardy and disastrous, turned on their heels and marched home. On the way they vented their spleen by killing a crippled plowman who refused to let them carry off one of his horses.

The country bristled with indignation over the news coming out of Kansas. Many people disbelieved the stories they heard, thinking they were grossly exaggerated. On the other hand, it was the tragedy of "bleeding Kansas" that gave impetus and purpose to the newly-founded Republican party, which was gaining recruits by the thousands in the Northern states. The terrorism existing in Kansas at this time was accurately described in this letter written by an eye-witness to a friend in Boston: "It may be that nothing short of a massacre of the suffering people of Kansas will arouse this nation to a sense of the inconceivable wickedness of the men at the head of affairs. You may imagine the feeling with which I read the cold blooded sneers, the diabolical sport which is made of our sufferings in the Boston Post, which I have just received. Are all the feelings of humanity, is all sense of decency dead in the minds of the men who uphold this infamous administration?"

In October of 1857 another election was held, and in spite of the ballot box stuffing, the free-staters won control of the territorial legislature by a large majority. In one district the pro-slavery advocates copied 1547 names directly out of the Cincinnati directory on to the fraudulent ballots. Governor Walker, although a native of Mississippi and an upholder of slavery, threw out the false returns, and for his honesty was removed from office. Lawrence was now freed from the menace of annihilation, the free-soil movement having become so strong that its ranks embraced about seventy per cent of the people.

In 1861 on the eve of the Civil War, Kansas was received as a free state into the Union. But the worst tragedy that ever struck Lawrence came suddenly and swiftly on the morning of August 21, 1863, when a guerrilla band of four hundred and fifty men, led by William Quantrill and the James brothers galloped into town about dawn and began to kill, burn, and plunder on an unprecedented scale. The people of Lawrence, unarmed and unsuspecting, had no time to organize resistance to the bloody ruffians who had burst in upon them while they slept. The work of slaughter and destruction was methodically planned. Squads of six or eight men were dispatched to every quarter of the town. No mercy was granted, and fortunate were they who sought safety in the cornfields and wooded areas outside of town. Not a house was unvisited, and the atrocities that were perpetrated by the blood-thirsty raiders upon an innocent citizenry almost pass belief. Orders were given to "kill every man and burn every house."

Every man seen on the streets was instantly shot. One woman, whose husband had been killed, begged to keep her wedding ring, but the ring was forcibly removed from her fingers. Some women who sought to shield their husbands by clinging tightly to them were pulled away and the men shot down in cold blood. Two clerks who were promised their lives if they opened the money safe in a department store, were felled as soon as the safe-door swung open. A sick man who had been carried out of a burning house was riddled with bullets as he lay on his mattress in the yard. Two wounded men were bound hand and foot and pitched into the raging flames of a burning store, even though they were piteously begging for mercy. Three old darkies, one of them about ninety years old and a cripple, were butchered almost beyond recognition. One raider asked for a drink of water. When the water carrier handed him the cup, the villain raised the cup to his mouth with one hand and shot the well-doer with his other.

Many escaped death, as if by a miracle. Dr. Robinson hid in the rafters of his barn. One woman posted herself near an outdoor cellar and steered all fugitives running in her direction toward this hide-away. The Episcopal minister's wife had no menfolks in her house, her husband being a chaplain in the Federal army, but she concocted an ingenious device for saving a hard-pressed friend. She and two other women shaved the man's whiskers, dressed him in a gingham wrapper, placed a bonnet on his head, and seated him in an easy chair, with pills and bottles at his side. When the outlaws entered, one of the ladies was fanning the patient. "Poor Aunt Betsie has a high fever and must be kept very quiet," said the minister's wife. The raiders took what they wanted and left without disturbing Aunt Betsie. One man was picked up later from the pavement as if he were dead, but there was no sign of a bullet wound about his body. He had fainted away when the bullets began to whistle on all sides of him. He was sure that he had been hit.

When the raiders galloped out of town at nine o'clock, after a stay of four hours, the survivors crept out of their hiding places to survey the wreckage of one of the most dastardly raids in history. One hundred and fifty people were dead, and thirty-two wounded. Homes had been looted from top to bottom. Everything in the stores had been turned topsy-turvy. Many buildings were burnt to the ground, but in most instances the fires had been extinguished by the women as soon as the savage fiends dashed elsewhere; yet seventy-five homes burned to the ground. About a million five hundred thousand dollars' worth of property had gone up in smoke. Two hundred and fifty children had been made orphans on that day, which left its "blackest mark on the fair shield of Southern chivalry," according to one of the raiders who privately stated that he had killed no one and had been persuaded to join Quantrill's forces to help recover some stolen horses.

The prostrate city laid its dead away, comforted by the thought—

The body they may kill,
God's truth abideth still.

The placid existence of Lawrence since 1865 is in marked contrast to the turbulent times previous to that date. The yells that resound from the heights overlooking the broad valleys of the Kansas and the Wakarusa arouse no fears, as they come from the campuses or the stadiums of the State University and the Haskell Institute, the latter being the largest Indian school in the United States.

Great numbers of young people from Kansas City and other parts of Missouri descend upon Lawrence each year, but they come to pursue their studies at the University, which claims among its alumni such distinguished figures as former Governor Alf Landon, William Allen White, Senator Borah, and General Funston.

In addition to the windmill and barns cut in the gold bowl of this particular spoon, the name of Kansas and the state seal are seen on the wave handle. The spoon, a product of the Williams Bros. Silver Company, bears the date of 1902 on the reverse side of handle. The length of spoon is 5½ inches.

No. 99   CHATTANOOGA VALLEY
No. 103 LOOKOUT MOUNTAIN

The Creeks had a word for it, Chat-to-to-noog-gee—meaning, the mountain that rises to a peaked summit—a sheer cliff that looks out over the Tennessee Valley, two thousand feet below. While the Indian name has been retained by the town lying at its base, the mountain goes by the modified English translation of the original Creek designation.

Various Indian tribes had inhabited this vicinity before the Creeks. The Muskhogean were living here when De Soto explored the region in 1541. During the Revolution the Cherokee, under their chieftain, Oconostota, united with other tribes in a confederation called the Chickamauga and strove in desperate but unsuccessful efforts to drive the white settlers back to the pales of civilization. In 1782 John Sevier, commander of some five hundred Tennessee Volunteers, defeated these Indians in a fiercely fought battle on Lookout Mountain. Later, during negotiations for a settlement of the conflict, Oconostota told Sevier that the mysterious old stone fortifications exisitng in this region "had been made by the White people who had formerly inhabited the country now called Carolina"—an allusion to the Welsh, who are now believed to have ventured into this area about the twelfth century. Whether it was the Welsh, some other white people, or even Indians, who settled here and built rugged fortifications, they must have realized the superior strategic values of this terrain in the matter of self-defense. Verily, history repeats itself, and many a battle has been fought for the military mastery of Lookout Mountain, which extends for eighty-three miles from its northern sheer end in Tennessee, through Georgia, to a flattened plateau in northeastern Alabama.

The city of Chattanooga on the Tennessee River was known as Ross Landing until 1838. At the time of the Civil War, it had already become an important railroad center. Many of the people living in the region, being non-slaveholders, sympathized with the Union and furnished a large quota of soldiers to the Northern armies.

The National government sent General Rosecrans into Tennessee during the summer of 1863, and by autumn all the state was virtually under Union control except for this southeastern section, which was held by the Confederate forces of General Braxton Bragg.

When it was learned that the Federal Army was heading for Chattanooga, General Joe Wheeler, then stationed at Gadsden, Alabama, hastened north to fortify every gap of Lookout Mountain that would thereby block the passage of any Federal troops. On September 9, 1863, the Northern forces entered Chattanooga and planted the Stars and Stripes above Mound Fort without firing a shot.

There were detachments of Union troops in several places. General Joe Hooker was stationed at Stevenson, Alabama; General John W. Geary, at Murfreesboro, Tennessee; General William T. Sherman, at Corinth, Mississippi. Generals Rosecrans, Crittenden, Wagner, Thomas, McCook, Baird, and Negley were located in or near Chattanooga. The over-all plan now was to converge and merge these forces for a vigorous attack on General Bragg, who seemed to be retreating toward Rome, Georgia.

The Southern commander, however, gaining reinforcements, decided it would be better to risk a battle now rather than later. He wheeled his men into position on the east side of Chickamauga Creek, ten miles south of Chattanooga. McCook's Corps had just arrived, after a strenuous march, in time to join the forces of General Thomas. On September 19th and 20th the two armies faced one another along a battlefront extending more than three miles in length, about 60,000 men being on either side.

The first day they seemed to be equally matched, and neither army gained any apparent advantage over the other. On the second day the Confederates swept through a gap, created by a mistaken reading of general orders on the Northern side, and Longstreet's command practically annihilated the exhausted forces of McCook. Only the left flank, under Thomas, held its ground and saved the Union army from an utter rout. A tremendous loss, totaling about 34,000 men, was suffered on both sides.

General Rosecrans withdrew to Chattanooga, where he was replaced in command by Grant. The northern army awaited the arrival of forces in charge of Generals Hooker and Sherman.

Grant shrewdly delayed any large action till he felt strong enough to storm the heights of Lookout Mountain, this "Gibraltar of America," where Bragg's men held all the vantage points. A packet of Confederate mail captured by the Federals at Pulaski, Tennessee, contained this communication from a Southern veteran, signed "Dan," to his wife: "I went on the point of Lookout Mountain yesterday to take a view of both armies and the surrounding country. It was the most sublime scene I have ever witnessed. I could see the whole Yankee army and ours at almost the same sight. My eyes had not grown weary of the magnificent view when we were greeted with shells from a Yankee battery on Moccasin Point, which soon shelled my old friend, Alf Davis, and myself off. I remarked to him when he heard the whistle of a shell, 'Do you like to hug the ground better than you do your wife?'"

General Thomas engaged in the opening skirmish of the battle now impending, when he advancd his men one mile to capture Orchard Knob. This general who had been dubbed the "Rock of Chickamauga" after his heroic stand at that battle, was, strangely enough, a Southerner—from Virginia—by birth and tradition. For five years preceding the War, he had been stationed in Texas with Lee, Hood, Kirby Smith and other close

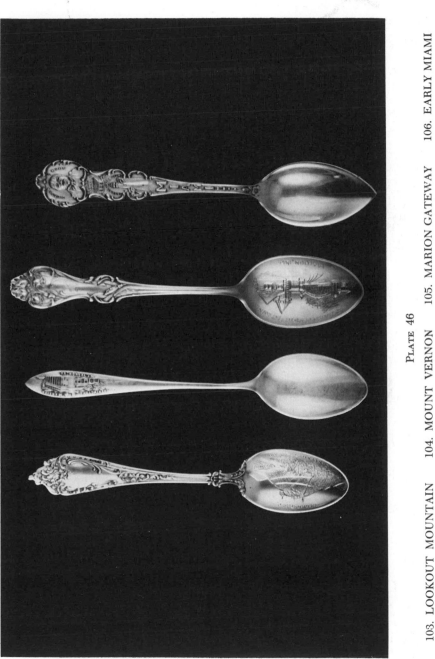

PLATE 46

103. LOOKOUT MOUNTAIN   104. MOUNT VERNON   105. MARION GATEWAY   106. EARLY MIAMI

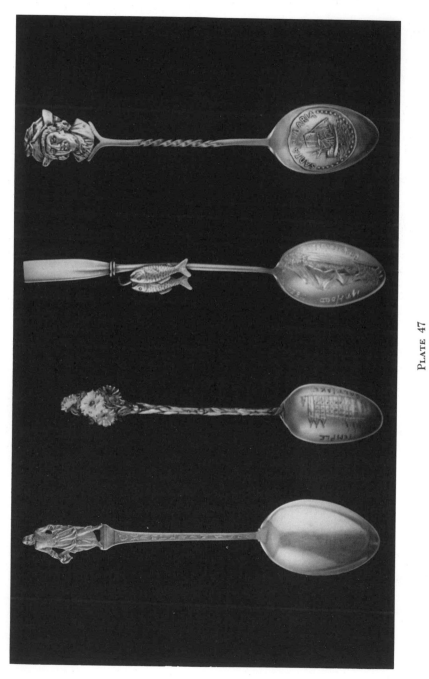

PLATE 47

107. CHAMPLAIN   108. SALT LAKE DAISIES   109. TWO SALMON   110. SANTA MARIA

PLATE 48

111. MOUNT HOOD   112. LURAY CAVERNS   113. ISLES OF SHOALS   114. HISTORIC WILMINGTON

PLATE 49

115. WEBSTER'S BIRTHPLACE   116. SOUTHERN PINES
117. GOLDEN GATE BEAR   118. PEORIA COURTHOUSE

Southern military associates, yet he chose to adhere to the Union cause. When his Virginia sisters heard he had accepted a commission in the Northern army, they sorrowfully turned his picture to the wall. A man greatly admired and loved by his subordinates, he performed signal achievements in the hard-fought struggle to preserve the Union.

The battle of Lookout Mountain, often called the "Battle of the Clouds," began on the evening of Novmber 23, 1863. Sharpshooters picked their way up and around the steep ledges, hiding frequently behind boulders for immediate protection. Through a cloud-like mist, General Geary's men clambered along vigorously, frequently on their hands and knees. Soon they were being attacked by Confederate pickets who had barricaded themselves behind boulders and in the pockets of rock-sheltered ravines. The hills were honeycombed with small detachments of Southerners, who fought desperately to stave off the Federal advance amid the bursting of hand grenades. Over the very ground where the whites and Indians had waged such a stubborn contest for mastery of this region in the Revolutionary War, two factions of the whites were now opposing each other in deadly combat.

Every foot of the up-hill struggle was made by men who refused to be repulsed. The Southerners as stubbornly defended their positions. The intermittent stretches of fog aided the Federal troops in their advance, and the higher they climbed the heavier became the fog. By two o'clock in the afternoon the Federals had wrested the greater part of the mountain from their enemies.

The Confederates quietly retreated from the summit of Lookout during the night of November 24th and took up positions on Missionary Ridge. Before daybreak of the 25th five volunteers from the Eighth Kentucky had scaled the peak of Lookout and planted the Stars and Stripes on the point where it could be seen waving when the sun rose.

The battle of Missionary Ridge lasted throughout the morning and afternoon of the twenty-fifth. Hooker withdrew from the slopes of Lookout across the Chattanooga Valley and attacked the Confederate left wing; Sherman kept up a continuous fire on the right. Bragg greatly weakened his center to protect both flanks. The Army of the Cumberland, under General Thomas, awaited the firing of six cannon at two-second intervals as a signal for attack. It came at three in the afternoon. "Without waiting for further orders, in the next few minutes, was made one of the most remarkable charges that has been recorded in military history," says Robert Sparks Walker, historian of the Lookout Mountain region. Within fifty-five minutes from the initial charge, the Union forces were in possession of the ridge, and Bragg's men, utterly exhausted after a heroic defense without any hope of reënforcements, broke their lines and fled toward the eastern hills of Georgia. The casualties amounted to over twelve thousand, the Confederates losing slightly more than the Federals.

Today Lookout Mountain attracts annually more than a half-million tourists, who enjoy the beauty of its many fine perspectives over the surrounding country, as well as the six waterfalls located amid picturesque scenes.

On the Chattanooga Valley spoon are discerned two mountain ridges, sharply separated by a deep valley, and these occupy the silvered right half of the bowl, which is executed in crinkled wave-lines. At the top of Lookout Mountain there is an observation tower, to which an inclined cable railway runs. Two electric cars travel concurrently on these tracks, one going up and one coming down, at a very slow rate of speed.

The handle is treated conventionally. This spoon, made by Gorham and Company, is 4½ inches long.

The Lookout Mountain spoon bears the name cut out on the left periphery of the bowl. The ridge itself is drawn at a closer perspective than on the previous spoon. The observation tower appears here somewhat more conspicuously, and three buildings are distinctly limned at the foot of the ridge.

The shaft is short, and the nave runs into the caput without any lineal interruption. The left and right borders of the caput differ from each other in floral design. The crown, bearing a chrysanthemum garniture, shows a Renaissance influence.

A product of Watson and Newell. Length, 5 inches.

No. 100 FORT WORTH

More millions have passed by the Worth monument at the intersection of Broadway and Fifth Avenue in New York than any other memorial in the world, yet very few of the passers-by could tell you anything of the man it commemorates. Ask any pedestrian on the streets of Fort Worth about General Worth and he will answer you, "Of what?" Tourists that walk the streets of Lake Worth in Florida have never heard of the general. No book has ever been written about him. A good but brief biography of his career appeared in the July, 1929, issue of *Americana*. But if we would know this enigmatic character, we must go to the annals of the Mexican War for the story.

William Jenkins Worth was born at Hudson, New York, on March 1, 1794, of Quaker parentage, his father being a seaman who wanted his son to be a business man. After a scant schooling, the boy was placed in a mercantile establishment in Albany. When the War of 1812 broke out, he was glad to grasp an opportunity that afforded him an escape from indoor work. He washed his hands of dry goods forever when he enlisted as a private under General Lewis.

He came to the general's notice in an indirect way. His bunk-mate had been called in to make an explanation of some misdemeanor he had committed. A letter replete with minor details, purportedly written by the culprit, was handed over to the general. Finding that the letter was not written by the one who had signed it, the general sent for the real author.

"Are you Private Worth?" he asked sternly.

"I am, sir," was the straightforward reply.

"Did you write this letter?" still more sternly.

"I did, sir."—in the same unhesitating manner.

A silence, then the general softened, "Henceforward, you are my private secretary."

Worth did not remain in this capacity very long, for after General Lewis's wounding and retirement, he returned to active service in the field with a commission as first lieutenant. After his outstanding action at the battle of Chippewa in August, 1814, he was made a captain and selected as aide-de-camp to General Winfield Scott, who lauded him in a citation to the War Department for his "unprecented gallantry and unequaled bravery in action." Scott took a particular liking to the twenty-year-old boy who was as handsome as Apollo, as heroic as Horatius, and as chivalrous as Bayard. Henceforth Scott kept his eye upon him and heaped superlatives on his military talents in many communiqués to the capital.

At the battle of Lundy's Lane, near Niagara, Worth was wounded and confined to his bed for a year, but he would not quit the service in spite of a slight limp. He was a major when he received an appointment to teach infantry tactics at West Point, where he remained from 1820 to 1828. These were the happiest years of his life, for he married and here two of his four children were born.

After he left West Point with a colonel's commission, he was stationed on a Canadian border patrol that moved back and forth as far west as Wisconsin. During the Seminole Wars he was sent to Florida, where his talents proved effective in bringing this troublesome issue to a successful conclusion. While there he was brevetted a brigadier-general by President Polk.

In 1846 he was called to the Mexican border and was second to General Taylor in command till Colonel David E. Twiggs appeared. Then arose an acrimonious debate between Twiggs and Worth over precedence in rank. The former actually held seniority of rank, but Worth insisted that he would not make way for a man whose chief merits lay in his huge bulk and his abilities to swagger and swear. The popular nicknames applied to Old Davy were the "Horse" and the "Bengal Tiger," and it is said that he "cussed his soldiers right out of their boots," thirsting more for the blood of his own men than that of the enemy. Angered at the delay in decision, for Taylor had referred the matter of rank to Washington, Worth offered his resignation. Taylor persuaded him to reconsider his withdrawal, but Twiggs meanwhile was assigned to the superior command.

This act turned Worth against Taylor and he vented his spleen by saying, "We are literally an anomalous body without a head." Taylor countered that Worth was an ambitious egotist who took no interest in the welfare of his men, "flies or no flies."

Back in Washington, Scott issued a ruling that placed brevet rank above a colonelcy. Scott's preference was only natural, for he believed in Worth's ability while he privately affirmed that Twiggs could not "command an army—either in the presence, or in the absence of an enemy."

Plans for the capture of Monterey were fast taking shape. Worth flamed with enthusiasm, for in battle he found his true element, and he inspired his men with his motto, "A grade or a grave." He was assigned to take Independence Hill and cut off access to the Saltillo highway whence came the Mexican source of supplies and their only avenue in case of retreat. Worth, whose expert horsemanship always thrilled his men, rode up and down before the lines at attention and exclaimed, "Men, you are to take that hill—and I know you will do it." And, as Justin Smith, the authority on the Mexican War, puts it,—"his bold magnetic way of speaking went straight to the soldier's heart."

Guarding the approaches to the Hill was a garrison stationed at the Bishop's Palace, thought to be impregnable because of its inaccessibility. A garrison with heavy guns was mounted at the top of the precipitous redoubt. The weather was wild, and the incessant rainfall loosened boulders that went crashing down the steep hillside. The Americans, wet through, without blankets, huddled in the darkness, shivered from the cold, and waited for orders to fall in and go forward. Very few dozed during the interminably long hours. At three o'clock the orders for action were whispered around. Numb hands clutched for their firearms, and the hazardous ascent of the gorge started. Those who pulled the heavy cannon after them had to hitch one hand around the thorny cactus and dig niches in the slippery soil for a toehold. At the most vertical part of the climb the storm burst into a maniacal fury that threatened at times to hurtle them from whatever heights they might have already attained.

Just as the first graying light seeped through the torrential downpour, a blaze of musketry from the picket guard startled the sleeping garrison. One cannon was pushed over the ramparts to impede the progress of the attackers who had not yet reached the parapets, but this was safely sidestepped. The Mexicans barricaded themselves inside the Palace and fought desperately. Worth, passing fearlessly from one detachment to another on horseback, shouted commands and exhorted his men on to victory. Other divisions of Taylor's army closed in, and there were fierce hand-to-hand encounters in every street. By noon the doors of the Bishop's Palace had been battered in, and the Stars and Stripes floated over its battlements. Less than twenty of Worth's men were killed.

Back in the States the praises of "Old Rough and Ready" were being sung and his name emblazoned in all the newspapers. To him went the

394

credit for the glorious victory at Monterey. But in camp he was criticized on all sides. "Worth won the laurels and Taylor receives them," one soldier wrote home. "Worth is the real cock-of-the-walk," said another. Opinions sailed like missiles through the air. Worth himself offered this criticism: "Twigg's volunteers were taken into action without order, direction, support, or command; in fact, murdered." Lt. Col. Hitchcock made this assertion: "Worth attacked too soon and without orders. Gen. Smith saved Worth and his reputation . . . He has striking manners and great felicity in conversation, but is utterly destitute of stability and judgment." While the Mexican general, Requeña, had this to say: "Worth made the real attack; Taylor blundered." Nevertheless, Taylor's popular reputation was made at Monterey, and ably upheld at Buena Vista.

In reward for his share of the victory, Worth was brevetted a major general and by resolution of Congress presented with a jeweled sword. Two states and his native county also offered their tribute with swords. He participated in other battles, and was now at the height of his popularity. In Vera Cruz a fellow-officer put a bee in his bonnet by saying: "One of the generals is coming out of this war to be the next president. It might well be you." A reporter added some substance to this wax by an article to the New York *Sun*. A few politicians espoused Worth's candidacy. The hats of Scott and Taylor had already been tossed into the ring, much to President Polk's chagrin. Worth's military advancements were owing chiefly to Scott's personal interest in him. His only son bore the name of Winfield Scott Worth. He could not break with his greatest benefactor, the big-hearted Scott, without good, justifiable reasons. But those reasons were not long in forthcoming.

When the Americans entered Puebla in May, 1847, Worth, as military governor, committed so many blunders in so short a time that Scott found it necessary to act. Half the soldiers were sick with dysentery and ague. Many died. Many also deserted because their pay was in arrears. Morale was at a low ebb. The native population felt insulted and refused to coöperate when they read this in a circular: "Doubtless there are among those with whom we are situated many who will not hesitate, as is the habit of cowards, to poison those from whom they habitually fly in battle—a resource familiar in Spanish history, legitimately inherited and willingly practiced by Mexicans." Thus, poison was suggested as a possible cause for the high death rate.

Dissatisfaction was rampant, and it was with the greatest sighs of relief that the commander-in-chief was received when he entered the town with fresh troops and set up a new military government.

Throughout 1847 certain scurrilous letters, anonymous most of them, found circulation in American newspapers. Scott was a lot of fuss and feathers, a bungler, a military mistake; the war had not been won by Scott but in spite of him; Worth had been the first to enter Mexico City, while Scott reaped the glory for that honor. An accumulation of evidence pointed to Worth, Duncan, and Pillow as the perpetrators of these notes. When accused, the three acted defiantly and wrote abusive letters about Scott to the President. Polk owed a great deal to Pillow. When the President's brother shot a man in Nashville, it was Pillow who helped him escape. It was Pillow who engineered Polk's nomination for the presidency. His record for diabolical machinations rivaled Iago's. He had been planted by Polk to spy on Scott and Taylor, and to discredit their actions by contemptible perversions of the truth.

Before the court-martial of the three conspirators could take place, the President relieved Scott of his command and cancelled the arrests. "Scott has manfully performed his duties and is now turned out like an old horse to die," commented Robert E. Lee.

Taylor won the presidency in 1848 and Scott resumed his former high position. To show that he bore no ill will, he generously placed Worth in command of the military department of Texas, even after he heard that Worth had changed his son's name from Winfield Scott to William Scott. A year later Worth died of the cholera, a disappointed man.

There is no doubt that Worth was a military genius with an inspiring presence on the battlefield. Off the battlefield his imperious, impetuous temperament displayed itself at its worst advantage. Lee, Grant, Meade, Semmes, Anderson, and other high ranking officers who had contact with him testified to his gallantry, courage, and ability. All were unanimous that his infirmities stemmed from a nervous impatience and a too active imagination that led him to barbed criticisms of others when results were not quickly obtained.

Yet there were thousands of people in his day who greatly admired General Worth. The women of New York City raised money to honor him with a monument. Many of his soldiers idolized him, and one of them, Major Arnold, who revered his memory, christened his Indian patrol-camp in Texas after him, not long after the General's death in 1849. Hence, the origin of Fort Worth.

Camp Worth, as it was first called, had to struggle for its existence from the very beginning. For years it fought for a railroad. One representative even went to London in 1873 and laid his plans before some English capitalists at a formal banquet. He had just about convinced them that his blueprints for Fort Worth's future had possibilities when a cablegram was placed on the banquet table—Jay Cooke & Company, biggest banking house in America, had collapsed. The panic of 1873 queered the railroad deal. It wrought havoc with deals all over the country, and it left the town of Fort Worth, just incorporated a few months before, so prostrate that a passer-through declared he had seen a panther lying asleep in the streets. A howl of protest from the civic patriots arose to combat this insinuating belittlement. As a result, the "Panther City" was adopted as a nickname and accepted as a source of local pride by the insulted citizens.

The railroad finally came to town in 1876 amid the ringing of bells, Comanche yells, flowing bowls, and discharging shells. No longer was the place just a dusty relay point along the Chisholm Trail.

Soon after the installation of gas lights, two Comanche chieftains, Yellow Bear and Quanah Parker, staying their first night at a hotel—Luke Short's White Elephant—blew the gas out and went to bed. Yellow Bear did not rise to learn of his error. Quanah Parker barely survived.

Fort Worth stands at a crossroads where East and West meet, where the tree-lands stop and the prairies start. It is popularly known as Cowtown, and being one of the Big Three livestock centers, has an inalienable right to that title.

But Fort Worth does more than shuttle herds of cattle through stockyard runways. It is a beehive of industry, a center of oil, metal, meat packing, livestock, grain, and steel companies. Seventy-five per cent of the wheat grown in Texas runs through its flour mills. Amon Carter, editor of the *Star-Telegram*, has done much to publicize the cowboy character of the town; incidentally he hands out twenty-gallon hats to famous visitors.

There are three seats of learning here: The Baptist Theological Seminary, Texas Christian University, and Texas Wesleyan College. A collection of invaluable old Bibles is housed at the Mary Couts Burnett Library, one of them being a Latin Bible printed at Basel, Switzerland, less than a quarter-century after the invention of the printing press.

In the bowl of the Fort Worth spoon the name is left uncut in the center of an incised cloud that has scalloped darts along its edges. The name is written in small, disconnected backhand letters. The handle, without deviation of general direction except for tiny nicks on the interior lines, gradually widens and is embellished profusely with a multiplicity of intertwining leaves, vines, twigs, and blossoms apparently of the magnolia genus. Encircling vines create an openwork of two machicolations in the caput.

Imprinted by R. Wallace & Sons. Length is 4¼ inches.

No. 102 JUMBO

In the summer of 1882 a great outcry arose in the London press, and repercussions of that alarm echoed in every provincial paper throughout England. The substance of the fanfare sounded something like this: "Jumbo is being stolen away from us . . . Save Jumbo for the enjoyment of our kiddies . . . That Yankee exploiter, Phineas Taylor Barnum, is about to buy Jumbo to ship off to America . . . Fling Barnum back his filthy lucre, and keep Jumbo in England."

The only creature who seemed not to be perturbed by this uproar was Jumbo himself, one of the most amiable elephants on record. What did it matter to him if he took another seafaring trip, this time to America?

He had similarly been brought on a long, circuitous voyage by sea from Ceylon years before, when he was nothing but a baby pachyderm, to the Royal Zoological Gardens of London, where he thrived and grew to mammoth proportions. He took to the learning of tricks, dances, and good manners as readily as the proverbial duck to water. And notwithstanding all his traits of showmanship, he was not conceited or theatrically temperamental, but as benignly gentle as a faithful lap dog. With his prehensile snout he had patiently and carefully lifted hundreds, yea thousands, of children, including the numerous progeny of the Queen unto the third and fourth generations, onto his lofty, broad ridgepole. He had become a national institution, a nationally known figure, familiarly dear to every child in the British capital. Hence, the uluation against his sale, especially to that Yankee publicity-seeker, P. T. Barnum.

Still, in spite of the mighty protest, the negotiations went through, and Jumbo was sold for ten thousand dollars of good Yankee money. It cost Barnum another twenty thousand till the big beast was duly installed in proper lodgings on the American continent. But what did Barnum care for this trivial expense? The newspapers had trumpeted abroad through the land every minute item in the procedure of the purchase, the preparations for the trip, the time of the departure, the crossing of the ocean, and the date of disembarcation. Jumbo's arrival in New York was heralded throughout these United States as an event of national importance and pride.

It took exactly two weeks for Barnum to be fully repaid for his lavish expenditures on Jumbo. New Yorkers streamed in multitudinous throngs to gaze at "the largest elephant ever known, either wild or in captivity." Thomas Nast drew a famous cartoon of master and mammal standing affectionately cheek to cheek. One glass company in Canton, Ohio, brought out an unusual Jumbo pattern in glassware for table service, having an elephant as finial on the lids of the sugar bowl, butter dish, and covered compote. A spoon-rack was also topped by an elephant. The butter dish was an extraordinarily elaborate affair resembling a Buddhist temple with ivory carvings, such as one sees in pictures from Ceylon, Siam, or India. Perched at the apex of this temple was a statuesque semblance of Jumbo. Another glass company, in Bellaire, Ohio, listed among its Christmas specialties, according to Mrs. Kamm, a covered punch bowl, having on its lid a Jumbo that was "a perfect imitation of Barnum's well-known animal, a bowl that will be an ornament to every sideboard, but a very attractive and useful article in saloons, where we are confident it will find a ready sale."

Other people in other places wanted to see this mammoth hunk of pachydermatous avoirdupois; so, Barnum graciously yielded to the clamor and took Jumbo for a swing around the country. At Cleveland occurred an incident typical of Barnum's own bigness. While showing his circus in that Ohio city, Barnum took time out to visit a five-year-old invalid, a little fellow called Trot, whom he had befriended on a previous tour. The child was overcome with joy that the busy man had not forgotten him, but unfortunately Trot was in no physical condition to attend the show under the big tent this time. "Never mind," Mr. Barnum assured him, "if you cannot go to the show, we must bring the show to you." Within half an hour Jumbo and other animal-actors were doing their stunts on the street and in the yard in front of Trot's home. The tiny boy from his bed by the window was allowed to call out commands, which Jumbo dutifully obeyed. After this matinee performance, the animals were marched back to the circus grounds, leaving the invalid child "wild with delight." Children in orphan homes were all given free passes, that they too might have the pleasure of seeing the mighty Jumbo perform in the "biggest show on earth."

Throughout the width and length of the nation—and beyond—Jumbo traveled, as far south as Havana, as far west as San Francisco, and as far north as the cities of Canada. He was popular everywhere, and drew record-crowds of children. But Jumbo's career came to an untimely end in the southwestern part of Ontario, Canada, when a fast train between Detroit and Buffalo upset his equilibrium as he was crossing some tracks at the town of St. Thomas on his return to his own specially-built freight car. The seven-ton mass of flesh came crashing from its height of eleven and a half feet to earth, never to rise again. He had been but three years in America, yet that period of time was sufficient to make his name a familiar word in every household where there were children. Stuffed and mounted, he continued to excite the curiosity of circus-goers for several more years. Today his hulking carcass may still be seen in the Barnum Museum of Natural History at Tufts College in Medford, Massachusetts. He thus survives his own celebrated history.

Long before the time of Jumbo, Barnum was obsessed with the idea of putting a drove of elephants in his "Great Asiatic Caravan Museum and Menagerie." In May, 1850, his agents, June and Nutter, were despatched to Ceylon on the chartered ship *Regatta* with the express orders to buy or capture, and bring back at least a half-dozen elephants. Five hundred tons of hay and the staves and hoops necessary for constructing water-kegs were taken along from New York and deposited at the island of St. Helena in readiness for the return trip.

The many obstacles that the expedition encountered were unforeseen. There were no living elephants standing around and waiting to be bought in Ceylon. The agents realized they would have to go into the jungles after them—or go home empty-handed. But before they could round up any elephants, they had to round up a hundred and sixty experienced elephant-hunters. Into the low-lying jungles plunged this assorted crew of natives with guns, clubs, stone-slings, drums and rattles; and aided by domesticated elephants, they drove a herd of the wild beasts into an Indian kraal at Anarajah Poora after a desperate and dangerous struggle.

Selecting ten of the choicest animals, they drove these onto the ship *Regatta* and sailed for New York. The elephants harnessed in pairs were marched up Broadway in a gala parade before throngs of gaping spectators.

Four years later Barnum sold all his elephants except one which he sent to his Connecticut farm. The New York and New Haven Railroad ran past this farm, and the keeper, dressed in his Ceylonese costume, was given a time-table and told to be hard at work plowing a six-acre tract near the railroad whenever the time approached for passenger trains to be going either way past the scene. Over and over, the little field was plowed. This advertising stunt soon attracted the attention of the public, and Barnum was credited with the introduction of elephant-power for heavy draft work on his farm. Passenger traffic on the railroad picked up; people were curious enough to make special trips by train past the place. Letters of inquiry poured in from presidents and secretaries of agricultural societies as to the merits of using elephants on American farms.

In his recollections the great enterpriser amusingly describes the reactions of the press: "Newspaper reports came from far and near, and wrote glowing accounts of the elephantine performances. One of them, taking a political view of the matter, stated that the elephant's sagacity showed that he knew more than any laborer on the farm, and yet, shameful to say, he was not allowed to vote. Another said that Barnum's elephant built all the stone wall on the farm; made all the rail fences; planted corn with his trunk, and covered it with his foot; washed my windows and sprinkled the walks and lawns, by taking water from the fountain-basin with his trunk; carried all the children to school, and put them to bed at night, tucking them up with his trunk; fed the pigs; picked fruit from branches that could not otherwise be reached; turned the fanning mill and corn-sheller; drew the mowing-machine and turned and cocked the hay with his trunk; carried and brought my letters to and from the post office (it was a male elephant); and did all the chores about the house, including milking the cows and bringing in eggs."

Barnum was once questioned closely by a neighboring landowner about the feasibility of using elephants to save labor on the farm, and the showman boasted that his elephant could draw more than forty yoke of oxen.

"I don't want to tell you that I doubt your word," declared the farmer stoutly, "but I would just like to know what he can draw."

Whereupon the circus-master solemnly asserted: "He can draw the attention of twenty millions of American citizens to Barnum's Museum."

The old man laughed heartily, and forewent his questioning with this comment: "Well, I give it up. I have been a farmer for thirty-five years and I have only just discovered that an elephant is a very useful and profitable animal on a farm—provided the farmer also owns a museum."

400

It is quite understandable why the Ceylon officials should have chosen a spoon with an elephant finial as their souvenir for the World's Fair in St. Louis in 1904. The elephant has always been considered a Ceylonese symbol; it is seen on their national arms and used in their flags, though not on their present one; it has been placed as a trademark on their products; and, moreover, most of the elephants in our museums have come from Ceylon—or India nearby. The African species has invariably sickened and died in captivity, while the Ceylonese type has proved to be the most intelligent, tractable, and receptive to training of various kinds.

The youthful-looking elephant on the finial of the Jumbo demi-tasse spoon is a sure-fire stealer of the show with his waggish, contagious grin, his snout up and mouth open, and his right foot resting with a histrionic pose on a stone beside an overturned forest tree. It must have been a whimsy of the artist to place at Jumbo's rear a budded floral stem which might be mistaken for his tail. The grotesquerie somehow resembles a lion's tail. In his present stance, so suggestive of a heraldic pose, we may thus behold the elephant rampant.

The bowl of this spoon pictures the Ceylon government pavillion at the St. Louis Fair. The embossed edifice adheres in general details to the type of architecture prevalent in this Indian Ocean island.

The handle-shaft is unornamented except for a reeding along the periphery. A four-petaled flower is tucked into the constricted waist between the shaft and nave.

The reverse side of spoon is barren of trademark or decor. Length is 4⅛ inches.

No. 104 MOUNT VERNON
No. 138 WASHINGTON'S MANSION

The original house at Mount Vernon was burned in 1739, and the present structure erected almost on the same site, by Lawrence Washington, in 1744. On the death of his brother and niece, George Washington acquired the estate and gradually imparted to it that atmosphere of domesticity, well-being, and largess that it still retains. It is said that Washington's dinner table was never without its visitors. Whether friend or stranger, every guest was made welcome.

After the deaths of the immediate family, the house fell into a slow decline. A half-century later it was badly in need of repairs. Then a campaign, organized by a group of patriotic women in 1853, raised a fund of two hundred thousand dollars to buy the estate and preserve it as a national museum for posterity. It is interesting to note that one of the initial promoters of this movement was the invalid Miss Pamela Cunningham, descendant of a prominent Tory family during the Revolution. Edward Everett, a famous lecturer of his day, presented such an effective eulogy of Washington on his platform tour around the country that record-breaking audiences came to hear him, and ninety-six thousand dollars were raised by this one means alone.

Owing to the simplicity of its colonial design, the symmetry of its chaste proportions, and the sentiments associated with the very name, the Mount Vernon spoon with its slender, ovoidal bowl and lancet-tipped handle is an exquisite treasure.

The bowl and handle are both barren of ornamentation as far as the caput. Then, in the widened crown we are given a miniature view of Mount Vernon from a southeasterly perspective. Along the slightly convexed periphery runs the wording: "Washington's Mansion" above, and "Mt. Vernon, Va." below the picture, thus focusing our attention as definitely as a tableau framed between curtains and footlights.

The east or river front, the one most frequently pictured, is shown here in its entirety. The imposing porch, measuring ninety-five feet in length and forty in width, is supported by eight square two-story columns, and is surmounted by a balustrade of lattice pattern with ornate turnings. Only a side door and five windows are visible on this front, the other apertures being shadowed. Considerable imagination must be used if one is to see the flagstone pavement clearly. On the hipped roof a distinctive cupola stands in the center of the ridge-pole, flanked on both ends by chimneys. Although dormer windows appear on every side of the roof, we have an unobstructed view of only one, that on the south slope.

The atmosphere of the Colonial period is nowhere better preserved than at Mount Vernon, and the spirit of the great Washington still seems to be hovering over the place. The visitor soon senses a feeling of heightened contact with the man who was "first in peace" and "first in the hearts of his countrymen" during a leisurely walk amid these quiet surroundings only sixteen miles away from the hubbub of the national capital. Owen Wister has most ably conveyed this feeling in these words: "Everything, every object, every corner and step, seems to bring him close. Turn into his garden and look at the walls and walks he planned, the box hedges, the trees, the flower beds, the great order and the great sweetness everywhere. You may spend an hour, you may spend a day, wandering, sitting, feeling this gentle power of the place; you may come back another time, it meets you, you cannot dispel it by familiarity."

Made by the Watson Company, the Mount Vernon spoon is 5 inches in length.

The Washington Mansion spoon gives practically the same view of this historic home as that exhibited on the first spoon, though transposed here to the bowl. There was an infinitude of souvenir spoons dealing with Washington and his home put out during the nineties of the last century and well into this one, because the mansion on the Potomac was long the number-one attraction of tourists, all of whom, if they came near the city of Washington, felt it a patriotic duty to visit Mount Vernon. In fact, there was one silver concern called the Mount Vernon Co., which specialized in making souvenir spoons on the "Father of His Country," though it is now long defunct.

This last spoon is fashioned in the best of Colonial traditions, with its acuminate-tipped bowl and its handle lines showing a pure Chippendale influence. It would have felt at home among the other pieces of flat silverware on the Washington table.

Pressed by the R. Wallace & Sons Mfg. Co.   Length, 5¾ inches.

No. 105 MARION GATEWAY

The Rufus Daggetts were going home, their destination roughly splotched in large, green lettering over their prairie-schooner. On one side was daubed "Back to God's Country," and on the other, "Back to Indiana."

The Daggetts had had all their illusions shattered in the western country by a rain of misfortunes in the guise of grasshoppers, cyclones, dust storms, cloudbursts, blizzards, blights, and sundry maladies of the flesh. One of their four children had sickened and died in the hostile environment.

They couldn't even sell the homestead. All they had besides the wagon and mules was a bird-dog, a few dollars in change, and high hopes of buying back their old farm near Emerald Grove, Indiana.

They camped along the way in the wide, open spaces, where they could cook their own meals and the mules could forage for themselves. If they ventured to pitch camp in a village, they were looked upon rather suspiciously as gypsies, and the constable sternly bade them move outside the village limits. Sometimes a farmer, scenting the smoke of their campfire, warned them not to trespass for wood on his premises. Occasionally a farmer's wife, feeling compassion for the children, handed out milk, eggs, or even a chicken to the campers.

At nights around the smouldering embers of the campfire the Daggetts mulled over their prospects of getting back the old farm, which they had sold to Joinville Haines, a former suitor for the hand of Mrs. Daggett. They were sure that Joinville Haines, being a kind-hearted, well-to-do man, would let them buy the old place back and pay for it as they could.

At a small town in Missouri, Daggett took the older children to see a performance of *Uncle Tom's Cabin* at the local Opera House, while Mrs. Daggett remained in camp with Bobbie, the youngest child, and Spot, the bird-dog. On the way back from the show, Daggett discovered to his sorrow that he had been relieved of his pocketbook. He now had less than five dollars in cash, and his destination still lay two hundred and fifty miles ahead.

On the road between St. Louis and Vincennes, with only a dollar and twenty cents left, Daggett very reluctantly had to sell the bird-dog. Of course, the children cried themselves sick over the loss of their faithful pet, but the price he brought meant the difference between starvation and survival for the Daggetts. Their hegira would soon be over, and they would be back among friendly faces—in God's country, old Indiana.

The scenery was becoming familiar to them—the hills, creeks, roads, and bridges. Their hearts pulsed faster as they approached Emerald Grove. They stopped just short of the old homestead for their last encampment. All through the night they heard a low, mysterious, chugging sound, inexplicably strange to their ears.

At the first peep of dawn the next morning, before the children were awake, Daggett and his wife climbed to the hilltop for a first view of the old homestead. What they saw brought an involuntary outburst of tears from Mrs. Daggett, while her husband stared, stonily silent, at the panorama before them.

"There was no farm! There was no cottage—no barn—no vineclad well house! All had been swept from the face of the earth as if by the besom of destruction. In their place were long, low, ugly brick buildings, with tin roofs; great tanks; tall towers of structural steel, a huge brick chimney, from which jetty smoke rolled forth; several rows of newly painted laborers' quarters; a railroad track and cars.

" 'Oil!' broke out Daggett, hoarsely, at last. 'They've struck oil!' "

This poignant piece of ironic tragedy, which I have briefly sketched here from the story, "Back to Indiana," by Elmore Elliott Peake, and published originally in 1905 in *Harper's Magazine*, might easily have been based on actual facts, so true to form were such incidents in many Indiana towns during the last two decades of the nineteenth century.

Not the least of these Hoosier towns to enjoy more than an equitable share of the transient boom was Marion, once dubbed the Queen City of that area which flourished so regally during the brief, dazzling period of spouting gas and oil wells.

Marion, founded in 1831, was named in honor of General Francis Marion, the Swamp Fox of the Carolinas during the Revolution. It became the county seat of Grant County, and grew slowly, having a few business houses clustered around the courthouse square, and hitching posts up and down its four streets to accommodate the farmers who constituted the chief source of trade in the small town.

The phenomenal growth of the city ended as abruptly as it started. The gas wells were not capped, and the gas soon blew itself to Kingdom Come. Then oil was discovered, and Marion experienced another period of wild-cat expansion. But the oil gave out more quickly than the gas had.

The city went into a doddering slump. Something had to be done or else the town would shrink back into its original four streets hugging the county courthouse. Enterprising business men in a rousing oratorical campaign raised more than one hundred thousand dollars to bring more mills and factories to Marion. Their promoting slogan was, that a city could prosper without gas and oil wells. And the slogan succeeded. Today Marion has more industries than in the flush era of gas and oil.

The gateway engraved in the gold-oxidized bowl of the Marion spoon was the entrance to a home established originally, in 1888, for aged veterans of the Civil War. After the passing of the Union veterans, the home was converted in 1921 into a sanctuary for the neuro-psychiatric victims of the First World War. Today this hospital houses nearly two thousand patients, about one-fourth of whom are veterans of the Second World War. It is expected that the number of these younger men will perceptibly increase with time.

This institution, covering an area of two hundred and ninety-nine acres and consisting of more than one hundred buildings, is noted for its remarkable success in rehabilitating the mentally-ill veterans, three out of every four now admitted being discharged within a year.

The newest techniques of treatment are employed. Electric and insulin shock treatments are widely used to redintegrate loss of mental balance. A narco-synthetic serum is often administered to the brooding, introvert type of person to compel him to talk easily and truthfully about his troubles. Pre-frontal lobotomies are often necessary operations to disconnect associational tissues of the brain.

Forms of physical therapy are popular. Nearly one hundred thousand of these are given each year. Occupational therapy is helpful in many cases to remove the patient's thoughts from his own distraught condition. Eating, reading, and recreational habits of each patient are analyzed, and changes of these often prove to have beneficial results. Doctors, nurses, psychiatrists, psychologists, sociologists, teachers and preachers all pool their expert knowledge and best efforts, in order to return as many as possible of the maladjusted veterans to society within the quickest possible time. In all, more than eleven hundred persons are employed at the hospital, which is worthy of our plaudits for rendering a new and distinctly-needed service to mankind.

The handle of the Marion Gateway spoon shows definite French Renaissance influences of the Francis the First era. A product of the Shepard Mfg. Co., the spoon measures 5¾ inches in length. Used through the courtesy of its owners, Mr. and Mrs. John Harland Downing, Marion, Indiana.

No. 106 EARLY MIAMI

How different from anything we would expect today in views of modernistic Miami is this orange spoon picturing scenes associated entirely with the Miami of the past! How quaint are the buildings here portrayed, every one of which has long since disappeared or been concealed by conversion to other purposes than originally designed! Nevertheless, these old landmarks are highly interesting, and serve to show the tourist of today that this mecca of sunshine-seekers is a little older than the latest mushrooms in the cow pastures back home.

Beginning in one section of the nave and running into a second is the picturesque old Cape Florida Light, the first building of any consequence in the region of Miami. It was erected in 1826 on the southern tip of Biscayne Key, offshore from what is now Matheson Hammock Park. The site had once been used as an Indian burial mound. The lighthouse stood peacefully amid its lonely surroundings until it was attacked in 1836 during the Seminole War.

John W. B. Thompson and his negro servant were working in a garden when they were surprised by the war whoop of onrushing Indians. They scurried into the lighthouse, barricaded the door and windows, and climbed the staircase ascending to the belfry light. The savages set fire to the woodwork and destroyed all avenues of escape for the two men who were perched on the platform at the top of the tower. A barrel of crude oil used for servicing the light in the belfry was set on fire, and the heat from the flames roasted the two men so severely that the negro died as a result of the burns he had incurred. Thompson was rescued the next day by a ship that carried him to Key West, where he eventually recuperated.

Evidence has come to light recently from an old diary that there were other people in the lighthouse at this time, or possibly during a second attack a few months later. According to this source, a family by the name of Duke was warned by a friendly Indian of an impending attack on their home, which was situated on the south bank of the Miami River. The Dukes, with a small son and daughter, had always lived on the best of terms with the Seminoles, but the few neighbors in the vicinity persuaded them to accompany the group to the lighthouse. They were there when the attack occurred, and boarded the boat to Key West also. After a few weeks they returned to their home to find it untouched. The Indians, remembering past kindnesses, had left the house unharmed. The watch dog warmly welcomed them back.

In 1846 the old stone tower was replaced by a higher structure of brick. During the Civil War a Federal gunboat fired on the lighthouse and demolished the upper part. It was recapped and used until 1876, when it was abandoned for a new building closer to the shipping lane. During the Spanish-American War the Old Florida was occupied by the U. S. Signal Corps.

A close-up of the lighthouse, as seen on the spoon, shows the entrance and one window. This building, at a more distant perspective, appears also in the bowl of the Osceola Soffkee spoon, where a frame house stands a few yards away from the lighthouse.

Old Fort Dallas, in the upper part of the nave, was built in 1834 during the Seminole War at the mouth of the Miami River. The original wooden stockade was replaced by a stone structure in 1849, at which time it was made the headquarters for the laborers clearing a highway to Lake Okeechobee. After this it became, for a while, the courthouse for Dade County. Today the Daughters of the American Revolution have established their headquarters here.

In the caput there is an Indian purporting to be Chief Osceola. By all appearances the Indian is a true Seminole but lacking in all verisimilitude to the actual features of the famous chieftain.

On the reverse of the handle a royal palm extends through the shank. The Royal Palm Hotel, a long rambling frame building, runs through both sections of the nave. Built by Henry Flagler in 1896, it was long a fashionable hotel overlooking the waters near the mouth of the Miami River. When excavations were being made for the foundations of the hotel, workmen brought to light some sixty skeletons and a great number of artifacts, evidence that the site had once been an Indian encampment.

At the time that Flagler built his pretentious hotel—painted a vivid yellow—the adjacent land was being used for pasturage. The first cow had been shipped to the town shortly before this, and was such a curiosity that school was dismissed for the day so that the youngsters could witness the animal's arrival. After Flagler's death the hotel became dilapidated and, having lost all its fashionable clientele, was razed in 1930.

Halcyon Hall, shown on the reverse caput, is a unique structure that might not look out of place along the Thames or on the Rhine as a townhall. Indeed, the sobriquet, the White Palace, by which it was once familiarly known, is somewhat reminiscent of the White Tower of London. Twin turrets cap each corner, and dormers are visible all along the roof above the fourth floor. There is an imposing array of windows, offset walls, and balconies in this piece of Gothic architecture, so exceptional in design. It is a pity that it had to give way to the American mania for the strictly modern, being replaced in 1939 by just another one of those streamlined skyscrapers.

There is no trademark to indicate the maker of this spoon, which probably dates from around the turn of the century. Length, 5¼ inches.

No. 107 CHAMPLAIN

The French, like the English, began a half-century later than the Spaniards and Portuguese to think of planting their flags over New World territories. And more than a century passed before either of them was able to found a permanently successful settlement. The South American continent having already been preëmpted by the Iberian nations, the

French and English both cast eager eyes toward the northern continent for ventures in colonization.

For a justification of their claims to land in the western hemisphere, the French, too, had their traditions of discovery prior to Columbus. In 1488 Cousin, a merchant navigator from Dieppe, while trading in the Azores, was blown by a violent tempest as far west as America, where, in a tropical climate, his bark skirted the shoreline of a vast jungle interior, presumably Brazil, and sailed past the estuaries of a mighty flood-crested river. On board the vessel was a well-born Spanish seaman by the name of Pinzón, whose insubordinate behavior all during the trying trip caused him to be dismissed from the maritime service by Cousin as soon as they reached Dieppe once more. Pinzón, it is said, returned straightway to Spain, aroused interest in his story, and even hoped for the command of the Spanish expedition headed by Columbus four years later.

Whether true or not, this accidental discovery of America by the French is entirely plausible. For the same thing happened to other mariners, the most notable instance being that of Cabral, the Portuguese navigator who was plying for the Orient around the Cape of Good Hope in 1500 and, blown by adverse winds, came quite by accident upon the richly forested shores of Brazil, thus establishing Portuguese claims for eventual possession of that land.

Those hardy French stocks, the Normans, Bretons, and Basques, were already fishing for cod along the Newfoundland banks when the Cabots, on their exploratory voyage in 1497, found the designation for this region to be Bacalaos, the Basque name for codfish. In 1565 the French king, Charles IX, in a discussion with an envoy from Madrid, stated that French fishermen from Brittany had been catching codfish off the northern coast of North America for more than a hundred years, hence the origin of the name for Cape Breton Island.

In 1523 Francis I took into his employ a Florentine sea-rover, John Verrazzano, born of an illustrious family, but sometimes rated as a gentleman pirate of no mean skill. Verrazzano in his efforts to find a short-cut route to India sailed along the North American coast beginning at the Carolinas or Florida, where the land was full of trees yielding "most sweete savours, farre from the shore," to Long Island Sound and Narragansett Bay, at which place he inspected the harbors where New York and Newport now stand. He visited the rock-bound coasts of Maine and Newfoundland before he returned to Europe. The first to use the title of New France, Verrazzano achieved no tangible results for France or for himself from this voyage, and it is believed that the Spaniards eventually hanged him as a pirate.

Jacques Cartier, from 1534 to 1536, made two exploratory trips to the New World, traveling as far up the St. Lawrence as Montreal, which was then the site of an Indian village known as Hochelaga. Cartier spent the winter here, but the terrible cold cast a blight over his men who, having insufficient clothing and shelter and a none too plentiful supply of food, fell ready victims to a fatal scurvy. The disease decimated two-thirds of his men before a friendly Indian apprised them of a healing concoction brewed from the leaves of a balsam fir. They drank copious drafts of the brew and were quickly cured, but they had endured enough from the hostile climate and were glad to lift anchor and head homewards.

Twice more the French attempted to make settlements in the New World, both times within the present boundaries of the United States. A group of Huguenots under Admiral Coligny in 1562 constructed a fort on the shores of South Carolina, but menacing Indians soon drove them away. In 1564 the Huguenots tried another location, this time at Fort Caroline on the St. John's River in Florida. The Spaniards at St. Augustine were angered by this encroachment on what they deemed to be their domains; so, the Spanish commander, Pedro Menéndez, attacking the small French garrison, captured and shot every one of the Huguenots after their hands had been tied behind their backs, placing above their common grave this inscription, "Not as Frenchmen, but as heretics." A band of Frenchmen, in high dudgeon at this cowardly deed, sailed for Florida and showed themselves to be equally as bloodthirsty when they had captured the defenders of Fort Caroline by hanging every one of the Spaniards and nailing this cynical epitaph over their gibbets: "Not as Spaniards, but as traitors, robbers, and murderers."

The first successful French colonizer and to all practical purposes the "Father of New France" was Samuel de Champlain, a man who is, as Sedgwick says, "particularly interesting to Americans because he is a Frenchman with those qualities which a wayward English tradition denies to the French—patience, sobriety, calm self-control, and a complete absence of vanity." Totally absent in his nature were the sanguinary tendencies all too frequently found in the early explorers and conquistadors, and in all his dealings he never failed to show those warmer traits of humanity— tolerance, good will, and tenderness of heart—yet combined with courage, tenacity of will, and resourcefulness in action. He pursued his course undeviatingly for founding French power on a permanent basis in the New World, "never looking for ease or asking for profit, loved by the wild people of the forest, respected by the courtiers of the king and trusted by the close-fisted merchants of the maritime cities of France."

Information about Champlain's youth have been meagerly preserved. Born in 1567 at Brouage, a small but flourishing port on the Bay of Biscay, now made an inland village through roving tidal sands, he early learned the ways of the sea by accompanying his father, an officer in the navy on expeditions to and fro from the Atlantic to the Mediterranean. That he desired to follow in his father's footsteps may be deduced from this statement made late in life: "Among the most useful and excellent arts, navigation has always seemed to me to take the first place . . . By this art we acquire knowledge of various lands, countries, and kingdoms . . .

It is this art that from my childhood has lured me to expose myself almost all my life to the rude waves of the ocean."

His ambitions, however, were diverted to a soldier's career by the dispute that arose over the succession to the French throne, and in the Civil War that ensued, Champlain, good Catholic though he was, served six years in the armies of the Huguenot, Prince Henry of Navarre, believing firmly the Prince best represented French interests free of Spanish domination. At the conclusion of this struggle the successful Prince, now King, rewarded Champlain for his services by granting him a commission in the naval transports conveying the Spanish soldiery back to their native country.

The young mariner must have taken full advantage of his trips to Spain, for we soon find him engaged as a captain on a Spanish caravel bound for the West Indies. Two years later he approached the King armed with a complete report on his voyage as well as with plans for cutting a canal through the narrow neck of Panama, which would "thus shorten by more than fifteen hundred leagues" the passage from Europe to the treasure-rich lands of Asia.

Champlain's chance came, however, when he met up with Aymar de Chastes, governor of Dieppe, and Francois Gravé, Sieur de Pont, the latter generally known as Pontgravé. These men had been granted a monopoly on the fur trade of Canada by the King, and as they were casting about for some one to head their enterprise, Champlain was only too happy to accept such an offer. Together with Pontgravé and a well-picked crew in two small boats, he sailed from France early in March of 1603 on a reconnoitering expedition. Having passed the island of Anticosti, he steered his vessel up the St. Lawrence as far as the mouth of the Saguenay River. The Indians, members of the Algonquin tribe, welcomed the strangers cordially and prepared in their honor a savory banquet of steaks sliced from the haunches of bear, beaver, elk, and seal. The natives ate with fingers from wooden bowls, and to get rid of excessive grease, wiped their hands on their hair or on the backs of dogs. Peace pipes were smoked during the long harangues made to confirm the treaty of perpetual friendship between the French and the Algonquins. The parley concluded with a native dance accompanied by tribal chants and the rattling of Iroquois skulls over their shoulders.

After stopping at the site of Quebec and passing around the Lachine Rapids, Champlain turned in his course and hastened to reach France ahead of the autumnal storms. De Chastes had died during his absence and was replaced by the Sieur de Monts as the director of the fur-trading syndicate. De Monts, a shrewd business man of the Huguenot faith, accompanied Champlain on his second voyage in the spring of 1604. Thinking the valley of the St. Lawrence too cold, according to all reports he had heard, de Monts determined to make a settlement somewhere on the warmer east coast. Sailing past Sable Island and around the Bay of

Fundy, looking for a favorable site, they came upon an island at the mouth of the St. Croix River (in New Brunswick), wooded with birch and pine, and inaccessible of entrance on account of its high, rocky shores, except for one harbor. This place looked to be easily defendable. They disembarked and went to work at once, constructing a fort with cannon mounted on an interior platform, cabins, a communal kitchen and bakery, a blacksmith shop, storage bins, and even lodgings for those sailors who wished to come ashore—on future commercial voyages.

This done, Champlain and Pontrincourt, a leader in the fur-trade enterprise, began to make explorations down the coast visiting the shores of Maine and Massachusetts, finding forests rich in timber, fields of ripening Indian corn, and natives so full of fleas that the whites had to change clothing after conversing with them.

The summer and fall were pleasant enough, but a severe winter came early and stayed late. There were no springs or wells on the island; fresh water had to be brought from the mainland. Food, except for dried meat, was scarce, and an infectious mouth disease, which swelled the gums over the teeth, made it well nigh impossible for them to eat the little they had. Scurvy and pneumonia were so prevalent and malignant that thirty-five of the seventy-nine settlers died. It was a happy day when Pontgravé sailed into port the following May with a varied assortment of fresh foods.

De Monts, vowing he would never spend another winter on this desolate island, sought a more hospitable region for his headquarters by moving across the Bay of Fundy in August, and locating at Port Royal, now Annapolis, in the thickly pine-wooded land of Acadia. Most of the buildings had been brought along piecemeal, and these were quickly made serviceable. Some ground was cleared; vegetables were sown, and grains planted in time to be safely harvested.

Although Port Royal did not suit the colonists as the seat for a capital, they deemed it advisable to wait until they were convinced, by further explorations, as to which would be the best locality. Champlain and Pontrincourt contemplated a trip to Florida, but their travels were delayed by skirmishes with the Indians, bad winds, and a broken rudder. Turning around at Martha's Vineyard, they repaired to Port Royal for another grueling winter.

To make the time pass more quickly and pleasantly, Champlain created an "Order of Good Times," whereby each one of the fifteen men sitting at Pontrincourt's table was, by rotation, to become Grand Master for the day, his duties demanding not only that he furnish the food but that he also prepare and serve it. A sort of rivalry arose among the members of this Order, each vying to outdo the other for a most sumptuous dinner by planning the bill of fare several days in advance. "Thus did Pontrincourt's table groan," says Parkman, "beneath all the luxuries of the winter forest: flesh of moose, caribou, and deer, beaver, otter, and hare, bears and wildcats; with ducks, geese, grouse, and plover; sturgeon, too, and trout, and fish innumerable, speared through the ice of the 'Equille or drawn from the depths of the neighboring bay." An elaborate ceremony preceded and followed the feast. When the bell for the banquet rang, the Grand Master would enter the hall gravely bearing a napkin on his shoulder, the collar of the Order on his neck, and the staff of office in his uplifted hand. The assembled guests formed a processional and filed in decorously, not least among whom were many Indians of both sexes and all ages, eagerly awaiting a portion of the bread or cake as they squatted on the floor and grunted their approbation of every little morsel. In the evening the changing of the Grand Masters was another punctilious ceremony. Few men in the new colony were sick that winter.

Bad news arrived at Port Royal in May of 1607. The charter granting a monopoly in the fur trade to de Monts had been revoked by the king. There was nothing the colonists could do except withdraw, as the profits in fur had provided all the funds for the maintenance of Port Royal. As soon as the wheat crop was harvested, the Acadians took ship and departed for France.

Pontrincourt and Champlain refused to be disheartened by this recall. Carrying specimens of grains raised in Acadia and five brant goslings in their colorful plumage before Henry IV, they delighted the Monarch so greatly that he extended the fur monopoly to de Monts for another year.

By the middle of June, 1608, Champlain was escorting two ships into the mouth of the St. Lawrence River. At the point where the river becomes constricted after passing around the Island of Orleans the two vessels anchored, and Champlain began the building of Quebec, July the fourth, on the walnut-covered flats dominated by high cliffs rising in the rear to a height of three hundred and fifty feet. Champlain was now well acquainted with all the methods for laying out and building a town, and the inevitable planting of fruit trees and gardens soon followed.

A few weeks later, while spading in his garden, Champlain was surprised by a revelation whispered in his ear that a conspiracy was afoot to kill him and deliver the struggling settlement into the hands of Basque Spaniards. Acting quickly, he induced the four conspirators, through intermediaries, to board a vessel for some social refreshments, and there they were arrested. Pontgravé banished three of them to France and hanged the ringleader.

The next summer Champlain accompanied three hundred warriors of the Algonquin and Huron tribes, who were going on the warpath against their hereditary enemies, the Iroquois, then dwelling in and controlling the rich valleys of upper New York State. This trip provided Champlain with an excellent means for exploring the country to the south, which territory, since it was possessed by strongly entrenched enemies, could not otherwise have been safely penetrated.

412

The canoes glided down the Richelieu River past sinuous islands rich in verdure, the Green Mountains peering up on the left and the Adirondacks on the right, until they reached the broad expanses of that lake, which ever since has paid honor to Champlain in bearing his name. Parkman pictures a sunset scene on the lake shores as Champlain saw it more than three centuries ago: "The glow of the vanished sun behind the western mountains, darkly piled in mist and shadow along the sky; near at hand, the dead pine, mighty in decay, stretching its ragged arms athwart the burning heaven, the crow perched on its top like an image carved in jet, and aloft, the nighthawk circling in his flight, and, with a strange whirring sound diving through the air each moment for the insects he makes his prey."

Near Ticonderoga, at the northern tip of Lake George, members of the two hostile Indian bands sighted each other almost at the same time. As dusk was deepening over the lake, the Iroquois hastily retreated from the waters to the adjacent forests, where they worked feverishly over the night to erect a barricade, all the while casting taunts and imprecations at Champlain's allies, who remained singing and dancing all night in their fragile canoes lashed fast to the tree-roots on shore.

The next morning the allies advanced, with Champlain and two other Frenchmen well out in front. "Champlain wore the doublet and long hose then in vogue. Over the doublet he buckled on a breastplate, and probably a back-piece, while his thighs were protected by cuisses of steel, and his head by a plumed casque. Across his shoulder hung the strap of his bandoleer, or ammunition-box; at his side was his sword, and in his hand his arquebus, which he had loaded with four balls."

The Iroquois emerged from their barricade and advanced about thirty paces before they paused to level their bows and arrows in aim. The allies loudly called upon the Frenchmen to use their magic weapons. Champlain took deliberate aim and while the arrows rained harmlessly around him, the discharge of his musket soon despatched two Indian chiefs. The Iroquois, seeing their arrows were ineffectual against the onslaught of such thundering firearms, fled in dismay. The allies hotly pursued them, killing quite a few and taking several prisoners.

The overwhelming triumph of the Algonquins and Hurons led them to perpetrate excessive cruelties on their prisoners. One of these poor wretches was so abused by having his fingernails plucked out, the tendons torn out of his wrists, his flesh seared by torches, and hot rosin poured on his head, that Champlain insisted on ending his misery with a bullet through the head. Even after the man was dead, his enemies lopped off his extremities and ripped out his entrails. Hacking his heart into small pieces, they even tried to force these gruesome tidbits down the throats of the other prisoners.

During the next few years Champlain devoted all his energies in strengthening his fortifications at Quebec, in cementing alliances with the

Indians north and west of that slowly-growing town, and in exploring the huge lakes and forests that lay west of the St. Lawrence Basin. On May 29, 1611, he started the construction of a stockade on the present site of Montreal, and in 1613 he made plans for a city to be built at Ottawa. On one of his frequent trips to France he contracted a marriage with Hélène Boullé, a girl of twelve who, because of her extreme youth, remained in her father's house till she was twenty-two, at which age she joined her husband in Quebec. Finding life in the wilderness distasteful, she returned to Paris after four years and spent the rest of her life there in saintly works of charity. The marriage was childless, and after her husband's death, Madame Champlain entered a convent.

In 1620 Champlain became the Lieutenant Governor of Canada. The following years were a period of struggle and uncertainty. In 1628 the English attempted to capture Quebec but were valiantly beaten off by the small French garrison. The English, however, returned the next year and, seizing the French food ships on the river, forced the city to capitulate rather than starve. Champlain was taken to England as a prisoner, but when Quebec and Acadia were restored by the peace treaty of 1633 to French rule, the indomitable old leader promptly came back bearing the title of Governor. In this capacity he encouraged the migration of entire families—husbands, wives, and children—to the Canadian wilderness. His many bitter experiences as a colonizer had taught him that no settlement could thrive without permanently established families, above all, those inclined toward agricultural pursuits. At the time of his death, on Christmas Day of 1635, New France was an unquestioned reality, with her roots thrust deeply into the virgin soil of the New World.

The Champlain spoon, of demi-tasse size, exhibits the great colonizer standing proudly erect on the finial-like caput, one foot forward, his plumed cap held in his right hand and his sword gripped firmly in his left. Down through the shaft runs his name and the date, 1609. On the reverse side of the shaft appears the name of Burlington, Vermont, the largest city and most flourishing port on Lake Champlain today.

This spoon, showing the earliest of the three trademarks used by the Robbins Company, of Attleboro, Massachusetts, is slenderly built, and four inches in length.

No. 109 TWO SALMON
No. 111 MOUNT HOOD

There could not be two spoons more disparate in handle design than these, although the bowls, both portraying Mount Hood, are almost identical except for unimportant details. The Mount Hood handle is rococo in general pattern, with definite Victorian influences obvious in the charming serpentine curves, elaborate scrolls around border and bonnet,

414

and pictorial fullness of finish. There is something indigenous about the handle of the Salmon spoon that leads me to suggest a native Indian influence, entirely relevant in this case.

Mount Hood, 11,932 feet high according to the spoons but a few hundred feet less than that figure today on account of erosion and glaciation, is the highest peak in Oregon and stands out because there are no rival peaks to mar its fine perspective. Lying forty-five miles from Portland, it is Oregon's chief tourist attraction.

The Hood River Indians and the Clackamas were the two main tribes dwelling in this region prior to the white man's arrival. The Hood River (or "canoe") Indians lived in apartment-like lodges constructed out of roughly-split cedar logs. Sometimes as many as fifteen or twenty families resided under one roof, having one main kitchen and dining room in common near the center. Beds were ranged along the walls on either side behind reeded curtains with a narrow corridor running between these private compartments.

The principal source of food was the Chinook or quinnat salmon which were scooped into wicker nets out of the Hood River, cleaned, cut into strips, hung on a framework to dry in the sun, pounded into a pulpy mash, and stored away in hampers for a reserve supply sometimes lasting untainted for several seasons.

Most of the salmon were caught in the spring—the time when these game fish begin their epic migration in gigantic silvery hordes, flashing, fighting, and leaping upstream in an inherent urge to gain the upper reaches of their spawning grounds in the quiet pools near the mouths of countless creeks and mountain freshets which pour into the rivers of the Northwest. No obstacle seems to deter their progress, as they push madly forward stemming currents, surmounting waterfalls, splashing through shallows, darting through cascades of rocks, plowing through whirlpool rapids, never resting on the journey and never veering in their course. So great is their exhilaration that they will keep on leaping and leaping to vault an unattainable height till overcome by death in the futile struggle. Instinctively they return, usually in pairs, to the same native haunts where they were spawned, sometimes after a journey of from two to four thousand miles.

The baby salmon and grilse feed on algae, worms, and slugs near the bottom of their native stamping ground till they are able to buck the stronger currents of midstreams. After two years they begin to move toward the sea, where they frolic for three or four years before they attempt to return inland. By this time the Chinook salmon has attained a weight of fifteen or twenty pounds. He will continue to grow, if he lives to the ripe old age of seven or eight, till he reaches the tremendous weight of a hundred pounds. The pink salmon, the smallest of the species, seldom exceeds five pounds.

Most of the early Indian wars in the Hood River region were occasioned by infringements on fishing rights and the trespassings of other Indians on the fishing grounds of the two local tribes. The "horse Indians" lived farther inland along the tributaries of the Columbia River. They depended for a livelihood chiefly on forest game, and carried on a thriving trade with the "canoe Indians." The Clackamas or "horse Indians" protected themselves against marauders by going underground. They built subterranean wigwams of wood, conical cells securely bolstered against cave-ins by a well-grooved brace of girders.

The first white men to perceive the summit of Mount Hood were the sailors on a flagship of the British navy in 1792. The captain of the ship named the peak in honor of his commander, Rear-Admiral Samuel Hood. The first Americans to sight Mount Hood were members of the Lewis and Clark expedition in 1805. They called it the Falls Mountain, a name suggested by the great falls of the Columbia River, which they had just passed.

The first white men known to reach the summit of the mountain were a group of hikers in the summer of 1857. A loop highway was completed and formally opened for the motoring public in 1926.

The handle of the Two Salmon spoon simulates a canoe paddle, around the flattened part of which is twisted a fish line. The hook at the end of this line has apparently snagged both salmon. The Two Salmon spoon was produced by the Alvin Corporation. It has been used here through the courtesy of its owner, Mrs. Gordon Scheimer. Length of spoon is 4¼ inches.

The Mount Hood spoon, which belongs to the wave-handle state seal series, was put out by the Shepard Manufacturing Company. It exhibits, in addition to the state seal and the date (1859) of Oregon's admission to the Union, an amusing sidelight on the fickle nature of Oregonian weather—an upright frog holding an umbrella over his head. Length, 5½ inches.

No. 110 SANTA MARIA
No. 136 THE VOYAGER
No. 143 LANDFALL OF COLUMBUS
No. 147 RETURN OF COLUMBUS

Nothing can stay the onward march of an idea implicitly believed. For two decades Columbus had been gathering material evidence tending to confirm his belief that by sailing due westward from Europe he could reach Asia. His open, inquiring mind drank in every sop of knowledge nourishing that dream. The time was ripe for the discovery of a new world lying beyond the western horizons of the Atlantic Ocean. He had read the accounts of Marco Polo and Sir John Mandeville concerning the marvels of the East, and believed they were more than entertaining fabrications. He had talked with seasoned sailors who vowed that the world was a rounded sphere. He had probably seen a copy of d'Ailly's *Imago Mundi,* printed in 1480, ascribing a global shape to the earth, and most certainly had read a letter addressed by the Florentine geographer, Paolo Toscanelli, to Fernando Martinez of Lisbon, in which Toscanelli's views were set forth in these terms: "Let it not create wonder that a westerly region is assigned for the country of spices, which have always been understood to grow in the East; for those who sail west will find those lands in the West, and those who sail East will find the same places in the East." Immediately upon reading this straightforward letter, Columbus engaged in a correspondence with Toscanelli, and was rewarded by the receipt of a nautical chart in which the Florentine had placed the island of Antillia some five to six hundred leagues west from Gibraltar. The land of Antillia was already marked, before the time of Toscanelli, on the Weimar Map of 1424, the Genoa Map of 1434, and the Florentine Map of 1436. Martin Behaim, of Nuremberg, also exhibited in Lisbon in the early part of 1492 a globe showing Antillia, as well as Brazil, though this latter place is made to be only one of the conjectural islands of Hesperides celebrated in Greek mythology.

Frequent allusion is found in the writings of the ancients to a "great island to the west." Theopompus, a Greek historian of the fourth century before Christ, mentions in a conversation between Silenus and Midas a "great continent beyond the Atlantic, larger than Asia, Europe, and Libya together." Aelian, a Roman author, repeats this assertion one hundred years later. Plato and Aristotle both refer to the lost continent of Atlantis. Diodurus Siculus, a Greek author flourishing in the island of Sicily a century before Christ, speaks in his *Bibliotheca Historica* of a "very great island in the vast ocean, many days' sail from Libya westward." And he continues: "The soil is very productive. It is diversified with mountains and pleasant vales, and the towns are adorned with stately buildings." And he describes how Phoenician sailors, plying to and forth from their established port of Gades (Cadiz) in Spain, were driven far westward upon the ocean by a fierce tempest of many days' duration till they came upon this fruitful country abounding in rich orchards, impenetrable forests, and endless rivers of water. Plutarch, the best of Greek biographers, living from 46 to 126 A.D., also speaks of this "great continent beyond the ocean."

It would be sciolistic on our part to believe that the ancients knew nothing about the nature of this world. Aristarchus of Samos discovered that the planets revolve around the sun. Claudius Ptolemy of Alexandria, although he erroneously believed that the sun moved and the earth remained stationary, yet rightly taught that the world had a global form. Eratosthenes, another Graeco-Egyptian, advanced cartography greatly not merely by indicating latitude and longitude with a cross-netting of lines on maps, but, also by his accurate computations of distance; he missed the true diameter of the earth by only fifty miles. Some early cartographers placed Atlantis in widely varying outlines on their maps in the western ocean. Certainly the ancient Egyptians must have had some intimate knowledge of the western hemisphere, since the Pyramid of the Sun in Mexico occupies a very unusual site: a straight line passing over both this pyramid and the Great Pyramid of Egypt touches the greatest amount of water on the surface of the northern hemisphere. This could not have happened by accident or mere coincidence.

There are many claims to the discovery of America prior to the time of Columbus. Most of these are purely legendary and present no shred of conclusive evidence. Whether Columbus had ever heard or read about any of these voyages it is difficult to ascertain, yet it is worth our while to mention the claims of American discoveries by the Chinaman Fou Sang in 499 A.D., the Norseman Leif Erikson in 1000, the Arab Ebn-al-Ouardi in 1146, and the Welsh prince Madoc in 1170, the Zeno brothers of Venice in 1380, Cortereal the Portuguese in 1463, Szkolny the Pole in Danish service in 1476, Martin Behaim the German in Portuguese service in 1483, and Cousin the Frenchman from Dieppe in 1488. Most of these claims sound pretty fictitious, and were evidently brought forward to bolster national pride after Columbus and later navigators had actually demonstrated the existence of the Western World. On the other hand, there is no reason for declaring those early voyages impossible. Dozens of Chinese junks have been blown by storms to our shores within the last century. Perhaps many a European vessel, likewise driven to America before the time of Columbus, was only too glad to venture back toward friendly native shores.

For only one group among the early navigators is there any concrete material evidence to substantiate their claims of discovery. Through the years an accumulation of data seems to prove the Norsemen visited our shores many times and actually attempted temporary settlements. It would be most logical to surmise that, as they had discovered Iceland and Greenland, they would inevitably have sailed on and touched the North American mainland lying so close to the shores of Greenland. That Leif Erikson's colony was known in Europe as far south as Rome is verified by the fact that Pope Paschal II appointed Erik Uppsi in 1112 to be bishop of Iceland, Greenland, and Vinland. Adam of Bremen in 1073 wrote in a book concerning the Christian religion in the North of Europe that besides the Scandanavian countries of Sweden, Norway, Denmark, Iceland, and Greenland "there is still another region, which has been visited by many, lying in the Ocean Sea (the Atlantic), which is called Vinland, because vines grow there spontaneously, producing very good wine; corn likewise springs up there without being sown . . . This we know not by fabulous conjecture, but from positive statements of the Danes."

The Icelandic sagas pertaining to Vinland, which John Fiske calls "quiet and sober narrative," bear all the earmarks of historical veracity

418

shorn of any fictional devices: the profusion of grapes; the abundance of foxes, bears, salmon and halibut; the "self-sown fields of wheat" (Indian corn); the torrid summers and mild winters; the scrawny Skraelings (small Indians in comparison with the tall Norsemen), who were swarthy of complexion and had broad cheek-bones and black, stringy hair; the murdered Thorbrand lying with a "flat stone sticking in his head" (the weapon being no doubt a tomahawk), and the attack of the Skraelings who in their skinboats "came up the river in a swarm yelling at the top of their voices."

A startling likeness of names to Vinland can be detected in Martha's Vineyard and Martin's Vineyard. The old Norse word *holl* for hill still survives in Powder Hole, Quick's Hole, Holmes' Hole, Butler's Hole, and Wood's Hole. An elderly gentleman of the latter place could explain this curious corruption of the word for hill only by saying that he "always understood that it came from the Indians." From what source had the Indians acquired this word if not from the Norsemen?

The Paul Knutson expedition, composed of both Norwegians and Swedes, whose explorations lasted from 1355 to 1364, seems to have left definite tokens of its different camp-sites, numerous enough to indicate the itinerary of a journey taken more than a thousand miles inland. Among these indicia may be noted the Kensington Stone, the runic inscriptions of which remained a mystery for so long a time; the Viking grave at Lake Nipigon; the Climax fire-steel; the Viking sword at Ulen; and a great number of axes, hatchets, spears, and mooring stones in widely separated places, south of Lake Winnipeg and west of Lake Nipigon. The old round tower at Newport, once thought to have been the remains of an early New England mill, is now regarded in all detail as an authentic Viking structure of the Middles Ages. The Arctic Expedition of Donald MacMillan in the summer of 1925, along the Labrador coastline near the fifty-sixth parallel of north latitude, found ruins that indicated clearly the region had once been explored by Viking adventurers. Another evidence that the Vikings had penetrated far into the interior of North America survived in the physical features of certain Indian tribes, notably the Mandans, whose predominantly light complexions, blue eyes, and fair hair were viewed with wonder by early French explorers.

The Norsemen abandoned Vinland for several reasons. They were attacked constantly by the ferocious Skraelings, and gunpowder not having yet been invented, their weapons of defense were in no wise superior to those of their assailants. They were also at a disadvantage in the matter of numbers; perhaps at no time did their strength ever exceed a hundred and fifty persons, including women and children. The perils of travel on stormy seas, the frequent loss of ships, and the great distances without benefit of compass or improved piloting devices discouraged a continuance of voyages to Vinland. Even the colony of Greenland, once a flourishing community of from six to seven thousand souls, was abandoned. The sparsity of population in all the Scandinavian countries precluded any necessity on the part of these peoples to migrate. Indeed, all during the Middle Ages the eyes and minds of Europeans were turned eastward, not westward. Not until the fall of Constantinople to the Turks in 1453, and the epochal voyages of the Portuguese around Africa to India did the desire to traverse the Ocean Sea rise to a feverish temperature. People were hungry for the coffee, tea, sugar, pepper, and spices which had been seeping into Europe, and though this mere trickle had been stopped, Europeans could not forget these things once they had acquired a taste for them. Courtly ladies and gentlemen yearned for the silks, laces, linens, pearls, golden ornaments, and other finery once obtainable from the East. How to get them now was the great problem.

A spirit of discovery was in the air. Columbus caught this infectious spirit and was obsessed by it for eighteen years before he succeeded in becoming an "admiral of the Ocean Sea." There are two lines of thought regarding the real objective of Columbus' first voyage. Was he looking for Asia or was he expecting to find a New World? On the surface, he was obviously searching for the Indies. He had to make it appear so anyway, in order to get a hearing at the courts of Castile and Portugal. The lure of the East and possession of its profitable trade would command the attention of any monarch. How could an unknown adventurer hope to persuade the Spanish sovereigns to finance an expedition in search of lands inhabited by ferocious, ignorant savages, barren of riches, and devoid of commercial profits? All evidence points out that Columbus was not interested in the Orient. He did not even engage himself for any trips down the coast of Africa, but he did manage to travel as far north as Iceland, as we are told by Columbus himself in later life. "In the month of February and in the year 1477 I navigated as far as the Island of Thule (Iceland) a hundred leagues. And to this island which is as large as England, the English, especially those of Bristol, go with merchandise; and when I was there the sea was not frozen over, although there were high tides—so much so that in some parts the sea rose twenty-five brazas (arm-lengths) and went down as much as twice during the day." His son and biographer, Fernando Colombo, relates specifically that his father on this trip sailed three hundred miles west of Iceland—for what reason we do not learn. Now it is obvious that Columbus learned a great deal from this voyage: first that the ocean freezes over in this high latitude; second, that the ocean is much rougher in the north around Iceland than farther south, and west from Portugal; and third, he verified the tales of Norse discoveries of lands to the west. This latter fact is not mentioned, but without such an ulterior purpose for making the voyage in mind, Columbus' trip to Iceland would become a schoolboy's feckless jaunt.

There are other very good reasons which lead us to believe that Columbus set out primarily to find a new continent other than Asia. In the Capitulation or contract that he signed with the Spanish monarchs,

420

there is one stipulation making him governor of all the lands that he discovered. Would he be foolish enough to reckon without the Great Chans, or the rulers of India, Cipango, and Cathay? Would they allow him to land peacefully on their shores and take possession of large hunks of their territory? Evidently he was convinced that the islands or continent directly to the west of Spain and Portugal were inhabited by half-savage, primitive peoples. The fact that the very first thing he did as soon as he disembarked on the new lands discovered during his first voyage was to kneel and take possession of the territory in the name of the King and Queen of Spain gives proof of his belief that he had found land outside the dominions of any established rulers. Had he landed upon the shores of England or France, would he have done the same? Common sense compels us to believe otherwise. He was simply taking possession of unclaimed territory, sparsely inhabited by people as barbaric or savage as the natives found along the coast of Africa.

Testimonials had also been made to Columbus by old sea dogs about strange bits of flotsam that had been seen around the Azores. Canes, probably of the bamboo plant, unlike anything known in Africa and with jointed sections large enough to hold a gallon of wine had frequently washed up on shore. Bits of carved wood "ingeniously wrought" had been picked up by a Portuguese mariner. But the strangest kind of physical proof borne in by the Gulf Stream current was two dead bodies, with facial features and coloration unlike either Europeans or Chinamen— the latter were not entirely unknown to experienced navigators. So far as Columbus could make out, the characteristics of these two stray corpses corresponded closely to the descriptions given of the natives encountered by the Norsemen in their "New World" adventures.

The story of Columbus prior to his embarkation at Palos, Spain, on his famous voyage of discovery reads like a crossword-puzzle, the parts of which do not always dovetail. It is wiser to pass over this period briefly without any comment that would give rise to argument. The time of his birth is uncertain. The year is given variously as 1436, 1446, 1451, or 1453. The place of his birth is also uncertain, though most biographers now let him be cradled at Genoa, Italy. It is puzzling, however, to learn that Columbus did not speak or write Italian. Even in letters written to a bank in Genoa, all communications back and forth were in Castilian Spanish. Considerable evidence has been adduced by recent scholars lending weight to the belief that he was of Spanish-Jewish descent. And no good reason can be given for his change of name from Cristoforo Colombo to Cristóbal Colón. His marriage (or marriages) remain shrouded in mist. His whereabouts till he turned up at the courts of Portugal and Spain could be anybody's guess. His agreements with various backers of his enterprise and with the Pinzón brothers, his fellow navigators, have never been clearly explained.

421

The first voyage of Columbus was made under the most favorable circumstances of weather. The trip which began on Friday, August 3, 1492, was held up for three weeks at Gomera, one of the Canary Islands, to make repairs on the rudder of the Pinta, the caravel under the command of Martin Alonzo Pinzón. The Niña, in charge of Martin's brother, Vicente Yañes, was changed from lateen to square-rigged sails to accelerate her speed. From September 6th till the dawn of October 12th the three vessels journeyed westward without sight of land, but with occasional evidences in the guise of birds, "large patches of herbs and weeds," a live crab (a creature that always lives near land), dolphins, flying fish, and finally a thorny branch containing a few unwithered roseberries.

Many fair hopes had been raised and then shattered by various sailors who believed they saw the pinnacles of mountains in the cumuli of cloud banks. There was plenty of murmuring and muttering by those who thought the favorable winds bearing them westward would in turn be just as unfavorable in bearing them homeward. Columbus, as admiral of the enterprise, kept a faithful log of each day's progress, but he deliberately falsified the records to keep his apprehensive crewmen ignorant of the great distances they were leaving behind them. In fact, he kept two records, the right one in private for his own information, the false one given out openly to the sailors. Some of these records run as follows: sailed sixty leagues, reckoned as forty-eight; fifty-five leagues, reduced to forty-eight; thirty-one, cut down to twenty-four; sixty-three, lessened to forty-six. About the 9th of October it became apparent to the admiral that they would soon be approaching the place where Toscanelli's map had located *terra firma*. He now promised his disgruntled seamen that he would reverse his course if land were not sighted within three days.

A sanguine sea and a benign atmosphere spiced with the "fragrance of aromatic groves" bolstered the morale of the sailors considerably. Land birds were becoming more numerous. It became increasingly apparent from all signs that they were not too far from land. It would have been catastrophic if they had encountered one of those seasonal hurricanes, so unpredictable in its course and fury, to drive them back upon their tracks in this wilderness of water. But the voyage continued westward on a trip requiring far fewer days than that of many another sailing vessel during the next three hundred years.

It was Columbus himself who, standing on the castle of the poop deck of his flagship, the Santa Maria, first descried a faint light afar off in the distance. The moon was shining brightly overhead in the early morning hours of Friday, October 12, 1492. The dawning of that day was the beginning of a new era in the world's history. The mists of medieval ignorance were cleared away, as if by a parting of curtains, when the sun on that morning rose to reveal new horizons of knowledge, hitherto contained in the courageous vision of only one man, to all mankind.

The first spoon in this group on Columbus represents the Santa Maria, the Admiral's own flagship stamped in the bowl. No authentic picture or accurate description of the vessel exists. Samuel Eliot Morison, the only biographer of Columbus concerned about his experiences as a navigator, confesses that "nobody knows what Niña, Pinta and Santa Maria really looked like. Every picture of them is about 50 per cent fancy, and almost all are demonstrably inaccurate in some important respect." Several reproductions, based on the best information available, give us a good idea of the appearance of these vessels.

Most of the restorers of the Santa Maria have rebuilt this *nao* (a kind of ship "round and chunky like the carracks of Venice," not a *carabela*) on the knowledge from an entry in Columbus' *Journal* referring to a five-fathom depth drawn by the boat. One restorer has accordingly given her a tonnage of 120 to 130; another, of 150 to 200; and another of 120. And the term tonnage or *tonelada* in the Spanish of 1492 did not mean the weight or displacement but the number of tons or hogshead of wine that a vessel could stow away below decks. Morison thinks the Santa Maria had a capacity for holding less than 100 tons of wine. It was not built, like the Niña and Pinta, in Palos but in Galicia, a province in the northwestern corner of Spain. Columbus thought the vessel was clumsy, and expressed no affection for her. When the Santa Maria ran aground off the island of Hispaniola, Columbus abandoned her without any tear-shedding or fond farewells.

The Santa Maria spoon rises on a slender, part-way twisted stem to a splayed pedestal, on which the admiral's bust is mounted as a finial. Made by the Howard Sterling Company. Length, 4 inches.

The Voyager spoon, plain of bowl, has a handsomely designed handle. On the foliated scroll, resembling a plume, that mounts somewhat like a question-mark through the lower part of the handle, appears in small letters "Columbian Exposition." In the caput, the admiral, standing in a seafaring cloak, is anxiously peering through a spyglass. Perhaps the time is meant to be the early morning of October 12, 1492. On the reverse of handle, the foliations simulate waves, and the admiral's foot is resting on the shank of an anchor. Length, 4¼ inches.

The third spoon represents the landing of Columbus, and is reproduced in the bowl, from one of the best of many paintings on the subject, that by John Vanderlyn, done in 1840 and now hanging in the rotunda of the Capitol at Washington, D. C. Washington Irving best describes this momentous scene:

"As he approached the shore, Columbus, who was disposed for all kinds of agreeable impressions, was delighted with the purity and suavity of the atmosphere, the crystal transparency of the sea, and the extraordinary beauty of the vegetation. He beheld also fruits of an unknown kind upon the trees which overhung the shores. On landing he threw himself on his knees, kissed the earth and returned thanks to God with tears of joy.

423

His example was followed by the rest, whose hearts indeed overflowed with the same feelings of gratitude. Columbus then rising drew his sword, displayed the royal standard, and, assembling round him the two captains and the rest who had landed, he took solemn possession in the name of the Castilian sovereigns, giving the island the name of San Salvador. Having complied with the requisite forms and cermonies, he called upon all present to take the oath of obedience to him as admiral and viceroy, representing the persons of the sovereigns.

"The feelings of the crew now burst forth in the most extravagant transports. They had recently considered themselves devoted men hurrying forward to destruction; they now looked upon themselves as favorites of fortune and gave themselves up to the most unbounded joy. They thronged around the admiral with overflowing zeal, some embracing him, others kissing his hands. Those who had been most mutinous and turbulent during the voyage were now most devoted and enthusiastic. Some begged favors of him, as if he had already wealth and honors in his gift. Many abject spirits, who had outraged him by their insolence, now crouched at his feet, begging pardon for all the trouble they had caused him and promising the blindest obedience for the future."

The handle-shaft of the Landfall of Columbus spoon is a fasces; the nave contains a globe showing the two continents of the Western Hemisphere; the caput is a laurel-bordered medallion enclosing an eagle, the wing tips and beak of which extend slightly outside the circular margins. C. D. Peacock, the Chicago jeweler whose name appears on the reverse of handle, grew up with Chicago. He was descended from a long line of craftsmen who prided themselves upon producing things of artistic values and intrinsic beauty. At the time of his death in 1903 Mr. Peacock's shop had long been a mecca for all lovers of fine silverware and exquisite jewelry.

Length of this spoon is 5¾ inches.

The last spoon of this group, depicting the reception of Columbus by Ferdinand and Isabella at Barcelona in April, 1493, is unique in shape, sturdy of workmanship, and replete with pictorial design. Rather then turn to the versions of Irving or Prescott here, let us instead follow the story given us by this exceptionally fine spoon itself.

The scene embossed on the bowl is explained for us by the words running vertically along the right margin, "Returning of Columbus and Reception of Court." On the left margin appears "World's Columbian Exposition."

Horizontally across the bowl may be seen twelve persons. At the extreme left a standard-bearer holds in his left hand the stanchion of the Spanish flag, surmounted by a Latin cross, the pennon of which is drooped through lack of a breeze in its folds. Next appear three Indians, apparently chieftains, for they are in full regalia of feathered head-dress and native robe. Two of them are facing the throne, and oddly enough, disport swords in hands, saber-sheaths on their hips, and crowns of feathers

424

resembling shuttle-cocks on their heads. The third, standing four-square with bare back turned to us, conveys a sling of arrows fastened to his waist and a bow in his hands, though only a portion of this bow can be seen. He is obviously of lower rank than the other two, perhaps only an "Indian page," for he has neither sword at side nor flowing robe on his shoulders.

Columbus occupies the central position in the scene, his right hand clasping that of one of the Indian chiefs, his left holding a plumed navigator's cap, and his face averted slightly toward the throne. Somewhat to the rear are two figures, rather obscured, but presumably those of two friars. To the right of the platformed throne stands a monk with folded hands. Next to him is a mitred bishop or abbot with a long crozier in his right hand.

On the dais sit King Ferdinand and Queen Isabella listening with rapt attention to the narration of Columbus. The king's right arm is resting on the chair-arm, his hand posed under his chin. The queen, with a cross pendant over her bodice, is resting her hands in her lap. Both monarchs are wearing their crowns, the backs of their chairs towering well above the diadems. The chairs have spooled posts and, rising to a triangular peak, display neweled embossments at the central angle and on the side-posts. Behind the sovereigns are curtains draped in loose overlapping folds. Above their heads hangs a lighted chandelier-lamp. On the extreme right is an indistinct figure, possibly that of a cowled monk, squatting, his face turned toward the monarchs.

Before the platform a spray of beribboned flowers lies on a ridged incline. The vertical part of the platform displays a minute ribbing and the horizontal part under the royal feet a fine stippling.

The handle shaft bears the name of Chicago vertically and the date 1893, horizontally.

The sides of the handle, both nave and caput together in one section becoming greatly enlarged at the waist, run parallel without indentations to break the linear contours from the waist till the crown is reached. On this portion of the handle, in the nave, appears the medallioned head of Columbus. The extension of this area shows the great navigator kneeling in a prayer of gratitude on ship-deck while a mariner points toward land. The beaded crown, convexed like a crescent moon, bears the words, "Discovery of America." Directly beneath the inverted crescent we read, "Friday, Oct. 12, 1492."

On the reverse side of handle there is a picture of the Administration Building at the Columbian Exposition, two small craft and a bridge in the river foreground.

This spoon bears the trademark of Rogers Sterling, now owned by the International Silver Company. Length, 6 inches.

No. 112 LURAY CAVERNS

Throughout the states bordering the Ohio and the central run of the Mississippi are numerous caves. Of course, the most famous of all is Mammoth Cave in western Kentucky. In the region adjacent to Mammoth Cave are many limestone caverns of smaller extent, visited extensively by the public. Southern Indiana also has two well-known caves, Marengo and Wyandotte; in Tennessee is found the interesting Nicajack. In some parts of Kentucky and Missouri small caves are so common that every good-size farm can boast of one or two. Mark Twain brings one of these subterranean passages into his story of *Tom Sawyer* as a hiding place for buried treasure. In New Mexico are located the beautiful Carlsbad Caverns. The present spoon brings to our attention the Luray Caverns in Virginia.

Encircled by the picturesque Blue Ridge Mountains and lying in the lap of the fertile Shenandoah Valley is the small town of Luray, much frequented by tourists in summer. Later in origin than most towns in this region, it became the county seat when Page County was formed in 1831. One of its chief attractions is the Luray Museum, a twelve-room log house, containing collections of Civil War relics, coins, stamps, buttons, fans, pipes, canes, books, letters, documents, antique furniture, bottles, vases, shoes, shawls, clothing, and all sorts of minerals, rocks, and fossils obtained from the underground cavern nearby. The gatherer of this immense collection, Mollie Zeiler Zirkel (1845-1933), was the wife of a former superintendent of Luray Caverns, but even before her marriage, she began at the age of twelve to collect the thousands of odd and unique articles in her educational displays.

Naturally, what brings most people to the town are the Luray Caverns. While there are many such underground passages in the valley, composed of huge limestone formations tinted with a phantasmagoric array of colors, Luray is by far the largest. Stalactites and stalagmites abound in gorgeous motley colorings and in an infinite variety of configurations. There are many chambers of these subterranean wonders: the Throne Room, the Ball Room, the Giants' Hall, and the Cathedral, the latter displaying the realistic likeness of a pipe organ.

In the gold bowl of this spoon is depicted the Fallen Column, which lies athwart a natural corridor. The stalactites overhead are simulated by silver splinter-cuttings on a gold background. On the wave-handle is embossed the name of Virginia. The nave contains typical products of the state: a peanut, a tobacco plant, a crab, and an oyster shell.

In the caput on the obverse side appears the state seal. An Amazon, representing Virtus (or Courage), stands with her left foot on the prostrate body of a man symbolizing Tyranny, a broken scourge fallen from his left hand and a crown lying on its upturned rim near his head. A Roman helmet with pendent feathers crowns the head of Virtus. In her left hand is a spear resting on the neck of the tyrant and in her right a sheathed sword touching the left knee of the prostrate figure. This seal differs somewhat from the latest official state seal adopted in 1930. The state motto SIC SEMPER TYRANNIS (Thus always to tyrants) forms an arc above the Amazon's head. A series of five mountain ranges is laminated in the background.

Made by the Shepard Manufacturing Company, this spoon is 5½ inches in length. Used through the courtesy of its owner, Professor Ralph Carter, Clinchport, Virginia.

No. 113 ISLES OF SHOALS

Off the coast of New Hampshire lie the Isles of Shoals. Their individual names are extremely picturesque: Appledore, Smutty Nose, Cedar, Star, White, Lunging, and Duck. These tiny bleak islands will always be associated in our literature with the name of Celia Leighton Thaxter, who came to live on White Island when she was five years old. Her father, his political ambitions thwarted on the mainland, moved to the islands as keeper of the lighthouse and manager of the hotel, a popular resort in summer for tourists.

Years later Celia Thaxter was to immortalize these islands in her poems and highly cadenced prose. Every aspect of the sea and every phase of human, plant, animal, and bird life on the islands were depicted faithfully—and felicitously—by her pen: "the sea fowl soaring aloft or tossing on the water;" "the soft skies and softer winds;" "the murmur of the encircling sea;" "the vessels scudding over the dark blue sea, all feather white where the short waves broke hissing in the cold;" "the first blades of grass that prick through the soil;" "tiny stars of crimson sorrel threaded on their long brown stems;" "the blackberry blossoms in bridal white, the blue-eyed grass, and the crow-foot flowers—like drops of yellow gold spilt over the moss . . . dandelions, buttercups, and clover . . . morning glories lifting their faces, all awake, to my adoring gaze;" "sunrise and sunset, the changing moon, the northern lights, the constellations wheeling in splendor through the winter night."

Her lines on the sunset, set to music, are now used as a vesper hymn by the Congregational and Unitarian Churches which hold summer conferences on the islands:

Good-by, sweet day, good-by!
I have so loved thee, but I cannot hold thee.
Departing like a dream, the shadows fold thee;
Slowly thy perfect beauty fades away:
Good-by, sweet day, good-by!

Good-by, sweet day, good-by!
All thy rich gifts my grateful heart remembers,
The while I watch thy sunset's smouldering embers
Die in the west beneath the twilight gray.
Good-by, sweet day, good-by!

Let us see the lighthouse, incised here on the gold bowl of this spoon, as Celia Thaxter first saw it: "It was at sunset that we put ashore on that lonely rock where the lighthouse looked down on us like some tall black-capped giant. The stars were beginning to twinkle, and the salt air blew cold from the sea." Ever afterwards to the impressionable child it was "a fresh excitement to watch the lighting of the lamps, and to see the colored rays shine out over the sea. In the great lantern there were fifteen lamps, ten of them golden and five red . . . It was a pleasure to think how far the lighthouse sent its rays and how many hearts it gladdened with its warning light of safety."

The child made friends with the curlew and sea gull, and crab and limpet, the grasshopper and cricket; and in one instance she was inspired to write her best-known lyric through her friendship with one tiny bird:—

Across the lonely beach we flit,
    One little sandpiper and I;
And fast I gather, bit by bit,
    The scattered driftwood bleached and dry.
The wild waves reach their hands for it,
    The wild wind raves, the tide runs high,
As up and down the beach we flit—
    One little sandpiper and I.

Above our heads the sullen clouds
    Scud black and swift across the sky;
Like silent ghosts in misty shrouds
    Stand out the white lighthouses high.
Almost as far as eye can reach
    I see the close-reefed vessels fly,
As fast we flit along the beach—
    One little sandpiper and I.

Comrade, where wilt thou be tonight
    When the loosed storm breaks furiously?
My driftwood fire will burn so bright!
    To what warm shelter canst thou fly?
I do not fear for thee, though wroth
    The tempest rushes through the sky;
For are we not God's children both,
    Thou, little sandpiper and I?

If you are not acquainted with Celia Thaxter, go back to the old readers of McGuffey, Appleton, Harper, Brooks, and others, and read "Little Gustava," "The Wounded Curlew," and the stories of her life on the Isles of Shoals.

428

On the handle, this spoon bears the seal of New Hampshire, the Old Man of the Mountain, and the picture of an angler. Made by the Shepard Mfg. Co., this spoon is 5½ inches in length.

No. 114 HISTORIC WILMINGTON

While closely knit together by an indigenous stock of people who have been "Tarheels" for so many generations that their original identity has been lost, the state of North Carolina is divided topographically into three distinct regions. In the east there is a coastal plain, the Tidewater region, that has been agrarian in its social and political concepts since the earliest clearings were hewn out of its pine forests. Running north and south through the center is the Piedmont region, the most thickly populated part and, by reason of its abundant water power, rapidly becoming industrialized. The western hinterland is composed of rugged highlands, which have produced a sturdy race of mountaineers. Although many of these westerners opposed secession in 1861, they went along with the rest of the state, which incidentally furnished "more privates and fewer generals" than any other Southern state. Roughly one-fourth of the Confederate soldiers lost in action were Tarheelers.

While North Carolina was the only seaboard state on either of our coasts that did not have a deep-water port until World War II, it had in Wilmington good harbor facilities for lighter seafaring craft. Founded in 1732, the settlement was first known as New Liverpool. Later the name was changed to its present one in honor of the Earl of Wilmington. Scotch Highlanders after 1745 made it one of their chief ports of entry.

Wilmington had a notable list of patriots during the Revolution. To the assembly at Philadelphia in 1776 the town sent William Hooper to sign the Declaration of Independence. Hooper, a public-spirited man of sterling character, performed many services for the American cause, and suffered loss of property and ill treatment of himself and family when the Tories held Wilmington over a long period in 1779-1781. Aristocratic, brilliant, with great charm of manner, he was called the "prophet of independence."

Cornelius Harnett was one of the first to denounce the Stamp Act in North Carolina. He was thrice a delegate to the Continental Congress and a wartime governor of the state. Taken prisoner of war when the British seized Wilmington, he was paroled, but died shortly before the final victory at Yorktown.

James Iredell, although English born, warmly espoused the patriot cause, thereby forfeiting a large fortune from a rich uncle in the West Indies. Later, he was appointed as associate-justice of the Supreme Court by Washington.

John Ashe took an active part in the Revolution. When he heard of the battle at Bunker Hill, he immediately raised a force of five hundred men and captured Fort Johnson. In 1778 his forces drove the British out of Augusta. Taken a prisoner at Wilmington in 1780, he lived just long enough to witness the successful termination of the war.

Counties in North Carolina have been named for Harnett, Iredell, and Ashe; the city of Asheville likewise honors the memory of John Ashe.

Shortly after he became president, Washington made a tour of the South, and described the road from New Bern to Wilmington as one of the loneliest and worst he had ever beheld. He had to detour around swamps, stumps, boulders, and steep hills. In some places his horse sank up to the saddle in mud. It is a far cry from that mode of travel to the fine motor highways that traverse the state today. North Carolina was one of the first states to inaugurate a better-roads program.

The first railroad built in the state was completed in 1840. It extended for a distance of one hundred and sixty-two miles from Wilmington to Weldon, and to celebrate the event one hundred and sixty-two cannon salutes were fired in the port. It was the longest railroad line in the world at the time, and the pine rails had been surfaced with iron sheeting to insure safety at the high speed of thirty miles an hour.

During the Civil War Wilmington became the last link to the outer world for the South. Blockade runners slipped in and out of the port, long after all other avenues of escape had been blocked, until very shortly before the end of hostilities.

Wilmington, for nearly two hundred years the largest city in North Carolina, has never glamorized itself in the same way as have other Southern cities with a storied past; the Tarheels have always lived too close to Mother Nature to puff and put on unnatural airs. And yet it has a history equal to that of any. It has entertained five presidents and many celebrities in their time, men like Lafayette, Calhoun, Webster, and Clay.

Some of the finest colonial mansions are to be found in Wilmington. Cornwallis chose one of them for his headquarters, now known as the McNary House. Theatricals flourished here before the Revolution, and Charles Godfrey, the only dramatist of any ability in colonial times, lies buried in St. James churchyard. A valuable Spanish painting of Christ, with the crown of thorns on his head, hangs on the vestry walls of this old church.

All styles of early American architecture may be studied here. Houses display every type of early roof: gambrel, gable, and mansard. The manor houses of outlying plantations exhibit much finely carved woodwork, fanlights, pedimented porticoes, Doric and Corinthian columns, ornate balconies of lacy ironwork, broad flights of entry stairs, and sculptured lions. Gothic, Greek, and Roman Revival styles abound.

Wilmington is one of the last places touched by the warming Gulf Stream on the Atlantic Coast. Consequently, it assumes a subtropical aspect in its gardens of magnolia, crape myrtle, and live oaks, the latter clad in long garlands of gray moss. Not far away are the marshes, sand dunes, and savannas, displaying a luxuriant growth of wild flowers, shrubs, and reeds: the pitcher plant, evening primrose, honeycup, sea lavender, oxeye, marsh dayflower, samphire, Venus's fly-trap (found only near Wilmington), parrot feathers, lizard tails, and others. Many kinds of trees, strange to the north, thrive here, safe from the cold; the yaupon, a wind-blown holly of the sand dunes, yields a berry formerly used in making tea. The whistling swan and the water turkey nest in the reeds along the marshes.

In the bowl of this spoon the Wilmington post office, constructed in 1889-1891, exhibits a Romanesque edifice with two pryamidal towers, horse-shoe-arched windows, and a substantial stone masonry.

This spoon belongs to the state seal series having the wave-handle. In addition to the seal, a bale of cotton and a red spruce appear on the handle. Two female figures symbolizing Well-Being and Liberty are represented in the seal. The former is seated; the latter is standing. Between them is a cornucopia opening downward and its contents pouring out in abundance upon the ground.

Made by the Shepard Mfg. Co., the spoon is 5½ inches in length.

No. 115 WEBSTER'S BIRTHPLACE

On the handle of the spoon before us appears a simple one-and-a-half story structure known as the birthplace of Daniel Webster. It is a careful reproduction of the sketch drawn by Webster's private secretary, Lanman, and approved by the great orator himself as a close likeness of the original which disappeared a few years after Webster's birth. The big elm tree to one side, the shrubs and the rocks in the foreground, and the rail fence running to the rear of the house depict the surroundings so typical of an old New England farm. Not visible on the spoon but shown in Lanman's sketch are the barn, a cow, and the rock-ribbed hills to the rear of the farmhouse. There is one minor difference of detail, however. Under the giant elm the spoon exhibits a well sweep, which the original shows to be a dog kennel.

This house once stood on the farm at Salisbury, near Franklin, New Hampshire, where Daniel Webster was born in 1782. A year before, the family had moved from a pioneer's log cabin not far away from this spot. The fact that he was not actually born in a log cabin may have lost Webster the nomination for president in 1840. William Henry Harrison won the nomination partly because his lowly birth in a log cabin was held up as a great asset appealing strongly to thousands of voters still living in this pioneer type of home.

Webster's father was married twice, and had five children by each wife, Daniel being the ninth child and the youngest son. He was evidently a favorite with his father, who relieved the boy of any heavy work about the farm. The story is told that, once when he was helping cut hay on his father's farm, he kept asking his father to hang the scythe-blade differently. Wearied by this constant importuning, the father suggested that Daniel hang it to suit himself. He accordingly hung it on a tree limb and left the field.

When Daniel was three years old the family moved close by to a more commodious house called the Elms, where in addition to the farm the father ran a tavern. Even at this early age the boy impressed the teamsters who frequented the tavern by the majestic tones of his voice, and at nights they would listen with rapt attention to his reading of portions of the Scriptures.

In his youth Daniel was slender and delicate in appearance. But as he grew older he became more thickset; the term applied to him as most characteristic was *massive*. His dark complexion he inherited from some of his Welsh forebears, and this swarthiness caused him to be mistaken once for an Indian while he was crossing the campus at Dartmouth, where he received his college education. The father mortgaged his farm so that Daniel and his older brother Ezekiel might finish their work in college.

Upon his graduation Daniel was admitted to the bar and practiced law for nine years before he moved to Marshfield, Massachusetts, which was to be his home for the rest of his life except for occasional vacations to the old farmstead in New Hampshire.

He rose rapidly in popular esteem as an orator, and served almost continuously from 1823 till his death in 1852, in one office or another, as congressman, senator, or secretary of state. The demands made upon him for public addresses were very heavy, and his Olympian presence commanded the respect and admiration not only of friends but also of the bitterest political adversaries. When he strode to the rostrum, an awed hush awaited his words. His movements were deliberate, and he used gestures charily. The occasion always seemed momentous when he began to speak. One who heard the Miltonic organ tones of his voice and saw the dilations of those eyes black as the ace of spades, describes him thus: "Such a figure, such an intellect, such a heart, were never before combined to awe the world. The vast plan of him: the front of Jove; the regal commanding air which cleared a path before him; the voice of thunder and of music which revealed the broad caverns of his crest; the unfathomable eye which no sculptor could render—all the external signs said, 'Here is a man!' "

His dress was impeccable. In his later years he clothed his ponderous figure of two hundred pounds in a formal dress suit, dark blue in color, and adorned with a double row of brass buttons. On the street he wore a tall silk top hat that added immeasurably to his height. An aura of majesty pervaded his person. "There goes a king!" exclaimed an English sailor on seeing him pass. Sidney Smith, the English essayist, compared him to a cathedral. Carlyle spoke of his "crag-like face," his "black eyes under their precipice of eyebrow, like dull anthracite furnaces, needing only to be *blown*," and the "mastiff-mouth, accurately closed."

When seated in Congress, he gave one the impression of dreamy indolence, as if he were little perturbed by transient outward events. Yet beneath the surface reposed a deeply emotional nature. Tears often welled into his eyes when he heard an expression of noble or generous sentiments. He often stood as stone when his eye swept over natural scenes of beauty. Cattle grazing on the rocky hillsides, a colt frolicking about its mother, sleigh bells giving off their sweet, silvery tones over a field of white, a lighthouse beaming in the darkness—all familiar, all beloved, in memories from his childhood—moved him to the core as he stood transfixed by the picture, heedless of himself or the conscious world around him.

Among his speeches these may be cited as masterpieces of the orator's art: The *Dartmouth College Case; Plymouth Oration; First Bunker Hill Oration;* speech on the *Murder of Captain White;* eulogy on *Adams and Jefferson; Reply to Hayne; Reply to Calhoun; Second Bunker Hill Oration;* and the *Seventh of March Speech.* Francis Lieber, student of political science, compared Webster's speeches with those of Demosthenes by the simple process of reading aloud, first from Demosthenes and then from Webster, or vice versa, and he concluded that Webster "stood the test" favorably every time. Another proof of the profound merits of Webster's oratory lies in the fact that he is quoted in Congressional debate "twenty times as often as any other public man in our history." The speeches of Clay, Calhoun, and Edward Everett, the other three most famous orators of Webster's day, rest embalmed like Egyptian mummies, dead beyond resurrection. The sap of life has departed from their utterances forever. But Webster's words still ring true to our ears. They are instinct with the salt and savor of genuine literature. Let us refresh our minds with a few sentences extracted here and there from his "unimpeachable rhetoric:"

"Sink or swim, live or die, survive or perish, I give my hand and my heart to this vote . . . whatever may be our fate, be assured, be assured that this Declaration will stand. It may cost treasure, and it may cost blood; but it will stand, and it will richly compensate for both. . . . We shall make this a glorious, an immortal day. When we are in our graves, our children will honor it. They will celebrate it with thanksgiving, with festivity, with bonfires, and illuminations. On its annual return they will shed tears, not of subjection and slavery, not of agony and distress, but of exultation, of gratitude, and of joy. Sir, before God, I believe the hour is come. My judgment approves this measure, and my whole heart is in it. All that I have, and all that I am, and all that I ever hope in this life, I am now ready here to stake upon it; and I leave off as I began, that live or die, survive or perish, I am for the Declaration. It is my living sentiment, and by the blessing of God it shall be my dying sentiment, Independence now, and INDEPENDENCE FOREVER." (From the supposed speech of John Adams).

"Let it rise, let it rise till it meet the sun in his coming; let the earliest light of morning gild it, and parting day linger and play on its summit." (Apostrophe to the Bunker Hill monument).

The greatest speech that Webster ever made was his *Reply to Hayne,* in which he spoke on the subject that lay closest to his heart, the defense of the Constitution and the indissolubility of the Union. As a boy of twelve, he had bought a cotton handkerchief with the Constitution printed on it at a county fair. He kept it about his person till he had memorized every word of that document. In the famous debate with Hayne in 1830 he not only epitomized his own lofty sentiments but also crystallized in luminous language the devotion which most of his fellow-countrymen felt only too vaguely for the nation as a whole:

"When my eyes shall be turned to behold for the last time the sun in heaven, may I not see him shining on the broken and dishonored fragments of a once glorious Union; on states dissevered, discordant, belligerent; on a land rent with civil feuds, or drenched, it may be, in fraternal blood! Let their last feeble and lingering glance rather behold the gorgeous ensign of the Republic, now known and honored throughout the earth, still full high advanced, its arms and trophies streaming in their original lustre, not a stripe erased or polluted, nor a single star obscured, bearing for its motto no such miserable interrogatory as 'what is all this worth?' nor those other words of delusion and folly, 'Liberty first and Union afterwards,' but everywhere, spread all over in characters of living light, blazing on all its ample folds, as they float over the sea and over the land and in every wind under the whole heavens, that other sentiment, dear to every true American heart,—'Liberty and Union, now and forever, one and inseparable!' "

Thirty years after this patriotic appeal was made, the unity of the nation was tested. Webster was gone, but his words were remembered by thousands of young men who gave their lives that the Union might remain, one and inseparable.

Webster failed in his highest ambition, to be president, and if any man ever deserved that coveted honor it was he. When, in 1852, he was rejected by his party in favor of a military hero, a hundred thousand voters, scattered in all sections of the country, wrote in his name on the ballot. But Webster never knew of this singular devotion; he died a few days before the election, his eyes turned toward the U. S. flag on his sailboat anchored close to his home at Marshfield.

"Yes, Dan'l Webster's dead—or at least, they buried him. But every time there's a thunderstorm around Marshfield, they say you can hear his rolling voice in the hollows of the sky. And they say that if you go to his grave and speak loud and clear, 'Dan'l Webster—Dan'l Webster!' the ground'll begin to shiver and the trees begin to quake. And after a while you'll hear a deep voice saying, 'Neighbor, how stands the Union?' Then you better answer the Union stands as she stood, rock bottomed and copper sheathed, one and indivisible, or he's liable to rear right up out of the ground." But that's the beginning of another story—*The Devil and Daniel Webster*, by Stephen Vincent Benet—a wonderful evocation of the magical powers inherent in the words of the greatest of our orators.

And, just for variation, to descend from the heights of the sublime to the depths of the ridiculous, let us recall that Mark Twain named the "celebrated jumping frog of Calaveras County" after Daniel Webster. Neither the famous orator nor the celebrated frog had a fair chance to win the greatest race of their lives. Both got set to go—and suffered a fatal setback.

This spoon is an early product of Durgin's. Length, 6 inches.

No. 116 SOUTHERN PINES

I know a very ancient range of hills
And on their pine-crowned crests the soughing wind
Is never still. They march in serried ranks
Away and yet away until the eye
Of the beholder faints and cannot reach
That last blue smoky line against the sky.
Immutable and ageless, awful, grand,
They still the ravaged, tortured soul
And fill it with a deep serenity.

The Indiana author of these lines, Mrs. F. B. Lewis, must have been thinking specifically of that delightful pine-region around Southern Pines and Pinehurst when she indicted her tribute to the state of North Carolina. No evergreen forests surpass those of the Carolina Sandhill country which is found halfway between the Alleghenies and the ocean. Who has not felt a deep sense of restfulness when passing through the "serried ranks" of longleaf pines that everywhere greet the eye in countless numbers, pointing undeviatingly upward toward the sky while their boughs, thick-studded with pale, slender leaves, hold converse in sweet undertones with the plaintive breezes? Who has ever heard the call of the mourning dove or the quail somewhere afar off when pine cones are dropping softly on sandy hillsides and not sensed a quickening of the pulse, a rejuvenation of the spirit, or a closer affinity with the elemental forces in nature like unto that which our pioneering forefathers experienced as the privilege of their birthright?

Something akin to this primal feeling that root-binds all of us to a timbered soil inspired John T. Patrick in 1883 to establish for those New Englanders becoming weary of their long rigorous winters a hospitable retreat among the Carolina pines. The thrifty local farmers thought Patrick a little unbalanced when he bought five hundred and seventy acres of land at the hitherto unheard-of price of two dollars and fifty cents an acre. At that time the land was considered practically worthless because the hard woods had been winnowed out, leaving only a scrub growth on the pine barrens.

Undaunted by local doubts, Patrick went ahead with his project. He laid off streets, staked off lots, constructed a hotel, and christened his dream-village "Southern Pines." He devised an unusual method of advertising. Hiring a minstrel troupe, he toured the North with his show and paid newspapers for ads with lots. Then the newspapers sold said lots through further advertising—at their own expense to get rid of the lots. By 1887 there were enough people in the town to warrant incorporation.

The Northerners, some of whom at first feared they might have been hoaxed, found Patrick's extravagant praises justified. There was plenty of sparkling winter sunshine; the weather might be crisp, but it rarely snowed. There was extraordinarily good water to drink, being filtered of impurities in the sandy soil. And the air was always redolent with the pleasing scent of pines, especially after a rain.

Today, people come to Southern Pines as much for recreation as for health. The winter residents look forward to a season with an endless variety of events: golf and tennis tournaments, horse shows, fox and deer hunts, gymkhanas, anglers' clubs, social affairs, cultural forums, lectures, concerts, historical exhibits, and literary gatherings. The town has become the rendezvous for writers and artists through the efforts of James Boyd, the author of *Drums*, who came to Southern Pines for many years before his death in 1944. Boyd organized the first fox hunts held here, and his interest drew lovers of the hunt from far-away places to follow the Moore County hounds, many of which have been developed to meet the requirements necessary in the Sandhills.

Among members of the writers' colony in Southern Pines are Struthers Burt and his wife, Katharine Newlin Burt, Lawrence B. Smith, Walter and Bernice Gilkyson, Manly Wade Wellman, Almet Jenks, and Maude Parker. Glen Rounds illustrates books, etches, and does woodcuts. But, being an ex-cowboy from Montana, he prefers to paint animal murals. He thinks the bare outside walls of American homes "constitute a challenge to the imagination" and call for picturesque murals conformable to their surroundings.

Winter residents, coming in greater numbers all the time, more than double the town's population. While Southern Pines was originally thought of as a New England village transplanted to Dixie, there are equally as many visitors from other Northern states. The streets bear witness to this fact in their names: Delaware, New Jersey, New York, Illinois, Indiana, Ohio, Pennsylvania, Maine, and Massachusetts. But regardless of their varied backgrounds, the visitors all succumb to the best traditions of Southern hospitality and a deference for good living.

In the gold-washed bowl of the Southern Pines spoon, engraved with an oxidized flare, is the passenger depot, one of the first buildings in the town. The handle is strikingly attractive. The shaft simulates the scaly, reflexed prickles of a pine cone, although in the handle drop the scales approach more nearly the likeness of nodules on pine stems. There is no separation of caput and nave, the sections being taken up with three huge cones set within a gleaming spray of beautiful needles or leaves. The reverse of handle shows only an irregular branch of needles without the cones.

The trademark of Watson and Newell is touched by a delicate cluster of leaves on the reverse handle drop. Length, 5¼ inches.

No. 117 GOLDEN GATE BEAR
No. 120 JOHN MARSH BEAR

"What a bear!" was the epithet frequently hurled at John Marsh, pioneer doctor and the first of the big cattle kings in the Golden Gate country. His Yankee inheritance endowed him with the ability to chase down a dollar, but his diabolical instincts straightway led him to hug it to death with ursine ferocity.

Marsh was born in Massachusetts the last year of the eighteenth century, and educated at several academies and at Harvard. His mother, a pious woman, prayed that her son would enter the ministry because of his scholarly proclivities. But young Marsh's penchant for reading and study contained no germ of affection for theology.

The father hoped that John would take to farming. But the boy would have none of it. "Poverty, ignorance, and the soil go hand in hand," he declared.

John returned home after an exciting affair at Harvard. He had placed gunpowder in some logs which were being stolen from his woodbox. The subsequent explosion wrecked the room of a young professor. John still wanted to continue his schooling. His father balked at the idea, refusing to advance the funds whereby he could study medicine at Baltimore. So young Marsh decided to go west.

He departed for the wilds of Minnesota, where he was engaged to tutor Colonel Snelling's children at Fort St. Anthony. Marsh parsimoniously hoarded every penny of his salary. To supplement his earnings he acted as a messenger once to carry some important mail through to government outposts. He was paid handsomely but he did not give his Indian guide anything more than a prevaricating report to the effect that he had been robbed of the payment. Meanwhile he was taking a practical course in medicine by helping a Doctor Purcell on his cases. Unfortunately the doctor died before Marsh had been given a medical diploma of any sort.

Lewis Cass, governor of the Northwest Territory, obtained for him an appointment as sub-agent of Indian affairs. Always adept in learning languages, he mastered the Sioux speech well enough to write a grammar and edit a dictionary of that language.

About this time he fell in love with Marguerite Decouteaux, the daughter of a French father and a Sioux mother. For seven years he lived happily with Marguerite, who was accepted as his common-law wife. The child of this irregular union, known as Charles Marsh, resembled his father in every way except that the boy had webbed toes on his right foot. He showed no trace of his Indian heritage.

When the agent for Indian affairs died and Marsh failed to be advanced to the top position, he was disgruntled and angry. To add to his embitterment Marguerite died. He placed his son with friends farther East when the Black Hawk War broke out around Prairie du Chien. He recruited volunteers for the American forces, but when evidence turned up that he was secretly selling stores of ammunition to the redskins, he had to flee hurriedly to avoid arrest and trial for treason.

With all the cash he could rifle from the government coffers, he traveled southward as far as Missouri. At Independence he set up a store trading in furs and selling general merchandise at a good profit to the Indians. Once more, to escape federal agents on his trail, he left his lucrative business and decamped under cover of darkness.

Weary of this hide-and-seek existence, he did not pause in his travels till he had reached California, then under Mexican rule. The American authorities could not hound him farther.

In Los Angeles he applied for permission to practice medicine. His Harvard letter of admission, a precious possession which he kept with him through all hazards, was accepted in lieu of a doctor's license, no one being able to read it or bothering to find out what it had to say. The priest who examined him was in all sincerity satisfied at his spiritual soundness, since he now professed the Roman Catholic faith.

Marsh soon had as many patients as he could tend to, there being no other doctor in all the adjoining territory. He displayed skill in surgery, and he read many volumes on medicine to improve his knowledge of the subject. His large, muscular figure and reserved, even somewhat haughty, manners appealed to the high-class gentry of the old stock, who paid liberally for his services.

But Marsh was dissatisfied. He felt humbled in having to wait on other people. His secret, fervent desire was for the opposite treatment: he wanted to be waited upon, looked up to, listened to, not for the gravity

438

of his medical opinion but for his wealth and the importance of his position as a mighty grandee in this land of sunshine and plenty.

He wandered north and asked questions concerning the richness of grass lands and the fertility of soil-crops. At San Francisco, then Yerba Buena, he stayed for a year sponging off the largess of a fellow-American, Jacob Leese. When the latter hinted that it was time for this free-of-charge social visit to come to an end, Marsh reminded his host that he owed his guest fifty cents for some fish he had bought and for which he had not yet been reimbursed. Leese paid the debt, glad to be rid of this ungrateful, greedy bear.

Soon after this he bought a great ranch of seventy thousand acres forty miles from San Francisco for a mere song because the Indians who lived adjacent to the ranch were always creating unpleasant episodes by their marauding expeditions. Marsh immediately stopped the Indian depredations and won the good will of the savages by going among them, speaking to them in their own language, and by speedily curing them of malarial complaints. He simply dosed them with quinine. They revered him as a miracle man. He extracted cattle from them in payment, plenty of the very best. For delivering a baby he demanded fifty head; for a surgical operation, a hundred. Cattle disappearing from the herds on the big haciendas were hardly missed, and the doctor had no time to question payments proffered in live beef by his patients.

The native Californians about this time were restive under Micheltorena, the governor appointed in Mexico City to rule over them. Every move he made was unpopular. When he transferred the capital from San Francisco to Los Angeles, the northerners were enraged. When he cut the salaries of many office-holders he lacerated the feelings of that sensitive group. He threatened to confiscate ranch lands once the property of the Church, and to legislate all foreigners out of California. Rebellion was in the air and it broke into open warfare before long.

Marsh was compelled to join Sutter's army in support of Micheltorena, or be arrested. This army of eight hundred men was a heterogeneous lot, including many Americans. Immediately Marsh set to work sowing the seeds of disloyalty in those who would lend a willing ear. His propaganda for an independent republic had its effect. After a battle with mock-heroics on both sides, the sole casualty being one horse, the governor's forces deserted en masse to the rebels. Private Marsh had defeated the Mexican army by treachery, and thus won an unfought war!

The Republic of California was proclaimed at Sonoma. The Mexican flag was pulled down and in its place was substituted a banner made from a meal sack, ever since known as the bear flag. In the upper half of a white field appeared a "California grizzly bear upon a grass plot, in the position of walking toward the left." A single red star was placed in the upper left corner. This has remained until today, except for modification of minor details, the state flag of California.

Marsh now conceived the grandiose idea of a republic on the Pacific coast embracing all the territory from the northern borders of Oregon to the southern end of California. He was evolving plans whereby he would be the first president of this republic, which in good time he would graciously hand over to the United States government. But he was never able to make his magnanimous gesture. Events moved too fast for him. The Bear Flag of the California Republic, which Marsh had a hand in devising, had a short-lived existence of one month. Then Fremont and Sloat arrived, and the American flag was hoisted first at Monterey, then in San Francisco harbor.

Marsh was disillusioned, frustrated, forgotten. His services were overlooked. Fremont was lionized, later to be chosen as a presidential candidate. Sloat's action was acclaimed as heroic in the East. Dozens of names in the new territories of Texas, Arizona, New Mexico, and California sprang into print, emblazoned in headlines of big capital letters. There was little or no mention of his name, the reputation of which remained purely local.

Marsh shut himself up like a clam. He rarely made trips now, not even to San Francisco. He sought solace in re-reading his favorite books: Johnson's *Lives of the Poets*, Anacreon's *Odes*, Paine's *Works*, and a set of Greek tragedies—volumes which he had cherished since his days in college.

Then he heard that gold had been discovered in the Sierras. He went wild. He was sick with desire, avid for that plenitude of gold, that precious spilth in running streams, free to the first comer. Visions of the Seven Cities of Cibola flitted through his Midas-like brain. The Indians had not lied to the conquistadores after all. California the Golden was become a lucid reality.

The hermit sloughed his shell of seclusion, leapt to his horse, and galloped off toward the Sierras.

For days Marsh panned gold on the banks of the Yuba. He dug, sifted, groveled, gloated, inveigled the Indians into bartering their nuggets for gauds of one sort of another. He neither slept nor rested till nature rebelled. He had to give up or break down.

With his pack mules loaded down with the precious dust, he went back to his ranch. There he buried his treasure. No bank was safe enough.

Shortly after returning from this gold-dust junket, the winds of romance blew their warming breath over his life again. A party of Baptist missionaries was passing his hacienda and a dismal rain was falling. Miss Abigail Tuck, one of the party, suggested they seek shelter for the night with Doctor Marsh. The Reverend William Smith hesitated, but the increasing downpour convinced him it was worth trying. "He has the reputation of being as hospitable as a grizzly bear," asserted the minister.

Contrary to their expectations, the Smiths and Miss Tuck were taken in with the most cordial greetings. And their visit extended beyond all

440

anticipation. At the end of two weeks Doctor Marsh and Miss Tuck were united in marriage by the Reverend Smith.

Abigail Tuck Marsh was an intelligent woman, with a penchant for the classics that dovetailed neatly with the doctor's literary tastes. For five years their life was one of great happiness together. Then Mrs. Marsh died, leaving the doctor with a small daughter named Alice, who was given over to the charge of a friend.

Again the doctor crawled into his shell, a hermit, lonelier than ever until he was summoned one night to his door and heard a young man announce himself as Charles Marsh, the doctor's son. The boy proved his identity by his webfoot and by the close physical likeness to his father. He was made welcome and acknowledged before the world as the doctor's son by a former marriage.

The two men got along well together. Charles proved to be a good assistant in running the ranch. Father and son agreed in all matters except that of wages for the hired help. The doctor would not always pay what he had stipulated to do, often finding some reason for docking his laborers. In a lawsuit over sheep-shearing fees, he made mortal enemies of three shearers. The doctor won the case but he lost his life through the animosity he had created. He was dragged from his buggy one night, his throat cut, and his body thrown into a dry creek bed.

The doctor had promised to divulge the cache for his hidden gold to his son, but death beat him to the draw. Charles and Alice, the two heirs, could never discover where their father had buried his money.

Thirty-six years later one of the murderers was pardoned. Soon after, on the old Marsh ranch, a pit was seen to have been opened and some chests removed. The contents of the chests always remained a mystery. But the pardoned murderer died an extraordinarily rich man.

The Golden Gate Bear spoon contains the familiar sunset scene over the Bay, in the bowl. On the handle-shaft are floral ornamentations, the name of San Francisco, and a miner's pan filled with nuggets and gold dust. A bear tops the handle as finial.

A product of the George C. Shreve & Co., of San Francisco. Used through the courtesy of its owner, Miss Evelyn Rogers, Hayward, California.

The John Marsh Bear spoon contains the same sunlit scene as the previous spoon, in the bowl. A cluster of grapes nestles in the handle drop. The name of California runs perpendicularly through the shaft in raised letters on a stippled background. The nave, of two sections, manifests ripening oranges still fastened to the branches above, and a contentious-looking bear below. The California state seal appears in the caput.

On the reverse of handle there is an eagle with wings uplifted to form an arch. An American flag is swirling breezily about its standard. Pressed by the Paye and Baker Co., the spoon is 5½ inches in length.

No. 119 UNIVERSITY OF CHICAGO

There have really been two universities in Chicago, with separate and distinct entities in time and place. The first, somewhat similar in its career to that of its founder, blossomed, decayed, and perished. The second, its career likewise resembling that of its creator, has continued to flourish like the proverbial tree planted by the rivers of water; its roots have not withered and its fruit has been goodly.

Stephen A. Douglas was at the apex of his fame and fortune in 1856 when he turned ten acres of his land and a considerable sum of money over to the Baptists for the construction of a university to be finished within a prescribed time. A total of one hundred thousand dollars was raised by public subscription and the work got under way. The whole edifice was to be built out of imposing Greek marble, with plenty of space for classrooms, libraries, chapel, and gymnasium. The panic of 1857 put a damper on the drive for further subscriptions to free the buildings of debt. A mortgage once incurred continued to grow till the property was doomed to foreclosure. Not even the interest could be paid, and at the demise of the institution in 1885, the mortgage amounted to more than three hundred thousand dollars. The doors to the marble halls swung open no more; weeds covered the campus; the walks were littered with trash. The institution which owed its existence to the magnanimity of Stephen A. Douglas had become a haunt of toads and lizards.

Not so the institution established in 1890, mainly through the generosity of John D. Rockefeller. It seems to have entered upon its existence fully grown like Eve or Minerva, having skipped over the first two acts of its seven ages. Mr. Rockefeller provided the millions and William Rainey Harper, the first president, procured the services of the best scholars by the simple device of offering these scholars better salaries than they could ever hope to obtain elsewhere.

Today the university is attended by thousands of students from all over the world, and the influence of its cultural life is felt by and large over the country as a whole fully as much as within the area of the city's own confines.

On the gold-washed bowl of this spoon is a midway quadrangle for one of the many campus-buildings, nearly all of which are constructed in Gothic style out of Indiana limestone. The shaft of the handle contains the Douglas monument. On the pedestal stands the bronze statue of the Little Giant. Around the base, not shown here, are four figures, symbolic of Illinois, Justice, History, and Eloquence, seated around the sarcophagus of Douglas, sculptured by Leonard W. Polk, the artist who is also noted for his statue of Lincoln.

The name of Chicago is embossed on a banderole just below a picture of Fort Dearborn in the nave. The caput bears an Indian in head-dress;

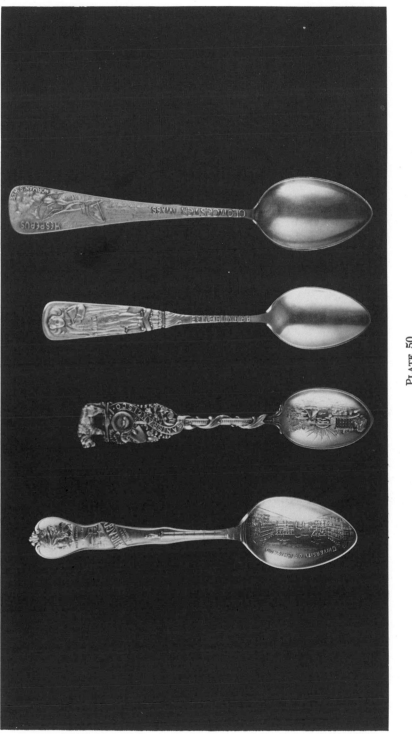

PLATE 50

119. UNIVERSITY OF CHICAGO   120. JOHN MARSH BEAR   121. ROGER WILLIAMS   122. WRECK OF THE HESPERUS

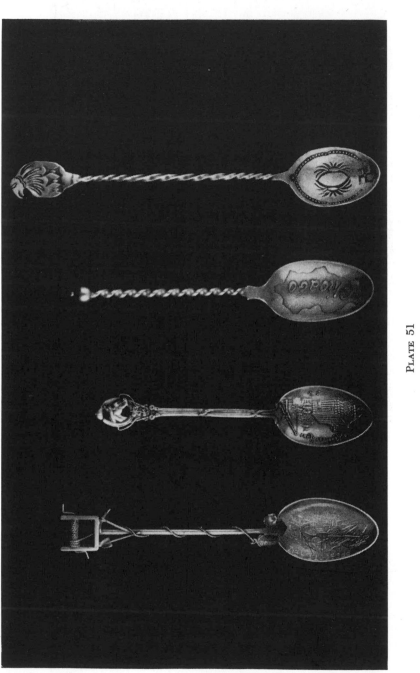

PLATE 51

123. PRESCOTT WINDLASS   124. HORSE-IN-HORSESHOE   125. CHICAGO KATE   126. NAVAHO SYMBOLS

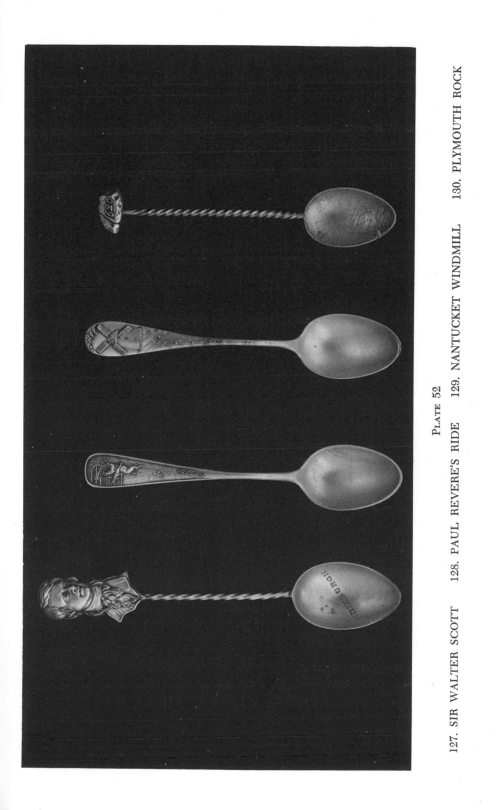

Plate 52

127. SIR WALTER SCOTT   128. PAUL REVERE'S RIDE   129. NANTUCKET WINDMILL   130. PLYMOUTH ROCK

PLATE 53

131. ALAMO FAÇADE   132. HAWKEYE   133. HUDSON-FULTON CELEBRATION
134. WILLIAM PITT

perhaps this is meant to be Black Partridge, but there is no inscription to tell us so.

The reverse of handle contains a wigwam and other Indian paraphernalia. A product, dating from about 1910, of the Watson Company. Length, 4¼ inches.

No. 122 WRECK OF THE HESPERUS

Love of the sea was born in Longfellow's blood. His ancestry on both sides of the family hailed from Yorkshire, on the northeast coast of England, an area originally settled by Viking seafarers from Scandinavia in the eighth and ninth centuries. These people, heathen pirates and marauders at first, were allowed to remain in England and engage in peaceful agricultural pursuits only after they had become Christianized. The earliest of the Longfellows to migrate to the New World were already townsmen, one of them being a blacksmith, but they never moved inland away from the sea.

The poet often refers to the sights and sounds of the ocean near his boyhood town of Portland, Maine. In "My Lost Youth" he evokes wistful memories of that town "seated by the sea" a quarter of a century after he had left it—

> I can see the shadowy lines of its trees,
>   And catch, in sudden gleams,
> The sheen of the far-surrounding seas,
> And islands that were the Hesperides
>   Of all my boyish dreams.

In swift succession come flooding back the vivid mental pictures of "the black wharves and the slips," "the sea-tides running free," "Spanish sailors with bearded lips," "bulwarks by the shore," "the fort upon the shore," and "the sea-fight far away" that "thundered o'er the tide."

On another visit to Portland, he says: "At sunrise caught a glimpse of the fair city of my birth, rising beautifully in terraces above the sea. . . . A glorious scene, with market-boats rowing cityward, rocks, promontories, lighthouses, forts, and wooded islands." While rambling around the city he lay down in one of the embrasures of old Fort Lawrence, and listened, as if held by magic, to the "lashing, lulling sound of the sea. . . . It was a beautiful afternoon, and the harbor was full of white sails, coming and departing."

How multitudinous are Longfellow's references to the "toiling surges" and the "flashing surf." Whole poems are redolent with the aroma and the salty tang of the lapping waves. In others there are frequent bits of imagery that unexpectedly dash the far-flung sea-spray straight into our eyes. The syrupy sweetness that nauseates modern readers of Longfellow's verse in so many of his more sentimental passages is notably absent in such poems as "The Building of the Ship," the climactic peroration of which has "raised thousands of American audiences to frenzies of patriotic enthusiasm." And Professor Pattee, who wrote the foregoing statement, proceeds to declare that it is "finer oratory than the finest of Webster or Sumner."

"The Skeleton in Armor," the first of the *Ballads and Other Poems*, reveals what strong, virile verse Longfellow could write when his subject justified it. The poet was in his true element when his hero, the bloodless, funereal-voiced Viking in armor, recites such galloping, red-blooded, masculine measures as these:

> And as to catch the gale
> Round veered the flapping sail,
> "Death!" was the helmsman's hail,
>   "Death without quarter!"
> Mid-ships with iron keel
> Struck we her ribs of steel;
> Down her black hulk did reel
> Through the black water!

The second ballad in this collection was "The Wreck of the Hesperus," elemental in tone, but in no wise elementary. The skill with which this ballad is wrought can be appreciated only after forming a re-acquaintance with several Old-World, medieval ballads. The one that most naturally springs to mind is "Sir Patrick Spens," because there are certain direct likenesses between these two ballads of the sea. The nature of the subject would obviously invite similarities, but occasionally we even find close echoes of wording in the two, such as: "A loud laugh laughèd he"—"And a scornful laugh laughed he" . . . "The ladyes wrang their fingers white, The maidens tore their hair"—"The maiden clasped her hands and prayed That savèd she might be" . . . "For I feir a deadlie storme"—"For I fear a hurricane."

Anyone who criticizes the shifting of the stress from the penultimate to the last syllable on such words as *daughter* and *sailor* in Longfellow's ballad may be surprised to learn that it was a legitimate practice for the medieval minstrel to do so, as we find this transposition of accent occurring in the first three stanzas of Sir Patrick's story, to wit, in *skipper, sailor,* and *letter.*

Another characteristic of the old ballad that Longfellow employed was the omission of the relative pronoun used as subject, a device permissible in the old days but forbidden in modern English. Compare, for instance—

> O up and spake an eldren knight,
> Sat at the king's right knee—

with

> Then up and spake an old sailor,
> Had sailed to the Spanish main . . .

448

Again, Longfellow has been needled for his extraordinary use of metaphorical personification in such expressions as "trampling surf," "whooping billow," "cruel rocks," and "ho! ho! the breakers roared!" John Ruskin, who found fault with Kingsley's expressive phrase, "the cruel, crawling foam," in *The Sands of Dee*, declared that it was a pathetic fallacy to ascribe human attributes to inanimate objects. By all odds, we know that Ruskin stands revealed here as a bad critic of poetry because he lacked the poetic imagination—and he was also a bad poet for the same reason. Good figures of speech give air, light, freedom, wings to the higher flights of poetry.

The Reef of Norman's Woe lies to the left of the entrance to Gloucester Harbor. Helen Archibald Clarke describes it thus: "The grimness of this cruel rock is never felt in all its possibilities of horror until some venturesome oarsman persuades you to row up to it and around it in the evening shadows after sunset. Though the bay be quiet as a mill-pond, and reflect in long, peaceful streaks the waning lights in the sky, yet about this reef the ocean seems to make vindictive thrusts at your boat, and the waves leaping upon the rocks moan and shudder like wraiths of the long-departed skippers." In calm weather the reef resembles a rat, humpbacked, with a long tail thrust straight out, barely above the water, easy enough to perceive and avoid when the tide rolls in lazily, but treacherous indeed in tumbling, foam-flecked billows.

During the middle of December, 1839, the newspapers carried enlarged headlines of many ships being swamped or dashed to pieces by hurricanes, with a consequent loss of many lives. In Longfellow's journal the entry for the 17th reads: "News of shipwrecks horrible on the coast. Twenty bodies washed ashore near Gloucester, one lashed to a piece of the wreck. There is a reef called Norman's Woe, where many of these took place; among others, the schooner *Hesperus* . . . I must write a ballad upon this."

The storm that lashed the New England coast for two or three days was a stinging northeaster, driving a blinding snowfall over the surf with a malevolent fury. The Gloucester evening paper for December 17th stated that no less than fifty persons must have perished; the coasts were strewn with the wrecks of twenty to twenty-five vessels, and scattered about them were mangled bodies of lifeless sailors. In Cape Ann Harbor twenty vessels were grounded, and sixteen of these were dashed to bits. Countless lives had been lost, and seventeen corpses had already been recovered. The newspaper adds that one body was that of a female who had been "lashed to the bitts of the windlass of a coastline schooner. The place where most of these vessels struck was a reef of rocks called Norman's Woe."

For ten days the thought of this direful catastrophe kept running through Longfellow's mind before the outline for a story on the subject unfolded itself clearly before him. Then on December 30th he relates in his journal the results of his ruminations: "I sat till twelve by the fire, smoking, when suddenly it came into my mind to write the 'Ballad of the Schooner Hesperus,' which I accordingly did. I went to bed, but could not sleep. New thoughts were running in my mind, and I got up to add them to the ballad. It was three by the clock. I then went to bed and fell asleep. I feel pleased with the ballad. It hardly cost me an effort. It did not come into my mind by lines but by stanzas."

For a while he was frenzied with the thought of becoming a sort of Icelandic scop or gleeman. He would have the ballad printed on individual sheets, with a picture of the wreck and the frozen girl appearing at the top of the sheet, above the poem. He would then distribute copies on the docks among the sailors. Hawthorne was also taken up with the idea and volunteered help in distributing the ballad-sheets. The plan fell through, however.

A few weeks later the poem was published in the *New World*. Park Benjamin, the editor, was delighted with the ballad, and paid the author twenty-five dollars for it. Since its first publication, "The Wreck of the Hesperus" has been sailing along smoothly, year after year, entering our school readers and anthologies far more easily than it ever entered Gloucester Harbor.

The spoon, colonial in form, is barren of ornament except for the outlines of the wrecked schooner lying on its port side against the reef of Norman's Woe. The names of the Hesperus, Norman's Woe, and Gloucester, Massachusetts, all stand in relief on the slightly-splayed, single-section handle. A product of the Williams Bros. Silver Company, the spoon is 4¼ inches long.

No. 123 PRESCOTT WINDLASS

The failure of many of the conquistadores to strike riches in their explorations may be attributed to the fact that they looked for precious metals in the finished product and overlooked a horn of plenty in the rough. Coronado, the earliest Spaniard to wander through the Southwest in search of gold, handed in a very sour report on the fruitless results of his expedition. Espejo, hearing about mines on the Verde River, did some prospecting in the territory and reported that the mines were "so worthless we did not find in any of them a trace of silver, as they were copper mines, and poor." Oñate drove sheep and cattle northward out of Mexico, opened up the first settlement in the arid country, but opened no mines. What little silver was obtained by Espejo and Oñate came from surface deposits not far west of Prescott.

Nearly three centuries elapsed before hardy American prospectors, their faithful burros loaded with grub kit and mining tools, appeared in the hills around Prescott looking for gold and taking out claims. The Civil War was in progress, and most of the miners were Southern sympathizers.

450

To make sure the region would be kept in the right hands, the government in Washington created the Territory of Arizona late in 1863, built barracks, and established a capital, naming it after the noted New England historian, William Hickling Prescott.

The first building in the new town was Fort Misery, a simple two-room log cabin, which was attacked by Indians during the first court session held there. Prisoners being tried rushed to the defense of the settlement, and in reward for their services were freed without further trial. Fort Misery acquired its lugubrious name while it was still a boarding house kept by the "Virgin Mary," a kind and motherly old woman who for years served venison steaks and coffee enriched by goats' cream to tickle the gullets of her customers. A replica of the old fort stands on the same site today.

In 1867 the capital was transferred to Tucson; then Prescott was again made the capital from 1877 to 1889. The rivalry between Tucson and Prescott ended when Phoenix, halfway between the two towns, was chosen as the permanent capital. Prescott might have languished and died after the first gold-rush fever had cooled, if Eastern promoters had not advertised the place as a distinctive New England village ideal for those people seeking to regain their lost health.

Mines were constantly being opened up in Yavapai County, of which Prescott was made the seat, and at one time, after new rich veins of silver had been discovered, the town became a wide-open gambling resort, belying the staid primness of its New England designation. Swarms of prospectors camped on the pine-clad hillsides, and some of them scraped fortunes from silver-rich lodes bursting out of rocky seams to the surface for easy pickings.

When the price of silver slumped, miners diverted their attention to gold, but gold mining was expensive and the hit-or-miss prospectors did not have the money to finance large undertakings. It took capital to move gold.

Then in 1916 the United Verde Copper Mines struck veins of ore that revealed the richest deposits of copper to be found anywhere in the world. The company could well afford the construction of a smelter costing two and a half millions. Other companies came in for a large share of the big profits in copper production. The ore is found here in cylindrical masses, and costs about ten cents a pound for extraction. Some two billion pounds have already been taken out by the United Verde, and probably twice that amount still remains in the teeming lodes.

Since 1907 Arizona has produced more copper than any other state. Much of the ore yields other metals as well, the chief of these being gold, silver, lead, and zinc, by-products which would not be profitable in themselves, but tremendously valuable when recovered along with the copper. One-fourth of the population of the state earns its livelihood from the mining industry. Gone are the days when miners employed the

451

primitive methods of pick and shovel, the Long Tom, arrastra and tailing dump for separating the valuable minerals from the gangue in placer workings. Diamond-point drills and shovels operated electrically delve deep into the bowels of rock to displace the rich assortment of ores.

Prescott, high in its mountain fastness, enjoys a dry, invigorating climate throughout the year. When Phoenix and Tucson are sweltering in summer temperatures reaching 100 degrees or above, Prescott sleepers can draw their blankets up about them for a comfortable night's rest. Many people from the low, heat-burdened sections flee to this haven of coolth for relief. The atmosphere, lacking humidity and laden with the pungent aroma of pines, is extremely beneficial to tuberculars. The beauty of its mountain vistas is awe-inspiring: the lofty peaks and precipitous chasms, the forest-girt ridges, the crystalline waters of filliping streams, the aura of clouds in the sapphire-blue skies; and permeating all with gladness, overhead, everywhere, is the beneficent sunshine.

In its plaza Prescott has erected a monument in bronze to one of its favorite sons, Bucky O'Neil, on horseback, in verisimilitude of his actions in busting a bronco. O'Neil, hero of endless tales in the days when outlaws needed taming, rode with Teddy Roosevelt's Rough Riders in the Spanish-American War and lost his life at San Juan Hill. Somehow it seems that he is the truest embodiment of that invigorating spirit which distinguishes Prescott from the towns of the Arizona lowlands.

In the gold-washed bowl of the Prescott Windlass spoon is the engraving of a smeltering plant and mountains in the background. Hardly perceptible in the bottom foreground is an ore-wagon drawn by two mules, the driver holding a whip in his hands.

The handle of this spoon is unique. It vividly represents a mine shaft, at the top of which is a winch or windlass with movable crank fastened to a rope that winds around the handle to the drop, where it is attached to an ore-bucket. A pick and shovel form the nave to support the winch-box in the caput.

No maker's name appears on the spoon. Length, 6 inches.

No. 125 CHICAGO KATE

It was the Columbian World's Fair and Exposition in Chicago in 1893 that gave the greatest impetus to the collecting of souvenir spoons and made it a national hobby. Every visitor to the Fair brought back a goodly number of spoons for gifts to friends at home. Today we invariably find spoons commemorating the Fair in every collection, large or small.

This particular spoon must have struck the fancy of a great many people, for it still appears in many collections. It is usually found with some familiar Christian name engraved on the reverse side of bowl. Of the three different sizes in which it was made, the largest appears here.

On the bowl in front, the space around the name of Chicago has been cut away, thus forming the semblance of an irregular-shaped cloud. The shaft begins on a short shelf, from which it proceeds to the top in a corkscrew twist resembling an auger. On the shaft-end rests a globular knop having a short protuberance like the blunted point of a pencil.

On the reverse side of this bowl the name "Kate" is engraved. Whether Kate was a denizen of Chicago, a visitor, or the recipient of a gift from the Windy City, we do not know, but let us hope she was not so shrewish as Petruchio's Kate, so unfortunate as Henry the Eighth's two Kates, or so imperious as Russia's Kate the Great. But what's in a name?

There is no indication as to the maker of this spoon. Length, 5¾ inches.

No. 126 NAVAHO SYMBOLS

The art of the silversmith is not an ancient one among the Navahos. Less than a century ago they learned the art from the Mexicans in an accidental manner. A horse that had thrown and killed its Mexican rider was found grazing by the Indians. Their eye was quickly diverted to the handsome silverwork on the bridle.

One of the first Navahos to imitate successfully the headstall, bridle-ring, bit, and dingle-dangles was Old Smith, an artisan who for years had been fashioning Indian bridle-bits out of iron. So great was the demand for Old Smith's work among his own tribesmen that he trained his four sons, Big Black, Red Smith, Little Smith, and Burnt Whiskers to follow in his footsteps. He would say to his sons as he said to many who asked him to teach them: "Watch me and I won't have to teach you." As yet, all of their work was hammered out of iron, there being no access to any silver.

In 1864 when the Navahos were herded into Fort Sumner, they were given coils of copper and brass with which to while away their time in devising bracelets. Unable to sell more than a few of these objects to the soldiers in the fort, the Indians used their handiwork to gamble with. Piles of bracelets, valued at twenty-five cents apiece, passed from hand to hand among the gamblers.

When they returned to the reservation, the Navahos received a small supply of silver from the whites, most of it already coined into money. With this meager dole of the white metal the Indians applied their craft in making bells, buttons, belts, squash blossom necklaces, and adornments for harness. Much of their handiwork was worn on their persons, and when they visited a trading post, they would detach an ornament or snip off a button in exchange for a manufactured article of the whites.

During the last three decades of the nineteenth century the best Navaho silver was made. The Indians followed their own bent in designing pieces that were simple but curiously original. Their productions, though tending to show rough edges, were practical and contained a rich content of silver.

Learning that they could obtain better results with Mexican pesos, they bartered American dollars for those coins. Eventually they became wiser, and paid only seventy-five cents for the pesos, later reducing the price to fifty cents.

In 1899 the Fred Harvey Company, realizing the great interest which sightseers to the Southwest were taking in Navaho silverwork, made contracts to secure regular supplies for its curio shops in Albuquerque and at the Grand Canyon. The commercialization of the art made certain changes necessary. While the quality of the silver remained substantially the same, the quantity was reduced to give lightness of weight. The company provided much of the material that went into these commercialized articles. Raw silver slugs were substituted for the Mexican pesos, and many designs, hitherto unknown to the Indians, were made possible by dies which stamped patterns on the silver while it was still ductile. Some craftsmen preferred, however, to fabricate their designs by hand on the malleable metal, and rubbed them down with buckskin to attain a soft, glowing finish.

The Indians learned quickly to cater to the tourist trade, which rose to a tremendous volume after the First World War. Travelers from the East carried back great quantities of low-priced souvenirs which the Harvey Company sold on trains and in station stands, curio shops, and resort hotels. Among the various articles made by the Navahos as souvenirs may be mentioned the conchas (plaques of silver worn on belts or hatbands), ketohs (bow guards), bridle adornments, necklaces and bracelets, rings and earrings, tobacco canteens and boxes, buttons and pins, ash trays and letter openers, forks and spoons.

The Zuñi, Hopi, and other Pueblo Indians, seeing the profits being made by the Navahos, have turned to silver making also. There is a tendency on the part of some people to deplore the mass production of souvenirs, believing that commercialized precision has killed the beauty inherent in a hand-wrought art. It is true that the personal touch is gone, but an increased skill compensates for the primitive crudeness of a former day. The Indian is willing to give up his originality if he is paid for it. Many of them have turned into artisans for the money. John Adair in his book on *The Navaho and Pueblo Silversmiths* quotes one Zuñi workman as saying, "My wife and I have fifty-five sheep and ten goats, an auto, and this new house. Seven years ago we didn't have anything."

The spoon pictured here is quite typical, as it contains four of the most popular and characteristic symbols.

The thunderbird at the top of the spiral handle is regarded as a supernatural bird by the North American Indians, able to create thunder and lightning by flapping its wings among the black clouds scudding through the upper regions of the sky. Actually the bird resembles the turkey vulture, familiar in the Southwest.

454

At the bottom of the bowl is seen the swastika, or whirling log. Unlike the Nazi Hakenkreuz, which bends its arms at right angles, clockwise, the Indian symbol turns its arms in the opposite direction, at left angles. The swastika is a very ancient character, having been thought by the peoples of early Persia and India to be a sign of good luck or benediction. Representations of the swastika have been unearthed in remains from the Bronze Age at Troy. The North American Indians have generally regarded the "whirling log" as a token of the benevolent rays of the sun.

In the center of the bowl appears a sand spider, a symbol of much significance on Navaho rugs and blankets. At one time there was always a hole left in a blanket by the weaver, and this outlet was called the spider hole.

According to the legend related by Dane and Mary Coolidge in their book on the Navahos, there happened to be a Kisani Woman whom no one wanted for a wife, for, although she was a comely, spirited wench, she wove very badly, and her blankets were the ugliest in the tribe. While out picking blueberries one day she walked toward a hole in the ground from which smoke was rising. Looking down into the hole, she saw the Spider Woman spinning a web of such intricate design and beautiful colors that the Kisani Woman asked permission to come down and watch. The Spider Woman granted this permission in return for a bucket of berries.

For days the Kisani Woman sat and patiently watched till she had learned to make three distinct designs in blankets, the Cloud Weave, the Lightning Weave, and the Ceremonial. She thanked the Spider Woman, who gave her one last warning before she departed: "Whenever you make a blanket, leave a hole in it or you will have dire misfortune. The hole is an escape for all that is ugly and bad."

So the Kisani Woman went back to her people and began to weave the most beautiful blankets they had ever seen. The women uttered exclamations of envy while the men were now all anxious to have her as a wife.

"But where did you learn to weave such wonderful designs?" queried every one.

"In the berry patch from a little spider," she answered honestly.

They laughed incredulously at this strange explanation, but ever since the Navahos have been careful to leave the spider hole in the middle of a blanket, just like the hole in the center of a spider web.

The beaded crescent that lies near the rim of the bowl is a variation of the *najahe* (or *naja*), a form of amulet originally suspended from the headstrap on bridles. Later it became a popular pendant on the squash blossom necklace, where it often resembles a horseshoe full of nails. Here again we have an emblem that was used in the Old World by the Romans and Moors. Yet it was known to several other widely scattered tribes of Indians besides the Navahos at an early date. It may not be, therefore, of European origin in this particular usage.

The Navaho Symbols spoon is much longer than usual, measuring 7 inches. It has been used through the courtesy of Captain Lloyd E. Miller, formerly of the Kentucky Military Institute, Lyndon, Kentucky. Captain Miller states that the spoon was bought in 1910 at Albuquerque.

No. 127 SIR WALTER SCOTT

The only British author who might be set up as a rival to Shakespeare for the extent of his influence upon American thought is Sir Walter Scott, romantic poet and founder of the historical school of fiction. In unlocking the world of the past, Scott created a widened circle of readers for the novel, which quickly surpassed drama and poetry in popular esteem. His romances were not only informative but extremely entertaining. The novel was not a new type of literature when Scott appeared upon the scene, but he gave it prestige and a more dignified position than it had hitherto enjoyed. The fiction of Elizabethan writers had been experimental in nature and full of conceits; Bunyan, Swift, and Defoe had written splendid narratives in a simple, straightforward style, yet devoid of suspense, mystery, or love interest; Richardson and Burney used the clumsy epistolary method to advance a love story; Fielding and Smollett, in making the novel more realistic, coarsened the form while they broadened it; Sterne and Goldsmith, though utterly lacking in the creation of plots, furnished pleasant reading; Horace Walpole and Mrs. Radcliffe aimed to give their readers the creeps with the supernatural elements of their Gothic romances; Maria Edgeworth and Jane Austen presented superb pictures of English manners and society. Still, fiction was not yet a widely accepted type of reading, and young ladies still had to hide novels under their pillows from parents concerned over the proper sort of reading pap for their dutiful offsprings.

It remained for Scott to change all this. He brought the novel out into the open, rejected all its worst elements, and by making people believe they were actually reading history in a sugar-coated form, overrode most of the time-honored objections to the novel.

Scott's influence was enormous, not only in England and on the Continent, but also here in America. As early as 1805 we find Americans among the most avid readers of Scott's poems. As soon as the *Lay of the Last Minstrel, Marmion,* and the *Lady of the Lake* appeared in Great Britain, they were whisked off to this country and published in popular editions, there being then no international copyright law to prevent such piracy. It was far more profitable for our presses to republish English books than to pay American writers for original works. In 1807 Noah Webster voiced a protest against the prevalence of English books on the American market, adding: "But there is another evil resulting from this dependence which is little considered; that is, that it checks improvement.

No one man in a thousand—not even the violent political opposers of Great Britain—reflects upon this influence. Our people look to English books as the standards of truth on all subjects, and this confidence puts an end to inquiry . . . We have opposed to us the publishers of most of the popular periodical works in our large towns."

The cause of American literary independence seemed all the more hopeless when Scott began his series of Waverley novels in 1814. During the next nine years five hundred thousand copies of his Scottish romances were sold in this country. In 1823 when Scott turned back to the Middle Ages and began to glamorize feudalism and the Crusades, his books reached an even wider sale on the American market. One publisher reported, a few years after this, that he had shipped a whole train-load of these novels south of the Potomac.

In 1818 John Bristed, while giving his reasons for Scott's great success in America, went on to say: "Of native novels we have no great stock, and none good; our democratic institutions placing all the people on a dead level of political equality; and the pretty equal diffusion of property throughout the country affords but little room for varieties, and contrasts of character; nor is there much scope for fiction, as the country is quite new, and all that has happened from the first settlement to the present hour, respecting it, is known to every one. There is, to be sure, some traditionary romance about the Indians; but a novel describing these miserable barbarians, their squaws and papooses, would not be very interesting to the present race of American readers."

Our native writers were not prone to take this challenge of Scott's supremacy lying down. Even though our history could boast of no Feudal Age, with its turreted towers or castles, titled lords or ladies, we had had two hundred years of Indian warfare and a struggle for political independence behind us. In 1821 James Fenimore Cooper published his first book, *The Spy*, and it soon became obvious that Scott had an American competitor with the power to create exciting stories out of native material. Cooper sustained his reputation with *The Pioneers*, *The Last of the Mohicans*, and *The Prairie*, all of which were as eagerly read by Europeans as by Americans. In his vivid tales of the sea, *The Pilot* and *The Red Rover*, Cooper clearly surpassed Scott in a field unexploited by the British author except for a single attempt. Scott's *Pirate* has been called a "mere daub" in comparison with Cooper's *Pilot*.

The two novelists met several times in Europe, and each recorded his reactions about the other. The entry in Scott's diary says that Cooper possessed "a good deal of the manner, or want of manner, peculiar to his countrymen." Cooper, on the other hand, believed that Scott lacked "the ease and *aplomb* of one accustomed to live with his equals." Both were overshadowed by Coleridge, the brilliant conversationalist, at a dinner party in London. When later they walked into the parlor, Scott was quickly surrounded by a "maze of petticoats"—so says Cooper—"and as in Paris let them play with his mane as they pleased." The American inherently disliked Scott's deference to rank and titles. When Cooper recognized Scott's carriage in the Pall Mall one day by its coat-of-arms, with the bloody hand and the mermaid combing her long hair before a dainty mirror, he was not disgusted by the points of the escutcheon so much as he was by the fact that Scott was thus slavishly aping the nobility in so conspicuously displaying his coat-of-arms.

Cooper protested against the sobriquet often applied to him, "the American Scott," as it betokened an imitation which he stoutly disclaimed. In fact, Scott's romances produced an adverse effect upon Cooper, and he penned three novels, *The Bravo, The Headsman,* and *The Heidenmauer,* on medieval European subjects primarily to rectify the false impressions created by Scott's glamorous pictures of the feudal world, and to "show the evil of institutions that throve on the ignorance of the masses and had no proper base in the will of the nation." He postulated the superiority of a democratic government in these three stories, in which "American opinion should be brought to bear on European facts." As it happened, these novels were the least successful of Cooper's performances. People did not like a realistic treatment of the Middle Ages.

The American author with whom Scott shared the greatest mutual admiration was Washington Irving. Shortly after the publication of *Knickerbocker's History of New York,* Scott wrote that he had never found anything more comical than the characters in this naïve account of early New York, and he declared Irving was already one of the surest masters of the English language. A few years later, when Irving was on his way to Melrose Abbey, he stopped at Abbotsford with a letter of introduction from Thomas Campbell, and was quite overwhelmed by the effusive welcome with which Scott received him. The "lord of the castle" hurriedly limped up the gravel walk on his cane and, surrounded by a nondescript pack of yelping dogs, grasped the young author's hand warmly. "Come, drive down, drive down to the house," he insisted. "Ye're just in time for breakfast, and afterwards ye shall see all the wonders of the Abbey." Although Irving had eaten one breakfast, he had to eat another with the Scott family.

This visit, intended for a half hour or so, lengthened into a stay of several days. With a discerning insight Irving paints a pleasing picture of the daily life at Abbotsford, and we find many democratic touches in the Scotchman who was eventually to become a baronet and flaunt a coat-of-arms on his carriage. Abbotsford was then in the process of being transformed into a lordly castle, and Irving saw Scott stop and ask for a pinch of snuff from one of the masons cutting stone from the quarry for the new edifice. All the laborers paused to have a "crack wi' the laird," and several pleasantries were exchanged between the master and his workmen.

458

The evenings were spent in a delightful old drawing room, where Scott was seated in a large armchair surrounded by his books, relics, and border trophies, and his favorite hound, Maida, lying at his feet. The eldest daughter, Sophia, sang quaint old Scotch ballads without the help of accompaniment in simple folksong style, and Scott related the story concerning a "whimsical picture" hanging on the wall. When Irving inquired into the nature of the oldest boy's studies, Scott replied: "Faith, I can't say much on that head. I am not over bent upon making prodigies of any of my children. As to Walter, I taught him, while a boy, to ride, and shoot, and speak the truth." Scott also confessed that he had taken "special care" to prevent his children from reading any of their "papa's follies" during their earlier years.

For us the most interesting feature of Irving's visit to Abbotsford was the graphic account he gave about an acquaintance of his, the beautiful Jewess, Rebecca Gratz, who had nursed his fiancée, Mathilda Hoffman, during her last illness. Scott was enthralled by the tragedy of the ailing Christian maiden who was so faithfully attended by her closest friend, a Jewish girl, who could not conscientiously forsake the religion of her ancestors to marry a Christian suitor whom she loved. Scott was so deeply affected by the story that he incorporated the American Jewess, even without changing her name, into the novel *Ivanhoe*, which he published the next year.

Since this is the only character from the New World ever used by Scott, let us pause to review his description of her: "The figure of Rebecca might indeed be compared with the proudest beauties of England. . . . Her form was exquisitely symmetrical, and was shown to advantage by a sort of Eastern dress, which she wore according to the fashion of the females of her nation. Her turban of yellow silk suited well with the darkness of her complexion. The brillancy of her eyes, the superb arch of her eyebrows, her well-formed aquiline nose, her teeth as white as pearl, and the profusion of her sable tresses, which, each arranged in its own little spiral of twisted curls, fell down upon as much of a lovely neck and bosom as a simarre of the richest Persian silk, exhibiting flowers in their natural colours embossed upon a purple ground, permitted to be visible—all these constituted a combination of loveliness, which yielded not to the most beautiful of the maidens who surrounded her. It is true, that of the golden and pearl-studded clasps, which closed her vest from the throat to the waist, the three uppermost were left unfastened on account of the heat, which somewhat enlarged the prospect to which we allude. A diamond necklace, with pendants of inestimable value, were by this means also made more conspicuous. The feather of an ostrich, fastened in her turban by an agraffe set with brilliants, was another distinction of the beautiful Jewess, scoffed and sneered at by the proud dames who sat above her, but secretly envied by those who affected to deride them."

Rebecca Gratz lived with her father for several years in Lexington, Kentucky, where two of her brothers married into Gentile families, descendants of whom are still prominent in that section of the state. Her father, who at one time owned Mammoth Cave, later moved back to Philadelphia, where Rebecca died, unmarried, like Irving, in the eighty-seventh year of her age, in 1869.

Because of its colorful pageantry, *Ivanhoe* has always been the favorite of Scott's novels among Americans, although some of his Scottish romances, particularly *Guy Mannering* and *The Heart of Midlothian* are relished more by those who do not mind Scott's use of a rich, racy vernacular.

Except for his inclusion of Rebecca Gratz in *Ivanhoe*, Scott introduced no other American characters into his writings. The only allusions he ever made to America were in *Peveril of the Peak*, where Major Bridgenorth relates some of his youthful experiences in New England. We know that Scott read a few American authors, such as Washington Irving and Charles Brockden Brown—he used two names from the latter's books in *Guy Mannering*. Then he also purloined a line, for inclusion in the third canto of *Marmion*, from Freneau's *Eutaw Springs*, a poem which he handsomely praised. Yet for all his lack of interest in things American, it is our countrymen who have paid him the greatest homage in our continued veneration. Nearly all the devotees who make the pilgrimage to the Scott countryside are Americans.

It may be that the English were more quickly disenchanted from Scott's spell than his far-away readers across the Atlantic. George Barrows, the Welshman, was an inveterate foe of Scott and soundly berated his "Scotch-gentility nonsense." Thackeray considered Cooper's Leatherstocking superior to any of the heroes in "Scott's lot." The influence of Scott was practically nil on the other members of the English Romantic movement, and to some, like Shelley and Keats, his subservience to royalty was anathema. Lord Morpeth was astonished when he visited Charleston, South Carolina, just before the Civil War and perceived the intense adulation of Scott among the Charlestonians. When he argued the merits of their native novelist, William Gilmore Simms, they in turn were astonished. But the honest, august British lord floored them with his swift retort: "If Simms is not a great man, then for God's sake, who is your great man?"

As for his readers in this country, we have only to turn the pages of biography to discover that Scott was the favorite youthful reading for many of our authors in all sections. Bryant, Longfellow, Lowell, N. P. Willis, Fitz-Greene Halleck, Daniel Pierce Thompson, Lanier, John Esten Cooke, Harriet Beecher Stowe, and George Ticknor all have testified to a penchant for Scott in their early days. Whitman perused all the Scott novels he could find in the library of a neighboring doctor, and carried a dirty copy of Scott's *Border Minstrelsy* in his lunch basket when he went about carpentering. Audubon slept with a Scott novel under his pillow.

460

Among novels obviously patterned after Scott's style or betraying his influence are Hawthorne's *Fanshawe,* Catherine Sedgwick's *Redwood,* John McClung's *Camden,* James Hall's *Harpe's Head,* Robert Montgomery Bird's *Calavar,* and William Alexander Caruthers' *The Cavaliers of Virginia.* Steamboats on the Mississippi and the Ohio were named "Marmion," "Lady of the Lake," and "Loch Katrine." Race horses were frequently christened "Rob Roy," "Ivanhoe," or "Redgauntlet." Manorial estates in the South bore such Scottish echoes as "Kenilworth," "Rokeby," "Waverley," "Woodstock," or "Deloraine."

In the North we find several spirits rebelling against this Scott idolatry. James Kirke Paulding often made thrusts at the inflated, stilted style of Scott and his followers. He burlesqued the poetic mannerisms of Scott in *The Lay of the Scottish Fiddle,* a rollicking poem in five cantos. In *Koningsmarke, the Long Finne,* he poked fun at the Waverley novels by taking a self-booster with heroic pretensions in the old Swedish colony of Delaware and eventually proving him to be just an ordinary fellow, only with a little less common sense than his more prosaic countrymen.

Emerson certainly was not swayed by the romantic tales of Scott, else he would not have written this admonition in his Journal of 1843: "Do not write modern antiques like Landor's *Pericles* or Scott's *Lay of the Last Minstrel.* They are paste jewels. You may well take an ancient subject where the form is incidental merely, like Shakespeare's plays, and the treatment and dialogue are simple, and most modern. But do not make much of the costume. For such things have no verity; no man will live or die by them. The way to write is to throw your body at the mark when the arrows are spent, like Cupid in Anacreon. Shakespeare's speeches in *Lear* are in the very dialect of 1843."

When we come to evaluate Scott's influence upon the South, often called "Sir Walter Scotland," we run into a tinderbox of conflicting opinions. His vogue persisted there longer than in the North, for certain of his virtues appealed to the heart of the Southerner, whether or not that Southerner was a big cotton planter, lawyer, a middle-class townsman, or the dweller of a humble country cabin. Scott depicted a Golden Age, long past, but fascinating, one that could be taken as an ideal for a present-day order that did not concern itself with immediate problems or look toward dubious changes in the future. Scott's main characters were brave, pure, high-minded, and infallibly righteous, with an intense veneration for the *status quo,* which in this instance meant a feudal system consisting of two social class-orders, inherent in the lord and his vassals.

We have evidence that Jefferson Davis and Robert E. Lee were both great admirers of the Wizard of the North. Henry Clay spellbound the members of the Virginia legislature, before which body he had carried the case of statehood for Kentucky, when he quoted that passage from *Marmion* beginning —

Breathes there a man with soul so dead,
Who never to himself hath said,
"This is my own, my native land"?

Hugh Swinton Legaré, of Charleston, spent hours, when he was studying law in Edinburgh, simply gazing at the great Sir Walter sitting at his
desk in the Parliament House. Grace King tells this pathetic story of a
victim to the plague which swept over New Orleans in 1832: A friend had
placed the latest Scott novel in the sick man's hands. "His cold fingers
could turn the leaves, but his eyes were growing dim. 'I am blind,' he
gasped. 'I cannot see. I must be dying, and leaving this new production
of immortal genius unread.'" When Scott died, it seemed like a time of
national mourning in the South. The *Richmond Enquirer* placed a heavy
margin of black around its pages.

On the other hand, not all Southerners fell victims to the prevalent
Scott-o-mania. Thomas Jefferson thought it reprehensible that Scott should
disinter the bones of feudalism and use them as puppets after Cervantes
had so effectually buried them two centuries before. John Randolph of
Roanoke preferred Fielding and Byron to Scott. William Childs, editor
of the *Charleston Courier,* would have let all the Waverley Novels perish,
if a choice had to be made, rather than lose anything of Shakespeare,
Milton, or Pope. The two chief novelists of the ante-bellum South, William
Gilmore Simms and John Pendleton Kennedy, reveal little or no influence
of Scott. Indeed, Kennedy writes as if the Scottish novelist had never
been, being more of an Elizabethan or Addisonian writer than a nineteenth-
century romanticist. "His vocabulary," says Parrington, "is saturated with
the homely old speech, and his characters talk as if they had culled all
the simples of English cottage gardens to garnish the staple of their wit.
He has a keener delight than Simms in the picturesque archaic. He far
surpasses Irving in easy mastery of the old-fashioned colloquial, as indeed
he surpasses all our early novelists."

Of course, the most vitriolic attack ever made upon Scott was that
penned by Mark Twain, in his *Life on the Mississippi*: "Then comes Sir
Walter Scott with his enchantments . . . sets the world in love with dreams
and phantoms; with decayed and swinish forms of religion; with decayed
and degraded systems of government; with the sillinesses and emptinesses,
sham grandeurs, sham gauds, and sham chivalries of a brainless and worthless long-vanished society. He did measureless harm; more real and lasting
harm, perhaps, than any other individual that ever wrote. Most of the
world has now outlived good part of these harms, though by no means
all of them; but in the South they flourish pretty forcefully still . . . There,
the genuine and wholesome civilization of the nineteenth century is
curiously confused and commingled with the Walter Scott-Middle Age
sham civilization, and so you have practical common sense, progressive
ideas, and progressive works, mixed up with the duel, the inflated speech,
and the jejune romanticism of an absurd past that is dead, and out of

charity ought to be buried . . . It was Sir Walter Scott that made every gentleman in the South a major or a colonel, or a general or a judge, before the war . . . For it was he that created rank and caste down there, and also reverence for rank and caste, and pride and pleasure in them."

Following hard on the heels of this indictment, Mark Twain charges that "Sir Walter had so large a hand in making Southern character, as it existed before the war, that he is in great measure responsible for the war." In the light of these pronouncements, Sir Walter might have toppled the world off its axis, had his influence on the other points of the compass been commensurate with that exercised on the South. Certainly there is a grain of truth in what Mark Twain says, but the diatribe is too jaundiced in its viewpoint to be wholly logical. And yet, to be sure, such blasts often act as good cathartics for the unthinking.

Miss Grace Landrum, of William and Mary College, made a very effectual refutation to Mark Twain's charges several years ago in the *American Literature* magazine by pointing out a large number of trenchant criticisms of Scott's work and influence, culled from the ante-bellum journals and reviews of the South. Scott had formidable rivals in Byron, Bulwer-Lytton, and a host of other English and American writers. One reviewer in 1851 says that Thackeray is "in all probability a greater benefactor to his kind than gentle Walter Scott or any other novelist in this century or the last." Bulwer's *Pelham,* she finds, took the South by storm, for readers "had grown weary of gallants pricking over the plain to the relief of distressed damsels. . . . We have no sympathy with these iron-clad knights of the olden time." Linton Stephens called Scott a "sycophant," and one critic in an issue of the *Southern Review* for 1829 spoke of Scott's poetry as "insufferable doggerel." A very discordant note was struck in the *Southern Literary Messenger* of 1835 when it was said that after the Radcliffe "dynasty" had come the Edgeworth, then the Scott, "each like the family of Caesars, passing from good to bad, and from bad to worse till each has run out." An essayist in the same magazine for 1860 suspects that admiration for Scott was something more "hereditary and dutiful" than profound or fundamental. Again, in his *Life of Napoleon,* Scott is charged with being a time-server with a "humble prostration of intellect becoming a courtly writer."

Walter Hines Page in 1881 wrote an article entitled "An Old Southern Borough" for the *Atlantic Monthly.* He proceeded to picture two types of individuals found in a small, lethargic North Carolina town: those who continued to feed on the opiates of the old classics, especially the writings of Sir Walter Scott, who had drugged them with the false notions of a long-outmoded chivalry; and those belonging to a new generation, alert, and conscious of the burning issues of the present order.

Whatever we might say further, pro or con, in regard to the great Scottish romancer, of this fact we must become increasingly aware—that he was read as no other writer was ever read in America, and that his influence was a very real and potent one over a long period of years. For some he was a great source of pleasure and happiness, a veritable necromancer who lifted thousands of ordinary people out of their humdrum existences and cast them into another world of dancing plumes and glittering lances; for others he was a source of prickly irritations, a wicked enchanter who brought harm and bedevilment to all those who read him.

Out of charity, let us end this discussion with the tribute of Mark Rutherford, one of his humble admirers: "If anywhere in another world the blessings which men have conferred here are taken into account in distributing reward, surely the choicest in store of the Most High will be reserved for His servant Scott!"

The Sir Walter Scott spoon, doubtless brought back from Edinburgh by some ardent admirer of the Northern bard and romancer, is of British make, and measures 5 inches in length. But for the name on the reverse side of the bust, which stands out prominently at the top of the spiraling handle, I would have assumed this were Bobbie Burns, the national poet of Scotland. As it is, I still think it resembles Burns more than Scott, although I have discovered one portrait of the latter, made in his earlier years, when he looks pretty much as he is imaged on this spoon. Even if it were Burns, it would still be a Scot(t)!

No. 128 PAUL REVERE'S RIDE

The famous ride of Paul Revere occurred, as we learn from Longfellow's poem, on the eighteenth of April, 1775, as soon as he saw the signal lights appear in the belfry of the Old North Church, indicating that the British were marching toward Lexington and Concord.

Events had moved swiftly during the immediately preceding months around Boston. General Gage, whose business it was to collect the taxes imposed by Parliament on the colonists, had a large contingent of regulars at his command ready to quell any open outbreak attempted by the fractious patriots, who for their part had been arming and drilling in groups known as Minutemen. Ammunition had been stored at Concord by the colonists, and General Gage figured that, if he seized control of this contraband means of war, he could cow the rebels into submission.

Paul Revere was waiting impatiently, "booted and spurred," on the Charlestown shore as he kept his eye on the church steeple—

> And lo! as he looks, on the belfry's height,
> A glimmer, and then a gleam of light!
> He springs in the saddle, the bridle he turns,
> But lingers and gazes till full on his sight
> A second lamp in the belfry burns!

Longfellow does not acquaint us with the fact that two other men, William Dawes and a Doctor Prescott, also rode forth with Paul Revere to

464

arouse the farmers and villagers from their sleep and to warn them that the Redcoats were marching. The poet singled out Revere to make the ride alone and the story, thus, was rendered more dramatic. Indeed, Revere and Dawes were captured and turned back, but Prescott evaded the British sentries by forcing his horse to vault a stone wall, and, by circumventing the danger point, succeeded in carrying the news on to Concord.

Even if he did not complete the ride he began on that fateful night, Paul Revere fully deserves the sobriquet thrust upon him, the "courier" or the "mercury of the Revolution." For years previous to 1775 he had been bearing messages from one colony to another. He had ridden regularly to Philadelphia and New York conveying plans for the establishment of a Continental Congress. Disguised as an Indian, he had participated in the Boston Tea Party. When the Congress was in session at Philadelphia, Revere rode once more to learn what was going on there. In December, 1774, four months before his Concord ride, he had journeyed to Portsmouth, New Hampshire, to warn the patriots that a British force was coming by sea from Boston to occupy Fort William and Mary near Portsmouth. The local Minutemen then surprised the fort, captured it, and carried away ninety-seven kegs of powder and several hundred muskets. This was the first direct seizure of royal firearms, and the King was angered. Again in January, 1775, Revere went to New Hampshire to attend a session of the provincial congress.

Paul Revere was an artist and industrialist as well as a patriot. Before the start of the Revolution, he had printed lampoons against the unjust measures of taxation forced upon the colonists. He made engravings of memorable scenes like the Boston Massacre. During the war he supervised the manufacture of cannon and gunpowder, repaired damaged muskets, printed the paper money needed by Congress, and even saw active service for a while in Rhode Island and Maine.

After the war he devised a new type of silver-plated false teeth helpful in speaking as well as in eating. In silverware he made tankards, tea and coffee pots, punch bowls, braziers, candlesticks, and dainty table pieces like cups and saucers—all long ago securely garnered into museums. He opened an iron foundry and experimented with metals of one sort or another for their practicability. He cast more than sixty bronze bells which were hung in church belfries throughout New England.

When he was nearing his seventieth year he discovered how to roll copper into sheets, and soon he was roofing state houses and coating the keels of ocean-going vessels with his new copper sheets. He sealed the boilers of Robert Fulton's steamboat, the *Raritan*, in copper.

When Washington died in 1799 a lock of the general's hair was cut from his head and placed in a golden receptacle designed by Paul Revere, who then prepared a cenotaph of white and black marble as a memorial to Washington. Revere survived until 1818, full of years well spent and honors well deserved.

The coffee spoon that shows Paul Revere on his midnight ride has a plain bowl and nothing but the rider on a galloping horse and the name of Boston on the handle. It is of a simple colonial type not unlike that designed so often by the artisan Revere himself. A full moon is rising behind the hills and several farm buildings are visible toward the left. As Revere gallops by, swinging his right arm like a beacon, a Minuteman stands in his doorway, a gun held in his right hand partly behind him.

This spoon was pressed by Durgin. The length is 4½ inches.

No. 129 NANTUCKET WINDMILL

From two limericks known to my childhood I learned two things about Nantucket: it was an island far away from the mainland, and the people who lived on this island were hardy seafaring folk. Limericks can make sense as well as nonsense. Nantucket, the Indian word for *Far-Away-Land,* is twenty miles from the "Continent." And once upon a time this small island, fourteen miles long and from two to four miles wide, was the umbilical cord of the whaling industry. When that cord was cut, Nantucket's prosperity dried up and the one town on the island became a miniature museum-piece.

The Indians had an ingenious way of explaining topographical peculiarities not known to our modern geologists. They said that a giant sleeping on Cape Cod could not rest one night because his moccasins were freighted with sand. So he tossed them off, one after the other, and they landed in the sea; one became Martha's Vineyard, the other Nantucket.

The first settlements on Nantucket were made about 1660. Originally a part of New York, the island was turned over to Massachusetts in 1692. A persuasive female preacher converted nearly all the people to Quakerism, and this religious influence lasted well down into the nineteenth century.

During the Revolution Nantucket was hard hit by the British blockade. Trade was strangled, and merchants went elsewhere. But business gradually revived, and by 1850 the island was a veritable beehive of industry, turning out candles, corsets, and perfumes—products derived from the spouting sperm whales which were harpooned in the far stretches of the seven seas. Two books that tell most graphically the exploits of these whaling days are Dana's *Two Years Before the Mast* and Melville's *Moby Dick.*

Spacious mansions of mansard, Victorian Gothic, and Neo-Greek styles attest the well-being of retired seamen in this golden era of the clipper ship. But a sharp decline in the number of whales captured set its seal of doom on this prosperity about the time of the Civil War. Within three decades two-thirds of the population had packed up their belongings and moved to the mainland, or set sail for California. Today the town of Nantucket derives its income chiefly from the tourist trade. Vacationers come to loiter, and to enjoy the beauty of the elm-shaded, cobblestone streets and the quietude of a picturesque, sea-girt countryside.

One of the principal landmarks near the town is the old mill pictured on the handle of this spoon. Built in 1746, it is the sole survivor of four mills once standing on the island. The arms of the mill can move only when the wind is from the west, but enough corn meal is ground to supply every one who wishes to take back a bag of meal with him to the mainland.

The mill is located on a high promontory that offers a splendid view of the surrounding area. All sorts of stories grown to legendary proportions are told of the old mill. During the Revolution a cannon ball came crashing through the walls and carried the miller's cap off his head. A daring young girl once attempted—a la Quijote—to stop the revolving arms, and was jounced up and over a few times before she called it quits. A boy once sighted, from the stair-window, a vessel floundering in a storm; he dispatched word around; all hands helped, and the entire crew was rescued only a few minutes before the ship sank.

The Nantucket spoon, pressed by Durgin, was patented April 2, 1891. The jeweler who controlled its sale was E. V. Hallett. Of demi-tasse size, the pattern is plain; the lines are curvaceous; there is not a single angle anywhere along the perimeter. The name Nantucket is carried in raised letters along the shaft, and on the crown, arched above the mill, is a cluster of wild spikenard. Length, 4¼ inches.

No. 132 HAWKEYE (BLACK HAWK)

The word "Hawkeye" as a sobriquet for Iowa or one of its inhabitants was coined by James G. Edwards, editor of the first newspaper in the state, the Fort Madison *Patriot*. Iowa, which had been first a part of the Territory of Michigan and then of Wisconsin, was set up as the Territory of Iowa in June, 1838. Three months previous, on March 24, 1838, Edwards had written editorially in his paper: "If a division of the territory is effected, we propose that the Iowans take the cognomen of Hawk-eyes. Our etymology can then be more definitely traced than can that of the Wolverines, Suckers, Gophers, etc., and we shall rescue from oblivion a memento, at least, of the name of the old chief." Readers of the Fort Madison *Patriot* took up the nickname that Edwards had suggested as a fine way for honoring "the old chief"—in this case, meaning Black Hawk.

The old Indian leader was still living, at the time, in that part of the Iowa Territory known as the Black Hawk Purchase, and he had always described that section of the Purchase along the Skunk River as "my old favorite hunting ground." Most of the lands considered as the special domain of the Sacs and Foxes, allied tribes to which Black Hawk belonged, were west of the Mississippi in Iowa, and only the capital town of Saukenuk, within a small adjacent area, was located east of the river in Illinois.

Saukenuk, at the mouth of the Rock River, was not the usual aggregate of wigwams indiscriminately set up in a clearing, but a stabilized settlement of five hundred families, with streets, a public square, rows of bark houses, a council lodge, brush ramparts, and gates of entrance. When the Sacs were not hunting wild game in the forests, they were employed in the cultivation of corn, potatoes, tobacco, beans, and melons on a rich strip of bottom land comprising about eight hundred acres. In their spare time the Indians turned their hands to composing tribal chants, songs, and speeches for pageants and plays glorifying their native traditions.

Black Hawk, who late in life dictated his autobiography, says that he was born in Saukenuk in 1767, but did nothing worthy of note till his fifteenth year, when he wounded an enemy, after which action he was elevated to the rank of a brave. Somewhat later he participated in a foray against the Osages, the hereditary enemies of the Sacs, and when he triumphantly displayed the scalp of a man he had killed, his father "said nothing, but looked pleased." After this exploit he was allowed to take part in the tribal scalp-dances.

For several years Black Hawk was constantly on the warpath, ostensibly for the purpose of defending the tribal possessions against predatory incursions. At one time he led a party of seven against one hundred Osages, killed one man, and beat a hasty retreat without incurring a single loss. When his father was killed by the Cherokees, he blackened his face, fasted, and prayed to the Great Spirit for five years before he was able to lead a party forth to avenge his father's death. When he ran upon and captured a party of five Cherokees, he felt compassion for them. He released the four men, but brought the squaw home. Not to be satisfied till he had humbled or annihilated the encroaching Osages, he recruited "five hundred Sacs and Foxes, and one hundred Ioways" to help carry out this grim determination. For several days he stalked the marauders till he discovered their encampment. Waiting till early dawn of the next day, he and his followers swooped down upon the forty lodges of the unsuspecting sleepers, and slew all of them except two squaws. This battle caused the surviving Osages "to remain on their own lands," relates Black Hawk, "and cease their aggressions upon our hunting grounds."

By the time he was thirty-five years old, Black Hawk, without the title or prerogatives of a chieftain, had become the accepted military leader of his people. He did not earn his commanding position through any physical attributes or military exploits so much as through his prepossessing personality. In height he was only about the average, nor was he stoutly built of frame. His bright, mild-mannered eyes and his persuasive voice gained for him an undue influence over his followers, who came to be known as the "British Band," because he was "firmly attached to the British and cordially hated the Americans." Governor Ford of Illinois, prejudiced though he was against Black Hawk, yet willingly conceded that this Indian enemy was "distinguished for courage, and for clemency to the vanquished. He was an Indian patriot, a kind husband and father, and was noted for his integrity in all his dealings with his tribe and with the Indian traders." Governor Reynolds, Benjamin Drake, Washington Irving, and others who saw him speak of his noble head and "Roman style of face."

The chief causes of the Black Hawk War resulted from a clause in the Treaty of 1804, made between the United States government and the Sac and Fox confederacy, wherein the Indians were allowed to hunt and fish over a domain of fifty million acres, ceded to the whites, so long as the property remained public lands of the government. But the encroachment of squatters, in subsequent years, on these lands made the Indians increasingly bitter. They did not mind the settlement of tracts on the eastern borders of their territory if the whites had not persisted in laying waste their cornfields, pillaging their village while they were away on the hunt, desecrating their cemeteries, beating their squaws and children, and even burning the wigwams of those Indians who ventured to live in isolated spots of the forest. The historian Thwaites remarks that it was "surprising that they acted so peacefully while the victims of such harsh treatment."

Keokuk, Rappello, and other leaders advocated a quiet removal to the Indian lands west of the Mississippi. Black Hawk might have acquiesced in this transfer also if, in the spring of 1830, he had not returned from his winter hunt to find some of the graves of his ancestors ploughed over. He immediately proceeded north to Malden in Canada, where his "British Father" listened sympathetically to a relation of his woes. He also visited White Cloud, the Prophet, who promised to enlist the aid of the Potawatomis and Winnebagos for his cause.

On his return from the hunt the next spring Black Hawk found squatters on his corn lands and threatened to use forceful measures if they did not decamp of their own will. The whites began to shower petitions upon Governor Reynolds appealing for protection. The governor issued a call for mounted volunteers, and in a short time sixteen hundred men, under the command of General Edmund P. Gaines, marched on Saukenuk. The night before their arrival the Indians withdrew during a terrible storm across the Mississippi and pitched camp about twelves miles below Rock Island. The volunteers entered the deserted village, and in spite of a heavy downpour of rain, left the place a smoldering heap of ruins. Not a single lodge-pole escaped the torch. A few days later the Indians signed a treaty in which they agreed never again to cross to the east banks of the Mississippi "without the permission of the President of the United States or the Governor of the State of Illinois."

Black Hawk's followers then settled on the north banks of the Iowa River, but being without food, they tried to steal roasting ears, beans, and pumpkins from the fields they had planted. In this they were unsuccessful, for at every attempt to "steal their own food," they were fired upon.

Black Hawk sat and brooded in his hut on the Iowa during the winter of 1831-32. He was visited by the malcontent, Neapope, said to have been a half-brother of White Cloud, both of whom intensely hated all Americans. Neapope acted as an intermediary envoy and spoke glowingly of the aid promised by the British Father, the Ottawas, Chippewas, Potawatomis, and Winnebagos if Black Hawk went on the warpath in the spring.

Early in April, 1832, Black Hawk assembled his warriors, about five hundred in number, and crossed the Mississippi into Illinois. The squaws followed in the rear with their children and belongings. At the Rock River they joined the Prophet and his band of four hundred and fifty men, intending to raise a crop and collect war supplies sufficient for a campaign in the fall. When General Henry Atkinson heard the news of Black Hawk's crossing into Illinois, he sent word to Governor Reynolds that he could not cope with the hostile forces assembled in White Cloud's camp, and asked for reënforcements. The governor was not slow in issuing another frenzied proclamation urgently calling for mounted volunteers.

The army that was organized amid the general excitement included many men who were to make their mark later in the nation's history, such as Abraham Lincoln, Jefferson Davis, Zachary Taylor, Winfield Scott, Robert Anderson, Allbert Sidney Johnston, and William S. Harney. The story is told that Jefferson Davis administered the oath of service to Lincoln on his enlistment. The story is interesting but not true, for Davis was at home in Mississippi on furlough at the time that Lincoln enlisted.

Discouraged by the lack of enthusiasm among the Potawatomis and Winnebagos for an all-out war against the whites, Black Hawk resolved to return to the west bank of the river after making his peace with General Atkinson. He consequently dispatched three of his men with a flag of true to bring the "White Beaver" into a council for peace negotiations. Five scouts followed at a distance to observe the treatment accorded the flag-bearers. While the emissaries were being looked upon suspiciously as spies by the whites, there being no interpreter present, some of the volunteers caught sight of the five observers, leapt to their saddles, and galloped off in swift pursuit. There was plenty of commotion in camp, and angry voices were raised. In the violence that ensued one of the truce-bearers was killed; two of the scouts were shot down before they could reach a wooded area.

When Black Hawk heard how dastardly mean had been the treatment of his envoys and scouts, he fairly choked with rage, tore to pieces the white flag which he had expected to carry with him on his mission of capitulation, and delivered a fiery speech to about forty of his braves, mostly the older men who had not gone away on a hunt. This small remnant of his band galloped off on their spotted ponies, and at no great distance saw an army of whites approaching. "Some of our people have been killed!" yelled Black Hawk, "wantonly and cruelly murdered! We must revenge their deaths!"

Hiding behind some bushes, the Indians waited till the Americans were within firing range. "I gave another yell," Black Hawk continues, "and ordered my brave warriors to charge upon them—expecting that we would all be killed! They did charge! Every man rushed and fired, and the enemy retreated in the utmost confusion and consternation before my little, but brave band of warriors!"

The three hundred fugitives in Stillman's corps did not stop in camp but dashed—it seems—toward all four points of the compass at once. Nightfall did not stay their flight. In the darkness some fell into bogs and briar patches. Many of them, straggling along on foot, headed for home and did not rest till they arrived there three or four days later.

The news of the rout created a panic of fear in the hearts of outlying settlers. Everywhere the ominous report that "Black Hawk and two thousand bloodthirsty warriors were sweeping all Northern Illinois with the besom of destruction" caused farm families to vacate their cabins and head for the settlements. Of one fleeing family it is told that the father was the only one strong enough to ford a certain rain-swollen creek. Upon him fell the burden of carrying the mother and children across, one at a time. "When they all, as they thought, had got over," an old chronicler relates, "they started, when the cry of poor little Susan was heard on the opposite bank, asking if they were not going to take her with them. The frightened father again prepared to plunge into the strong current for his child, when the mother, seeing it, cried out, 'Never mind Susan; we have succeeded in getting ten over, which is more than we expected at first—and we can better spare Susan than you, my dear.' So poor Susan, who was only about four years old, was left to the mercy of the frightful savages. But poor little Susan came off unhurt; one of the neighbors who was out hunting came along and took charge of little Susan, the eleventh, who had been so miserably treated by her mother."[1]

The "reign of terror," though mostly imaginary, that followed Stillman's defeat caused the governor to issue a call for two thousand more men. There were skirmishes and sporadic Indian raids on the stockaded villages, but no decisive engagements.

As the summer wore on, the American volunteers became more and more disgruntled, even mutinous, at army routine and the pursuit of Black Hawk's Band, which was leading them on a will-o'-the-wisp chase

---

[1] Wakefield, *History of the Black Hawk War.*

northward along the Rock River to the Four Lakes in a clock-wise operation that began to veer southward shortly above Madison, Wisconsin. By
this circular movement Black Hawk hoped to elude his pursuers and thus
be able to cross the Mississippi without detection. Governor Reynolds
and several other political figures who had been following the army
gave up the pursuit as a bad job and returned home. Some of the
volunteers, worrying about their untended crops, did likewise.

On the twenty-first of July occurred the Battle of Wisconsin Heights.
The Americans had caught up with the Indians about twenty-five miles
northwest of Madison. "We were now compelled to fight," relates Black
Hawk, "or sacrifice our wives and children to the fury of the whites!
I met them with fifty warriors (having left the balance to assist our
women and children in crossing) about a mile from the river, when an
attack immediately commenced. I was mounted on a fine horse, and
was pleased to see my warriors so brave. I addressed them in a loud
voice telling them to stand their ground and never yield it to the enemy."
The fifty Indian warriors did stand their ground so effectively that the
main body of their people were able to cross the Wisconsin without serious
opposition. Only six braves were killed or wounded.

Jefferson Davis, years afterwards, in speaking of this battle, says:
"This was the most brilliant exhibition of military tactics that I ever
witnessed—a feat of most consummate management and bravery in the
face of an enemy of greatly superior numbers. I never read of anything
that could be compared with it. Had it been performed by white men,
it would have been immortalized as one of the most splendid achievements
in military history."

The night after this battle Black Hawk made another gesture to
achieve a peaceful settlement of the war. Toward dawn of the twenty-
second a voice was heard coming from the heights where the battle had
taken place the day before. It was Neapope speaking in the Winnebago
tongue, a language that no one in camp understood, as the Winnebagos
who had been with the Americans were absent at the time. Afterwards
it was learned that the war might have ended here if the nature of
Neapope's mission had become known. Instead, the soldiers in camp
were aroused from their slumbers to make ready for combat, thinking the
voice on the hills was Black Hawk's, and his words an exhortation to battle.

The pursuit dragged on. The Indians were in desperate straits,
weakened by the fatigue of travel, the pangs of hunger, and the toll of
incessant fighting. Sometimes the miserable creatures had to seek nourish-
ment from bark, roots, a few scant berries, and the meat of fagged-out
ponies. Their only hope was to race for the Mississippi and cross over
into the wilderness country still left open to the Indians. Many of the
sick and wounded were abandoned by the way, and the weary squaws and
children trudged along on foot for twelve or more hours at a stretch.

The final battle came on the second of August when the Indians, having gone down the Bad Axe River, attempted to escape across the Mississippi at a point directly opposite the northern border-line of present-day Iowa. Black Hawk describes the carnage that took place after his people were overtaken by the Americans. "They tried to give themselves up—the whites paid no attention to their entreaties—but commenced slaughtering them! Our braves, finding that the enemy paid no regard to age or sex, and seeing that they were murdering helpless women and little children, determined to *fight until they were killed!* As many women as could, commenced swimming the Mississippi, with the children on their backs. A number of them were drowned, and some shot, before they could reach the opposite shore." The historian Thwaites says that the sharpshooters regarded these non-combatants as "rats instead of human beings."

Those who were fortunate enough to reach the Iowa bank of the Mississippi met further misfortunes. Sioux tribesmen, summoned for the purpose of wreaking vengeance on hereditary enemies, tomahawked a large number of defenseless Sacs and Foxes before the latter could climb up the river banks to shore. More than two hundred fugitives were butchered by the Sioux.

The Battle of the Bad Axe brought the Black Hawk War to an end. It was not so much a battle, says Cyrenus Cole, as a "massacre of red men, women, and children in rags, by white soldiers, some of them in uniform." Of the one thousand or more people whom Black Hawk led forth in April on this disastrous expedition, about one hundred and fifty survived the trail's end in August. Armstrong estimates that at least twelve thousand men were employed in the task of "driving Black Hawk and his band back across the Mississippi." The American casualties amounted, at most, to two hundred and fifty men.

After his surrender Black Hawk was kept first at Fort Crawford and then at Jefferson Barracks. His transfer escort was led by Jefferson Davis, and between the fallen chieftain and the future president of the Confederacy there sprang up a mutual friendship. On his arrival at Jefferson Barracks, Black Hawk was forced to wear a ball and chain, but such humiliating treatment did not lower his status as a hero in the eyes of the hosts of curious people who thronged in to see him.

Instead of releasing him at once, President Jackson ordered Black Hawk and his fellow-prisoners to Washington to impress the fallen warriors with the multiple wonders of our country. By steamboat the entourage proceeded past Louisville and Cincinnati to Wheeling; thence by stage through Hagerstown and Frederick; and on by railroad to Washington, Baltimore, Philadelphia, New York, Albany, Buffalo, and Detroit on the way back home. In the nation's capitol he stood facing President Jackson a few moments in silence before he uttered that amazing concept of equality that must be recognized before two men can discuss straightforwardly any transaction: "I am a man and you are another." Everywhere he was acclaimed as a great fallen hero. There were fireworks, balloon ascensions, theatrical entertainments, and banquet festivities in his honor. The white "squaws" showered him with many presents. All this attention flattered not a little the vanity of the now grizzled warrior and brought him to look upon his white conquerors with less bitterness of heart.

Back in his simple cabin on the Iowa River, Black Hawk dictated the story of his life through an interpreter. Of this autobiography Cyrenus Cole, who spent thirty-five years of research on the life and times of Black Hawk, says that the Indian leader's descriptions of battle events have never been contradicted by the critics. "They are models of good description . . . The *Autobiography* is more than a narration of events, it is an exposition of the traditions, myths, and legends of the Indians. . . . Other Indians have since written autobiographies, but most of them were written by men who had learned to think after the manner of the white men. Black Hawk's *Autobiography* is distinct and distinguished because it is the product of an Indian who was still thinking as Indians thought in their native haunts of forests and prairies. It is this fact that makes Black Hawk's book one of its own kind: indeed, the only one of its kind."

The few remaining years of his life, Black Hawk lived quietly and on the best of terms with his white neighbors. At the fourth of July celebration in 1838 at Fort Madison he was the honor guest of the city. In the pleasant summer weather and under the trees, with a panoramic view of the Mississippi in the distance, Black Hawk ate with a large assembly of whites and heard his name toasted on every tongue.

Three months later Black Hawk was dead at the age of seventy-one. He was survived by his wife—the only one he ever had—and by two sons and a daughter. An enormous statue, of stone and concrete, and forty-two feet high, commemorates the name of Black Hawk on the steep banks of the Rock River in Ogle County, Illinois. The statue, dedicated in 1911, is not carved in the likeness of Black Hawk; it is simply a "draped male figure, standing with folded arms, looking down the river which was part of the Indian's last trail." Lorado Taft, the sculptor, called it "a spirit unconquered while still belonging to a conquered race."

The Hawkeye or Black Hawk spoon bears the state seal of Iowa in the caput. An eagle is pictured holding in his beak a scroll on which is inscribed the state motto: "Our liberties we prize, and our rights we will maintain." A volunteer soldier, with a plow behind him in the background, is holding the American flag in one hand and a gun in the other. The profiled face of an Indian chief occupies the nave; a bundle of wheat, the name of Iowa, and a floral decoration are seen in the shank.

This spoon is a product of the Baker-Manchester Mfg. Co. Its length is 5 inches.

474

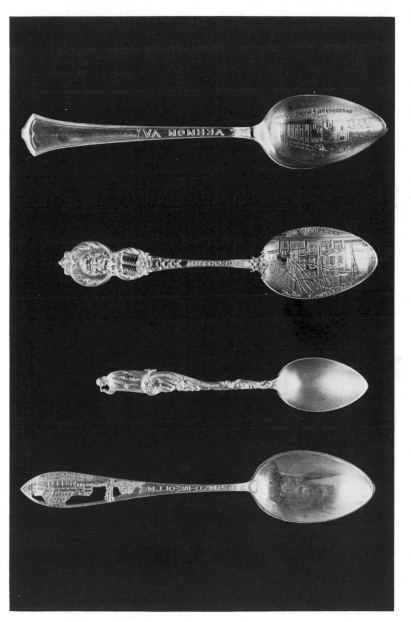

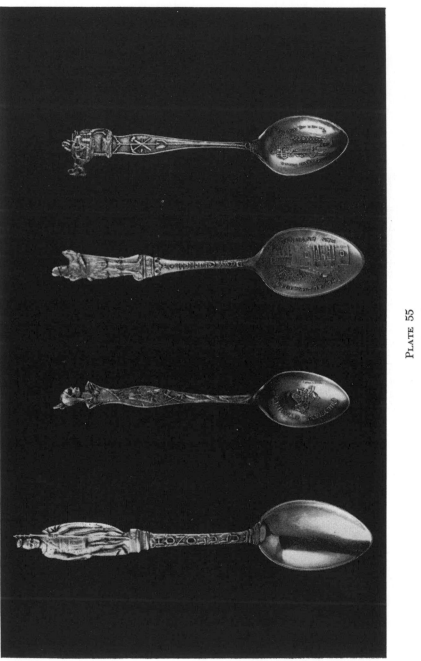

Plate 55

139. KAMEHAMEHA   140. CHEYENNE BRONCO BUSTER   141. DAVY CROCKETT   142. DYNAMITE

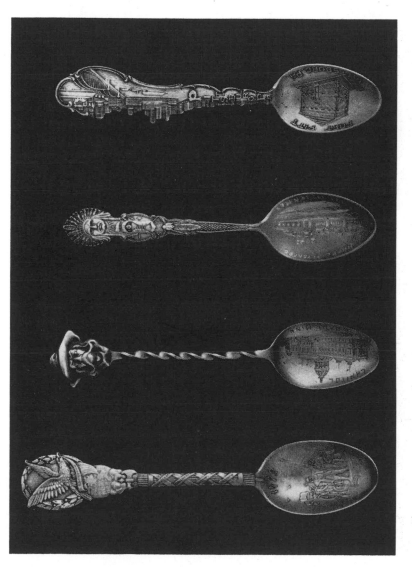

PLATE 56

143. LANDFALL OF COLUMBUS   144. MINNESOTA PIONEER
145. NEW MEXICO INDIANS   146. FORT PITT

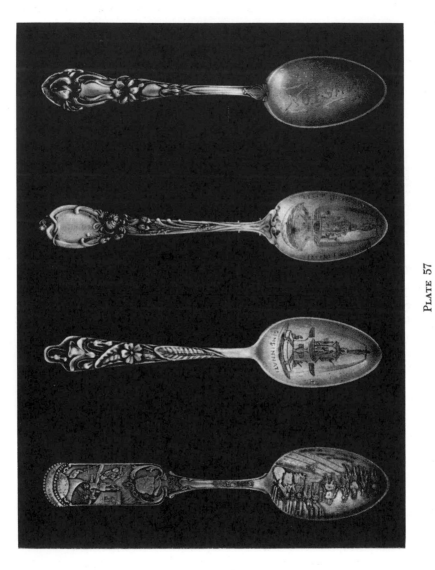

PLATE 57

147. RETURN OF COLUMBUS   148. CINCINNATI FOUNTAIN
149. TYLER DAVIDSON FOUNTAIN   150. HOUSTON

No. 134 WILLIAM PITT
No. 146 FORT PITT

Our school histories picture the Revolutionary War for us as a muscular bout between liberty-loving Americans and liberty-loathing Englishmen, the latter epitomized in a boorish, dictatorial king and his subservient prime ministers. The colonists rose as a man to fight for their independence; their patriotic fervor, noble ideals, and firmly-knit unity were the deciding factors in the David-Goliath contest.

Actually the war was fratricidal in nature, not only in America but to a lesser degree also in England—certainly on the political front. In the colonies one-third of the people harbored Tory sympathies; in England, Whig party members openly expressed pro-American sentiments. Burke's *Speech on Conciliation with America* defends constitutional government and condemns the policy of taxation without representation as wholeheartedly as the most zealous of Americans. Thomas Paine came from England to the New World on the eve of the Revolution to lock horns with "British tyranny" in the imminent struggle. Generals Effingham, Amherst, and Oglethorpe, holding the best interests of America at heart, refused to participate in any plans for the subjugation of the colonies. The Marquis of Rockingham, Lord Shelburne, the Duke of Richmond, and Charles James Fox, all Whig leaders, advocated a conciliatory peace, and defended American opposition to the Stamp and Tea Acts in Parliament. Eight signers of the Declaration of Independence were born in the British Isles; four of them arrived here less than twenty years before the beginning of the armed conflict.

Just how did people in England feel toward the American war during its progress? Samuel Rogers, the London banker-poet who might have been laureate but refused the honor, gives us an insight into such an attitude when he wrote J. P. Kennedy on his Revolutionary romance *Horseshoe Robinson*: "Your story in my eyes has a double charm; for, delightful as it is in itself, the time was the time of my childhood, and the turns of fortune in that cruel war are as fresh in my memory as the events of yesterday. My earliest pulses beat in your favor; and, little as I was then, I can well remember what we felt, when, as we sat around the fire, my father, before he opened his Bible, announced to us the Battle of Bunker Hill. I need not, I am sure, repeat how happy I shall be to see you here, and to thank you, face to face, for all I owe you."

This pro-American viewpoint was widespread, and the war to squash the colonial rebellion was so unpopular up and down the English countrysides that few young men volunteered for military service; foreign mercenaries had to be bought.

Not the least among those who "rejoiced that America resisted" was William Pitt the elder, the Great Commoner, the first Earl of Chatham, prime minister of England, and leader of the opposition when not in office. Frederic Harrison places Pitt among the four "great creative statesmen" of England: William the Conqueror made the country an organic union; Edward the First created the concept of Great Britain; Cromwell knit the pattern for a United Kingdom and established her strength on the sea; Pitt devised the colonial system out of which evolved the Empire. "For good and for evil, through heroism and through spoliation, with all its vast and far-reaching consequences, industrial, economic, social, and moral," says Harrison, "the foundation of the Empire was the work of Chatham. He changed the course of England's history—nay, the course of modern history." Lord Brougham calls Pitt "the most successful statesman and the most brilliant orator" that his country could boast of. John Cuthbert Long summarizes Pitt's achievements in a few very pithy sentences: "He raised a nation from the dust and democracy from the scrap heap . . . brought honesty to the Army, integrity to the State, and dignity to the common people. He defined the philosophy of democracy and trained men to defend it."

To the biographer Pitt presents the same problem as does Shakespeare; a problem that is at the same time a temptation—to by-pass the personal facts because those known count for little, and to concentrate on studies of those "brain-children," which lend themselves so aptly to quotable lines and phrases.

Born in 1708, the second son in a family of six children he had many of the eccentricities and little illnesses which led people to call his family the "mad Pitts." He entered the army as a "cornet of horse," but resigned his commission after his nomination to Parliament from the borough of Old Sarum.

Already the inherent dislike of Horace Walpole, the prime minister, toward Pitt rose to the surface, for, to keep him out of Parliament, Walpole offered the young man a higher commission in the army and the neat sum of twelve hundred pounds to relinquish the seat to another. The money was refused, and Pitt took his seat in Parliament in 1735.

The hostility engendered by this effort of Walpole's to sidetrack Pitt continued to grow through the years. Pitt's rising reputation as an orator likewise gained him the ill-will of George II, because he criticized the policies of the Crown, which were subservient to the King's interests on the Continent, whereby England was involved in many bickering quarrels of a petty nature, though important enough to burden the exchequer with mounting deficits.

Pitt foresaw that the real enemy of England was France under the imperialistic policies of the Bourbons. In North America the French possessions covered five times as much territory as the Spanish and twenty times as much as the English. "France by her influence and her arms means to undo England and all Europe," he said. In 1757, during the worst reverses of the Seven-Years War, Pitt became prime minister, and he set about at once to demolish French power and influence in the New World. At home his competence soon became apparent, for he dismissed corrupt officials, punished the giving and taking of bribes, appointed commanders according to their abilities, and not according to their seniority or their rank in the peerage. He placed around him in the cabinet those men who performed their duties most efficiently.

He found himself ardently supported by the common people at home and by the English colonists in America. A series of brilliant campaigns in the New World ousted the French from their fortified strongholds one by one, and at the end of the war England was master of the North American continent. The straggling colonies along the eastern coast were not to be circumscribed in growth by a French arc of demarcation hedging in their western borders. "Pitt laid the foundation of the great republic of the West," declared John Richard Green in his *Short History of the English People.*

Clive's victories in India also occurred during Pitt's ministry, and British rule extended into the far reaches of Asia. The fleet was strengthened, and merchant vessels were beginning to carry English goods into all the seven seas. Pitt was venerated by the common people and respected abroad as the most noted of Englishmen. Still, there existed a great deal of covert opposition among the Tory circles who surrounded the new king, George III, and eventually they devised ways and means to rid themselves of the popular idol. Pitt was growing gouty, and it was suggested that he retire on the boon of a pension and a seat in the peerage. This proposal he accepted, and henceforth he was to be known also as the Earl of Chatham. In addition to his pension, Pitt was comfortably fixed by two legacies that had fallen to him as pleasant surprises. The aged Duchess of Marlborough, a great admirer of his "patriotism," left him ten thousand pounds, at a time when he was living meagerly on one hundred pounds a year. Then an erratic old fellow without close relatives, Sir William Pynsent, left him a huge estate yielding nearly four thousand pounds a year. The donor of this legacy had never even seen Mr. Pitt but admired him for his staunch advocacy of government by constitutional processes.

The best friend and defender that America has ever had in England was William Pitt. His public utterances from 1765 until his death were mainly on the subject of unjust acts inflicted by the Crown on the colonies. It was Pitt's voice, raised in righteous condemnation, that brought repeal of the Stamp and Tea Acts. His fervor caught fire. "It is my opinion," he said, "that this kingdom has no right to lay a tax upon the colonies . . . They are the subjects of this kingdom, equally entitled with yourselves to all the natural rights of mankind, and the peculiar privileges of Englishmen, equally bound by its laws, and equally participating of the Constitution of this free country. The Americans are the sons, not the bastards of England . . . There is an idea in some, that the colonies are virtually represented in this House. I would fain know by whom an American is here represented? . . . The idea of a virtual representation of America in this House is the most contemptible idea that ever entered into the head of man; it does not deserve a serious refutation."

When Pitt heard what Patrick Henry had said at the First Continental Congress in Philadelphia the previous September, he rose in the House of Lords on January 20, 1775, and declared: "The Americans will never be in a temper or state to be reconciled—they ought not to be—till the troops are withdrawn. The way must be immediately opened for reconciliation. It will soon be too late . . . What foundation have we for our claims over America? What is our right to persist in such cruel and vindictive measures against that loyal, respectable people? They say you have no right to tax them without their consent. They say truly . . . For genuine sagacity, for singular moderation, for everything respectable and honorable, the Congress at Philadelphia stands unrivaled . . . They do not ask you to repeal your laws as a favor: they claim it as a right—they demand it . . . I tell you the acts must be repealed—you cannot enforce them."

When Grenville denounced the Americans as open rebels and accused Pitt of preaching insurrection, the latter sprang to his feet to refute the charges: "Gentlemen, I have been charged with giving birth to sedition in America . . . But the imputation shall not discourage me . . . The gentleman tells us, America is obstinate; America is almost in open rebellion. I rejoice that America has resisted. Three millions of people so dead to all the feelings of liberty, as voluntarily to submit to be slaves, would have been fit instruments to make slaves of the rest."

Worried with gout and scarcely able at times to walk except with a cane, Pitt appeared more and more infrequently in Parliament. In May, 1777, he rose with difficulty on his crutches, his knees swathed in flannels, and made a motion without result for calling a halt to hostilities: "If an end be not put to this war, there is an end to this country. America has carried us through four wars, and will now carry us to our death, if things be not taken in time. You may ravage—you cannot conquer the Americans. I might as well talk of driving them before me with this crutch!"

Before he had received the news of Burgoyne's defeat at Saratoga, he upheld American resistance as *noble* in the face of Parliament: "If I were an American, as I am an Englishman, while a foreign troop was landed in my country, I never would lay down my arms—never—never—never!"

In January, 1778, after he had heard the report of the disastrous British defeat at Saratoga, he lamented: "Where is this ruin to end? Heaven only knows. I hold out without gout hitherto; perhaps I may last as long as Great Britain."

Three months later he attempted to speak again, but after a few introductory remarks, he sat down, pressed a hand to his heart, and fell to the floor in a heap. He lay abed for another month, gradually becoming weaker till his death on May 11, 1778.

William Pitt was always a beloved name in America. Pittsburgh, Pennsylvania, and Pittsfield, Massachusetts, bear testimony to the esteem in which he was held. In many colonial homes his portraits were on the walls and Chelsea statuettes of him on mantels, both before and during the Revolution. A statue of him was erected in Charleston, South Carolina, in 1766. Fourteen years later a British grapeshot, "by an incredible irony of history"—says John Cuthbert Long—"broke off the right arm, and shattered the right hand which held a copy of the Magna Carta."

The cradle of Pittsburgh was Fort Pitt, a key-link in the chain of fortresses on the western frontier. The spit of land where the Allegheny and Monongahela Rivers merge to form the Ohio was a strategic point long before it became Pittsburgh's Golden Triangle. Frenchmen and Englishmen vied for its possession. During the French and Indian War there was a sudden flurry of concern in the seaboard colonies over the encroachment of the French in this territory. Governor Dinwiddie of Virginia sent young Major George Washington in the fall of 1753 on a mission to warn the French that they were trespassing. Washington in his report to the governor described the land at the Forks of the Ohio in favorable terms: "I spent some time in viewing the rivers, and the land in the fork, which I think extremely well situated for a fort, as it has the absolute command of both rivers."

The Ohio Company of Virginia started a fort at this location, but it was only half finished when a French contingent of eight hundred men from Montreal swooped down upon it and, seizing it, proceeded to build a triangular stockade, two sides flanking the river banks and a third exposed side twelve feet thick bordered by a moat, and an abatis beyond that. Here the French remained firmly entrenched for four years behind the bulwarks of Fort Duquesne, as they called it, till the colonists built a road westward, over which they could bring sufficient men and supplies to blast the French out of their stronghold.

In September, 1758, the colonists arrived in full strength over their new road, but the French had wisely withdrawn a few days before, leaving their fortress a smoking ruins. When William Pitt, then prime minister in England, heard that Fort Duquesne had been destroyed, he ordered a new fort constructed on the same site and of such insuperable strength that it could command mastery of the entire Ohio terrain.

Fort Pitt, the new structure, was a five-walled stockade, two years in the building. A lively settlement, called Pittsburgh, grew up around the fort, and the townsmen were of good service when the fort was besieged for two months in 1763 during the Pontiac uprising.

Fort Pitt was one of three forts able to withstand the concerted onslaught of the Indians. In charge of the fort was a tough Swiss mercenary, Captain Simeon Ecuyer, while the town militia were commanded by

William Trent, who kept a journal of day-by-day events. These entries, without due regard for literary niceties, present an accurate picture of a grave situation faced with a stoical, undaunted attitude of mind. Samplings of them run as follows:

May 30th. All the inhabitants moved into the fort.

June 1st. This morning an order was issued by the commandant to pull down and burn all the out-houses.

3rd and 4th. All the garrison were employed in repairing and strengthening the fort.

24th. The Turtles Heart a principal Warrior of the Delaware and Mamaltree a chief came within a small distance of the Fort. Mr. McKee went out to them and they made a Speech letting us know that all our Posts at Ligonier were destroyed, that great numbers of Indians were coming out and that out of regard to us, they had prevailed on 6 Nations not to attack us but give us time to go down the Country and they desired we would set out immediately. The Commanding Officer thanked them, let them know we had everything we wanted, that we could defend it against all the Indians in the Woods, that we had three large Armys marching to Chastise those Indians that had struck us.

July 3rd. At 10 o'clock this morning as a party went to the Garden for greens, etc. they were fired upon by Indians who had hid within 60 yards of the Fort. Our people pursued em till they were ordered back. At 1 o'clock 2 Guns were heard on the opposite side of the Allegheny and immediately four Indians appeared naked and their Bodies painted with different Colours singing as they came along according to their Custom when appearing as friends.

11th. All quiet. 12th Ditto. 13th Ditto. The first night I have striped since the beginning of the allarm.

29th. Continued firing on the Fort the whole day from the Ohio Bank they kep up a very smart fire . . . The Roofs of the Governours House and the Barracks much hurt by the Enemys fire.

August 3rd. Six Nights the whole Fort have been under Arms, the Garrison having two Reliefs.

10th. At break of day in the Morning Miller who was sent Express the 5th with two others came in from Col. Boquet, who he left at the Nine Mile Run, he brings an Account that the Indians engaged our Troops for two days, that our People beat them off . . . The following is the best Account I have been able to learn of the Action which happened the 5th about a Mile beyond Bushy Run. Our Advanced Guard discovered the Indians where they were lying in Ambush and fired on them about 3 o'clock in the Afternoon this brought on a General Engagement which continued the rest of the next day and night our people behaved with the greatest Bravery as well as the Indians who often advanced within a few steps of our People. The Action continued doubtful till the Enemy by a stratagem was drawn into an Ambuscade when they were entirely routed, leaving a great many of their People dead on the Spott. Our loss in this Affair is about 50 killed and 60 wounded. Its thought by our People the Enemy lost as many.

The significance of this victory can hardly be over-estimated. "The Battle of Bushy Run—little known in comparison with dozens of lesser engagements," says R. E. Banta, historian of the Ohio, "was one of the greatest victories won over the North American Indians to its time . . . Bouquet's victory may be said to have broken the back of organized Indian resistance to the settlement of the Ohio."

Within two years following this battle the forces under Colonel Bouquet had risen in numbers to such strength that the domination of Fort Pitt over the area was never seriously questioned again by the Indians. Pittsburgh was well on its way toward becoming "the Smoky City," "the Steel Queen," and "the Citadel of Learning"; as well as being the nest where the Mellons, Carnegies, Schwabs, Schenleys, Heinzes, and Fricks found their golden eggs.

The William Pitt spoon, of plain bowl and acuminate-tipped handle, manifests a severely chaste colonial style. Through the shank runs the name of Pittsburgh. The bust of Pitt and the armorial bearings of his house occupy the nave. The blockhouse of old Fort Pitt surmounted by an ogival arch in the crown, appears in the caput. A product of the Robbins Company, Attleboro, Massachusetts. Length, 5½ inches.

The Fort Pitt spoon contains the old blockhouse of the fort not only in the bowl but also on the reverse side of handle in the caput. Here, some of the old cabins and the powder magazine are visible in the background. The handle offers an extremely impressive panorama of the Pittsburgh skyline, but among the skyscrapers the forty-two story Cathedral of Learning (the University) is conspicuously absent, not having been erected yet at the time this spoon was pressed. The Allegheny County Courthouse and the Carnegie Library also appear on the reverse side of handle. Made by the Paye and Baker Company. Length, 5¼ inches.

No. 139 KAMEHAMEHA

"The most savage face I have ever seen," remarked an early voyager after gazing at the visage of Kamehameha, the first king to unite all the Hawaiian Islands under one rule. The king was a young man when this observation was made about his facial aspect. He still had a strenuous struggle ahead of him before he was able to establish the sovereignty of Hawaii securely over the other seven smaller islands. Fate may have given him many lucky breaks, but most of his successes can be attributed not alone to his superior physical strength and courage but equally as well to his great mental endowments aul the sheer force of his personality.

485

At his birth, which occurred about the year 1737 during a fierce autumnal storm, the soothsayers decreed death for the tiny babe because he belonged to a rival branch of chieftains, and some day might prove to be a disturbing factor to the reigning line of kings. He was smuggled out of his mother's bed and carried off to a cave, where he lived in concealment for five years before his father thought it safe to bring the child into his own house.

He grew up at the royal court of Hawaii and was instructed by Kekuhaupio, a wise old man well versed in the military arts, how to toss sling stones, throw a javelin, parry as many as a half-dozen spears thrown simultaneously at his body; how to hollow out canoes, catch fish, swim, dive, and ride surf boards; how to coast on sleds safely down the steepest slopes of lava; and how to play the maika and other native games of skill. The young warrior repaid this capable instructor by becoming his devoted friend and saving his life once when the aged man had been overcome in battle.

When Kamehameha was about twenty years old, the king, his great-uncle, died, and a long period of civil war followed. Hawaii was split up among three rival chieftains. For years these forces fought indecisively. Five leaders from the Kona region, fearing the ruin or confiscation of their lands, acknowledged Kamehameha as their king and looked to him for protection and guidance.

During a raid on the Puna coast Kamehameha leapt out of a canoe to attack some wading fishermen. They fled, and he pursued them till his foot lodged in a coral crevice. One of the fishermen turned and struck Kamehameha such blows on the cranium that the oar broke into splinters. When the fishermen were apprehended later and hauled before him, Kamehameha not only granted them their lives but also gave them small farms, saying he had no one to blame except himself for the severe beating he had received.

At a New Year's celebration held always in honor of Lono, the god of harvest, Kamehameha first met Kaahumanu the Feather Mantle, daughter of one of his Kona supporters. He instantly fell in love, and soon married this seventeen-year-old maiden who was "lovely as a lauhala blossom." It was she who, after her husband's death, destroyed the tabu system of the old gods and introduced Christianity to the islands.

Great excitement prevailed when a British expedition under Captain James Cook was sighted off the shores of Oahu and Kauai by the astonished natives in 1778. Cook was at first regarded as a reincarnation of the god Lono, but on a second visit several very human quarrels took place, and Cook, now no longer held in reverential awe, was stabbed to death in a disorderly scuffle.

In the next few years more and more ships visited Hawaii. Two Americans, John Young and Isaac Davis, who were left stranded on the islands, became trusted advisors to Kamehameha, and eventually they

486

came to hold responsible positions in the government. There were other Americans to be found now among the natives but the king had enough perspicuity to discern the discreditable character of most of them, and rejected their offers of service. Captain George Vancouver, who had been with Cook thirteen years before, brought animals, plants, and seeds that were useful, but refused to sell any guns or ammunition.

When Vancouver saw Kamehameha again after the long interval since his visit with Cook, he was "agreeably surprised to find that the king's riper years had softened that stern ferocity which his younger days had exhibited, and had changed his general deportment to an address characteristic of an open, cheerful, and sensible mind, combined with great generosity and goodness of disposition."

Kamehameha built up a gradual supply of guns and cannon from the foreign ships that now passed more often. His only opposition on the island of Hawaii came from Keona, a former ally who once set out to invade Hilo, the king's home district, while he was absent. This army on its way across the hills camped near the muttering volcano Kilauea. One morning, after a clear sunrise, there came a violent eruption, and darkness closed in except for intermittent flares of spectral, gaseous lights. When the atmosphere cleared, about one third of the invading army lay motionless on the ground. These had been asphyxiated.

A truce was made, and a conference arranged for Kamehameha and Keona to meet each other. When Keona's boat neared shore, Kamehameha hailed him: "Rise and come here, that we may know each other." As Keona walked up the beach, he was pierced by a spear and fell dead. This base treachery, whether done with or without the foreknowledge of the king, will always remain to tarnish his otherwise honorable record.

The next five years Kamehameha spent in subduing Maui, Oahu, and Kauai. The other smaller islands gradually came into the confederation by peaceful negotiations. Then for twenty-three years Kamehameha bent all his energies toward improving conditions and promoting prosperity in his kingdom. The devastated areas were soon under cultivation, not only of the native tuberous plants, but also of the foreign importations of pineapples, sugar cane, coffee, rice, tobacco, potatoes, and a variety of garden vegetables.

Kamehameha set an example for industry to his people by working like a common laborer in the fields. He ate only what he raised on his own farm or the fish he caught for himself. He made strict laws against crime. Any one doing violence to peaceful or innocent persons was subject to the death penalty. "The aged, the weak, and the helpless must be able to lie in safety along the road," he said.

He observed faithfully all the rites of his ancient religion, saying, "My gods have always stood by me and so I shall always stand by them." Most of the foreigners, nominally Christians, by their example led him to have a low opinion of their religion.

Political refugees coming from Australia taught the natives the art of distilling liquor. Kamehameha, seeing its effects were evil, ordered every distillery on the islands destroyed. During his last illness his attendants, hoping to alleviate his suffering, offered him an eggnog seasoned with brandy. The king, perceiving the alcoholic odor so disagreeable to his nostrils, dashed the drink to the floor, angered at the deceptive method employed to make him violate unwittingly his pledge of abstinence. He died that night, being in the eighty-second year of his age. Mourned greatly by the people, this "Napoleon of the Pacific" was carried into the mountains of northern Kona and there buried at a lonely spot never made known by the one man who bore him to his last destination.

He still lives enshrined in the hearts of Hawaiians as their greatest hero. A statue of him, set up to commemorate the centennial of Hawaii's discovery by Cook, stands in front of the Territorial Office Building in Honolulu. It represents the king in his red-feather robe and helmet, one hand clasping the pololu, the barbed spear of peace, the other lifted outward and upward as a sign of leadership to his people.

The Kamehameha spoon shows a fine likeness of the monarch similar to the aforementioned statue, though the right hand is not elevated but reaches downward and grasps one side of the mantle thrown back to reveal a bare arm and shoulder; nor is the spear extended forward.

The king graces a pedestal with his name at its base. HONOLULU runs perpendicularly down the shaft.

This coffee spoon was made by the Charles M. Robbins Company. Length, 4¼ inches. Used through the courtesy of its owner, Miss Evalyn Rogers, Hayward, California.

No. 140 CHEYENNE BRONCO BUSTER

About the time that I was cutting my baby teeth I was likewise singing a certain song—which must have been a sort of theme-song with me, repeated often enough to have stuck indelibly in my memory, as I have never heard the song since or seen the words in print. The chorus runs like this:

> Cheyenne, Cheyenne, hop òn my pony,
> There's room here for two, dear,
> And after the ceremony
> We'll both ride back home, dear, as one,
> On my pony from old Cheyenne.

During my college days, while traveling with a glee club group, I stood shivering on the streets of Cheyenne. A blizzardy wind was whipping wisps of snow around street corners. Hardly a soul was venturing forth on the sidewalks, but coming down the street was a single cowboy on his pony, both bravely facing the wind. In the distance, at the end of the avenue, stood out the cold, white outlines of the State Capitol building. So this was Cheyenne, the city of song and story.

The beginnings of Cheyenne were coëval with the coming of the Union Pacific Railway. It had been only an indistinguishable spot on the sagebrush plains until General Grenville Dodge, in blueprinting a route for the railroad line westward through the hills, camped on Crow Creek for several weeks in the summer of 1865. Two years later he decided to select this camping place as a terminal and operational point for the new railroad already in the process of building. He named the site Cheyenne, as much to honor the courageous fighting spirit of these Plains Indians as to commemorate the shameful massacre of a friendly tribe of Cheyennes asleep in their tepees at Sand Creek three years previous.

The railroad did not reach Cheyenne till November of 1867. But that human flotsam so typical of the early Wild West mining centers drifted in before the railroad arrived, and began to play the game of "all's fair in love, war—and a new town" for all the chances of a big rake-off. Cheyenne sparkled like the sun by day and the moon by night. A theatrical troupe came to town before a theatre was there. Beer cost a dollar a quart, two eggs about the same. Still, prices were called "reasonable."

Malcolm Campbell, later a sheriff with the sort of hair-raising reputation that young boys love to read about, showed up in Cheyenne about this time, and his account of the bustling embryo town is incomparably vivid: "There were tents set everywhere without alignment, and the scaffoldings of new buildings were being erected to the tune of many hammers, the lumber having been hauled all the way from Denver. There were tents where men sat on benches before long plank tables wolfing meals; tents with rough shelves of canned goods piled to the eaves, and many others where sat gamblers playing faro, roulette and monte. Saloons were everywhere with their bourbons, whiskeys, brandies and beers. Hurdy-gurdies could be heard in any block at any time of the day or night. Along the banks of Crow Creek were grouped the canvas-covered wagons of emigrants. Camp fires blazed continuously and shelters had been erected on ropes stretched from wheel to wheel. The aisles between the tents in the town were swarming with the roughest of the population. Idlers sauntered from gambling table to dance hall, then on to saloons. Others stood in groups debating the probable boom in real estate values within the next few days. Water wells were being dug at four of the corners of what was to be a business block. Everywhere was expectancy and alertness."

For a while the mushroom city was the mecca for all the lawless elements of the West, and nearly everybody toted a gun. That didn't always provide the adequate protection because many people were slugged in the head from the rear, robbed, and left dazed, sometimes half-dead. Stray bullets formed a habit of killing innocent persons. Drunken, reckless ruffians abounded. "Hell must have been raked to furnish them," commented a reporter of this early scene. General Dodge dubbed Cheyenne the gambling hub of the world.

But the railroad went on its way westward and some of the worst elements of the population went along. Groups of vigilantes were formed, and a county organization, strong enough to enact and enforce laws, was set up with Cheyenne as the county seat. Then, with the formation of Wyoming Territory in 1869, Cheyenne, as the largest town, was selected as the territorial capital. It continued in that capacity after Wyoming was made a state in 1890. Although located off and away, in the extreme southeastern corner of the state, Cheyenne today wields a strong influence as a cattle, railroad, and industrial center over an area extending far beyond the confines of Wyoming.

Every year in July, since 1897, Cheyenne has been holding its rodeo celebration, known as the Frontier Days, to keep alive the early traditions of the cattleman and the cowboy. The colorful old costumes of the cow country are donned by spectators and performers alike. A prominent feature of the celebration is a parade highlighting all the various means of transportation known to have been used by the people of Wyoming at one time or another.

There are all kinds of interesting events scheduled for each day of the show, such as calf roping, team roping, bucking-horse riding, wild-cow milking contest, wild-horse race, cowboy-pony race, bulldogging of steers, steer riding, bronco busting, Indian war dance, squaw foot-race, dress parades and trick drills, the last two features being staged by military detachments from Fort Francis E. Warren, located a mile outside of Cheyenne.

John K. Rollinson has graphically described, from the cowboy's viewpoint, a Frontier Days celebration around the turn of the century in his *Pony Trails in Wyoming*. Trainloads of people from Denver, Laramie, and other points poured into the town. Flags and bright streamers fluttered overhead in welcome. The band repeatedly struck up "Casey Jones," the popular tune of the day. Rollinson participated in the calf-roping event. "The calves were good-sized and rollicky," he says, "and a rider had to be mounted on a fast pony in order to make a catch in front of the grandstand. The calf must be caught with one loop, and when tied the judge had to see that three feet were securely hog-tied. Each rider carried a tie string of soft twisted rope about his waist in a loose knot, or between his teeth.

"I was feeling pretty nervous when my turn came, and I took my place. Old Blue was pretty calm, or quieter than I thought he would be. He had never been ridden in a contest, though he had helped rope hundreds of calves. My calf was made ready and he bounded out like a streak, heading for the opening in the wing fence, and the man holding a light rope across in front of me dropped the rope. When the calf got clear, he ran straight, which was fortunate for me, as I had noted that many ran in a dodging manner. I held my loop ready to swing, as old Blue began to close up the distance, and when I figured it was time, I made the loop stand out in a few steady circles. It dropped over the calf's head, and old Blue set himself back. When I piled off, a dust cloud prevented me from seeing the calf for a fraction of a second as I went down the rope. The calf had busted himself, but was up when I reached him, and he bawled and reared back as I caught a foreleg in one hand and his flank in the other. As he lunged and bucked, I tripped him in the air off his balance, and had my tie line wrapped around the three feet. I threw up my hands as a signal; the judge examined the tie and made a signal to the timer, and as I climbed back on old Blue, some of the men threw off my rope with the tie and handed it to me, and the calf galloped off toward the corral.

"The judge announced my time, which was not fast by any means, and I knew that my catch was due more to luck than expert training. At the end of the afternoon I found I stood third in that event for the day, and so was eligible for the next day's contest, and I felt pretty proud."

Today the Frontier Days celebration draws many thousands of people from the Western states and from Canada, and has become an event of national importance for those who like to see the typical features of the old West preserved and reënacted in authentic style.

The gold-washed bowl of the spoon in hand pictures a cowboy holding on for dear life to the reins of a bucking bronco. The handle portrays in the lower shank two ears of corn, and higher up, a peace pipe and tomahawk crossed diagonally; in the nave, a wigwam; and in the caput, the bust of a Plains Indian of the Cheyenne type, his face being in profile as a finial.

Pressed by Paye and Baker, this spoon is only 3½ inches in length.

No. 141 DAVY CROCKETT

More than any other American, Davy Crockett measures up most proportionately to an epical stature. He had his prototypes in the half-legendary heroes of Homer, or better yet, in the half-god-half-man warriors of the early Teutons. Like Beowulf, Davy Crockett was known mainly for three exploits, though Parrington, the literary historian, prefers to call them *exploitations,* after this fashion: "The exploitation of Davy's canebrake waggery, the exploitation of his anti-Jackson spleen, and the exploitation of his dramatic death at the Alamo."

Composited in his nature were all the virtues and vices of half a dozen other frontiersmen, that is, of men like Daniel Boone, Mike Fink, Sam Houston, Jim Bowie, Kit Carson, and Paul Bunyan. Standing among men of his own kind, and in his own time, he was, in flesh and spirit, already, as John M. Myers states, "a living legend; one, furthermore, that had jumped the borders of the remarkable into the unshackled realm of myth. He was a national and an international figure, the inspiration of a whole school of hacks, and the godfather of America's most purely indigenous literary movement. He was also, and above all, the apotheosis of frontiersmen."

We need not go to second-hand sources for our knowledge of Davy Crockett; he wrote, or, more than likely, dictated his own epic story in four books, by far the most genuine of these being *A Narrative of the Life of David Crockett, of the State of Tennessee*, published two years before his death, in 1834. Parrington calls it the "great classic of the southern frontier," and proceeds to say: "In its backwoods vernacular it purveys the authentic atmosphere of the cabin and the canebrake; it exhibits the honesty, the wit, the resourcefulness, the manly independence of a coon-skin hero; it reveals, in short, under the rough exterior of a shiftless squatter and bear-hunter, qualities that are sterling in every society where manhood is held in repute. It is an extraordinary document, done so skillfully from life that homespun becomes a noble fabric and the crudest materials achieve the dignity of an epic." It is to the pages of this auto-biography that we must resort, then, if we would know the aliquot parts of this substantial figure.

Davy Crockett was the fifth son in a family of six sons and three daughters. His Irish-born father, John Crockett, married a Maryland girl, Rebecca Hawkins, and had first migrated to the western confines of North Carolina before he set up as a farmer and miller at the mouth of the Limestone where it empties into the Nolichucky River, at which place Davy was born on the seventeenth of August, 1786. Some years before this, Creek Indians had murdered both the Crockett grandparents and taken Joseph, Davy's uncle, a prisoner. Joseph Crockett, a deaf and dumb child, remained among the red men for nearly eighteen years before he was discovered by his family, who paid a goodly ransom for his freedom. When a flood washed John Crockett's mill away, he pulled up stakes and moved farther west, to Jefferson County, Tennessee, where, as a crossroads tavernkeeper, he made a livelihood keeping the drovers and waggoners who moved back and forth through the western country.

One of Davy's earliest recollections was that of seeing his father draw a silk handerchief through the body of a man who had been mistakenly shot for a bear while he was gathering wild grapes in a thicket. The man incidentally recovered under the crude but resourceful treatment tendered by this backwoodsman as efficaciously as if he had been privileged to have the best of care from surgical experts.

By the time he was twelve years old Davy already had to help eke out his portion for the family larder. A Dutchman driving a herd of cattle to Virginia stopped at the Crockett hostelry one night and very soon had Davy hired to assist him. For five weeks the boy worked for the Dutchman, and then set out for home in a heavy snow-storm. So anxious was he to see his parents again that he traveled most of the four hundred miles without stopping for rest at nights.

The next fall he started to acquire some education at a small school conducted in the neighborhood by a man named Benjamin Kitchen. For four days he attended without mishap, but on the fifth day he had "a falling out with one of the scholars"—a boy much larger and older than he was. After school the two antagonists fought it out in the bushes by the wayside, and Davy flew at his adversary like a wild cat, "scratched his face all to a flitter jig, and soon made him cry out for quarters in good earnest." Instead of going to school the next few days for fear of a thrashing from the master, Davy loitered in the woods. When his father heard about this state of affairs, he demanded a reason for the truancy. Davy said that he was afraid of old Kitchen, who might "cook him to a cracklin" if he turned up. His father, who had been "taking a few horns," was in a fit mood to "make the fur fly." Picking up a hickory stick, he vowed he'd whip the boy an "eternal sight worse than the master" would if he didn't start for school. Davy started, but in the opposite direction from school. Then began a hard chase, but Davy kept far enough ahead of the old man to gain the top of a hill and slip out of sight behind some bushes till his father passed, puffing like a bellows in a forge.

Davy did not go home that night. Nor did he venture near home for the next three years. He worked at various employments, and even contemplated going to sea as a sailor. Once, while working for a waggoner who was hauling barrels of flour, Davy was nearly mashed to death by toppling barrels when the team ran away. For eighteen months he worked without pay for a hatter, who finding himself overwhelmed with debts, skipped the country. Now penniless and with only a few clothes left, Davy decided to return home. He arrived late in the evening and was not recognized by any members of his family, as he had changed so greatly in three years. While he was sitting among several strangers at the supper table, his oldest sister suddenly "recollected" him, grasped him around the neck, and cried to her mother and sisters, "Here is our long-lost brother!" The welcome home was very effusive.

A short time later he went to work for a man from whom his father had borrowed thirty-six dollars. It took six months to pay off this debt, and Davy dutifully carried the cancelled note to his father. Then for another six months he was hired out to a Quaker who held a forty-dollar note from his father. When he handed over this cancelled note, the old man shed a "heap of tears," but being too poor could give Davy nothing in return.

He was still working for the Quaker when the latter's niece came from North Carolina for a visit. Then he fell head over heels in love, and was so flabbergasted at the sight of her that he couldn't say a thing in her presence; whenever he tried to talk his heart would begin to "flutter like a duck in the puddle." But the Quaker girl told him very honestly that she was engaged to another man, and could not receive his attentions. It was hard for him to cool off, as he had "hardly safety pipes enough," but he saw it was well nigh useless to press his suit further.

He was sharp enough to perceive that his lack of education placed him at a disadvantage, not only in love but in the ordinary concerns of life as well. So he decided to improve matters by going back to school. He now worked two days a week for the Quaker, and attended school on four. In six months he had learned to read a little, write his name, and "cypher some in the three first rules in figures." And that was the extent of his formal education. He quit going to school because he concluded that he "couldn't do any longer without a wife."

From a family of very pretty girls he selected the one he liked best and made a proposal. At first she was evasive, but as he gave her no peace of mind she finally consented. The day before the wedding he set out for the girl's house, but on the way he stopped at a shooting match and won a beef, which he sold for five dollars. The extra cash made him particularly happy, and in a good humor he proceeded on his way. Before he even arrived, he met his fiancée's sister, who immediately burst into tears and told him the intended bride had gone off with another man to buy their wedding license. This news sounded to Davy like a "clap of thunder on a bright sunshiny day." He returned to his work at the Quaker's, lost his appetite, became morose, and felt a great sickness "around the tender parts of his heart."

Davy continued in "this down-spirited situation for a good long time," but at a barn dance he was introduced to a girl with whom he was "plaguy well pleased." He danced a couple of reels with her, and paid special attention to her mother, going on the old assumption that to "catch the calf you must salt the cow." Matters moved very smoothly for a while with this match, but the old lady didn't want her daughter to marry at all; so, whenever he broached the subject of marriage, she looked at him "as savage as a meat axe," and all but drove him out of the house. The father, however, was favorably disposed, and brought his wife around to his viewpoint so completely that, as a dowry, she gave the young couple two "likely cows and calves."

Davy rented a farm and cabin, but had nothing to put in his new dwelling. His old Quaker friend came forward, then, with a loan of fifteen dollars. With that neat sum Davy and his wife were "fixed up pretty grand." Three children, two sons and a daughter, were born to this marriage, but Davy gradually came to the conclusion that he was better at "increasing his family than his fortune."

He moved several times, and at the outbreak of the Creek War, he was living in Franklin County, near the Alabama border, in south-central

494

Tennessee. He decided to join up, under the over-all command of General Jackson, although his wife objected to his going and cried a little. He argued with her that, if he and others like him didn't go, the Indians would murder and scalp all of them in their beds.

At one place Davy's company set out to capture an Indian town, and when they approached, many of the squaws ran out and gave themselves up. One of them, however, sat in the doorway of a large frame building, into which Davy had seen forty-six warriors run for concealment. The squaw in the doorway aimed with bow and arrow, and "raising her feet she drew with all her might." One of the white invaders fell over dead. This act so enraged his comrades that they sent at least twenty balls flying through the old squaw. "We now shot them like dogs," says Davy, "and then set the house on fire, and burned it up with the forty-six warriors in it."

Rations being cut into half, the soldiers went back to search for provisions the next day in the Indian village, "where many of the carcases were still to be seen. They looked very awful, for the burning had not entirely consumed them, but gave them a very terrible appearance. It was somehow or other found out that the house had a potato cellar under it, and an immediate examination was made, for we were all as hungry as wolves. We found a fine chance of potatoes in it, and hunger compelled us to eat them, though I had a little rather not if I could have helped it, for the oil of the Indians we had burned up on the day before had run down on them, and they looked like they had been stewed with fat meat."

During the winter months food became scarce, and the men suffered for want of heavier clothing. They asked General Jackson's permission to go home on a furlough, as they had volunteered for only sixty days and had already been in service for ninety. He refused, and issued an order against their departure. The men were just as determined, and prepared for a start. "The general went and placed his cannon on a bridge we had to cross, and ordered out his regulars, and drafted men to keep us from crossing. . . . When the militia started to guard the bridge, they would holler back to us to bring their knapsacks along when we came, for they wanted to go as bad as we did. . . . We got ready and moved on till we came near the bridge, where the general's men were all strung along on both sides. . . . But we all had our flints ready picked, and our guns ready primed, that if we were fired on we might fight our way through, or all die together. . . . When we came still nearer the bridge we heard the guards cocking their guns, and we did the same. . . . But after all, we marched boldly on, and not a gun was fired, nor a life lost." Old Hickory had to admit that those were "the damndest volunteers he had ever seen in his life; that we would volunteer to go out and fight, and then at our pleasure would volunteer to go home again, in spite of the devil."

Still, Davy was not satisfied to stay at home. When Jackson sent word of further Indian troubles, Davy felt it was his bounden duty to go, and could not rest at home. So, back he went, and even reënlisted for a campaign in the South under Old Hickory.

Glad when his "career as a warrior" was over with, Davy settled down with his family to the business of running his farm. "But Death, that cruel leveller of all distinctions," he says, "entered my humble cottage, and tore from my children an affectionate mother, and from me a tender and loving wife."

He placed his children, for a while, with an older brother's family, but feeling that this arrangement was not too satisfactory, he set out to woo a widow bereft of her husband in the late war. She was a "good, industrious woman, owned a snug little farm, and lived quite comfortable." Davy paid her his most ardent respects but went about it "as sly as a fox when he is going to rob a hen-roost." This second wife already had a good-sized brood of children, but she nevertheless took care of Davy's progeny on equal terms with her own. "In a great deal of peace we raised our first crop of children, and they are all married and doing well. But we had a second crop together; and I shall notice them as I go along, as my wife and myself both had a hand in them, and they therefore belong to the history of my second marriage."

The Crocketts again moved westward, this time into Giles County, and they settled on land recently purchased from the Indians. It was here that he began to be bitten by the political bug. Selected by his neighbors to be first a magistrate and then a squire, he made an excellent record in this judicial capacity. "My judgments were never appealed from, and if they had been, they would have stuck like wax, as I gave my decisions on the principles of common justice and honesty between man and man, and relied on natural born sense, and not on law-learning to guide me; for I had never read a page in a law book in all my life."

Squire Crockett's zest for politicking and electioneering increased more and more, although it was a "bran-new business" for him. He was begged to run for major in a regiment by a certain well-to-do man who was running for colonel. He objected a little at first, but when he discovered that the well-to-do man's son was being secretly groomed to make the race against him, Squire Crockett organized his own ticket, ran for the appointment himself, and carried his whole slate to victory.

Some time afterwards Colonel Crockett offered himself for the state legislature. His opponent did not take the bear-hunting Colonel seriously till the election was over, and the Colonel had won twice over with nine votes to spare. Crockett had discovered that the best way for him to campaign was not to talk about government or laws, but to tell rip-roarin' good jokes on the rostrum, and trail off afterwards to the nearest liquor-stand for a general treat.

While he was serving in the legislature, he met with a dire misfortune at home in the nature of a flood, that swept away his grist mill, his powder

496

mill, and his distillery, for all of which he had gone deeply into debt. His wife advised him to pay up, and "shuffle for more." Crockett declared that this was "just such talk" as he "wanted to hear," came home from the legislature with a clear conscience and an empty purse, and set out once more for another location farther west.

The new home selected was in the northwest corner of Tennessee, on the Obion River, not far from the Reel Foot Lake, in a richly-wooded country spotted by canebrake clearings. It was an ideal "happy hunting ground" for Davy, who loved his rifle, Old Betsey, far more than he did a hoe, and thus did a great deal more hunting than farming. Many pages of his autobiography are now filled with accounts of his hunting expeditions and the large amount of game he killed. In half an hour he brought down three bears; in one week, seventeen; in one month, forty-seven; in one year, a hundred and five. He generously gave a thousand pounds of meat to a needy neighbor. Elk, deer, panthers, wolves, turkeys, and squirrels were also plentiful, but buffalo did not frequent this territory.

Crockett's name, without his knowledge, was placed among the candidates for the legislature from this new region of Tennessee. His chief opponent was a Doctor Butler, a nephew of Old Hickory's by marriage. It was a spirited contest, in which the Colonel declared that, even if he did not have carpets on the floors like the Doctor, he had "industrious children and the best of coon-dogs, and they would hunt every night till midnight to support my election." The Colonel also won the support of the voters, and came through with a majority of two hundred and forty-seven votes.

He served two terms in the state legislature from this district, and then ran for Congress. His opponent, a Colonel Alexander, had the wind blowing his way, however, and took credit for the high price of cotton, then bringing twenty-five dollars a hundred, since he had voted for the tariff law of 1824. The voters believed Alexander enough to give him an edge of two votes over Crockett.

The political winds veered in Crockett's favor the next Congressional election. Cotton having dropped to six cents a pound hurt Alexander. Crockett spoke with his two opponets, General Arnold and Colonel Alexander, from the same platform at one gathering. The General had been holding forth for a long time, explaining one thing or another in great detail when "a large flock of guinea-fowls came very near where he was, and sat up the most unmerciful chattering that was ever heard, for they are noisy little brutes anyway. They so confused the general that he made a stop and requested that they might be driven away. I let him finish his speech, and then walking up to him, said aloud, 'Well, General, you are the first man I ever saw that understood the language of fowls.' I told him that he had not had the politeness to name me in his speech, and that when my little friends had come up and began to holler 'Crockett,

Crockett, Crockett,' he had been ungenerous enough to stop and drive them away. This raised a universal shout among the people for me, and the general seemed mighty bad plagued. But he got more plagued than this at the polls in August." The guinea-fowls may have gone to the polls also; anyhow, Crockett beat both his competitors by nearly twenty-eight hundred votes.

On his way to the capital, Colonel Crockett stopped over for the night in Raleigh, North Carolina. "I was rooting my way to the fire, not in a very good humor," he explains, "when some fellow staggered towards me, and cried out, 'Hurrah for Adams!' Said I, 'Stranger, you had better hurrah for hell, and praise your own country.' Said he, 'And who are you?' 'I'm that same David Crockett, fresh from the backwoods, half-horse, half-alligator, a little touched with the snapping-turtle; can wade the Mississippi, leap the Ohio, ride upon a streak of lightning, and slip without a scratch down a honey locust; can whip my weight in wild cats—and if any gentleman pleases, for a ten-dollar bill, he may throw in a panther! I can hug a bear too close for comfort, and eat any man opposed to Jackson'."

Davy in coonskin cap, buckskin britches, and bearskin coat stalking along the streets of Washington became a much talked-of figure. And when he refused to wear the "dog collar" of King Andrew around his neck, he became the popular idol of the newly-formed Whig party. He was just the man to help give color and character to the up-and-coming Whigs in their opposition to the Jackson regime. He belonged to the new "coonskin democracy" of the West—he was a native of Jackson's own state and at first a partisan of Old Hickory's. He possessed the rugged individualism and independence of spirit that appealed so strongly to the straight-shooting frontiersmen who were adding strength to strength in the lately-devised electoral college. And Crockett, gifted with gab, spiced his yarns with the redolence and tang of the authentic Western vernacular. Hyperbole was his natural and most effective figure of speech; the factual tall-tale was his forte. What could sound more credible than this utterance from a politic old raccoon to an infallibly certain marksman, "Don't shoot, Davy, I'll come down!"?

Crockett served his first term in the House under Adams, and was a mild sort of Jacksonian democrat. He was reëlected by an overwhelming majority. But he differed with Jackson, first on the Indian sovereignty bill, and then later on the question of rechartering the United States Bank. "I will pledge myself to support no administration," declared the staunchly independent Crockett. "I would rather be politically dead than hypocritically immortalized."

The government, that is, Andrew Jackson, took cognizance of the champion bear-hunter's attitude; it neither forgot nor forgave. The beads of every high-powered gun in the government's arsenal were drawn on Crockett when he came up for reëlection in 1830. "I was hunted down like a wild varmint," he admits. Ten days before the election men went around making engagements for Crockett to speak everywhere in defense of his stand againt Jackson's measures in Congress. At the appointed time, when a large crowd had gathered, Crockett did not appear but his enemies were on hand with ready-made speeches against the "gentleman of the canebrake" who was too ashamed of his record to stand up before the public and defend it. News traveled slowly in those days, and Crockett knew nothing of the skullduggery till it was too late. He lost by the narrow margin of seventy votes.

Davy did not dawdle away his time during the next two years. When he was not bear hunting, he was regaling his erstwhile constituents with ring-tailed twisters and distillery tonic in the local taverns. Nothing could stop Davy from going back to Washington again. In spite of all the gerrymandering that the state legislature could do, Crockett came off victoriously in the election of 1832, although Jackson carried the state by a landslide.

Colonel Crockett was becoming an outstanding figure, mentioned by some as the next president. The Whigs took up the Colonel's apothegm, "Be sure you are right, then go ahead," as their national slogan. Davy himself decided on a tour around the country, and the Whigs joyously accorded him the greatest amount of publicity possible. His passage on a steamboat up the Chesapeake Bay was agreeably pleasant, and a ride on a train for seventeen miles was a strange, new experience. At Philadelphia a group of Whigs presented him with a shining new rifle to replace Old Betsey, a gift he highly prized and which was to serve him well to the last, at the defense of the Alamo. He visited the waterworks and the mint, and then was taken to an asylum for the insane, at which place he felt "monstrous solemn, and could not help thanking God" that he was not one of the poor, unfortunate inmates.

Another train ride brought him to New York. "I can only judge of the speed," he says, "by putting my head out to spit, which I did, and overtook it so quick, that it hit me smack in the face." He was cheered by crowds everywhere, and welcomed even at whistle stops. His triumphs continued to gather momentum as he passed on to Providence, Boston, Pittsburgh, Cincinnati, and Louisville. It was a progress intended to broaden his knowledge of various sections of the country besides his own, in preparation for his candidacy as president.

There was only one hurdle yet before him, and that was the election of 1834 in his own district. He was certain that his own constituents would return him again to the halls of Congress. He repeated his stories, treated more generously than usual, and listened to the jubilant huzzas of "Crockett forever!" His confidence remained unshaken till the votes were all in, and he lost by two hundred and thirty votes to a peg-legged veteran of the War of 1812. He could not believe that any political machine had enough power and money to defeat him. Later he wrote: "I have suffered myself to be politically sacrificed to save my country from ruin and disgrace, and if I am never again elected, I will have the gratification to know that I have done my duty. . . . I confess the thorn still rankles."

The third period of Davy Crockett's life is short but dramatic. A completely accurate account of his westward wanderings undertaken to give "the Texians a helping hand on the high road to freedom" will never be known, but the climax of that story, reached in the defense of the Alamo, has epic elements in it unsurpassed by anything in Homer's *Odyssey*. Crockett arrived in the nick of time to be one in that immortal band of one hundred and eighty-three men who fought to the last man, gave no quarter, and asked for none in return. Tradition has it that Crockett fired the first shot and the last in that gallant defense. Nobody can gainsay it, and nobody would want it otherwise. Had he survived the Alamo, the presidency would have easily been within his grasp; perhaps the bear-hunting philosopher from the backwoods of Tennessee would be enshrined today in the same Pantheon with the rail-splitting philosopher from the backwoods of Kentucky. But it is a big *perhaps*. As it is, to those who love a hero, whether they be such as dwell "deep in the heart of Texas" or just deep in the universal world-heart, aye, to them Davy Crockett will always be a well-beloved and glorious figure.

The small coffee spoon commemorating this hero pictures the Alamo embossed in the bowl. Along the shank runs the name of Davy Crockett. On a pedestal stands Crockett himself in his backwoods costume, both of his hands holding onto "Old Betsey," or, more than likely, the rifle presented to him by his admirers in Philadelphia. The date, 1836, represents the year of his death.

The provenance of this spoon is not indicated. Length, 3¾ inches.

No. 148 CINCINNATI FOUNTAIN
No. 149 TYLER DAVIDSON FOUNTAIN

The hub of Cincinnati for four score years has been Fountain Square between Vine and Walnut Streets. In the center of this square is the Tyler Davidson Fountain, at the dedication of which in 1871 Rutherford B. Hays, then governor of Ohio, was the speaker.

Tyler Davidson was the proprietor of a hardware store, and upon the marriage of his sister to Henry Probasco in 1840 made his brother-in-law a partner in the business. The sales of the company increased tremendously under the enterprising management of these two men. When Mr. Davidson died in 1865, Mr. Probasco soon disposed of the business and devoted the remainder of his life to various public-minded projects and to the embellishment of his suburban estate at Clifton. He erected a beautiful mansion of limestone and sandstone with embroidered wrought-iron approaches that have not been equaled elsewhere in the country. He landscaped the grounds with rare trees and shrubs from abroad. In his travels he acquired a large number of paintings by the old masters, and assembled a valuable library of fine gift books and first editions.

The topic once arose in a conversation between the two brothers-in-law of the need in Cincinnati for a public fountain. Shortly after the death of the senior partner, Mr. Probasco decided to bring about the realization of this idea by erecting a memorial to Mr. Davidson. While he was passing through Munich in 1866 he was shown various fountain designs at the Royal Bavarian Bronze Foundry. He soon engaged two famous artists, Kaulbach and his son-in-law, August Kreling, to set to work on the design he had selected. Not until after the Franco-Prussian War was the monument ready for shipment to this country. The bronze in the statue had been converted from cannon captured by Prussia from the Danes in 1866.

The nine-foot bronze figure of the "Spirit of Water" stands aloft on a high pedestal, her arms extended horizontally as if showering blessings on a wide area below. Jets of water are being emitted from her hands. Lola Montez, the famous dancer and the favorite of King Ludwig of Bavaria, posed as the model for this figure.

Beneath the pedestal in a canopied open-crypt are four figures dramatizing the indispensable uses of water. In the central panel, as shown in both spoons, a mother is leading her young son to the bath. In the right panel a man trapped on the top of a burning building is calling for water to extinguish the flames. On the left side, a farmer kneels in prayer for rain to save his crops from a searing drouth. The west side is not visible here, but the panel exhibits a girl proffering a cup of water to a crippled beggar.

Around the base are three children riding, one a turtle, one a dolphin, and one a bird; a fourth child is trying to escape from a serpent wound around one of his legs. The Cincinnati Fountain spoon shows only two of these children; the other does not show any of them.

Both fountains are in reverse positions on the bowls. The Tyler Davidson spoon is a Reed and Barton product, made in 1892. The Cincinnati Fountain spoon, pressed and patented in 1889 by George H. Shiebler Company, bears the sales imprint of H. Lange. The Lange Jewelry Company, founded by Herman Lange in 1864, is still in business. The firm has an effective slogan: "Remember, your grandmother's wedding ring came frome Lange's."

The *Cincinnati* volume of the *American Guide Series* has this to say of the Fountain Square: "Through the years it has been the core of Cincinnati's civic, social, and commercial life. People come here to meet friends, to feed the pigeons, to loll in the sun, and to catch bus and trolley cars nearby. Holiday events crowd the esplanade with sightseers, and most public appeals for worthy causes begin and end here."

Length of the Tyler Davidson spoon is 6 inches; that of the Cincinnati Fountain spoon, 5¾ inches.

No. 150 HOUSTON

Here are the salient facts in the life of General Sam Houston in the briefest sort of outline: Born near Lexington, Virginia, in 1793. Removed to Tennessee, 1807. Soldier in the War of 1812. Member of Congress from Tennessee, 1823-27. Governor of Tennessee, 1827-29. Removed to Texas, 1832. Commander-in-chief of the Texan army, winning independence from Mexico, 1836. President of Texas, 1836-38 and 1841-44. United States senator from Texas, 1845-59. Governor of Texas, 1859-61. Died July 25, 1863.

Informed only by this summary account, the reader would gather that Houston spent an active life concerned mainly with political and military affairs, and enjoyed a great measure of success in his undertakings. But such a skeletal brief gives us no clues to Houston's colorful personality or the reasons which make him the popular hero of Texas. Let us fill in the gaps of the outline.

At the age of thirteen he journeyed over the Alleghenies with his widowed mother and her brood, settling near the borders of the Cherokee nation in eastern Tennessee. Taking a liking to the Indian mode of life, he lived among the redskins and was virtually accepted as one of their braves. Overwhelmed by gambling debts, he returned to the whites and soon after opened a school that had a short, hectic existence. During the War of 1812 he joined Jackson's army and won commendation for his courageous stand at the battle of Horseshoe Bend, where his wounds proved almost fatal. He resigned from the armed forces with the rank of ensign after being rebuked by Calhoun, then Secretary of War, for appearing before him in the garb of an Indian.

He studied law in Nashville and practiced in Lebanon. His sententious rhetoric, spiced with bluff, good humor, punctuated with double exclamatory points, and terminating invariably with dramatic climaxes, made him popular with the backwoodsmen, and he was soon elected governor of Tennessee. He wore the dazzling outfit of a dandy at his inauguration, and was the "observed of all observers."

While running for reëlection, he suddenly married and as suddenly separated from the lady. He received so many congratulations after he had already parted company from his wife that, to avoid embarrassments, he resigned from office, quit the state, and went to live with the Cherokees in their new home on the Arkansas River.

For three years he lived on the reservation, latched onto an Indian squaw, and dissipated to such a degree that the savages labeled him the "Big Drunk." Still, they adopted him into the tribe, and he went to Washington to intercede with the President in their behalf. In the Capital he astonished everybody by wearing the picturesque Indian dress.

When the Texans began their struggle for independence, he set out for their territory. He was soon given command of a small unruly band of volunteers with an insubordinate group of officers, who were more determined on the invasion of Mexico than the defense of Texas. Houston was practically left a general without an army while the Alamo was being besieged by the Mexicans under General Santa Anna. The volunteer army and their leaders refused to budge from their intentions of invading Mexico and continued to dally on the Texan coast waiting for their ships of embarcation, callously indifferent to calls for help from the Alamo. There they remained while the defenders of the Alamo fought and fell. Houston, however, was not idle. He performed one good service, during the siege, by moving about among the Indians and smoking the peace pipe with chiefs to keep them off the warpath just when the way lay open for them to wipe out the defenseless white settlements.

The Texan volunteers soon realized their serious mistake, and, after the fall of the Alamo, rallied under Houston's banner. At San Jacinto on April 21, 1836, the newly-organized army dealt the Mexicans a crushing defeat in a battle that lasted eighteen minutes, killing six hundred and thirty of the enemy and capturing the remaining seven hundred and thirty. Santa Anna himself was among the prisoners. The American losses amounted to only eight men killed and twenty-five wounded. The independence of Texas was assured.

By general acclamation the Texans elected Houston their president. But the new republic had no capital. Two enterprising brothers, John and A. C. Allen, decided to create one, and the new town, more properly a mud hole, was named for the new president. When the immaculate Audubon called at the executive mansion, he was showered with mud splattering up from interstices in the loose board walk.

The members of the legislature were great whittlers, and Houston, to keep down expenses and save the furniture, ascertained beforehand what sort of wood, hard or soft, the whittlers preferred, and he provided sticks for everybody while the legislature was in session. A bill was passed, making Houston the Dictator, but he vetoed it as a "presumptuous piece of nonsense."

The panic of 1837 made hard times, and Houston got his share of the blame. So, at the next election a newcomer Mirabeau Buonaparte Lamar squeezed into the presidency. Houston gave a farewell brawl and every one got rip-roarin' drunk. The weather turned exceedingly cold all of a sudden, and there was no surplus firewood in the rude executive mansion.

503

The ingenious president ripped up the floor boards and kept the fire blazing on the hearth. The affair was a great success, liquidly speaking. So was the farewell address the next day. Sam jerked out every stop in the gamut of emotion, and the crowd by turns shed gobs of tears or burst into gales of laughter. After an hour and a half of this, the reaction to Lamar's address that followed was callously apathetic.

Lamar's head was puffy with grandiose ideas. His first gesture was to remove the capital to Nova New Orleans, that is, in modern terms, Austin. He could not settle on a name vilifying enough for the former capital; so it remained the same, fit enough for a stinking mud hole. The name of the republic itself would have been changed if he could have only thought of something to match its hills and plains in sublimity. Mirabeau Buonaparte was also a poet by fits and starts. When he fell, humpty-dumpty for a South American beauty, he felt constrained to warble forsoothly:—

> O lend to me, sweet nightingale,
>   Your music by the fountains!
> And lend to me your cadences,
>   O river by the mountains!
> That I may sing my gay brunette,
> A diamond spark in coral set,
> Gem for a prince's coronet—
>   The daughter of Mendoza.
>
> How brilliant is the morning star!
>   The evening star how tender!
> The light of both is in her eye,
>   Their softness and their splendor.
> But for the lash that shades their light,
> They are too dazzling for the sight.
> And when she shuts them, all is night—
>   Sweet daughter of Mendoza.

Mirabeau Buonaparte would have fain perched a coronet on the head of the "beguiling gazelle," likewise one on his own. But first he must needs emulate his namesake, the great Napoleon. He toyed with schemes of conquest, and expedited an army to bring Santa Fe under his yoke. Never was a campaign more touted—and more bungled. The whole outfit landed in lion cages, and were shuttled off to Mexican prisons. When Lamar found it necessary to treble the taxes, the would-be victims of said taxes stepped on board the teetering ship, deodorized the deck of Napoleonitis, and turned the rudder over to their former pilot, Sam Houston.

By this time Houston, now affectionately known as Old Grizzly, had straightened out considerably. His third wife was a good disciplinarian who remodeled his drinking habits. He did not become a teetotaler but he did learn the virtues of abstemiousness. He joined the Baptist Church, attended services, and read the Bible. His wild pulse and warm heart were steadied henceforth in their course by a wise feminine influence.

504

He performed his subsequent public duties with much dignity. As the last president of Texas, he steered the bark of state safely into the Union. His name was frequently mentioned for the presidency of the United States, but that distinction failed to fall his way. He strenuously opposed secession, and left the governor's chair on account of it. He died in poverty amid the shambles of a war that he had so vigorously discountenanced. As long as there breathes a true-blooded Texan, the name and fame of Sam Houston will never grow dim.

The city of Houston perpetuates that remembrance. The story of its phenomenal growth is as fantastically amazing as any tall tale by that surprise-ending short-story writer, O. Henry, who lived for a while in the city. The plans for the future metropolis of Houston were mapped out on the inside of a postmarked envelope by one of the Allen brothers employing his hat as an office desk. No "dream town" was ever more widely bruited abroad throughout the land, luring promoters, grafters, gamblers, nobodies hoping to become big cattlemen, and floaters of all kinds to the new settlement, which briefly held the honor of being the capital of the lately-created Texan republic. No judiciary court existed, and consequently there were no trials by jury. Disputes that could not be arbitrated by mutual agreement were settled by the trigger.

The first steamboat to negotiate Buffalo Bayou missed the town and had to back-track three miles. Railroads, providing a quicker means of transportation, linked the struggling city to the outside world and brought increasing prosperity. Dredging a channel to the coast made Houston one of the chief Gulf ports for the outflow of cotton from the fast-developing plantations of the inland area.

Today Houston is the hub of a huge petroleum industry. Cotton, lumber, garden vegetables, fruit, sulphur, and pig iron move steadily toward the freight liners anchoring in the port. Chemical industries have been centering their plants here, for easy access to the rich resources of oil, natural gas, sulphur, and salt in the hinterland. Businesses of all sorts have mushroomed, and Jesse Jones, the real estate magnate, has erected skyscraper office buildings to accommodate the limitless expansions.

The name etched in big capital letters in the gold bowl of the Houston spoon sports as many flourishes as the signature of the "Southwest Wind, Esquire" in Ruskin's *King of the Golden River*. The handle of the spoon bears blooms of the swamp magnolia, one of the most characteristic trees in Houston, in three varying stages of development. The reverse side of handle embodies the leaves of the magnolia in spiraling formations.

This spoon is a Watson and Newell product. As the pennant, here used, was the trademark of the company from 1879 to 1905, after which it was discarded, it is reasonable to suppose that the Houston spoon, heavy in the caput and nave, was made fairly early. Length, 5¾ inches.

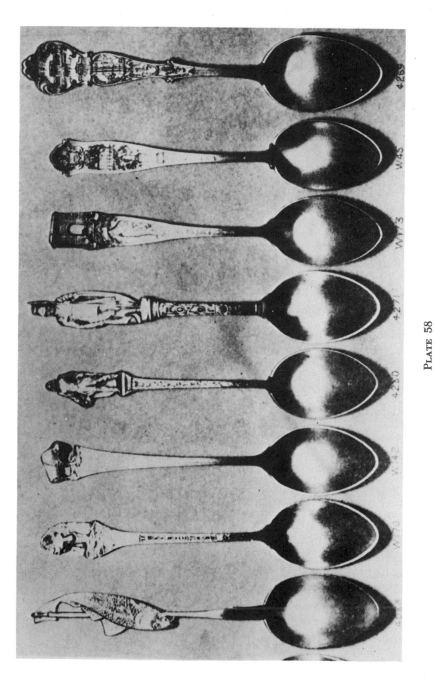

PLATE 58

Spoons from an early Robbins Company catalogue

Watson MARK Sterling

1879 to 1905

1905 to 1929

1910 to 1938

The above marks indicate the date of manufacture

MAIN OFFICE AND WORKS AT ATTLEBORO

THE WATSON COMPANY

ATTLEBORO, MASSACHUSETTS

Makers of Sterling Silver Exclusively

PLATE 59

A page from a Watson Company catalogue showing various trademarks used by the company

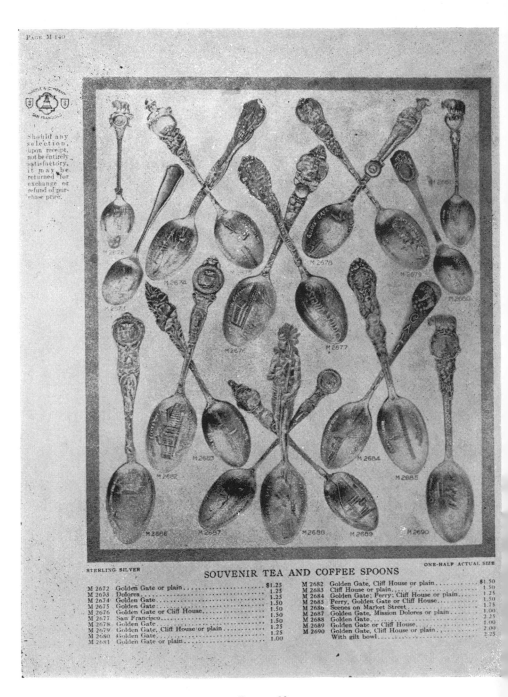

PLATE 60

A page from the Shreve Company catalogue of 1910

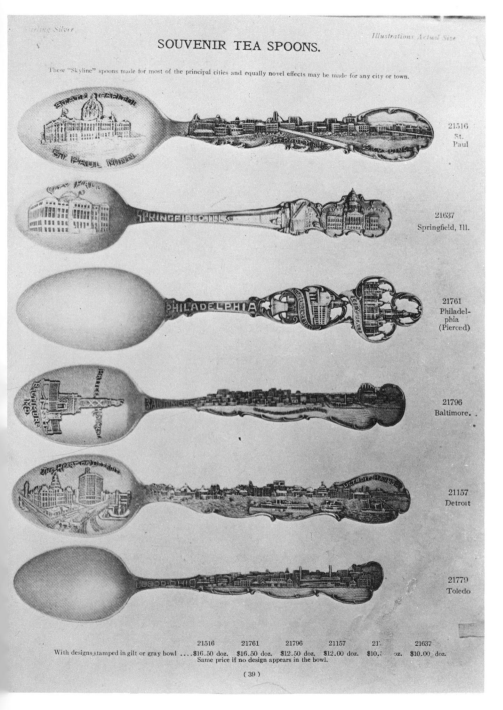

SOUVENIR TEA SPOONS.

Sterling Silver *Illustrations Actual Size*

These "Skyline" spoons made for most of the principal cities and equally novel effects may be made for any city or town.

21516
St.
Paul

21637
Springfield, Ill.

21761
Philadel-
phia
(Pierced)

21796
Baltimore.

21157
Detroit

21779
Toledo

	21516	21761	21796	21157	21...	21637
With designs stamped in gilt or gray bowl	$16.50 doz.	$16.50 doz.	$12.50 doz.	$12.00 doz.	$10.. oz.	$10.00 doz.

Same price if no design appears in the bowl.

(39)

PLATE 61

Souvenir teaspoons from the Paye and Baker catalogue of 1906

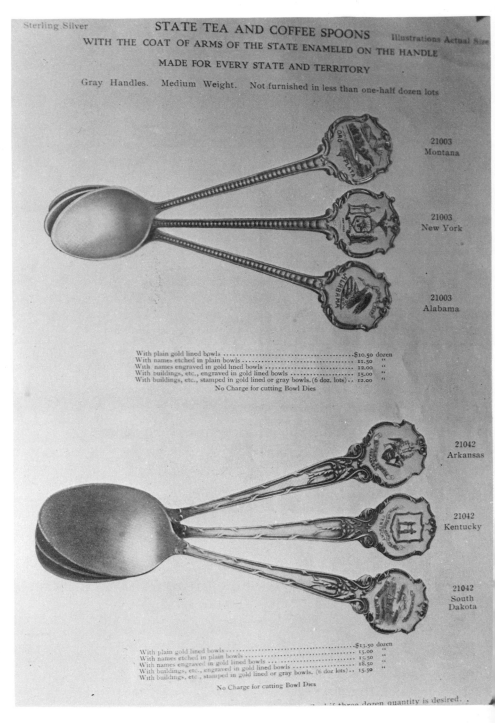

STATE TEA AND COFFEE SPOONS

Sterling Silver

Illustrations Actual Size

WITH THE COAT OF ARMS OF THE STATE ENAMELED ON THE HANDLE

MADE FOR EVERY STATE AND TERRITORY

Gray Handles.   Medium Weight.   Not furnished in less than one-half dozen lots

21003
Montana

21003
New York

21003
Alabama

With plain gold lined bowls .... $10.50 dozen
With names etched in plain bowls .... 11.50 "
With names engraved in gold lined bowls .... 12.00 "
With buildings, etc., engraved in gold lined bowls .... 15.00 "
With buildings, etc., stamped in gold lined or gray bowls.(6 doz. lots) .. 12.00 "

No Charge for cutting Bowl Dies

21042
Arkansas

21042
Kentucky

21042
South
Dakota

With plain gold lined bowls .... $13.50 dozen
With names etched in plain bowls .... 15.00 "
With names engraved in gold lined bowls .... 15.50 "
With buildings, etc., engraved in gold lined bowls .... 18.50 "
With buildings, etc., stamped in gold lined or gray bowls. (6 doz lots) .. 15.50 "

No Charge for cutting Bowl Dies

if three dozen quantity is desired.

PLATE 62

State, tea, and coffee spoons from the Paye and Baker catalogue of 1909

PLATE 63

Fruit and flower spoons from the Robbins Company catalogue of 1911

BIBLIOGRAPHY

ABBOTT, JOHN S. C. *Miles Standish: Captain of the Pilgrims.* Dodd, Mead & Co., New York, 1872.

ABBOTT, LYMAN. *Silhouettes of My Contemporaries.* Doubleday, Page & Co., Garden City, N. Y., 1920.

ADAIR, JOHN. *Navajo and Pueblo Silversmiths.* University of Oklahoma Press, Norman, Okla., 1944.

ADAMS, HENRY. *Historical Essays.* Charles Scribner's Sons, New York, 1891.

ADAMS, J. DONALD. "The American Ulysses" in *Literary Frontiers.* Duell, Sloan & Pearce, New York, 1951.

ADAMS, SAMUEL HOPKINS. *The Godlike Daniel.* Sears Publishing Co., New York, 1930.

AIKMAN, DUNCAN. *Taming of the Frontier.* Minton, Balch & Co., New York, 1925.

ALBEE, LOUELLA B. *Doctor and I.* S. J. Bloch Publishing Co., Detroit, Michigan, 1951.

ALBRIGHT and TAYLOR. *Oh, Ranger!* Stanford University Press, Stanford University, California, 1928.

ALDRICH, CHARLES. "Jefferson Davis and Black Hawk" in *The Midland Monthly.* Des Moines, Iowa, Vol. V, 1913.

ALEXANDER, MARY CHARLOTTE. *Story of Hawaii.* American Book Co., New York, 1912.

ALGER, WILLIAM R. *Life of Forrest.* J. B. Lippincott & Co., Philadelphia, 1877.

AMERICAN GUIDE SERIES. Compiled by the Workers of the Writers' Program of Work Projects Administration. Includes volumes on: *Alabama. Arizona. Arkansas. California. Cincinnati. Colorado. Florida. Georgia. Illinois. Indiana. Iowa. Kansas. Kentucky. Louisiana. Louisville. Maine. Maryland. Massachusetts. Miami and Dade County. Michigan. Minnesota. Missouri. Mount Hood. New Hampshire. New Mexico. New York. New York City. North Carolina. Ohio. Oregon, Pennsylvania. Rhode Island. San Francisco. Savannah. South Carolina. Tennessee. Texas. Utah. Vermont. Virginia. Washington. West Virginia. Wisconsin. Wyoming.* Various publishers.

ANDERSON, C. W. *Thoroughbreds.* Macmillan Co., New York, 1942.

ANDERSON, MARY. *A Few Memories.* Harper & Brothers, New York, 1896.

ANDERSON, MARY SAVAGE, *et al. Georgia: A Pageant of Years.* Garrett & Massie, Inc., Richmond, Va., 1933.

ANDERSON, RASMUS B. *America Not Discovered by Columbus* (8th ed.). Leif Erikson Memorial Association, Madison, Wisconsin, 1930.

ANDREWS, GEN. C. C. *History of St. Paul.* D. Mason & Co., Syracuse, N. Y., 1890.

ANDREWS, C. L. *The Story of Alaska.* Caxton Printers, Ltd., Caldwell, Idaho, 1938.

512

ANTHONY, IRVIN. *Ralegh and His World.* Charles Scribner's Sons, New York, 1934.

ARLISS, GEORGE. *My Ten Years in the Studio.* Little, Brown & Co., Boston, 1940.

ARMSTRONG, ZELLA. *Who Discovered America?* Lookout Publishing Co., Chattanooga, Tenn., 1950.

ATHERTON, GERTRUDE. *Golden Gate Country.* Duell, Sloan & Pearce, New York, 1945.

Author not given. *A History of the City of Chicago.* Inter Ocean Press, Chicago, 1900.

Author not given. *Orange: The City of Your Future.* Brochure, publisher not given, 1947.

Author not given. *Paul Revere.* Towle Manufacturing Co., Newburyport, Mass., 1901.

AXELRAD, JACOB. *Patrick Henry.* Random House, New York, 1947.

BACON, EDGAR MAYHEM. *Henry Hudson: His Times and His Voyages.* G. P. Putnam's Sons, New York, 1907.

BAKELESS, JOHN. *Daniel Boone.* William Morrow & Co., Inc., New York, 1939.

BALDWIN, LELAND D. *Pittsburgh: The Story of a City.* University of Pittsburgh Press, Pittsburgh, Pa., 1937.

BANCROFT, GEORGE. *History of the United States* (10 vols.). Little, Brown & Co., Boston, 1848-1875.

BANTA, R. E. *The Ohio.* Rinehart & Co., New York, 1949.

BARNARD, HARRY. *Eagle Forgotten: The Life of John Peter Altgeld.* Duell, Sloan & Pearce, New York, 1938.

BARNUM, P. T. *Struggles and Triumphs.* Courier Company, Buffalo, N. Y., 1875.

BARTHOLOMEW, Ed. *The Houston Story.* Frontier Press, Houston, Texas, 1951.

BELL, MARGARET. *Women of the Wilderness.* E. P. Dutton & Co., New York, 1938.

BELLOY, AUGUSTE. *Christopher Columbus and the Discovery of the New World.* Gebbie & Barrie, Philadelphia, 1878.

BENET, STEPHEN VINCENT. *Selected Works of Stephen Vincent Benet.* Rinehart & Co., New York, 1936.

BICKEL, KARL A. *Mangrove Coast.* Coward-McCann, Inc. New York, 1942.

BIGELOW, FRANCIS HILL. *Historic Silver of the Colonies and Its Makers.* Macmillan Co., New York, 1917.

BIGHAM, HON. CLIVE. *Prime Ministers of Britain.* E. P. Dutton & Co., New York, 1924.

BINGAY, MALCOLM W. *Detroit is My Own Home Town.* Bobbs-Merrill Co., Indianapolis, Ind., 1946.

BINNS, ARCHIE. *Northwest Gateway.* Doubleday, Doran & Co., Garden City, N. Y., 1941.

BLAU, JOSEPH L. (ed.). *Cornerstones of Religious Freedom in America.* Beacon Press, Boston, 1949.

BOLTON, HERBERT E. *Spanish Borderlands.* Yale University Press New Haven, Conn., 1921.

BOYNTON, HENRY W. *Washington Irving.* Houghton Mifflin Co., Boston, 1901.

BOYNTON, PERCY H. *Literature and American Life.* Ginn & Co., New York, 1936.

BRADFORD, GAMALIEL. *American Portraits.* Houghton Mifflin Co., Boston, 1922.

BRADFORD, GAMALIEL. *Damaged Souls.* Houghton Mifflin Co., Boston, 1923.

BRADLEY, HUGH. *Such Was Saratoga.* Doubleday, Doran & Co., Garden City, N. Y., 1940.

BRADY, CYRUS TOWNSEND. *Indian Fights and Fighters.* Doubleday, Page & Co., Garden City, N. Y., 1904.

BRITT, ALBERT. *Great Indian Chiefs.* Whittlesey House, New York, 1938.

BROOKE, TUCKER. *Essays on Shakespeare.* Yale University Press, New Haven, Conn., 1948.

BROOKS, VAN WYCK. *The Flowering of New England.* E. P. Dutton & Co., New York, 1936.

BROOKS, VAN WYCK. *The World of Washington Irving.* E. P. Dutton & Co., New York, 1944.

BROOKS, WILLIAM E. *Grant of Appomattox.* Bobbs-Merrill Co., Indianapolis, Ind., 1942.

BROWN, HENRY COLLINS. *In the Golden Nineties.* Valentine's Manual, Inc., Hastings-on-Hudson, N. Y., 1928.

BROWN, JOHN P. *Old Frontiers.* Southern Publishers, Inc., Kingsport, Tenn., 1938.

BROWN, SAMUEL GILMAN. *Life of Rufus Choate.* Little, Brown & Co., Boston, 1881.

BROWN, SARA SHELLENBERGER. "The Kentucky Thoroughbred" in *The Filson Club History Quarterly,* January, 1951.

BROWNE, WALDO. *Altgeld of Illinois.* Viking Press, Inc., New York, 1924.

BROWNE, WILLIAM HAND. *George Calvert and Cecilius Calvert.* Dodd, Mead & Co., New York, 1890.

BROWNE, WILLIAM HAND. *Maryland: The History of a Palatinate.* Houghton Mifflin Co., Boston, 1884 & 1899.

BRUCE, H. ADDINGTON. *Daniel Boone and the Wilderness Road.* Macmillan Co., New York, 1910.

BRUCE, HENRY. *Life of General Houston.* Dodd, Mead & Co., New York, 1891.

BUCK, J. H. *Old Plate.* Gorham Mfg. Co., New York, 1888.

BURGESS, FRED W. *Silver, Pewter, Sheffield Plate.* Tudor Publishing Co., New York, 1947.

BURT, STRUTHERS. *Powder River.* Farrar & Rinehart, Inc., New York, 1938.

CABELL, J. B. and HANNA, A. J. *The St. Johns.* Farrar & Rinehart, Inc., New York, 1943.

CAJUN, ANDRE. *Stories of New Orleans, Louisiana.* Twin City Printing Co., Monroe, La., 1941.

CAMERON, MARGUERITE. *This is the Place.* Caxton Printers, Ltd., Caldwell, Idaho, 1939.

CARLTON, MABEL MASON. *Ulysses Simpson Grant.* Houghton Mifflin Co., Boston, 1923.

CARMER, CARL. *The Hudson.* Farrar & Rinehart, Inc., New York, 1939.

CHAMBERLAIN, SAMUEL. *Historic Salem.* Hastings House, New York, 1938.

CHAMBRUN, CLARA LONGWORTH DE. *Cincinnati, the Queen City.* Charles Scribner's Sons, New York, 1939.

CHAMPLAIN, SAMUEL DE. *Voyages and Explorations* (tr. by Annie Nettleton Bourne). A. S. Barnes & Co., New York, 1906.

CHATTERTON, E. KEBLE. *Captain John Smith.* Harper & Brothers, New York, 1927.

CHIDSEY, DONALD BARR. *Sir Humphrey Gilbert.* Harper & Brothers, New York, 1932.

CHIDSEY, DONALD BARR. *Sir Walter Raleigh.* John Day & Co., New York, 1931.

CHOATE, RUFUS. *Addresses and Orations of Rufus Choate.* Little, Brown, & Co., Boston, 1887.

CLARK, THOMAS D. *The Kentucky.* Farrar & Rinehart, Inc., New York, 1942.

CLARKE, HELEN ARCHIBALD. *Longfellow's Country.* Baker & Taylor Co., New York, 1909.

CLEAVES, FREEMAN. *Rock of Chickamauga.* University of Oklahoma Press, Norman, Okla., 1948.

CLEVELAND, HENRY R. "Henry Hudson" in *These Splendid Explorers.* J. H. Sears & Co., New York, 1926.

COLBY, MERLE. *Alaska.* American Guide Series. Macmillan Co., New York, 1939.

COLE, CYRENUS. *I Am a Man: The Indian Black Hawk.* State Historical Society of Iowa, Iowa City, 1938.

COLE, HARRY ELLSWORTH. *Stage-Coach and Tavern Tales of the Old Northwest.* Arthur H. Clark Co., Cleveland, Ohio, 1930.

COLEMAN, J. WINSTON, JR. *Stage-Coach Days in the Bluegrass.* Standard Press, Louisville, Ky., 1936.

COLOMBO, CRISTOFORO. *Journal of First Voyage to America.* Albert & Charles Boni, New York, 1924.

COLOMBO, FERNANDO. *History of Admiral Cristopher Colon,* in the General John Pinkerton Collection, Vol. 12. Longman, Hurst, Rees, and Orme, London, 1804-1814.

CONNELLEY, WILLIAM E. *Quantrill and the Border Wars.* Torch Press, Cedar Rapids, Iowa, 1910.

COOLIDGE, D. and M. R. *Navajo Indians.* Houghton Mifflin Co., Boston, 1930.

COOPER, JAMES FENIMORE. *History of the Navy of the United States of America.* Thomas, Cowperthwait & Co., Philadelphia, 1846.

CORBY, JANE. *The Story of David Crockett.* Barse & Hopkins, New York, 1922.

CORDLEY, REVEREND RICHARD. *History of Lawrence, Kansas.* Lawrence Journal Press, Lawrence, Kansas, 1895.

COWIE, ALEXANDER. *The Rise of the American Novel.* American Book Co., New York, 1948.

CRAWFORD, MARY CAROLINE. *Romance of the American Theatre.* Little, Brown & Co., Boston, 1925.

CRISS, MILDRED. *Pocahontas.* Dodd, Mead & Co., New York, 1943.

CROCKETT, DAVY. *A Narrative of the Life of Davy Crockett, of the State of Tennessee, by Himself.* Philadelphia, 1834. Reprinted in the Modern Student's Library, Charles Scribner's Sons, New York, 1923.

CROCKETT, W. S. *The Scott Originals.* Charles Scribner's Sons, New York, 1912.

CROWLEY, MARY. *Daughter of New France.* Little, Brown & Co., Boston, 1901.

CUTTEN, GEORGE BARTON. *The Silversmiths of North Carolina.* State Department of Archives and History, Raleigh, N. C., 1948.

DARROW, FLOYD M. *Masters of Science and Invention.* Harcourt, Brace & Co., New York, 1923.

DARROW, GEORGE M. *Strawberry Culture: Eastern United States.* U. S. D. A. Farmers' Bulletin 1028, Washington, D. C., 1944.

DARROW, GEORGE M. and WALDO, GEORGE F. *Strawberry Varieties in the United States.* U. S. D. A. Farmers' Bulletin 1043, Washington, D. C., 1946.

DAVID, ROBERT B. *Malcolm Campbell, Sheriff.* Wyomingana, Inc., Casper, Wyoming, 1932.

DAVIS, CLYDE BRION. *The Arkansas.* Farrar & Rinehart, Inc., New York, 1940.

DAWSON, DOCTOR SAMUEL E. *Canada and New Foundland.* Stanford's Compendium of Geography, Vol. I. Stanford & Co., London, 1897.

DAY, DONALD. *Big Country: Texas.* Duell, Sloan & Pearce, New York, 1947.

DESMOND, ALICE CURTIS. *Martha Washington.* Dodd, Mead & Co., New York, 1942.

DICKINSON, THOMAS H. *The Making of American Literature.* Century Co., New York, 1932.

DODGE, GRENVILLE. *How We Built the Union Pacific.* Government Printing Office, Washington, D. C., 1910.

DONNELLEY, IGNATIUS. *Atlantis.* Harper & Brothers, New York, 1882.

DOS PASSOS, JOHN. *The Ground We Stand On.* Houghton Mifflin Co., Boston, 1941.

DOUGLAS, MARJORY STONEMAN. *The Everglades.* Rinehart & Co., New York, 1947.

DRINKWATER, JOHN. *Shakespeare.* Macmillan Co., New York, 1933.

DRURY, AUBREY. *California: An Intimate Guide.* Harper & Brothers, New York, 1947.

DUFF, CHARLES. *Truth About Columbus and the Discovery of America.* Random House, New York, 1936.

DUFFUS, R. L. *Santa Fe Trail.* Longmans, Green & Co., New York, 1930.

DUHOUSSET, CHARLES. *L'Art Pour Tous.* Paris, 1879.

DUNN, ESTHER CLOUDMAN. *Shakespeare in America.* Macmillan Co., New York, 1939.

DURRETT, COLONEL REUBEN T. *Traditions of the Earliest Visits of Foreigners (Filson Club Publications,* No. 23). John P. Morton & Co., Louisville, Ky., 1908.

EARLE, ALICE MORSE. *Stage Coach and Tavern Days.* Macmillan Co., New York, 1900.

EARLY, ELEANOR. *New Orleans Holiday.* Rinehart & Co., New York, 1947.

EASTON, EMILY. *Roger Williams: Prophet and Pioneer.* Houghton Mifflin Co., Boston, 1930.

EBERLEIN AND McCLURE. *Practical Book of American Antiques.* Halcyon House, Garden City, N. Y., 1948.

ECKENRODE, H. J. "Sir Walter Scott and the South" in *North American Review,* Vol. CCVI, pp. 598-603.

EDWARDS, EDWARD. *Life of Sir Walter Raleigh* (2 vols.). Macmillan Co., London, 1868.

ELIOT, T. S. *Selected Essays.* Harcourt, Brace & Co., New York, 1932.

ELLIOTT, G. R. *The Cycle of Modern Poetry.* Princeton University Press, Princeton, N. J., 1929.

ELLIS, EDWARD P. *Life of Colonel David Crockett.* Porter & Coates, Philadelphia, 1884.

ERNST, JAMES. *Roger Williams: New England Firebrand.* Macmillan Co., New York, 1932.

FARIS, JOHN T. *Historic Shrines of America.* George H. Doran Co., New York, 1918.

FARIS, JOHN T. *Romance of Forgotten Men.* Harper & Brothers, New York, 1928.

FERGUSON, HARVEY. *Rio Grande.* Alfred A. Knopf, Inc., New York, 1933.

FERGUSSON, ERNA. *Albuquerque.* Merle Armitage Editions, Albuquerque, N. Mex., 1947.

FERGUSSON, ERNA. *Our Southwest.* Alfred A. Knopf, Inc., New York, 1940.

FERRIS, MARY P. "Chapter on Some Old Spoons" in *Harper's Bazaar,* September, 1890.

FINLAY, IAN. *Scottish Crafts.* Oxford University Press, London and New York, 1948.

FISHER, DOROTHY CANFIELD. *Paul Revere and the Minute Men.* Random House, New York, 1930.

FISHER, SYDNEY GEORGE. *The True Daniel Webster.* J. B. Lippincott Co., Philadelphia, 1911.

FISKE, JOHN. *Discovery of America.* Houghton Mifflin Co., Boston, 1891.

FISKE, JOHN. *Dutch and Quaker Colonies in America.* Houghton Mifflin Co., Boston, 1899.

FISKE, JOHN. *Old Virginia and Her Neighbors.* Houghton Mifflin Co., Boston, 1897.

FLETCHER, JOHN GOULD. *Arkansas.* University of North Carolina Press, Chapel Hill, N. C., 1947.

FLETCHER, JOHN GOULD. *John Smith—Also Pocahontas.* Brentano's, Inc., New York, 1928.

FLEXNER, JAMES THOMAS. *Steamboats Come True.* Viking Press, New York, 1944.

FOOTNER, HULBERT. *Rivers of the Eastern Shore.* Farrar & Rinehart, Inc., New York, 1944.

FORBES, ESTHER. *Paul Revere and the World He Lived In.* Houghton Mifflin Co., Boston, 1942.

FORD, PAUL LEICESTER. *The True George Washington.* J. B. Lippincott Co., Philadelphia, 1896.

FORD, GOVERNOR THOMAS. *History of Illinois.* S. C. Griggs & Co., Chicago, 1854.

FOREMAN, GRANT. *Pioneer Days in the Southwest.* Arthur H. Clark Co., Cleveland, Ohio, 1926.

FOREMAN, GRANT. *Sequoyah.* University of Oklahoma Press, Norman, Okla., 1938.

FOX, HELEN MORGENTHAU. *Gardening for Good Eating.* Macmillan Co., New York, 1943.

FREEDLEY AND REEVES. *History of the Theatre.* Crown Publishers, New York, 1941.

FREEMAN AND BEAUMONT. *Early American Plated Silver.* Century House, Watkins Glen, N. Y., 1947.

FREEMAN, LEWIS R. *The Colorado River.* Dodd, Mead & Co., New York, 1923.

FUESS, CLAUDE M. *Rufus Choate.* Minton, Balch & Co., New York, 1928.

GALTER, JUAN SUBIAS. *El Arte Popular en España.* Barcelona, Spain, 1948.

GAMBLE, THOMAS. *Savannah Duels and Duellists.* Review Publishing and Printing Co., Savannah, Georgia, 1923.

GARDINER, DOROTHY. *West of the River.* Thomas Y. Crowell Co., New York, 1941.

GELLER, JAMES J. *Grandfather's Follies.* Macaulay Co., New York, 1934.

GIBB, GEORGE S. *The Whitesmiths of Taunton: A History of Reed and Barton.* Harvard University Press, Cambridge, Mass., 1946.

GILBERT AND BRYSON. *Chicago and Its Makers.* Felix Mendelsohn, Chicago, 1929.

GILDER, RODMAN. *Statue of Liberty Enlightening the World.* New York Trust Co., New York, 1943.

GOING, MAUD. *With the Trees.* Baker and Taylor Co., New York, 1903.

GOODALE, KATHERINE. *Behind the Scenes with Edwin Booth.* Houghton Mifflin Co., Boston, 1931.

GORMAN, HERBERT S. *A Victorian American.* George H. Doran Co., New York, 1926.

GOVERNMENT DOCUMENT. "U. S. Frigate *Constitution.*" Bureau of Construction and Repair, Navy Department, Washington, D. C., 1932.

GRAHAM, LLOYD. *Niagara Country.* Duell, Sloan & Pearce, Inc., New York, 1949.

GRANT, FREDERICK J. *History of Seattle, Washington.* American Publishing and Engraving Co., New York, 1891.

GRANT, J. FRANCIS. *Manual of Heraldry.* John Grant, Ltd., Edinburgh, 1948.

GRATZ, REBECCA. *Letters of Rebecca Gratz.* Edited by Rabbi David Philipson. Jewish Publications of America, Philadelphia, 1929.

GRAY, JAMES. *The Illinois.* Farrar & Rinehart, Inc., New York, 1940.

GREEN, H. C. and M. W. *Pioneer Mothers of America.* G. P. Putnam's Sons, New York, 1932.

GREEN, WALFORD DAVIS. *William Pitt, Earl of Chatham.* G. P. Putnam's Sons, New York, 1901.

GRIFFIS, WILLIAM ELLIOT. *The Pilgrims in Their Three Homes.* Houghton Mifflin Co., Boston, 1900.

GRINNELL, GEORGE BIRD. *The Fighting Indians.* Charles Scribner's Sons, New York, 1915.

GRISMER, KARL H. *The Story of Sarasota.* M. E. Russell, Sarasota, Fla., 1946.

GUEDALLA, PHILIP. *Fathers of the Revolution.* Garden City Publishing Co., Garden City, N. Y., 1926.

GUERNSEY, CHARLES. *Wyoming Cowboy Days.* G. P. Putnam's Sons, New York, 1936.

HALL, CLAYTON COLMAN. *The Lords Baltimore.* Theodore A. Arnold, Baltimore, Md., 1905.

HALL, EDWARD HAGAMAN. *Hudson-Fulton Celebration.* State of New York, Albany, N. Y., 1909.

HALLECK, REUBEN POST. *History of American Literature.* American Book Co., Cincinnati, 1911.

HANNA, A. J. AND K. A. *Lake Okeechobee.* Bobbs-Merrill Co., Indianapolis, 1948.

HANSEN, HARRY. *The Chicago.* Farrar & Rinehart, Inc., New York, 1942.

HANEY, JOHN LOUIS. *The Story of Our Literature.* Charles Scribner's Sons, New York, 1923.

HARBAUGH, THOMAS C. *Troy, Piqua, and Miami County.* Richmond-Arnold Publishing Co., Chicago, 1909.

HARDEN, WILLIAM. *History of Savannah and South Georgia* (2 vols.). Lewis Publishing Co., Chicago, 1913.

HARLOW, ALVIN T. *Weep No More, My Lady.* Whittlesey House, New York, 1942.

HARPSTER, JOHN W. (ed.). *Pen Pictures of Early Western Pennsylvania.* University of Pittsburgh Press, Pittsburgh, Pa., 1938.

HARRISON, FREDERIC. *Chatham.* Macmillan Co., New York, 1905.

HATCHER, HARLAN. *The Great Lakes.* Oxford University Press, New York, 1944.

HATCHER, HARLAN. *Lake Erie.* Bobbs-Merrill Co., Indianapolis, Ind., 1945.

HATFIELD, JAMES TAFT. *New Light on Longfellow.* Houghton Mifflin Co., Boston, 1933.

HAWTHORNE, HILDEGARDE. *Romantic Cities of California.* D. Appleton-Century Co., New York, 1939.

HAYDEN, ARTHUR. *Chats on Old Silver.* A. A. Wyn Inc., New York, 1949.

HELLMANN, GEORGE S. *Washington Irving, Esquire.* Alfred A. Knopf, Inc., New York, 1925.

HENRY, W. W. *Patrick Henry* (3 vols.). Charles Scribner's Sons, New York, 1891.

HERNDON, BOOTON. "America's Only Diamond Mine" in *Collier's,* August 25, 1951.

HERWIG, WES. "Spring Has a Sweet Tooth" in *The Highway Traveler,* Vol. 21, No. 1, February-March, 1949.

HESSELTINE, WILLIAM B. *Ulysses S. Grant, Politician.* Dodd, Mead & Co., New York, 1935.

HIGGINSON, THOMAS WENTWORTH. *Henry Wadsworth Longfellow.* Houghton Mifflin Co., Boston, 1902.

HOLAND, HJALMAR R. *America 1355-1364.* Duell, Sloan & Pearce, New York, 1946.

HOLAND, HJALMAR R. *Westward from Vinland.* Duell, Sloan & Pearce, New York, 1940.

HOLLIS, IRA NELSON. *The Frigate Constitution.* Houghton Mifflin Co., Boston, 1900.

HOLMES, OLIVER WENDELL. *Complete Poems.* Houghton Mifflin Co., Boston, 1928.

HORNBLOW, ARTHUR. *History of the Theatre in America* (2 vols.). J. B. Lippincott Co., Philadelphia, 1919.

HOUGH, EMERSON. *Way to the West.* Bobbs-Merrill Co., Indianapolis, 1903.

HUBBARD, ELBERT. *Little Journeys to the Homes of Eminent Orators.* G. P. Putnam's Sons, New York, 1907.

HUTTON, LAWRENCE. *Curiosities of the American Stage.* Harper & Brothers, New York, 1891.

IRVING, WASHINGTON. *History of the Life and Voyages of Christopher Columbus.* J. B. Lippincott Co., Philadelphia, 1880.

IRVING, WASHINGTON. *Knickerbocker's History of New York.* Doubleday, Doran & Co., Garden City, N. Y., 1928.

IVES, J. MOSS. *The Ark and the Dove.* Longmans, Green & Co., New York, 1936.

JACKSON, SIR CHARLES JAMES. *Illustrated History of English Plate* (2 vols.). Country Life, Limited, London, 1911.

JACKSON, HELEN HUNT. *Bits of Travel.* Roberts Brothers, Boston, 1878.

JACKSON, HELEN HUNT. *Ramona.* Little, Brown & Co., Boston, 1903.

JACKSON, PHYLLIS W. *Golden Footlights.* Holiday House, New York, 1949.

JAMES, GEORGE P., JR. *Souvenir Spoons.* A catalog-brochure. A. W. Fuller & Co., Boston, 1891.

JAMES, GEORGE WHARTON. *Arizona the Wonderland.* Page Co., Boston, 1917.

JAMES, GEORGE WHARTON. *Our American Wonderlands.* Page Co., Boston, 1915.

JAMES, GEORGE WHARTON. *Utah, the Land of Blossoming Valleys.* Page Co., Boston, 1922.

JAMES, MARQUIS. *The Raven: A Biography of Sam Houston.* Bobbs-Merrill Co., Indianapolis, 1929.

JEFFERSON, JOSEPH. *Rip Van Winkle: The Autobiography of Joseph Jefferson.* A revision of the 1890 edition. Appleton-Century-Crofts, New York, 1950.

JENKINS, CHARLES FRANCIS. *Button Gwinnett.* Doubleday, Page & Co., Garden City, N. Y., 1926.

JOHNSTON, SIR HARRY. *Pioneers in Canada.* Blackie & Son., Ltd., London and Glasgow, n. d.

JONES, CHARLES CALCOCK. "Sergeant William Jasper" in *Magazine of History with Notes and Queries,* vols. VIII and IX, 1908-1909.

JULIEN, CARL. *Ninety Six.* University of South Carolina Press, Columbia, S. C., 1950.

KAEMPFFERT, W. *A Popular History of American Inventions* (2 vols.). Charles Scribner's Sons, New York, 1924.

KAMM, MINNIE WATSON. *Pattern Glass Pitcher Books* (6 vols.). Published by the author, Grosse Pointe Farms, Michigan, 1939-48.

KANE, HARNETT T. *Queen New Orleans.* William Morrow & Co., New York, 1949.

KATKOV, NORMAN. "Embattled Twins" in *Holiday,* Curtis Publishing Co., Philadelphia, February, 1951.

KENNEDY, JOHN PENDLETON. *Horseshoe Robinson.* American Book Co., Cincinnati and New York, 1937.

KENNEDY, W. SLOANE. *Henry Wadsworth Longfellow.* Moses King, Cambridge, Mass., 1882.

KING, THOMAS STARR. *Patriotism and Other Papers.* Tompkins & Co., Boston, 1864.

KINGSLEY, CHARLES. *Poems.* Macmillan Co., New York, 1887.

KNIGHT, GRANT C. *American Literature and Culture.* Ray Long & Richard R. Smith, Inc., New York, 1932.

KNIPE, E. B. AND A. A. *The Story of Old Ironsides.* Dodd, Mead & Co., New York, 1929.

KNOX, THOMAS W. *Life of Robert Fulton.* G. P. Putnam's Sons, New York, 1887.

KREYMBORG, ALFRED. *A History of American Poetry: Our Singing Strength.* Tudor Publishing Co., New York, 1934.

KUYKENDALL, RALPH S. *History of Hawaii.* Macmillan Co., New York, 1926.

KUYKENDALL AND DAY. *Hawaii: A History.* Prentice-Hall, Inc., New York, 1948.

KUNZ, GEORGE FREDERICK. *Ivory and the Elephant in Art, Archaeology and Science.* Doubleday, Page & Co., Garden City, N. Y., 1916.

LAKE CHAMPLAIN TERCENTENARY COMMISSION. *The Champlain Tercentenary*. State of New York, Albany, N. Y., 1911.

LANDRUM, GRACE W. "Sir Walter Scott and His Literary Rivals in the Old South" in *American Literature*, Vol. II, November, 1930, and Vol. III, March, 1931.

LATHROP, ELISE. *Early American Inns and Taverns*. Tudor Publishing Co., New York, 1935.

LAUT, AGNES C. *Cadillac: Knight Errant of the Wilderness, Founder of Detroit, Governor of Louisiana from the Great Lakes to the Gulf*. Bobbs-Merrill Co., Indianapolis, 1931.

LAWSON, MARIE. *Pocahontas and Captain John Smith*. Random House, New York, 1950.

LAZARUS, EMMA. *Poems*. Houghton Mifflin Co., Boston, 1888.

LEE, RUTH WEBB. *Early American Pressed Glass*. Published by the author, Northboro, Mass., 1931.

LEE, RUTH WEBB. *Victorian Glass*. Published by the author, Northboro, Mass., 1944.

LEE, SIDNEY. *Great Englishmen of the Sixteenth Century*. Charles Scribner's Sons, New York, 1904.

LEISY, ERNEST E. *American Literature: An Interpretative Survey*. Thomas Y. Crowell Co., New York, 1929.

LEISY, ERNEST E. *The American Historical Novel*. University of Oklahoma Press, Norman, Okla., 1949.

LEWIS, LLOYD. *Captain Sam Grant*. Little, Brown & Co., Boston, 1950.

LIMBACH, RUSSELL. *American Trees*. Random House, New York, 1942.

LINDSEY, BESSIE M. *Lore of Our Land Pictured in Glass* (2 vols.). Published by the author, Forsyth, Ill., 1948-50.

LOCKRIDGE, RICHARD. *Darling of Misfortune: Edwin Booth*. Century Co., New York, 1932.

LONG, J. C. *Mr. Pitt and America's Birthright*. Frederick A. Stokes Co., New York, 1940.

LONG, WILLIAM J. *American Literature*. Ginn & Co., New York, 1913.

LONGACRE, CHARLES S. *Roger Williams: His Life, Work and Ideals*. Review and Herald Publishing Co., Washington, D. C., 1939.

LONGFELLOW, HENRY WADSWORTH. *Complete Poetical Works*. Houghton Mifflin Co., Boston, 1922.

LONGFELLOW, SAMUEL. *Life of Henry Wadsworth Longfellow* (2 vols.). Ticknor & Co., Boston, 1886.

LOSSING, BENSON J. *Mary and Martha Washington*. Harper & Brothers, New York, 1885.

LOWES, EMILY LEIGH. *Chats on Old Silver*. Frederick A. Stokes Co., New York, 1909.

LYMAN, GEORGE D. *John Marsh, Pioneer*. Charles Scribner's Sons, New York, 1930.

McCANTS, ELLIOTT. *Ninety Six*. Thomas Crowell & Co., New York, 1930.

McCLUNG, JOHN A. *Sketches of Western Adventure*. L. F. Claflin & Co., Dayton, Ohio, 1854.

MacCORKLE, WILLIAM A. *White Sulphur Springs.* Neale Publishing Co., New York, 1916.

McCRADY, EDWARD. *South Carolina in the Revolution.* (2 vols.). Macmillan Co., New York, 1901-1902.

McLAUGHLIN, A. C. *Lewis Cass.* Houghton Mifflin Co., Boston, 1899.

McMEEKIN, ISABEL M. *Louisville.* Julian Messner, Inc., New York, 1946.

McMURRY, CHARLES A. *Pioneers on Land and Sea.* Macmillan Co., New York, 1905.

MADARIAGA, SALVADOR DE. *Christopher Columbus.* Macmillan Co., New York, 1940.

MADISON, CHARLES A. *Critics and Crusaders.* Henry Holt & Co., New York, 1948.

MARTIN, JOHN BARTLOW. *Indiana: An Interpretation.* Alfred A. Knopf, Inc., New York, 1930.

MASTERS, EDGAR LEE. *The Sangamon.* Rinehart & Co., New York, 1942.

MASTERS, EDGAR LEE. *The Tale of Chicago.* G. P. Putnam's Sons, New York, 1933.

MATHEWS, J. BRANDER and HUTTON, LAWRENCE. *Edwin Booth and His Contemporaries.* L. C. Page & Co., Boston, 1886.

MATTHIESEN, F. O. *American Renaissance.* Oxford University Press, New York, 1941.

MAY, EARL CHAPIN. *A Century of Silver.* Robert M. McBride & Co., New York, 1947.

MEANY, EDMOND S. *History of the State of Washington.* Macmillan Co., New York, 1909.

MEDSGER, OLIVER PERRY. *Edible Wild Plants.* Macmillan Co., New York, 1939.

MERIWETHER, COLYER. *Raphael Semmes.* G. W. Jacobs & Co., Philadelphia, 1913.

METCALF, JOHN CALVIN. *American Literature.* Johnson Publishing Co., Richmond, Va., 1925.

MEYER, FRANZ SALES. *Handbook of Ornament* (tr. from the German). London, 1888. Reprinted by Wilcox & Follett Co., Chicago, 1945.

MOORE, CHARLES. *Family Life of George Washington.* Houghton Mifflin Co., Boston, 1922.

MOORE, N. HUDSON. *Old China Book.* Frederick A. Stokes Co., New York, 1903. Reprinted by Tudor Publishing Co., New York, 1944.

MOORE, N. HUDSON. *Old Furniture Book.* Frederick A. Stokes Co., 1903. Reprinted by Tudor Publishing Co., New York, 1935.

MORGAN, GEORGE. *Patrick Henry.* J. B. Lippincott & Co., Philadelphia, 1929.

MORISON, SAMUEL ELIOT. *Admiral of the Ocean Sea.* (2 vols.). Little Brown & Co., Boston, 1942.

MORISON and COMMAGER. *Growth of the American Republic* (2 vols.). Oxford University Press, New York, 1942.

MORRIS, CHARLES. *Autobiography of Commodore Charles Morris, U. S. Navy.* DeWolfe & Fiske Co., Boston, 1880.

MORRIS, CLARA. *Life on the Stage.* McClure, Phillips & Co., New York, 1901.

MOSES, MONTROSE J. *Famous Actor-Families in America.* Thomas J. Crowell & Co., New York, 1906.

MOSES, MONTROSE J. and BROWN, JOHN MASON (editors). *American Theatre.* W. W. Norton & Co., New York, 1934.

MUZZEY, DAVID SAVILLE. *History of Our Country.* Ginn & Co., Boston, 1947.

MYERS, JOHN MYERS. *The Alamo.* E. P. Dutton & Co., New York, 1948.

NEILSON, JOSEPH. *Memories of Rufus Choate.* Houghton Mifflin Co., Boston, 1884.

NETTELS, CURTIS P. *The Roots of American Civilization.* F. S. Crofts & Co., New York, 1938.

NEUENBURG, EVELYN. *California Lure: The Golden State in Pictures.* California Lure Publishers, Pasadena, Calif., 1946.

NEVINS, WINFIELD S. *Witchcraft in Salem Village.* Lee & Shepard, Boston, 1892.

NEWCOMB, REXFORD. *The Old Mission Churches and Historic Houses of California.* J. B. Lippincott Co., Philadelphia, 1925.

NOYES, ETHEL J. R. C. *Women of the Mayflower and Women of Plymouth Colony.* Memorial Press, Plymouth, Mass., 1921.

O'CONNOR, RICHARD. *Thomas: Rock of Chickamauga.* Prentice-Hall, Inc., New York, 1948.

ODELL, GEORGE C. D. *Annals of the New York Stage* (3 vols.). Columbia University Press, New York, 1936.

ODELL, RUTH. *Helen Hunt Jackson.* D. Appleton-Century Co., New York, 1939.

O'HIGGINS, HARVEY. *The American Mind in Action.* Harper & Brothers, New York, 1924.

ORMSBEE, THOMAS H. *Story of American Furniture.* Macmillan Co., New York, 1943.

PARKER, JEAN (ed.). *The Story of Sterling.* Sterling Silversmiths Guild of America, New York, 1947.

PARKMAN, FRANCIS. *A Half-Century of Conflict* (2 vols.). Little, Brown & Co., Boston, 1905.

PARKMAN, FRANCIS. *Pioneers of France in the New World.* Little, Brown & Co., Boston, 1894.

PARKS, EDD WINFIELD. *Segments of Southern Thought.* University of Georgia Press, Athens, Ga., 1938.

PARRINGTON, VERNON A. *Main Currents in American Thought.* Harcourt, Brace & Co., New York, 1927.

PATTEE, FRED LOUIS. *History of American Literature.* Silver, Burdett & Co., New York, 1909.

PAUL, H. and GEBBIE, G. *The Stage and Its Stars* (2 vols.). Gebbie Co., New York, n. d.

PAYNE, LEONIDAS W., JR. *History of American Literature.* Rand McNally & Co., New York, 1919.

PEATFIELD, J. J. "Around the Garden of the Gods" in *The Californian,* October, 1893.

PEATTIE, DONALD CULROSS. *Trees of North America.* Whitman Publishing Co., Racine, Wis., 1934.

POCHMANN, HENRY A. *Washington Irving.* American Book Co., New York, 1934.

POOLE, ERNEST. *Giants Gone: Makers of Chicago.* Whittlesey House, New York, 1943.

POPE, ARTHUR UPHAM. *Masterpieces of Persian Art.* Dryden Press, New York, 1945.

POPE-HENNESSEY, UNA. *The Laird of Abbotsford.* G. P. Putnam's Sons, New York, 1932.

POTTER, REUBEN MARMADUKE. *The Fall of the Alamo.* Herald Press, San Antonio, Texas, 1860.

POUND, ARTHUR. *Detroit: The Dynamic City.* D. Appleton-Century Co., New York, 1940.

POWELL, LYMAN P. (ed.). *Historic Towns of the Southern States.* G. P. Putnam's Sons, New York, 1904.

POWERS, JAMES T. *Twinkle Little Star.* G. P. Putnam's Sons, New York, 1939.

PRENTICE, GEORGE DENNISON. *Poems.* Clarke Co., Cincinnati, 1875.

PRESCOTT, WILLIAM HICKLING. *History of Ferdinand and Isabella* (3 vols.). Estes & Co., Boston, 1872.

PRINDIVILLE, KATHLEEN. *First Ladies.* Macmillan Co., New York, 1932.

QUAIFE, MILO M. *Checagou.* University of Chicago Press, Chicago, 1933.

QUAIFE, MILO M. (ed.). *Life of Black Hawk.* R. R. Donnelley & Sons Co., Chicago, 1916.

RASMUSSEN, C. A. *History of Red Wing.* Published by author, Red Wing, Minn., 1934.

RAWSON, M. NICHOLL. *Little Old Mills.* E. P. Dutton & Co., New York, 1935.

RICE, JAMES M. *Peoria City and County.* S. J. Clarke, Chicago, 1912.

RIES, ESTELLE H. *The Human Side of Decorative Metals.* Haldeman-Julius Publications, Girard, Kansas, 1948.

ROBERTS, BRIGHAM H. *A Comprehensive History of the Church of Jesus Christ of Latter-Day Saints* (6 vol.). Deseret News Press, Salt Lake City, Utah, 1930.

ROBERTS, W. ADOLPHE. *Semmes of the Alabama.* Bobbs-Merrill Co., Indianapolis, 1938.

ROBERTSON, SIR CHARLES GRANT. *Chatham and the British Empire.* Macmillan Co., New York, 1948.

ROBINS, EDWARD. *Twelve Great Actors. Twelve Great Actresses.* G. P. Putnam's Sons, New York, 1900.

RODD, SIR RENNELL. *Sir Walter Raleigh.* Macmillan Co., New York, 1905.

ROGERS, CAMERON. *Colonel Bob Ingersoll.* Doubleday, Page & Co., Garden City, N. Y., 1927.

ROGERS, JULIA ELLEN. *Tree Guide.* Doubleday, Doran & Co., Garden City, N. Y., 1926.

ROLLINSON, JOHN K. *Pony Trails in Wyoming.* Caxton Printers, Ltd., Caldwell, Idaho, 1944.

ROURKE, CONSTANCE M. *Davy Crockett.* Harcourt, Brace & Co., New York, 1934.

ROURKE, CONSTANCE M. *Troupers of the Gold Coast, or The Rise of Lotta Crabtree.* Harcourt, Brace & Co., New York, 1928.

ROURKE, CONSTANCE M. *Trumpets of Jubilee.* Harcourt, Brace & Co., New York, 1927.

ROWSE, A. L. *The England of Elizabeth.* Macmillan Co., New York, 1951.

RUCKER, MAUDE A. *West Virginia.* Walter Neale Co., New York, 1930.

RUGGLES, ELEANOR: *Prince of Players: Edwin Booth.* W. W. Morton & Co., New York, 1953.

RUPERT, CHARLES G. *Apostle Spoons.* Oxford University Press, London, 1929.

RUSTERHOLTZ, WALLACE P. *American Saints and Heretics.* Manthorne & Burack, Inc., Boston, 1938.

SABATINI, RAFAEL. *Heroic Lives.* Houghton Mifflin Co., Boston, 1934.

SAINTSBURY, GEORGE. *Prefaces and Essays.* Macmillan Co., London, 1933.

SALE, EDITH TUNIS. *Interiors of Virginia Houses of Colonial Times.* William Byrd Press, Inc., Richmond, Va., 1927.

SANCHEZ, NELLIE VAN DE GRIFT. *Stories of the States.* Thomas Y. Crowell Co., New York, 1941.

SCARBOROUGH, W. J. "William Jenkins Worth—Soldier" in *Americana,* July, 1929.

SEAGER, ALLAN. *They Worked For a Better World.* Macmillan Co., New York, 1939.

SEDGWICK, HENRY D., JR. *Samuel de Champlain.* Houghton Mifflin Co., Boston, 1902.

SEITZ, DON C. *The "Also Rans."* Thomas Y. Crowell Co., New York, 1928.

SEITZ, DON C. *Famous American Duels.* Thomas Y. Crowell Co., New York, 1929.

SELINCOURT, HUGH DE. *Great Ralegh.* G. P. Putnam's Sons, New York, 1908.

SEMMES, RAPHAEL. *Cruise of the Alabama and of the Sumter.* Carleton Publishers, New York, 1864.

SEMMES, RAPHAEL. *Memoirs of Service Afloat.* Kelly, Piet & Co., Baltimore, 1869.

SHANKLE, GEORGE EARLIE. *State Names, Flags, Seals, Songs, Birds, Flowers.* H. W. Wilson Co., New York, 1941.

SIMON, HENRY W. *The Reading of Shakespeare in American Schools.* Simon & Schuster, Inc., New York, 1932.

SIMONS, RICHARD S. "Veterans are not Forgotten" in the *Indianapolis Star,* June, 1950.

SINGMASTER, ELSIE. *Gettysburg Stories.* Houghton Mifflin Co., Boston, 1913.

SKINNER, CONSTANCE L. *Pioneers of the Old Southwest.* Yale University Press, New Haven, Conn., 1919.

SMITH, BERTHA H. *Yosemite Legends.* Paul Elder & Co., San Francisco, n. d.

SMITH, JOHN. *True Travels, Adventures, and Observations of Captaine John Smith in Europe, Asia, Africke, and America.* Franklin Press, Richmond, Va., 1819.

SMITH, JOSEPH. *Reminiscences of Saratoga.* Knickerbocker Press, New York, 1897.

SMITH, JUSTIN H. *War with Mexico* (2 vols.). Macmillan Co., New York, 1919.

SMITH, MOSES. *Naval Scenes in the Last War* (War of 1812). Reprinted in part in the *Golden Book*, October, 1927, with the title, "A Gunner on *Old Ironsides.*"

SMITH, SOL. F. *Theatrical Management in the West and South.* Harper & Brothers, New York, 1868.

SNOW, EDWARD R. *Mysteries and Adventures Along the Atlantic Coast.* Dodd, Mead & Co., New York, 1948.

SNOW, ELLIOTT and GOSNELL, A. H. *On the Decks of "Old Ironsides."* Macmillan Co., New York, 1932.

STARKEY, MARION L. *The Devil in Massachusetts.* Alfred A. Knopf, Inc., New York, 1949.

STEBBING, WILLIAM. *Sir Walter Raleigh.* Oxford University Press, London, 1891.

STEBBINS, EMMA. *Charlotte Cushman: Her Letters and Memoirs of Her Life.* Houghton Mifflin Co., Boston, 1878.

STEDMAN, EDMUND C. *Poets of America.* Houghton Mifflin Co., Boston, 1896.

STEGNER, WALLACE. *Mormon Country.* Duell, Sloan & Pearce, New York, 1942.

STEVENS, WILLIAM O. *Discovering Long Island.* Dodd, Mead & Co., New York, 1941.

STEVENS, WILLIAM O. *Nantucket.* Dodd, Mead & Co., New York, 1936.

STOKES, THOMAS L. *The Savannah.* Rinehart & Co., New York, 1951.

STONG, PHIL. *Horses and Americans.* Frederick A. Stokes Co., New York, 1939.

STONG, PHIL. "Hot Springs" in *Holiday*, Vol. 9, No. 1, January, 1951.

STRANG, LEWIS C. *Players and Plays of the Last Quarter Century* (2 vols.). L. C. Page & Co., Boston, 1902.

STRUNSKY, SIMEON. *No Mean City.* E. P. Dutton & Co., New York, 1944.

STUCKEY, H. P. *Southern Horticulture.* Turner E. Smith & Co., Atlanta, Ga., 1944.

SUTCLIFFE, ALICE C. *Robert Fulton and the "Clermont."* Century Co., New York, 1909.

SWEETSER, KATE D. *Book of Indian Braves.* Harper & Brothers, New York, 1913.

TALLANT, ROBERT. *Mardi Gras.* Doubleday & Co., Garden City, N. Y., 1948.

TALLANT, ROBERT. *The Romantic New Orleanians.* E. P. Dutton & Co., New York, 1950.

TAYLOR, EMERSON. *Paul Revere.* Dodd, Mead & Co., New York, 1930.

THAXTER, CELIA. *Among the Isles of Shoals.* Osgood & Co., Boston, 1873; Houghton Mifflin Co., Boston, 1901.

THAXTER, CELIA. *Poems.* Houghton Mifflin Co., Boston, 1906.

THOMPSON, EDWARD. *Sir Walter Ralegh: Last of the Elizabethans.* Yale University Press, New Haven, Conn., 1936.

THOMPSON, JOHN R. *Poems.* Charles Scribner's Sons, New York, 1920.

THWAITES, REUBEN G. *Daniel Boone.* Appleton & Co., New York, 1902.

THWAITES, REUBEN G. *Essays in Western History.* A. C. McClurg & Co., Chicago, 1904.

TICKNOR, FRANCIS O. *Poems.* J. B. Lippincott Co., Philadelphia, 1879; Walter Neale, New York, 1911.

TILDEN, FREEMAN. *The National Parks.* Alfred A. Knopf, Inc., New York, 1951.

TILLOTSON, M. R. and TAYLOR, F. J. *Grand Canyon Country.* Stanford University Press, Stanford University, Calif., 1929.

TOWSE, JOHN RANKEN. *Sixty Years of the Theater.* Funk & Wagnalls Co., New York, 1916.

TRENT, ERSKINE, SHERMAN, and VAN DOREN (eds.). *The Cambridge History of American Literature.* Macmillan Co., New York, 1944.

TRUMBULL, WILLIAM. *The White Canoe.* G. P. Putnam's Sons, New York, 1894.

TUCKERMAN, HENRY T. *Life of John Pendleton Kennedy.* G. P. Putnam's Sons, New York, 1871.

TWAIN, MARK. *Life on the Mississippi.* Harper & Brothers, New York, 1883.

TYLER, MOSES COIT. *Patrick Henry.* Houghton Mifflin Co., Boston, 1898.

UNDERWOOD, FRANCIS H. *Henry Wadsworth Longfellow.* James R. Osgood & Co., Boston, 1882.

VAN DE WATER, FREDERIC F. *Lake Champlain and Lake George.* Bobbs-Merrill Co., Indianapolis, 1946.

VERNON, ARTHUR. *History and Romance of the Horse.* Halcyon House, Garden City, N. Y., 1941.

WAKEFIELD, JOHN A. *History of the Black Hawk War.* Jacksonville, Illinois, 1834.

WALKER, ROBERT S. *Lookout: The Story of a Mountain.* Southern Publishers, Kingsport, Tenn., 1930.

WARNER, CHARLES DUDLEY. "Captain John Smith" in *Complete Writings,* Vol. VI, American Publishing Co., Hartford, Conn., 1904.

WARNER, CHARLES DUDLEY. *Life of Washington Irving.* Houghton Mifflin Co., Boston, 1882.

WARNER, CHARLES DUDLEY. *Their Pilgrimage.* Harper & Brothers, New York, 1886.

WASSERMAN, JACOB. *Columbus, Don Quixote of the Seas.* Little, Brown & Co., Boston, 1930.

WATERS, FRANK. *The Colorado.* Rinehart & Co., New York, 1946.

WAY, FREDERICK, JR. *The Allegheny.* Farrar & Rinehart, Inc., New York, 1942.

WEEMS, MASON. *A History of the Life and Death, Virtues and Exploits of General George Washington.* Latest reprint by Macy-Masius, Publishers, n. p., 1927.

WERNER, ROBERT MORRIS. *Barnum.* Harcourt, Brace & Co., New York, 1923.

WERTENBAKER, T. J. *The Founding of American Civilization.* Charles Scribner's Sons, New York, 1938.

WESTFALL, ALFRED VAN RENSSELAER. *American Shakespearean Criticism.* H. W. Wilson Co., New York, 1939.

WESTMAN, HABAKKUK O. "The Spoon: Primitive, Egyptian, Roman, Medieval and Modern" in *The Transactions of the Society of Literary and Scientific Chiffoniers,* New York, 1844.

WHARTON, ANNE H. *Martha Washington.* Charles Scribner's Sons, New York, 1897.

WHIPPLE, E. P. *Recollections of Eminent Men.* Ticknor & Co., Boston, 1887.

WHIPPLE, MAURINE. *This is the Place: Utah.* Alfred A. Knopf, Inc., New York, 1945.

WHITE, STUART EDWARD. *Daniel Boone: Wilderness Scout.* Garden City Publishing Co., Garden City, N. Y., 1922.

WHITE, TRUMBULL. *Manitou, Colorado's Great Resort.* B. L. Winchell, Denver, Colo., 1896.

WHITMAN, WALT. *Leaves of Grass.* Doubleday & Co., New York, 1948.

WHITTIER, JOHN GREENLEAF. *Poems.* Houghton Mifflin Co., Boston, 1930.

WILKINSON, ALBERT E. *Encyclopedia of Fruits, Nuts, and Berries.* Blakiston Co., Philadelphia, 1945.

WILLIAMS, A. M. *Sam Houston and the War of Independence in Texas.* Houghton Mifflin Co., Boston, 1893.

WILLIAMS, ROGER. *The Bloudy Tenent of Persecution for Cause of Conscience.* O. S. Straus, New York, 1894.

WILLIAMS, S. T. *The American Spirit in Letters* (Vol. XI in the *Pageant of America* series). Yale University Press, New Haven, Conn., 1926.

WILLITS, C. O. "Crops from the Maple Trees" in *Crops in Peace and War.* U. S. Department of Agriculture, Washington, D. C., 1950-51.

WILSON, ADELAIDE. *Historic and Picturesque Savannah.* Boston Photogravure Co., Boston, 1889.

WILSTACH, PAUL. *Mount Vernon.* Bobbs-Merrill Co., Indianapolis, 1930.

WILSTACH, PAUL. *Tidewater Maryland.* Bobbs-Merrill Co., Indianapolis, 1931.

WIMSATT, GENEVIEVE. "Apostle Spoons in America" in *American Home,* 35: 50-52, March, 1946.

WIMSATT, GENEVIEVE. "Strange Case of the Monkey Spoon" in *American Home,* 42: 34-35, October, 1949.

WINSHIP, GEORGE P. (ed.). *Journel of Francisco Vásquez de Coronado.* San Francisco, 1933.

WINTER, WILLIAM. *Life and Art of Edwin Booth.* Macmillan Co., New York, 1893.

WINTER, WILLIAM. *Life and Art of Joseph Jefferson.* Macmillan Co., New York, 1894.

WINTER, WILLIAM. *Old Friends.* Moffat, Yard & Co., New York, 1909.

WINTER, WILLIAM. *Shadows of the Stage* (3 vols.). Macmillan Co., New York, 1895.

WINTER, WILLIAM. *Vagrant Memories.* George H. Doran Co., New York, 1915.

WINTER, WILLIAM. *Wallet of Time.* Moffat, Yard & Co., New York, 1913.

WINWAR, FRANCES. *Puritan City.* Robert McBride & Co., New York, 1938.

WIRT, WILLIAM. *Life of Patrick Henry.* Andrus, Gauntlett Co., Ithaca, N. Y., 1850.

WIRTH, FREMONT P. *The Development of America.* American Book Co., Cincinnati, 1948.

WISTER, OWEN. *The Seven Ages of Washington.* Macmillan Co., New York, 1907.

WOODFORD, FRANK B. *Lewis Cass: The Last Jeffersonian.* Rutgers University Press, New Brunswick, N. J., 1950.

WOODS, KATHARINE P. *True Story of Captain John Smith.* Doubleday, Page & Co., New York, 1901.

WOODWARD, W. E. *Meet General Grant.* Horace Liveright Co., New York, 1928.

WYLER, SEYMOUR. *The Book of Old Silver.* Crown Publishers, New York, 1937.

YARD, ROBERT STERLING. *The Book of the National Parks.* Charles Scribner's Sons, New York, 1937.

YOUNG, COLONEL BENNETT H. *Prehistoric Men of Kentucky (Filson Club Publications,* No. 25). John P. Morton & Co., Louisville, Ky., 1910.

INDEX

534